SEMINAL GRAPHICS
Pioneering Efforts that Shaped the Field

Editor
Rosalee Wolfe, DePaul University

Jury
Jim Blinn, Microsoft Research
Michael F. Cohen, Microsoft Research
Donald P. Greenberg, Cornell University
Jim Foley, ITA – Mitsubishi Electric Information Technology Center America
Carl Machover, Machover Associates Corporation
Stephen Spencer, The Ohio State University
Turner Whitted, Microsoft Research

SIGGRAPH 98 History Chair
Carl Machover, Machover Associates Corporation

SIGGRAPH 98 Chair
Walt Bransford, Thrillistic

ACM SIGGRAPH Chair
Steve Cunningham, California State University Stanislaus

Contents

Foreword vii

Credits viii

Introduction ix

Visibility

Algorithm for Computer Control of a Digital Plotter
    J. Bresenham 1-6

Be Vision, a Package of IBM 7090 FORTRAN Programs to Drive Views of
Combinations of Plane and Quadric Surfaces
    R. Weiss 7-18

The Notion of Quantitative Invisibility and the Machine Rendering of Solids
    A. Appel 19-26

A Solution to the Hidden Surface Problem
    M. Newell, R. Newell and T. Sancha 27-34

Computer Display of Curved Surfaces
    E. Catmull 35-42

Hierarchical Geometric Models for Visible Surface Algorithms
    J. Clark 43-50

Casting Curved Shadows on Curved Surfaces
    L. Williams 51-56

Antialiasing

The Antialiasing Problem in Computer-Generated Shaded Images
    F. Crow 57-64

Pyramidal Parametrics
    L. Williams 65-76

Distributed Raytracing
    R. Cook, T. Porter and L. Carpenter 77-86

Shading

Continuous Shading of Curved Surfaces
H. Gouraud 87-94

Illumination for Computer Generated Pictures
B. Phong 95-102

Models of Light Reflection for Computer Synthesized Pictures
J. Blinn 103-110

Simulation of Wrinkled Surfaces
J. Blinn 111-118

An Improved Illumination Model for Shaded Display
T. Whitted 119-126

Shade Trees
R. Cook 127-136

Modeling the Interaction of Light Between Diffuse Surfaces
C. Goral, K. Torrence, D. Greenberg and B. Battaile 137-146

An Image Synthesizer
K. Perlin 147-156

The Rendering Equation
J. Kajiya 157-164

Ray Tracing JELL-O™ Brand Gelatin
P. Heckbert 165-166

A Progressive Refinement Approach to Fast Radiosity Image Generation
M. Cohen, S. Chen, J. Wallace and D. Greenberg 167-176

Modeling

Behaviour of Recursive Division Surfaces Near Extraordinary Points
D. Doo and M. Sabin 177-182

Recursively Generated B-spline Surfaces on Arbitrary Topological Meshes
E. Catmull and J. Clark 183-188

Computer Rendering of Stochastic Models
A. Fournier, D. Fussell and L. Carpenter 189-202

Particle Systems: A Technique for Modeling a Class of Fuzzy Objects
W. Reeves 203-220

Global and Local Deformations of Solid Primitives
A. Barr 221-230

Animation

A System for Computer Generated Movies
    E. Catmull 231-240

Computer Generated Animation of Faces
    F. Parke 241-248

Interactive Skeleton Techniques for Enhancing Motion Dynamics in Key Frame Animation
    N. Burtnyk and M. Wein 249-254

Computational Modeling for the Computer Animation of Legged Figures
    M. Girard and A. Maciejewski 255-262

Principles of Animation as Applied to 3D Character Animation
    J. Lasseter 263-272

Flocks, Herds and Schools: A Distributed Behavior Model
    C. Reynolds 273-282

Architecture

Real-Time Display of Computer Generated Half-Tone Perspective Pictures
    G. Romney, G. Watkins and D. Evans 283-288

On the Design of Display Processors
    T. Myer and I. Sutherland 289-294

A Head-Mounted Three-Dimensional Display
    I. Sutherland 295-302

Scanned Display of Computer Graphics
    M. Noll 303-310

Distributing A Visible Surface Algorithm Over Multiple Processors
    H. Fuchs 311-314

A Random-Access Video Frame Buffer
    J. Kajiya, I. Sutherland and E. Cheadle 315-320

The Geometry Engine: A VLSI Geometry System for Graphics
    J. Clark 321-328

Rendering from Samples

Texture and Reflection in Computer Generated Images
    J. Blinn and M. Newell 329-334

Color Image Quantization for Frame Buffer Display
    P. Heckbert 335-346

Marching Cubes: A High Resolution 3D Surface Construction Algorithm
    W. Lorensen and H. Cline 347-354

Compositing Digital Images
    T. Porter and T. Duff 355-362

Volume Rendering
    R. Drebin, L. Carpenter and P. Hanrahan 363-372

Feature-Based Image Metamorphosis
    T. Beier and S. Neely 373-380

View Interpolation for Image Synthesis
    S. Chen and L. Williams 381-390

Foundations

Sketchpad: A Man-Machine Graphical Communication System
    I. Sutherland 391-408

A System for Interactive Graphical Programming
    W. Newman 409-416

The Art of Natural Graphic Man-Machine Conversation
    J. Foley and V. Wallace 417-426

Paint
    A. Smith 427-441

Bibliography 443-444

Index 445

Foreword

Early in the planning for the 25th SIGGRAPH Conference celebration, we decided that we wanted to bring together the significant seminal papers that shaped Computer Graphics.

This fascinating but daunting task involved soliciting, gathering and organizing recommendations from the Computer Graphics community and convening a prestigious jury to make some exceedingly difficult decisions. Once the papers were selected, the challenge became one of locating high quality copy from individuals and archives around the world, and shepherding this volume through the editing and production process. And look at the result! I believe this is the first time these influential papers have been assembled in a single volume. This should provide to be an immensely valuable reference tool for students, teachers, researchers, practitioners and anyone else interested in our roots.

Thanks to Rosalee Wolfe and her associates for making this important contribution to Computer Graphics.

Carl Machover
SIGGRAPH 98 History Chair

Credits

Many people generously contributed time, expertise, materials and support to the effort of creating this book. The book began as a gleam in the eye of Carl Machover, Machover Associates and chair of the SIGGRAPH 98 History Committee. He and his administrative assistant Alyce Branum have lent their unflaggingly enthusiastic support on all matters great and small; from finding contact information to patiently answering all of my "what ifs." It has been a pleasure being a part of his committee.

The Seminal Graphics Jury, consisting of Jim Blinn, Michael F. Cohen, Jim Foley, Donald Greenberg, Carl Machover, Stephen Spencer and Turner Whitted, selected the list of articles, which was no mean feat given the wealth of excellent papers that have been published. They took time and care in choosing and organizing their selections and pointed out the paths of inheritance from one contribution to another.

Patrick McCarren and Deborah Cotton of ACM and Ralph Teague at the University of Washington were instrumental in obtaining copies of ACM publications. This book contains articles from a variety of other sources and t was Deb and Pat who guided me through the process of gaining publishers' permissions. William Hagen and Brian David, IEEE, Jennifer Goff, IBM, Plamen Nedkov, IFIP and Jean Pimm, Elsevier were most responsive in expediting our reprint requests.

Many Chicago area libraries were generous in their time and expertise in finding articles from back issues. John Rininger at DePaul University was enormously helpful in tracking down sources from as far away as France, and in obtaining clean photocopies, which is a challenging task. Teauria Brown, University of Illinois-Chicago Math Library spent several afternoons patiently and cheerfully answering questions about publications including one that had undergone at least two name changes. The staff at Northwestern and Illinois Institute of Technology offered help and sympathy in finding several arcane volumes.

A big thank you goes to the CMG team of Jennifer Anderson, Betsy Johnsmiller and Dino Schweitzer, the folks at Smith Bucklin including Leona Caffey, Sheila Hoffmeyer, Peggy Sloyan and Cindy Stark, and the designers at Q Ltd. including Jeff Callender, Erin Mulcahy and Tom "Word Guy" Rieke. They worked all sorts of magic, from arranging the "Seminole Papers" jury meeting to creating the cool artwork for the book cover.

The following researchers took time out from their schedules to answer questions, donate materials, supply information and pointers to information: Jim Blinn, Rob Cook, Tom DeFanti, John Dill, Gerald Farin, Alain Fournier, Henry Fuchs, Bertram Herzog, Dave Kasik, Kimberly Kelly, Ken Perlin, Tom Porter, Judson Rosebush, Malcolm Sabin, Dino Schweitzer, Harry Smith, Andries van Dam, Turner Whitted and Mary Whitton.

Shelley Weiss, the administrative assistant on this project, cheerfully and effectively aided with all aspects of this book, including assembling the response list from researchers, performing cut-and-paste the old fashioned way and toting library books all over town. She and Flora Barbussi retyped several of the articles for which we simply could not find clean copy. It was most enjoyable to work with her.

For myriad reasons in addition to all the proofreading he did, many thanks go to my husband, Alain Wolfe.

Introduction

This book began as a gleam in the eye of Carl Machover. Early in the planning for the 25th anniversary of the SIGGRAPH conference, he decided that a fitting part of the festivities would be to assemble a volume of significant papers that have shaped computer graphics. The goal of this book is to distribute a set of outstanding, but out-of-print papers, not just as an archival compendium, but as a resource for future researchers. Young scholars aspiring to a career in computer graphics are in the processing of starting their personal libraries and do not have easy access to a long "black shelf" of past SIGGRAPH proceedings. This book provides reprints of some of the important papers that broke new ground and still serve as guideposts for current work.

Jim Blinn, Michael Cohen, Jim Foley, Don Greenberg, Carl Machover, Stephen Spencer and Turner Whitted agreed to serve as members of the selection jury. In preparation for the jury meeting, email was sent to researchers asking them to list important papers that had influenced their work. The replies to this request generated over 178 Kbytes of email and listed 534 different citations. Jury members received summaries of these responses.

Many took time in their responses to include a summary of a paper's influence in addition to listing the citation. Some of these descriptions bordered on the poetic. One person wrote of a paper that "forms the basis of my existence. Its publication has made the world a better place." Another comment emphasized how compressed our history really is. One researcher began with the statement, "… the papers that come to mind are very old," and proceeded to list citations from 1988. In what other discipline would a publication from ten years ago be deemed very old? The field moves at a blazing pace.

As many researchers predicted in their email messages, choosing the final set of papers was an extremely difficult task, not only because there are so many subfields of computer graphics, but because there are so many excellent papers. The jury wanted to include more, but space limitations prevented them from doing so.

Through these papers one can witness the discipline's progress as new researchers take their inspiration from contributors who came before them. The papers are organized into eight groups based on paths of inheritance. The eight sections are entitled Visibility, Antialiasing, Shading, Modeling, Animation, Architecture, Rendering from Samples and Foundations.

Visibility

When rendering an image, perhaps the most fundamental question is "What is visible at this location?" This section covers different approaches to answering this question and includes hidden surface methods, which determine interobject relationships with respect to a viewpoint.

In 1965 Bresenham contributed a fast drawing algorithm capable of displaying line segments of any slope [BRES 65]. Its speed stemmed from the fact that it used only integer arithmetic. If you investigate any of today's graphics packages, most likely you will find that its line-drawing routine is based on Bresenham's algorithm.

Early line drawings of three-dimensional objects were not very realistic due to the fact that every edge of every object was visible. As a result, viewers often found it difficult to understand displayed objects. Weiss' BE VISION package, written in 1964, was the first to use hidden-line removal when displaying objects made from planes and quadric surfaces [WEIS 64]. The software computed and displayed lines of intersection among objects. A side note: at the time, a program size of 60K bytes was considered large.

Appel introduced a general-purpose hidden-line algorithm that could render isolated polygons as well as polyhedra [APPE 67]. To determine visibility, Appel made use of a point's *quantitative invisibility*, which he defined to be the number of front-facing polygons obscuring the point. A line segment is visible only when its quantitative invisibility is zero.

Compared to hidden-line removal, hidden-surface removal offers a greater degree of visual realism. One of the earliest hidden-surface methods was Newell, Newell and Sancha's depth-sort algorithm [NEWE 72]. It began by ordering polygons from back to front. Starting with the polygon furthest from the viewer, it proceeded to draw each polygon into the frame buffer. Subsequent polygons could obscure polygons drawn earlier in the process. It used a list of rules to resolve any ambiguities in depth, splitting polygons when necessary.

Catmull's z-buffer algorithm represented a significant contribution because it was (and still is) one of the easiest hidden-surface methods to implement [CATM 75]. It made use of a memory called a z-buffer that stored depth information for each pixel. Almost all of today's graphics workstations come equipped with hardware that performs z-buffering.

In the same paper, Catmull also introduced image-based texture mapping. His method mapped pixels of an image onto a bicubic patch by treating the parameters of the patch as normalized device coordinates.

To improve the performance of surface algorithms, Clark introduced the concept of a hierarchical geometric model as a means of capitalizing on object coherence [CLAR 76]. It allowed for multiple object definitions at varying levels of detail and the hierarchical structure facilitated extremely fast clipping. Whole subtrees representing scores of polygons could be eliminated with a single clip test. He also presented a special case of a binary space partitioning tree.

Shadows add visual realism to a scene, and while some shadow algorithms existed before William's work, none of them could accurately display shadows of curved surfaces. To achieve this goal Williams extended the z-buffer algorithm by introducing a shadow buffer [WILL 78]. The scene is first rendered from the "viewpoint" of the light source, but only the depth information is computed. This information is stored in the shadow buffer. The scene is then rendered using the z-buffer algorithm. If a polygon is found to be visible at a given pixel, the corresponding location in the shadow buffer is examined to determine if the polygon is visible to the light source. If not, the light source does not play a role in the color calculation and the pixel is in shadow.

Antialiasing

Not long after researchers first drew lines on display devices, they noticed that many of the lines were jagged. Aliasing is a common problem in computer-generated imagery and is caused by the undersampling that occurs when attempting to display a continuous object with a discrete set of pixels. In still images, aliasing manifests itself in various forms, including "jaggies", disintegrating textures and the disappearance of small objects. In animation, aliasing can cause an object's disappearance and sudden reappearance in a subsequent frame, resulting in the object's popping in and out of view.

Antialiasing attempts to minimize these undesirable effects. In 1977, Crow introduced area filtering as an antialiasing method [CROW 77]. Each pixel is treated as an area, and a polygon's influence on a pixel's color depends on the area of overlap between polygon and pixel.

Crow's technique was extremely effective in combating aliasing effects, but it added significantly to the overall rendering cost, especially when performing texture mapping. This was due to the fact that a pixel on an object may correspond to an area in the texture map that encompasses hundreds of pixels. Computing one color to represent this large area is costly.

Williams developed a fast method of filtering texture maps [WILL 83]. His technique precomputed a series of mipmaps. A pixel in the Ith level mipmap corresponded to an area of 2^I pixels in the original texture map. Instead of using a brute force approach to compute a representative color for an area within a texture map, William's algorithm looked up the answer in the mipmaps.

In contrast to area filtering which treats a pixel as an area, the supersampling approach takes multiple point samples per pixel and averages them. Cook, Porter and Carpenter extended the idea of spatial supersampling to sample motion, camera lenses and entire shading functions [COOK 84b]. Their distributed raytracing method provided the means to render motion blur, depth of field, penumbras and translucency. Part of their innovation involved jittering, or adding a slight displacement to the regularly spaced supersamples. A problem with supersampling is that it does not prevent all aliasing. Jittering produces noise in the final image, but noise is less objectionable to a viewer than aliasing artifacts.

Shading

After determining visibility at a pixel location, rendering software must grapple with the fundamental question, "What color is it?" This responsibility falls to shading algorithms. While some of the papers in this section present refinements that more accurately simulate the interaction of light and surfaces, others focus on reducing cost.

In early renderings, the underlying polygon structure of an object was readily apparent because each polygon received only one color, and discontinuities in shade were clearly evident. Gouraud's smooth shading technique calculated the color at each vertex and used bilinear interpolation to blend the colors along a polygon's edges and interior [GOUR 71]. He noted that a hardware implementation was feasible, and many of today's graphics cards offer Gouraud shading as a feature.

As an alternative to interpolating color across a polygon's surface, Phong interpolated normal vectors instead and performed a color calculation at each pixel [BUIT 75]. This technique improved the appearance of specular highlights. In addition to a more sophisticated shader, Phong introduced a simple illumination model that effectively simulated objects made from shiny plastic.

Blinn introduced a more accurate model when he adapted the physically based Torrance-Sparrow illumination model for use in computer graphics [BLIN 77]. Specular highlights from the Blinn model resemble those from the Phong model when the light source is in the vicinity of the viewpoint. However, when the light is positioned to the side or to the rear of the object, the new model more accurately simulates recorded observations of a highlight's behavior.

Blinn also introduced bump mapping, a technique that adds visual interest or complexity to a surface without the expense of generating a myriad of tiny polygons [BLIN 78]. By perturbing the surface normal, bump mapping fools the color calculation into producing a shade that is different from what the surface geometry would imply.

Early illumination models are categorized as local illumination models because they only consider light that is directly emitted from a source and that light's interaction with an isolated surface. Indirectly reflected and transmitted light is approximated by a constant ambient term. Whitted introduced the first global illumination model [WHIT 80]. His recursive raytracing algorithm was the first to simulate specular reflection and refractive transparency. An object's color could now be influenced not only by direct light, but also by light reflecting from other objects.

By the early 1980s, researchers had created a rich assortment of shading algorithms and illumination models. To give a user the freedom to choose and combine shading techniques, Cook designed a special purpose language in which users could specify shade trees [COOK 84a]. A shade tree describes a shader in terms of an illumination model. Users could use built-in terms that described surface properties, or they could create custom behaviors of their own. This flexibility of expression was a precursor to some of the features available in Pixar's Renderman Interface.

Another economical and effective shading method that introduces visual interest is texture mapping. Although image-based or two-dimensional texture mapping techniques had been in use since 1974, they had several drawbacks, including the appearance of visible seams, distortion and the necessity of trapping singularities. In 1985, Perlin introduced the concept of three-dimensional or solid texturing [PERL 85]. Solid texturing techniques do not have the same drawbacks as image-based techniques. He also described a cheaply computed noise function suitable for rendering and animation. Perlin demonstrated how solid texture could create convincing depictions of marble, wood, stone and clouds.

Further refinements of illumination models occurred in the mid-1980s. Although Whitted's illumination model effectively simulated specular reflection and transmission, it still used a constant ambient term to account for other reflected light. Goral, Torrance, Greenberg and Battaile adapted engineering models of radiation emission and reflection to create radiosity, a technique that replaces the constant ambient term with a more accurate model of interobject reflection [GORA 84]. This was the first time that an illumination model accounted for light emitted from diffuse surfaces. Images created with this method accurately depict color bleeding and variations in depth of shadow.

Although images produced with radiosity are enormously realistic, they required a great deal of computation for the radiosity calculation. This meant a long wait between renderings. Cohen, Chen, Wallace and Greenberg developed a progressive radiosity technique that opened the door to interactive rendering with radiosity [COHE 88]. It begins with an estimate of incident energy for each surface, and each successive refinement step yields a more accurate approximation. Eventually the progressive approach will yield the same results as the original method. The advantage stems from the fact that it is possible to render an image after each refinement step, and a viewer is usually satisfied with an image long before the algorithm reaches the final refinement step.

To accurately portray such surfaces as hair or burnished metal, Kajiya generalized the Cook-Torrance illumination model to derive an anisotropic illumination model whose reflective properties are not symmetric about the surface normal. In this model Kajiya extended bump mapping to perturb the tangent in addition to perturbing the surface normal [KAJI 86]. These can be used to form a coordinate system that determines the orientation of the surface relative to the light source.

When nominating Heckbert's raytracing article [HECK 87], one researcher wrote, "I will never forget this presentation". As one of the jury members commented, "There's always room for JELL-O."

Modeling
Before software can create an image, a user must *model* or specify a representation of the objects that will appear in the image. The modeling techniques presented here all address some aspects of specifying or modifying the shape or behavior of an object.

For modeling objects, Bicubic B-spline surface patches offer significant advantages over polygon meshes. They are more compact, more manipulable and require less storage. They also provide an arbitrary level of precision in defining an object. A surface patch can be subdivided into four subpatches, and the subdivision process can be repeated until the surface reaches a desired level of refinement. Care must be taken that adjoining patches in a surface are continuous in tangent and curvature. If the underlying control mesh is rectangular, this is not hard to achieve, but problems arise when the control mesh is not rectangular.

To address this issue, Catmull and Clark generalized the B-spline subdivision algorithm [CATM 78]. It still produced standard B-spline surfaces for rectangular meshes, but for nonrectangular meshes, it generated surfaces that reduced to standard B-spline surfaces except at a small number of points called extraordinary points.

Doo and Sabin characterized the behavior of surfaces in the neighborhood of these points and modified the subdivision computation to compensate [DOO 78]. As a result they eliminated the possibility of the appearance of flat spots and zero-radius curvatures.

The term "detail" can imply accuracy as in the case of modeling curved surfaces, but detail can also refer to the rich variety of irregularity found in such natural phenomena as mountain terrain and coastlines. Drawing on Mandelbrot's work, Fournier, Fussel and Carpenter created a visually satisfying approximation of fractional Brownian motion that required less time to compute than the exact calculation [FOUR 82]. Because the approach uses recursive subdivision to reach the desired level of detail, it obviates the need to store massive quantities of polygons. This early work with fractals formed the basis for later simulations of fire, clouds, grass and a variety of other natural phenomena.

Fire and smoke differ from mountains in that they are not rigid and they change substantially in a relatively short time. Reeves developed particle systems to model such fuzzy, ephemeral objects [REEV 83]. Objects are defined as clouds of primitive particles. Particles are not static, but can change form and position. This approach generates a high level of detail without requiring large amount of human design time. Further, it facilitates easy motion blurring, and because it is procedurally based, can generate detail to any specified level. This method formed the basis for creating the Genesis Demo sequence from the movie *Star Trek II: The Wrath of Khan*.

The last paper in this group presented a set of modeling operations that were cheap to compute, easy to implement, and offered a user an easier way to specify some commonly-used deformations. Barr extended the use of the conventional transformation matrix to perform twisting, bending and tapering [BARR 84]. His method had the advantage of providing a speedy way of computing the surface normals of the deformed object.

Animation

In all likelihood future historians will declare animation to be the most significant art form of the twentieth century. The past three decades have seen computer animation rise from modest albeit exciting beginnings to a level of excellence equaling the best of conventional animation.

In 1972 Catmull presented a groundbreaking animation of a smooth shaded hand that lasted a little more than a minute [CATM 72]. To express complexities of movement, he created a scripting language that allowed a user to specify concurrent motions. This language specified events in terms of a start frame, a stop frame and an action taking place during the interval. In addition to expressing concurrent motion, the language provided a user the opportunity to specify accelerations and decelerations that imparted a more natural quality to the animation.

Parke created the first computer animation of a human face [PARK 72]. Since no appropriate three-dimensional input devices existed at the time, he captured the complex structure by painting a set of lines on an assistant's face. He took photographs from the front and the side as the assistant assumed a series of different facial expressions. He measured the position of each polygon vertex as it appeared in the two photographs, and from this he derived a three-dimensional polygon model for each expression. To animate the face, he interpolated the position of the polygon vertices.

When the goal is achieving the kind of fluidity seen in the best of conventional animation, it is too cumbersome to rely on analytic functions to specify motion. Burtnyk and Wein realized this and drew upon the traditions of conventional animation to introduce the keyframe technique [BURT 76]. This allowed computer animators the freedom to express motion by means of a few important or "key" frames. A computer then took on the responsibility of generating the in-between frames. To make life easier for the animator, Burtnyk and Wein introduced the use of a stick figure, or skeleton representation of an object. An animator could develop complex motion by manipulating the skeleton. Peter Foldes used Burtnyk and Wein's work to create the movies *Visage* and *Hunger*.

Although the keyframe technique helped simplify the process of specifying motion, animating a human figure via keyframes can be fiendishly complex. Girard and Maciejewski simplified the process of animating legged figures through inverse kinematics, which capitalizes on the inherent limitations of motion in jointed figures [GIRA 85]. It gave animators a new way to control motion at higher levels of complexity and abstraction. Girard used this technique in his movie *Eurhythmy*.

Lasseter opened up new possibilities for creative expression when he brought the traditions of two-dimensional character animation to the technology of three-dimensional computer animation [LASS 87]. He emphasized that the venerable, time-tested principles of hand animation are as essential as the physically based rules for motion, lighting and shading. In his paper, he used figures from the animations *Luxo, Jr.* and *Wally B.* to demonstrate such principles as squash and stretch, anticipation, staging, appeal and personality.

Reynolds gave animators a new potential for creativity when he harnessed the dramatic impact found in the surging motion of a school of fish or a flock of birds [REYN 87]. Before his work on flocking behavior, animators were forced to specify a path of motion for every object, which discouraged experimentation with large numbers of figures. His innovation was to treat each object as an actor imbued with the ability to set its own path of navigation according to a few simple rules. This self-organizing behavior allowed animators to create enormously complex motion without the tedium of specifying it explicitly. The 1987 film *Stanley and Stella: Breaking the Ice* by Wahrman shows several examples of flocking behavior.

Architecture
Architecture is what puts the term "computer" into "computer graphics." In the span of less than forty years, the state of the art has progressed from black ink on white paper to full color interactive displays. This constitutes one of the most exciting aspects of technology development in the latter half of the twentieth century.

In 1968 Romney, Watkins and Evans created a renderer capable of hidden surface removal, perspective scaling and shading [ROMN 68]. It created shaded images of solid objects without the aid of a frame buffer or z-buffer. The software drew images one scan line at a time, starting at the top of an image and working its way down. While drawing a line, it considered only those polygon edges that intersected with the current scan line. Speed also came from capitalizing on scan line coherence, which is the quality of similarity between two adjacent scan lines. This system ran on a Univac 1108 connected to a DEC PDP-8 that acted as the display controller. The PDP-8 sent intensity information through a DAC (digital-to-analog converter) to a Tektronix 453 oscilloscope. A camera captured the image as a time exposure.

In Romney's rendering system, the screen refresh responsibilities were offloaded from the main computer and placed on a simpler, cheaper auxiliary computer. Myers and Sutherland noted that this configuration was part of the "wheel of reincarnation" for the design of display processors [MYER 68]. A small simple processor is added to reduce the computational load of the main computer. Over subsequent design iterations, the small processor grows in capacity and complexity until it seems reasonable to offload some of its responsibility onto a small simple processor.

While Virtual Reality came into its own in the 1990s, it got its start in 1968, when Sutherland created a three-dimensional head mount display [SUTH 68]. The display system consisted of two miniature cathode ray tubes (CRTs) positioned in front of a viewer's left and right eyes. The CRTs displayed a pair of stereo images to the user. A sensor tracked head movements and sent the motion information to the computer. As the user moved about in an environment, the images on the CRTs changed to reflect the current position and direction of the viewer's head.

Due to severe constraints of real-time rendering, early interactive systems including Sutherland's head-mount display were limited to drawing wireframe renderings. In 1971, Noll described the use of core memory to store a digital representation of an image [NOLL 71]. This first use of a frame buffer freed researchers from the necessity of rendering images in real time, and it become possible to explore slower, but more sophisticated rendering algorithms.

As memory continued to drop in price, Kajiya, Sutherland and Cheadle used hardware to implement the z-buffer algorithm introduced by Catmull [KAJI 75]. Having a hardware z-buffer not only made rendering faster, but also removed the need to implement one of the more complex surface algorithms.

Fuchs incorporated both a frame buffer and a z-buffer in his multiprocessor graphics system, which was the first to partition an image into rectangular regions and distribute them to multiple processors [FUCH 77]. Despite the fact that the image was partitioned, object coherence could still be utilized to reduce the required number of calculations. Because multiple processors labored in parallel to determine visibility and shading, the images could be rendered in a fraction of the time required by a uniprocessor system.

Clark's Geometry Engine constituted an important turn of the wheel of reincarnation in that it shouldered the bulk of the computational load for rendering, thus freeing a CPU for other work [CLAR 82]. The Geometry Engine was a special-purpose VLSI processor capable of processing floating-point vectors. It provided three of the operations essential to rendering: matrix operations, clipping and conversion to device coordinates. Equally important was the fact that the entire graphics pipeline had been implemented on a small number of VLSI chips, thus paving the way to a startling jump in the performance/price ratio.

Rendering from Samples
It is not always practical or even possible to define a model in terms of surfaces. In the case of medical imaging applications, raw data sets are not comprised of polygons but of n-dimensional arrays of numbers. In order to visualize this data, one must first determine a geometric interpretation of the data. Another application of sample rendering is as a means of reducing the computation demands of a project. It offers a method of summarizing geometric information from a potentially massive number of polygons and avoids the time requirements of the brute force approach.

Blinn and Newell spearheaded this approach when they extended the texture mapping idea first presented by Catmull to create the environment mapping method [BLIN 76]. Environment mapping simulates specular reflections among objects without the need to compute them explicitly. Conceptually, the scene surrounding a reflective object is painted onto the surface of a large sphere that surrounds the object. Instead of computing a specular reflection directly from the scene's geometry, environment mapping finds the corresponding color on the surrounding sphere.

Another early example of rendering from samples is color quantization, which is the process of representing a full-color image with a very small number of colors. The resulting quantized image should match the original in appearance but will require far fewer system resources for storage and display. The challenge is to choose the colors that will best represent the original image. Heckbert's color quantizer was the first such algorithm where color choice was based on an error-minimization criterion [HECK 82].

Lorensen and Cline's marching cubes algorithm was a boon to the medical profession because it was the first simple, robust method for extracting isosurface models from three-dimensional medical data [LORE 87]. Once it had extracted polygons, conventional rendering methods created images of the selected surface in isolation. The marching cubes algorithm gave doctors and researchers the ability to select tissue types and see them clearly without interference, something which had been difficult or impossible to do with previous methods.

Porter and Duff's compositing technique drew its inspiration from traditional cel animation, where foreground figures are rendered separately from the background, and the final image is created by compositing foreground and background together when the frame is shot [PORT 84]. To achieve this effect digitally, Porter and Duff created images whose pixels had four elements. In addition to the conventional RGB information, a fourth element, called the alpha channel, contained matte information. The matte information and a set of compositing operators provide a wide range of possibilities, including darkening, attenuation and transparency.

In contrast to Lorensen and Cline's approach, Drebin, Carpenter and Hanrahan did not attempt to extract surfaces from three-dimensional data sets but capitalized instead on the alpha channel concept of Porter and Duff [DREB 88]. This approach assigns a color and opacity to each voxel. Opacity is analogous to the alpha channel data of Porter and Duff's algorithm. The second step of Drebin's method treats each two-dimensional slice of voxels as a layer and creates an image from a composite of the layers.

Beier and Neely's morphing algorithm also operates on two-dimensional images, but the goal is to give the illusion that one image is transforming itself into another over time [BEIE 92]. It is a combination of compositing, cross-dissolve and warping, which distorts one image into another. Lines drawn by an animator in the 'before' and 'after' images guide the morph. The result is a convincing animation at a fraction of the cost of rendering three-dimensional models.

Chen and Williams' innovation of image-based rendering is based partly on Beier and Neely's morphing technique and is capable of producing walkthroughs of static environments at a cost that is basically independent of scene complexity [CHEN 93]. Image-based rendering uses morphing to create animated walkthroughs of three-dimensional scenes from a few pre-existing images. The intermediate frames derived by morphing can be used to approximate three-dimensional transformations of the scene.

Environment mapping was the first algorithm that reduced rendering time by summarizing scene geometry in two-dimensional images. In a certain sense, this concept is brought to its logical extreme by image-based rendering.

Foundations
This last group of papers discusses innovations and understandings of interactive technique. Some of these are so ubiquitous that today's computer graphics practitioners benefit from them in their everyday routines.

Sutherland's Sketchpad demonstrated the exciting promise of interactive computer graphics [SUTH 63]. Before Sketchpad, users expressed object geometry by typing numbers on a keyboard and then waited to see the result as a paper plot. In contrast, Sketchpad gave users the ability to express geometric shapes by positioning a light pen at the face of a cathode ray tube. Results were immediately visible, enabling a user to accomplish in minutes a variety of tasks that had previously required hours to complete. Some of the innovations presented in this paper included the concept of instancing from a master object, rubber band lines, zooming, grouping, ungrouping and constraint-based animation. Sutherland also demonstrated the feasibility of applying interactive computer graphics to a variety of applications that ranged from circuit design to animation.

Newman was the first to model the interaction of user and application as an event-driven finite state machine [NEWM 68]. User interface designers still use this approach to specify screen transitions, and all of today's application development environments support programmer-written "event handlers". Another important idea introduced in this paper was the concept of device independence, which looks beyond the characteristics of a physical input device and classifies user input based on its purpose.

Foley and Wallace took the concept of categorizing user input even further and presented a taxonomy of logical input devices including pick (select), button, locator and evaluator [FOLE 74]. Their paper surveyed the lore of man-machine communication and presented a foundation to encourage the development of design rules for effective interactive systems. They discussed the qualities that can facilitate full user involvement and they also listed impediments that cause user boredom, panic, frustration, confusion and discomfort. This is one of the first papers to emphasize how important it is for designers to "know the user."

Many early interactive graphics efforts were in computer-aided design and other technically oriented fields, but the efforts of Alvy Ray Smith made computer graphics more accessible to artist and graphic designers [SMIT 82]. He designed his Paint program to be as similar as possible to the experience of applying actual paints to a physical canvas. His system allowed for a choice of brush size, shape and color; it had menus that popped out from the borders of the canvas; it provided various fill types and a facility to create custom brushes. Paint allowed a user to create and save custom palettes and gave users the chance to user a color system other than RGB for specifying color.

Conclusion
Newton once wrote, "If I have seen further it is by standing on the shoulders of giants." This book contains monumental pioneering efforts of many researchers. May it help you to see far into the future.

An algorithm is given for computer control of a digital plotter. The algorithm may be programmed without multiplication or division instructions and is efficient with respect to speed of execution and memory utilization.

Algorithm for computer control of a digital plotter
by J. E. Bresenham

This paper describes an algorithm for computer control of a type of digital plotter that is now in common use with digital computers.[1]

The plotter under consideration is capable of executing, in response to an appropriate pulse, any one of the eight linear movements shown in Figure 1. Thus, the plotter can move linearly from a point on a mesh to any adjacent point on the mesh. A typical mesh size is 1/100th of an inch.

The data to be plotted are expressed in an (x, y) rectangular coordinate system which has been scaled with respect to the mesh; i.e., the data points lie on mesh points and consequently have integral coordinates.

It is assumed that the data include a sufficient number of appropriately selected points to produce a satisfactory representation of the curve by connecting the points with line segments, as illustrated in Figure 2. In Figure 3, the line segment connecting

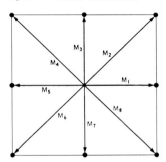

Figure 1 Plotter movements

Figure 2 Curve defined by linear segments joining data points

Reprinted by permission from *IBM Systems Journal* copyright 1965 by Intenational Business Machines Corporation

Figure 3 Sequence of plotter movements

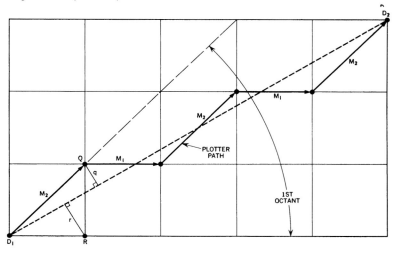

the two adjacent data points $D_1(x_1, y_1)$ and $D_2(x_2, y_2)$ is shown on the mesh, drawn on an enlarged scale. Also shown is the path actually taken by the plotter in accordance with the algorithm. In each instance, the mesh point nearest the desired line segment is selected. For example, since Q is closer to the line segment than R, Q is chosen as the second mesh point in the path taken by the plotter in approximating the desired segment joining D_1 and D_2.

algorithm for first octant

In the first case to be considered, it is assumed that D_2 lies in the first octant, relative to a rectangular coordinate system obtained by translation of the origin to D_1. It is apparent that the plotter movement can be accomplished by a sequence of moves involving only M_1 and M_2, as illustrated in Figure 3.

In Figure 4, an (a, b) coordinate system obtained by translation of the origin to D_1 is shown. Consequently, the new coordinates of D_2 are $(\Delta a, \Delta b) = (x_2 - x_1, y_2 - y_1)$.

When the plotter has progressed to the point P_{i-1}, as indicated in Figure 4, the next movement is either M_1 (to the point R_i) if $r_i < q_i$, or M_2 (to the point Q_i) if $r_i \geq q_i$.

It follows from similar triangles that $r'_i - q'_i$ has the same sign as $r_i - q_i$. Since the segment $D_1 D_2$ lies in the first octant, $\Delta a > 0$. Thus, $\nabla_i = (r'_i - q'_i)\Delta a$ also has the same sign as $r_i - q_i$ and may be used for computational convenience in selecting the appropriate movement, either M_1 or M_2. Later in the paper, ∇_i is shown to satisfy the recursive relation:

$$\left. \begin{aligned} \nabla_1 &= 2\Delta b - \Delta a \\ \nabla_{i+1} &= \begin{cases} \nabla_i + 2\Delta b - 2\Delta a & \text{if } \nabla_i \geq 0 \\ \nabla_i + 2\Delta b & \text{if } \nabla_i < 0 \end{cases} \end{aligned} \right\}, \quad (1)$$

where

$$\Delta a = x_2 - x_1, \quad \Delta b = y_2 - y_1. \quad (2)$$

The values of ∇_i computed by means of (1) and (2) are used to determine the movement of the plotter:

$$\text{if } \begin{cases} \nabla_i < 0, & \text{execute } m_1 \\ \nabla_i \geq 0, & \text{execute } m_2 \end{cases}, \quad i = 1, \cdots, \Delta a, \quad (3)$$

where

$$m_1 = M_1 \quad \text{and} \quad m_2 = M_2. \quad (4)$$

Expressions (1), (2), (3), and (4) constitute the algorithm for the present case. For other octants, the right members of each equality in (2) and (4) must be modified.

Before indicating this modification, the recursive relation (1) is shown to hold. The notation employed in Figure 4 is as follows: $(a_{i-1}, \hat{b}_{i-1})$ is used to denote the coordinates of P_{i-1}. Consequently, the coordinates of R_i and Q_i are, respectively, $(a_i, \lfloor b_i \rfloor)$ and $(a_i, \lceil b_i \rceil)$, where "$\lfloor \ \rfloor$" and "$\lceil \ \rceil$" are used to denote the *floor* and *ceiling* operators.[2] Denoting the ordinate of S_i by b_i, the coordinates of S_i are (a_i, b_i).

proof of the recursive relation

This notation is used to rewrite the expression for ∇_i:

$$\nabla_i = (r'_i - q'_i)\Delta a = [(b_i - \lfloor b_i \rfloor) - (\lceil b_i \rceil - b_i)]\Delta a.$$

By noting that $b_i = (\Delta b/\Delta a)a_i$,

$$\nabla_i = 2a_i \Delta b - (\lfloor b_i \rfloor + \lceil b_i \rceil)\Delta a.$$

Since the line segment $D_1 D_2$ lies in the first octant, $a_i = a_{i-1} + 1$. By definition, $\lceil b_i \rceil = \hat{b}_{i-1} + 1$ and $\lfloor b_i \rfloor = \hat{b}_{i-1}$. These relations are used to rewrite the latter expression for ∇_i in a form free of a_i and b_i:

$$\nabla_i = 2a_{i-1}\Delta b - 2\hat{b}_{i-1}\Delta a + 2\Delta b - \Delta a.$$

Figure 4 Notation for the algorithm

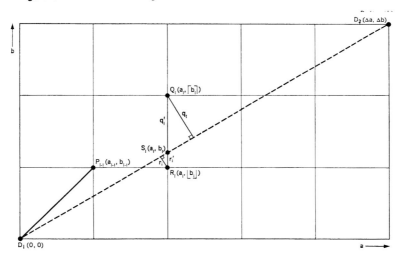

Applying the initial condition for the coordinates of P_0, $a_0 = 0$ and $\hat{b}_0 = 0$,

$$\nabla_1 = 2\Delta b - \Delta a.$$

If $\nabla_i \geq 0$,

$$\hat{b}_i = \hat{b}_{i-1} + 1,$$

so that

$$\nabla_{i+1} = 2(a_{i-1} + 1)\Delta b - 2(\hat{b}_{i-1} + 1)\Delta a + 2\Delta b - \Delta a$$
$$= \nabla_i + 2\Delta b - 2\Delta a.$$

If $\nabla_i < 0$,

$$\hat{b}_i = \hat{b}_{i-1},$$

so that

$$\nabla_{i+1} = 2(a_{i-1} + 1)\Delta b - 2\hat{b}_i\Delta a + 2\Delta b - \Delta a$$
$$= \nabla_i + 2\Delta b.$$

Thus (1) has been shown to hold.

other octants   The second data point has been assumed to be in the first octant with respect to the first data point. If the second data point lies in another octant, an (a, b) rectangular coordinate system is again chosen with origin at the first data point, but with the axes oriented individually for each octant, as shown in Figure 5. Directions associated with the plotter movements m_1 and m_2 are also indicated. This information is summarized in the left columns of Table 1 together with the assignments made to m_1 and m_2. Thus, the variants of Equations (1) and (4) have been specified for each of the eight octants, and the reader may verify that, in conjunction with (2) and (3) as previously stated, they comprise a correct formulation for the general case.

To complete the algorithm, a computational procedure is needed to determine the applicable octant for an arbitrary pair of data points so that the appropriate forms of (2) and (4) can be determined. The form of (2) depends on the sign of $|\Delta x| - |\Delta y|$.

Table 1   Determination of form of Equations 2 and 4

Δx	Δy	$|\Delta x| - |\Delta y|$	OCT	Δa	Δb	X	Y	Z	m_1	F	m_2	G
≥ 0	≥ 0	≥ 0	1	$|\Delta x|$	$|\Delta y|$	1	1	1	M_1	(1, 0, 0, 0)	M_2	(1, 0, 0, 0)
≥ 0	≥ 0	< 0	2	$|\Delta y|$	$|\Delta x|$	1	1	0	M_3	(0, 1, 0, 0)	M_2	(1, 0, 0, 0)
≥ 0	< 0	≥ 0	8	$|\Delta x|$	$|\Delta y|$	1	0	1	M_1	(1, 0, 0, 0)	M_8	(0, 0, 0, 1)
≥ 0	< 0	< 0	7	$|\Delta y|$	$|\Delta x|$	1	0	0	M_7	(0, 0, 0, 1)	M_8	(0, 0, 0, 1)
< 0	≥ 0	≥ 0	4	$|\Delta x|$	$|\Delta y|$	0	1	1	M_5	(0, 0, 1, 0)	M_4	(0, 1, 0, 0)
< 0	≥ 0	< 0	3	$|\Delta y|$	$|\Delta x|$	0	1	0	M_3	(0, 1, 0, 0)	M_4	(0, 1, 0, 0)
< 0	< 0	≥ 0	5	$|\Delta x|$	$|\Delta y|$	0	0	1	M_5	(0, 0, 1, 0)	M_6	(0, 0, 1, 0)
< 0	< 0	< 0	6	$|\Delta y|$	$|\Delta x|$	0	0	0	M_7	(0, 0, 0, 1)	M_6	(0, 0, 1, 0)

Figure 5 Axes orientation

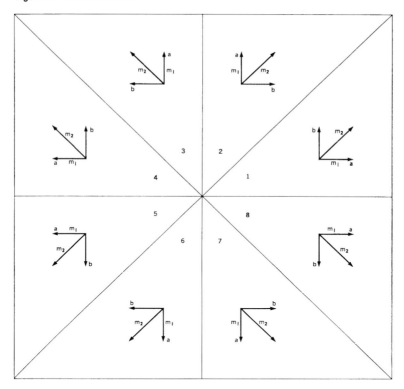

To find the form of (4), Boolean variables X, Y, and Z, corresponding to Δx, Δy, and $|\Delta x| - |\Delta y|$, are introduced. As shown in Table 1, these variables assume the value 0 or 1, depending on whether or not the correspondent is negative. To determine the assignment of m_1, the function

$$F(X, Y, Z) = (XZ, Y\bar{Z}, \bar{X}Z, \bar{Y}\bar{Z}),$$

found by inspection of Table 1, is introduced. Correspondence between values assumed by F and the assignment of m_1 is indicated by columns headed F and m_1. Similarly,

$$G(X, Y) = (XY, \bar{X}Y, \bar{X}\bar{Y}, X\bar{Y})$$

is used in conjunction with the G- and m_2-columns of Table 1 to make the appropriate assignment to m_2.

concluding remarks

The algorithm can be programmed without the use of multiplication or division. It was found that 333 core locations were sufficient for an IBM 1401 program (used to control an IBM 1627). The average computation time between successive incrementations was approximately 1.5 milliseconds.

A functionally similar algorithm reported in the literature[3] is described as requiring 513 core positions and 2.4 milliseconds between successive incrementations.[4]

ACKNOWLEDGMENT

The suggestions of the author's colleagues, D. Clark and A. Hoffman, were of considerable assistance.

CITED REFERENCES AND FOOTNOTES

1. This paper is based on "An incremental algorithm for digital plotting," presented by the author at the ACM National Conference at Denver, Colorado, on August 30, 1963.
2. The *floor* ($\lfloor\ \rfloor$) and *ceiling* ($\lceil\ \rceil$) operators are defined as follows: $\lfloor x \rfloor$ denotes the greatest integer not exceeding x, and $\lceil x \rceil$ denotes the smallest integer not exceeded by x. This notation was introduced by Iverson; see, for example: K. E. Iverson, "Programming notation in systems design," *IBM Systems Journal* **2**, 117 (1963).
3. F. G. Stockton, Algorithm 162, XMOVE PLOTTING, *Communications of the ACM* **6**, Number 4, April 1963. Certification appears in **6**, Number 5, May 1963.
4. F. G. Stockton, *Plotting of Computer Output*, Bulletin No. 139, California Computer Products, May 1963.

BE VISION, A Package of IBM 7090 FORTRAN Programs to Draw Orthographic Views of Combinations of Plane and Quadric Surfaces

RUTH A. WEISS

Bell Telephone Laboratories, Inc., Murray Hill, New Jersey

Abstract. BE VISION is a package of FORTRAN programs for drawing orthographic views of combinations of plane and quadric surfaces. As input, the package takes rectangular coordinate equations specifying the surfaces plus a three-angle specification of the viewing direction. Output is a drawing on the Stromberg Carlson 4020 Microfilm Recorder. Many views of one scene may be obtained simply by changing the viewpoint.

The various subroutines of the package and their functions are described in this paper. It also gives numerous examples of pictures that were produced by BE VISION. The package has been in use since April 1964.

I. *Introduction*

The choice of quadric surfaces for the general program was made for practical and esthetic reasons. While there are many geometrical figures consisting of planes alone, the vast majority of objects in the real world contain some curved surfaces. A program for drawing pictures would not be very useful if it did not at least include a provision for the simplest of these, namely quadric surfaces. In drawing the curves of the picture it was found that a great many calculations for each point had to be made. If surfaces of higher degree than two were considered, the storage space and the machine time used would become too large to be practical; however, the program for drawing quadrics has proved versatile enough to produce some quite complicated pictures.

A quadric surface is the locus of the general second-degree equation in three variables:

$$Q(x, y, z) = a_1 x^2 + a_2 y^2 + a_3 z^2 + b_1 yz + b_2 xz + b_3 xy + c_1 x + c_2 y + c_3 z + d = 0.$$

The program can handle any Q including planes. To handle complex objects, not only complete surfaces but also bounded quadric surfaces were included in the vocabulary of the program. Indeed, since many quadrics, such as planes or cylinders, are unbounded, some limits must be provided to obtain a picture at all. Thus, the program accepts two kinds of surfaces as input; namely, (1) the principal equations, which define the surfaces themselves, and, (2) the bounding inequalities which limit the extension of the surfaces of type (1). The type (1) and type (2) equations are alike in that they are of the same form (plane or quadric surfaces), but they also have these important differences:

(a) *A principal surface* may stand alone without boundaries, is defined by an equation, is a visible, opaque surface, and has visible intersections with other principal surfaces and with its own bounds.

(b) *A bounding surface* must be associated with a principal surface, is defined by an inequality, is an invisible, transparent surface, and has visible intersections only with its associated principal surfaces.

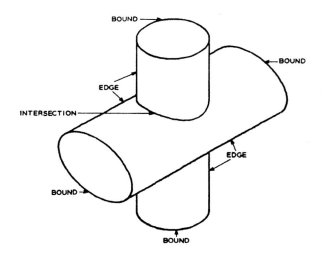

Fig. 1. Intersecting cylinders

The lines appearing in a drawing are of three kinds: the intersection of two surfaces, the intersection of a surface and one of its bounds, and the extremal points of a surface which are not a boundary, referred to hereafter as intersections, bounds and edges, respectively (see Figure 1).

No matter which of the three kinds of curves is being calculated, its coordinates are obtained numerically by incrementing one of the three variables x, y or z from a minimum to a maximum value and solving for the other two; therefore before anything else can be done these minima and maxima have to be found.

The intersections and bounds of a picture remain the same for any view; edges do not. All the intersections and bounds are calculated and stored as ordered lists of the coordinates of the curves. When a particular view is requested, the edges are calculated afresh. Then the lists are tested one at a time. Each point is tested for visibility. If two adjacent points are visible, a segment is drawn connecting their projections in the picture plane.

All the illustrations in this paper were drawn with BE VISION except for labels, arrows and dotted lines.

II. General Explanation of the Program

A. *General Notation*. The following notations are used throughout this paper.

The equation of the general quadric surface is:

$$Q(x, y, z) = a_1x^2 + a_2y^2 + a_3z^2 + b_1yz + b_2xz + b_3xy + c_1x + c_2y + c_3z + d = 0.$$

The quadratic part of Q is:

$$q(x, y, z) = a_1x^2 + a_2y^2 + a_3z^2 + b_1yz + b_2xz + b_3xy.$$

The partial derivatives of Q are:

$$Q_x \equiv Q_1(x, y, z) = 2a_1x + b_3y + b_2z + c_1,$$
$$Q_y \equiv Q_2(x, y, z) = 2a_2y + b_3x + b_1z + c_2,$$
$$Q_z \equiv Q_3(x, y, z) = 2a_3z + b_2x + b_1y + c_3.$$

Two intersecting quadric surfaces are:

$$Q'(x, y, z) = a_1x^2 + a_2y^2 + a_3z^2 + b_1yz + b_2xz + b_3xy + c_1x + c_2y + c_3z + d = 0,$$

$$Q''(x, y, z) = A_1x^2 + A_2y^2 + A_3z^2 + B_1yz + B_2xz + B_3xy + C_1x + C_2y + C_3z + D = 0.$$

B. *Minima and Maxima.* A minimum and a maximum value for each of the three variables, x, y, z must be calculated for every surface in the picture. Any portion of a curve on a surface will be discarded with no further investigations, if it lies outside the limits for that coordinate on that surface.

These limits are obtained either from the bounding equations provided as input or from the natural bounds of the surface itself or from a combination of these two. The simplest bounds which may be placed on a surface are the six inequalities $x_{min} \leq x \leq x_{max}$, $y_{min} \leq y \leq y_{max}$ and $z_{min} \leq z \leq z_{max}$. If any of these is provided as input, it is left untouched. If a minimum or a maximum of a variable has *not* been provided as input, it is obtained in the following way: The equation of the surface itself and the equations of all its bounds are examined for natural limits. From these the lowest value of a variable is taken as its minimum and the highest value of a variable is taken as its maximum.

Let us take one of the variables, say x, and show how its natural limits are determined.

Case 1. If, for example,

$$Q = f(x) = ax + c = 0,$$

then $x_{min} = -c/a = x_{max}$.

Case 2. If

$$Q = f(x) = ax^2 + bx + c = 0,$$

then x_{min} and x_{max}, respectively, equal the lesser and greater of $-b \pm \sqrt{(b^2 - 4ac)}/2a$.

Case 3. If

$$Q = f(x, y) = a_1x^2 + a_2y^2 + b_3xy + c_1x + c_2y + d = 0,$$

the discriminant is set to 0 and solved for x:

$$(b_3x + c_2)^2 - 4a_2(a_1x^2 + c_1x + d) = 0 \tag{1}$$

where x_{min} is equal to the lesser of the roots of (1) and x_{max}, the greater of the roots of (1).

Case 4. If

$$Q = f(x, z) = a_1x^2 + a_3z^2 + b_2xz + c_1x + c_3z + d = 0,$$

the same process is used as was used for case 3.

Case 5. If

$$Q = f(x, y, z) = a_1x^2 + a_2y^2 + a_3z^2 + b_1yz + b_2xz + b_3xy + c_1x + c_2y + c_3z + d = 0,$$

the z discriminant is set to 0 and solved for y, the y discriminant is then set to 0 and solved for x. Then the two roots are x_{min} and x_{max}.

The x_{min} and x_{max} obtained by processes 3, 4 and 5 are not necessarily the actual minimum and maximum values of x for the surface Q. They *are* limits for the surface Q but they may well be the values between which the surface Q does not exist (this is the case for a hyperboloid of two sheets). This is useful information for determining visibility but it is not what is desired for minima and maxima. To forestall such cases where no natural limits exist, it is necessary for the user to supply clear limits to the program.

C. *Curves of Intersection.* An intersection or a bound is a curve of intersection of two quadric or planar surfaces, Q' and Q''. The points on a curve are obtained by varying one of the coordinates from its minimum to its maximum and solving the equations Q' and Q'' for the other two coordinates at each point. The minima and maxima of x, y and z for the curve are obtained by taking the larger minimum and the smaller maximum for each variable for Q' and Q''. Every point on the curve is tested for these bounds and eliminated if it does not lie within them. However, these bounds only enclose a rectangular parallelepiped and are not stringent enough. Each point must also be tested to make sure it meets the inequality requirements of all the bounds of the surface or surfaces. If a point does not fall within bounds, it is flagged as invisible.

If Q' and Q'' contain the same variable in the second degree, there will be more than one branch of the curve of intersection. In the case where Q' and Q'' contain at least two of the same variables in the second degree, we wish to eliminate one of the variables, say x, between the equations and get one equation $F(y, z) = 0$.

By using Sylvester's method we obtain an eliminant which furnishes a necessary and sufficient condition that the two equations have a root in common.

If Sylvester's method is applied to the equations for the quadric surfaces, namely, $Q'(x, y, z) = 0$ and $Q''(x, y, z) = 0$ with

$$Q'(x,y,z) = a_1 x^2 + a_2 y^2 + a_3 z^2 + b_3 xy + b_2 xz + b_1 yz + c_1 x + c_2 y + c_3 z + d = 0$$

and

$$Q''(x,y,z) = A_1 x^2 + A_2 y^2 + A_3 z^2 + B_3 xy + B_2 xz + B_1 yz + C_1 x + C_2 y + C_3 z + D = 0,$$

the resultant becomes

$$\begin{vmatrix} a_1 & (b_3 y + b_2 z + c_1) & (a_2 y^2 + a_3 z^2 + b_1 yz + c_3 z + d) & 0 \\ 0 & a_1 & (b_3 y + b_2 z + c_1) & (a_2 y^2 + a_3 z^2 + b_1 yz + c_2 y + c_3 z + d) \\ A_1 & (B_3 y + B_2 z + C_1) & (A_2 y^2 + A_3 z^2 + B_1 yz + C_3 z + D) & 0 \\ 0 & A_1 & (B_3 y + B_2 z + C_1) & (A_2 y^2 + A_3 z^2 + B_1 yz + C_2 y + C_3 z + D) \end{vmatrix} = 0.$$

The value of this determinant is the required equation $F(y, z) = 0$. Either y or z, say z, is varied in increments of delta from its minimum to its maximum and substituted in $F = 0$. Since F is in general quartic [5], this gives the possibility of four real solutions for y at each value of z. Four separate lists are kept for these curves if they should exist. At each point, y and z are substituted in $Q' = 0$ and $Q'' = 0$ to get a solution for x; if $Q' = 0$ and $Q'' = 0$ have common real roots, these roots are entered into the lists.

It may occur that a curve does not extend clear across from the lower to the upper limit of the varying coordinate. In this case two branches must terminate by joining instead of by running out of bounds. Unless the point of meeting appeared in the list for each branch, a gap would occur at the junction. This point of meeting is calculated by using one of the methods 3, 4 or 5, for determining natural bounds as explained in the section on minima and maxima.

The subroutine for calculating intersections contains many subsections for special cases. It was divided in this way to avoid unnecessarily lengthy calculations.

D. *Edges* [1]. In general any quadric surface will have visible curves (herein known as edges) which are not intersections with other surfaces. Every surface is tested for second degree terms to find these extremal points which are not a boundary. These extremal points are points at which the line of view is tangent to the quadric surface. The following theorem is used to obtain these points.

THEOREM. *If the point (α, β, γ) lies on the quadric surface $Q(x, y, z)$, the line $x = \alpha + \lambda s, y = \beta + \mu s, z = \gamma + \nu s$ will be the tangent to the surface at the point (α, β, γ) if and only if its direction cosines, λ, μ and ν satisfy the equation*

$$\lambda Q_1(\alpha, \beta, \gamma) + \mu Q_2(\alpha, \beta, \gamma) + \nu Q_3(\alpha, \beta, \gamma) = 0,$$

where Q_1, Q_2 and Q_3 are the partial derivatives of Q with respect to x, y and z respectively.

If the line is the line of view and its direction cosines are λ_0, μ_0, ν_0, and if $Q(x, y, z)$ is the surface for which an edge is wanted and (x, y, z) is the point we are looking for, the equation to be solved is

$$\lambda_0(2a_1 x + b_3 y + b_2 z + c_1) + \mu_0(b_3 x + 2a_2 y + b_1 z + c_2)$$
$$+ \nu_0(b_2 x + b_1 y + 2a_3 z + c_3) = 0,$$
$$x(2a_1 \lambda_0 + b_3 \mu_0 + b_2 \nu_0) + y(b_3 \lambda_0 + 2a_2 \mu_0 + b_1 \nu_0)$$
$$+ z(b_2 \lambda_0 + b_1 \mu_0 + 2a_3 \nu_0) + (c_1 \lambda_0 + c_2 \mu_0 + c_3 \nu_0) = 0.$$

This gives us a linear equation in x, y and z. We already have a second degree equation (the equation of the surface) and we solve these numerically for edges just as we did for intersections.

E. *Visibility* [1]. When considering the feasibility of writing BE VISION, one of the first problems to be encountered was that of deciding whether a line is visible or not. For a picture with a fixed number of known surfaces and a predetermined view, large sections of curves are known to be visible or invisible; but the whole point of writing BE VISION was to have a general program for drawing *any* reasonable number of quadric surfaces from *any* view. In order to decide on the visibility of a curve (say of the intersection of surfaces Q' and Q'') or any arbitrarily small part of that curve, all the surfaces including Q' and Q'' have to be examined to see if any of them hides it from view. (Two good examples of this difficulty can be seen in Figure 9, the ellipsoidal coordinates, and Figure 6c, an oblique view of Mickey Mouse.) Changing the angle of the picture plane even slightly may make a large difference in the amount of visibility of a curve (as much as from completely visible to completely invisible or vice versa as in Figure 2). To assure an accurate and general way of deciding on the visibility of a curve, the author chose the following method; namely, calculate it point by point and test each point against all the surfaces to see if any of them is hiding it from view. Unfortunately this is a time-consuming process.

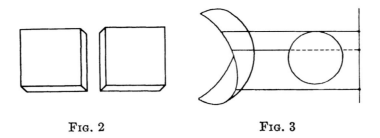

Fig. 2   Fig. 3

Suppose all the points of a curve have been calculated; that is, the x, y, z coordinates for each point are in storage in order. It is now necessary to decide which points are visible. BE VISION uses orthographic projection only, which means that all the lines of view are parallel. The direction cosines, λ, μ and ν of the lines of view are obtained from the input parameters of the picture plane (see Section IIF) and these are constant for one picture. By solving a quadratic equation it can be determined if a line through the point (x, y, z) with direction cosines λ, μ and ν (a) pierces a quadric surface in two places, (b) is tangent to the surface, or (c) does not touch the surface. However, this depends on whether there are (a) two real roots, (b) a double root, or (c) no real roots (Figure 3).

If there are real roots, the piercing points are calculated and tested to see if they actually exist; for they may have been cut off by a boundary. If they are real points, a simple inequality is used to determine whether either one lies nearer the picture plane than the point (x, y, z). This test is made against all the surfaces in the picture for each point (x, y, z) on the line. When two adjacent points in the list are visible they are connected. If a point P_n is visible and its adjacent point P_{n+1} is not visible, one twentieth of the difference between them is added to P_n until the first invisible point is found. The last visible point is then connected to P_n.

F. *Point of View.* In its canonical form the picture plane is assumed to be parallel to the y-z plane and the $\bar{x}$ and $\bar{y}$ axes of the picture plane, parallel to the y and z axes respectively.

Then if α is the azimuth of the vantage point measured counterclockwise from the x-axis about the vertical z-axis in the horizontal x-y plane, β is the elevation of the vantage point above the x-y plane, and γ is the counterclockwise rotational position of the picture about the vantage direction, the direction cosines of the line of view, λ, μ and ν and the coordinates, $\bar{x}$, $\bar{y}$ in the picture plane corresponding to the point x, y, z in three-space are derived from the three input angles α, β, γ in the following way:

$$\lambda = \cos\alpha\cos\beta, \qquad \mu = \sin\alpha\cos\beta, \qquad \nu = \sin\beta,$$

$$\bar{x} = x(-\sin\alpha\cos\gamma - \cos\alpha\sin\beta\sin\gamma) + y(\cos\alpha\cos\gamma - \sin\alpha\sin\beta\sin\gamma)$$
$$+ z(\cos\beta\sin\gamma),$$

$$\bar{y} = x(\sin\alpha\sin\gamma - \cos\alpha\sin\beta\cos\gamma) + y(-\cos\alpha\sin\gamma - \sin\alpha\sin\beta\cos\gamma)$$
$$+ z(\cos\beta\cos\gamma).$$

Figure 4 shows the orientation of the axes and the angles of the picture plane.

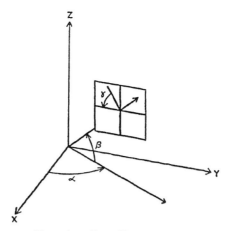

Fig. 4. Coordinate system

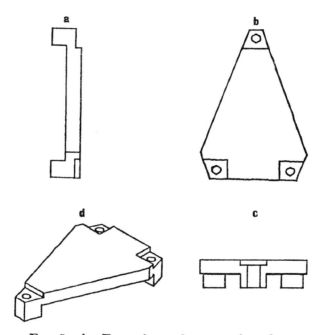

Fig. 5a-d. Four views of a mounting plate

III. *Discussion*

1. At the time BE VISION was written literature on the subject of drawing quadric surfaces was rather sketchy. The most important treatises on the subject of the analytic geometry of 3 dimensions did not cover such practical problems (for BE VISION) as which coordinate to vary for a curve, how to get the general numerical solution for the intersection of two quadric surfaces, or how to find the exact point at which the solution of the two equations becomes imaginary. These rules had to be derived and this fact undoubtedly made the subroutines which calculate the intersection of curves the most difficult to write.

More recently several papers have been written suggesting solutions to some of these problems. Luh and Krolak [6] use a pair of inequalities to obtain the intersection of a pair of quadric surfaces, but they do not explain how to get the exact end points of this intersection. Roberts [7, 8] has done extensive work in the field

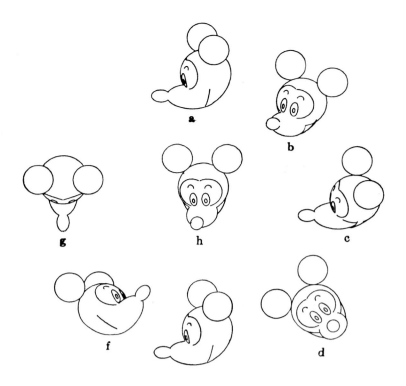

Fig. 6a–h (© Walt Disney)

of drawing 3-dimensional solids, but in his May 1965 paper he does not tackle the problem of the intersection of two quadric surfaces.

2. The roundoff error had to be bypassed if good points were not to be discarded (for instance, if the error made a point appear to be slightly behind a surface instead of in front of it). Every coordinate was given a tolerance limit when tested for its minimum or maximum or when tested for visibility. It would not be too intolerable to drop one point perhaps, but even this would leave a gap in the curve; there are cases, however, where a whole curve might be missed if, for example, one of the coordinates is a constant.

3. Right from the beginning it was obvious that machine time would be a problem. It takes time to calculate every single point of every curve, but it was necessary to do this because of the visibility problem. The time for calculating the points (a maximum of 1 millisecond per point and very much less than this where Q' and Q'' both are linear in all three variables) turned out to be surprisingly low. Even this time can be appreciable in a picture with several thousand points, however. The time for all the other operations necessary to get a picture takes anywhere from 3 to 15 times that for getting the points alone, depending on the number of surfaces involved. Most of this time is spent in testing for visibility.

4. The program is large. It occupies almost all of the approximately 60,000 octal locations available to a program running under the Bell Laboratories monitor, BESYS7. It includes the microfilm and mathematical functions subroutines but not the input-output which is included in BESYS7. The program can draw a picture with as many as 50 principal surfaces and a total of 180 principal and bounding surfaces. Experience has shown that this is a good ratio.

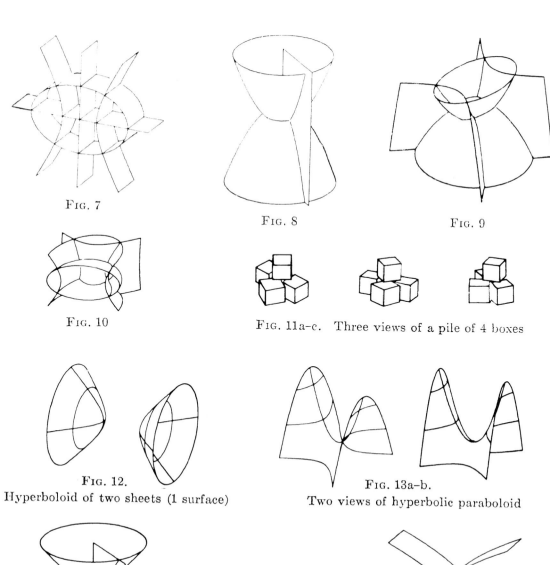

Fig. 7

Fig. 8

Fig. 9

Fig. 10

Fig. 11a–c. Three views of a pile of 4 boxes

Fig. 12.
Hyperboloid of two sheets (1 surface)

Fig. 13a–b.
Two views of hyperbolic paraboloid

Fig. 14

Fig. 15

Fig. 16

Fig. 17

Fig. 18

The subprogram which gets the curves of intersection is by far the longest and most complex, and it does not include the use of Sylvester's Method which is in a separate subprogram.

5. Originally BE VISION was rather difficult to use as this involved writing out all the equations of the surfaces in rectangular form. Now there is a picture drawing language written by M. D. McIlroy of Bell Telephone Laboratories, which greatly facilitates the task of specifying the surfaces. The two programs are available as a single system on a single run.

IV. *Pictures Produced by BE VISION*

This section contains a few examples of pictures produced by BE VISION (see Figures 5–18).

In the case of Mickey Mouse all the views were produced with the same equations of type (1) and type (2); only the picture plane parameters were changed for different views. Mickey's head and ears are spheres, his snout and nose are ellipsoids, and the jaw which connects the head and snout is a piece of an ellipsoid. All the intersections (as defined in the Introduction) were omitted to give the artistic effect (see Figures 6a–g).

The general equations for the various coordinate systems were taken from *Field Theory Handbook* [4]. They were chosen as illustrations of the many ways in which quadric surfaces can be combined.

All the bounds of the mounting plate were omitted. If they were included superfluous lines would be drawn between sections of the same surface. The subroutine for getting intersections ignores parallel planes. In general, if a picture represents a completely enclosed solid body whose surfaces consist of planes, it is not necessary and indeed undesirable to draw the bounds.

Acknowledgments. The author wishes to thank M. D. McIlroy for suggesting such a fascinating project and to thank M. D. McIlroy and H. O. Pollak for their encouragement and interest throughout its implementation.

RECEIVED APRIL, 1965; REVISED SEPTEMBER, 1965

REFERENCES

1. DRESDEN, A. *Solid Analytical Geometry and Determinants*. John Wiley & Sons, New York City, 1930.
2. ROEVER, W. H. Fundamental theorems of orthographic axonometry and their value in picturization. Washington U. Studies—New Series, St. Louis, Mo., 1941.
3. WEISNER, L. *Introduction to the Theory of Equations*. The MacMillan Co., New York, 1938.
4. MOON, P., AND SPENCER, D. E. *Field Theory Handbook; Including Coordinate Systems, Differential Equations and Their Solutions*. Springer-Verlag, Berlin, Gottinger, Heidelberg, 1961.
5. GRAY, M. C. QUARTC, a 7090 subroutine to get the roots of a quartic equation with real coefficients. Bell Telephone Laboratories Program Library, Murray Hill, N. J.
6. LUH, J. Y. S., AND KROLAK, R. J. A mathematical model for mechanical part description. *Comm. ACM 8* (Feb. 1965), 125–129.
7. ROBERTS, L. G. Machine perception of three-dimensional solids. Tech. Rep. No. 315, Lincoln Laboratory, MIT, May 1963.
8. ROBERTS, L. G. Homogeneous matrix representation and manipulation of N-dimensional constructs. MS-1405, Lincoln Laboratory, MIT, May 1965.

APPENDIX

Theorem Used to Determine Visibility

Theorem. (1) $Q(x, y, z) = 0$ is the equation of a quadric surface; (2) Q_1, Q_2, Q_3 are the partial derivatives of Q with respect to x, y, z; and (3) $q(x, y, z)$ is the part of Q which is homogeneous in the second degree. Then the parameter values of the points in which the line $x = \alpha + \lambda s$, $y = \beta + \mu s$, $z = \gamma + \nu s$ meets the quadric surface $Q(x, y, z) = 0$, are the roots of the equation

$$L_0 s^2 + 2L_1 s + L_2 = 0,$$

where

$$L_2 = Q(\alpha, \beta, \gamma),$$
$$L_1 = \tfrac{1}{2}[\lambda Q_1(\alpha, \beta, \gamma) + \mu Q_2(\alpha, \beta, \gamma) + \mu Q_3(\alpha, \beta, \gamma)],$$
$$L_0 = q(\lambda, \mu, \nu).$$

Corollary. The line $x = \alpha + \lambda s$, $y = \beta + \mu s$, $z = \gamma + \nu s$ (a) will meet the quadric surface Q in two distinct real points iff $L_1^2 - L_0 L_2 > 0$; (b) will be tangent to Q iff $L_1^2 = L_0 L_2$; and (c) will not have any real points in common with the surface iff $L_1^2 - L_0 L_2 < 0$.

If (α, β, γ) is a point being tested for visibility, (x, y, z) is one of the points of (a) above and λ_0, μ_0, ν_0 are the direction cosines of the line of view; then (α, β, γ) is hidden by the surface $Q(x, y, z) = 0$ and not drawn if

$$[(\lambda_0 \alpha + \mu_0 \beta + \nu_0 \gamma) - (\lambda_0 x + \mu_0 y + \nu_0 z)] < 0.$$

The notion of quantitative invisibility and the machine rendering of solids

by ARTHUR APPEL

International Business Machines Corporation
Yorktown Heights, New York

INTRODUCTION

Line drawings are the most common type of rendering used to convey geometrical description. This is due to the economy of preparing such drawings and the great information density obtainable. On a pure line drawing, that is where no attempt is made to specify or suggest shadows, tone or color, the lines rendered are either the intersection curves of surfaces or the contour curves of surfaces. The nature of these curves are adequately discussed in the literature[1] and in a previous report.[2] In order to convey a realistic impression of an object or an assembly of objects, the segments of lines which cannot be seen by an observer are not drawn or are drawn dashed. Without specification of visibility a drawing is ambiguous. This paper presents a recently developed scheme for the determination of visibility in a line drawing which enables comparitively high speed calculation and excellent resolution.

Visibility tests

There have been varied approaches to the determination of line drawing visibility. All schemes that have been implemented to date have assumed a limited vocabulary of solids or surfaces. E. E. Zajac and, more recently, P. Loutrel have discussed determining the hidden edges of a convex polyhedron.[3,4] By their techniques if the angle between the local line of sight and the outward normal to a face of a convex polyhedron is greater than 90° the face is declared invisible, and any line which is the intersection of two invisible faces is declared invisible. This is essentially a surface visibility test, where the basic element tested for visibility is a surface element. Such testing is valid only for convex polyhedra because on other types of solids a surface can be partially hidden. Because surface visibility testing applied to a single convex polyhedral object determine the visibility of a complete line segment, there is no resolution problem. The line connecting two vertex points is either completely visible or completely invisible. Also since only one test is made on every surface the time to determine visibility of an object does not vary significantly with the viewpoint. Schemes for handling convex polyhedra are very fast, usually requiring only two to five times as much calculation time as a wire frame drawing.*

L. G. Roberts has done the most advanced work for convex polyhedra by determining not only the hidden edges in a single object but also the segments of visible edges that are hidden by other objects in the same scene[5]. The very important aspect of his strategy was that two procedures are implemented.

Edges which are the intersection of hidden surfaces are determined and suppressed, and then all other edges are tested to determine to what extent they are hidden by other objects. The prime limitation of his work is that is is applicable only to solids which are assemblies of convex polyhedra modules. This is a severe limitation on the vocabulary of shapes which can be rendered.

A far greater vocabulary of solids have been handled in the point visibility determination or "brute force" schemes but at very high calculation times. These schemes essentially have the following strategy: a curve is broken down into many small segments and a small segment is drawn if a test point on the segment is not hidden by any surface in the scene. The author has developed a scheme for the perspec-

---

*A good machine independent measure of visibility versus nonvisibility rendering is the ratio of calculation time required for rendering. The ratios mentioned in this paper are based upon measurements of the author's programs run on an IBM 7094 and are meant to provide an approximate comparison of schemes and are not indicative of limitations of the state-of-the-art. In general, it is not possible to exactly specify a ratio of visibility to non-visibility time since this ratio varies from object to object and from viewpoint to viewpoint for the same object.

tive rendering of assemblies of planes in space which are bounded by straight line segments.[2] This work takes into account internal boundaries (holes), and external boundaries. Y. Okaya has applied the point visibility scheme to assemblies of spheres and cylinders which are used to form a molecular model.[6] R.A. Weiss has developed a very powerful system for rendering combinations of planes and quadric surfaces in orthographic projection.[7] Point visibility schemes are applicable to a large vocabulary of surfaces, combinations of surfaces and projection schemes. These schemes are very docile, since computation errors are not cumulative and usually affect only a small curve segment. The main disadvantage of point visibility tests is the large computation times required for high resolution renderings. For renderings of engineering usefulness of about 40 surfaces and 150 lines, computation time for visibility determination can exceed fifteen minutes on an IBM 7094. This cost increases directly with the size of the picture, the resolution required, and the complexity of the scene. Rendering assemblies of planes bounded by line segments with visibility determined at points costs about 100 to 1000 times as much as the wire frame rendering.

Quantitative invisibility

The rationale behind the scheme to be presented in this paper is that there ought to be a visibility determination scheme which would be midway in characteristics between the surface visibility and the point visibility schemes. Obviously the scheme should be based upon determining the change in visibility on a curve. The fundamental notion of quantitative invisibility is that it is not sufficient to specify a curve invisible or visible, but that the total number of visible surfaces that hide a point on the curve should be measured and when no surface hides points on the curve, the curve is rendered. This notion is useful because techniques developed for detecting changes in quantitative invisibility along a line are more economical than measuring quantitative invisibility at a point. Algorithms for detecting changes in quantitative invisibility have only been developed for straight lines and planes but the strategy should be applicable to higher order curves and surfaces. Procedures for line visibility determination have been implemented, and calculation times of about 10 to 20 times the wire frame calculation time resulted.

Define a *material line* as having specific end points and that this line does not pierce any bounded surface with the surface boundary. From a practical viewpoint, only material lines are manufactured and since we are interested in rendering real objects only material lines need be dealt with. When a volume is completely enclosed by flat surfaces, assign to every surface a *material vector* which points into the volume or into the material of the object. When the angle between a material vector and the line of sight to the origin of that vector is less than 90° then the surface associated with that material vector can never be seen and the surface must be invisible. Lines which are the intersection of two invisible surfaces are obviously invisible. Surfaces whose material vectors form angles of greater than 90° with the local line of sight may be completely or partially visible or even completely invisible. Define a *contour line* as being a line along which the line of sight is tangent to the surface. For polyhedra, given a specific viewpoint, a contour line is a material line which is the intersection of two surfaces, only one of which is invisible. For a given viewpoint, the quantitative invisibility of a material line can change only when it passes behind a contour line. Figure 1A illustrates the variation in quantitative invisibility as a line passes behind two overlap-

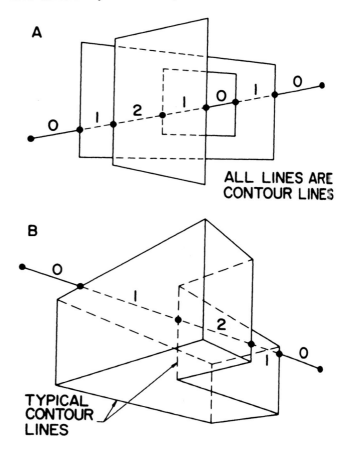

Figure 1 — Changes in quantitative invisibility

ping surfaces. Figure 1B illustrates how quantitative invisibility varies as a line pases behind a solid. Notice that quantitative invisibility can change as it crosses a hidden contour line which is a concave corner. Only surfaces that are viewed from the spatial side should affect the measurement of quantitative invisibility.

Implied vorticity

There are two basic mathematical procedures required in order to utilize the notion of quantitative invisibility: detecting when a material line passes behind a contour line, and determining whether the material line is going behind or coming from behind the visible surface of which the contour line is a boundary. Economic techniques developed for these two procedures make use of a property of closed plane boundaries which can be called *implied vorticity*. This property is a consequence of the order in which the vertex points of a plane bounded by line segments are entered and stored. From the order in which vertex points are stored it can be determined whether a point coplaner with the bounding line segments is on the interior or exterior side of the line. Referring to Figure 2, where the vertex points P_n are entered in a counterclockwise manner, when point A or B are on the interior side of

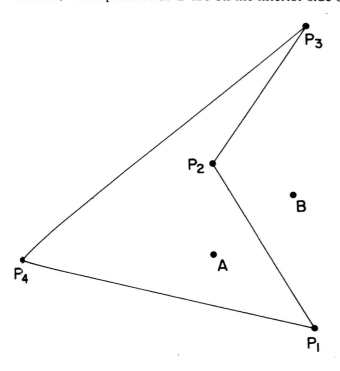

Figure 2 – A bounded plane and two points

a line P_nP_{n+1} the sense of rotation about A or B from P_n to P_{n+1} is counterclockwise. When A or B is on the exterior side of a line the sense of rotation from P_n to P_{n+1} is clockwise. In essense then, the vector from P_n to P_{n+1} has a moment or an implied vorticity about a point not colinear with the vector. When the sense of the vorticity is compared to the sense in which the vertex points of the plane containing P_n are listed, the location of the point relative to the line can be quickly deduced. When the sense of vorticity and the sense of listing are the same then the point lies on the interior side of the line. If the senses disagree the point is on the exterior side. This does not necessarily mean the point lies within the boundary. For example, in Figure 2, point A lies on the exterior side of line P_2P_3 and point B lies on the interior side on line P_3P_4. However, when the surface boundary is a triangle and if the sense of implied vorticity of all three sides are identical about a coplaner point, that point must lie within the triangular boundary. This test for whether a point lies within a triangle is very fast and for reference we can call this a *tri-sense test*. Another application of implied vorticity is that it can be used to determine whether a vector is pointing into or out of a surface boundary as it crosses the boundary. For example, referring again to Figure 2, if we take the vector A to B which crosses line P_1P_2, the sense of P_1P_2 about point B disagrees with the implied vorticity of the vertex points so the vector AB points out of the boundary as it crosses line P_1P_2. The vector BA points into the boundary as it crosses P_1P_2 because the sense of implied vorticity about point A agrees with the implied vorticity of the vertex points. This notion of implied vorticity and its applications can be applied to holes in a surface if the direction in which the vertex points which describe the hole is opposite to the outer boundary direction.

A rapid method to determine the sense of rotation of a vector $P_i P_{i+1}$ about a point O is to take the sign of the matrix equation for the area of the triangle (P_i, P_{i+1}, O).

This matrix equation is:

$$A = \pm a/2 \begin{vmatrix} y_0 & z_0 & 1 \\ y_i & z_i & 1 \\ y_{i+1} & z_{i+1} & 1 \end{vmatrix} \quad (1a)$$

$$A = \pm b/2 \begin{vmatrix} z_0 & x_0 & 1 \\ z_i & x_i & 1 \\ z_{i+1} & x_{i+1} & 1 \end{vmatrix} \quad (1b)$$

$$A = \pm c/2 \begin{vmatrix} x_0 & y_0 & 1 \\ x_i & y_i & 1 \\ x_{i+1} & y_{i+1} & 1 \end{vmatrix} \quad (1c)$$

where a, b, c, are the direction cosines of a line perpendicular to the plane of the triangle (P_i, P_{i+1}, O). At least one of the equations (1) can be used for any plane since $a^2+b^2+c^2 = 1$. In the usual application of the matrix equations (1) the indeterminancy of sign is treated as a nuisance, but for purposes of indicating the direction of rotation it is essential. Since the sign of a matrix is changed if any two rows are interchanged, a change in the order in which the points are entered in the matrix equations (1) will change th sign of the matrix. For example, the matrix A/a is positive when evaluated for a triangle in the first quadrant which is not perpendicular to the $x = 0$ plane when the points are entered in a counterclockwise sense, and the matrix is negative if the points are entered in a clockwise sense. This is illustrated for a simple triangle in Figure 3.

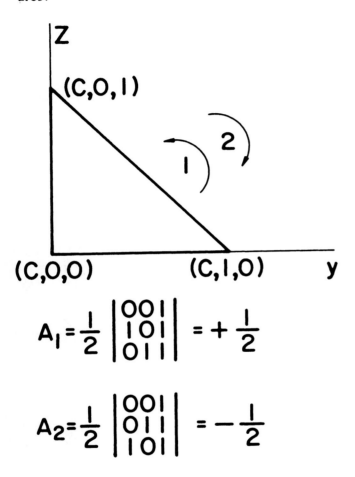

Figure 3 — Sign change of area with direction

The *sweep plane* of a line to be drawn is the plane which contains this line and the viewpoint. This plane is bounded by a triangle whose vertex points are the eye of the observer and the end points of the line to be drawn. The line to be drawn passes behind a contour line for a specific viewpoint when (i) the piercing point of the contour line in the sweep plane lies within the limits of the contour line and (ii) the piercing point lies within the triangular boundary of the sweep plane. Condition (i) can easily be determined by a distance test or evaluation of the parametric variable of the piercing point when all line equations are in parametric form. Condition (ii) can be determined by a tri-sense test of the three vertex points of the sweep line about the piercing point. Referring to Figure 4, contour line 1 satisfies both conditions on sweep plane SP_1, contour line 2 fails condition (i) and contour line 3 fails condition (ii).

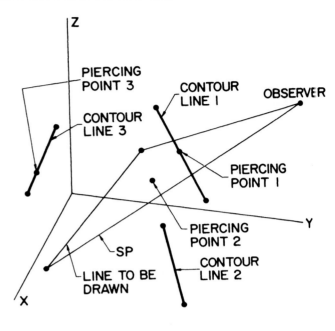

Figure 4 — Determining when a line to be drawn passes behind a contour line

After determining that a line to be drawn has passed behind a contour line, it is necessary to determine what effect this had on the count of quantitative invisibility. Referring to Figure 5, the procedure for determining this effect is as follows:

1. Determine piercing point of line to be drawn (P_1P_2) in sweep plane (SP_2) of the contour line (CL). The line to be drawn starts at point P_1.
2. Locate preceding point (K) on the line to be drawn which is a small distance (usually 10^{-5} units) closer to the starting end of the line (P_1) to be drawn than the piercing point.
3. Project this preceding point (K) onto the plane (S) which contains the contour line (CL). The projected point (J) is the piercing point of the line of sight to the preceding point (K).
4. Determine the sense (CL/J) of implied vorticity of the contour line (CL) about the projected point (J). When the sense (CL/J) agrees with the sense of implied vorticity of the surface (S) then the line (P_1P_2) is coming out from behind surface (S) and the count of quantitative invisibility is to be decreased by one. When the sense (CL/J) disagrees with the sense of implied vorticity of the surface (S) then the line (P_1P_2) is go-

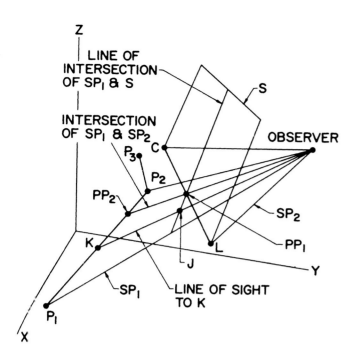

Figure 5 — Determining the change of quantitative invisibility

ing behind surface (S) and the count of quantitative invisibility is increased by one. Those segments of line (P_1P_2) which have a zero count of quantitative invisibility are rendered.

Since all the lines to be rendered on a drawing are in contact with other lines, for example the line (P_1P_2) has a common vertex P_2 with line (P_2P_3), an initial measurement of quantitative invisibility need not be made very often, as the count of quantitative invisibility is valid for both intersecting lines at their common vertex point. This initial measurement of quantitative invisibility is a count of all those surfaces which hide the starting point. The starting point is connected to all other vertex points on a completely described object by material lines so that the changes in quantitative invisibility can be rapidly determined by the methods of implied vorticity. An initial measurement of quantitative invisibility need be undertaken only once for every object in a scene or, where the list processing becomes time consuming, once for every internal or external surface boundary.

Initial measurement

A bounded surface hides a point when the line of sight to that point pierces the surface within the surface boundaries, and the piercing point is closer to the observer than the point being tested for visibility. The essential problem of point visibility testing is the determination of when a point lies within a surface boundary. The author has previously described in another report a test of this kind,[2] but J. Rutledge has suggested a scheme which has proven to be more economical. If we connect a point, whose relative location to a surface boundary is unknown, to a point which is outside the boundary by a curve (usually a line), and if the number of times this connecting curve (line) crosses the boundary is odd, the point being tested lies within the boundary. In order to make an initial measurement of quantitative invisibility at a point the piercing points of the line of sight to that point on all surfaces are determined and a count is made of those piercing points which are:
  i) closer to the observer than the point being measured.
  ii) within a surface boundary as detected by Rutledge's scheme.

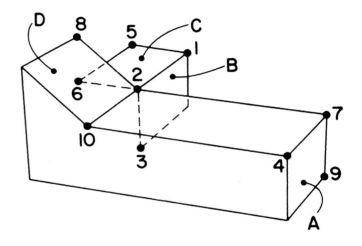

Figure 6 — Singularities

Corners

Several singularities arise in the implementation of the notion of quantitative invisibility and techniques of implied vorticity. These are illustrated in Figure 6. In drawing the boundary of surface A, as line 4-7 is completed, contour line 2-7 is crossed at vertex point 7. There should be no change in quantitative invisibility at point 7. In rendering surface B, as the boundary turns at vertex point 2 from line 1-2 to line 2-3 the count of quantitative invisibility should increase by one, which in this single object picture will make line 2-3 invisible. When drawing surface C as the boundary turns at vertex point 2 from line 6-2 to line 2-1, the count of quantitative invisibility should decrease by one. If surface C is being drawn in the opposite direction, as line 2-6 leads to line 6-5 at vertex point 6, no change should occur at the vertex point as the far segment of line 6-5 will become visible as it crosses contour line 8-2. Obviously, the rules to specify changes in quantitative invisibility when a contour line passes thru a vertex point are:

a) when an external corner line leads at a common vertex point to an internal corner line, quantitative invisibility increases by one only when a contour line exists at the common vertex and the internal corner is a contour line.

b) When an internal corner line leads at a common vertex point to an external corner line, quantitative invisibility decreases by one only when a contour line exists at the common vertex and the internal corner is a contour line.

c) When no contour line exists at a common vertex no change in quantitative invisibility can take place.

What these rules essentially detect is the instance when an internal corner line is hidden from view. When an internal corner line is not a contour line, we are looking into the corner. For example in drawing surface D as line 8-2 leads to line 2-10 at vertex point 2, the internal corner 2-10 is not a contour line so no change in quantitative invisibility occurs.

All of the procedures discussed in this paper have been reduced to practice. Coding has been in Fortran IV and is executed on an IBM 7094 with graphic output on an IBM 1627 (CalComp) plotter. Figures 7 thru 12 are examples of the graphic output. When appropriate, the captions specify calculation time and the number of surfaces and surface boundary lines in a scene. All computer generated pictures in this article were rendered under the control of the same computer program.

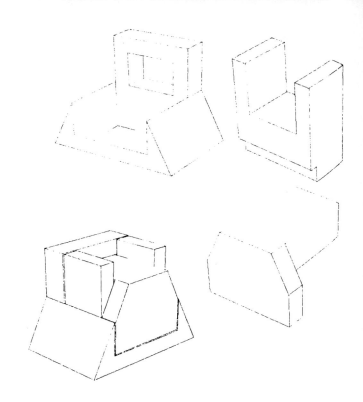

Figure 8 — Assembly of three machine parts 41 surfaces 104 lines 7094 calculation time per view: about 9.3 seconds

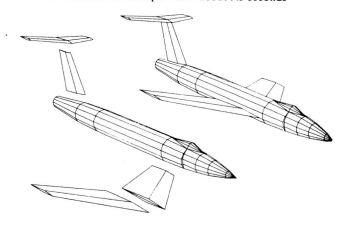

Figure 9 — Assembly of a transonic aircraft from five components each of which may be altered independently, 143 surfaces, 226 lines 7094 calculation time per view: about 41.5 seconds

ACKNOWLEDGMENTS

The author is grateful to Dr. J. D. Rutledge for many helpful discussions, and to P. Loutrel for a helpful conversation. J.A. Dobbs, L. E. Harrington, Mr. & Mrs. E. P. McGilton, S. L. Tramaglini, and R. M. Warner among others were especially helpful with plotter output problems and the maintenance of a high computer thruput which contributed significantly to this project. The author is deeply indebted to J. P. Gilvey and F. L. Graner for their continuing encouragement and support of this work.

Figure 7 — Assembly of two objects, 32 surfaces, 84 lines, 7094 calculation time per view: about 6.5 seconds

A Solution to the Hidden Surface Problem

M.E. Newell, R.G. Newell, T.L. Sancha
The Computer-Aided Design Center

A method for producing half-tone pictures by computer is presented. The basic method, which is very simple, works well in most cases, but does not handle all objects correctly. The extended method, which copes with all cases, is also described. The functions used for calculating the intensity of parts of objects, and the method for handling transparency, are discussed. Examples of pictures produced by this method are included, and the times taken to generate them are tabulated. The extended algorithm compares favourably in speed and storage requirements with other published algorithms.

KEY WORDS AND PHRASES: graphics, computer-aided design, computer art, curved surfaces, hidden-line, hidden-surface, visible-surface, half-tone, greyscale, shading, raster scan, video-disc

CR CATEGORIES: 3.41, 4.9, 8.2

INTRODUCTION

The computer production of shaded images is a further attempt to improve the realism of computer-produced pictures. This subject has received increasing attention in recent years and it has become apparent that images can be produced with an acceptable amount of computation.

The solution to the hidden-surface problem involves comparisons of chosen parts of the scene with other parts to determine those which are visible. Previous approaches have carried out these comparisons on a point by point basis [1], a scan-line basis [2,3,4,5], or on an area basis [6].

The approach described in this paper tackles the problem by identifying areas of complexity in the image, then resolving the difficulty by dividing the planar faces of the object until the difficulty has disappeared. Although no direct machine trials have been undertaken, it seems that this method compares favourably with other published methods. The cost of software methods is coming down, but it is probably true to say that the time taken to produce an image precludes the possibility of using shaded pictures in a truly interactive way in the design process.

The method outlined in this paper is relatively fast as a software approach, and has the advantage that a major part of the computational load can be offloaded onto a fairly cheap hardware device.

THE BASIC METHOD

Input for the present implementation is a series of conceptually opaque quadrilateral faces. Although the faces are nominally planar, the algorithm will handle cases where the faces are slightly twisted, thus allowing approximations to curved surfaces to be handled.

Initially the object is transformed into the viewer's coordinate system, this being x horizontal and y vertical, the negative z axis being the line of sight. The transformed object is then clipped to remove any portion behind a plane placed just in front of the viewing point. After the half-space clip the object is further transformed into screen (or perspective) space, by applying a single perspective divide to each of the x,y and z coordinate values. The reason for working in 3D perspective space is to simplify many of the 2D and 3D tests involving pairs of faces.

At this stage, any face lying completely outside the viewing area is discarded. For a solid object, any face of the surface that faces away from the eye can be discarded. This simplification cannot be applied to surfaces that do not represent solids or closed shells. In all cases faces that are viewed edge-on can also be rejected. The resulting object description is processed by the main body of the hidden surface procedure.

The approach to be described centres around a screen map, which may be considered as a software simulation of a digital video disc. The screen map holds sufficient information to determine the intensity of every raster point in the image. Portions of the object are written to the screen map in an ordered manner such that those faces furthest from the eye are written first, the map being successively overwritten by each succeeding face.

An advantage of this method over most others is that if the correct relative ordering of groups of faces is known, then only one group need be handled at a time. The overwriting capability of the screen map handles the obscuring of one group by another. Using this method, scenes can be produced containing many more faces than can be held in core at once.

Figure 17 shows an example of the use of this technique. There are 10,870 faces in the scene, whereas the program considered only one pawn of 720 faces at any one time. The ordering of groups of faces is at present done manually, though in some cases it could be automated.

An early implementation of the algorithm takes the planar faces of the object, orders them according to the z coordinates of their centroids and then writes them to the screen map in this order. This approach is remarkably simple to implement, but although the resulting algorithm is fast it is not able to solve all cases correctly. The correct order for writing faces does not necessarily depend on the position of the centroids; in such cases a more elaborate scheme is required to find the ordering. Worse cases arise when no ordering exists to solve the hidden-surface problem correctly. This happens when faces intersect, or obscure one another cyclically. However this approach has the advantage of simplicity, and it has been found that it caters for a large class of objects. It works well when the object consists of a large number of small quadrilateral faces. The basic method has been extended to cater for the failing cases.

THE EXTENDED ALGORITHM

The simple algorithm described above was augmented by providing a control section to order the faces correctly and split those faces that cause problems in the ordering. The flowchart in Figure 1 gives a broad outline of the augmented procedure. Prior to entering the procedure certain frequently-used data items are computed and stored in linear arrays. These data items consist of such things as plane equations in screen space, and extremum values of x and y on the screen. In addition to these, an ordered list is initialised to contain references to faces in decreasing order of their minimum z values. The minimum z value of the face corresponds to the point furthest from the eye. The face at the top of the list has a good chance of not obscuring any other, and so it is potentially the first face to be written to the screen map. Whenever a face is written to the screen map it is removed from the top of the list and is no longer considered. However the current top face in the list, P, must first be checked against each face, Q, that could possibly be obscured by P. Such faces are those whose furthest point is further from the eye than the nearest point of P. This usually involves only a small proportion of the total number of faces in the scene, and since the list is ordered on minimum z value these always appear at the top of the list.

The comprehensive routine that tests whether P can definitely be written to the screen map before Q answers the question 'does P obscure Q?'. This consists of a sequence of tests of increasing severity, the result of which is either a definite negative answer or an indication of failure to prove a negative answer, in which case there is a possibility that a part of P obscures Q.

In the event of failure the program investigates the possibility of writing Q to the

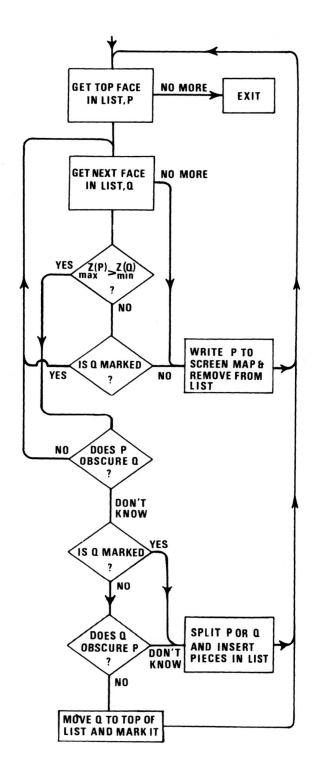

Fig.1 Outline Flowchart of Method

screen map before P, thereby forcing Q out of the previous ordering to the top of the list. This attempt is only permissible if Q has not been forced out of order previously, otherwise the program could loop interminably. The test for writing Q before P is very similar to the test for writing P before Q and can utilise some of the intermediate results of the former test. If it can be proved that Q does not obscure P, then Q is moved to the top of the list and marked. The list is collapsed to fill the gap created.

Should the attempt to reorder Q fail, the program enters a face-splitting procedure that slices P or Q into two pieces and then inserts the resulting fragments in their correct positions in the list, according to their minimum z values.

An earlier implementation of the extended algorithm entered the face-splitting routine without any attempt to reorder faces. This worked well for many cases, but occasionally the program would split faces into smaller and smaller pieces without sorting out the difficulty until fragments the size of raster points resulted. Such cases were considerably improved by the reordering enhancement, and in all examples tested it led to an improvement in computation time.

THE ORDERING TEST IN DETAIL

The routine that tests whether it is permissible to write face P to the screen map before Q must be made as efficient as possible, since it will be entered frequently for all faces in the object. In the current implementation the following sequence of tests is made. Although they are not the only set of tests that could be devised, they have been designed so that the program can exit after a minimal amount of computation. As mentioned previously, the routine answers the question 'does P obscure Q?', and exits with a negative answer should any of the following tests be satisfied:

1. Extreme screen values of x of two faces do not overlap

2. Extreme screen values of y of two faces do not overlap

3. P is contained wholly in the back half-space of Q

4. Q is contained wholly in the front half-space of P

5. Faces do not overlap on the screen

   (Any face divides space into two half-spaces, and the front half-space is defined to contain the eye.)

Should all five tests fail then it is still possible that the ordering is satisfactory, but the further computation needed to prove this conclusively is considered unjustified. Hence in these circumstances the program assumes that P obscures Q. In the event of failure then only the equivalent of tests 3 and 4 need be repeated for the converse test for writing Q before face P. If it is shown that Q does not obscure P, and Q has not been previously displaced, then it is moved to the top of the list and marked. This new top member of the list is now treated as the new P.

THE FACE-SPLITTING ROUTINE

If all attempts to find a correct ordering of a pair of faces fail, then either face P or Q (not both) is sliced in two in the hope that reducing the face size will enable an ordering of the resulting fragments to be found. The procedure is as follows:

1. If parts of P lie in both half-spaces of Q then slice P in two with the plane of Q and exit

2. If parts of Q lie in both half-spaces of P then slice Q in two with the plane of P and exit

3. Slice P in half through the mid-points of the longest pair of opposite sides.

After one face has been split, the resulting fragments and the other unsplit face are inserted in their correct positions in the list, this being below any marked faces which have been previously forced out of order to the top of the list. Again, as in the case of the ordering tests, this splitting strategy is not the only one possible.

THE REPRESENTATION OF THE SCREEN MAP

The basis of this whole method of solving the hidden-surface problem is the screen map with its overwrite capability. This occupies most of the time used in producing an image. As mentioned earlier, only very simple logic is required to implement a restricted hidden-surface routine that will work for a large class of cases; the very nature of the screen map solves the hidden-surface problem.

In the first implementation of the screen map, 3 bits are held for each raster point on a grid of 256 by 256. Hence pictures are limited to 8 intensity levels, and the resolution is poor. If one tries to improve the situation by increasing the resolution and using more intensities, then the escalation in storage requirements becomes excessive. For example the original screen map occupies 4k of 48 bit words on the ATLAS 2. Doubling the resolution and allowing 16 intensities would increase this to about 21k. Thus an alternative approach has been used that does not require such a large amount of store.

The second implementation consists of a buffer area that holds a string of data 'beads'. Each bead holds the list of line segments for a particular raster line, and the beads are accessed via a directory based on the y values of the raster lines. When a new face of the object is to be written to the screen map, it is first processed into horizontal line segments at the required intensity. When one of these line segments is added to the screen map, its corresponding raster line bead is copied to the top of the buffer area, simultaneously merging the new line with line segments already there. Thus the raster line pointer has to be updated and the original bead nullified. When the buffer area gets filled, which in some cases can be frequently, the program enters a simple 'garbage collection' procedure to remove the nullified beads. Investigations were made into methods of reducing the amount of garbage collection required, and although large reductions were achieved, the net result was to increase the overall computing time, and so it transpires that the simple approach is the best yet found.

The algorithm, considered as a software method, could be regarded as a scan-line method with a preprocessor that allows the logic to solve the 2D hidden-line problem on each scan-line to be greatly simplified. In fact, extensions along these lines are the subject of current investigations. The idea is to produce a list of faces and face fragments which, if written to the screen map in order, would produce the correct picture. A back end consisting of a much simplified scan-line method could then be used to produce the picture. Intersections and orderings would thus be handled on a face by face basis, thereby improving line to line coherence. It is hoped that an improved performance will be achieved by this method.

PICTURE DISPLAY

The device used at the CAD Centre for displaying shaded pictures is a PDP9 computer with 340 display unit. The PDP9 is an 8K machine and the 340 is capable of displaying approximately 2000 inches of line per second. In order to display a shaded picture, the screen map is converted (in ATLAS) into a compressed format display file that is processed interpretively by the PDP9 for display on the 340. The compressed format allows three horizontal line segments to be held in two PDP9 18 bit words. The DEC 340 display has been enhanced to 64 intensities, thus 6 bits are used to define the intensity of a line segment, and 6 bits are used to hold its length. To overcome the limited speed at which the 340 can display lines, the picture can be interlaced. Raster lines are not displayed in order of increasing y value. In the case of a picture of 512 raster lines, the nth raster line displayed has a y value of (n.p)modulo 512, where p is prime to 512. In practice a value of p of 97 has been found to give good results, in some cases nearly freezing the picture. For the purposes of taking photographs, the picture is displayed an integral number of times while the camera shutter is open, thereby ensuring that all parts of the film are exposed for an equal amount of time.

FUNCTIONS USED FOR SHADING

Several authors [3,6,7] have discussed methods of computing the intensity of a particular face of the object for a given light condition. Usually the problem is limited to cases where the light source is at the eye and a uniform mean intensity is computed over the whole face. One of the reasons for this restriction is to avoid the complexity of solving the shadow problem. However, interesting effects can be obtained with oblique lighting even if the shadow problem is ignored. The most interesting objects to investigate with different lighting functions are those that consist of a large number of small faces derived from some curved surface definition. The large number of differing orientations arising in the scene lead to interesting reflection patterns. For instance, consider the simple intensity function

$$I = r.\cos^n(a)+b$$

where r is the intensity range, n is some arbitrary power, a is some measure of the angle between the incident light and the face normal and b is the ambient level of lighting.

For n=1 this function simulates diffuse reflection, but if n is increased to a high value, say 20, then this leads to most of the object appearing dark, with a few critical faces appearing at the brightest intensity. This gives the effect of a black shiny object.

Observations in the real world show that many curved surfaces, for example bottles and other solids of revolution, are characterised by having longitudinal reflection patterns. This effect is easily simulated by having a component in the lighting function of the form

$$s.\sin^m(a)$$

where again m is a high power. In this case the brightest faces appear where the light is nearly tangential, which in the case of a bottle produces a white streak right down the side of the bottle.

A third effect that picks out the silhouette of a dark object has been used. This is done by having a light source of the 'sine' type at the viewing point.

Transparent materials can be simulated by using a small extension to the screen map routine. When a line segment is to be added to the map, instead of completely overwriting the map, some function of the intensity of what it would obscure and of its own intensity is used. The form of this function determines the apparent transparency of the material. The function used at present defines the resulting intensity, I, as:

$$I_1 < I_0 : I = w.I_1 + (1-w).I_0$$
$$I_1 > I_0 : I = I_1$$

Where I_1 and I_0 are the intensities of the new and obscured line segments respectively, and w is a weighting factor.

These functions do not attempt to simulate the real world, though a judicious use of them can considerably enhance the appearance of some objects. Examples of various combinations of these effects can be found in the accompanying illustrations.

PERFORMANCE OF THE METHOD

Watkins [4] has classified published hidden-surface algorithms according to three criteria; deterministic or non-deterministic, area subdivision or scan-line subdivision, and object space or sample space. It is relevant to see where the current algorithm fits into this classification.

The non-deterministic front end of the current algorithm works in object space and is also of the area subdivision type. The fundamental difference from Warnock's approach is that area subdivision is carried out on the planar faces of the object in an intelligent manner, instead of on areas of the screen in a fixed manner. However, the deterministic back end, namely the screen map, works in sample space on a scan-line basis.

The present algorithm has not been directly tested against any other published methods and so accurate assessments cannot be given of the performance relative to these methods. The current implementation is written wholly in FORTRAN except for the screen map routines, which are written in machine code. The program runs in 24k of core in ATLAS 2 and up to 800 faces and 1000 points can be accomodated in this core space. The time taken to produce an image can be broken down into four parts as follows:

1. Object transformation, preliminary data calculations and initialisation of ordered list.

2. Preparation of faces for the screen map including ordering tests and face splitting.

3. Writing of faces to the screen map.

4. Conversion of screen map into compressed format display file.

Items 1 and 4 make a relatively insignificant contribution to the total computation time, usually taking less than 2 seconds. The time taken for item 2 is largely dependent on how good the initial ordering is. If few faces intersect then this time is usually short, but cases can arise where it becomes significant.

Item 3 takes most of the time, and clearly this is a part of the algorithm that can be isolated and implemented with fairly cheap hardware. However, the software method used still makes this approach to the hidden-surface problem a feasible proposition.

The table in Figure 2 gives a breakdown of the times taken for a series of test objects. For comparison with other machines, it is estimated that equivalent FORTRAN programs take 3 times longer on ATLAS 2 than on a UNIVAC 1108. All times quoted in the table are based on a picture of 512 by 512 raster points.

Figure 3 shows a cube and an octahedron intersecting. The intersections were handled completely by the program. This picture

FIGURE	COMPLEXITY				TIME SPENT (SECONDS)			
	TOTAL FACES	FACES CONSIDERED BY PROGRAM	FACE FRAGMENTS WRITTEN TO SCREEN MAP	LINE SEGMENTS IN PICTURE	TRANSFORMING AND INITIALISING	ORDERING AND SLICING FACES	WRITING FRAGMENTS TO SCREEN MAP	CONVERTING SCREEN MAP TO DISPLAY FILE
3	14	7	18	2431	0.1	0.2	1.4	1.2
4	225	106	410	5474	0.7	10.6	10.6	1.8
5	140	62	158	3860	0.2	3.9	8.6	1.6
6	140	140	409	7197	0.6	12.6	33.4	2.4
7	63	27	449	3258	0.2	27.0	12.0	1.3
8	625	599	600	7182	2.8	6.2	14.8	2.4
9	625	625	626	6333	3.0	6.4	12.4	2.2
10	720	406	408	4503	2.5	3.2	5.7	2.0
11	450	444	444	4224	2.1	3.5	14.5	1.5
12	393	180	180	7107	1.3	1.1	9.8	2.5
13	195	98	118	2532	0.6	1.5	4.4	1.6

Figure 2

illustrates the program's capability of assigning different material functions to parts of an object. Up to six different materials can be specified.

Figures 4 to 7 are included for comparison with similar objects given as examples in previous papers. Figure 4 is taken from Bouknight [5], and figures 5 and 7 are from Watkins [4].

Figure 6 shows the same object as figure 5, rendered in a transparent material.

Figures 8 to 10 are examples of objects designed with a solids of revolution program.

Figure 11 is an example of an object generated with THINGS [8]. It is necessary to consider all but the edge-on planes in this object, because it is not a solid.

Figure 12 is another object generated with THINGS. The picture was generated on its side since the horizontal complexity is far greater than the vertical.

Figure 13 shows a representation of a crematorium modelled using THINGS.

Figures 14 to 17 are further examples of output from the program. Figures 14 and 15 were designed using bi-cubic patches.

APPLICATIONS OF SHADED PICTURES IN COMPUTER AIDED DESIGN

Any department that invests time developing a shaded picture facility should show that the result is not merely a sophisticated paint brush with relevance only to the cosmetics of CAD. For this reason effort has been devoted to evolving a generalized input system for the production of shaded pictures using the results of design programs as input [9]. The central part of this input system is THINGS - THree dimensional INput of Graphical Solids. THINGS is implemented as a set of subroutines that can be called from a user's FORTRAN design program. The function of this package is to enable a user to assemble objects at different positions and orientations in space and store these on a file for future use by the shaded picture program. This system is capable of taking object definitions from a number of sources, including two surface design systems, a highway design system, and a solids of revolution design system, together with standard objects such as prisms, spheres and boxes.

One of the main potential uses of shaded pictures is in the assessment of the aesthetics of a new piece of architecture or a proposed product. This potential has not yet been realized, although the cost of producing a sequence of views from one object definition is cheap.

Another application is data verification. Small errors in objects defined with curved surfaces often become blatantly obvious in a shaded picture, despite the approximation by planar faces. An example of such an error occurs when two surfaces unintentionally intersect, such as a car engine fouling the body. This type of error is very obvious in a shaded picture. Another error is the existence of ridges or grooves in a surface. Although at every quadrilateral face boundary there is a discontinuity in the slope of the approximated surface, it is surprising how obvious discontinuities in the original definition can be. Errors of this nature have already been found by using shaded pictures.

CONCLUSIONS

A number of methods of solving the hidden-surface problem now demonstrate that a variety of pictures can be produced economically. The main area of use seems to be in the final stages of computer-aided design. A further reduction in cost is needed before shaded pictures can become fully integrated with the design process itself.

The method described in this paper compares favourably both in speed and storage requirements with other published methods. An advantage of the method lies in the fact that a large part of the computational load can be removed by using a hardware screen map. This device could be either a digital video disc or a solid state memory.

ACKNOWLEDGEMENTS

To R. M. Williamson for designing and implementing the display routines enabling the production of the pictures on an 8K PDP9 with 340 display.

REFERENCES

1. Appel A.,'On Calculating the Illusion of Reality', IFIP Congress 68 Proc., E79, August 1968.
2. Wylie C., Romney G., Evans D.C., Erdahl A., 'Halftone Perspective Drawings by Computer', AFIPS Proc. FJCC 31 November 1967.
3. Romney G.W.,'Computer Assisted Assembly and Rendering of Solids', RADC Contract AF30(602)-4277.
4. Watkins G.S.,'A Real Time Visible Surface Algorithm', UTECT-CSC-70-101,University of Utah, June 1970.
5. Bouknight W.J.,'A Procedure for Generation of Three-Dimensional Half-toned Computer Graphics Presentations', CACM Vol 13, 9, September 1970.
6. Warnock J.E.,'A Hidden Surface Algorithm for Computer Generated Halftone Pictures', RADC-TR-69-249, University of Utah, 1969.
7. Gouraud H.,'Continuous Shading of Curved Surfaces', IEEE Transactions on Computers, Vol. c-20,6, June 1971.
8. CAD Centre, Cambridge, England,'THINGS - THree dimensional INput of Graphical Solids'.
9. Newell M.E., Newell R.G. and Sancha T.L. 'The Economic Application of a Half-tone Picture Generating Algorithm', Computer Aided Design, IEE Conference Publication 86, Southampton April 1972.

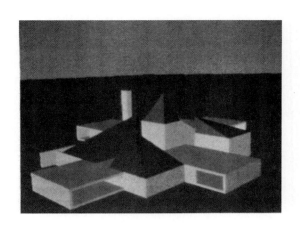
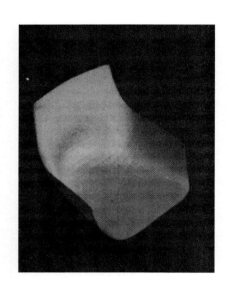
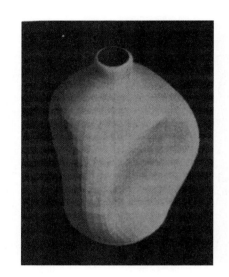

COMPUTER DISPLAY OF CURVED SURFACES
Edwin Catmull
New York Institute of Technology
Old Westbury, New York

Summary

This paper presents a method for producing computer shaded pictures of curved surfaces. Three-dimensional curved patches are used, as contrasted with conventional methods using polygons. The method subdivides a patch into successively smaller subpatches until a subpatch is as small as a raster-element, at which time it can be displayed. In general, this method could be very time consuming because of the great number of subdivisions that must take place; however, there is at least one very useful class of patches—the bicubic patch—that can be subdivided very quickly. Pictures produced with the method accurately portray the shading and silhouette of curved surfaces. In addition, photographs can be "mapped" onto patches thus providing a means for putting texture on computer generated pictures.

Introduction

A method for creating shaded pictures of curved surfaces is presented in this paper. A motivation for the method is that we wish to produce high quality computer-generated images of surfaces and curved solid objects on a raster-scan output device. We would not only like the images to accurately represent the surfaces we choose but in addition we would like control over shading and texture. There has already been significant research directed toward these ends, especially on the hidden-surface [1,2] and shading [3,4] aspects of the problem. All such methods must address the questions of how to model objects and then how to render them.

Polygons, and sometimes quadric patches, are used to model objects in current shaded-picture methods. There are some difficulties with using these simple pieces to model or approximate free-form curved surfaces. Approximation with polygons gives a faceted effect and a silhouette made up of straight-line segments. Quadric patches [5,6] while smooth in appearance, are not suitable for modeling arbitrary forms, since they don't provide enough degrees of freedom to satisfy slope continuity between patches.

Curved surface segments or "patches" can be used instead of polygons to model free-form curved surfaces. If such patches can be joined together with slope continuity across the boundaries then a picture of a surface can be made to appear "smooth" both in shading and at the silhouette. For patches to be useful in modelling a curved surface, techniques must be found for describing and manipulating the patches and for connecting them together with slope continuity across boundaries. An example of such a patch is the widely used bicubic patch.

Generating pictures of curved patches requires techniques for
(1) establishing a correspondence between points on the surface and the elements of the display raster,
(2) removing hidden or, more generally, the "not seen" parts of patches, and
(3) calculating light intensities to be displayed on the raster.

Definitions

A "raster-scan device" or "raster-display" is the device that we will consider for final output of an image. The rectangular array of "dots" that is produced on a raster-display is called the "raster." Each dot will usually be called a "raster element." The raster-element covers a very small area of the raster; however, it should not be thought of as a point. Each raster-element has a brightness that is determined by the intensity value for that raster-element. The process of taking the intensity values and putting the dots on the raster with the corresponding intensities is called "displaying."

A "frame buffer" is a memory large enough to store all of the intensity values prior to displaying. An intensity value in the frame-buffer can be addressed in a way that corresponds to the position where the value will be displayed on the raster. Locations in the frame-buffer will also be called "raster-elements" since there is a strong one-to-one correspondence between those locations and the geometric locations of the raster-elements and because the distinction between the two is not important here. For our purposes, the frame buffer is made with random-access memory so that values can be written into it in any order, as opposed to scan-line order only. The size of the frame-buffer is determined by the resolution of the raster-display and the number of "bits" used to store intensity values. For the most part we will ignore the raster-display and address ourselves to the issue of putting the right intensity values in the raster-elements of the frame-buffer.

The terms relating the original description of an object to its image will now be defined. "Object-space" is the three-dimensional space in which objects will ordinarily be described. In order to generate realistic pictures of objects we make a perspective transformation [1,7,8] of the object from object-space to "image-space." Image-space is also three-dimensional but the objects have undergone a perspective distortion so that an orthogonal projection of the object onto the x-y plane would result in the expected perspective image. We want the image-space to be three-dimensional in order to preserve depth information which will later be used to solve the hidden-surface problem. The orthogonal projection of the image-space object onto the x-y plane is called the "projected image." That part of the x-y plane which will be associated with the raster is called the "screen."

We must define the relationship between the image-space and the raster in order to transfer information from the projected image to the raster. Recall that the screen is the portion of the x-y plane of the image-space that corresponds to the raster. The area of the screen is divided into small squares called "raster element squares." There is, of course, a one-to-one correspondence between raster-element squares and raster elements. The center of each raster-element square will be called a "sample point." A diagram depicting the relationships of the above terms is shown in figure 1.

1975 IEEE. Reprinted, with permission, from Proceedings of the IEEE Conference on Computer Graphics, Pattern Recognition and Data Structures; Los Angeles, California, May 1975; 11-17.

The Subdivision Algorithm

The algorithm for establishing the correspondence between a patch and the raster-elements will now be presented. The algorithm, hereafter called the "subdivision algorithm," works for either patches or segments of patches, called "subpatches." Figure 2 illustrates a portion of the screen where the dots represent the sample points. (The outlines of the raster-element squares are not shown.) The curved lines represent the edges of a protected patch. Even though only the projection is shown, we assume that enough information about the patch is maintained so that the light intensity for any location on the patch can be calculated.

A statement of the algorithm is:

If the patch (subpatch) is small enough so that its projection covers only one sample-point, then compute the intensity of the patch and write it into the corresponding element of the frame buffer; otherwise, subdivide the patch into smaller subpatches; and repeat the process for each subpatch.

Figure 3 shows a patch subdivided into four subpatches where most of the subpatches still cover more than one sample-point. In Figure 4 the subpatches that are too large are again subdivided. Subdivision continues until no subpatch covers more than one sample-point.

Readers familiar with other computer generated shaded-picture efforts will recognize a similarity between the method presented here and Warnock's hidden surface algorithm [9]. Warnock solved the hidden surface problem for polygons by recursively subdividing the screen space into successively smaller sections until all questions about the ordering of polygons left in a section were easy to answer. Warnock's algorithm differs from the one presented here in that the former subdivides the screen, while the latter subdivides the surface being rendered.

Termination

The decision as to whether or not a subpatch should be subdivided is based on termination conditions. Two termination conditions will be discussed—size and clipping. For the purpose of this discussion we note that the terms "patch" and "subpatch" can be used interchangeably, hence we will usually use the word "patch."

As specified in the algorithm, subdivision terminates when a patch covers only one sample-point. Since the edges of a patch are curved, the test as to whether or not a patch covers only one sample-point may be time consuming. However, for the purpose of this test, a patch can be approximated by a polygon formed by connecting the four corners of the patch with straight line segments. The size of that polygon can then be checked to determine whether or not it covers at most one sample-point.

Clipping

A second termination condition might be a check to see if the patch is on the screen. If part of the projection of a patch in image-space onto the x-y plane lies off the screen or the patch is behind the eye then that part of the projection should not be displayed. The process of eliminating the portion of the projection that should not be on the screen is called clipping [7, 8]. A clipping termination condition requires that there be some method for determining if a patch is totally on or totally off the screen. If the patch is totally on the screen then the subdivision may proceed for that patch with no further need of clipping checks for the subpatches generated from that patch. If the patch is totally off the screen then that patch may be discarded. If it cannot be determined that the patch is totally on or totally off the screen then that patch should be subdivided and the clipping check should be made for each new patch resulting from the subdivision.

Number of Subdivisions

The number of times a patch must be subdivided to get down to the size of a raster-element is proportional to the area of the patch on the screen. The number of subdivisions is somewhat greater than 1/3 the number of raster-element squares covered by the patch.

The Sampling Problem

There are some problems encountered when using sample points. The most obvious is the "staircase-effect" or "jaggies" seen on the silhouettes of objects. In addition, a patch might be so small that it doesn't cover any sample-point, causing it to disappear. The latter problem can be solved by assigning a patch to the nearest sample-point if it doesn't cover any sample-point. The problems of sampling are inherent with the use of a raster display. An alternative to point sampling is presented in [15].

Application

The subdivision algorithm presented above was first applied to bicubic patches. Bicubic patches are convenient on several counts: they are widely used, they can be compactly specified in several different ways, and they can be easily joined with first derivative continuity at the boundaries. The author has discovered a very fast method for subdividing bicubic patches reported in [15]. It should be emphasized at this point however that the subdivision algorithm is by no means limited to bicubic patches but can be applied to other kinds of surfaces.

The Hidden Surface Problem

In order to display surface patches it is necessary to determine which surfaces are visible. The method used to solve the hidden surface problem for this research is the "z-buffer algorithm."

The z-buffer is an extension of the frame-buffer idea in that the z value from the image-space of the visible object is stored at every raster-element as well as the intensity. The z value of any new point to be written into the buffer is compared with the z value of the point already there. If the new point is behind, it is discarded. If it is in front it replaces the old value.

There are several advantages to using the z-buffer. Hidden surface problems and intersection of arbitrary surfaces are handled trivially. Pictures can be of any complexity. Except as noted below, surfaces may be written into the buffer in any order, thus saving the time-consuming sorting of highly complex surfaces.

There are of course some disadvantages to the z-buffer. A 512 by 512 buffer with 8 bits of intensity and 20 bits of z uses a quarter of a million 28 bit words. At the current cost of memory this means an expensive implementation. A more serious problem is that of "anti-aliasing," or getting rid of the "staircase effect." Any algorithm for getting rid of the staircase effect requires that on the silhouette of objects the intensity at the corresponding raster-elements will be some combination of intensities from at least two objects—namely the object being displayed and the object being partially obscured, which may of course be simply background. If all of the objects have been rendered in random order, then it is possible that the intensities from the wrong objects will be combined, giving a local error. This means that it may sometimes be necessary to sort the objects to eliminate the staircase effect.

The author implemented the z-buffer algorithm by paging the z-buffer onto disk. Thirty-two pages could be resident in core where each page contained a 16 by 16 square section of the raster. The time needed for swapping was small compared to the time spent by the software implementation of the subdivision algorithm. All of the pictures in this paper were made using the z-buffer.

Intensity

When a patch has been subdivided into subpatches small enough to cover only one sample-point it is necessary to associate an intensity with the corresponding point. There are several ways of getting the intensity at each point.
1. Use the normal to the surface to calculate intensity.
2. Use some intensity function of u and v.
3. Map the intensities from some picture.

There are good examples where each of the above might be applicable, so they will each be discussed.

Using Surface Normals

The normal to a surface is frequently needed to calculate the intensity. Phong has already shown [4] several ways of calculating intensity if the surface normal and the light sources are known. A typical way of doing it would be to use as the intensity the dot product of a light vector and the surface normal. One needs to use the normal from the object-space surface before the perspective transformation is performed instead of the image-space surface because perspective distorts the surface and hence falsifies the intensity.

Using an Intensity Function

The intensity at a raster-element is represented by a number and any useful way of deriving that number is legitimate. Instead of being a function of the orientation of the surface, the intensity might be a function of pressure, strain, height, density, artistic whim etc.

Mapping

Photographs, drawings, or any picture can be mapped onto bivariate patches. This is one of the most interesting consequences of the patch splitting algorithm. It gives a method for putting texture, drawings, or photographs onto surfaces. It also allows one to have reflections in pictures, as in flat or curved mirrors.

One can make a correspondence between any point on a patch and an intensity on a picture. If a photograph is scanned in at a resolution of x times y then every element can be referenced by $u \cdot x$ and $v \cdot y$ where $0 \leq u, v \leq 1$. In general, one could think of the intensity as a function $I(u, v)$ where I references a picture.

In practice the above method for getting intensities from pictures can fall afoul of sampling errors. This will occur when the number of points to be displayed on a patch is less than the number of elements in the stored picture, resulting in less information being put on the patch than is in the picture.

One way to alleviate this is to map areas onto areas rather than points onto points. Every time the patch is subdivided, the picture is also subdivided. When the algorithm determines that a subpatch is to be displayed, the corresponding area on the picture is known. The average intensity of that area can be found and used as the intensity of the piece. While this reduces considerably the sampling problem it does not completely solve it.

Conclusion

The subdivision algorithm has been implemented in software on a PDP-10 at the University of Utah. Several pictures generated by the program are included in this paper.

Table 1 lists some timing information about the generation of a few of the pictures. The initialization of the frame buffer took about 7 seconds and displaying the frame buffer took about 28 seconds. The times listed below do not include initialization and display time.

Object	Time (minutes: seconds)
glass	1:55
bottle	4:15
klein bottle	15:00

Table 1

List of References

[1] I.E. Sutherland, R.F. Sproull, R.A. Schumacker, "A Characterization of Ten Hidden-Surface Algorithms." ACM Computing Surveys, Volume 6, number 1, March 1974.

[3] H. Gouraud, "Computer Display of Curved Surfaces," Department of Computer Science, University of Utah, UTEC-CSc-71-113, June 1971. Also in IEEE, TC-20 June 1971, page 623.

[4] Bui Tuong-Phong, "Illumination for Computer-Generated Images," Department of Computer Science, University of Utah, UTEC-CSs-73-129, July 1973.

[5] MAGI, Mathematical Applications Group Inc., "3-D Simulated Graphics," Datamation, February 14, 1968, p. 69.

[6] R.Mahl, "Visible Surface Algorithm for Quadric Patches," IEEE, TC-21, p.1, January. 1972.

[7] W.M. Newman and R.F. Sproull, *Principles of Interactive Graphics*, Chapter 12, McGraw-Hill, 1973.

[8] I.E. Sutherland and G.W. Hodgman, "Reentrant Polygon Clipping," CACM, page 43, January, 1974.

[9] J.E. Warnock, "A Hidden-Line Algorithm for Halftone Picture Representation," Department of Computer Science, University of Utah, TR 4-15, 1969.

[10] M.E. Newell, R.G. Newell, T.L. Sancha, "A New Approach to the Shaded Picture Problem," Proceedings of the ACM, 1973 National Conference.

[11] R.E. Barnhill and R.F. Riesenfeld, *Computer Aided Geometric Design,* Academic Press, 1975.

[12] A.R. Forrest, "On Coons and Other Methods for the Representation of Curved Surfaces." Computer Graphics and Image Processing, page 341, 1972. (Contains an extensive bibliography.)

[13] A.R. Forrest, "Appendix 2—Coons' Surfaces," *Numerical Control – Mathematics and Applications* P.E. Bésier, London: John Wiley and Sons, 1972.

[14] J.H. Clark, "B-spline Surface Design," Dissertation, Computer Science Department, University of Utah, December 1974.

[15] E.E. Catmull, "A Subdivision Algorithm for Computer Display of Curved Surfaces," Technical Report, Computer Science Department, University of Utah, December, 1974.

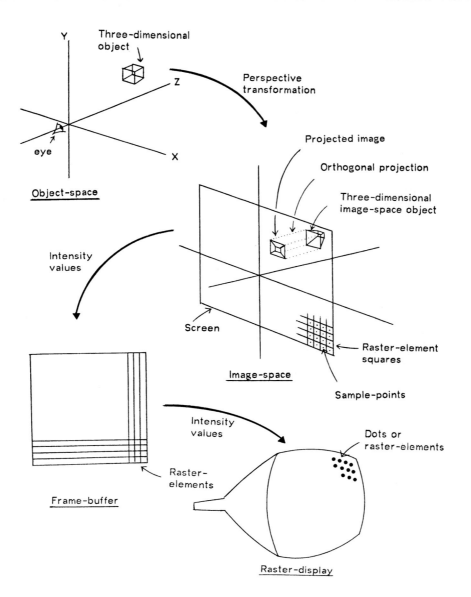

Figure 1

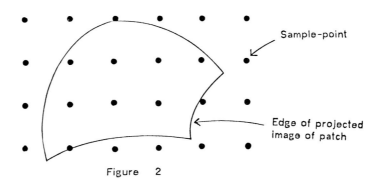

Sample-point
Edge of projected image of patch

Figure 2

Patch divided into four sub-patches

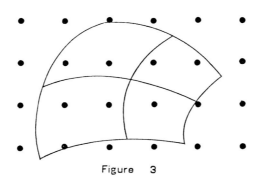

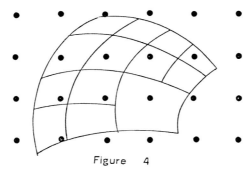

Figure 3

Patch subdivided so that no sub-patch covers more than one sample-point

Figure 4

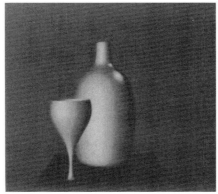

Picture 1

A bottle and glass. The bottle has 32 patches.

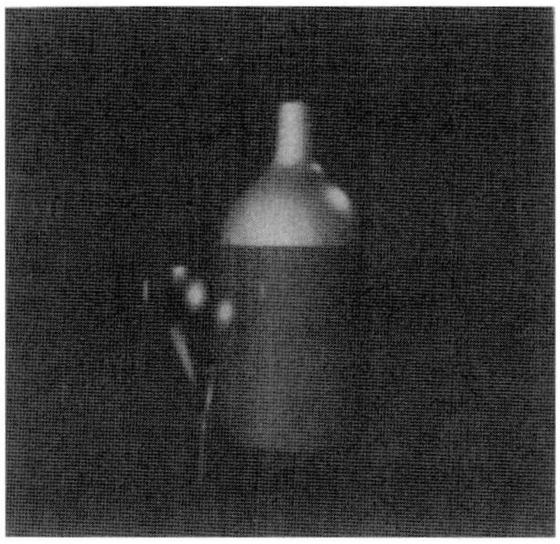

Picture 2

The bottle and glass with transparency added to the glass and "color" to the bottle.

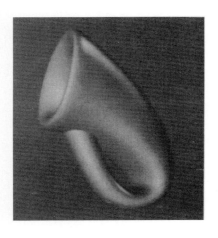

Picture 3

Klein bottle. Designed by Dr. James Clark using B-Splines.

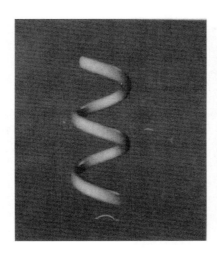

Picture 4

A spiral tube.

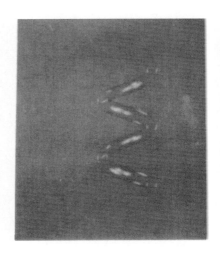

Picture 5

A transparent spiral tube.

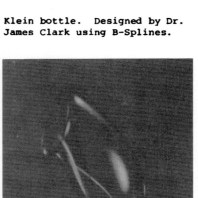

Picture 6

Klein bottle with transparency.

Picture 7

142 bottles and glasses.

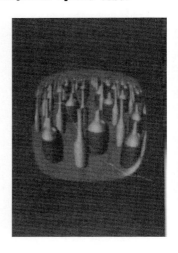

Picture 8

The bottles scene mapped onto a curved patch.

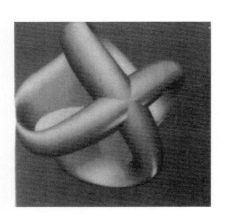

Picture 9

A sphere midway through its eversion. Designed by Dr. Nelson Max at Carnegie-Mellon University using bicubic Coons patches.

Picture 10

A photograph of a hill mapped onto a curved patch.

Picture 11

Winnie the Poo and Tigger on a curved patch.

Picture 12

The brick image mapped respectively onto a single rounded patch, a stretched patch, an S curved patch, and a cylinder of four patches.

Graphics and
Image Processing

Hierarchical Geometric Models for Visible Surface Algorithms

James H. Clark
University of California at Santa Cruz

The geometric structure inherent in the definition of the shapes of three-dimensional objects and environments is used not just to define their relative motion and placement, but also to assist in solving many other problems of systems for producing pictures by computer. By using an extension of traditional structure information, or a geometric hierarchy, five significant improvements to current techniques are possible. First, the range of complexity of an environment is greatly increased while the visible complexity of any given scene is kept within a fixed upper limit. Second, a meaningful way is provided to vary the amount of detail presented in a scene. Third, "clipping" becomes a very fast logarithmic search for the resolvable parts of the environment within the field of view. Fourth, frame to frame coherence and clipping define a graphical "working set," or fraction of the total structure that should be present in primary store for immediate access by the visible surface algorithm. Finally, the geometric structure suggests a recursive descent, visible surface algorithm in which the computation time potentially grows linearly with the visible complexity of the scene.

Key Words and Phrases: visible surface algorithms, hidden surface algorithms, hierarchical data structures, geometric models
CR Categories: 5.31, 8.2

Copyright © 1976, Association for Computing Machinery, Inc. General permission to republish, but not for profit, all or part of this material is granted provided that ACM's copyright notice is given and that reference is made to the publication, to its date of issue, and to the fact that reprinting privileges were granted by permission of the Association for Computing Machinery.
A version of this paper was presented at SIGGRAPH 76: The Third Annual Conference on Computer Graphics, Interactive Techniques, and Image Processing, The Wharton School, University of Pennsylvania, July 14–16, 1976.
Author's address: Information Sciences, University of California, Santa Cruz, CA 95064.

1. Introduction

1.1 Background

Early research in computer graphics was concerned with the organization and presentation of graphical information in the form of real-time line drawings on a CRT. Many of the concepts of structuring graphical information were developed by Sutherland in Sketchpad [19], and the line-drawing graphical displays that resulted from his early research remain the most widely used today. With the development of integrated circuit technology, research interests shifted to producing very realistic, shaded, color pictures of the visible parts of complex three-dimensional objects. Because of the desire to utilize television technology, the algorithms for producing these pictures generated output for a raster CRT. The pioneering works in this area were by Schumacker et al. [18] and Wylie et al. [23].

Computer produced pictures now provide one of the most direct and useful ways of communicating with the computer. The ability to produce shaded pictures that illustrate mathematical functions and physical properties of mathematical models is of incontestable value in both research and education. With the development of computer controlled simulators, a real-time computer displayed environment is now used to train pilots of aircraft [11, 16], spacecraft [9] and ocean vessels [2]. Other significant uses of computer pictures include computer aided design [4], modeling of chemical structures [22], and computer animation [7, 12]. With this increased value of computer generated pictures, comes an increasing need to devise efficient algorithms that improve the realism and enhance the descriptive power of these pictures.

1.2 Motivation for New Research

The underlying motivation for new research on computer produced pictures is to either enhance the realism of the pictures or improve the performance of the algorithms that generate them. Most recent research has addressed a combination of these issues.

There are three basic approaches to improving picture quality. The first is to devise clever ways to add information value to a scene without significantly increasing the total amount of information in the database for the scene, for example, without increasing the number of polygons used in representing the objects. Approaches of this type usually make subtle changes to the visible surface and shading algorithms that result in greatly improved pictures. Examples are the improvements to shading algorithms devised by H. Gouraud [10] and Bui-Tuong Phong [15].

The second approach is to employ more refined mathematical models for the objects being rendered and to devise algorithms that can find the visible surfaces using these models. The goal of these methods is to model smooth surfaces with surface patches, such as Coons patches [5] or B-splines [4, 17], rather than with clusters of polygons, and still not increase the size of the database. Catmull's [3] ingenious algorithm is an example of this approach. The benefit of these methods is that an arbitrarily refined description of the model is present, thus allowing much better renditions of contours and shading. The disadvantage is that because of nonlinear mathematics, the algorithms are less efficient than polygon-based algorithms.

The third approach is to increase the information in the database and employ more structured methods for handling the increased information. The motivation for this approach is that the information value of a scene grows in proportion to the amount of information in the database for the scene. Newell's [13] algorithm is an example of this approach.

The structured approach appears to be the most promising of these approaches since it potentially improves both picture quality and algorithm performance. However, there are several problems associated with this approach. First, increased complexity of a scene, or increased information in the database, has less value as the resolution limits of the display are approached. It makes no sense to use 500 polygons in describing an object if it covers only 20 raster units of the display. How do we select only that portion of the data base that has meaning in the context of the resolution of the viewing device? Second, how do we accommodate the increased storage requirements of this additional information? We might, for example, wish to model a human body to the extent that a closeup view of the eye shows the patterns of the iris, yet such a fine description of the entire body will indeed require large amounts of store. Third, how much information must be presented to convey the information content of the scene? In other words, we would like to present the minimal information needed to convey the meaning of what is being viewed. For example, when we view the human body mentioned above from a very large distance, we might need to present only "specks" for the eyes, or perhaps just a "block" for the head, totally eliminating the eyes from consideration. The amount of information "needed" can be the subject of psychological debate, but it is clear that even coarse decisions will yield more manageable scenes than attempting to use all of the available information.

These issues have not previously been addressed in a unified way. The research described here represents an attempt to solve these and related problems.

2. Summary of Existing Algorithms

Visible surface algorithms may be categorized according to whether they employ polygons, parametric surface patches, or procedures as the underlying method of modeling the surfaces they render. The most thoroughly studied types of algorithms use polygons. However, because of the shortcomings of representing smooth surfaces with faceted clusters of polygons, some research interest has recently been devoted to parametric surface algorithms, which allow higher degrees of continuity than just positional continuity. The algorithms for these different modeling methods will be discussed separately.

2.1 Polygon-Based Algorithms

A highly informative survey of existing polygon-based visible surface algorithms has been written by Sutherland et al. [20]. As they point out, a convenient way to classify these algorithms is according to the order in which they sort the image space polygons that are potentially visible in a scene. The basic difference between the major algorithms is in whether they sort in depth (from the viewpoint) before the vertical-horizontal sort, or vice versa.

Depth-first sort. The most significant algorithms to use this sorting order are due to Schumacker et al. [18] and Newell et al. [14]. Schumacker utilizes this order along with a polygon clustering concept to achieve a coherence from one frame to the next, while Newell utilizes it to render translucent images. By first computing a priority ordering of polygons according to their image space distance from the screen, they are able to establish which polygon *segments* on a given scan line have visibility priority.

Newell uses this information to write those segments with a lesser priority into a scan-line buffer before writing in those with a greater priority. Thus greater priority segments which are from translucent polygons only modify the intensity values in the buffer rather than completely overwriting them. While there is clearly a considerable overhead in writing into the buffer segments that might eventually be obscured, some beautiful pictures have resulted from this work.

Schumacker's goal is to produce real-time picture sequences. Rather than writing the polygon segment information for a scan-line into a buffer according to its priority, a set of priority-ordered hardware registers are simultaneously loaded with the priority-ordered segment information. Then as the scan line is displayed, the register information is counted down and a combinational-logic network selects the appropriate highest priority register according to its lateral displacement on the screen. This approach requires a separate set of registers for each polygon segment that intersects the scan line. Nonetheless, it represents the first real-time solution to the visible surface problem [9].

There are two very significant features to Schumacker's work. First, he makes use of a priori knowledge of the database to compute fixed priorities for clusters of polygons. If the polygons in a group of polygons are not subject to changes in relative placement, they form a *cluster* and may be assigned fixed priorities which work no matter from where the cluster is viewed. Thus part of the priority ordering is fixed with the environment and need not be recomputed each frame. Second, he shows that if the environment is restricted so that the clusters are linearly separable, an intercluster priority can be established that does not change unless the viewpoint crosses one of the separating planes; hence, the priority ordering remains fixed from one frame to the next unless one of the planes is crossed.

This work by Schumacker and coworkers represents the only visible surface algorithm to make use of both structured information (clustering) and frame to frame coherence (relatively constant intercluster priority). These very important concepts will be discussed in more detail later.

Depth-last sort. The algorithms that use this sorting order have been devised by Watkins [21], Bouknight [1], and Wylie et al. [23]. They are referred to as scan-line algorithms and differ only in their use of various image-space coherence properties. All three first perform a vertical bucket (radix) sort of polygon edges according to their uppermost vertices. Then for each scan line, the various polygon segments on that scan line are sorted according to their horizontal displacements. The depth sort is deferred until last under the assumption that the initial two sorts will decrease the number of depth comparisons needed to determine final visibility.

Of the three approaches, Watkins' is the most economical because of its uses of scan-line coherence and a logarithmic depth search. The assumption of scan-line coherence is that in going from one scan line to the next, the number of changed polygon segments is small; hence the horizontal sort may be optimized to take advantage of this. Watkins' is the only other algorithm besides Schumacker's that has been implemented in hardware.

2.2 Parametric Surface Algorithms

Modeling smooth surfaces with collections of polygons leads to problems both in shading the surface and in rendering the contour edges. While there have been a number of very clever improvements to the quality of such pictures without significantly increasing the amount of information used, notably those of Gouraud [10], Phong [15], and Crow [6], the most direct approach is to employ a more refined model, such as parametric surface patches. Such patches can be used to define the surface using no more, and usually even less, information than is required with polygons. Yet they can join together with tangent or even higher continuity, thus eliminating the above problems. The difficulty with this method is that the mathematics is no longer linear; to explicitly solve for such things as the curve of intersection of two bi-cubic patches or of a patch and a clipping plane are very difficult problems.

Catmull [3] solves such problems, but not explicitly. Rather, he does so by employing the discrete character of the image space, a recursive algorithm, and what he calls a Z-buffer. For each patch in the environment his algorithm asks: does the patch extend over more than a single raster unit? If the answer is yes, the patch is subdivided (by a very fast algorithm for bi-cubic patches) into four patches and the same question is *recursively* asked of these patches. When the answer finally is no, an attempt is made to write the intensity and depth coordinates for the resulting "patch" into a buffer for the raster unit, or *pixel*, in question. The attempt fails if the pixel buffer already has in it a depth coordinate nearer to the observer (with some minor modifications to allow for translucent patches).

A very significant feature of Catmull's algorithm is that, despite the more complex mathematics, it will actually work faster than polygon-based algorithms if the object being rendered occupies a very small area of the screen. Because of the recursive structure of the algorithm, it will "structure" the surface no more finely than the resolution of the display dictates, whereas current polygon-based algorithms keep the same structural description, i.e. the same number of polygons, no matter how much of the screen area is occupied. This notion of structuring will be extended to include polygon-based algorithms in the next section.

2.3 Procedurally Modeled Objects

Newell [13] has recently employed procedural modeling to solve the visible surface problem for complex scenes. According to this approach, objects are modeled using procedures which "know how" to render themselves in terms of their own primitives, which might include activations of other object procedures; such knowledge includes rendering only their visible parts. This is a very general way to represent objects.

Although the underlying philosophy of this approach is very general, in the actual implementation Newell user polygons as the basic primitives for the objects. The object procedures are activated according to a priority ordering so that more distant objects are activated first. Each procedure renders the object it represents by activating the Watkins process, the results of which are written into a frame buffer. The net result is therefore a "hybrid" Watkins/Newell priority algorithm.

The significant point about this algorithm is not the procedural modeling but that it represents another example of structuring to simplify the total sorting problem, namely that the geometric primitives of one object need be compared with those of another only when the objects overlap.

3. Hierarchical Approach

It was indicated in the previous section that, aside from uses of image-space coherence to reduce the amount of sorting required, the most fruitful gains in visible surface algorithm research have resulted from structuring the environments being rendered. However, the structures employed take a diverse variety of forms, from Catmull's implicit structuring of surface patches to Newell's procedural objects. What is needed is a single, unified, structural approach that embodies all of the ideas from these algorithms. Before presenting one such approach it is instructive to consider two ways in which structure has been utilized to prepare objects for visible surface processing.

3.1 Existing Uses of Structure

Defining relative placement. The benefits of a position or motion structure have been realized for some time. Sutherland used such concepts in two dimensions in Sketchpad, and a number of graphics hardware companies incorporate transformation hardware in their display devices to accommodate structural descriptions. Most of the visible surface algorithms presented used a position or motion structure to describe positions and orientations of objects relative to each other. However, all but the few mentioned in Section 2 disregard the structure at the visible surface algorithm level. That is, all polygons of the objects are transformed into a common screen coordinate system in which the visible surface algorithm works.

An example of such a structure is shown in Figure 1. Each node in the hierarchy represents a set of geometric primitives (e.g. polygons) defining the node and the arc leading to the node represents a transformation defining the orientation and placement of the node relative to its "parent." Because each node has its own unique transformation defining it, it may represent one of many "instances" of the same primitive description, or data set. This is a very convenient and general way to define and place objects.

Decreasing clipping time. When simulating a camera in a computer-generated environment, some parts of the environment must be "clipped" to the field of view of the simulated camera. This can be done either by transforming all of the geometric primitives of each object into the camera, or screen, coordinate system and clipping each of them separately or by first clipping some bounding volume of the object to see if it intersects the boundaries of the field of view. If it does not, then the parts of the object lie either totally within or totally outside of the field of view and thus need not be separately clipped. This utilization of the above mentioned position hierarchy is implicitly assumed, although this author does not know if the authors of the various algorithms actually made such use of it.

3.2 New Uses of Structure

Varying environment detail. By choosing to represent an object with a certain amount of detail, one fixes the minimum distance from which the object may be displayed with a realistic rendering. For example, a dodecahedron looks like a sphere from a sufficiently large distance and thus can be used to model it so long

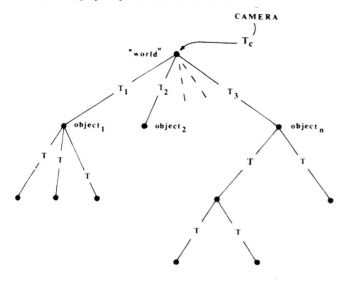

Fig. 1. The traditional motion structure used to position objects relative to the "world" and subobjects relative to objects. Each arc in the graph represents a transformation.

as it is viewed from that or a greater distance. However, if it must ever be viewed more closely, it will look like a dodecahedron. One solution to this is simply to define it with the most detail that will ever be necessary. However, then it might have far more detail than is needed to represent it at large distances, and in a complex environment with many such objects, there would be too many polygons (or other geometric primitives) for the visible surface algorithms to efficiently handle.

As mentioned in Section 2, the solution to this problem has been to define objects relatively coarsely and employ clever algorithms that smooth appropriate contours or improve shading to make the object look more realistic at close observation. The difficulty with these approaches is that at best the range of viewing depth is only slightly improved, and the problem of too much detail at large distances usually remains. Although these approaches have yielded results of unquestionable value, it seems evident that multiple levels of description must be used to adequately represent complex environments.[1]

How does one represent these multiple levels of description? A solution is to define "objects" in a hierarchy like that of Figure 2. The entire environment is itself an "object" and is represented as a rooted tree. ("Object" is a generic term for the things represented by nodes of the tree. This generic term will be used for the remainder of this paper.) There are two types of arcs in the tree, those that represent transformations as before and those that represent pointers to more detailed structure (the identity transformation). Each nonterminal node represents a "sufficient" description of the "object" if it covers no more than some small

---

[1] Actually, Evans and Sutherland made use of a three-level description of the New York skyline in its Maritime simulation, but in an ad hoc way [2].

area of the display; the arcs leading from the node point to more detailed "objects" which collectively define a more detailed version of the original object if its description is insufficient because it covers a larger area of the screen. The terminal nodes of the tree represent either polygons or surface patches (or other primitives) according to whether they are primitive elements of a faceted or a smooth object.

As an example of such a description, consider a model of the human body. When viewed at a very large distance, for example when the body covers only 3 or 4 display raster units, it is sufficient to model the body with a single rectangular polyhedron with appropriate color. Therefore the uppermost node, or "object," for this body represents this simple description. If the body is viewed from a closer distance—for example, if its topmost node's description covers 16 raster units—then this topmost description is no longer sufficient, and the next level of more refined description is needed. At this next level the body is now perhaps described as a collection of rectangular polyhedra appropriately attached to each other, for example using one polyhedron for each of the arms and legs, the head and the torso. Then so long as each of these "objects" covers only a few raster units of the display, their description is "sufficient." When the viewing distance decreases such that any of them covers a critical maximum area of the display, its more detailed subobjects are used to replace its description. This process is carried out to whatever maximum level of detail will be needed. For example, a terminal level of description of the fingertip might be several surface patches (which could be implicitly structured even more finely using Catmull's algorithm).

The body described is just one "object" of an environment, or larger hierarchy. There might be many such bodies, or other objects. The significant point, however, is that in a complex environment, the amount of information presented about the various objects in the environment varies according to the fraction of the field of view occupied by these objects.

It is worth noting again that Catmull's algorithm, described in the previous section, implicitly built such a structure. His algorithm used this structure in such a way that, despite the more complex mathematics of surface patches, it outperforms polygon-based algorithms if the surface occupies a small area of the screen. Thus it seems that such a structure should lead to improvements in polygon-based algorithms as well.

Clipping: a truncated logarithmic search. The choice of this structural representation poses another problem. How does one select only that portion of a potentially very large hierarchy that is meaningful in the context of the viewpoint and the resolution of the viewing device? In other words, clipping in a broader sense must mean selecting not only that part of the environment within the field of view (the usual meaning) but also just the *resolvable* part. This implies finding the visible nodes of the tree, as shown in Figure 2. The contour shown in the figure represents a possible set of objects that are within the field of view and are both not too large and not too small for the screen areas they occupy.

In order to efficiently perform this clipping operation some minimal description of object sizes must be available. For example, a bounding rectangular box or a bounding sphere would be sufficient information to test whether an object is totally within or totally outside of the field of view. The minimum necessary information is the center and radius of a bounding sphere.

This general structure therefore suggests a very fast clipping algorithm which recursively descends the tree, transforming (if necessary) this minimal information into perspective viewing coordinates and testing both the area occupied by the bounding sphere and its intersection with the boundaries of the field of view. The criterion for descending a level is the area test, while the criterion for inclusion/rejection is the field of view boundary test. Only after either the area test terminates the descent or the terminal level of representation is reached is it necessary to actually transform and possibly clip the polygons or surface patches represented by the node. Clipping therefore resembles a logarithmic search that is truncated by the area (resolvability) test.

This relatively simple mechanism for varying the detail in a scene suggests several other interesting possibilities. Since the center of attention of a scene is often its geometric center, one might effectively render the scene with a center-weighting of detail. In other words, the maximum area an object is allowed to cover before splitting it into its subobjects becomes larger towards the periphery of the field of view. This is somewhat analogous to the center-weighted metering systems of some cameras. Likewise, since moving objects are less resolved by both the human eye (because of saccadic suppression) and a camera (because of blurring), one can render them with an amount of detail that varies inversely with their speeds. Indeed, an entire scene might be rendered with less detail if the camera is moving. Thus "clipping" can be extended to include these concepts as well.

Graphical working set. Since the problems addressed by this model are those associated with producing pictures and picture sequences of very complex environments, the excessive storage needed for the geometric description of these environments must somehow be accommodated. Denning's "working set" model for program behavior provides a useful analogy [8]. According to this model, a computer program that makes excessive demands on immediate-access store is structured or segmented, and its storage demands are managed in such a way that only those segments most recently in use are actually kept in immediate-access store. The remaining potentially large number of segments are kept on a slower, secondary store, such as a disk. The "working set" is that set of segments

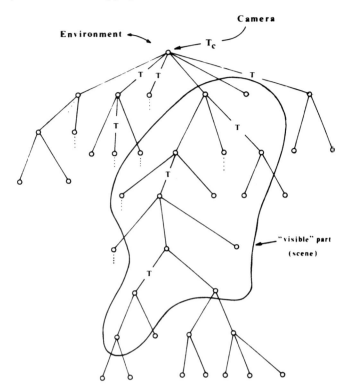

Fig. 2. A very deep hierarchy that structures the environment much more than the traditional motion structure. Arcs in this graph represent either transformations or pointers to more refined definitions of the node. The visible part contour represents a possible result of clipping.

available for immediate access, and is usually defined by a time average of past program reference patterns. Reference to an unavailable segment causes that segment to become part of the working set, and segments not accessed after some period of time are deleted from the working set.

This working set model coupled with the broader sense of clipping mentioned above suggests a suitable way to accomplish a particular type of frame coherence. The working set in this context is that set of objects in the hierarchy that are "near" to the field of view, inside it, or "near" to the resolution of the image space. Only if an object is a member of this set is its description kept in immediate-access store. The set membership will change slowly since the differences between one scene and the next are usually small. Those cases in which the differences are large due to fast camera (or object) motion are easily accommodated by rendering the scene (or object) with less detail, as mentioned above. Moreover, the minimal description of node size needed for clipping suffices as the graphical analog of the segment table used in the computer program context. That is, this minimal clipping description must always be available in immediate-access store to facilitate determining the working set. This working set model therefore seems particularly well suited to the graphics context.

Improving existing algorithms. There are two ways in which a geometric hierarchy should lead to improvements in existing algorithms. The first is by reducing the number of comparisons needed to sort objects and the second is by eliminating from potential consideration an entire portion of the environment because an object obscures it.

Since sorting is the central problem of visible surface algorithms, the performance of these algorithms improves with improved sorting methods. Indeed, many of the fast visible surface algorithms that have been discussed have resulted from clever utilization of image-space coherences, such as scan-line coherence, to improve sorting speeds. In the present hierarchical framework, the geometric proximity of the subobjects of an object provides an object-space coherence that can also be utilized to decrease sorting time.

For example, consider an ideal case of a binary tree as shown in Figure 3. Each node of the tree has associated with it a bounding volume, but since this ideal tree is the result of clipping, only the terminal nodes actually represent geometric primitives, e.g. polygons or patches. Assuming that there are n levels in the tree, not counting the root node, there are $m = 2^n$ terminal nodes.

If the structure is ignored, then the fastest possible sort of these terminal nodes is accomplished with proportional to $m \log_2 m$ comparisons using a quicksort. However, if the structure is utilized and if the bounding volumes of siblings do not overlap, which is admittedly an optimum arrangement, then the number of required operations is $p2^0$ for the first level, $p2^1$ for the second level, $p2^2$ for the third, etc., where p is a proportionality factor. Summing the number of operations performed at all levels yields $p\sum_{i=0}^{n-1} 2^i = p(2^n - 1)$, or roughly pm. In other words, by using the structure, in the optimum situation of no overlap, the sorting time grows linearly rather than as $m \log_2 m$.

Of course, this analysis holds only for a binary hierarchy in which none of the siblings' bounding volumes overlap, which is an idealized situation. A binary hierarchy might not be appropriate, and any complex environment will no doubt have some overlap, although presumably not a very large amount. However, the point here is that sorting methods which utilize the geometric structure can yield a considerable performance improvement over those which do not, even under less than ideal conditions.

The other improvement provided by a deeply structured geometric hierarchy is that of eliminating a potentially large part of the structure from consideration because an object obscures it. Such an improvement requires defining for each object (in the generic sense) both a simple occluded volume, Δ, such that if Δ is obscured then the entire object is obscured, and a simple occluding volume, δ, such that if δ obscures something then that thing is sure to be obscured by the object. Clearly, Δ exists for all objects, whereas δ might not exist for some objects, such as an open-ended cylinder or a transparent object. Δ can be just the bounding sphere used in clipping, but δ is in general additional information that must be kept for each object.

Recursive descent, visible surface algorithm. The above considerations suggest a totally new recursive-descent visible surface algorithm in which at each level all objects are sorted according to their bounding volumes. If any of the bounding volumes overlap both laterally and vertically then the occlusion test potentially allows one (or more) of the objects, and hence all of its descendents, to be totally eliminated from consideration.

Using the ordering thus obtained, the same sorting and occlusion tests are recursively applied to each of the descendants of these objects; in those cases where two or more objects' bounding volumes overlap in all three dimensions, indicating potential intersections, the descendents of these objects are treated as if they have the same parent nodes at the next level of recursion. Of course, recursion terminates when a terminal node is reached, and the net result of descending the tree is a very rapid sort of the primitives represented by these terminal nodes. Under ideal conditions, the computation time of this algorithm grows linearly with the *visible* complexity of the scene.

Since both this algorithm and the clipping algorithm described above recursively descend a tree structure, it seems natural to combine them. Doing so not only potentially eliminates area tests on occluded objects but also potentially decreases the size of the working set. If all processing is performed by a single pro-

Fig. 3. An ideal binary hierarchy in which none of the terminal nodes overlap. The first $p2^0$ comparison sorts all objects into two classes, the second $p2^1$ comparisons sort them into 4 classes, etc. Summing all comparisons from all levels yields $p(2^n - 1)$ comparisons.

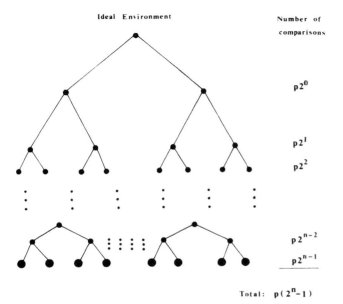

cessor, such as a general purpose computer, then the algorithms are probably most conveniently integrated into a single algorithm. However, if multiple processors are available, whether special purpose hardware or general purpose computers, then the algorithms might be left separate or combined according to whether parallelism is achieved by pipelining or otherwise.

Building structured databases. Obtaining a good graphical database is a very time consuming and difficult part of computer picture research. Databases obtained by careful measurement of real objects, by "building" objects from collections of simple mathematical objects, or by sculpturing surfaces in three dimensions [4] are at least as valuable as the visible surface algorithms that render them.

At first glance it appears that the structural framework multiplies the dimensions of this problem since multiple descriptions of the same object must be defined. However, in the case of carefully measured real objects, the multiple descriptions can be produced by judicious "bottom-up" pruning of existing definitions of the objects in their most detailed form. Therefore use can be made of all objects that have already been defined.

Those existing objects modeled with surface patches also present no problem. The coarser, high-level descriptions of these objects can be obtained by replacing the patches themselves with polygons and proceeding with the "bottom-up" pruning mentioned above to obtain even coarser descriptions. The finer, low-level descriptions of the objects can be obtained by "top-down" splitting of the surface patches, as in the Catmull algorithm. This can be done either at display time or beforehand in building the database; the difference is the traditional time/space tradeoff.

4. Conclusions

All of the recent major advances in computer picture research have resulted from either explicitly or implicitly incorporating structure information in the geometric modeling techniques. This research represents an attempt to encompass all of these advances in a more general structural framework as a unified approach to solving a number of the important problems of systems for producing computer pictures.

The proposed hierarchical models potentially solve a number of these problems. They provide a meaningful way to vary the amount of detail in a scene both according to the screen area occupied by the objects in the scene and according to the speed with which an object or the camera is moving. They also extend the total range of definition of the object space and suggest convenient ways to rapidly access objects by utilizing a graphical working set to accomplish frame coherence.

An important aspect of the hierarchical models is that by providing a way to vary detail they can yield an incremental improvement to existing systems for producing computer pictures without modifying their visible surface algorithms. Another incremental improvement is then possible by incorporating the structure in the sorting phases of existing algorithms. A final improvement is suggested by a totally new recursive descent visible surface algorithm in which the computation time potentially grows linearly with the visible complexity of a scene rather than as a worse than linear function of the object-space complexity.

References
1. Bouknight, W.J. A procedure for generation of three-dimensional half-toned computer graphics representations. *Comm. ACM, 13*, 9 (Sept. 1970), 527.
2. Computer Aided Operations and Research Facility, U.S. Maritime Service Simulator (principal contractor Philco-Ford, visible-surface processor by Evans and Sutherland Comptr. Corp.)
3. Catmull, E. A subdivision algorithm for computer display of curved surfaces. Tech. Rep. UTEC-CSc-74-133, U. of Utah, Salt Lake City, Utah, Dec. 1974.
4. Clark, J.H. 3-D design of free-form B-spline surfaces. UTEC-CSc-74-120, Ph.D. Th., U. of Utah, Salt Lake City, Utah, (abridged version Designing surfaces in 3-D. *Comm. ACM 19*, 8 (Aug. 1976), 464–470.)
5. Coons, S.A. Surfaces for computer-aided design of space forms. Project MAC TR-41., M.I.T., Cambridge, Mass., June 1967.
6. Crow, F.C., and Bui-Tuong Phong. Improved Rendition of Polygonal Models of Curved Surfaces. Proc. Second USA-Japan Comptr. Conf., Aug. 1975, p. 475.
7. Csuri, C. Computer animation, Computer Graphics 9, 1 (1975), 92–101 (Issue of Proc. Second Ann. Conf. Comptr. Graphics and Interactive Techniques).
8. Denning, P.J. The working set model for program behavior. *Comm. ACM, 11*, 5 (May 1968), 323–333.
9. Electonic scene generator expansion system. Final Rep., NASA Contract NAS 9-11065, Defense Electronic Div., General Electric Corp., Syracuse, N.Y., Dec. 1971.
10. Gouraud, H. Computer display of curved surfaces. *IEEE Trans. Computers C-20* (June 1971), 623.
11. Nasa-Ames Short Take-off and Landing Simulator (built by Evans and Sutherland Comptr. Corp.).
12. New York Inst. Tech., Comptr. Animation Dep.
13. Newell, M. The utilization of procedure models in digital image synthesis. Ph.D. Th., Comptr. Sci., U. of Utah, Salt Lake City, Utah, 1975.
14. Newell, M.E., Newell, R.G., and Sancha, T.L. A new solution to the hidden-surface problem. Proc. ACM 1972 Ann. Conf., pp. 443–448.
15. Bui-Tuong Phong. Illumination for computer generated pictures. *Comm. ACM 18*, 6 (June 1975), 311–317.
16. Rediflow Flight Simulation, Ltd., NOVOVIEW Visual Systems (video system provided by E&S Comptr. Corp.).
17. Riesenfeld, R.E. Applications of B-spline approximation to geometric problems of computer aided design. Ph.D. Th., Syracuse U., Syracuse, N.Y., 1972.
18. Schumacker, R.A., Brand, B., Gilliland, M., and Sharp, W. Study for applying computer-generated images to visual simulations. AFHRL-TR-69-74, US Air Force Human Resources Lab., Washington, D.C., Sept. 1969.
19. Sutherland, I.E. Sketchpad: a man-machine graphical communication system. TR 296, M.I.T Lincoln Labs, M.I.T., Cambridge, Mass., Jan. 1963.
20. Sutherland, I.E., Sproull, R.F., and Schumacker, R.A. A characterization of ten hidden-surface algorithms. Computing Surveys, *6*, 1 (March 1974), 1–55.
21. Watkins, G.S. A real-time visible-surface algorithm. UTECH-CSc-70-101, Ph.D. Th., Comptr. Sci. Dep., U. of Utah, Salt Lake City, Utah, June, 1970.
22. Wipke, T., et al. *Computer Representation and Manipulation of Chemical Information*. Wylie Interscience, New York, 1974.
23. Wylie, C., Romney, R.S., Evans, D.C., and Erdahl, A. Halftone perspective drawings by computer. Proc. AFIPS 1967 FJCC, Vol. 31, AFIPS Press, Montvale, N.J., pp. 49–58.

CASTING CURVED SHADOWS ON CURVED SURFACES

Lance Williams
Computer Graphics Lab
New York Institute of Technology
Old Westbury, New York 11568

Abstract

Shadowing has historically been used to increase the intelligibility of scenes in electron microscopy and aerial survey. Various methods have been published for the determination of shadows in computer synthesized scenes. The display of shadows may make the shape and relative position of objects in such scenes more comprehensible; it is a technique lending vividness and realism to computer animation.

To date, algorithms for the determination of shadows have been restricted to scenes constructed of planar polygons. A simple algorithm is described which utilizes Z-buffer visible surface computation to display shadows cast by objects modelled of smooth surface patches. The method can be applied to all environments, in fact, for which visible surfaces can be computed. The cost of determining the shadows associated with each light source is roughly twice the cost of rendering the scene without shadows, plus a fixed transformation overhead which depends on the image resolution. No extra entities are added to the scene description in the shadowing process. This comprehensive algorithm, which permits curved shadows to be cast on curved surfaces, is contrasted with a less costly method for casting the shadows of the environment on a single ground plane.

In order to attain good results, the discrete nature of the visible-surface computations must be treated with care. The effects of dither, interpolation, and geometric quantization at different stages of the shadowing algorithm are examined. The special problems posed by self-shadowing surfaces are described.

Key words: shadows, hidden surface algorithms, computer animation, computer graphics.

CR classification: 8.2

Introduction

The Z-buffer visible surface algorithm, first published by Catmull [1], was the first method to make possible computer generated shaded pictures of bicubic surface patches. The algorithm is extremely general and quite simple to implement but requires substantial memory.

A "frame buffer," in the current computer graphics parlance, is a memory that stores a complete digital picture. It may serve as an intermediary between the computer that produces the picture and a video driver which continuously refreshes a display. Some visible surface algorithms (e.g. [2]) require a frame buffer in order to compute an image. In this case, the frame buffer mediates the display process in a more substantial way.

The Z-buffer is an extension of this mass-memory approach to computer graphics which resolves the visible surfaces in a scene by storing depth (Z) values at each point in the picture. As objects are rendered, their Z values are compared at each point with the stored Z values to determine visibility. Since this determination requires only that a measure exist which orders the surfaces to be displayed, it is not too strong a statement to say that the Z-buffer algorithm provides a discrete solution to all scenes for which visible surfaces can be computed.

Z-buffer visible surface computation is of particular interest because it exhibits limiting-case properties [3]. The objects to be rendered do not have to be sorted beforehand, so indefinitely complex scenes can be handled. At the pixel level, the Z-buffer implicitly executes radix sorts in X and Y and simple indexing in Z. In X and Y, the sorts are bucket sorts, the special case of the radix sort where the radix encompasses the range of the keys, obviating all comparisons. In Z, the index of the sort is reduced to one, necessitating only a single comparison for each item.

Radix sorting is the only sorting method which grows only linearly in expense with the number of randomly-ordered items to be sorted, and the Z-buffer is the only visible surface algorithm the cost of which grows only linearly with the average depth complexity of the environment (that is to say, with the total screen area of all surfaces rendered, whether visible in the final image or not).

Thus the Z-buffer algorithm enjoys two key advantages over all other existing visible surface algorithms:

1. indefinitely large environments;

2. linear cost growth.

In addition, the final image computed has an associated Z partition, a "depth map" [4] of the scene. This extra information permits a great many interesting post-processes on a computed image. Such algorithms are noteworthy because their expense does not vary with the size or complexity of the environment, but depends only on the image resolution. The shadow algorithm described here is one attempt to exploit the Z partition.

Shadow Information

The display of shadows may make the shape and relative position of objects in computer generated scenes more comprehensible. Shadows emphasize and may serve to clarify the three dimensional nature of the forms displayed.

The shadows cast by a point source of light onto a flat surface represent, like a perspective transformation, a projection of the scene onto a plane. This simplified situation offers a convenient way of understanding the information that shadows convey. A scene rendered with shadows contains two views in one image. If we are content to cast shadows on a single wall or ground plane, these two views are simple projections. In general, of course, shadows may fall across any surface in the scene. Two views are still sufficient to compute the shadows, however, if they are Z-buffer views.

The proposed algorithm works as follows:

1. A view of the scene is constructed from the point of view of the light source. Only the Z values and not the shading values need be computed and stored.

2. A view of the scene is then constructed from the point of view of the observer's eye. A linear transformation exists which maps X,Y,Z points in the observer's view into X,Y,Z coordinates in the light source view. As each point is generated in the observer's view, it is transformed into the computed view in the light source space and tested for visibility to the light source before computing its shading value. If the point is not visible to the light source, it is in shadow and is shaded accordingly.

Step (2) as defined is the "correct" form of the proposed algorithm, but in the ensuing discussion and pictures a modified procedure is assumed. The complete scene is computed from the observer's viewpoint, and the point-by-point transformation to the light source space and consequent shadowing is undertaken as a post-process. This modified algorithm incorrectly shades the hilights in the scene, since they appear in the shading process and then are merely darkened if they are found to lie in shadow; hilights should not appear in shadowed areas at all. The modified algorithm may also suffer more severely from quantization problems, since the Z coordinates of the visible points will have been quantized to the resolution of the Z buffer (16 bits in the cases illustrated here) before transformation. On the other hand, the expense of the transformation in the modified version does not depend on the complexity of the scene, as it does when all points are transformed as they are computed. Operating as a post process, the transformation is applied only to the points that are visible in the final picture. The expense is thus dependent only on the resolution of the image. Like most point-by-point operations, expense increases with the square of the resolution.

Limitations of Image Space

The generalization to curved surfaces and the linear cost growth which distinguish the proposed algorithm are both attributable to the fact that all computations are performed in image space. This approach carries with it certain limitations, however, which must be weighed against the advantages.

Since shadow determination is based on transformation between two images, the user must take care to ensure that all objects which may cast a shadow in the observer's image be within the field of view of the light source image. The assumption is that points transformed into the light source space which lie outside the viewing volume of the light source are illuminated. Shadows may only be cast within the viewing volume of the light source.

While it is not precisely true that the light source must lie outside the observer's field of view, it can cast shadows only within its own field. If a light source within the observer's viewing volume is to cast shadows in all directions, its sphere of illumination must be sectored into multiple views as suggested by Crow [5]. Computing these views in the Z-buffer is only slightly more expensive than computing a single view containing all the objects in the scene. Transforming points from the observer's image into the light source space becomes more expensive, however. Either each point must be transformed into each light source view (the correct approach in computing shadows for multiple light sources), or clipped against the light source viewing volumes in the observer's space and transformed into the coordinates of the light source view in which it falls. The major difficulty with this method is the increased memory required.

Severe perspective, either in the observer's view or required by a light source close to the scene, may increase the quantization problems attendant in transforming from one image to the other. In any case, quantization and aliasing are the chief drawback of image space algorithms. The aliasing problem must be addressed vigorously whenever image space techniques are applied. This is a large and complicated issue, outside the scope of this paper; for a general treatment of aliasing and visible surface algorithms, see [1], [6], and especially [7]. [3] will treat the special topic of aliasing, geometric quantization and the Z-buffer.

Self-shadowing surfaces rendered by the proposed technique constitute an excellent case study in image space sampling problems. When we transform a point from a surface in the observer's space onto a surface in the light source space, it should ideally lie right on the surface of which it is a part. Due to the imprecision of machine arithmetic and more particularly to the quantization of Z-buffer surfaces, it will fall above or below the surface. Since we want the point to appear illuminated if it lies on a visible surface, we subtract a bias from

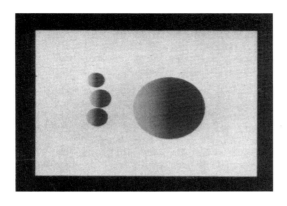

fig. 1
The observer's view of four spheres.

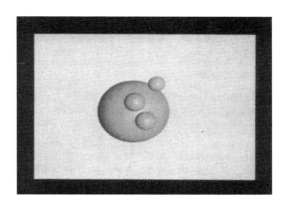

fig. 2
The four spheres viewed from the position of the light source.

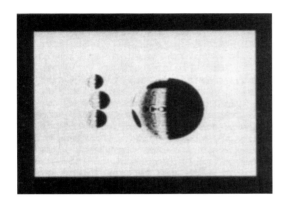

fig. 3
Shadow with reduced surface bias reveals quantization moire.

fig. 4
Increased bias and dither applied to shadow computation.

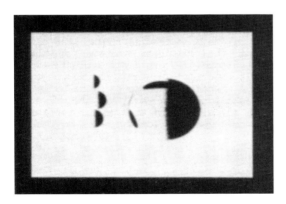

fig. 5
Low-pass filtering applied to shadow.

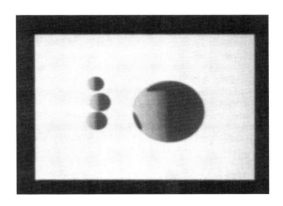

fig. 6
Shadow applied to the image of fig. 1

the Z value of the point after it has been transformed into the light source space (actually, of course, this bias is incorporated into the general linear transformation employed). The bias may move the shadow line slightly, but it has the desired effect of keeping surfaces from shadowing themselves where they are plainly visible to the light source.

As a surface curves smoothly away from the light, however, it must ultimately shadow itself. This is not a problem with polygons, the sharp edges of which make shadowing a rather sharply defined proposition. A smooth surface shadowing itself in a shallow curve may switch from light to dark on the strength of a least significant bit in the Z-buffer. Worse, it may switch back and forth as the quantizing error beats with the sampling grid, producing a vivid moire.

Figures 1 and 2 illustrate a simple scene from the point of view of an observer and from the point of view of the light source, respectively. The Z bias subtracted from the transformed points in computing the shadows of figure 3 has been deliberately reduced to reveal the quantizing moire. The light source is at infinity, rotated one hundred degrees about the vertical axis to the left of the observer's bearing. Note that the quantizing error is greatest in two areas: at the edge of the vertical solid shadow line, and in a dark curved band to the left of it. These correspond to, respectively, the right edge of the spheres in the light source view, and the right edge of the spheres in the untransformed observer's view. These edges are aliased in the original views, discrete periodic samples of non-bandlimited images. Another way of viewing the problem is that the edges are quantized in the original views, quantized to the nine bits of resolution available in X and Y. Clearly the problem is much greater than in Z, where sixteen bits are available. Unfortunately, extra lateral resolution is purchased at square law expense.

Bandlimiting the Z partition before sampling, if it were practical, would not improve matters. Z values at the edges of the spheres would be a smooth blend of the depth of the edge and the depth of the far clipping plane, meaningless points as far as the scene is concerned. The aliasing effects observed are local, however, and it is reasonable to treat the smooth surfaces within the ragged edges as correctly sampled. This assumption implies that a filter to reconstruct the surface between samples is in order. Indeed, interpolating the Z values of the light source image to derive Z values at the exact X,Y coordinates of the transformed observer points (rather than using the Z value of the nearest neighbor for comparison) improves matters somewhat, reducing shadow noise in the form of isolated pixels.

Treating shadow noise as a quantizing rather than an aliasing problem improves the image further. The error signal in a quantizing system correlates quite strongly with the signal. Addition of random noise in the range of a single quantum breaks up this correlation, reduces the resulting periodicities (moire) to which the human eye is so sensitive, and whitens the spectrum of the error. Figure 4 illustrates the sphere shadows with increased negative Z bias and bilinear interpolation of light source Z values to the X,Y of the transformed observer points, which have been dithered by the addition of normally distributed random values in the range -.5 to +.5. The shadow image is subsequently dejagged by an edge dequantizing filter similar to one advanced by Freeman [8], then low pass filtered to further smooth the contours and merge the dithered edge of self shadowing (figure 5).

As a final, not unimportant observation, figure 6 illustrates that the problem of self shadowing surfaces may not be terribly significant in practice. Figures 3 through 5 were of the computed shadows alone; figure 6 displays the shaded surfaces with their shadows. Shading the spheres according to the position of the light source casting the shadows causes a smooth shadow transition which obscures the quantization error. In practice, translucent shadows (their translucency corresponding to the additive "ambient" term in most surface shading formulations) generally look better than deep black shadows, and low pass filtering of the shadows before they are applied to the image subjectively approximates the soft penumbra cast by real light sources.

Conclusions

The algorithm described operates successfully on scenes of curved surface patches, and does so with a cost that increases only linearly with the complexity of the environment. The cost is roughly twice the cost of rendering the scene normally, plus the cost of transforming the points of the observer's image into the light source image. In the originally stated algorithm, the cost of transformation increases linearly with the depth complexity of the scene. The cost of transformation in a modified version of the algorithm which performs shadowing strictly as a post-process is fixed by the resolution of the screen, and corresponds to a scene with an average depth complexity of one. The rendering cost is only "roughly" twice the cost of rendering the scene normally, since the light source view requires no shading computation. Depending on the complexity of the shading rules applied [9], this may represent a substantial savings.

Speed does not directly correspond to "computational expense" when special hardware can be applied. The enormous interest in real-time graphics has led to the development of specialized transformation hardware, specifically, digital devices to multiply four by four transformation matrices by four element homogeneous point coordinates [10]. The modified version of the shadow algorithm, developed for animation purposes, is particularly suited to pipelining of the coordinate transforms. The intent at NYIT is to apply the Floating Point Systems AP120-B array processor to such problems.

The complexity of software necessary to implement the shadow algorithm is minimal if the necessary memory is available. Although it has long been suggested that two passes of a visible surface algorithm is sufficient to compute shadowing [5], relating the data provided by the two passes is very difficult for many algorithms. The Z-buffer provides a straightforward means of relating data in different views since the visible surfaces are three dimensional and hence subject to general three dimensional transformations.

The bright outlook for memory technology bodes well for mass-memory graphics. The shadow algorithm discussed here is one simple example of a wide class of extremely general algorithms which exhibit very desirable cost growth properties. The challenge of this approach to computer graphics is to cope successfully with the problems posed by the discrete nature of image space scene representations.

References

[1] Catmull, E., "A Subdivision Algorithm for Computer Display of Curved Surfaces," PhD. thesis, Dept. of Computer Science, University of Utah, 1974.

[2] Newell, M. G., Newell, R. G., and Sancha, T. L., "A Solution to the Hidden Surface Problem," Proceedings of the 1972 ACM National Conference.

[3] Williams, L., forthcoming PhD. thesis, University of Utah.

[4] For the application of this representation to scene analysis, see: Levine, M. D., O'Handley, D. A., and Yagi, G. M., "Computer Determination of Depth Maps," Computer Graphics and Image Processing, No. 2, 1973.

[5] Crow, F. C., "Shadow Algorithms for Computer Graphics," Siggraph 1977 Proceedings, Vol. 11, No. 2, Summer 1977.

[6] Blinn, J. F., "A Scan-Line Algorithm for the Display of Bicubic Surface Patches," PhD. thesis, Dept. of Computer Science, University of Utah, 1978.

[7] Crow, F. C., "The Aliasing Problem in Computer-Synthesized Shaded Images," PhD. thesis, Dept. of Computer Science, University of Utah, 1976.

[8] Freeman, H., "Computer Processing of Line Drawing Images," ACM Computing Surveys, Vol. 6, No. 1, March 1974.

[9] Blinn, J. F., "Models of Light Reflection for Computer Synthesized Pictures," Siggraph 1977 Proceedings, Vol. 11, No. 2, Summer 1977.

[10] Sutherland, I.E., "A Head-Mounted Three-Dimensional Display," Fall Joint Computer Conference 1968, Thompson Books, Washington, D.C., 757.

fig. 7a
3d smile sculpted by Alvy Ray Smith.

fig. 7b
evinces the shadow of a smile.

fig. 8
The robot casting his shadow on the wall and floor is composed of over 350 bicubic surface patches.

Especial thanks are due David DiFrancisco and Garland Stern for photographic assistance.

Graphics and Image Processing — J. Foley, Editor

The Aliasing Problem in Computer-Generated Shaded Images

Franklin C. Crow
The University of Texas at Austin

Certain defects, such as jagged edges and disappearing detail, have long been an annoyance in digitally generated shaded images. Although increasing the resolution or defocusing the display can attenuate them, an understanding of these defects leads to more effective methods. This paper explains the observed defects in terms of the aliasing phenomenon inherent in sampled signals and discusses prefiltering as a recognized cure. A method for evaluating filters is presented, the application of prefiltering to hidden-surface algorithms is discussed, and an implementation of a filtering tiler is shown accompanied by examples of its effectiveness.

Key Words and Phrases: aliasing, computer graphics, convolutional filtering, hidden-surface removal, sampling

CR Categories: 8.2

Copyright © 1977, Association for Computing Machinery, Inc. General permission to republish, but not for profit, all or part of this material is granted provided that ACM's copyright notice is given and that reference is made to the publication, to its date of issue, and to the fact that reprinting privileges were granted by permission of the Association for Computing Machinery.

The work reported in this paper took place at the University of Utah and was supported in part by the Advanced Research Projects Agency of the Department of Defense under Contracts DAHC15-73-C-0363 and F30602-80-C-0300. Author's address: Department of Computer Sciences, Painter Hall 3.28, The University of Texas at Austin, Austin, TX 78712.

Reprinted with permission from *Communications of the ACM* Vol. 20, No. 11, November 1977, 799-805.

Introduction

Shaded computer-synthesized images of opaque objects with only visible surfaces displayed have become relatively common in recent years. The primary commercial use of such images has been visual simulators, which require the most realistic possible image obtainable at real-time rates. To create realistic images, relatively complicated scenes must be depicted, and defects due to the quantization necessary for computer generation must be minimized.

A close look at virtually any shaded synthetic image reveals that major problems exist in the rendition of detail (Figures 1 and 4). These problems characteristically occur in three specific situations: (1) along edges on the silhouette of an object or a crease in a surface, (2) in very small objects, and (3) in areas of complicated detail. The most obvious problems occur on object silhouettes, where edges often have an annoyingly jagged appearance. If computer-synthesized images are to achieve a greater degree of realism, it will be necessary to generate images of arbitrarily complicated scenes which contain many potentially jagged edges, small objects, and details.

Small objects pose a problem because they can disappear between the dots. This occurs because each dot in the image represents a sample point in the scene, an infinitely small spot on some surface being depicted. If an object is small enough it is possible that no part of it will coincide with a sample point. Therefore a very small object may disappear entirely; a long thin object may appear in some places and not in others, giving the appearance of a string of beads; and a highly detailed object such as a human face may lose some of its features.

In animated sequences of images these problems become very obvious. Armies of ants appear to run along edges as their slopes change; small objects and details flash on and off distractingly; slightly larger objects appear to change shape and size without reason; even a simple horizontal edge which looks fine in a still picture can be seen to jump from one raster line to another as it moves vertically in the display.

There are essentially three techniques for improving the rendition of detail. The first is to increase the resolution, causing sample points to occur more frequently. This allows representation of finer details and

Fig. 1. Jagged edges can be attenuated by convolutional filtering. The horizontal resolution in this image is approximately 128 samples.

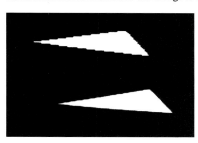

diminishes the obtrusion of jagged edges. However, it is impractical to increase the resolution sufficiently to accommodate small, bright objects owing to the increased cost of image production. The expense of the most commonly used hidden-surface algorithms is proportional to the resolution, and the number of dots which must be produced grows as the square of the resolution.

The second technique is to process the output image by blurring it or applying contour-smoothing algorithms such as those suggested by Freeman [3]. Although this approach can lessen the impact of jagged edges, it can do nothing to restore objects or details which have been lost. Furthermore, the image loses sharpness which may be retained by other methods.

The third and most attractive technique is to make each sample point represent a finite area in the scene rather than an infinitesimal spot. Thus a very small object would occupy a part of such a small area, causing the intensity of the corresponding dot in the output image to be computed as a weighted average of the colors of the small object and its local background. This approach corresponds closely to what actually takes place in television and screen printing processes [5, 10]. While the first two techniques offer somewhat ad hoc approaches to improving rendition of detail, it will be seen that the third technique is based on sound principles.

Making each sample represent a finite area has the effect of applying a convolutional filter before the scene is sampled. It is well known that a signal may be faithfully reproduced from digital samples only if the highest frequency in the signal does not exceed one-half the sampling frequency [7]. Convolutional filtering may be used to satisfy this condition closely enough to greatly improve the output image.

The consequence of failing to filter the signal properly before sampling is known as "aliasing." Aliasing occurs when a lower frequency signal appears as an "alias" of a high frequency signal after sampling (Figure 2). Therefore highly periodic images of scenes involving, for example, picket fences or venetian blinds may appear, when sampled, to be made up of a few broad strips rather than many fine lines.

Reproducing the signal involves representing each sample in such a way that the reproduced signal has no frequencies higher than the original signal. This can be accomplished by representing each sample as a rectangular pulse and then low-pass filtering the resulting signal. In the two-dimensional case, the result of failing to filter the signal properly during reconstruction is known as "rastering." Rastering is an artifact of the structure of the displayed image. If the beam in a television monitor is incorrectly focused, the resulting effects are due to rastering.

Filtering Shaded Synthetic Images

To produce an image by computer, the scene is first modeled by approximating all surfaces with easily handled entities (e.g. line segments, polygons, or bicubic patches). These entities are then stored in memory at a precision determined by the available word size. If N bits of precision are available, the scene is defined to a resolution of 2^N elements (R_s). To produce an image, the scene definition is sampled at the image resolution (R_i).

To ensure that the high frequencies in the scene do not exceed one-half the sampling rate, the scene must be convolved with a two-dimensional filter. Fast convolution methods [8] involving the two-dimensional fast Fourier transform (FFT) are impractical since taking the FFT would require producing an image of resolution R_s, not to mention the $2R_s^2 \log R_s$ operations each FFT would require. Direct convolution can be much more easily applied since the convolution need only be evaluated at the sample points. This requires R_i^2 times R_f^2 operations, where R_f is the resolution of the filter. If R_f is chosen to be $2R_s/R_i$ (empirically found by us to be adequate), then the number of operations needed to compute the direct convolution is $4R_s^2$, much less than a single FFT. Nevertheless, this is still an excessive amount of computation. In the following discussion, an algorithm which simplifies the computation by approximating direct convolution is presented.

This algorithm assumes a filter which is nonzero over a square region two sample intervals wide and separable into functions in x and y. The scene is abstracted so that all features within the compass of a single superposition of the filter are modeled as rectangular areas of constant intensity. This allows the intensity of an image element to be calculated as a weighted average of the contributions of the rectangular areas. The weighting is, of course, determined by the filter function.

Two-dimensional discrete convolution can be expressed as follows:

$$G(i,j) = \sum_{k=-\infty}^{\infty} \sum_{m=-\infty}^{\infty} F(k,m)H(i-k, j-m). \qquad (1)$$

Since H must be separable, it can be expressed as

$$H(i,j) = H_i(i)H_j(j). \qquad (2)$$

With this restriction, the discrete convolution becomes

Fig. 2. Aliasing. x's represent a sampling rate of 10 samples per unit on 12 cycle and 2 cycle signals. Samples are the same in both cases.

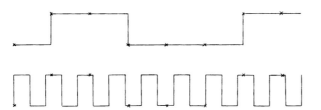

$$G(i,j) = \sum_{k=-\infty}^{\infty} \sum_{m=-\infty}^{\infty} F(k,m) H_i(i-k) H_j(j-m) \quad (3)$$

where G represents the filtered scene produced by convolving the scene F with the filter H.

Furthermore, if the function F is approximated by rectangular blocks, then the function over any such block becomes constant. This greatly simplifies evaluation of the filtered function. The summation can now be rearranged so that the contribution of each rectangular block is independent. The function G then becomes

$$G(i,j) \simeq \sum_{k=p_1}^{q_1} \sum_{m=r_1}^{s_1} C_1 H_i(i-k) H_j(j-m) + \cdots \\ + \sum_{k=p_n}^{q_n} \sum_{m=r_n}^{s_n} C_n H_i(i-k) H_j(j-m) \quad (4)$$

where $[p_n, q_n]$ and $[r_n, s_n]$ represent the bounds of a given rectangular block of intensity C_n and n such blocks give the approximation to the filtered scene at (i,j).

To allow H_i and H_j to be considered separately for a given rectangular block, the summation can be rearranged as follows:

$$\sum_{k=p_n}^{q_n} \sum_{m=r_n}^{s_n} C_n H_i(i-k) H_j(j-m) \\ = C_n \sum_{k=p_n}^{q_n} H_i(i-k) \sum_{m=r_n}^{s_n} H_j(j-m). \quad (5)$$

The implementation of an algorithm for discrete convolution over the scene description becomes relatively easy as a result of this rearrangement. Note that by making the rectangular blocks arbitrarily small an arbitrarily good approximation to G can be obtained.

Implementing the algorithm involves building lookup tables for summations over the functions H_i and H_j. Since H is always of limited nonzero extent, two finite tables can be built, one for H_i and the other for H_j (in practice these have usually been the same). Each table will consist of entries which represent partial sums across the function from the lower nonzero bound to each point below the upper nonzero bound. To obtain the sum over the function between any two nonzero points, it is sufficient to find the difference between the table entries for these two points. With the help of lookup tables, any of the independent summations (see eq. (5)) giving the approximation to G for a given i and j can be found with four lookups, two subtractions, and two multiplications.

To evaluate the filter functions used with the convolution algorithm, a test pattern which emphasizes the defects due to aliasing may be used. A test pattern has been invented which generates moire patterns in response to improperly represented edges and detail.

The pattern is produced by generating almost parallel sections of parabolas by using second-order differences (Figure 3). The curvatures of the parabolas

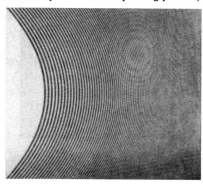

Fig. 3. Test pattern consisting of closely spaced parabolic arcs (moire patterns in this figure and some of those in Figures 5–8 are caused by the half-tone printing process).

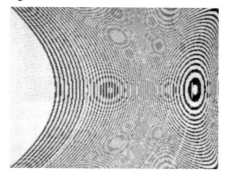

Fig. 4. Test pattern synthesized at a resolution of 256 samples by using techniques similar to those of conventional hidden-surface algorithms.

decrease linearly from a maximum on the left to zero on the right. In addition, the distance between any two adjacent parabolas decreases linearly from left to right across the pattern, causing jaggedness along edges to be repeated with slight variation from curve to curve. The effects along groups of curves form elliptical patterns which are much easier to detect than jaggedness along a single edge. Furthermore, toward the right side of the pattern where the detail is too fine to be resolved by the display, similar patterns are caused by improper summing of the details represented in a sample (Figure 4).

A program has been developed to display the pattern convolved with various filters. An interactive filter design routine allows quick design and modification of a filter. The pattern can then be regenerated in a few minutes to allow visual evaluation. Equipment calibration routines are also included; the test pattern sensitivity is great enough to make consistent calibration an absolute necessity.

Figures 5–8 illustrate the effectiveness of various filters. In each figure, the curve at the lower left represents the presampling filter while the upper left curve represents the calibration function.

Having developed a method for applying convolutional filters and having found effective filters, we must find methods to restrict filtering to those parts of the image where it is necessary. In other words, the filtering process must be made adaptive.

Fig. 5. Pattern convolved with a filter consisting of nine equally weighted discrete points (equivalent to tripling the resolution).

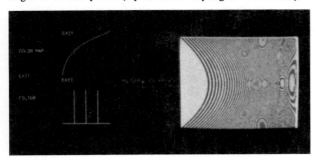

Fig. 6. Pattern convolved with a filter consisting of 25 unequally weighted discrete points.

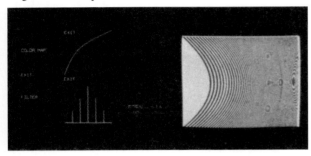

Fig. 7. Pattern convolved with a roughly triangular filter having a base width of one sample interval.

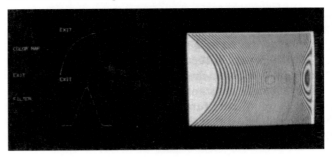

Fig. 8. Pattern convolved with a roughly triangular filter having a base width of two sample intervals.

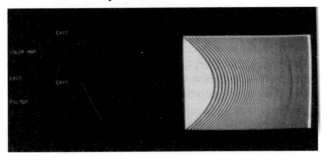

Improved Efficiency Through Selective Filtering

To isolate most of the conditions which contribute to aliasing before the hidden-surface computation is begun, certain parts of the data can be tagged for special treatment. Tagging the data allows the hidden-surface routine to operate normally over most of the image, applying the more expensive convolution techniques only where necessary.

Nearly all the difficulties in shaded images appear where abrupt changes in intensity and thus high spatial frequencies occur. If the elements of the scene description which cause these occurrences can be tagged, the difficulties can be localized. As noted above, the abrupt intensity changes typically occur in the following three cases: (1) along the silhouette of an object, (2) along creases, corners, or other sharp changes in the direction of a surface, and (3) at the edges of colored patches on a surface.

If polyhedral objects are represented, every polygon edge is a potential source of aliasing problems. On the other hand, if curved surfaces are represented by a polygonal approximation, shading techniques may be used to conceal the polygon boundaries over smooth areas [1, 4]. A curved surface approximated by polygons can be made to look smooth by calculating intensities based on the orientation of the surface at the vertices of the polygons and then using interpolation to find the intensities for the rest of the surface. The data structure for describing the polygons is usually arranged so that adjacent polygons can share data where they have common vertices. If there is a sharp change of surface orientation or color across a polygon border, there can be two sets of vertices defining the edge which joins the two polygons. Therefore creases and color changes define two different edges over the same position, and this property can be used to isolate such edges.

Since the most noticeable jaggedness occurs on the silhouettes of objects, it is clearly necessary to find those edges which lie on the silhouettes. Any edge which lies on the silhouette must join a polygon facing the viewer to one facing away from the viewer. Of course an edge associated with only one polygon may also lie on the silhouette of an object. In this case the edge must be a surface edge as opposed to a silhouette edge. A surface edge occurs wherever the surface halts, for example, at the edge of a sheet of paper or a hole in a surface (Figure 9).

To save space, polygons facing away from the viewer (backfacing polygons) are often discarded before the hidden-surface computations are done, in which case silhouette edges become surface edges (and therefore belong to only one polygon). Note that this step cannot be taken until all vertex coordinates have been transformed into the perspective space in which the image will be computed. After backfacing polygons have been discarded, creases, color changes, and silhouette edges occur at edges belonging to only one polygon, a characteristic which can be used to find and tag all such edges.

Although an exhaustive search could be used to find all the edges associated with a single polygon, a far more attractive alternative is to add an adjacent polygons list to the data for each object, providing a pointer to the adjacent polygon for each polygon edge.

Fig. 9. Silhouette edges and surface edges.

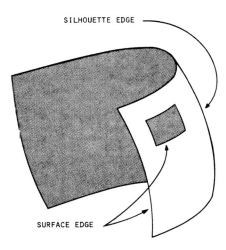

Fig. 10. Tiling a convex polygon.

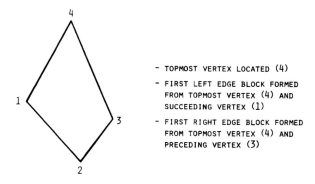

All neighboring polygons are then immediately accessible. With this arrangement, a null pointer immediately indicates an edge associated with a single polygon. Without the adjacent polygons list, tagging edges which are adjacent to polygons facing away from the viewer is a difficult task. With the list, a graph in which all adjacent nodes are bidirectionally linked is provided and tagging silhouette edges by nullifying appropriate adjacent polygon pointers is straightforward.

It is then necessary to consider the problem of small objects. It is quite possible to encounter a sharp change in intensity which is not caught by edge tagging. Consider the case of a cube with rounded corners defined by three or four polygons running the length of each edge. When the image of such a cube is large enough that each edge polygon spans several dots in the output image, no problems occur; the rounded edges appear rounded. However, when the cube is viewed from a considerable distance, the total span of the edge polygons may be considerably less than a single dot. In this case, the edge will appear as jagged as it would if the cube were made from the usual six square polygons. Therefore, in addition to tagging edges, it would be wise to tag small or thin polygons.

Having developed a method for efficient application of adaptive convolutional filtering, we must now integrate this method into ordinary hidden-surface algorithms. The following discussion outlines this integration with respect to different classes of hidden-surface algorithms.

Application of Filtering to Hidden-Surface Algorithms

Hidden-surface algorithms for shaded images can be reduced, for this discussion, to three classes: scanning algorithms, in which the image is generated scan line by scan line; depth-priority algorithms, in which the image is generated from the rear forward, without regard to vertical or horizontal order; and depth-buffer algorithms, in which the order of generation is immaterial [9].

In order to properly compute the intensity at a sample point, all visible surfaces which lie under nonzero areas of the superposed filter must be taken into account. Of the three classes of hidden-surface algorithms, only the scanning algorithms make all necessary information simultaneously available. Both the depth-priority algorithms and depth-buffer algorithms deliver the necessary information for a given sample at intervals while accumulating the image in a frame buffer, and there is no way of knowing whether two surfaces involved in the same sample lie next to each other or overlap.

By using pointers to neighboring polygons, some of these problems can be resolved since neighboring polygons must lie next to each other. This allows creases to be handled correctly. However, where silhouette and surface edges are involved, a correct intensity cannot be guaranteed. If surfaces are rendered in strictly back-to-front order as in some depth-priority algorithms [6], an acceptable edge can be obtained under most conditions. However, the depth-buffer algorithms, which render surfaces in any order, clearly violate this constraint. To be able to calculate the proper intensities where a surface appears behind a previously rendered edge, the intensity of the edge and the extent of its contribution to the sample must be recorded. A more complete discussion of these problems can be found in [2].

It should be noted that where scanning algorithms are used with a frame buffer to achieve greater image complexity by separating foreground and background objects, all the problems of the depth-priority algorithms can be expected. Therefore, if a correct intensity must be guaranteed at every sample point, a single-pass scanning algorithm is required. However, if an occasional error may be accommodated or sufficient memory space and processor time may be devoted to maintaining records on all filtered samples, the frame-buffer-based algorithms can be used.

In the interests of simplicity, the results obtainable with convolutional filtering are demonstrated by using a filtering tiler (a tiler is a procedure which generates the individual dots, or "tiles," from the description of a polygon). The tiler is simple enough to be described in this space yet demonstrates generally applicable techniques for displaying surfaces.

Implementation of a Filtering Tiler

Only convex polygons are considered in this implementation; thus each scan line intersects a polygon in a single segment. Therefore it is sufficient to establish the position and intensity of the end points for each scan segment and pass them to a shader-interpolator routine which generates the intensity for each sample point. Assuming the tiler proceeds from top to bottom, the polygon is first searched for its highest vertex. The vertices of the polygon are known to be stored in a given order (usually clockwise or counterclockwise). If the vertices are stored clockwise the vertex preceding the top vertex defines an edge which lies to the left of an edge defined by the topmost vertex and the succeeding vertex (Figure 10).

Thus a left-edge block is formed which stores attributes for the left edge; similarly a block is formed for the right edge. The attributes for each block include present position, increments yielding the position at the next scan line, and shading attributes associated with their increments. Each block also includes a count of the number of scan lines remaining until the bottom of the line segment is reached. The increments are used to update the edge blocks after each invocation of the shader-interpolator routine. When a vertex is reached, the appropriate edge block must be recalculated to reflect the attributes of the edge below. The algorithm terminates when the next vertex for a block lies above the current one, when both edge blocks reach the same vertex, or when the lowest extent of the polygon, determined by the bottom-most vertex, is reached.

Figure 11 shows a flowchart for the tiler just described, and Figure 12 shows the tiler extended to include a presampling filter. One important difference between the filtering and nonfiltering tilers is that the filtering tiler may not "ignore" edges with a vertical range of less than one scan line. In particular, an edge block which lies along the top or bottom of a polygon, and thus may have considerable horizontal extent, must be properly filtered.

The filtering and nonfiltering tilers also differ in their treatment of edge blocks. In the nonfiltering tiler, edge blocks which may be "ignored" are immediately marked "done" and a new edge block made. The filtering tiler, on the other hand, must keep track of as many edge blocks as may affect intensities on a given line. Therefore a queue of edge blocks must be provided for both the left and right sides. In practice, the length of these queues rarely exceeds two edge blocks, and images can usually be made by using queues restricted to that length.

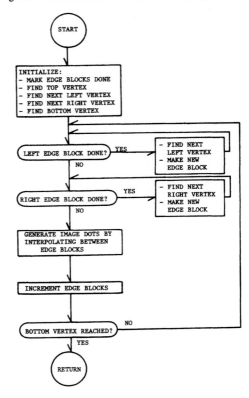

Fig. 11. Conventional tiler for convex polygons.

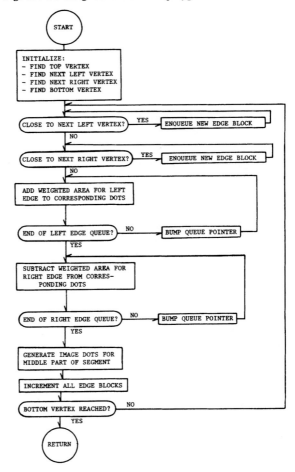

Fig. 12. Filtering tiler for convex polygons.

Fig. 13. Calculating the weighted area of a small polygon.

Left Areas   Right Areas   Area

Fig. 14. Three images each from the filtering tiler (left side), the conventional tiler (middle, top to bottom), and a doubled-resolution tiler (lower right) displayed together.

Fig. 15. A particularly difficult object, a slender, nearly horizontal triangle, rendered by the conventional tiler (top four), the filter tiler (middle five) and the doubled-resolution tiler (bottom four).

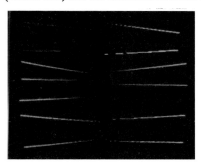

The process of filtering the left and right edges proceeds as described earlier. The approximate area lying to the right of each left edge in each intersecting filtered area is weighted and then added to the intensity for the corresponding image dot. Conversely, the areas lying to the right of right-hand edges are subtracted from the intensity for the affected image dots. Note that since the final sum is the weighted area covered by the polygon, very small polygons are treated correctly (Figure 13). Figures 14 and 15 compare the filtering tiler with conventional tilers.

A detailed evaluation of the performance of the filtering tiler in comparison with conventional tilers awaits further research. However, observed execution times were two to five times longer for the filtering tiler than for a conventional tiler working at the same resolution. Such figures can be expected to range widely, varying inversely with the size of the polygons displayed and the amount of computing overhead included.

Conclusion

The intention here has been to provide a discussion of the aliasing problem and to offer a solution based on the theory of sampling and reproduction of two-dimensional signals. The examples shown here have been chosen to illustrate aliasing at its worst. Although such cases can sometimes be avoided in still pictures, animated sequences virtually always exhibit obvious defects due to aliasing. It follows that genuinely realistic images will require more than token efforts at resolving the problems discussed above. A general approach to a solution has been offered here. Further ideas and more specific suggestions are offered in [2].

Acknowledgments. This paper has been greatly improved by the helpful comments of the referees. They deserve praise for their careful reading of an earlier version. It should also be noted that the presence of excellent research groups in both computer graphics and signal processing at the University of Utah made this work possible.

References
1. Bui Tuong Phong. Illumination for computer-generated images. UTEC-CSc-73-129, Dept. Comptr. Sci., U. of Utah, Salt Lake City, Utah, July 1973. Abridged in *Comm. ACM 18*, 6 (June 1975), 311-317.
2. Crow, F.C. The aliasing problem in computer-synthesized shaded images. UTEC-CSc-76-015, Dept. Comptr. Sci., U. of Utah, Salt Lake City, Utah, March 1976.
3. Freeman, H. Computer processing of line-drawing images. *Computing Surveys 6*, 1 (March 1974), 57-97.
4. Gouraud, H. Computer display of curved surfaces. UTEC-CSc-71-113, Comptr. Sci., U. of Utah, June 1971. Abridged in *IEEE Trans. Comptrs. C-20* (June 1971).
5. Hunt, R.W.G., *The Reproduction of Colour in Photography, Printing and Television*. Fountain Press, England, 3rd Ed., 1975.
6. Newell, M.G., Newell, R.G., and Sancha, T.L. A solution to the hidden-surface problem. Proc. ACM 1972 Annual Conf., Boston, Mass., Vol. I, pp. 443-450.
7. Oppenheim, A.V., and Schafer, R.W. *Digital Signal Processing*. Prentice-Hall, Englewood Cliffs, N.J., 1975.
8. Stockham, T.G. Jr., High-speed convolution and correlation. Proc. AFIPS 1966 SJCC, Vol. 28, AFIPS Press, Montvale, N.J., pp. 229-233.
9. Sutherland, I.E., Sproull, R.F., and Schumaker, R.G. A characterization of ten hidden-surface algorithms. *Computing Surveys 6*, 1 (March 1974), 1-55.
10. Zworykin, V.K., and Morton, G.A. *Television*. Wiley, New York, 2nd Ed., 1954.

Pyramidal Parametrics

Lance Williams

Computer Graphics Laboratory
New York Institute of Technology
Old Westbury, New York

Abstract

The mapping of images onto surfaces may substantially increase the realism and information content of computer-generated imagery. The projection of a flat source image onto a curved surface may involve sampling difficulties, however, which are compounded as the view of the surface changes. As the projected scale of the surface increases, interpolation between the original samples of the source image is necessary; as the scale is reduced, approximation of multiple samples in the source is required. Thus a constantly changing sampling window of view-dependent shape must traverse the source image.

To reduce the computation implied by these requirements, a set of prefiltered source images may be created. This approach can be applied to particular advantage in animation, where a large number of frames using the same source image must be generated. This paper advances a "pyramidal parametric" prefiltering and sampling geometry which minimizes aliasing effects and assures continuity within and between target images.

Although the mapping of texture onto surfaces is an excellent example of the process and provided the original motivation for its development, pyramidal parametric data structures admit of wider application. The aliasing of not only surface texture, but also highlights and even the surface representations themselves, may be minimized by pyramidal parametric means.

General Terms: Algorithms.

Keywords and Phrases: Antialiasing, Illumination Models, Modeling, Pyramidal Data Structures, Reflectance Mapping, Texture Mapping, Visible Surface Algorithms.

CR Categories: I.3.3 [Computer Graphics]: Picture/Image Generation--display algorithms; I.3.5 [Computer Graphics]: Computational Geometry and Object Modeling--curve, surface, solid and object representations, geometric algorithms, languages and systems; I.3.7 [Computer Graphics]: Three-Dimensional Graphics and Realism--color, shading, shadowing, and texture.

1. Pyramidal Data Structures

Pyramidal data structures may be based on various subdivisions: binary trees, quad trees, oct trees, or n-dimensional hierarchies [17]. The common feature of these structures is a succession of levels which vary the resolution at which the data is represented.

The decomposition of an image by two-dimensional binary subdivision was a pioneering strategy in computer graphics for visible surface determination [15]. The approach was essentially a synthesis-by-analysis: the image plane was subdivided into quadrants recursively until analysis of a subsection showed that surface ordering was sufficiently simple to permit rendering. Such subdivision and analysis has been subsequently adopted to generate spatial data structures [5], which have been used to represent images [9] both for pattern recognition [13] and for transmission [10], [14]. In the field of computer graphics, such data structures have been adopted for texture mapping [4], [16], and generalized to represent objects in space [11].

The application of pyramidal data to image storage and transmission may permit significant compression of the data to be stored or transmitted. This is so because highly detailed features may be localized within an otherwise low-frequency image, permitting the sampling rate to be reduced for large sections of the image. Besides permitting bandwidth compression, the representation orders data in such a way that the general character of images may be recalled or transmitted before the specific details.

Pattern recognition and classification often require the comparison of a candidate image against a set of canonical patterns. This is an operation the expense of which increases as the square of the resolution at which it is performed. The use of pyramidal data structures in pattern recognition and classification permits the comparison of the gross features of two-dimensional functions preliminary to the minute particulars; a good general reference on this application is [12].

In computer graphics, pyramidal texture maps may be used to perform arbitrary mappings of a function with minimal aliasing artifacts and reduced computation. Once again, images may be represented at different spatial bandwidths. The concern is that inappropriate resolution misrepresents the data; that is, sampling high-resolution data at larger sample intervals invites aliasing.

2. Parametric Interpolation

By a pyramidal parametric data structure, we will mean simply a pyramidal structure with both intra- and inter-level interpolation. Consider the case of an image represented as a two-dimensional array of samples. Interpolation is necessary to produce a continuous function of two parameters, U and V. If, in addition, a third parameter (call it D) moves us up and down a hierarchy of corresponding two-dimensional functions, with interpolation between (or among) the levels of the pyramid providing continuity, the structure is pyramidal parametric.

The practical distinction between such a structure and an ordinary interpolant over an n-dimensional array of samples is that the number of samples representing each level of the pyramid may be different.

3. Mip Mapping

"Mip" mapping is a particular format for two-dimensional parametric functions, which, along with its associated addressing scheme, has been used successfully to bandlimit texture mapping at New York Institute of Technology since 1979. The acronym "mip" is from the Latin phrase "multum in parvo," meaning "many things in a small place." Mip mapping supplements bilinear interpolation of pixel values in the texture map (which may be used to smoothly translate and magnify the texture) with interpolation between prefiltered versions of the map (which may be used to compress many pixels into a small place). In this latter capacity, mip offers much greater speed than texturing algorithms which perform explicit convolution over an area in the texture map for each pixel rendered [1], [6].

Mip owes its speed in compressing texture to two factors. First, a fair amount of filtering of the original texture takes place when the mip map is first created. Second, subsequent filtering is approximated by blending different levels of the mip map. This means that all filters are approximated by linearly interpolating a set of square box filters, the sides of which are powers-of-two pixels in length. Thus, mapping entails a fixed overhead, which is independent of the area filtered to compute a sample.

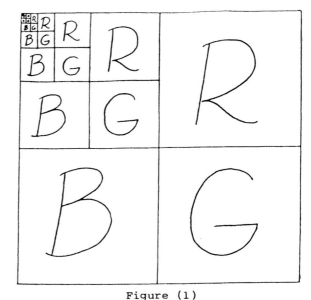

Figure (1)
Structure of a Color Mip Map
Smaller and smaller images diminish into the upper left corner of the map. Each of the images is averaged down from its larger predecessor.

(Below:)
Mip maps are indexed by three coordinates: U, V, and D. U and V are spatial coordinates of the map; D is the variable used to index, and interpolate between, the different levels of the pyramid.

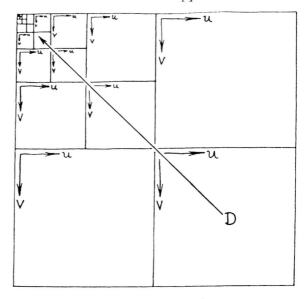

Figure (1) illustrates the memory organization of a color mip map. The image is separated into its red, green, and blue components (R, G, and B in the diagram). Successively filtered and down-sampled versions of each component are instanced above and to the left of the originals, in a series of smaller and smaller images, each half the linear dimension (and a quarter the number of samples) of its parent. Successive divisions by four partition the frame buffer equally among the three components, with a single unused pixel remaining in the upper left-hand corner.

The concept behind this memory organization is that corresponding points in different prefiltered maps can be addressed simply by a binary shift of an input U, V coordinate pair. Since the filtering and sampling are performed at scales which are powers of two, indexing the maps is possible with inexpensive binary scaling. In a hardware implementation, the addresses in all the corresponding maps (now separate memories) would be instantly and simultaneously available from the U, V input.

The routines for creating and accessing mip maps at NYIT are based on simple box (Fourier) window prefiltering, bilinear interpolation of pixels within each map instance, and linear interpolation between two maps for each value of D (the pyramid's vertical coordinate). For each of the three components of a color mip map, this requires 8 pixel reads and 7 multiplications. This choice of filters is strictly for the sake of speed. Note that the bilinear interpolation of pixel values at the extreme edges of each map instance must be performed with pixels from the opposite edge(s) of that map, for texture which is periodic. For non-periodic texture, scaling or clipping of the U, V coordinates prevents the intrusion of an inappropriate map or color component into the interpolation.

The box (Fourier) window used to create the mip maps illustrated here, and the tent (Bartlett) window used to interpolate them, are far from ideal; yet probably the most severe compromise made by mip filtering is that it is symmetrical. Each of the prefiltered levels of the map is filtered equally in X and Y. Choosing a value of D trades off aliasing against blurring, which becomes a tricky proposition as a pixel's projection in the texture map deviates from symmetry. Heckbert [8] suggests:

$$d = \max\left(\sqrt{\left(\frac{\partial u}{\partial x}\right)^2 + \left(\frac{\partial v}{\partial x}\right)^2}, \sqrt{\left(\frac{\partial u}{\partial y}\right)^2 + \left(\frac{\partial v}{\partial y}\right)^2}\right)$$

where D is proportional to the "diameter" of the area in the texture to be filtered, and the partials of U and V (the texture-map coordinates) with respect to X and Y (the screen coordinates) can be calculated from the surface projection.

Illustrations of mapping performed by the mip technique are the subject of Figures (2) through (10). The NYIT Test Frog in Figure (2) is magnified by simple point sampling in (3), and by interpolation in (4). The hapless amphibian is similarly

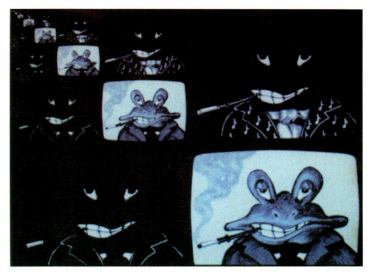

Figure (2)
Mip map of the flexible NYIT Test Frog.

compressed by point sampling in (5) and by mipping in (6).

The more general and interesting case -- continuously variable upsampling and downsampling of the original texture -- is illustrated in (7) on a variety of surfaces. Since the symmetry of mip filtering would be expected to show up badly when texture is compressed in only one dimension, figures (8) through (10) are of especial interest. These pictures, created by Ed Emshwiller at NYIT for his videotape, "Sunstone," were mapped using Alvy Ray Smith's TEXAS animation program, which in turn used MIP to antialias texture. As the panels rotate edge-on, the texture collapses to a line smoothly and without apparent artifacts.

Figure (7)
General mapping: interpolation and pyramidal compression.

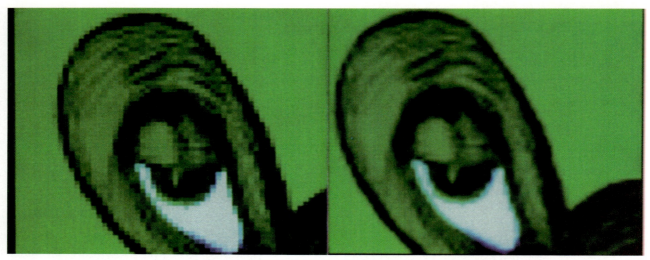

Figure (3)
Upsampling the frog: magnification by point sampling.

Figure (4)
Upsampling the frog: magnification by bilinear interpolation.

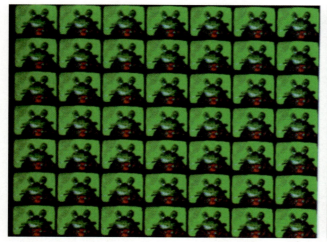

Figure (5)
Downsampling the frog: compression by point sampling (detail, right).

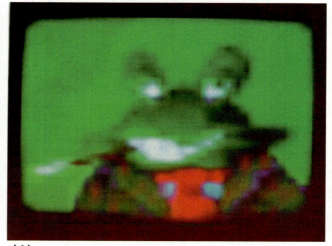

Figure (6)
Downsampling: compression by pyramidal interpolation (detail, right).

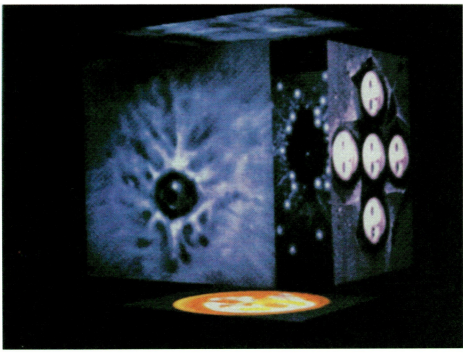

Figures (8)-(9)
"Sunstone" by Ed Emshwiller, segment animated by Alvy Ray Smith
Pyramidal parametric texture mapping on polygons.

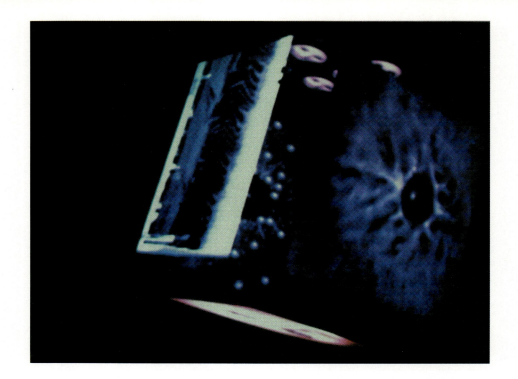

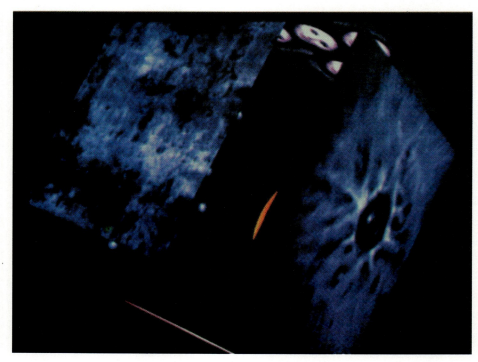

Figures (10)-(11)
"Sunstone" by Ed Emshwiller, segment animated by Alvy Ray Smith
Pyramidal parametric texture mapping on polygons.

4. Highlight Antialiasing

As small or highly curved objects move across a raster, their surface normals may beat erratically with the sampling grid. This causes the shading values to flash annoyingly in motion sequences, a symptom of illumination aliasing. The surface normals essentially point-sample the illumination function.

Figure (12) illustrates samples of the surface normals of a set of parallel cylinders. The cylinders in the diagram are depicted as if from the edge of the image plane; the regularly-spaced vertical line segments are the samples along a single axis. The arrows at the sample points indicate the directions of the surface normals. Depending on the shading formula invoked, there may be very high contrast between samples where the normal is nearly parallel to the sample axis, and samples where the normal points directly at the observer's eye.

Figure (12)

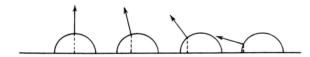

The shading function depends not only on the shape of the surface, but its light reflection properties (characterized by the shading formula), the position of the light source, and the position of the observer's eye. Hanrahan [7] expresses it in honest Greek:

$$\int_x \int_y \varphi(E,N,L) \frac{\partial(u,v)}{\partial(x,y)} \, dx\, dy$$

where the normal, N, the light sources, L, and the eye, E, are vectors which may each be functions of U and V, and the limits of integration are the X, Y boundaries of the pixel.

Figure (13) illustrates highlight aliasing on a perfectly flat surface. The viewing conventions of the diagram are the same as in Figure (12). "L" is the direction vector of the light source; the surface is a polygon at an angle to the image plane; the dotted bump is a graph of the reflected light, characteristic of a

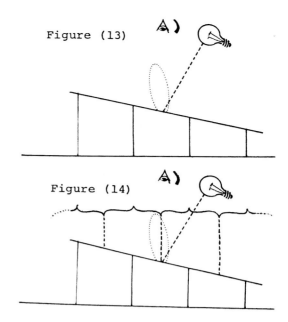

specular surface reflection function. The highlight indicated by the bump falls entirely between the samples. (Note that this is only possible on a flat surface if either the eye or the light is local, a point in space rather than simply a direction vector. Some boring shading formulae exclude the possibility of highlight aliasing on polygons by requiring all flat surfaces to be flat in shading.)

A first attempt to overcome the limitations of point-sampling the illumination function is to integrate the function over the projected area represented by each sample point. This approach is illustrated in Figure (14). The brackets at each sample represent the area of the surface over which the illumination function is integrated. This procedure is analogous to area-averaging of sampled edges or texture [3].

In order to generalize this approach to curved surfaces, the "sample interval" over which illumination is integrated must be modified according to the local curvature of the surface at a sample. In Figure (15), the area of a surface represented by a pixel has been projected onto a curved surface. The solid angle over which illumination must be integrated is approximated by the volume enclosed by the normals at the pixel corners. The distribution of light within this volume will sum to an estimate of the diffuse reflection over the pixel. If the surface exhibits undulations at the pixel level, however, aliasing will result.

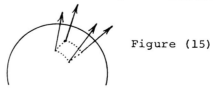

Figure (15)

Figure (16)
Michael Chou (right) poses with an imaginary companion. Reflectance maps can enhance the realism of synthetic shading.

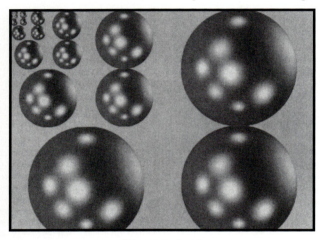

Figure (17)
A pyramidal parametric reflectance map, containing 9 light sources. The region outside the "sphere" is unused.

We might divide the surface up into regions of relatively low curvature (as is done in some patch rendering algorithms), and rely on "edge antialiasing" to integrate the different surfaces within a pixel. Alternatively, we may develop some mechanism for limiting the local curvature of surfaces before rendering. This possibility is explored in the next section.

If we represent the illumination of a scene as a two-dimensional map, highlights can be effectively antialiased in much the same way as textures. Blinn and Newell [1] demonstrated specular reflection using an illumination map. The map was an image of the environment (a spherical projection of the scene, indexed by the X and Y components of the surface normals) which could be used to cast reflections onto specular surfaces. The impression of mirrored facets and chrome objects which can be achieved with this method is striking; Figure (16) provides an illustration. Reflectance mapping is not, however, accurate for local reflections. To achieve similar results with three dimensional accuracy requires ray-tracing.

A pyramidal parametric illumination map permits convenient antialiasing of highlights as long as a good measure of local surface curvature is available. The value of "D" used to index the map is proportional to the solid angle subtended by the surface over the pixel being computed; this may be estimated by the same formula used to compute D for ordinary texture mapping. Nine light sources of varying brightness glint raggedly from the test object in Figure (18); the reflectance map in Figure (17) provided the illumination. In Figure (19), convincing highlight antialiasing results from the full pyramidal parametric treatment.

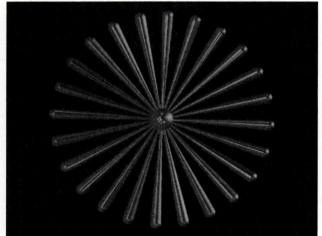

Figure (18) Before

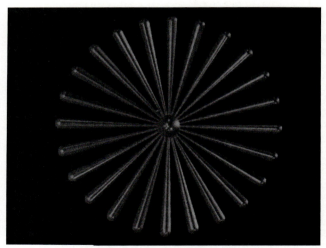

Figure (19) After

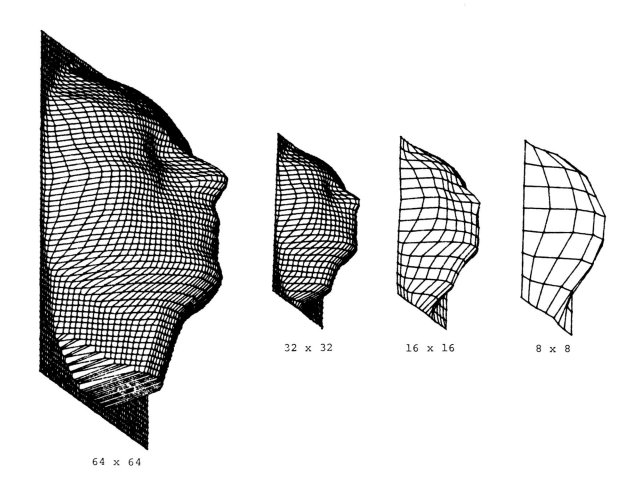

64 x 64   32 x 32   16 x 16   8 x 8

Figures (20-23) Different resolution meshes.

5. Levels of Detail in Surface Representation

In addition to bandlimiting texture and illumination functions for mapping onto a surface, pyramidal parametrics may be used to limit the level of detail with which the surface itself is represented. The goal is to represent an object for graphic display as economically as its projection on the image plane permits, without boiling and sparkling aliasing artifacts as the projection changes.

The expense of computing and shading each pixel dominates the cost of many algorithms for rendering higher-order surfaces. For meshes of polygons or patch control points which project onto a small portion of the image, however, the vertex (or control-point) expense dominates. In these situations it is desirable to reduce the number of points used to represent the object.

A pyramidal parametric data structure the components of which are spatial coordinates (the X-Y-Z of the vertices of a rectangular mesh, for example, as opposed to the R-G-B of a texture or illumination map) provides a continuously-variable filtered instance of the surface for sampling at any desired degree of resolution.

Figures (20) through (23) illustrate a simple surface based on a human face model developed by Fred Parke at the University of Utah. As the sampling density varies, so does the filtering of the surface. These faces are filtered and sampled by the same methods previously discussed for texture and reflectance maps. Pyramidal parametric representations such as these appear promising for reducing aliasing effects as well as systematically sampling very large data bases over a wide range of scales and viewing angles.

6. Conclusions

Pyramidal data structures are of proven value in image analysis and have interesting application to image bandwidth compression and transmission. "Pyramidal parametrics," pyramidal data structures with intra- and inter-level interpolation, are here proposed for use in image synthesis. By continuously varying the detail with which data are resolved, pyramidal parametrics provide economical approximate solutions to filtering problems in mapping texture and illumination onto surfaces, and preliminary experiments suggest they may provide flexible surface representations as well.

7. Acknowledgments

I would like to acknowledge Ed Catmull, the first (to my knowledge) to apply multiple prefiltered images to texture mapping: the method was applied to the bicubic patches in his thesis, although it was not described. Credit is also due Tom Duff, who wrote both recursive and scan-order routines for creating mip maps which preserved numerical precision over all map instances; Dick Lundin, who wrote the first assembly-coded mip map accessing routines; Ephraim Cohen, who wrote the second; Rick Ace, who translated Ephraim's PDP-11 versions for the VAX assembler; Paul Heckbert, for refining and speeding up both creation and accessing routines, and investigating various estimates of "D"; Michael Chou, for implementing highlight antialiasing and high-resolution reflectance mapping on quadric surfaces.

I owe special thanks to Jules Bloomenthal, Michael Chou, Pat Hanrahan, and Paul Heckbert for critical reading and numerous helpful suggestions in the course of preparing this text. Photographic support was provided by Michael Lehman.

8. References

[1] Blinn, J., and Newell, M., "Texture and Reflection on Computer Generated Images," CACM, Vol. 19, #10, Oct. 1976, pp. 542-547.

[2] Bui-Tuong Phong, "Illumination for Computer Generated Pictures," PhD. dissertation, Department of Computer Science, University of Utah, December 1978.

[3] Crow, F.C., "The Aliasing Problem in Computer Synthesized Shaded Images," PhD. dissertation, Department of Computer Science, University of Utah, Tech. Report UTEC-CSc-76-015, March 1976.

[4] Dungan, W., Stenger, A., and Sutty, G., "Texture Tile Considerations for Raster Graphics," SIGGRAPH 1978 Proceedings, Vol. 12, #3, August 1978.

[5] Eastman, Charles M., "Representations for Space Planning," CACM, Vol. 13, #4, April 1970.

[6] Feibush, E.A., Levoy, M., and Cook, R.L., "Synthetic Texturing Using Digital Filters," Computer Graphics, Vol. 14, July, 1980.

[7] Hanrahan, Pat, private communication, 1983.

[8] Heckbert, Paul, "Texture Mapping Polygons in Perspective," NYIT Computer Graphics Lab Tech. Memo #13, April, 1983.

[9] Klinger, A., and Dyer, C.R., "Experiments on Picture Representation Using Regular Decomposition," Computer Graphics and Image Processing, #5, March, 1976.

[10] Knowlton, K., "Progressive Transmission of Gray-Scale and Binary Pictures by Simple, Efficient, and Lossless Encoding Schemes," Proceedings of the IEEE, Vol. 68, #7, July 1980, pp. 885-896.

[11] Meagher, D., "Octree Encoding: A New Technique for the Representation, Manipulation, and Display of Arbitrary 3D Objects by Computer," IPL-TR-80-111, Image Processing Lab, Electrical and Systems Engineering Dept., Rensselaer Polytechnic Institute, October 1980.

[12] Tanimoto, S.L., and Klinger, A., Structured Computer Vision, Academic Press, New York, 1980.

[13] Tanimoto, S.L., and Pavlidis, T., "A Hierarchical Data Structure for Picture Processing," Computer Graphics and Image Processing, Vol. 4, #2, June 1975.

[14] Tanimoto, S.L., "Image Processing with Gross Information First," Computer Graphics and Image Processing 9, 1979.

[15] Warnock, J.E., "A Hidden-Line Algorithm for Halftone Picture Representation," Department of Computer Science, University of Utah, TR 4-15, 1969.

[16] Williams, L., "Pyramidal Parametrics," SIGGRAPH tutorial notes, "Advanced Image Synthesis," 1981.

[17] Yau, M.M., and Srihari, S.N., "Recursive Generation of Hierarchical Data Structures for Multidimensional Digital Images," Proceedings of the IEEE Computer Society Conference on Pattern Recognition and Image Processing, August 1981.

Distributed Ray Tracing

Robert L. Cook
Thomas Porter
Loren Carpenter

Computer Division
Lucasfilm Ltd.

Abstract

Ray tracing is one of the most elegant techniques in computer graphics. Many phenomena that are difficult or impossible with other techniques are simple with ray tracing, including shadows, reflections, and refracted light. Ray directions, however, have been determined precisely, and this has limited the capabilities of ray tracing. By distributing the directions of the rays according to the analytic function they sample, ray tracing can incorporate fuzzy phenomena. This provides correct and easy solutions to some previously unsolved or partially solved problems, including motion blur, depth of field, penumbras, translucency, and fuzzy reflections. Motion blur and depth of field calculations can be integrated with the visible surface calculations, avoiding the problems found in previous methods.

CR CATEGORIES AND SUBJECT DESCRIPTORS: I.3.7 [**Computer Graphics**]: Three-Dimensional Graphics and Realism;

ADDITIONAL KEY WORDS AND PHRASES: camera, constructive solid geometry, depth of field, focus, gloss, motion blur, penumbras, ray tracing, shadows, translucency, transparency

1. Introduction

Ray tracing algorithms are elegant, simple, and powerful. They can render shadows, reflections, and refracted light, phenomena that are difficult or impossible with other techniques[11]. But ray tracing is currently limited to sharp shadows, sharp reflections, and sharp refraction.

Ray traced images are sharp because ray directions are determined precisely from geometry. Fuzzy phenomenon would seem to require large numbers of additional samples per ray. By distributing the rays rather than adding more of them, however, fuzzy phenomena can be rendered with no additional rays beyond those required for spatially oversampled ray tracing. This approach provides correct and easy solutions to some previously unsolved problems.

This approach has not been possible before because of aliasing. Ray tracing is a form of point sampling and, as such, has been subject to aliasing artifacts. This aliasing is not inherent, however, and ray tracing can be filtered as effectively as any analytic method[4]. The filtering does incur the expense of additional rays, but it is not merely oversampling or adaptive oversampling, which in themselves cannot solve the aliasing problem. This antialiasing is based on an approach proposed by Rodney Stock. It is the subject of a forthcoming paper.

Antialiasing opens up new possibilities for ray tracing. Ray tracing need not be restricted to spatial sampling. If done with proper antialiasing, the rays can sample motion, the camera lens, and the entire shading function. This is called *distributed ray tracing*.

Distributed ray tracing is a new approach to image synthesis. The key is that no extra rays are needed beyond those used for oversampling in space. For example, rather than taking multiple time samples at every spatial location, the rays are distributed in time so that rays at different spatial locations are traced at different instants of time. Once we accept the expense of oversampling in space, distributing the rays offers substantial benefits at little additional cost.

- Sampling the reflected ray according to the specular distribution function produces gloss (blurred reflection).
- Sampling the transmitted ray produces translucency (blurred transparency).
- Sampling the solid angle of the light sources produces penumbras.

- Sampling the camera lens area produces depth of field.
- Sampling in time produces motion blur.

2. Shading

The intensity I of the reflected light at a point on a surface is an integral over the hemisphere above the surface of an illumination function L and a reflection function R[1].

$$I(\phi_r,\theta_r) = \int_{\phi_i}\int_{\theta_i} L(\phi_i,\theta_i)R(\phi_i,\theta_i,\phi_r,\theta_r)d\phi_i d\theta_i$$

where

(ϕ_i,θ_i) is the angle of incidence, and

(ϕ_r,θ_r) is the angle of reflection.

The complexity of performing this integration has been avoided by making some simplifying assumptions. The following are some of these simplifications:

- Assume that L is a δ function, i.e., that L is zero except for light source directions and that the light sources can be treated as points. The integral is now replaced by a sum over certain discrete directions. This assumption causes sharp shadows.
- Assume that all of the directions that are not light source directions can be grouped together into an ambient light source. This ambient light is the same in all directions, so that L is independent of ϕ_i and θ_i and may be removed from the integral. The integral of R may then be replaced by an average, or ambient, reflectance.
- Assume that the reflectance function R is a δ function, i.e., that the surface is a mirror and reflects light only from the mirror direction. This assumption causes sharp reflections. A corresponding assumption for transmitted light causes sharp refraction.

The shading function may be too complex to compute analytically, but we can point sample its value by distributing the rays, thus avoiding these simplifying assumptions. Illumination rays are not traced toward a single light direction, but are distributed according to the illumination function L. Reflected rays are not traced in a single mirror direction but are distributed according to the reflectance function R.

2.1. Gloss

Reflections are mirror-like in computer graphics, but in real life reflections are often blurred or hazy. The distinctness with which a surface reflects its environment is called *gloss*[5]. Blurred reflections have been discussed by Whitted[11] and by Cook[2]. Any analytic simulation of these reflections must be based on the integral of the reflectance over some solid angle.

Mirror reflections are determined by tracing rays from the surface in the mirror direction. Gloss can be calculated by distributing these secondary rays about the mirror direction. The distribution is weighted according to the same distribution function that determines the highlights.

This method was originally suggested by Whitted[11], and it replaces the usual specular component. Rays that reflect light sources produce highlights.

2.2. Translucency

Light transmitted through an object is described by an equation similar to that for reflected light, except that the reflectance function R is replaced by a transmittance function T and the integral is performed over the hemisphere behind the surface. The transmitted light can have ambient, diffuse, and specular components[5].

Computer graphics has included transparency, in which T is assumed to be a δ function and the images seen through transparent objects are sharp. Translucency differs from transparency in that the images seen through translucent objects are not distinct. The problem of translucency is analogous to the problem of gloss. Gloss requires an integral of the reflected light, and translucency requires a corresponding integral of the transmitted light.

Translucency is calculated by distributing the secondary rays about the main direction of the transmitted light. Just as the distribution of the reflected rays is defined by the specular reflectance function, the distribution of the transmitted rays is defined by a specular transmittance function.

2.3. Penumbras

Penumbras occur where a light source is partially obscured. The reflected intensity due to such a light is proportional to the solid angle of the visible portion of the light. The solid angle has been explicitly included in a shading model[3], but no algorithms have been suggested for determining this solid angle because of the complexity of the computation involved. The only attempt at penumbras known to the authors seems to solve only a very special case[7].

Shadows can be calculated by tracing rays from the surface to the light sources, and penumbras can be calculated by distributing these secondary rays. The shadow ray can be traced to any point on the light source, not just not to a single light source location. The distribution of the shadow rays must be weighted according the projected area and brightness of different parts of the light source. The number of rays traced to each region should be proportional to the amount of the light's energy that would come from that region if the light was

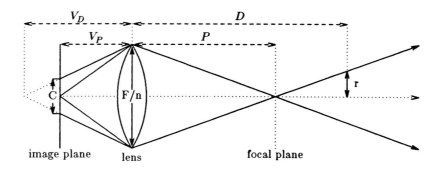

Figure 1. Circle of Confusion.

completely unobscured. The proportion of lighted sample points in a region of the surface is then equal to the proportion of that light's intensity that is visible in that region.

3. Depth of Field

Cameras and the eye have a finite lens aperture, and hence their images have a finite depth of field. Each point in the scene appears as a circle on the image plane. This circle is called the circle of confusion, and its size depends on the distance to the point and on the lens optics. Depth of field can be an unwanted artifact, but it can also be a desirable effect.

Most computer graphics has been based on a pinhole camera model with every object in sharp focus. Potmesil simulated depth of field with a postprocessing technique. Each object is first rendered in sharp focus (i.e., with a pinhole camera model), and later each sharply rendered object is convolved with a filter the size of the circle of confusion[8]. The program spends most of its time in the focus postprocessor, and this time increases dramatically as the aperture decreases.

Such a postprocessing approach can never be completely correct. This is because visibility is calculated from a single point, the center of the lens. The view of the environment is different from different parts of the lens, and the differences include changes in visibility and shading that cannot be accounted for by a postprocessing approach.

For example, consider an object that is extremely out of focus in front of an object that is in focus. Visible surface calculations done with the pinhole model determine the visibility from the center of the lens. Because the front object is not in focus, parts of the focused object that are not visible from the center of the lens will be visible from other parts of the lens. Information about those parts will not available for the postprocessor, so the postprocessor cannot possibly get the correct result.

There is another way to approach the depth of field problem. Depth of field occurs because the lens is a finite size. Each point on the lens "looks" at the same point on the focal plane. The visible surfaces and the shading may be different as seen from different parts of the lens. The depth of field calculations should account for this and be an integral part of the visible surface and shading calculations.

Depth of field can be calculated by starting with the traditional ray from the center of the lens through point p on the focal plane. A point on the surface of the lens is selected and the ray from that point to p is traced. The camera specifications required for this calculation are the focal distance and the diameter of the lens $\frac{F}{n}$, where F is the focal length of the lens and n is the aperture number.

This gives exactly the same circle of confusion as presented by Potmesil[8]. Because it integrates the depth of field calculations with the shading and visible surface calculations, this method gives a more accurate solution to the depth of field problem, with the exception that it does not account for diffraction effects.

Figure 1 shows why this method gives the correct circle of confusion. The lens has a diameter of $\frac{F}{n}$ and is focused at a distance P so that the image plane is at a distance V_P, where

$$V_P = \frac{FP}{P-F} \text{ for } P>F.$$

Points on the plane that is a distance D from the lens will focus at

$$V_D = \frac{FD}{D-F} \text{ for } D>F$$

and have a circle of confusion with diameter C of[8]

$$C = |V_D - V_P| \frac{F}{nV_D}$$

For a point I on the image plane, the rays we trace lie inside the cone whose radius at D is

$$r = \frac{1}{2} \frac{F}{n} \frac{|D-P|}{P}$$

The image plane distance from a point on this cone to a point on the axis of the cone is r multiplied by the magnification of the lens.

$$R = r\left(-\frac{V_P}{D}\right).$$

It is easily shown that

$$R = \frac{C}{2}.$$

Hence any points on the cone have a circle of confusion that just touches the image point *I*. Points outside the cone do not affect the image point and points inside the cone do.

4. Motion Blur

Distributing the rays or sample points in time solves the motion blur problem. Before we discuss this method and how it works, let us first look in more detail at the motion blur problem and at previous attempts to solve it.

The motion blur method described by Potmesil[9] is not only expensive, it also separates the visible surface calculation from the motion blur calculation. This is acceptable in some situations, but in most cases we cannot just calculate a still frame and blur the result. Some object entirely hidden in the still frame might be uncovered for part of the the time sampled by the blur. If we are to blur an object across a background, we have to know what the background is.

Even if we know what the background is, there are problems. For example, consider a biplane viewed from above, so that the lower wing is completely obscured by the upper wing. Because the upper wing is moving, the scenery below it would be seen through its blur, but unfortunately the lower wing would show through too. The lower wing should be hidden completely because it moves with the the upper wing and is obscured by it over the entire time interval.

This particular problem can be solved by rendering the plane and background as separate elements, but not all pictures can easily be separated into elements. This solution also does not allow for changes in visibility within a single object. This is particularly important for rotating objects.

The situation is further complicated by the change in shading within a frame time. Consider a textured top spinning on a table. If we calculate only one shade per frame, the texture would be blurred properly, but unfortunately the highlights and shadows would be blurred too. On a real top, the highlights and shadows are not blurred at all by the spinning. They are blurred, of course, by any lateral motion of the top along the table or by the motion of a light source or the camera. The highlights should be blurred by the motion of the light and the camera, by the travel of the top along the table, and by the precession of the top, but not by the rotation of the top.

Motion blurred shadows are also important and are not rendered correctly if we calculate only one shade per frame. Otherwise, for example, the blades of a fan could be motion blurred, but the shadows of those blades would strobe.

All of this is simply to emphasize the tremendous complexity of the motion blur problem. The prospects for an analytic solution are dim. Such a solution would require solving the visible surface problem as a function of time as well as space. It would also involve integrating the texture and shading function of the visible surfaces over time. Point sampling seems to be the only approach that offers any promise of solving the motion blur problem.

One point sampling solution was proposed by Korein and Badler[6]. Their method, however, point samples only in space, not in time. Changes in shading are not motion blurred. The method involves keeping a list of all objects that cross each sample point during the frame time, a list that could be quite long for a fast moving complex scene. They also impose the unfortunate restriction that both vertices of an edge must move at the same velocity. This creates holes in objects that change perspective severely during one frame, because the vertices move at drastically different rates. Polygons with edges that share these vertices cannot remain adjoining. The algorithm is also limited to linear motion. If the motion is curved or if the vertices are allowed to move independently, the linear intersection equation becomes a higher order equation. The resulting equation is expensive to solve and has multiple roots.

Distributing the sample points in time solves the motion blur problem. The path of motion can be arbitrarily complex. The only requirement is the ability to calculate the position of the object at a specific time. Changes in visibility and shading are correctly accounted for. Shadows (umbras and penumbras), depth of field, reflections and intersections are all correctly motion blurred. By using different distributions of rays, the motion can be blurred with a box filter or a weighted filter or can be strobed.

This distribution of the sample points in time does not involve adding any more sample points. Updating the object positions for each time is the only extra calculation needed for motion blur. Proper antialiasing is required or the picture will look strobed or have holes[4].

5. Other Implications of the Algorithm

Visible surface calculation is straightforward. Since each ray occurs at a single instant of time, the first step is to update the positions of the objects for that instant of time. The next is to construct a ray from the lens to the sample point and find the closest object that the ray intersects. Care must be taken in bounding moving objects. The bound should depend on time so that the number of potentially visible objects does not grow unacceptably with their speed.

Intersecting surfaces are handled trivially because we never have to calculate the line of intersection; we merely have to determine which is in front at a given location and time. At each sample point only one of the surfaces is visible. The intersections can even be motion blurred, a problem that would be terrifying with an analytic method.

The union, intersection, difference problem is easily solved with ray tracing or point sampling[10]. These calculations are also correctly motion blurred.

Transparency is easy even if the transparency is textured or varies with time. Let τ be the transparency of a surface at the time and location it is pierced by the ray, and let R be the reflectance. R and τ are wavelength dependent, and the color of the transparency is not necessarily the same as the color of the reflected light; for example, a red transparent plastic object may have a white highlight. If there are $n-1$ transparent surfaces in front of the opaque surface, the light reaching the viewer is

$$R_n \prod_{i=1}^{n-1} \tau_i + R_{n-1} \prod_{i=1}^{n-2} \tau_i + \cdots + R_2 \tau_1 + R_1 = \sum_{i=1}^{n} R_i \prod_{j=1}^{i-1} \tau_j.$$

If the surfaces form solid volumes, then each object has a τ, and that τ is scaled by the distance that the transmitted ray travels through that object. The motion blur and depth of field calculations work correctly for these transparency calculations.

The distributed approach can be adapted to a scanline algorithm as well as to ray tracing. The general motion blur and depth of field calculations have been incorporated into a scanline algorithm using distributed sampling for the visible surface calculations. Special cases of penumbras, fuzzy reflections, and translucency have been successfully incorporated for flat surfaces.

6. Summary of the Algorithm

The intensity of a pixel on the screen is an analytic function that involves several nested integrals: integrals over time, over the pixel region, and over the lens area, as well as an integral of reflectance times illumination over the reflected hemisphere and an integral of transmittance times illumination over the transmitted hemisphere. This integral can be tremendously complicated, but we can point sample the function regardless of how complicated it is. If the function depends on n parameters, the function is sampled in the n dimensions defined by those parameters. Rather than adding more rays for each dimension, the existing rays are distributed in each dimension according to the values of the corresponding parameter.

This summary of the distributed ray tracing algorithm is illustrated in Figure 2 for a single ray.

- Choose a time for the ray and move the objects accordingly. The number of rays at a certain time is proportional to the value of the desired temporal filter at that time.

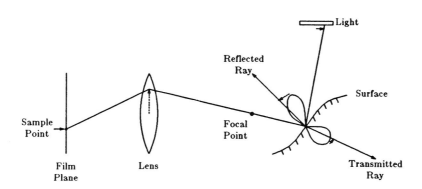

Figure 2. Typical Distributed Ray Path

- Construct a ray from the eye point (center of the lens) to a point on the screen. Choose a location on the lens, and trace a ray from that location to the focal point of the original ray. Determine which object is visible.
- Calculate the shadows. For each light source, choose a location on the light and trace a ray from the visible point to that location. The number of rays traced to a location on the light should be proportional to the intensity and projected area of that location as seen from the surface.
- For reflections, choose a direction around the mirror direction and trace a ray in that direction from the visible point. The number of rays traced in a specific direction should be proportional to the amount of light from that direction that is reflected toward the viewer. This can replace the specular component.
- For transmitted light, choose a direction around the direction of the transmitted light and trace a ray in that direction from the visible point. The number of rays traced in a specific direction should be proportional to the amount of light from that direction that is transmitted toward the viewer.

Figure 3. Motion Blurred Intersection.

7. Examples

Figure 3 illustrates motion blurred intersections. The blue beveled cube is stationary, and the green beveled cube is moving in a straight line, perpendicular to one of its face. Notice that the intersection of the faces is blurred except in in the plane of motion, where it is sharp.

Figures 4 and 5 illustrate depth of field. In figure 4, the camera has a 35 mm lens at f2.8. Notice that the rear sphere, which is out of focus, does not blur over the spheres in front. In figure 5, the camera is focused on the center of the three wooden spheres.

Figure 6 shows a number of moving spheres, with motion blurred shadows and reflections.

Figure 7 illustrates fuzzy shadows and reflections. The paper clip is illuminated by two local light sources which cast shadows with penumbras on the table. Each light is an extended light source (i.e., not a point light source) with a finite solid angle, and the intensity of its shadow at any point on the table is proportional to the amount of light obscured by the paper clip. The table reflects the paper clip, and the reflection blurs according to the specular distribution function of the table top. Note that both the shadows and the reflection blur with distance and are sharper close to the paper clip.

Figure 4. Depth of Field.

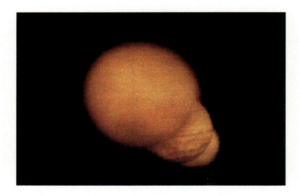

Figure 5. Depth of Field.

Figure 6. Balls in Motion.

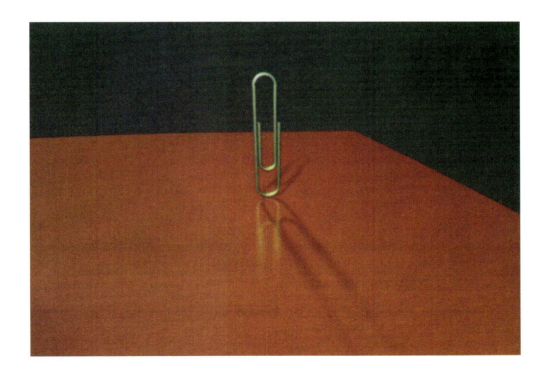

Figure 7. Paper Clip.

Figure 8 shows 5 billiard balls with motion blur and penumbras. Notice that the motion is not linear: the 9 ball changes direction abruptly in the middle of the frame, the 8 ball moves only during the middle of the frame, and the 4 ball only starts to move near the end of the frame. The shadows on the table are sharper where the balls are closer to the table; this most apparent in the stationary 1 ball. The reflections of the billiard balls and the room are motion blurred, as are the penumbras.

Figures 3, 5, and 7 were rendered with a scanline adaptation of this algorithm. Figures 4, 6, and 8 were rendered with ray tracing.

8. Conclusions

Distributed ray tracing a new paradigm for computer graphics which solves a number of hitherto unsolved or partially solved problems. The approach has also been successfully adapted to a scanline algorithm. It incorporates depth of field calculations into the visible surface calculations, eliminating problems in previous methods. It makes possible blurred phenomena such as penumbras, gloss, and translucency. All of the above can be motion blurred by distributing the rays in time.

These are not isolated solutions to isolated problems. This approach to image synthesis is practically no more expensive than standard ray tracing and solves all of these problems at once. The problems could not really be solved separately because they are all interrelated. Differences in shading, in penumbras, and in visibility are accounted for in the depth of field calculations. Changes in the depth of field and in visibility are motion blurred. The penumbra and shading calculations are motion blurred. All of these phenomena are related, and the new approach solves them all together by sampling the multidimensional space they define. The key to this is the ability to antialias point sampling.

9. Acknowledgements

Rodney Stock proposed the approach to antialiased point sampling that formed the basis of the paradigm explored in this paper. John Lasseter drew the environment map of the pool hall for "1984". Ed Catmull worked with us in the image synthesis working group and helped develop and refine these ideas. He and Alvy Ray Smith provided invaluable suggestions along the way. Tom Duff wrote the ray tracing program that we adapted to distributed ray tracing.

References

1. COOK, ROBERT L., TURNER WHITTED, AND DONALD P. GREENBERG, *A Comprehensive Model for Image Synthesis.* unpublished report
2. COOK, ROBERT L., "A Reflection Model for Realistic Image Synthesis," Master's thesis, Cornell University, Ithaca, NY, December 1981.
3. COOK, ROBERT L. AND KENNETH E. TORRANCE, "A Reflection Model for Computer Graphics," *ACM Transactions on Graphics*, vol. 1, no. 1, pp. 7-24, January 1982.
4. COOK, ROBERT L., "Antialiased Point Sampling," Technical Memo #94, Lucasfilm Ltd, San Rafael, CA, October 3, 1983.
5. HUNTER, RICHARD S., *The Measurement of Appearance,* John Wiley & Sons, New York, 1975.
6. KOREIN, JONATHAN AND NORMAN BADLER, "Temporal Anti-Aliasing in Computer Generated Animation," *Computer Graphics*, vol. 17, no. 3, pp. 377-388, July 1983.
7. NISHITA, TOMOYUKI, ISAO OKAMURA, AND EIHACHIRO NAKAMAE, *Siggraph Art Show*, 1982.
8. POTMESIL, MICHAEL AND INDRANIL CHAKRAVARTY, "Synthetic Image Generation with a Lens and Aperture Camera Model," *ACM Transactions on Graphics*, vol. 1, no. 2, pp. 85-108, April 1982.
9. POTMESIL, MICHAEL AND INDRANIL CHAKRAVARTY, "Modeling Motion Blur in Computer-Generated Images," *Computer Graphics*, vol. 17, no. 3, pp. 389-399, July 1983.
10. ROTH, S. D., "Ray Casting for Modeling Solids," *Computer Graphics and Image Processing*, no. 18, pp. 109-144, 1982.
11. WHITTED, TURNER, "An Improved Illumination Model for Shaded Display," *Communications of the ACM*, vol. 23, pp. 343-349, 1980.

Figure 8. 1984.

Continuous Shading of Curved Surfaces

HENRI GOURAUD

Abstract – A procedure for computing shaded pictures of curved surfaces is presented. The surface is approximated by small polygons in order to solve easily the hidden-parts problem, but the shading of each polygon is computed so that discontinuities of shade are eliminated across the surface and a smooth appearance is obtained. In order to achieve speed efficiency, the technique developed by Watkins is used which makes possible a hardware implementation of this algorithm.

Index terms – Coons patches, curved surfaces, halftone, hidden-line removal, shading.

INTRODUCTION

Since computers have been used to produce perspectives of three-dimensional objects, one of the main problems has been the tradeoff between the speed at which a picture could be produced and the realism of this picture. On one hand, cathode-ray tubes are able to display line drawings very efficiently; on the other hand, images with hidden parts removed and with shading take a long time to compute. In 1963 Roberts [1] developed the first program capable of removing hidden lines. Since then other algorithms performing the same task have been developed by Galimberty [2], Kubert [3], and Loutrel [4], among others. Their algorithms solve the hidden-line problem for structures composed of planar polygons. Two algorithms developed by Comba [5] and Weiss [6] remove hidden lines for objects made of quadric surfaces. In 1967 shaded images were introduced by the University of Utah (Romney [7], Warnock [8], Watkins [9]), General Electric (Rougelot [10]), MAGI [11], and IBM (Appel [12]). More recently, Bouknight and Kelley [17], [18] presented an algorithm producing shaded pictures with shadows and movable light sources. General Electric built for NASA the first hardware capable of generating real-time shaded pictures. Combining the work of both Warnock and Romney, Watkins recently developed a fast algorithm which will shortly be implemented in hardware at the University of Utah.

Realism beyond the obvious hidden-surface removal is obtained by shading each object in black and white or in color. In the General Electric system a fixed color is assigned by hardware to each of the different polygons composing the scene. The potential for changing this color from frame to frame exists, but the author is not aware of its use. This scheme gives a "cartoon-like" appearance to the generated images. Appel developed a system to produce shaded images on a digital plotter. The shading of a particular polygon is computed only as a function of the orientation of this polygon. This could become confusing in the case of parallel polygons, but is avoided in this particular case since the visible edges are drawn on top of the shading. Warnock and Romney were the first to use a shading rule in which both the orientation of the object and its distance from the observer are taken into consideration. Warnock uses the rule

$$S = \left| \frac{\cos \theta}{R} \right|$$

Romney uses the rule

$$S = \frac{\cos^2 \theta}{R^4} * \text{(normalization factor)}$$

Where $\cos \theta$ is a measure of the orientation of the polygon and R a measure of its distance from the observer. In both cases, the light source was located at the observer's position to avoid any need to show shadows. In the case of color pictures, Warnock also introduced the notion of specular reflectance as a term of the form

$$\frac{\cos^m \theta}{R} \quad 6 \leq m \leq 10$$

added to each of the three basic color components.

The essence of shaded pictures is to generate a different shade of gray for each resolution point on the projection screen, and each of the programs mentioned above has tried to reduce the time spent in computing a new shading for each point. The requirement that the objects be composed of planar polygons was mainly made to facilitate the hidden-parts computations, but it also permitted simplicity in the computation of the shading for each polygon because a part of this computation is done in common for all the points of this polygon. In the General Electric system the shading is the same on the entire projection of a given polygon. Warnock, Romney, and Watkins compute the shading at some particular points of the polygon and use linear interpolation to compute the shading at other points.

As an example, let us examine in more detail how the computation of the shading is performed in Watkins' algorithm. During a quick preprocessing of the description of the object, the orientation of each polygon is computed and stored in the data structure. The final image is then computed scan line by scan line. For each scan line the hidden parts are first eliminated and then each visible portion of a polygon is shaded according to its orientation and distance.

The distance has been introduced in the shading rule in order to make a distinction in shade between two overlapping separated parallel planes. Our experience has shown that the method used to compute this distance is not critical as long as the relative ordering of the objects is preserved.

The perspective transformation has this property, and the perspective coordinates which have already been used to solve the hidden-parts problem can be used again to compute the shading. If XYZ are the coordinates of a point, its projection has the coordinates

$$\frac{X}{Z} \quad \frac{Y}{Z} \quad \frac{1}{Z}$$

if the observer is located at the origin of the coordinate system looking in the Z direction. The coordinate $1/Z$ is a good monotonic approximation of the distance, and we can compute the shading as

$$S = \cos^2 \theta * \frac{1}{Z}$$

Since the value of $1/Z$ is known only at the vertices of the polygons, it is necessary to perform a linear interpolation between two vertices to obtain the value of $1/Z$ along one edge. Once this interpolation has been performed, it is possible to compute the shading among the scan line as (Fig. 5)

$$S = (1 - \alpha)\frac{1}{Z_E}\cos^2 \theta + \alpha\frac{1}{Z_F}\cos^2 \theta \quad (1)$$

Where α goes from 0 to 1 between E and F. It is remarkable to notice that the exact computation should be

$$S = \frac{\cos^2 \theta}{(1 - \alpha)Z_E + \alpha Z_F} \quad (2)$$

But the use of (1) does not show any noticeable degradation in the shading produced.

THE MACH BAND EFFECT

In attempting to represent a scene, the shading technique is subject to all the psychological illusions present in the visual process. Of interest to this discussion is a phenomenon thoroughly investigated by Mach [13] which explains how the retina performs some kind of two-dimensional filtering on the shading function of a scene. Each neuron, depending on the intensity of the light it receives, interacts with its neighbors and modifies their performances. The result of this interaction will be an attenuation of the low spatial frequencies and an amplification of the high spatial frequencies present in the shading. An example which is best suited to the discussion of this paper is shown in Fig. 1. Fig. 1(a) shows how the discontinuities in the value of the shading give a "fluted" aspect to each of the steps. Fig. 1(b) shows how a discontinuity in the first derivative of the shading gives the illusion of a small bump along the edge between two differently shaded surfaces.

CURVED SURFACES

In an effort to extend the class of objects that can be modeled by the computer, some techniques allowing the definition and the representations of curved surfaces have been developed. Coons introduced the Coons patch in 1964 [14]. At that time such surfaces were displayed by showing a grid of curves overlaid on the surface (Fig.2). This method presented all the disadvantages of wire frame perspectives, and no hidden-line removal method existed for this class of surfaces. At Cambridge, England, Armit [15] developed a system based on Coons patches. One of the facilities of the system was a modulation of the intensity of each segment of the curves by the distance from the segment to the observer. Without removing the hidden lines this method produced good looking pictures. At about the same time, Lee [16] developed an extension of the Coons patch called the rational Coons patch. The author is presently working at the University of Utah on the

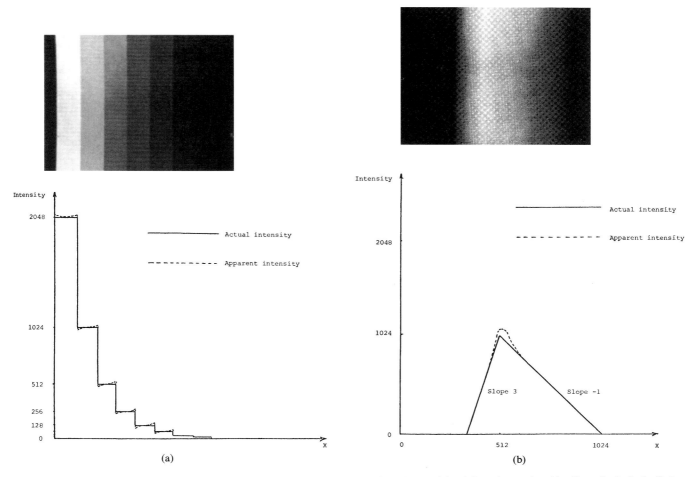

Fig. 1. (a) Mach band distortion produced by discontinuities in the value of the shading. (b) Mach band distortion produced by discontinuity in the first derivative of the shading.

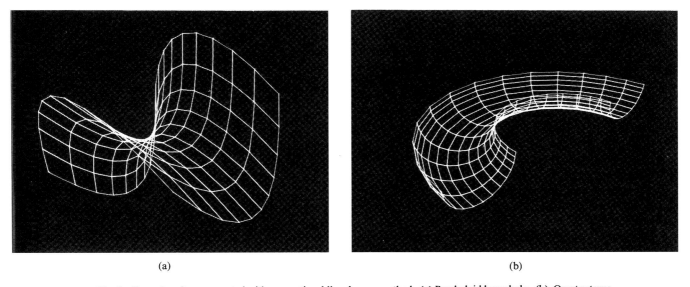

Fig. 2. Curved surfaces presented with conventional line drawng method. (a) Paraboloid hyperbole. (b) Quarter torus.

problems arising in the interactive design of rational Coons patches.

One of the properties of the rational Coons patch is the ability to reparametrize the patch without modifying its geometric shape. This can be viewed as a swashing of the grid of curves overlaid on the surface in one direction or another. In the two-dimensional perspective of such a patch, the spacing of the curves on the surface can give a cue of the depth properties of the surface. Since the reparametrization modifies the spacing it modifies also the depth cues; therefore one of the first problems the author was faced with was finding an automatic way of discovering the best parameterization for a given patch. It became rapidly evident that one should get rid of the grid on the surface by using a shading method in order to obtain the best depth representation of the surface.

Warnock and Romney had produced pictures of curved surfaces by approximating them with a large number of small planar polygons. Because of the Mach band phenomenon, this method produced pictures in which each small polygon was distinctly visible. Using Watkins' algorithm the author produced pictures of rational Coons patches, treating each grid element as a polygon (Fig. 3). The polygons thus obtained were not necessarily planar, but the fact that Watkins' algorithm accepts nonplanar polygons was very helpful at that point. As in the case of Warnock's and Romney's pictures, each polygon was very clearly visible and the grid had not disappeared.

From the explanation of the Mach band distortion it appears that in order to represent correctly the smooth aspect of a curved surface, the shading rule on this surface has to be continuous in value and if possible, in derivative. One way to achieve this would be to increase the number of polygons approximating the surface, but this is impractical for storage and time reasons. The approach described in this paper is to keep the polygon approximation of the surface, but to modify slightly the computation of the shading on each polygon so that continuity exists across polygon boundaries (Fig. 4).

Let us now examine how this continuity can be achieved. A typical data structure contains information about a certain number of lines and some more information connecting these lines into closed polygons. At a particular vertex common to several polygons, one might compute a normal for each polygon as a vector perpendicular to the plane of that polygon. To achieve continuity of the shading we have to have only one possible normal at any particular vertex. This normal could be computed as, for example, the average of the normals to each polygon associated with this particular vertex; but in the examples described in this paper an analytical description of the surface is available and it is possible to compute an exact normal at each vertex of the grid of polygons approximating the surface. Each polygon has a different shading for each of its vertices, and the shading at any particular point inside the polygon has to be computed as a continuous function of the shading at the vertices of the polygon.

If we now look at the projection of the polygon on the viewing plane, we see that one way to achieve this continuity is to compute the shading inside the polygon as two successive linear interpolations of the shading at the projection of the vertices. Given the projection of two edges AB and CD, and the scan line (Fig. 5), we assumed that the normal to the surface would be known at points A, B, C, D, which permits us to compute the shading at those four points. If E and F are the intersection of the scan line with AB and CD, respectively, and P is any point on the scan line between E and F, the shading at point E can be computed as a linear interpolation of S_A and S_B of the form

$$S_E = (1 - \alpha) * S_A + \alpha * S_B$$

where α is the coefficient ($0 \leq \alpha \leq 1$) expressing the position of E on the segment AB. If E is identical to A then $\alpha = 0$, and if E is identical to B then $\alpha = 1$. In a very similar fashion we can compute S_F as a linear interpolation of S_C and S_D and S_P as a linear interpolation of S_E and S_F.

$$S_F = (1 - \beta) * S_D + \beta * S_C \quad (0 < \beta < 1)$$
$$S_P = (1 - \alpha) * S_E + \alpha * S_F \quad (0 < \alpha < 1)$$

It can be easily verified from the equations above that if

$$P \equiv A, \quad \text{then} \quad S_P \equiv S_A$$
$$P \equiv B, \quad \text{then} \quad S_P \equiv S_B$$
$$P \equiv C, \quad \text{then} \quad S_P \equiv S_C$$
$$P \equiv D, \quad \text{then} \quad S_P \equiv S_D$$

In order to reduce the computation of a new shade for each point to a minimum, the very efficient technique developed by Watkins was extended to include this computation. The following is a very concise description of Watkins' algorithm (for complete understanding of the mechanisms, refer to Watkins' Ph.D. thesis [9]). If the picture is scanned from top of bottom the following information is computed for each polygon edge:

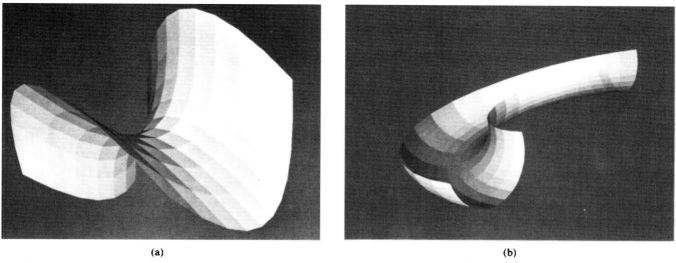

Fig. 3. Same curved surfaces presented with Watkins algorithm. (a) Computation time: 1 min 30 s. (b) Computation time: 1 min 20 s.

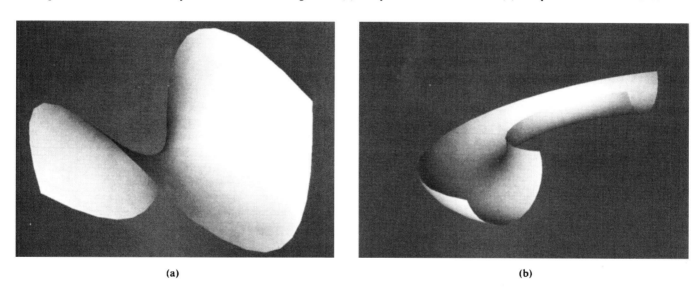

Fig. 4. Same curved surfaces presented with author's method. (a) Computation time: 1 min 45 s. (b) Computation time: 1 min 35 s.

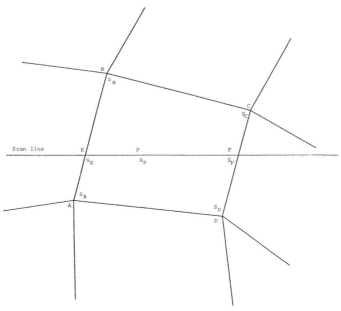

Fig. 5. Projection of one polygon intersected by the scan line.

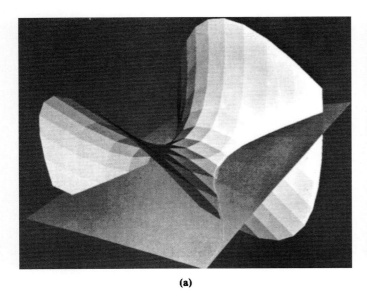 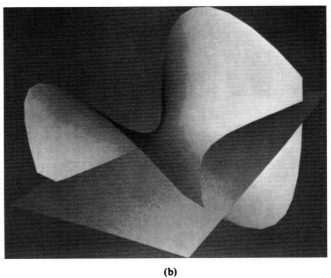

Fig. 6. Curved surface intersected by a plane presented with (a) Watkins' method (computation time 2 min), and (b) the author's method (computation time 2 min 15 s).

1) the number of the first scan line this edge will intersect;
2) how many scan lines below this one it will intersect;
3) the X and Z coordinates of the highest point of the edge;
4) 4) the slope in X and Z of this edge.

We can very easily add the following information:
5) the shading S of the surface at the highest point of this edge:
6) a "slope" of this shading along this edge.

This "slope" is computed as

$$\Delta S = \frac{S_2 - S_1}{n}$$

Where S_2 and S_1 are the shading at the two endpoints of the edge and n is the number of scan lines intersecting this edge.

Given this information it is now very easy to compute the shading on a given scan line. As the computation proceeds, an edge will become "active" when its first point is reached by a scan line. At that stage, we know the XYZ coordinates of this point and the value of the shading at the point on the surface. For the next scan line it is sufficient to add the "slope" to the coordinate information of the point as well as of the shading to find a new point and a new shading. Given a scan line and all the edges intersecting this scan line, edges belonging to the same polygon are paired to form segments (a segment could be viewed as the intersection of one of the polygons and the scan plane). A segment is created when an edge becomes "active." The segment contains the coordinates of its endpoints, the value of the shading at its endpoints, and the different slopes necessary to update this information from scan line to scan line. When an edge leaves the "active" list, it is necessary to rearrange the segments by deleting or merging some blocks of information. The hidden-lines computation is performed at that point and we are left with a number of segments totally or partially visible. For each point of the scan line on the visible part of a segment, we can compute a coefficient

$$\alpha = \frac{X_P - X_E}{X_F - X_E} \quad \text{(Fig. 5)}$$

and the shading as

$$S = (1 - \alpha) * X_E + \alpha * S_F$$

The linear interpolation which has been used here produces a shading which is continuous in value but not in derivative across polygon boundaries. The resulting Mach band effect can be observed mostly in the vicinity of the silhouette curves and where the surface bends sharply. Interpolation schemes more powerful that the linear interpolation could probably be used but the improvement obtained with such schemes would not compensate the loss of efficiency of the present algorithm and would make a hardware implementation unpracticable.

TIMING

At this point it is important to consider the time degradation we have imposed on Watkins' algorithm. Our modifications can be split into two categories. The first category is the extra information that is requested about each edge or segment. The second is the point-by-point computation of the shading of a scan line.

The first category adds hardware cost but should not slow down the process since all segment information is handled in parallel. Indeed, this is true only for a hardware implementation and it puts some more burden on the memory requirements. In the software simulation, about 40 percent of the time is spent in the routine which creates and updates segments from scan line to scan line. The amount of information attached to each segment was previously the X and Z coordinates of the endpoints of the segments, and is now augmented by the shading value of those two points. This multiplies the time spent in this routine by 1.5, or the total time taken by the modified algorithm by less than 1.2.

As for the second category, the proposed modification uses exactly the same hardware and does not take more time than the old method since the computation to be performed at that point is still a linear interpolation between two values provided by the segment handling routine.

INTERSECTIONS

The shading rule which we have described gives the illusion of a smooth curved surface when, in fact, this surface is described by a set of small polygons. It was necessary to keep this polygon approximation so that the computation of intersections could be handled easily using existing methods. As can be seen in Fig. 6, there is no difference here between the intersection computed by Watkins and the one computed with the modified algorithm. This does not seem to be a serious drawback and the final appearance of the picture remains good even when there are intersecting surfaces.

ACKNOWLEDGMENT

The author would like to thank I.E. Sutherland for the discussions that initiated the ideas presented here and G. Watkins for his help in explaining and modifying his algorithm.

REFERENCES

[1] L. G. Roberts, "Machine perception of three-dimensional solids." M.I.T. Lincoln Lab., Cambridge, Mass. Tech. Rep. 315, May 22, 1963.

[2] R. Galimberty and U. Montanari. "An algorithm for hidden line elimination." Istituto di Electtrotechnica ed Elettronica. Relazione interna, Apr. 1968.

[3] P. R. Kubert. "A computer method for perspective representation of curves and surfaces." Aerospace Corp., San Bernardino. Calif., Dec. 1968.

[4] P. Loutrel, "A solution to the 'hidden-line' problem for computer drawn polyhedra," New York Univ., New York, N.Y., Tech. Rep. 400-167, Sept. 1967.

[5] P. G. Comba, "A procedure for detecting intersections of three-dimensional objects," IBM New York Scientific Center, New York, N.Y., Rep. 39,020, Jan. 1967.

[6] R. A. Weiss, "Be vision, a package of IBM 7090 Fortran programs to draw orthographic views of combinations of plane and quadric surfaces." *J. Ass. Comput. Mach.* vol. 13, Apr. 1966, pp. 194-204.

[7] G. W. Romney, "Computer assisted assembly and rendering of solids," Dep. Comput. Sci., Univ. of Utah, Salt Lake City, Tech. Rep. TR 4-20, 1970.

[8] J. E. Warnock, "A hidden surface algorithm for computer generated halftone pictures." Dep. Comput. Sci., Univ. of Utah, Salt Lake City, Tech. Rep. 4-15, June 1969.

[9] G. S. Watkins, "A real time visible surface algorithm." Dep. Comput. Sci., Univ. of Utah, Salt Lake City. Tech. Rep. UTEC-CSc 70-101, July 1970.

[10] R. S. Rougelot and R. Shoemaker, "G. E. real time display." General Electric Co., Syracuse, N.Y., NASA Rep. NAS 9-3916.

[11] MAGI, Mathematical Applications Group, Inc., "3-D simulated graphics," *Datamation*, vol. 14, Feb. 1968, p. 69.

[12] A. Appel, "The notion of quantitative invisibility and the machine rendering of solids," *Ass. Comput. Mach. Conf. Proc.*, p. 387, 1967.

[13] F. Ratliff, *Mach Bands: Quantitative Studies on Neural Networks in the Retina*. San Francisco: Holden-Day, 1965

[14] S. A. Coons, "Surface for computer-aided design of space forms," M.I.T., Cambridge, Mass., Project MAC. Tech. Rep. MAC-TR-41, June, 1967.

[15] A. P. Armit, "A multipatch design system for Coons' patches, Univ. of Cambridge Computer Aided Design Group, Dec. 1968.

[16] T. M. P. Lee, "Three-dimensional curves and surfaces for rapid computer display," Harvard Univ., Cambridge, Mass., Tech. Rep. ESD-TR-69-189, Apr. 30, 1969

[17] W. J. Bouknight, "A procedure for generation of three-dimensional half-toned computer graphics presentations," *Commun. Ass. Comput. Mach.*, vol. 13, 1970.

[18] J. Bouknight and K. Kelley, "An algorithm for producing half-tone computer graphics presentations with shadows and movable light sources," in *1970 Spring Joint Computer Conf., AFIPS Proc.*, vol. 36. Montvale, N. J.: AFIPS Press, 1970, pp. 1-10.

Graphics and Image Processing

W. Newman
Editor

Illumination for Computer Generated Pictures

Bui Tuong Phong
University of Utah

The quality of computer generated images of three-dimensional scenes depends on the shading technique used to paint the objects on the cathode-ray tube screen. The shading algorithm itself depends in part on the method for modeling the object, which also determines the hidden surface algorithm. The various methods of object modeling, shading, and hidden surface removal are thus strongly interconnected. Several shading techniques corresponding to different methods of object modeling and the related hidden surface algorithms are presented here. Human visual perception and the fundamental laws of optics are considered in the development of a shading rule that provides better quality and increased realism in generated images.

Key Words and Phrases: computer graphics, graphic display, shading, hidden surface removal.
CR Categories: 3.26, 3.41, 8.2

Introduction

This paper describes several approaches to the production of shaded pictures of solid objects. In the past decade, we have witnessed the development of a number of systems for the rendering of solid objects by computer. The two principal problems encountered in the design of these systems are the elimination of the hidden parts and the shading of the objects. Until now, most effort has been spent in the search for fast hidden surface removal algorithms. With the development of these algorithms, the programs that produce pictures are becoming remarkably fast, and we may now turn to the search for algorithms to enhance the quality of these pictures.

In trying to improve the quality of the synthetic images, we do not expect to be able to display the object exactly as it would appear in reality, with texture, overcast shadows, etc. We hope only to display an image that approximates the real object closely enough to provide a certain degree of realism. This involves some understanding of the fundamental properties of the human visual system. Unlike a photograph of a real world scene, a computer generated shaded picture is made from a numerical model, which is stored in the computer as an objective description. When an image is then generated from this model, the human visual system makes the final subjective analysis. Obtaining a close image correspondence to the eye's subjective interpretation of the real object is then the goal. The computer system can be compared to an artist who paints an object from its description and not from direct observation of the object. But unlike the artist, who can correct the painting if it does not look right to him, the computer that generates the picture does not receive feedback about the quality of the synthetic images, because the human visual system is the final receptor.

This is a subjective domain. We must at the outset define the degree of realism we wish to attain, and fix certain goals to be accomplished. Among these goals are:

1. "Real time" display of dynamic color pictures of three-dimensional objects. A real time display system is one capable of generating pictures at the rate of at least 30 frames a second.
2. Representation of objects made of smooth curved surfaces.
3. Elimination or attenuation of the effects of digital sampling techniques.

The most important consideration in trying to attain these goals is the object modeling technique.

Existing Shading Techniques

Methods of Object Modeling

Image quality depends directly on the effectiveness of the shading algorithm, which in turn depends on the method of modeling the object. Two principal methods of object description are commonly used:
1. Surface definition using mathematical equations.
2. Surface approximation by planar polygonal mosaic.

Several systems have been implemented to remove hidden parts for mathematically defined curved surfaces [1, 2, 3, 4, 5]. With these systems, exact information at each point of the surface can be obtained, and the result-

---

Copyright © 1975, Association for Computing Machinery, Inc. General permission to republish, but not for profit, all or part of this material is granted provided that ACM's copyright notice is given and that reference is made to the publication, to its date of issue, and to the fact that reprinting privileges were granted by permission of the Association for Computing Machinery.

This research was supported in part by the University of Utah Computer Science Division and the Advanced Research Projects Agency of the U.S. Department of Defense, monitored by the Rome Air Development Center, Griffiss Air Force Base, NY 13440, under Contract F30602-70-C-0300. Author's address: Digital Systems Laboratory, Stanford University, Stanford, CA 94305.

ing computer generated pictures are most realistic. The class of possible surfaces is restricted, however, and the computation time needed to remove the hidden parts and to perform shading is very large. Up to the present time, these systems have usually considered the class of surfaces represented by quadric patches. Although higher degree surfaces are desirable and are sometimes necessary to model an object, they have not been taken into consideration due to an increase in computation time to remove hidden surfaces and to perform shading computations. Even when only quadric surfaces are considered, the implementation of a real time display system using this type of model is too expensive and complex.

A simple method of representing curved surfaces and objects of arbitrary shape is to approximate the surfaces with small planar polygons; for example, a cone might be represented as shown in Figure 1. This type of representation has the advantage that it avoids the problem, posed by mathematically curved surface approaches, of solving higher order equations.

Planar approximation also offers the only means of reducing hidden surface computation to within reasonable bounds, without restricting the class of surfaces that can be represented. For this reason, all recent attempts to devise fast hidden surface algorithms have been based on the use of this approximation for curved surfaces; these algorithms have been summarized and classified by Sutherland et al. [6]. The next section discusses their influence on the way shading is computed.

While planar approximation greatly simplifies hidden surface removal, it introduces several major problems in the generation of a realistic displayed image. One of these is the *contour edge* problem: the outline or silhouette of a polygonally approximated object is itself a polygon, not a smooth curve. The other problem is that of shading the polygons in a realistic manner. This paper is concerned with the shading problem; the contour edge problem is discussed by the author and F.C. Crow in [7].

Influence of Hidden Surface Algorithms

The order in which a hidden surface algorithm computes visible information has a decided influence on the way shading is performed. For example Warnock, who developed one of the first such algorithms [8], computed display data by a binary subdivision process: this meant that the order of generating display data was largely independent both of the order of scanning the display and of the order of the polygons in memory. This made it difficult to perform effective shading on curved objects.

The two major advances in the development of fast hidden surface algorithms have been made by Watkins [9] and by Newell, Newell, and Sancha [10]. Watkins generates the displayed picture scan line by scan line. On each scan line he computes which polygons intersect the scan line, and then computes the visible *segment* of each polygon, where this segment is the visible strip of

Fig. 1. A cone represented by means of planar approximation.

the polygon, one screen resolution unit in height, that lies on the scan line.

Newell, Newell, and Sancha adopt a different approach, using a *frame buffer* into which the object is painted, face by face. The hidden surface problem is solved by painting the farthest face first, and the nearest last. Each face is painted scan line by scan line, starting at the top of the face.

From the shading aspect, the important attribute of these algorithms is that they both generate information scan line by scan line in order to display the faces of an object. This information is in the form of segments, one screen resolution unit high, on which the shading computation may then be performed. The main differences between the algorithms, from the point of view of shading, are (a) the order in which the segments are generated, and (b) the fact that Watkins generates each screen dot only once, whereas the Newell-Sancha algorithm may overwrite the same dot several times.

Shading with the Polyhedral Model

When planar polygons are used to model an object, it is customary to shade the object by using the *normal vectors* to the polygons. The shading of each point on a polygon is then the product of a shading coefficient for the polygon and the cosine of the angle between the polygon normal and the direction of incident light. This cosine relationship is known in optics as the "cosine law," and allows us to compute the shading S_p for a polygon p as

$$S_p = C_p \cos(i), \qquad (1)$$

where C_p is the reflection coefficient of the material of p relative to the incident wavelength, and i is the incident angle.

Fig. 2. An example of the use of Newell, Newell, and Sancha's shading technique, showing transparency and highlight effects.

Fig. 3. Computation of the shading at point R using the Gouraud method. There are two successive linear interpolations: (1) across polygon edges, i.e. P between A and B, Q between A and D; and (2) along the scan line, i.e. R between P and Q.

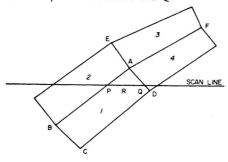

Fig. 4. Gouraud shading, applied to approximated cone of Fig. 1.

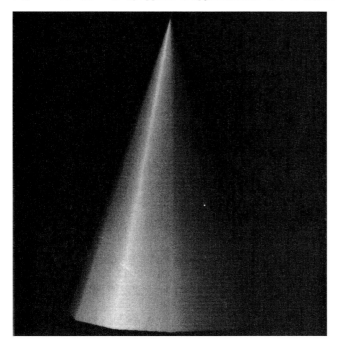

This shading offers only a very rough approximation of the true physical effect. It does not allow for any of the *specular* properties of the material, i.e. the ability of the material to generate highlights by reflection from its outer surface, and the position of the observer, which is ignored. A more serious drawback to this method, however, is the poor effect when using it to display smooth curved surfaces. The cosine law rule is appropriate for objects that are properly modeled with planar surfaces, such as boxes, buildings, etc., but it is inappropriate for smoothly curved surfaces such as automobile bodies. This does not mean, however, that we should abandon the use of such a polygon-oriented shading rule and search for a different rule for curved surfaces. Recent research in shading techniques demonstrates that significant results can be achieved by using the basic shading rule of eq. (1) and modifying the results to reduce the discontinuities in shading between adjacent polygons.

1. Warnock's shading. As three-dimensional objects are projected onto the cathode-ray tube screen, the depth sensation is lost, and the images of those objects appear flat. In order to restore the depth sensation, two effects were simulated by Warnock:

1. Decreasing intensity of the reflected light from the object with the distance between the light source and the object.

2. Highlights created by specular reflection.

Warnock placed the light source and the eye at the same position, so that the shading function was the sum of two terms, one for the normal "cosine" law, and the other term for the specularly reflected light. The resulting pictures have several desirable attributes; for example, identical parallel faces, located differently in space, will be shaded at different intensities, and facets which face directly toward the light source are brighter than adjacent facets facing slightly away from the incident light. However, the polygonal model gives a discontinuity in shading between faces of an approximated curved surface. When a curved surface is displayed, the smoothness of the curved surface is destroyed by this discontinuity. This is clearly visible in Figure 1.

2. Newell, Newell, and Sancha's shading. Newell, Newell, and Sancha presented some ideas on creating transparency and highlights. From observations in the real world, they found that highlights are created not only by the incident light source but also by the reflection of light from other objects in the scene; this is especially true in the case of objects made of highly reflective or transparent materials. In the Newell-Sancha model, curved surfaces are approximated with planar polygons. Unfortunately, the ability to generate highlights is severely limited due to the inability to vary light intensity over the surface of any single polygon. This problem is apparent in Figure 2.

3. Gouraud's shading. While working on a technique to represent curved objects made of "Coons surfaces" or "Bezier patches," Gouraud [11] developed an algorithm to shade curved surfaces. With his algorithm, a surface represented by a patch is approximated by polygonal planar facets. Gouraud computes information about the curvature of the surface at each vertex of each of these facets. From the curvature, a shade intensity is computed and retained. For example, the shade intensity may be computed for each vertex using eq. (1), with i as the angle between the incident light and the normal to the surface at this vertex. When the surface is displayed, this shade intensity is linearly interpolated along the edge between adjacent pairs of vertices of the object. The shade at a point on the surface is also a linear interpolation of the shade along a scan line between intersections of the edges with a plane passing through the scan line (Figure 3). This very simple method gives a continuous gradation of shade over the entire surface, which in most cases restores the smooth appearance. An example of Gouraud's shading is shown in Figure 4.

With the introduction of the Gouraud smooth shading technique, the quality of computer-generated images improved sufficiently to allow representation of a large variety of objects with great realism. Problems still exist, however, one of which is the apparent discontinuity across polygon edges. On surfaces with a high component of specular reflection, highlights are often inappropriately shaped, since they depend upon the disposition and shape of the polygons used to approximate a curved surface and not upon the curvature of the object surface itself. The shading of a surface in motion (in a computer generated film) has annoying frame to frame discontinuities due to the changing orientation of the polygons describing the surface. Also the shading algorithms are not invariant under rotation.

Frame-to-frame discontinuities of shade in a computer generated film are illustrated in the following situation. A curved surface is approximated with planar facets. When this surface is in motion, all the facets which are perpendicular to the direction of the light take on a uniform shade. In the next frame the motion of the object brings these facets into a different orientation toward the light, and the intensity of the shade across their surfaces varies continuously from one end to the other. Thus the surface appears to change from one with highlights to one of uniform shade. Moreover, the position of these highlights is not steady from frame to frame as the object rotates.

Mach Band Effect

Many of the shading problems associated with planar approximation of curved surfaces are the result of the discontinuities at polygon boundaries. One might expect that these problems could be avoided by reducing the size of the polygons. This would be undesirable, of course, since it would increase the number of polygons and hence would increase both the memory requirements for storing the model and the time for hidden surface removal.

Fig. 5. Normal at a point along an edge.

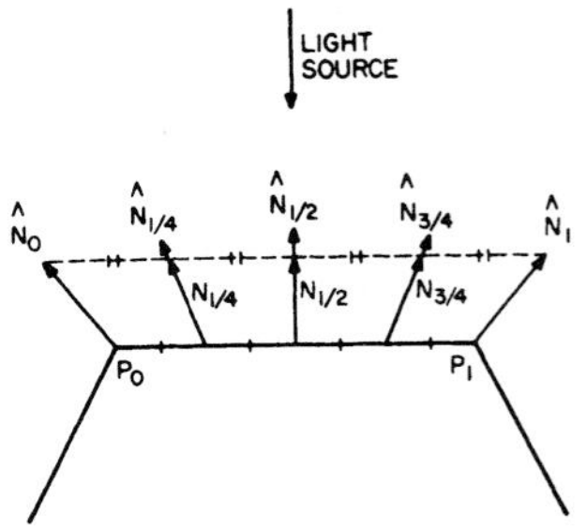

Fig. 6. Shading at a point.

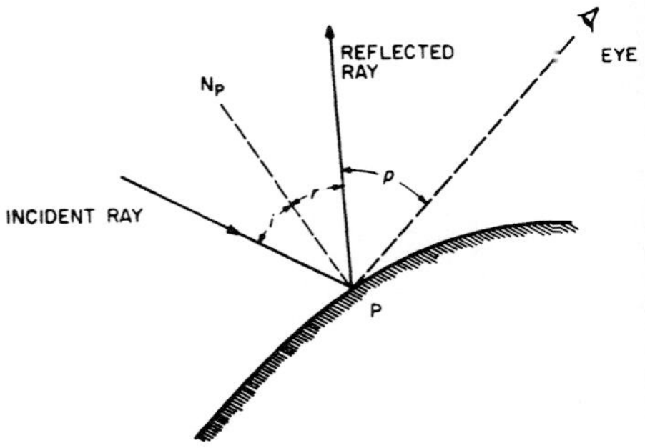

Unfortunately, because of visual perception effects, the reduction of polygon size is not as beneficial as might be expected. The particular effect responsible is the *Mach Band* effect. Mach established the following principle:

Wherever the light-intensity curve of an illuminated surface (the light intensity of which varies in only one direction) has a concave or convex flection with respect to the axis of the abscissa, that particular place appears brighter or darker, respectively, than its surroundings [E. Mach, 1865].

Whenever the slope of the light intensity curve changes, this effect appears. The extent to which it is noticeable depends upon the magnitude of the curvature change, but the effect itself is always present.

Without the Mach Band effect, one might hope to achieve accurate shading by reducing the size of polygons. Unfortunately the eye enhances the discontinuities over polygon edges, creating undesired areas of apparent brightness along the edges. Therefore unless the size of the displayed facets is shrunk to a resolution point, increasing the number of facets does not solve the problem. Using the Gouraud method to interpolate the shade linearly between vertices, the discontinuities of the shading function disappear, but the Mach Band effect is visible where the slope of the shading function changes. This can be seen in Figure 4. The subjective discontinuity of shade at the edges due to the Mach Band effect then destroys the smooth appearance of the curved surface.

A better shading rule is therefore proposed for displaying curved surfaces described by planar polygons. This new technique requires the computation of the normal to the displayed surface at each point. It is therefore more expensive in computation than Gouraud's technique; but the quality of the resulting picture, and the accuracy of the displayed highlights, is much improved.

Using a Physical Model

Specular Reflection

If the goal in shading a computer-synthesized image is to simulate a real physical object, then the shading model should in some way imitate real physical shading situations. Clearly the model of eq. (1) does not accomplish this. As mentioned before, it completely

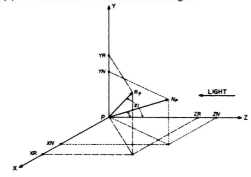

Fig. 7(a). Determination of the reflected light.

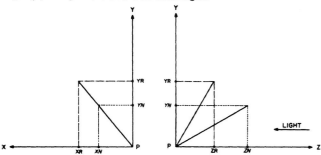

Fig. 7(b). Projections of the reflected light.

ignores both the position of the observer and the specular properties of the object. Even with the improvements introduced by Gouraud, which provide remarkably better shading, these properties are still ignored.

The first step in accounting for the specular properties of objects and the position of the observer is to determine the normal to the surface at each point to be shaded, i.e. at each point where a picture element of the raster display projects onto the surface. It is only with this knowledge that information about the direction of reflected rays can be acquired, and only with this information can we model the specular properties of objects. It is evident from the preceding discussion, however, that our polyhedral model provides information about normals only at the vertices of polygons. Thus the first step in improving our shading model is to devise a way to obtain the normal to the surface for each raster unit.

Computation of the Normal at a Point on the Surface

The normal at each vertex can be approximated by either one of the methods described by Gouraud [10]. It is now necessary to define the normal to the surface along the edges and at a point on the surface of a polygon.

The normal to the surface at a point along the edge of a polygonal model is the result of a linear interpolation to the normals at the two vertices of that edge. An example is given in Figure 5: the normal N_t to the surface at a point between the two vertices P_0 and P_1 is computed as follows:

$$N_t = tN_1 + (1-t)N_0, \qquad (2)$$

where $t = 0$ at N_0 and $t = 1$ at N_1.

The determination of the normal at a point on the surface of a polygon is achieved in the same way as the computation of the shading at that point with the Gouraud technique. The normal to the visible surface at a point located between two edges is the linear interpolation of the normals at the intersections of these two edges with a scan plane passing through the point under consideration. Note that the general surface normal is quadratically related to the vertex normal.

From the approximated normal at a point, a shading function determines the shading value at that point.

The Shading Function Model

In computer graphics, a shading function is defined as a function which yields the intensity value of each point on the body of an object from the characteristics of the light source, the object, and the position of the observer.

Taking into consideration that the light received by the eye is provided one part by the diffuse reflection and one part by the specular reflection of the incident light, the shading at point P (Figure 6) on an object can be computed as:

$$S_p = C_p[\cos(i)(1-d)+d] + W(i)[\cos(s)]^n, \qquad (3)$$

where:
- C_p is the reflection coefficient of the object at point P for a certain wavelength.
- i is the incident angle.
- d is the environmental diffuse reflection coefficient.
- $W(i)$ is a function which gives the ratio of the specular reflected light and the incident light as a function of the incident angle i.
- s is the angle between the direction of the reflected light and the line of sight.
- n is a power which models the specular reflected light for each material.

The function $W(i)$ and the power n express the specular reflection characteristics of a material. For a highly reflective material, the values of both $W(i)$ and n are large. The range of $W(i)$ is between 10 and 80 percent, and n varies from 1 to 10. These numbers are empirically adjusted for the picture, and no physical justifications are made. In order to simplify the model, and thereby the computation of the terms $\cos(i)$ and $\cos(s)$ of formula (3), it is assumed that:

1. The light source is located at infinity; that is, the light rays are parallel.
2. The eye is also removed to infinity.

With these two considerations, the values of $\cos(i)$ and $\cos(s)$ of the shading function in (3) can be rewritten as: $\cos(i) = kN_p / |N_p|$ and $\cos(s) = uR_p / |R_p|$ where k and u are respectively the unit vectors in the direction of the light and the line of sight, N_p is the normal vector at P, and R_p is the reflected light vector at P.

The quantity $kN_p / |N_p|$ can be referred to as the projection of a normalized vector N_p on an axis parallel to the direction of the light. If $|N_p|$ is unity, the previous

Fig. 8. Improved shading, applied to approximated cone of Fig. 1.

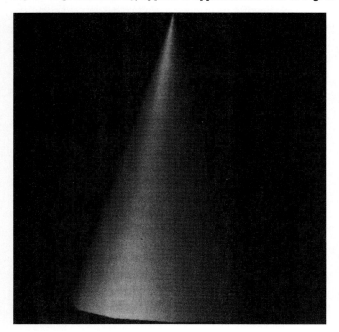

Fig. 9. Improved shading, applied to the example of Figure 2.

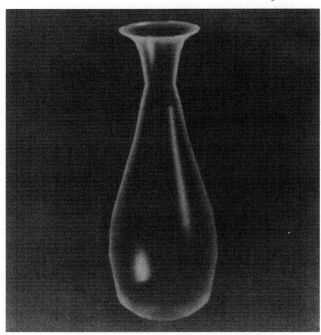

quantity is one component of the vector N_p in a coordinate system where the direction of light is parallel to one axis. In this case, the quantity $uR_p/|R_p|$ can be obtained directly from the vector N_p in the following way.

Let us consider a Cartesian coordinate system having the origin located at point P and having the z axis parallel to the light but opposite in direction (Fig. 7(a)).

We have the following assumptions about the model:

1. The normalized vector N_p makes an angle i with the z axis, and the reflected light vector R_p makes an angle $2i$ with the same axis.
2. Only incident angles less than or equal to 90 degrees are considered in the shading computation. For a greater angle, this means that the light source is behind the front surface. In the case where a view of the back surface is desired when it is visible, it can be assumed that the normal will always point toward the light source.
3. If k is the unit vector along the PZ axis, then by simple geometry, it may be shown that the three vectors k, N_p, and R_p are coplanar.
4. The two vectors N_p and R_p are of unit length.

From assumption (3), the projections of the vectors N_p and R_p onto the plane defined by (PX,PY) are merged into a line segment (Figure 7(b)). Therefore,

$$X_r/Y_r = X_n/Y_n, \qquad (4)$$

where X_r, X_n, Y_r, and Y_n are respectively the components of R_p and N_p in the x and y directions.

From assumptions (1) and (2), the component Z_n of N_p is:

$$Z_n = \cos(i), \qquad (5)$$

where $0 \leq i \leq 90$ degrees.

By simple trigonometry, we obtain the following expressions:

$$Z_r = \cos(2i) = 2[\cos(i)]^2 - 1 = 2Z_n^2 - 1, \qquad (6)$$

$$X_r^2 + Y_r^2 = [\sin(2i)]^2 = 1 - [\cos(2i)]^2. \qquad (7)$$

From (4) and (7), we obtain:

$$X_r = 2Z_n X_n, \quad Y_r = 2Z_n Y_n, \quad 0 \leq Z_n \leq 1.$$

The three components of R_p are then known in the light source coordinate system. The projection of the vector R_p onto the z-axis of the eye coordinate system may be found by a simple dot product of the reflected vector with this z-axis. The component of R_p on an axis parallel to the line of sight is the value of the cosine of the angle between the reflected light and the line of sight. The value of this cosine will be used in the simulation of the specular reflection.

This method of calculating the direction of the reflected light for each point from the orientation of the normal is preferred over the computation of the reflected light vector at vertices and the subsequent interpolation of them in the same way as the normal. It is faster and it requires less storage space than the interpolation scheme.

With the described method, the shading of a point is computed from the orientation of the approximated normal; it is not a linear interpolation of the shading values at the vertices. Therefore, a better approximation of the curvature of the surface is obtained, and highlights due to the simulation of specular reflection are properly rendered. Examples of application of the shading technique are shown in Figures 8 and 9. Figure 10 compares a display generated by this technique with a photograph of a real object.

Fig. 10(a). A sphere displayed with the improved shading.

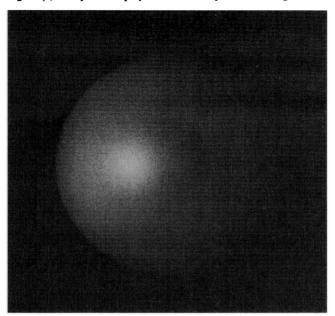

Fig. 10(b). A photograph of a real sphere.

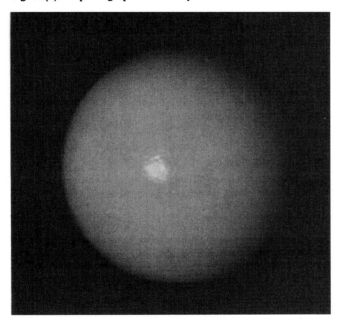

Conclusion

The linear interpolation scheme used here to approximate the orientation of the normal does not guarantee a continuous first derivative of the shading function across an edge of a polygonal model. In extreme cases where there is an abrupt change in the orientation of two adjacent polygons along a common edge, the subjective brightness due to the Mach Band effect will be visible along this edge. However, this effect is much less visible in the described model than in the Gouraud smooth shading model. Also, an interesting fact discussed previously on Mach Band effect shows that this effect is visible whenever there is a great change in the slope of the intensity distribution curve, even if the curve has a continuous first derivative. When a higher degree interpolation curve is used, it will make the presence of the edges unnoticeable, although it will still give some Mach Band effect.

When a comparison was made of pictures of the same object generated with different shading techniques, it was found that little difference existed between pictures generated with the new shading and the ones created with a cubic interpolant curve for the shading computation. Furthermore, as time is the critical factor in a real time dynamic picture display system, the use of a high degree interpolation curve does not seem to be possible at the moment with the current techniques to compute the coefficients of such a function.

A hardware implementation of this shading model would of course require more hardware than the simpler Gouraud method. The Gouraud model needs one interpolator for the shading function. It must compute a new shading value for each raster unit, and hence must be very high speed to drive a real time display. The model proposed here requires three of these interpolators operating in parallel. In addition, since the results of the interpolation do not yield a unit vector, and since eqs. (6), (7), and (8) require a unit normal vector, some extra hardware is necessary to "normalize" the outputs of the interpolators. This requires a very fast mechanism for obtaining square roots. None of these problems is too difficult to solve; and judging from the improvements in image quality obtained using the new model, it may well be worth the extra expense to provide such hardware in applications for which real time display is important.

Received November 1975; revised March 1975

References
1. MAGI, Mathematical Applications Group Inc. 3-D simulated graphics. *Datamation 14* (Feb. 1968), 69.
2. Comba, P.G. A procedure of detecting intersections of three-dimensional objects. Rep. 39,020, IBM New York Scientific Center, Jan. 1967.
3. Weiss, R.A. BE VISION, a package of IBM 7090 FORTRAN programs to draw orthographic views of combinations of plane and quadric surfaces. *J. ACM 13*, 2 (Apr. 1966), 194-204.
4. Mahl, R. Visible surface algorithm for quadric patches. *IEEE Trans. C-21*, (Jan. 1972), 1-4.
5. Catmull, E.E. A subdivision algorithm for computer display of curved surfaces. Ph.D th., Dep. of Comput. Sci., U. of Utah.
6. Sutherland, I.E., Sproull, R.F., and Schumacker, R.A. A characterization of ten-hidden surface algorithms. *Computing Surveys 6* (Mar. 1974), 1-56.
7. Bui Tuong Phong and Crow, F.C. Improved rendition of polygonal models of curved surfaces. To be presented at the joint USA-Japan Computer Conference.
8. Warnock, J.E. A hidden-line algorithm for halftone picture representation. Dep. of Comput. Sci., U. of Utah, TR 4-15, 1969.
9. Watkins, G.S. A real-time visible surface algorithm. Dep. of Comput. Sci., U. of Utah, UTEC-CSc-70-101, June 1970.
10. Newell, M.E., Newell, R.G., and Sancha, T.L. A new approach to the shaded picture problem. Proc. ACM 1973 Nat. Conf.
11. Gouraud, H. Computer display of curved surfaces. Dep. of Comput. Sci., U. of Utah, UTEC-CSc-71-113, June 1971. Also in *IEEE Trans. C-20* (June 1971), 623-629.

MODELS OF LIGHT REFLECTION

FOR COMPUTER SYNTHESIZED PICTURES

James F. Blinn

University of Utah

ABSTRACT

In the production of computer generated pictures of three dimensional objects, one stage of the calculation is the determination of the intensity of a given object once its visibility has been established. This is typically done by modelling the surface as a perfect diffuser, sometimes with a specular component added for the simulation of hilights. This paper presents a more accurate function for the generation of hilights which is based on some experimental measurements of how light reflects from real surfaces. It differs from previous models in that the intensity of the hilight changes with the direction of the light source. Also the position and shape of the hilights is somewhat different from that generated by simpler models. Finally, the hilight function generates different results when simulating metallic vs. nonmetallic surfaces. Many of the effects so generated are somewhat subtle and are apparent only during movie sequences. Some representative still frames from such movies are included.

Key Words and Phrases: computer graphics, graphic display, shading, hidden surface removal.

CR Categories: 3.17, 5.12, 8.2

INTRODUCTION

In producing computer generated pictures of three dimensional objects, two types of calculation must be performed. The first, and most popularly discussed, is the hidden surface problem; determining which object is visible where on the screen and what is the normal vector to the object at that point. The second is the intensity calculation; given the normal vector and the position of the light sources, what is the proper intensity for the corresponding spot on the picture. Very simple models are typically used which simulate ideal diffuse reflectors. This uses the, so called, Lambert's law which states that the surface will diffuse incident light equally in all directions. Differences in intensity are then caused by the different amounts of incident light per unit area intercepted by portions of the surface at various angles to the light source. This will be proportional to the cosine of the angle between the normal to the surface, N, and the vector to the light source, L. This cosine is evaluated by computing the dot product of the two vectors after normalizing them to a length of 1. If this dot product is negative it indicates that the viewer is on the opposite side of the surface from the light source. The intensity should then be set to zero.

In addition, some constant value is usually added to the intensity to simulate the effects of ambient light on the surface. This assumes that a small amount of light falls on the surface uniformly from all directions in addition to the main point light source. The integral of this ambient light from all directions yields a constant value for any normal direction. The net function is:

$$d = \max(0, N \cdot L)$$
$$i = p_a + d\, p_d$$

where

i = percieved intensity

p_a = proportion of ambient reflection

p_d = proportion of diffuse reflection

d = amount of diffuse reflection

N = Normal vector to surface

L = Light direction vector

This model is simple to compute and quite adequate for many applications.

SIMPLE HILIGHT MODELS

A more realistic lighting model was introduces by Phong [2] as part of a technique for improving the appearance of images of curved surfaces. The function makes use of the fact that, for any real surface, more light is reflected in a direction making an equal angle of incidence with reflectance. The additional light reflected in this direction is referred to as the specular component. If the surface was a perfect mirror light would only reach the eye if the surface normal, N, pointed halfway between the source direction, L, and the eye direction, E. We will name this direction of maximum hilights H, where

$$H = \frac{L+E}{\text{len}(L+E)}$$

Reprinted with permission from *Computer Graphics* Vol. 11, No. 2, July 1977, 192-198.

For less than perfect mirrors, the specular component falls off slowly as the normal direction moves away from the specular direction. The cosine of the angle between H and N is used as a measure of the distance a particular surface is away from the maximum specular direction. The degree of sharpness of the highlights is adjusted by taking this cosine to some power, typically 50 or 60. The net Phong shading function is then:

$$d = \max(0, N \cdot L)$$
$$s = (N \cdot H)^{c_1}$$
$$i = p_a + d\, p_d + s\, p_s$$

where

i = percieved intensity
p_s = proportion of specular reflection
s = amount of specular reflection
c_1 = measure of shininess of surface
other values as defined above

In addition, when simulating colored surfaces, there is a different intensity value for each primary. These should be calculated by scaling only the diffuse and ambient components by the color of the object. The highlights then appear desaturated or white.

TORRANCE-SPARROW MODEL

The reflection of light from real surfaces has been the subject of much theoretical and experimental work by physicists [5], [6] and illumination engineers [4]. The experimental results generally match the Phong shading function but some differences do arise. The main one is the fact that the height of the specular bump, represented by the parameter p_s above, varies with the direction of the light source. Also the direction of peak specular reflection is not always exactly along H. In 1967 Torrance and Sparrow [7] derived a theoretical model to explain these effects. The match between their theoretically predicted functions and experimentally measured data is quite impressive. In this section we derive the Torrance-Sparrow highlight function in terms of the vectors N, L, H and E, all of which are assumed to be normallized.

The surface being simulated is assumed to be composed of a collection of mirror like micro facets. These are oriented in random directions all over the surface. The specular component of the reflected light is assumed to come from reflection from those facets oriented in the direction of H. The diffuse component comes from multiple reflections between facets and from internal scattering. The specular reflection is then a combination of four factors:

$$s = \frac{DGF}{(N \cdot E)}$$

D is the distribution function of the directions of the micro facets on the surface. G is the amount by which the facets shadow and mask each other. F is the Fresnel reflection law. Each of these factors will now be examined in turn.

The light reflected specularly in any given direction can come only from the facets oriented to reflect the light in that direction. That is, the facets whose local normal vectors point in the direction of H. The first term in the specular reflectance is the evaluation of the distribution of the number of facets pointing in that direction. The distribution used by Torrance and Sparrow was a simple Gaussian:

$$D_2 = e^{-(\alpha c_2)^2}$$

D_2 is the proportionate number of facets oriented at an angle α from the average normal to the surface. The factor c_2 is the standard deviation for the distribution and is a property of the surface being modelled. Large values yield dull surfaces and small values yield shiny surfaces. We are interested in the number of facets pointing in the direction of H so the angle α here is $\cos^{-1}(N \cdot H)$.

Since the intensity is proportional to the number of facets pointing in the H direction, we must take into account the observer sees more of the surface area when the surface is tilted. The increase in area is inversely proportional to the cosine of the angle of tilt. The tilt angle is is the angle between the average surface normal, N, and the eye, E. This explains the division by $(N \cdot E)$.

Counteracting this effect is the fact that some of the facets shadow each other. The degree to which this shadowing occurs is called the "geometrical attenuation factor", G. It is a value from 0 to 1 representing the proportionate amount of light remaining after the masking or shadowing has taken place. Calculation of G assumes that the micro facets exist in the form of V shaped grooves with the sides at equal but opposite angles to the average surface normal. We are interested only in grooves where one of the sides points in the specular direction H. For differing positions of the light source and eye position we can have one of three cases illustrated in Figure 1.

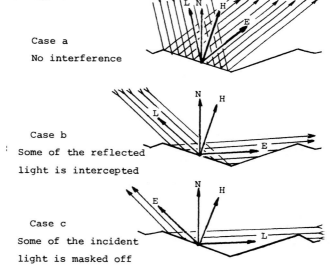

Case a
No interference

Case b
Some of the reflected light is intercepted

Case c
Some of the incident light is masked off

Figure 1

Note that the vectors L and E do not necessarily lie in the plane of the figure (i.e. the plane containing N and H). We can see this by considering a top view as in Figure 2.

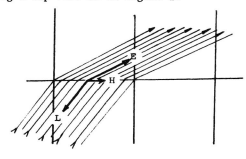

Figure 2 - Top view of reflection from a micro-facet

The value of G for case a of Figure 1 is 1.0, signifying no attenuation.

To compute G for case b we need to compute the ratio $1-(m/\ell)$ which is the proportionate amount of the facet contributing to the reflected light. See Figure 3.

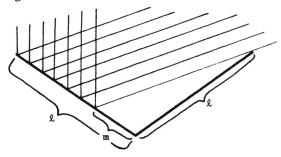

Figure 3 - Light which escapes is $1-(m/\ell)$

We can reduce the problem to two dimensions if we project E onto the plane containing N and H (the plane of the diagram). Calling this projection E_p and labeling relevant angles we have Figure 4.

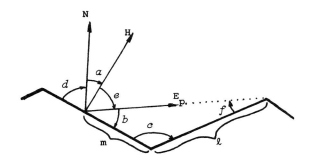

Figure 4 - Measurement of m/ℓ

Applying the law of sines we have

$$m/\ell = \sin f / \sin b$$

Then we note that

$$\sin b = \cos e$$
$$\cos b = \sin e$$

Since the angles of the triangle must sum to 2π we have

$$\sin f = \sin(b+c)$$
$$= \sin b \cos c + \cos b \sin c$$

Due to the symmetry of the groove and the complementarity of d and a

$$c = 2d$$
$$\cos c = 1-2\sin^2 d = 1-2\cos^2 a$$
$$\sin c = 2\cos d \sin d = 2\sin a \cos a$$

Plugging these into the expression for $\sin f$

$$\sin f = \cos e(1-2\cos^2 a) + 2\sin e \cos a \sin a$$
$$= \cos e - 2\cos a(\cos e \cos a - \sin e \sin a)$$
$$= \cos e - 2\cos a \cos(e+a)$$
$$= (H \cdot E_p) - 2(N \cdot H)(N \cdot E_p)$$

Since E_p is the projection of E onto the N,H plane then $N \cdot E_p = N \cdot E$ and $H \cdot E_p = H \cdot E$ so that

$$G_b = 1 - \frac{m}{\ell} = 2(N \cdot H)(N \cdot E)/(E \cdot H)$$

Examining the diagram for Gc we see that it is the same as that for G_b but with the roles of L and E exchanged. Thus

$$G_c = 2(N \cdot H)(N \cdot L)/(H \cdot L) = 2(N \cdot H)(N \cdot L)/(E \cdot H)$$

For a particular situation, the effective value of G will be the minimum of G_a, G_b and G_c.

The final factor in the specular reflection is the Fresnel reflection. This gives the fraction of the light incident on a facet which is actually reflected as opposed to being absorbed. This is a function of the angle of incidence on the micro facet and the index of refraction on the substance. It is given by

$$F = \frac{1}{2}\left(\frac{\sin^2(\phi-\theta)}{\sin^2(\phi+\theta)} + \frac{\tan^2(\phi-\theta)}{\tan^2(\phi+\theta)}\right)$$

where $\sin\theta = \sin\phi/n$
ϕ = angle of incidence
n = index of refraction

In our case, the angle of incidence is $\phi = \cos^{-1}(L \cdot H) = \cos^{-1}(E \cdot H)$. The interesting thing about this function is that it has a substantially different form for metallic vs. nonmetallic substances. For metals, corresponding to large values of n, $F(\phi,n)$ is nearly constant at 1. For nonmetals, corresponding to small values of n, it has a more exponential appearance, starting out near zero for $\phi=0$ and going to 1 at $\phi=\pi/2$.

FACET DISTRIBUTION FUNCTIONS

One thing in the above model can be improved upon. This is the facet distribution function. This function takes an angle, α, and a measure of the shininess of the surface and computes the proportionate area of facets pointing in that direction. The angle α is the angle between H and N; we can evaluate its cosine as $(N \cdot H)$.

The Phong model effectively uses the distribution function of the cosine raised to a power.

$$D_1 = \cos^{c_1}\alpha$$

The Torrance Sparrow model uses the standard Gaussian distribution already mentioned.

$$D_2 = e^{-(\alpha c_2)^2}$$

A third function has been proposed by Trowbridge and Reitz [8]. They showed that a very general class of surface properties could be generated by modelling the microfacets as ellipsoids of revolution. This leads to the distribution function

$$D_3 = \left(\frac{c_3^2}{\cos^2\alpha(c_3^2-1)+1}\right)^2$$

Where c_3 is the eccentricity of the ellipsoids and is 0 for very shiny surfaces and 1 for very diffuse surfaces.

Each of these functions has a peak value of 1 at $\alpha=0$ (for facets pointing along the average surface normal) and falls off as α increases or decreases. The rate of fall off is controlled by the values c_1, c_2 and c_3. In comparing the functions it is necessary to specify this rate in a uniform unit. A convenient such unit is the angle at which the distribution falls to one half. In terms of this angle, β, the three coefficients are:

$$c_1 = -\frac{\ln 2}{\ln \cos\beta}$$

$$c_2 = \frac{\sqrt{\ln 2}}{\beta}$$

$$c_3 = \left(\frac{\cos^2\beta-1}{\cos^2\beta-\sqrt{2}}\right)^{1/2}$$

If these three functions are plotted with equal values of β it can be seen that they are very similar in shape. However, since there is some experimental as well as theoretical justification for D_3 and since it is the easiest to compute, it is the one we shall choose.

COMPUTATIONAL CONSIDERATIONS

There are several observations which can be made to speed up the computation of the hilight function.

If β does not change within a frame the function D_3 can be calculated using the intermediate values (calculated once per frame):

$$k_1 = 1/(c_3^2-1)$$
$$k_2 = k_1+1$$

whereupon

$$D_3 = \left(\frac{k_2}{\cos^2\alpha+k_1}\right)^2$$

A simplification which is often made is to assume that the light source is at infinity. Thus the vector L is a constant for each point of the picture. We may also model the eye as being far away from the object so that $E = (0\ 0\ -1)$. This allows the calculation of the direction of H to be done once per change in light direction.

It is possible to avoid a potential division by zero when computing G by combining it with the term $1/(N \cdot E)$ and finding the minimum of Ga, Gb and Gc before doing the divisions:

```
if(N·E)<(N·L) then
    if 2(N·E)(N·H)<(E·H) then G:=2(N·H)/(E·H)
                         else G:=1/(N·E)
else
    if 2(N·L)(N·H)<(E·H) then G:=2(N·H)(N·L)/(E·H)(N·E)
                         else G:=1/(N·E)
```

The Fresnel reflection is a function only of the index of refraction and the dot product $(E \cdot H)$. If E is assumed constant at $(0\ 0\ -1)$ then this calculation needs to be made only once per change in light source direction. In addition, by some trigonometric identities it can be shown that the Fresnel formula can be calculated by:

$$F = \frac{(g-c)^2}{(g+c)^2}\left(1 + \frac{(c(g+c)-1)^2}{(c(g-c)+1)^2}\right)$$

where $c = (E \cdot H)$
$g = \sqrt{n^2+c^2-1}$

COMPARISON WITH PHONG SHADING

Now that we have derived this hilight function we should compare it with the Phong function to see where and by how much they differ. Figure 5 shows a plot of the amount of light reflected from a surface as a result of an incident ray at 30 degrees from the surface normal. The distance of the surface in a particular direction from the center represents the amount of light reflected in that direction. The incoming ray is from the right. A vector pointing to the left at the specular direction is shown for reference. The hemispherical portion of the function is the diffuse reflection; equal amounts in each direction. The bump is the specular reflection. For this angle of incidence the functions are almost identical. Figure 6 shows the same function for an incident ray at 70 degrees. Note that the specular bump is much larger for the Torrance

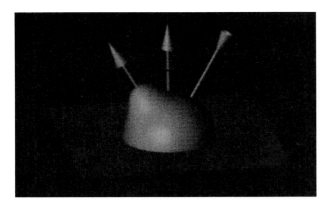
Phong Model

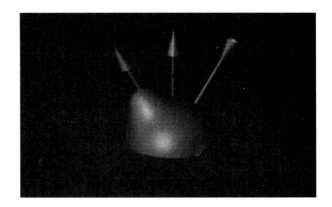
Torrance-Sparrow Model

Figure 5

Comparison of Phong and Torrance-Sparrow reflection distributions for incident light at 30° from normal

Sparrow function and not in quite the same direction. This indicates that the new function will be materially different only for shallow angles of incident light and that the specular reflection will be much higher there. This may be verified by the simple experiment of holding a matte sheet of paper edge on to a light and noting that it looks quite shiny.

Figure 7 shows images of an object made using the two hilight functions with both an edge-on lighting direction and a front-on direction. Figure 7a simulates an aluminum metallic surface using the experimentally measured parameters:

$$p_s = .4$$
$$p_d = .6$$
$$n = 200$$
$$c_3 = .35$$

Figure 7b simulates a Magnesium Oxide ceramic (a standard diffuse reflector) using the experimental parameters:

$$p_s = .667$$
$$p_d = .333$$
$$n = 1.8$$
$$c_3 = .35$$

Note that the ceramic looks quite diffuse for light hitting it almost perpendicularly and very specular (even more so than the aluminum) for light hitting it almost tangentially.

VARYING SURFACE SHININESS

In [1] and [3] a technique for mapping texture patterns onto bicubic surfaces was described. The object was defined as a biparametric surface and the parameter values were

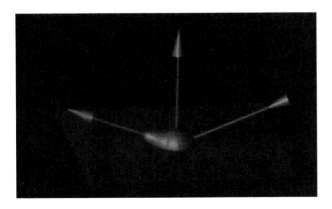
Phong Model

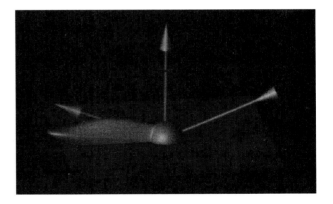
Torrance-Sparrow Model

Figure 6

Comparison of Phong and Torrance-Sparrow reflection distributions for incident light at 70° from normal

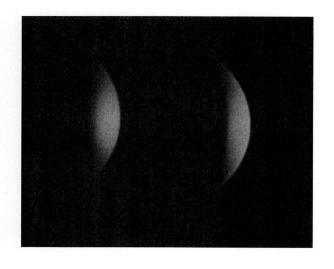 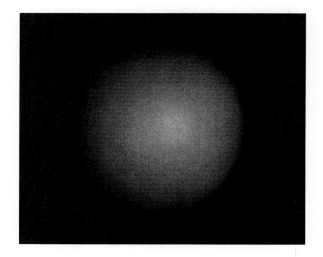

Phong   Torrance-Sparrow   Both Models Essentially Same
Edge Lit   Front Lit

Figure 7a
Simulation of Aluminum Surface

 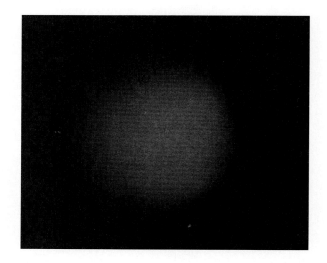

Phong   Torrance-Sparrow   Both Models Essentially Same
Edge Lit   Front Lit

Figure 7b
Simulation of Magnesium Oxide Surface

Figure 8
Surface shininess varying as a function
of two different texture patterns

used as input to a texture function which scaled the diffuse component of the reflection. This form of mapping is good for simulating patterns painted on the surface but attempts to simulate bumpy surfaces were disappointing. This effect can, however, be better approximated by using the same texture mapping approach applied to the local surface roughness c_3.

If c_3 is going to change from place to place on the surface we must worry about normallization of the D_3 function. In its original derivation in [8] D_3 differed from that shown here by a factor of c_3^2. This additional factor was included here as a normallizing constant to make $D_3(0)=1$. Since, now, c_3 is varying across the surface, we wish to use a constant normallizing factor based on its minimum value over the surface. The texture modulated distribution function should then be:

$$c_3 = c_{min} + (1-c_{min})\, t(u,v)$$

$$D_3 = \left\{ \frac{c_{min}\, c_3}{\cos^2\alpha(c_3^2-1)+1} \right\}^2$$

where $t(u,v)$=texture value

Figure 8 shows some images made with various texturing functions.

CONCLUSIONS

The Torrance-Sparrow reflection model differs from the Phong model in the inclusion of the G, F and $1/(N \cdot E)$ terms. This has a noticable effect primarily for non-metallic and edge lit objects. The use of the D_3 micro facet distribution function provides a better match to experimental data and is, happily, easier to compute than D_1 or D_2. This savings effectively offsets the extra computation time for G and F yielding a hilight generation function having a high degree of realism for no increase in computation time.

REFERENCES

1. Blinn, J. F. and Newell, M. E. Texture and reflection in computer generated images. Comm ACM 19, 10(Oct 1976), 542-547

2. Bui-Tuong Phong. Illumination for computer generated images. Comm ACM 18, 6(June 1975) 311-317

3. Catmull, E. A. Computer display of curved surfaces. Proc. Conf. on Comptr. Graphics. May 1975 (IEEE Cat. No. 75CH0981-1C) 11-17

4. Gilpin, F. H. Effect of the variation of the incident angle on the coefficient of diffused reflection. Trans. Illum. Eng. Soc. Vol 5, 1910 854-873

5. Middleton, W. E. K. and Mungall, A. G. The luminous directional reflectance of snow. J. Opt. Soc. Am. 42, 8(Aug 1952) 572-579

6. Torrance, K. E. and Sparrow, E. M. Polarization directional distribution, and off-specular peak phenomena in light reflected from roughened surfaces. J. Opt. Soc. Am. 56, 7(Jul 1966) 916-925

7. Torrance, K. E. and Sparrow, E. M. Theory for off-specular reflection from roughened surfaces J. Opt. Soc. Am. 57, 9(Sep 1967) 1105-1114

8. Trowbridge, T. S. and Reitz, K. P. Average irregularity representation of a roughened surface for ray reflection. J. Opt. Soc. Am. 65, 5(May 1975) 531-536

SIMULATION OF WRINKLED SURFACES

James F. Blinn

Caltech/JPL

Abstract

Computer generated shaded images have reached an impressive degree of realism with the current state of the art. They are not so realistic, however, that they would fool many people into believing they are real. One problem is that the surfaces tend to look artificial due to their extreme smoothness. What is needed is a means of sim{ulating the surface irregularities that are on real surfaces. In 1973 Ed Catmull introduced the idea of using the parameter values of parametrically defined surfaces to index into a texture definition function which scales the intensity of the reflected light. By tying the texture pattern to the parameter values, the texture is guaranteed to rotate and move with the object. This is good for showing patterns painted on the surface, but attempts to simulate rough surfaces in this way are unconvincing. This paper presents a method of using a texturing function to perform a small perturbation on the direction of the surface normal before using it in the intensity calculations. This process yields images with realistic looking surface wrinkles without the need to model each wrinkle as a separate surface element. Several samples of images made with this technique are included.

1. INTRODUCTION

Recent work in computer graphics has been devoted to the development of algorithms for making pictures of objects modelled by other than the conventional polygonal facet technique. In particular, several algorithms [4,5,7] have been devised for making images of parametric surface patches. Such surfaces are defined by the values of three bivariate functions:

$$X = X(u,v)$$
$$Y = Y(u,v)$$
$$Z = Z(u,v)$$

as the parameters vary between 0 and 1. Such algorithms basically consist of techniques for inverting the X and Y functions. That is, given the X and Y of a picture element, the corresponding u and v parameter values are found. This parameter pair is then used to find the Z coordinate of the surface to perform depth comparisons with other objects. The intensity of the resultant picture element is then found by a simulation of the light reflecting off the surface. Functions for performing this computation are described in [3].

The prime component in the calculation of the intensity of a picture element is the direction of the surface normal at that picture element. To calculate the surface normal we first examine the derivatives of the surface definition functions. If the coordinates of a point on the patch is represented by the vector P:

$$\vec{P} = (X,Y,Z)$$

The partial derivatives of these functions form two new vectors which we will call Pu and Pv.

$$\vec{P}u = (Xu,Yu,Zu)$$
$$\vec{P}v = (Xv,Yv,Zv)$$

These two vectors define a plane tangent to the surface at that point. Their cross product is thus a vector normal to the surface.

$$\vec{N} = \vec{P}u \times \vec{P}v$$

These vectors are illustrated in figure 1. Before using the normal in intensity calculations it must first be scaled to a length of 1.0 by dividing by its length.

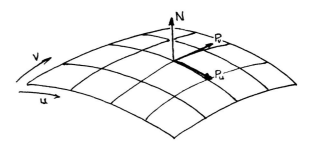

Figure 1 - Definition of Normal Vector

Images of smooth surfaces made directly from the patch description do not have the usual artifacts associated with polygonal facets, they do indeed look smooth. In fact they sometimes look too smooth. To make them look less artificial it is necessary to simulate some of the surface irregularities of real surfaces. Catmull [5] made some progress in this direction with process called texture mapping. Effectively the color of the surface was defined as a fourth bivariate function, C(u,v), and was used to scale the intensity of the generated picture at each point. This technique was good a generating pictures of objects with patterns painted on them. In order to simulate bumpy or wrinkly surfaces one might use, as the defining texture pattern, a digitized photograph of a bumpy or wrinkly surface. Attempts to do this were not very sucessful. The images usually looked like smooth surfaces with photographs of wrinkles glued on. The main reason for this is that the light source direction when making the texture photograph was rarely the same as that used when synthesizing the image. In fact, if the surface (and thus the mapped texture pattern) is curved, the angle of the light source vector with the surface is not even the same at different locations on the patch.

2. NORMAL VECTOR PERTURBATION

To best generate images of macroscopic surface wrinkles and irregularities we must actually model them as such. Modelling each surface wrinkle as a separate patch would probably be prohibitively expensive. We are saved from this fate by the realization that the effect of wrinkles on the perceived intensity is primarily due to their effect on the direction of the surface normal (and thus the light reflected) rather than their effect on the position of the surface. We can expect, therefore, to get a good effect from having a texturing function which performs a small perturbation on the direction of the surface normal before using it in the intensity formula. This is similar to the technique used by Batson et al. [1] to synthesize aerial picutres of mountain ranges from topographic data.

The normal vector perturbation is defined in terms of a function which gives the displacement of the irregular surface from the ideal smooth one. We will call this function $F(u,v)$. On the wrinkled patch the position of a point is displaced in the direction of the surface normal by an amount equal to the value of $F(u,v)$. The new position vector can then be written as:

$$\vec{P}' = \vec{P} + F\ \vec{N}/|N|$$

This is shown in cross section in figure 2.

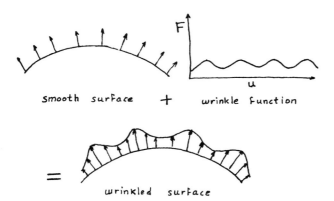

Figure 2 - Mapping Bump Function

The normal vector to this new surface is derived by taking the cross product of its partial derivatives.

$$\vec{N}' = \vec{P}u' \times \vec{P}v'$$

The partial derivatives involved are evaluated by the chain rule. So

$$\vec{P}u' = d/du\ \vec{P}' = d/du(\vec{P} + F\ \vec{N}/|N|)$$
$$= \vec{P}u + Fu\ \vec{N}/|N| + F\ (\vec{N}/|N|)u$$

$$\vec{P}v' = d/dv\ \vec{P}' = d/dv(\vec{P} + F\ \vec{N}/|N|)$$
$$= \vec{P}v + Fv\ \vec{N}/|N| + F\ (\vec{N}/|N|)v$$

The formulation of the normal to the wrinkled surface is now in terms of the original surface definition functions, their derivatives, and the bump function, F, and its derivatives. It is, however, rather complicated. We can simplify matters considerably by invoking the approximation that the value of F is negligably small. This is reasonable for the types of surface irregularities for which this process is intended where the height of the wrinkles in a surface is small compared to the extent of the surface. With this simplification we have

$$\vec{P}u' \approx \vec{P}u + Fu\ \vec{N}/|N|$$
$$\vec{P}v' \approx \vec{P}v + Fv\ \vec{N}/|N|$$

The new normal is then

$$\vec{N}' = (\vec{P}u + Fu\ \vec{N}/|N|) \times (\vec{P}v + Fv\ \vec{N}/|N|)$$
$$= (\vec{P}u \times \vec{P}v) + Fu\ (\vec{N} \times \vec{P}v)/|N|$$
$$+ Fv\ (\vec{P}u \times \vec{N})/|N| + Fu\ Fv\ (\vec{N} \times \vec{N})/|N|^2$$

The first term of this is, by definition, N. The last term is identically zero. The net expression for the perturbed normal vector is then

$$\vec{N}' = \vec{N} + \vec{D}$$

where $\vec{D} = (\ Fu\ (\vec{N} \times \vec{P}v) - Fv\ (\vec{N} \times \vec{P}u)\ ) / |N|$

This can be interpreted geometrically by observing that (N x Pv) and (N x Pu) are two vectors in the tangent plane to the surface. An amount of each of them proportional to the u and v derivatives of F are added to the original, unperturbed normal vector. See figure 3

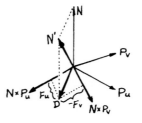

Figure 3 - Perturbed Normal Vector

Another geometric interpretation is that the vector N' comes from rotating the original vector N about some axis in the tangent plane to the surface. This axis vector can be found as the cross product of N and N'.

$$\vec{N} \times \vec{N}' = \vec{N} \times (\vec{N}+\vec{D}) = \vec{N} \times \vec{D}$$

$$= \frac{Fu\ (\vec{N} \times (\vec{N} \times \vec{Pv})) - Fv\ (\vec{N} \times (\vec{N} \times \vec{Pu}))}{|N|}$$

Invoking the vector identity $Qx(RxS) = R(Q.S) - S(Q.R)$ and the fact that $N.Pu = N.Pv = 0$ this axis of rotation reduces to

$$\vec{N}x\vec{N}' = |N|(Fv\ \vec{Pu} - Fu\ \vec{Pv}) \equiv |N|\ \vec{A}$$

This vector, A, is just the perpendicular to the gradient vector of F, (Fu,Fv) when expressed in the tangent plane coordinate system with basis vectors Pu and Pv. Thus the perturbed normal vector will be tipped "downhill" from the slope due to F. Note that, since NxD=|N| A and since N is perpendicular to D then

$$|NxD| = |N|\ |D|$$

so

$$|D| = |A|$$

Next, since the vectors N, D and N' form a right triangle, the effective angle of rotation is

$$\tan\vartheta = |D|/|N|$$

this is illustrated in figure 4.

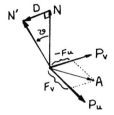

Figure 4 - Rotated Normal Vector

In summary, we can now calculate the perturbed normal vector, N', at any desired u and v parameter value. This vector must still be scaled to a length of 1 by dividing by its length. The result is then passed to the intensity calculation routines in place of the actual normal N.

3. TEXTURE FUNCTION DEFINITION

The formulation of the perturbed normal vector is in terms of the position functions X, Y, and Z and the bump displacement function F. To perform calculations we only need a means of evaluating the u and v derivatives of F(u,v) at any required parameter value. In this section we discuss some ways that such functions have been defined, means of evaluating them and show some resultant pictures.

The function F could, of course, be defined analytically as a bivariate polynomial or bivariate Fourier series. In order to generate a function with a sufficient amount of complexity to be interesting, however, an excessive number of coefficients are required. A much simpler way to define complex functions is by a table lookup. Since F has two parameters, this table takes the form of a doubly indexed array of values of F at various fractional parameter values. If the array is 64 by 64 elements and the parameters are between 0 and 1 a simple means of evaluating F (using Fortran style indexing) at u and v would be

```
FUNCTION FVAL(U,V)
   IU = IFIX(64*U)
   IV = IFIX(64*V)
   FVAL = FARRAY(IU+1,IV+1)
```

(We will duscuss the problem of overflow of the indices shortly). This will yield a function made of a checkerboard of constant valued squares 1/64 on a side. A smoother function can be obtained by interpolating values between table entries. The simplest interpolation technique is bilinear interpolation. Such an algorithm would look like

```
FUNCTION FVAL(U,V)
   IU=IFIX(64*U)
   DU=64*U - IU
   IV=IFIX(64*V)
   DV=64*V - IV
   F00 = FARRAY(IU+1,IV+1)
   F10 = FARRAY(IU+2,IV+1)
   F01 = FARRAY(IU+1,IV+2)
   F11 = FARRAY(IU+2,IV+2)
   FU0 = F00 + DU*(F10-F00)
   FU1 = F01 + DU*(F11-F01)
   FVAL= FU0 + DV*(FU1-FU0)
```

This yields a function which is continuous in value but discontinuous in derivative. Since the function F appears in the calculation only in terms of its derivative we should use a higher order interpolation scheme which is continuous in derivative. Otherwise the lines between function samples may show up as creases in the surface. Third order interpolation schemes (e.g. B-splines) are the standard solution to such a situation, but their generality is not really needed here. A cheaper, continuous interpolation scheme for derivatives consists of differencing the (bilinearly interpolated) function along the parametric directions. The increment between which differencing occurs is the distance between function sample values. The function generated by this interpolation scheme has continuity of derivative but not of value. The values of F are not used anyway. Thus

```
E = 1/64.
FU = (FVAL(U+E,V )-FVAL(U-E,V )) / (2*E)
FV = (FVAL(U ,V+E)-FVAL(U ,V-E)) / (2*E)
```

This is the form used in the pictures shown here. It is about as simple as can be obtained and has proven to be quite adequate.

In the above examples, the integer part of the scaled up parameter values were used directly as indices into the F array. In practive, one should protect against array overflow occurring when the parameter happens to be slightly less than 0 or greater than 1. In fact, for the bilinear interpolation case, all parameter values between 63/64 and 1 will attempt to interpolate to a table entry at index 65. The question of what is the function value at parameters outside the range of the table can be answered in a variety of ways. A simple method is to make the function periodic, with the table defining one period.

This is easily accomplished by masking off all but the low 6 bits of the IU and IV values. This also makes it easy to have the table represent a unit cell pattern to be replicated many times per patch. The function values U and V are merely scaled up by the replication count before being passed to FVAL.

Now that we know what to do with the table entries we turn to the question of how to generate them in the first place. Some simple geometric patterns can be generated algorithmically. One such is a gridwork of high and low values. The table entries of the F function for such a grid are shown plotted as a 3D line drawing in figure 5. The result when mapped onto a flat patch with one corner bent back is also shown.

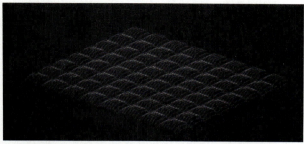

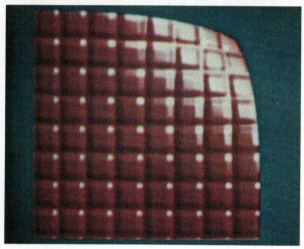

Figure 5 - Simple Grid Pattern

Embossed letters can be generated by using a bit-map character set as used to display text on a raster scan display. Such a texture array appears in figure 6. This pattern was used to make the title on the ribbon on the logo of the cover of these proceedings.

Figure 6 - Embossed Letter Pattern

Another method of generating bump functions derives from image synthesis algorithms which use Z-buffers or depth buffers to perform the hidden surface comparisons [5]. The actual Z values left in the depth buffer after running such an algorithm can be used to define the table entries for a bump function. In figure 7 an image of a sphere was generated using such an algorithm and the resultant Z-buffer replicated several times to generate the rivet-like pattern. This is the pattern mapped onto the cube on the cover logo. Similarly, a 3D character set was used with a Z-buffer algorithm to generate the pattern showing the date also in figure 7. This was used on the ribbon on the cover.

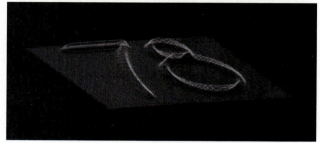

Figure 7 - Z-Buffer Patterns

The most general method of generating bump functions relies on video frame buffer technology and its standard tool, the painting program. Briefly, a frame buffer is a large digital memory with one word per picture element of an image. A video signal is continually synthesized from this memory so that the screen displays an image of what is in memory. A painting program utilizes a digitizing tablet to control the alteration of the values in the memory to achieve the effect of painting on the screen. By utilizing a region of the frame buffer as the defining table of the F function, a user can actually paint in the function values. The interpretation of the image will be such that black areas produce small values of F and white areas produce large values. Since only the derivatives of F are used in the normal vector perturbation, any area of constant intensity will look smooth on the final image. However, places where the image becomes darker will appear as dents and places where it becomes brighter will appear as bumps. (This correspondance will be reversed if the base patch is rotated to view the back side). The generation of interesting patterns which fit together end-to-end to form a continuous join between patches then becomes primarily an artistic effort on the part of the drawer. Figure 8 shows some sample results that can be achieved with this technique. The first pattern, a hand drawn unit cell of bricks was mapped onto the sphere on the cover.

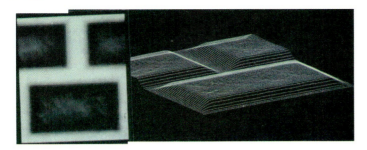

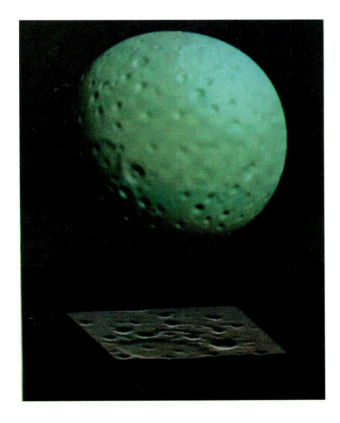

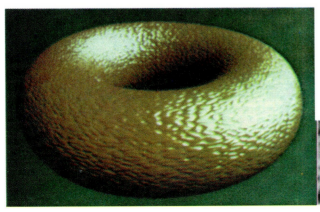

Figure 8 - Hand Drawn Bump Functions

4. DEPENDANCE ON SCALE

One feature of the perturbation calculation is that the perturbation amount is not invariant with the scale at which the object is drawn. If the X, Y, and Z surface definiton functions are scaled up by 2 then the normal vector length, $|N|$, is scaled up by a factor of 4 while the perturbation amount, $|D|$, is only scaled by 2. This effect is due to the fact that the object is being scaled but the displacement function F is not. (Scale changes due to the object moving nearer or farther from the viewer in perspective space do not affect the size of the wrinkles, only scale shanges applied directly to the object.) The net effect of this is that if an object is scaled up, the wrinkles flatten out. This is illustrated in figure 9.

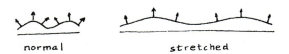

Figure 9 - Stretched Bump Texture

This effect might be desirable for some applications but undesirable for others. A scale invariant perturbation, D', must scale at the same rate as N. An obvious choice for this is

$$D' = a\, D\, |N|/|D|$$

so

$$|D'| = a\, |N|$$

where a is independant of scales in P. The value of a is then the tangent of the effective rotation angle.

$$\tan\theta' = |D'|/|N| = a$$

This can be defined in various ways. One simple choice is a generalization from the simple, flat unit square patch

$$X(u,v) = u$$
$$Y(u,v) = v$$
$$Z(u,v) = 0$$

For this patch the original normal vector perturbation gives

$$N = (0,0,1)$$
$$D = (-F_u, -F_v, 0)$$
$$\tan\theta = \sqrt{F_u^2 + F_v^2}$$

Here the value of a is purely a function of F. Use of the same function for arbitrary patches corresponds to a perturbation of

$$a = \sqrt{F_u^2 + F_v^2}$$
$$D' = a\, D\, |N|/|D|$$
$$N'' = N + D'$$

The texture defining function F is now no longer being used as an actual displacement added to the position of the surface. It just serves to provide (in the form if its derivatives) a means of defining the rotation axis and angle as functions of u and v.

5. ALIASING

In an earlier paper [2], the author described the effect of aliasing on images made with color texture mapping. The same problems can arise with this new form. That is, undesirable artifacts can enter the image in regions where the texture pattern maps into a small screen region. The solution applied to color textures was to average the texture pattern over the region corresponding to each picture element in the final image. The bump texture definition function, however, does not have a linear relationship to the intensity of the final image. If the bump texture is averaged the effect will be to smooth out the bumps rather than average the intensities. The correct solution to this problem would be to compute the intensities at some high sub-pixel resolution and average them. Simply filtering the bump function can, however, reduce the more offensive artifacts of aliasing. Figure 10 shows the result of such an operation.

Before

After

Figure 10 - Filtering Bump Texture

6. RESULTS

Surfaces appearing in images made with this technique look quite convincingly wrinkled. An especially nice effect is the interaction of the bumps with calculated highlights. We must realize, however, that the wrinkles are purely illusory. They only come from some playing with the parameters used in intensity calculations. They do not, for example, alter the smooth silhouette edges of the object. A useful test of any image generation algorithm is to see how well the objects look as they move in animation sequences. Some sample frames from such an animation sequence appear in figure 11. The illusion of wrinkles continues to be convincing and the smoothness of the silhouette edges is not overly bothersome.

Some simple timing measurements indicate that bump mapping takes about 4 times as long as Phong shading and about 2 times as long as color texture mapping. The pictures in this paper took from 3 to 7 minutes each to produce.

The author would like to thank Lance Williams and the New York Institute of Technology Computer Graphics Laboratory for providing some of the artwork and assistance in preparing the logo on the cover made with the techniques described in this paper.

REFERENCES

[1] Batson, R. M., Edwards, E. and Eliason, E. M. "Computer Generated Shaded Relief Images", Jour, Research U.S. Geol. Survey, Vol. 3, No. 4, July-Aug 1975, p. 401-408.

[2] Blinn, J. F., and Newell, M. E., "Texture and Reflection in Computer Generated Images", CACM 19, 10, Oct 1976, pp 542-547.

[3] Blinn, J. F., "Models of Light Reflection for Computer Synthesized Pictures", Proc. 4th Conference on Computer Graphics and Interactive Techniques, 1977.

[4] Blinn, J. F., "A Scan Line Algorithm for Displaying Parametrically Defined Surfaces", Proc. 5th Conference on Computer Graphics and Interactive Techniques, 1978.

[5] Catmull, E. E., "Computer Display of Curved Surfaces", Proc. IEEE Conf. on Computer Graphics, Pattern Recognition and Data Structures, Los Angeles (May 1975)11.

[6] Whitted, J. T., "A Scan Line Algorithm for Computer Display of Curved Surfaces", Proc. 5th Conference on Computer Graphics and Interactive Techniques, 1978.

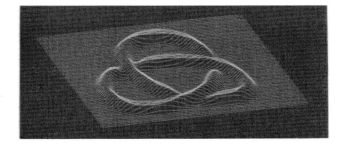

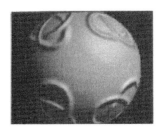
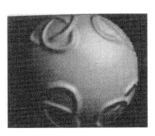

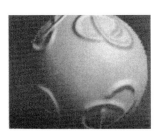

Figure 11 - Rotating Textured Sphere

Graphics and Image Processing

J.D. Foley Editor

An Improved Illumination Model for Shaded Display

Turner Whitted
Bell Laboratories
Holmdel, New Jersey

To accurately render a two-dimensional image of a three-dimensional scene, global illumination information that affects the intensity of each pixel of the image must be known at the time the intensity is calculated. In a simplified form, this information is stored in a tree of "rays" extending from the viewer to the first surface encountered and from there to other surfaces and to the light sources. A visible surface algorithm creates this tree for each pixel of the display and passes it to the shader. The shader then traverses the tree to determine the intensity of the light received by the viewer. Consideration of all of these factors allows the shader to accurately simulate true reflection, shadows, and refraction, as well as the effects simulated by conventional shaders. Anti-aliasing is included as an integral part of the visibility calculations. Surfaces displayed include curved as well as polygonal surfaces.

Key Words and Phrases: computer graphics, computer animation, visible surface algorithms, shading, raster displays

CR Category: 8.2

Introduction

Since its beginnings, shaded computer graphics has progressed toward greater realism. Even the earliest visible surface algorithms included shaders that simulated such effects as specular reflection [19], shadows [1, 7], and transparency [18]. The importance of illumination models is most vividly demonstrated by the realism produced with newly developed techniques [2, 4, 5, 16, 20].

Permission to copy without fee all or part of this material is granted provided that the copies are not made or distributed for direct commercial advantage, the ACM copyright notice and the title of the publication and its date appear, and notice is given that copying is by permission of the Association for Computing Machinery. To copy otherwise, or to republish, requires a fee and/or specific permission.
Author's address: Bell Laboratories, Holmdel, NJ 07733.
© 1980 ACM 0001-0782/80/0600-0343 $00.75.

The role of the illumination model is to determine how much light is reflected to the viewer from a visible point on a surface as a function of light source direction and strength, viewer position, surface orientation, and surface properties. The shading calculations can be performed on three scales: microscopic, local, and global. Although the exact nature of reflection from surfaces is best explained in terms of microscopic interactions between light rays and the surface [3], most shaders produce excellent results using aggregate local surface data. Unfortunately, these models are usually limited in scope, i.e., they look only at light source and surface orientations, while ignoring the overall setting in which the surface is placed. The reason that shaders tend to operate on local data is that traditional visible surface algorithms cannot provide the necessary global data.

A shading model is presented here that uses global information to calculate intensities. Then, to support this shader, extensions to a ray tracing visible surface algorithm are presented.

1. Conventional Models

The simplest visible surface algorithms use shaders based on Lambert's cosine law. The intensity of the reflected light is proportional to the dot product of the surface normal and the light source direction, simulating a perfect diffuser and yielding a reasonable looking approximation to a dull, matte surface. A more sophisticated model is the one devised by Bui-Tuong Phong [8]. Intensity from Phong's model is given by

$$I = I_a + k_d \sum_{j=1}^{j=ls} (\bar{N} \cdot \bar{L}_j) + k_s \sum_{j=1}^{j=ls} (\bar{N} \cdot \bar{L}_j')^n, \qquad (1)$$

where

I = the reflected intensity,
I_a = reflection due to ambient light,
k_d = diffuse reflection constant,
$\bar{N}$ = unit surface normal,
$\bar{L}_j$ = the vector in the direction of the jth light source,
k_s = the specular reflection coefficient,
$\bar{L}_j'$ = the vector in the direction halfway between the viewer and the jth light source,
n = an exponent that depends on the glossiness of the surface.

Phong's model assumes that each light source is located at a point infinitely distant from the objects in the scene. The model does not account for objects within a scene acting as light sources or for light reflected from object to object. As noted in [6], this drawback does not affect the realism of diffuse reflection components very much, but it seriously hurts the quality of specular reflections. A method developed by Blinn and Newell [5] partially solves the problem by modeling an object's environment and mapping it onto a sphere of infinite radius. The technique yields some of the most realistic computer generated pictures ever made, but its limitations preclude its use in the general case.

In addition to the specular reflection, the simulation of shadows is one of the more desirable features of an illumination model. A point on a surface lies in shadow if it is visible to the viewer but not visible to the light source. Some methods [2, 20] invoke the visible surface algorithm twice, once for the light source and once for the viewer. Others [1, 7, 12] use a simplified calculation to determine whether the point is visible to the light source.

Transmission of light through transparent objects has been simulated in algorithms that paint surfaces in reverse depth order [18]. When painting a transparent surface, the background is partially overwritten, allowing previously painted portions of the image to show through. While the technique has produced some impressive pictures, it does not simulate refraction. Kay [17] has improved on this approach with a technique that yields a very realistic approximation to the effects of refraction.

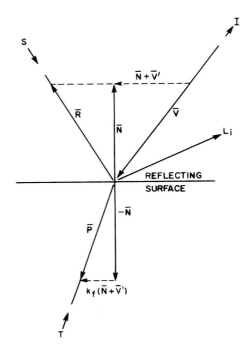

Fig. 1.

2. Improved Model

A simple model for reflection of light from perfectly smooth surfaces is provided by classical ray optics. As shown in Figure 1, the light intensity, I, passed to the viewer from a point on the surface consists primarily of the specular reflection, S, and transmission, T, components. These intensities represent light propagated along the $\bar{V}$, $\bar{R}$, and $\bar{P}$ directions, respectively. Since surfaces displayed are not always perfectly glossy, a term must be added to model the diffuse component as well. Ideally the diffuse reflection should contain components due to reflection of nearby objects as well as predefined light sources, but the computation required to model a distributed light source is overwhelming. Instead, the diffuse term from (1) is retained in the new model. Then the new model is

$$I = I_a + k_d \sum_{j=1}^{j=ls} (\bar{N} \cdot \bar{L}_j) + k_s S + k_t T, \qquad (2)$$

where

S = the intensity of light incident from the $\bar{R}$ direction,
k_t = the transmission coefficient,
T = the intensity of light from the $\bar{P}$ direction.

The coefficients k_s and k_t are held constant for the model used to make pictures in this report, but for the best accuracy they should be functions that incorporate an approximation of the Fresnel reflection law (i.e., the coefficients should vary as a function of incidence angle in a manner that depends on the material's surface properties). In addition, these coefficients must be carefully chosen to correspond to physically reasonable values if realistic pictures are to be generated. The $\bar{R}$ direction is determined by the simple rule that the angle of reflection must equal the angle of incidence. Similarly, the $\bar{P}$ direction of transmitted light must obey Snell's law. Then, $\bar{R}$ and $\bar{P}$ are functions of $\bar{N}$ and $\bar{V}$ given by

$$\bar{V}' = \frac{\bar{V}}{|\bar{V} \cdot \bar{N}|},$$
$$\bar{R} = \bar{V}' + 2\bar{N},$$
$$\bar{P} = k_f(\bar{N} + \bar{V}') - \bar{N},$$

where

$$k_f = (k_n^2 |\bar{V}'|^2 - |\bar{V}' + \bar{N}|^2)^{-1/2},$$

and

k_n = the index of refraction.

Since these equations assume that $\bar{V} \cdot \bar{N}$ is less than zero, the intersection processor must adjust the sign of $\bar{N}$ so that it points to the side of the surface from which the intersecting ray is incident. It must likewise adjust the index of refraction to account for the sign change. If the denominator of the expression for k_f is imaginary, T is assumed to be zero because of total internal reflection.

By making k_s smaller and k_d larger, the surface can be made to look less glossy. However, the simple model will not spread the specular term as Phong's model does by reducing the specular exponent n. As pointed out in [3], the specular reflection from a roughened surface is produced by microscopic mirrorlike facets. The intensity of the specular reflection is proportional to the number of these microscopic facets whose normal vector is aligned with the mean surface normal value at the region being sampled. To generate the proper looking specular reflection, a random perturbation is added to the surface normal to simulate the randomly oriented microfacets.

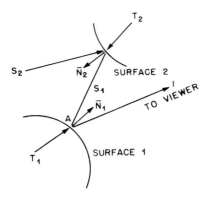

Fig. 2.

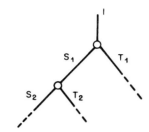

Fig. 3.

(A similar normal perturbation technique is used by Blinn [4] to model texture on curved surfaces.) For a glossy surface, this perturbation has a small variance; with greater variances the surface will begin to look less glossy. This same perturbation will cause a transparent object to look progressively more frosted as the variance is increased. While providing a good model for microscopic surface roughness, this scheme relies on sampled surface normals and will show the effects of aliasing for larger variances. Since this scheme also requires entirely too much additional computing, it is avoided whenever possible. For instance, in the case of specular reflections caused directly by a point light source, Phong's model is used at the point of reflection instead of the perturbation scheme.

The simple model approximates the reflection from a single surface. In a scene of even moderate complexity light will often be reflected from several surfaces before reaching the viewer. For one such case, shown in Figure 2, the components of the light reaching the viewer from point A are represented by the tree in Figure 3. Creating this tree requires calculating the point of intersection of each component ray with the surfaces in the scene. The calculations require that the visible surface algorithm (described in the next section) be called recursively until all branches of the tree are terminated. For the case of surfaces aligned in such a way that a branch of the tree has infinite depth, the branch is truncated at the point where it exceeds the allotted storage. Degradation of the image from this truncation is not noticeable.

In addition to rays in the $\bar{R}$ and $\bar{P}$ direction, rays corresponding to the $\bar{L}_j$ terms in (2) are associated with each node. If one of these rays intersects some surface in the scene before it reaches the light source, the point of intersection represented by the node lies in shadow with respect to that light source. That light source's contribution to the diffuse reflection from the point is then attenuated.

After the tree is created, the shader traverses the tree, applying eq. (2) at each node to calculate intensity. The intensity at each node is then attenuated by a linear function of the distance between intersection points on the ray represented by the node's parent before it is used as an input to the intensity calculation of the parent. (Since one cannot always assume that all the surfaces are planar and all the light sources are point sources, square-law attenuation is not always appropriate. Instead of modeling each unique situation, linear attenuation with distance is used as an approximation.)

3. Visible Surface Processor

Since illumination returned to the viewer is determined by a tree of "rays," a ray tracing algorithm is ideally suited to this model. In an obvious approach to ray tracing, light rays emanating from a source are traced through their paths until they strike the viewer. Since only a few will reach the viewer, this approach is wasteful. In a second approach suggested by Appel [1] and used successfully by MAGI [14], rays are traced in the opposite direction—from the viewer to the objects in the scene, as illustrated in Figure 4.

Unlike previous ray tracing algorithms, the visibility calculations do not end when the nearest intersection of a ray with objects in the scene is found. Instead, each visible intersection of a ray with a surface produces more rays in the $\bar{R}$ direction, the $\bar{P}$ direction, and in the direction of each light source. The intersection process is repeated for each ray until none of the new rays intersects any object.

Because of the nature of the illumination model, some traditional notions must be discarded. Since objects may be visible to the viewer through reflections in other objects, even though some other object lies between it and the viewer, the measure of visible complexity in an image is larger than for a conventionally generated image of the same scene. For the same reason, clipping and eliminating backfacing surface elements are not applicable with this algorithm. Because these normal preprocessor stages that simplify most visible surface algorithms cannot be used, a different approach is taken. Using a technique similar to one described by Clark [11], the object description includes a bounding volume for each item in the scene. If a ray does not intersect the bounding volume of an object, then the object can be eliminated from further processing for that ray. For simplicity of representation and ease of performing the intersection calculation, spheres are used as the bounding volumes.

Since a sphere can serve as its own bounding volume, initial experiments with the shading processor used spheres as test objects. For nonspherical objects, additional intersection processors must be specified whenever a ray does intersect the bounding sphere for that object. For polygonal surfaces the algorithm solves for the point of intersection of the ray and the plane of the polygon and then checks to see if the point is on the interior of the polygon. If the surface consists of bicubic patches, bounding spheres are generated for each patch. If the bounding sphere is pierced by the ray, then the patch is subdivided using a method described by Catmull and Clark [10], and bounding spheres are produced for each subpatch. The subdivision process is repeated until either no bounding spheres are intersected (i.e., the patch is not intersected by the ray) or the intersected bounding sphere is smaller than a predetermined minimum. This scheme was selected for simplicity rather than efficiency.

The visible surface algorithm also contains the mechanism to perform anti-aliasing. Since aliasing is the result of undersampling during the display process, the most straightforward cure is to low-pass filter the entire image before sampling for display [13]. A considerable amount of computing can be saved, however, if a more economical approach is taken. Aliasing in computer generated images is most apparent to the viewer in three cases: (1) at regions of abrupt change in intensity such as the silhouette of a surface, (2) at locations where small objects fall between sampling points and disappear, and (3) whenever a sampled function (such as texture) is mapped onto the surface. The visible surface algorithm looks for these cases and performs the filtering function only in these regions.

For this visible surface algorithm a pixel is defined in the manner described in [9] as the rectangular region whose corners are four sample points as shown in Figure 5(a). If the intensities calculated at the four points have nearly equal values and no small object lies in the region between them, the algorithm assumes that the average of the four values is a good approximation of the intensity over the entire region. If the intensity values are not nearly equal (Figure 5(b)), the algorithm subdivides the sample square and starts over again. This process runs recursively until the computer runs out of resolution or until an adequate amount of information about the detail within the sample square is recovered. The contribution of each single subregion is weighted by its area, and all such weighted intensities are summed to determine the intensity of the pixel. This approach amounts to performing a Warnock-type visibility process for each pixel [19]. In the limit it is equivalent to area sampling, yet it remains a point sampling technique. A better method, currently being investigated, considers volumes defined by each set of four corner rays and applies a containment test for each volume.

To ensure that small objects are not lost, a minimum radius (based on distance from the viewer) is allowed for bounding spheres of objects. This minimum is chosen so

Fig. 4.

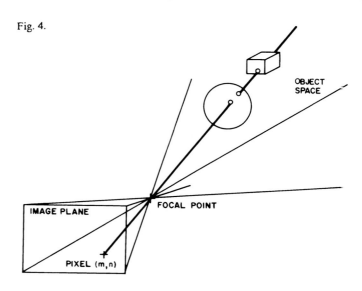

Fig. 5.

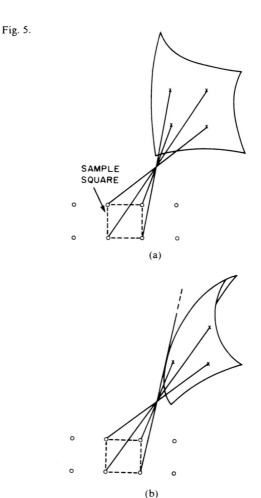

that no matter how small the object, its bounding sphere will always be intersected by at least one ray. If a ray passes within a minimum radius of a bounding sphere but does not intersect the object, the algorithm will know to subdivide each of the four sample squares that share the ray until the missing object is found. Although

Fig. 6.

Fig. 7.

Fig. 8.

Fig. 9.

adequate for rays that reach the viewer directly, this scheme will not always work for rays being reflected from curved surfaces.

4. Results

A version of this algorithm has been programmed in C, running under UNIX[1] on both a PDP-11/45 and a VAX-11/780. To simplify the programming, all calculations are performed in floating point (at a considerable speed penalty). The pictures are displayed at a resolution of 480 by 640 pixels with 9 bits per pixel. Originally color pictures were photographed from the screen of a color CRT so that only three bits were available for each of the three primary colors. Ordered dither [15] was applied to the image data to produce 111 effective intensity levels per primary. For this report pictures are produced by a high-quality color hardcopy camera that exposes each color separately to provide eight bits of intensity per color.

For the scenes shown in this paper, the image generation times are

Figure 6: 44 minutes,
Figure 7: 74 minutes,
Figure 8: 122 minutes.

All times given are for the VAX, which is nearly three times faster than the PDP-11/45 for this application. The image of Figure 6 shows three glossy objects with shadows and object-to-object reflections. The texturing is added using Blinn's wrinkling technique. Figure 7 illustrates the effect of refraction through a transparent object. The algorithm has also been used to produce a short animated sequence. The enhancements provided by this illumination model are more readily apparent in the animated sequence than in the still photographs.

A breakdown of where the program spends its time for simple scenes is:

Overhead—13 percent,
Intersection—75 percent,
Shading—12 percent.

For more complex scenes the percentage of time required to compute the intersections of rays and surfaces increases to over 95 percent. Since the program makes almost no use of image coherence, these figures are actually quite promising. They indicate that a more efficient intersection processor will greatly improve the algorithm's performance. This distribution of processing times also suggests that a reasonable division of tasks between processors in a multiprocessor system is to have one or more processors dedicated to intersection calculations with ray generation and shading operations performed by the host.

---

[1] UNIX is a trademark of Bell Laboratories.

5. Summary

This illumination model draws heavily on techniques derived previously by Phong [8] and Blinn [3–5], but it operates recursively to allow the use of global illumination information. The approach used and the results achieved are similar to those presented by Kay [16].

While in many cases the model generates very realistic effects, it leaves considerable room for improvement. Specifically, it does not provide for diffuse reflection from distributed light sources, nor does it gracefully handle specular reflections from less glossy surfaces. It is implemented through a visible surface algorithm that is very slow but which shows some promise of becoming more efficient. When better ways of using picture coherence to speed the display process are found, this algorithm may find use in the generation of realistic animated sequences.

Received 12/78; revised 1/80; accepted 2/80

References
1. Appel, A. Some techniques for shading machine renderings of solids. AFIPS 1968 Spring Joint Comptr. Conf., pp. 37–45.
2. Atherton, P., Weiler, K., and Greenberg, D. Polygon shadow generation. Proc. SIGGRAPH 1978, Atlanta, Ga., pp. 275–281.
3. Blinn, J.F. Models of light reflection for computer synthesized pictures. Proc. SIGGRAPH 1977, San Jose, Calif., pp. 192–198.
4. Blinn, J.F. Simulation of wrinkled surfaces. Proc. SIGGRAPH 1978, Atlanta, Ga., pp. 286–292.
5. Blinn, J.F., and Newell, M.E. Texture and reflection in computer generated images. *Comm. ACM* 19, 10 (Oct. 1976), 542–547.
6. Blinn, J.F., and Newell, M.E. The progression of realism in computer generated images. Proc. of the ACM Ann. Conf., 1977, pp. 444–448.
7. Bouknight, W.K., and Kelley, K.C. An algorithm for producing half-tone computer graphics presentations with shadows and movable light sources. AFIPS 1970 Spring Joint Comptr. Conf., pp. 1–10.
8. Bui-Tuong Phong. Illumination for computer generated images. *Comm. ACM* 18, 6 (June 1975), 311–317.
9. Catmull, E. A subdivision algorithm for computer display of curved surfaces. UTEC CSc-74-133, Comptr. Sci. Dept., Univ. of Utah, 1974.
10. Catmull, E., and Clark, J. Recursively generated B-spline surfaces on arbitrary topological meshes. *Comptr. Aided Design* 10, 6 (Nov. 1978), 350–355.
11. Clark, J.H. Hierarchical geometric models for visible surface algorithms. *Comm. ACM* 19, 10 (Oct. 1976), 547–554.
12. Crow, F.C. Shadow algorithms for computer graphics. Proc. SIGGRAPH 1977, San Jose, Calif., pp. 242–248.
13. Crow, F.C. The aliasing problem in computer-generated shaded images. *Comm. ACM* 20, 11 (Nov. 1977), 799–805.
14. Goldstein, R.A. and Nagel, R. 3-D visual simulation. *Simulation* (Jan. 1971), 25–31.
15. Jarvis, J.F., Judice, C.N., and Ninke, W.H. A survey of techniques for the display of continuous tone pictures on bilevel displays. *Comptr. Graphics and Image Proc.* 5 (1976), 13–40.
16. Kay, D.S. Transparency, refraction, and ray tracing for computer synthesized images. Masters thesis, Cornell Univ., Ithaca, N.Y., January 1979.
17. Kay, D.S., and Greenberg, D. Transparency for computer synthesized images. Proc. SIGGRAPH 1979, Chicago, Ill., pp. 158–164.
18. Newell, M.E., Newell, R.G., and Sancha, T.L. A solution to the hidden surface problem. Proc. ACM Ann. Conf., 1972, pp. 443–450.
19. Warnock, J.E. A hidden line algorithm for halftone picture representation. Tech. Rep. TR 4-15, Comptr. Sci. Dept., Univ. of Utah, 1969.
20. Williams, L. Casting curved shadows on curved surfaces. Proc. SIGGRAPH 1978, Atlanta, Ga., pp. 270–274.

Shade Trees

Robert L. Cook

Computer Division
Lucasfilm Ltd.

Shading is an important part of computer imagery, but shaders have been based on fixed models to which all surfaces must conform. As computer imagery becomes more sophisticated, surfaces have more complex shading characteristics and thus require a less rigid shading model. This paper presents a flexible tree-structured shading model that can represent a wide range of shading characteristics. The model provides an easy means for specifying complex shading characteristics. It is also efficient because it can tailor the shading calculations to each type of surface.

CR CATEGORIES AND SUBJECT DESCRIPTORS: I.3.7 [**Computer Graphics**]: Three-Dimensional Graphics and Realism; E.1 [**Data Structures**]: *Graphs, Trees.*

ADDITIONAL KEY WORDS AND PHRASES: color, computer graphics, illumination, lighting, reflection, shading, shadows, texture

1. Introduction

Making synthetic images look realistic is an important goal in computer imagery for two reasons. First, some applications require a high degree of realism as an end in itself. Second and more generally, realism acts as a measure of our techniques and understanding. To the degree that we lack the ability to make pictures look realistic, we also lack some artistic control.

Making a realistic image involves solving a number of different problems. This paper addresses the problem of shading, or selecting colors for points on each surface, and more specifically the problem of controlling and directing the shading calculations. Other problems, such as constructing a model and animating it, are equally important to realistic image synthesis but are not addressed in this paper.

At the heart of the shading calculations is the simulation of the way light interacts with objects. Early work in reflection models was done by Henri Gouraud[10] and by Phong[16], with more accurate models being developed by Jim Blinn[2] and by the author[7], who applied the shading model to the simulation of specific materials. Blinn has developed a separate shading model for clouds[5]. Turner Whitted included reflection and refraction[18].

Textures allow us to map shading properties onto a surface mathematically, greatly increasing the visual complexity and richness of an image without the overhead of explicitly modeling those properties. Texturing was first used in computer graphics by Ed Catmull[6]. Jim Blinn later extended the use of texturing to surface bumps, roughness, and reflections[1, 4, 3]. Geoff Gardner included texturing of transparency[9].

The trend in shaders has been toward more flexibility and generality, as evidenced by Blinn's generalization of texturing[1] and Whitted's shader dispatcher[19]. What has been lacking is an overall system that integrates the various shading and texturing techniques. This paper introduces such a system, one that is based on a more general approach to shading. The new approach provides a language for describing surfaces and allows traditional shading techniques to be combined in novel ways.

Previous shaders have been limited by the use of fixed models of light reflection into which all surfaces must be fit. The new approach is modular and assumes that no single shading model is appropriate for all surfaces. In some cases utter simplicity is desired, while in others we may require a complexity that would normally be a burden. Because of its modular nature, the new shader can handle both of these extremes in the same image; it performs only the calculations needed for the simple cases while allowing arbitrarily complex calculations where they are required.

Permission to copy without fee all or part of this material is granted provided that the copies are not made or distributed for direct commercial advantage, the ACM copyright notice and the title of the publication and its date appear, and notice is given that copying is by permission of the Association for Computing Machinery. To copy otherwise, or to republish, requires a fee and/or specific permission.

© 1984 ACM 0-89791-138-5/84/007/0223 $00.75

2. Appearance Parameters

A number of different geometric, material, and environmental properties together determine the color of a surface. Any value that is used in the shading calculation is called an *appearance parameter*. Appearance parameters include the surface normal, the color of the light source, the shininess of the surface, bump maps, etc.

The traditional approach to shading is to divide the calculations into two stages:
1. Determining the values of the appearance parameters.
2. Using those values to evaluate the fixed shading equation.

This approach can offer a great deal of generality in the first stage but is inflexible in the second. Appearance parameters may be determined in a number of ways, including texture mapping and normal interpolation. The shading equation itself, however, is fixed. All surfaces must be fit into it, no matter how complex and no matter how simple. Little allowance is made for the extremely diverse ways in which objects interact with light.

3. Shade Trees

A more general approach is to eliminate the fixed shading equation and the entire two stage approach. Rather than attempt to describe all possible surfaces with a single equation, the shader orchestrates a set of basic operations, such as dot products and vector normalization. The shader organizes these operations in a tree.

Each operation is a node of the tree. Each node produces one or more appearance parameters as output, and can use zero or more appearance parameters as input. For example, the inputs to a "diffuse" node are a surface normal and a light vector, and the output is an intensity value. The normal might come from the geometric normal, a bump map, or a procedural texture. The output might be the input to a "multiply" node, which would multiply the intensity by its other input, a color.

The shader performs the calculations at the nodes by traversing the tree in postorder. The output of the root of the tree is the final color. Basic geometric information, such as the surface normal and the location of the object, are leaves of the tree. (In general, the nodes actually form a directed acyclic graph, because a single appearance parameter can be used as input to more than one node.)

Even an appearance parameter that is usually thought of as the final shade can itself be treated as an intermediate step. This is particularly useful in rendering a surface that consists of different materials. The final shade can be a combination of the shades of the various materials, with the amount of the various materials based perhaps on a texture map.

Shade trees can describe a wide range of shading situations from simplest to the most complex. Different types of shading calculations can coexist in a single image, with each surface using as many or as few operations as it requires.

4. Light Trees

The appearance parameters used in the shading calculations include the light source direction and color. These appearance parameters are described by their own tree. Light trees are separate from shade trees so that each light tree can be grafted onto several different shade trees.

Different types of lights require different calculations[17, 11]. The intensity of a local light source changes as the square of the distance from the light. Spotlights have a goniometric curve that describes their intensity as a function of direction. Some lights have flaps that abruptly restrict their illumination. All of these lights are easily described by light trees. For example, the inputs to the "spotlight" tree are the direction of the central axis of the light beam and the rate at which the intensity of the beam decreases with angle, in addition to the position of the light and the location of the point being illuminated. It uses the relevant formulas to calculate the intensity of the light at that location. These calculations, which are so specific to this one particular type of light source, are isolated from the rest of the shading, communicating only through the appearance parameters.

5. Atmosphere Trees

The final output of a shade tree is the *exitance*, the color and intensity of the light leaving the surface. But this is not necessarily the same color and intensity as the light that reaches the eye. Atmospheric effects are described by a tree that has the exitance as one of its inputs and the light actually reaching the eye as its output.

Atmospheric effects are often described by procedural models. For example, haze is an exponential function of distance[14, 13] and can vary with direction. Loren Carpenter simulated sky and haze in his film *Vol Libre* and developed a general atmosphere model for the Genesis sequence in *Star Trek II*. These models are easily incorporated into atmosphere trees.

Rainbows can also be described by an atmosphere tree, with light being added in the primary and secondary bows and subtracted in Alexander's dark band[15, 12]. The color and intensity are a function of the angle between the light direction and the viewing direction.

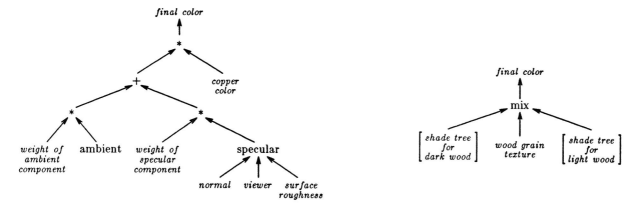

Figure 1a. Shade tree for copper.

Figure 1b. The mix node in a shade tree for wood.

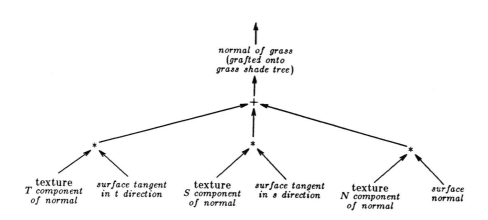

Figure 1c. Textured grass normal.

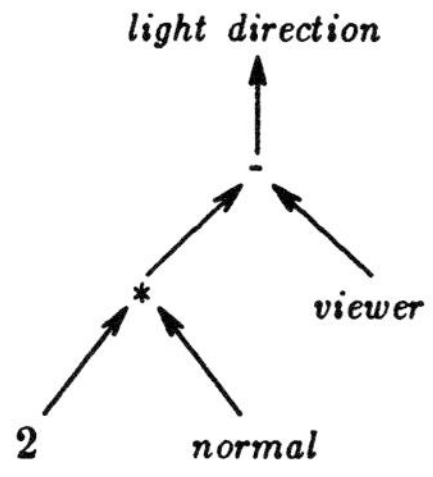

Figure 1d. "Highlight at" branch of a light tree.

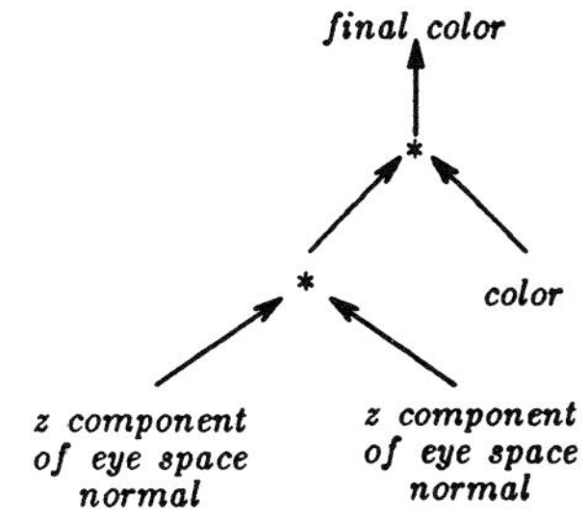

Figure 1e. Simple shade tree.

6. Implementation

To facilitate describing shade trees and building up a library of surfaces, we have developed a special shade tree language. A program written in this language is compiled into an internal representation of a shade tree. Programs in this language are also used to describe light trees and atmosphere trees.

A number of keywords, such as *normal* and *location*, refer to the basic geometric information provided as input to the shader. The final results are referred to by the keywords *final_color* and *final_opacity*.

Several types of nodes are built into the language, including mathematical functions such as *square root* and *normalize* and shading functions such as *diffuse* and *specular*. Other more specialized nodes can be added dynamically; when such a node is declared in the language, the shader searches for a file by that name and loads it. This provides enough flexibility to add new and exotic shading functions easily.

Variables in the language represent appearance parameters, and statements describe how to connect the nodes with appearance parameters. For example, the following program describes metallic shading and defines the shade tree shown in Figure 1a. Note that the ambient and specular nodes are built into the language, and that the output of the light trees is available to all nodes.

```
float a=.5, s=.5 ;
float roughness=.1 ;
float intensity ;
color metal_color=(1,1,1) ;
intensity = a*ambient() +
            s*specular(normal,viewer,roughness);
final_color = intensity * metal_color ;
```

Point variables can be specified in eye space or in world space, whichever is more convenient. World space coordinates are indicated by preceding them with the keyword "world_space".

This language works in conjunction with a modeling language to associate surfaces and light sources with objects. A light can be assigned to the group of objects because some lights affect only part of the environment. Its light tree calculations are performed only for the objects it affects.

The *surface* command in the modeling language designates a shade tree for an object. The values of variables in the surface language can be overridden here. For example, for the above "metal" surface, the statement

```
surface "metal",
        "metal_color", material bronze,
        "roughness", .15
```

in the modeling language initializes the variable "roughness" to be .15 instead of the default .1 and "metal_color" to be the color of bronze instead of white.

7. Experience with Shade Trees

This section presents several specific examples of shade trees and discusses the benefits of this new way of thinking about shading. Since we first started using shade trees, we have discovered many more uses for them than originally expected.

One surprise was the new uses of textures. For example, we rendered some leaves of grass generated by Bill Reeves by creating a texture map of transparency that could be mapped onto a polygon. Instead of using the texture to store the color of the blades for a particular orientation relative to the light source, the surface normal can be encoded in the texture and used in a shade tree as shown in figure 1c. The shading uses the correct normal and changes appropriately as the lights move.

Shadows, including penumbras, can be calculated or painted ahead of time and stored as textures that are accessed by the light tree. The ambient light is a separate light source; it is usually a constant, but it can also be textured to account for the dimming of the ambient light in corners.

Perhaps the most useful shade tree node has been the "mix" node, which uses one of its inputs to interpolate between the other two. This can be used to select between two types of materials, so that a pattern of one material can be inlaid into another. The mix node can also be used for a single material that is not homogeneous, such as wood. Many types of wood have a grain pattern of a light and dark wood. The light and dark wood are really separate materials, with separate sets of appearance parameters such as color and shininess. The grain is a single channel of texture that selects between these two materials. We compute the color of light oak and the color of the dark oak and then mix the two based on the grain texture. Figure 1b shows how the mix node is used in a shade tree for wood.

Metal fleck paint has flecks are oriented in random directions about the surface normal. A special node generates the location of each fleck on the surface and the orientation of each fleck relative to the surface normal. We add this relative normal to the surface normal and renormalize to get the true fleck normal, which is used to shade the fleck. The final color of the surface is a mixture of the color of the base paint and the color of the flecks, based on the procedural texture for the location of the flecks. Because the reflection from the flecks is highly directional, the "mix" node is essential. We can not simply shade a blend the appearance parameters (including the normals) of the flecks and the paint.

The input to the "texture" node is a set of texture coordinates. Texture coordinates are traditionally the same as the object's natural coordinates u and v. But once we regard the texture coordinates as an appearance parameter, we see that they do not need to be identical to u and v. We call the texture coordinates s and t to distinguish them from patch coordinates u and v. If we choose s and t properly, a single texture can extend over several patches without seams.

One of the more exotic uses of shade trees is an extension to bump maps called *displacement maps*. Since the location is an appearance parameter, we can actually move the location as well as perturbing the surface normal. Displacement maps began as a solution to the silhouette problems that arise when bump maps are used to make beveled edges. They are useful in many situations and can almost be considered a type of modeling. This use of shade trees, however, depends on performing the shading calculations (or at least the displacement map part of them) before the visible surface calculations.

In many cases, we are interested not in the actual location of a light source, but in the position of its highlight on a particular surface. The position of the desired highlight can be an input to the light tree, which calculates the light direction that would make a highlight appear at that given location. The tree for this calculation is shown in Figure 1d. It has proved useful in setting up the lighting for a scene.

Unusual shading functions can added to the library of shades easily. "Cat's eye" reflectors on highways reflect light back toward the light source. They are essentially a specular reflection with the normal pointed toward the light source. Marble has a textured diffuse component and a mirror-like specular component. The glowing shock wave in the Genesis sequence in *Star Trek II* was rendered by Loren Carpenter using a special purpose shading function he developed. This function was later easily described as a shade tree.

Other shade trees are used just for debugging. For example, a shade tree that assigns each patch a different random color can be useful in detecting bugs in the patch splitting code. The surface normal can be encoded in the color to look for discontinuities. It is easy to use a simple shading model, such as the one shown in Figure 1e, for trial images and to switch to more elaborate calculations for the final image.

Intermediate results can be computed by one shade tree and stored in a texture for later use by another shade tree. This is useful in calculating shading information that does not change from frame to frame within the scene.

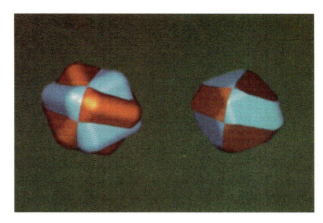

Figure 2. Union and Intersection of Two Cubes Beveled With Displacement Maps.

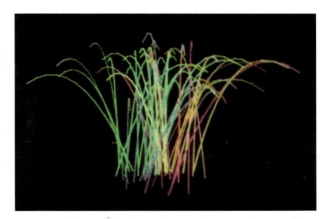

Figure 3a. Grass Normal Texture Map.

Figure 3b. Grass Rendered with Textured Normals.

8. Examples

Figure 2 shows the union and intersection of a plastic and a copper beveled cube. Each cube is described by 6 polygons that are beveled in the shader according to a procedural texture. The beveling is a displacement map that moves the locations as well as the normals.

Figure 3a is a grass texture map generated Bill Reeves. This texture was used to generate Figure 3b, which consists of a single polygon with texture mapped transparency. In addition, the red, green, and blue components of the texture are used to encode the three components of the normal relative to the normal of the surface. The resulting picture has highlights that are appropriate to the local lighting environment.

Figure 4 is *Road to Point Reyes* [8] The road lines, asphalt, and oil spots are each described by shade trees; the outputs of these trees are grafted to a "mix" node and mixed according to a texture map. The wooden fence posts and bronze chain links are described with shade trees. The hills are rendered with a three channel color texture map generated procedurally by Tom Porter. The rainbow is described by an atmosphere tree. During the early stages of design, texture maps were used to render the grass, the bushes, and the puddles quickly; these were later replaced by more exact models.

Figure 5c, *Bee Box*, illustrates light trees, displacement maps, and the "mix" node. The light is a spotlight, and its shadow (including penumbra) is produced by a texture map in a light tree. The regions of wood, ivory, copper, and bronze are selected by three channels of the texture map shown in figure 5a. Another channel controls the surface roughness in the copper and bronze regions. By contrast, figure 5b shows the same box rendered with diffuse blue shading and no displacement maps or shadows.

9. Efficiency

The overhead involved in using shade trees is small since the tree construction and traversal is done ahead of time by the shade tree compiler. At run time there is just a list of routines to call for each surface and a list of arguments (i.e., appearance parameters) for each routine.

Some of the surfaces described by shade trees are complex, and the shading time increases with the complexity of the shade tree. Shade trees are very useful in optimizing the shading calculations, however, because it is easy to adjust surface descriptions to the appropriate level of computation. If a surface is perfectly diffuse, the specular shading calculations are never used. If the geometrical attenuation of the Torrance-Sparrow[2] shading model is not necessary for a particular surface, it can easily be avoided. Reflections can be calculated with a "trace a ray" node or with an an environment map, as appropriate. Color maps, bump maps, or displacement maps can be used depending on the distance to the object.

Notice that in *Bee Box*, the wood uses only one channel of texture (the amount of grain) instead of the three one would expect (red, green, and blue). This one channel controls an entire set of appearance parameters, including color and roughness. Since wood is a mixture of surfaces, based on a texture map, only one branch of the shade tree need be descended in places where the texture calls for only one of surfaces.

10. Conclusions

Shade trees offer a way to specify and change shading properties quickly and easily. They are flexible because they are not based on a fixed shading formula; instead they provide a general way to connect basic shading operations. They are efficient because they customize the shading calculations for each type of surface.

11. Acknowledgements

Many of the ideas in this paper came out of discussions with Loren Carpenter. In some cases it is hard to say exactly who thought of what, because many of the ideas came out in the course of brainstorming sessions. Our discussions included displacement maps and shadow textures, which led to the extension of shade trees to light trees.

Tom Duff provided the nugget of code (a run time loader) that inspired a flexible implementation of shade trees. The modeling language that provides all of the hooks for lights and surfaces was written by Bill Reeves and Tom Duff. John Lasseter painted the texture of the bee. Discussions with Dan Silva were helpful in the early stages. This work began as a continuation of work done at the Program of Computer Graphics at Cornell University.

Figure 4. Road to Point Reyes.

References

1. BLINN, JAMES F. AND MARTIN E. NEWELL, "Texture and Reflection in Computer Generated Images," *Communications of the ACM*, vol. 19, pp. 542-547, 1976.
2. BLINN, JAMES F., "Models of Light Reflection for Computer Synthesized Pictures," *Computer Graphics*, vol. 11, no. 2, pp. 192-198, 1977.
3. BLINN, JAMES F., "Simulation of Wrinkled Surfaces," *Computer Graphics*, vol. 12, no. 3, pp. 286-292, August 1978.
4. BLINN, JAMES F., "Computer Display of Curved Surfaces," PhD dissertation, University of Utah, Salt Lake City, 1978.
5. BLINN, JAMES F., "Light Reflection Functions for Simulation of Clouds and Dusty Surfaces," *Computer Graphics*, vol. 16, no. 3, pp. 21-29, July 1982.
6. CATMULL, EDWIN, "A Subdivision Algorithm for Computer Display of Curved Surfaces," Phd dissertation, University of Utah, Salt Lake City, 1974.
7. COOK, ROBERT L. AND KENNETH E. TORRANCE, "A Reflection Model for Computer Graphics," *ACM Transactions on Graphics*, vol. 1, no. 1, pp. 7-24, 1982.
8. COOK, ROBERT L., LOREN CARPENTER, THOMAS PORTER, WILLIAM REEVES, DAVID SALESIN, AND ALVY RAY SMITH, "Road to Point Reyes," *Computer Graphics*, vol. 17, no. 3, July 1983. title page picture
9. GARDNER, GEOFFREY Y., EDWIN P. BERLIN JR., AND BOB GELMAN, "A Real-Time Computer Image Generation System Using Textured Curved Surfaces," *The 1981 Image Generation/Display Conference II*, pp. 60-76, June 1981.
10. GOURAUD, HENRI, "Computer Display of Curved Surfaces," PhD dissertation, University of Utah, Salt Lake City, 1971.
11. HALL, ROY A. AND DONALD P. GREENBERG, "A Testbed for Realistic Image Synthesis," *IEEE Computer Graphics and Applications*, vol. 3, no. 8, pp. 10-20, November 1983.
12. HULST, H. C. VAN DE, *Light Scattering by Small Particles,* pp. 228-266, Dover, New York, 1957.
13. MCCARTNEY, EARL J., *Optics of the Atmosphere,* pp. 1-49, John Wiley & Sons, New York, 1976.
14. MINNAERT, M., *The Nature of Light and Color in the Open Air,* Dover, New York, 1954.
15. NUSSENZVEIG, H. MOYSES, "The Theory of the Rainbow," *Scientific American*, vol. 236, no. 4, pp. 116-127, April 1977.
16. PHONG, BUI TUONG, "Illumination for Computer Generated Pictures," *Communications of the ACM*, vol. 18, pp. 311-317, 1975.
17. WARN, DAVID R., "Lighting Controls for Synthetic Images," *Computer Graphics*, vol. 17, no. 3, pp. 13-21, July 1983.
18. WHITTED, TURNER, "An Improved Illumination Model for Shaded Display," *Communications of the ACM*, vol. 23, pp. 343-349, 1980.
19. WHITTED, TURNER AND DAVID M. WEIMER, "A Software Testbed for the Development of 3D Raster Graphics Systems," *ACM Transactions on Graphics*, vol. 1, no. 1, pp. 44-58, January 1982.

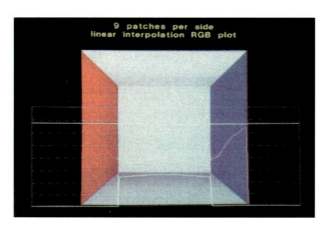
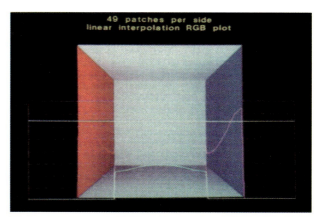

(a)   Figure 8. Simulated Cube with Two Wall Subdivisions and Linear   (b)
                   Interpolation Over each Element (Patch).

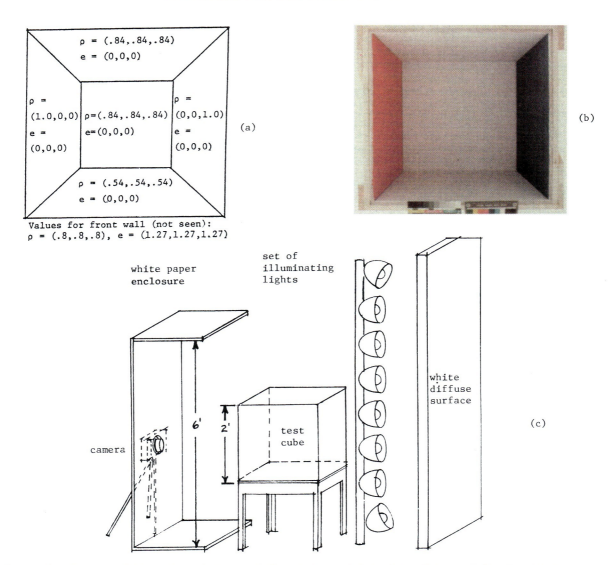

Figure 9. Diagram of Experimental Test. Reflectivity and Emissivity Values of Simulated Model
           are Shown in (a). Photograph of Real Model (b). Schematic of Environment (c).

145

quantitative comparison between simulated and real models.

For the physical model, the open face of the test cube was illuminated with diffuse white light. A second larger enclosure with white inside walls and an open side faced the cube. The diffuse white light was obtained by illuminating this second enclosure with white lights (Fig. 9c). Through a small hole cut in the second enclosure, photographs of the cube's interior were taken. This allowed the pictures to be taken without interfering with the diffuse lighting requirements for the experiment. The illuminating wall was isotropic and uniform to approximately ten percent.

A photograph of the real model is shown in Figure 9b. The most significant observation is the color-bleeding on the top, bottom, and back walls. This color-bleeding is apparent in the simulated images using the radiosity approach (Figures 6 and 8), but not in Figure 7a, which displays the effect of neglecting object-to-object multiple reflections.

6 Conclusions

A method has been described which models the correct interaction and object-to-object reflections between diffusely reflecting surfaces. Current light reflection models used in computer graphics do not account for this interaction, and thus incorrectly compute the global illumination effects. The procedure explicitly contains the effects of diffuse light sources of finite area, as well as the "color-bleeding" effects which are caused by the diffuse reflections.

Although computationally expensive, the procedure has a major advantage in that the results are independent of the observer position. Once the intensities have been computed for a static environment, the scene can be displayed from any position without recomputing intensity values. Thus, environmental intensities can be preprocessed for dynamic sequences. Furthermore, since small specularly reflecting objects may contribute little to the total light energy, the effects of such specular reflections can be superimposed on the diffuse solutions with minimal error.

Future work should include creating a smarter subdivision algorithm to obtain finer meshes in regions of high intensity gradients and considering occluded surfaces and non-polygonal objects.

7 Acknowledgements

This research was performed at the Program of Computer Graphics at Cornell University and supported by the National Science Foundation under grant number MCS8203979. Thanks go to Michael Cohen, Kevin Koestner, and Tim McCorry for their assistance in the model building, to Dottie Harrelson for typing, to Phil Brock for drawings, and to Emil Ghinger for photography. Thanks also go to an anonymous reviewer for providing many helpful comments.

8 References

[1] Abramowitz, Milton and Stegun, Irene (Ed.). Handbook of Mathematical Functions with Formulas, Graphs, and Mathematical Tables. US Dept of Commerce National Bureau of Standards, Applied Mathematics Series 55, June 1964.

[2] Blinn, James F. Models of light reflection for computer synthesized pictures. ACM Computer Graphics (Siggraph Proc '77) 11, 2, (Summer 1977), 192-198.

[3] Cook, Robert L. and Torrance, Kenneth E. A reflectance model for computer graphics. ACM Computer Graphics (Siggraph Proc '81) 15, 3, (August 1982), 307-316.

[4] Gouraud, Henri. Computer display of curved surfaces. PhD dissertation, University of Utah, Salt Lake City, 1971.

[5] Haber, Robert, Shepard, Mark, Abel, John, Gallagher, Richard and Greenberg, Donald. A generalized graphic preprocessor for two-dimensional finite element analysis. ACM Computer Graphics (Siggraph Proc '78) 12, 3, (August 1978), 323-329.

[6] Hall, Roy and Greenberg, Donald P. A testbed for realistic image synthesis. IEEE Computer Graphics and Applications 3, 8, (November 1983), 10-20.

[7] Phong, Bui Tuong. Illumination for computer-generated images. PhD dissertation, University of Utah, Salt Lake City, 1973.

[8] Siegel, Robert and Howell, John R. Thermal Radiation Heat Transfer. Hemisphere Publishing Corporation, Washington, 1981.

[9] Sparrow, E.M. A new and simpler formulation for radiative angle factors. Transactions of the ASME, Journal of Heat Transfer 85, 2, (1963), 81-88.

[10] Sparrow, E.M. and Cess, R.D. Radiation Heat Transfer. Hemisphere Publishing Corporation, Washington, 1978.

[11] Torrance, Kenneth E. and Sparrow, Ephraim M. Theory for off-specular reflection from roughened surfaces. Journal Optical Society of America 57, 9, (September 1967), 1105-1114.

[12] Verbeck, Channing P. and Greenberg, Donald P. A comprehensive light source description for computer graphics. submitted for publication, 1984.

[13] Whitted, Turner. An improved illumination model for shaded display. Communications of the ACM 6, 23, (June 1980), 343-349.

[14] Wiebelt, John A. Engineering Radiation Heat Transfer. Holt, Rinehart and Winston, Inc., New York, 1966.

An Image Synthesizer

Ken Perlin

Courant Institute of Mathematical Sciences
New York University

Abstract

We introduce the concept of a Pixel Stream Editor. This forms the basis for an interactive synthesizer for designing highly realistic Computer Generated Imagery. The designer works in an interactive Very High Level programming environment which provides a very fast concept/implement/view iteration cycle.

Naturalistic visual complexity is built up by composition of non-linear functions, as opposed to the more conventional texture mapping or growth model algorithms. Powerful primitives are included for creating controlled stochastic effects. We introduce the concept of "solid texture" to the field of CGI.

We have used this system to create very convincing representations of clouds, fire, water, stars, marble, wood, rock, soap films and crystal. The algorithms created with this paradigm are generally extremely fast, highly realistic, and asynchronously parallelizable at the pixel level.

CR CATEGORIES AND SUBJECT DESCRIPTORS: I.3.5 [Computer Graphics]: Three-Dimensional Graphics and Realism

ADDITIONAL KEYWORDS AND PHRASES: pixel stream editor, interactive, algorithm development, functional composition, space function, stochastic modelling, solid texture, fire, waves, turbulence

Introduction

This work arose out of some experiments into developing efficient naturalistic looking textures. Several years ago we developed a simple way of creating well behaved stochastic functions. We found that combinations of such functions yielded a remarkably rich set of visual textures. We soon found it cumbersome to continually rewrite, recompile, and rerun programs in order to try out different function combinations.

This motivated the development of a Pixel Stream Editing language (PSE). Cook [1] has proposed an expression parser for this purpose. We have taken the same idea somewhat farther by providing an entire high level programming language available at the pixel level. Unlike [1], The PSE contains general flow of control structures, allowing arbitrarily asynchronous operations at different pixels.

With the PSE we may interactively compose functions defined over modelling space. By starting with the right choice of primitive functions we can build up some rather convincing naturalistic detail with surprisingly simple and efficient algorithms.

We will first describe the PSE language and environment. Then we will introduce the concept of *solid texture*, together with our well behaved stochastic functions. Finally we will give some examples of how these concepts work together in actual practice.

A Pixel Stream Editing Language

Consider any list of variable names. We will call any list of corresponding values for these variables a "pixel". For example, one possible pixel for the variable list [red green blue] is [0.5 0.3 0.7]. We will call any list of names together with a two dimensional array of pixels an "image".

A Pixel Stream Editor (PSE) is simply a filter which converts input images to output images by running the same program at every pixel. We always read and write image pixels in some canonical order. At any one pixel, all that the program "knows" about each image are its variable names and their current values.

The PSE we have designed has a rather high level language. All of the familiar programming constructs are supported, including conditional and looping control structures, function procedure definitions, and a full compliment of arithmetic and logical operators and mathematical functions. Assignment and the equality operator are denoted by "=" and "==", respectively, as in the C programming language [2]. For any infix operator op, $a\ op=\ b$ denotes $a = a\ op\ b$.

Variables may be scalars, or else vectors of scalars and/or vectors (recursively). Typing is implicit, determined by assignment. Program blocks are indicated by indenting. All operators will work on scalars or vectors. For example $a+b$ is a scalar sum if a and b are scalars, and a vector sum if a and b are vectors.

The following simple example will illustrate. Suppose the input image contains the variable list [surface point normal], where *surface* is a surface identifier, *point* is the location in space of the surface visible at this pixel, and *normal* is the surface normal direction at *point*. This image in particular would generally be the output of some visible surface finding algorithm.

Let the output image consist of [color]. If we interpret color as a [red green blue] vector, then the procedure :

```
if surface == 1
    color = [1 0 0] * max(0.1, dot(normal, [1 0 0]))
else
    color = [0 0 0.1]
```

will produce an image of a diffusely shaded red object lit from the positive x direction against a dark blue background. The function "*dot*()" is simply a built in function returning the dot product of two vectors.

Spotted Donut

Bumpy Donut

Stucco Donut

Disgusting Donut

Bozo's Donut

Wrinkled Donut

Note that in the above example, "[1 0 0]" is used in one place to denote the color red, and in another to denote a direction in space. Such looseness and ambiguity was a deliberate design decision in creating the language. In using the system we obtained some of the most striking visual effects only by stepping over (real or imagined) semantic distinctions.

We find that the PSE is most useful as a design tool when used as interactively as possible. For this reason we have placed it in an interactive design cycle :

1. Edit PSE program
2. Run it on a *low* resolution image
3. View the results on a color monitor

Design resolution is generally chosen to allow a design cycle time of under one minute.

Space Functions and Solid Texture

A number of researchers have proposed procedural texture, notably [3], [5], and [6]. As far as we know all prior work in this direction has been with functions which vary over a two dimensional domain.

Suppose we extend this to functions which vary over a three dimensional domain. We call any function whose domain is the entirety of (x,y,z) space a "space function".

Any space function may be thought of as representing a solid material. If we evaluate this function at the visible surface points of an object then we will obtain the surface texture that would have occured had we "sculpted" the object out of the material. We will call a texture so formed a "solid texture".

This approach has several advantages over texture mapping :

1. Shape and texture become independent. The texture does not need to be "fit" onto the surface. If we change the shape or carve a piece out of it, the appearance of the solid material will accurately change.

2. As with all procedural textures, the database is extremely small.

Although it is not immediately obvious, this paradigm is a superset of conventional texture mapping techniques. Any stored texture algorithm may be cast as a table lookup function composed with a projection function from three dimensions to two.

We will use solid texture repeatedly over the course of this paper to simulate a variety of materials.

Noise()

In order to get the most out of the PSE and the solid texture approach we have provided some primitive stochastic functions with which to bootstrap visual complexity. We now introduce the most fundamental of these.

Noise() is a scalar valued function which takes a three dimensional vector as its argument. It has the following properties :

> Statistical invariance under rotation
> (no matter how we rotate its domain,
> it has the same statistical character)
>
> A narrow bandpass limit in frequency
> (its has no visible features larger or smaller
> than within a certain narrow size range)

> Statistical invariance under translation
> (no matter how we translate its domain,
> it has the same statistical character)

Noise() is a good texture modeling primitive since we may use it in a straightforward manner to create surfaces with desired stochastic characteristics at different visual scales, without losing control over the effects of rotation, scaling, and translation. This works well with the human vision system, which tends to analyze incoming images in terms of levels of differently sized detail [4].

The author has developed a number of surprisingly different implementations of the *Noise*() function. Some real tradeoffs are involved between time, storage space, algorithmic complexity, and adherence to the three defining statistical constraints.

Because of space limitations, we will describe only the simplest such technique. Although generally adequate, this procedure only approximately conforms to the bandwidth and rotational invariance constraints.

1. Consider the set of all points in space whose x, y, and z coordinates are all integer valued. We call this set the *integer lattice*.

   Associate with each point in the integer lattice a pseudo-random value and x, y, and z gradient values. More precisely, map each ordered sequence of three integers into an uncorrelated ordered sequence of four real numbers: $[a,b,c,d] = H([x,y,z])$, where $[a,b,c,d]$ define a linear equation with gradient $[a,b,c]$ and value d at $[x,y,z]$. $H()$ is best implemented as a hash function.

2. If $[x,y,z]$ is on the integer lattice, we define $Noise([x,y,z]) = d_{[x,y,z]}$.

   If $[x,y,z]$ is not on the integer lattice we compute a smooth (eg. cubic polynomial) interpolation between lattice equation coefficients, applied first in x (along lattice edges), then in y (within lattice z-faces), then in z. We then evaluate this interpolated linear equation at $[x,y,z]$.

We will now show some of the simpler uses of *Noise*(). We will assume that "*point*" and "*normal*" are vector valued input image variables.

By evaluating *Noise*() at visible surface points of simulated objects we may create a simple "random" surface texture (figure Spotted.Donut) :

   color = white * Noise(point)

The above texture has a band-limited character to it; there is no detail outside of a certain range of size. This is equivalent to saying that the texture's frequency spectrum falls off away from some central peak frequency.

Through functional composition we may do many different things with the value returned by the *Noise*() function. For example, we might wish to map different ranges of values into different colors (figure Bozo's.Donut) :

   color = Colorful(Noise(k * point))

In the above example we have scaled the texture by multiplying the domain of *Noise*() by a constant k. An nice feature of the functional composition approach is the ease with which such modifications may be made.

Another convenient primitive is the vector valued differential of the *Noise*() signal, defined by the instantaneous rate of change of *Noise*() along the x, y, and z directions, respectively. We will call this function *Dnoise*().

Water Crystal

Art Glass

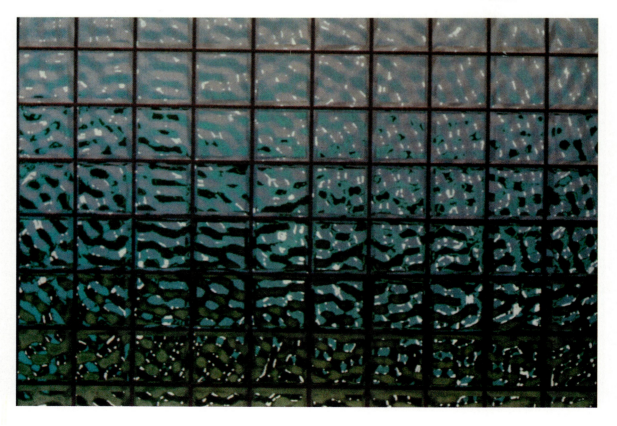

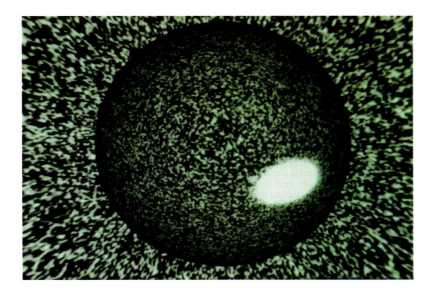

Dnoise() provides a simple way of specifying normal perturbation [7] (figure Bumpy.Donut) :

    normal += Dnoise(point)

By using functions of *Noise*() to control the amount of *Dnoise*() perturbation, we may simulate various types of surface (figure Stucco.Donut), and use these in turn to design other types of surface (figure Disgusting.Donut).

As another example, a 1/*f* signal over space can be simulated by looping over octaves (powers of 2 in frequency) :

$$\sum_i \frac{Noise(point * 2^i)}{2^i}$$

In order to create 1/*f* texture we observe that the differential of a function with a 1/*f* frequency spectrum is a vector valued function with a flat frequency spectrum (ie. gradients of 1/*f* functions are similar at all scales). This means that we must create similar normal perturbation in all octaves (figure Wrinkled.Donut) :

    f = 1
    while f < pixel_freq
        normal += Dnoise(f * point)
        f *= 2

Note that the calculation stops at the pixel level. In this way unwanted higher frequencies are automatically clamped.

Unlike subdivision based [5] or Fourier space [14] fractal simulations, the above algorithm proceeds independently at all sample points. There is no need to create and modify special data structures in order to provide spacial coherence. This results in a considerable time savings. As with all of the algorithms we will present, the calculation at different pixels can be done in any order, in parallel, or even on different machines.

Marble - An Example of a Solid Texture

We can use *Noise*() to create function *turbulence*() which gives a reasonable visual appearance of turbulent flow (see Appendix). We may then use *turbulence*() to simulate the appearance of marble.

We observe that marble consists of heterogeneous layers. The "marble" look derives from turbulent forces which create deformations before these layers solidify.

The unperturbed layers alone can be modeled by a simple color-filtered sine wave :

    function boring_marble(point)
        x = point[1]
        return marble_color(sin(x))

where *point*[1] denotes the first (ie. x) component of the *point* vector and *marble_color*() has been defined as a spline function mapping scalars to color vectors. To go from this to realistic marble we need only perturb the layers :

    function marble(point)
        x = point[1] + turbulence(point)
        return marble_color(sin(x))

By invoking this procedure at visible surface points we can create quite realistic simulations of marble objects (figure Marble.Vase).

Fire

We can create fire using *turbulence*() whenever we have a well defined flow.

For example, suppose we wish to simulate a solar corona. We will assume that the following entities :

norm()	scalar length (ie. norm) of a vector
direction()	the (unit length) direction of a vector
frame	global time variable (ie. one frame click)

have already been defined.

A corona is hottest near the emitting sphere and cools down with radial distance from the sphere center. At any value of radius, and hence of temperature, a particular spectral emission is visible. Assume we have defined a function *color_of_emission*() which models emission color as a function of radius.

Modeled as a smooth flow, the corona would be implemented by :

    smooth_corona(point - center)

    function smooth_corona(v)
        radius = norm(v)
        return color_of_emission(radius)

By adding turbulence to the radial flow we can turn this into a realistic simulation of a corona (figure Corona) :

    function corona(v)
        radius = norm(v)
        dr = turbulence(v)
        return color_of_corona(radius + dr)

To animate this we linearly couple the domain of turbulence to time :

    function moving_corona(v)
        radius = norm(v)
        dr = turbulence(v - frame * direction(v))
        return color_of_corona(radius + dr)

Water

Suppose we wish to create the appearance of waves on a surface. To simplify things we will use normal perturbation [7] instead of actually modifying the surface position.

Max [8] approached this problem by using a collection of superimposed linear wave fronts. Linear fronts have a notable deficiency - they form a self-replicating pattern when viewed over any reasonably large area.

To avoid this we use spherical wave fronts eminating from point source centers [17]. More precisely, suppose at a given pixel a particular surface point is visible. For any wave source center, we will perturb the surface normal towards the center by a cycloidal function of the center's distance from the surface point :

    normal += wave(point - center)

    function wave(v)
        return direction(v) * cycloid(norm(v))

We can create multiple centers, let's say distributed randomly around the unit sphere, by using the direction of *Dnoise*() over any collection of widely spaced points. This works because (by definition) the value of *Dnoise*() is uncorrelated for *any* two points which are spaced widely enough apart :

    function makewaves(n)
        for i in [1 .. n]
            center[i] = direction(Dnoise(i * [100 0 0]))
        return center

To make a wave model with 20 sources we would enter :

```
if begin_frame
    center = makewaves(20)
for c in center
    normal += wave(point - c)
```

Note that the surface need not be planar. By making our wave signal defined over 3-space we have ensured shape independence. This means that we can run the above procedure on *any* shape. The illustration "Water Crystal" was made using 20 sources (figure Water.Crystal). A similar procedure was used to simulate an "Art Glass" partition (figure Art.Glass).

Waves of greater realism are created by distributing the wavefront spacial frequencies using a $1/f$ relationship of amplitude to frequency. If we assign a random frequency f to each center, the last line of the procedure then becomes :

```
normal += wave((point - c) * f) / f
```

Using this refinement (again with 20 sources) we can realistically simulate ocean surfaces (figure Ocean.Sunset).

Since each wave front moves outward linearly with time we may animate these images by adding a linear function of time to the argument passed to *cycloid*() :

```
function moving_wave(v, Dphase)
    return direction(v) * cycloid(norm(v) - frame * Dphase)
```

where *Dphase* is the rate of phase change. For greatest realism we make *Dphase* proportional to $f^{1/2}$ [9]. The wave images pictured are actually stills from such animations.

Other Examples - Clouds and Bubbles

The two bubble images were designed by Carl Ludwig using the PSE. The various elements were all created and assembled by functional composition in the PSE.

For example, in the topmost bubble image the background clouds were created by composing a color spline function with *turbulence*(). The reflection and refraction from the bubble surface were done by using simple vector valued functions to modify an incoming direction vector in accordance with the appropriate physical laws. These were composed with the cloud function and added together.

In the center image, a function corresponding to the shape of an illuminated window was composed with reflection and refraction functions.

The appearance of variable bubble thickness was simulated by multiplying *turbulence*() by each of a red, green, and blue frequency and using *sin*() of this to create constructive and destructive interference fringes. In the PSE this looks like :

```
color *= 1 + sin([rfreq gfreq bfreq] * turbulence(point))
```

Compositing

We can use the PSE simply as a digital image compositor, in which case it functions as a generalization of [10]. We can also use it to combine and modify images in more unusual ways.

Suppose for example that we wish to synthesize some flame on the PSE, knowing that later we will receive some other animation to be composited with our synthetic flame.

We may defer the aesthetic decision of how to color the flame until after looking at this footage. We do this by computing the flame in two passes. The first pass outputs only a scalar flame value. The second and simpler pass maps this scalar quantity to the appropriate color vector.

Note that this process involves no recalculation of the flame itself. The second pass through the PSE is being used only as a general color splining filter, at a small fraction of the total computing cost.

In an actual commercial production this ability to split computation costs and defer post-production decisions adds enormously to throughput.

In more unusual cases we may use the scalar flame to modulate the frequency distribution or height of water waves, or the amount of rocklike character to give to a surface. In this context our approach is similar to that of [1] and [10], the difference being the extra flexibility we gain by the ability to specify arbitrary asynchronous pixel operations.

Considerations of Efficiency

The efficiency of an implementation is a rather elusive thing. This is because it consists of three fairly different considerations. Most familiar is time efficiency. There is also space efficiency, which often is inversely proportional to time efficiency (as in "should we use a procedure or a lookup table?").

The third consideration, often overlooked, is flexibility. Many of us are familiar with archaic and monolithic "dinosaur" programs that nobody dare modify lest they fall apart altogether. Such programs must be used "as is" or else scrapped and rewritten from scratch.

The approach we offer here does not always produce the most efficient algorithms. What it does offer is the opportunity to try out new approaches quickly and painlessly. For CGI in particular this is of the utmost importance. We generally want to see what the picture looks like before proceeding with optimization. Once implemented, PSE algorithms lend themselves readily to optimization by virtue of their simplicity and high degree of modularity.

In addition, a number of effects are ideally suited to a functional composition paradigm; generally when there is interplay between a simple regular structure and a complex stochastic structure. This is because we can use nonlinear functional composition to model the stochastic part of the structure. This will result in both good time efficiency and good space efficiency.

The flame model constitutes such a "best case" for our approach. The final motion picture quality animation ran in about 10 minutes a frame, written entirely in an unoptimized interpreted pseudo-code implementation of the design language on a Gould SEL 3287 Minicomputer. This appears to be much faster than the particle system approach of Reeves [11]. With optimization and true compilation a speedup of a factor of 5 is indicated. The marble vase, with twice as large an area of visible turbulence, took about 20 minutes to compute.

In all cases, the low resolution interactive design loop took between 15 seconds and 1 minute per iteration.

Now What?

We plan to make a number of improvements to the system. We are developing an optimized compiler for the design language which recognizes quantities that vary slowly over the image stream and computes quantities dependent these only as necessary. We are also adding a general facility for direct insertion of large data bases into the image prior to pixel streaming.

We are currently using the same paradigm of composition with stochastic functions for motion and shape modelling.

We have applied our approach to modelling stochastic motion not only for continuous turbulence models, but also for such things as falling leaves, swaying trees, flocks of birds, and muscular

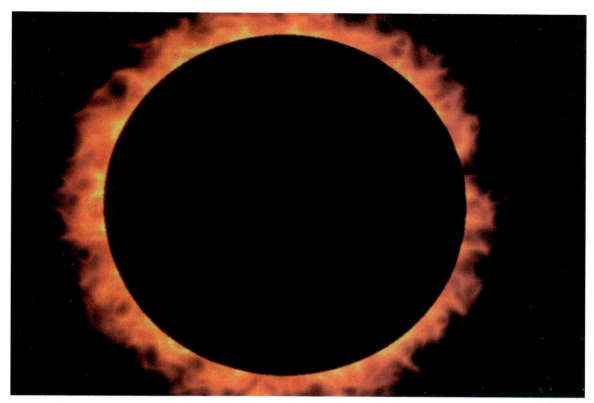

Corona

Ocean Sunset

rippling. In general the paradigm is appropriate whenever a regular, well defined macroscopic motion contains some stochastic component.

To create interesting stochastic shapes, we have generalized on the work of Blinn [15]. Given any space filling scalar valued function, we may consider the shape formed by any isosurface (surface of constant value) of the function. It turns out that a very rich class of shapes may be created in this manner (for example, we can actually build the three dimensional structure of the flame shown in figure Corona). We understand that Lance Williams of NYIT [16] is pursuing a similar line of research.

Conclusions

We have shown a new approach to the design of realistic CGI algorithms. We have introduced the concepts of the Pixel Stream Editor and of solid texture. We have demonstrated a number of effects which would have been considerably more difficult and expensive, and in some cases impossible, to generate by previously known techniques.

Appendix - Turbulence

A suitable procedure for the simulation of turbulence using the *Noise*() signal is :

```
function turbulence(p)
    t = 0
    scale = 1
    while (scale > pixelsize)
        t += abs(Noise(p / scale) * scale)
        scale /= 2
    return t
```

This is actually a simplified approximation to the magnitude of the deformation which results from swirling around the isosurfaces of the *Noise*() domain along the instantaneous vector field :

$$e^{-Noise(point)^2} (normal \times Dnoise(point))$$

This formulation is part of a synthetic turbulence model developed by the author [12]. We use the simplified *turbulence*() procedure because it is fast and the pictures it produces look good enough.

Even so it is interesting to examine, with only minimal comment, the algorithmic structure of *turbulence*(). Note the expression

Noise(p / scale) * scale

inside the loop. This says that at each scale the amount of *Noise*() added is proportional to its size. Thus we obtain a self-similar, or $1/f$, pattern of perturbation. This will give a visual impression of brownian motion. Also, while the deformation is continuous everywhere, the *abs*() at each iteration assures that its gradient will have discontinuous boundaries at all scales. This will give a visual impression of discontinuous flow, which will be interpreted by the viewer as turbulent.

Acknowledgements

The management of MAGI very graciously allowed me the use of its facilities for this research. Frank Crow got me to publish. I'd also like to thank my Ph.D. advisor David Lowe, the faculty of the Courant Institute at NYU, and R/Greenberg Associates for their continuing support.

Gene Miller at MAGI designed "Bozo's Donut" and made a number of valuable suggestions for this paper.

Carl Ludwig made the bubbles and the lovely ocean sunset image. He also codeveloped the wave algorithm, made countless good suggestions for the system and for this paper, and performed the all important service of being the first *user* of the system other than the author.

Mike Ferraro originated the crucial concept of using functional composition to create texture [13]. Much of this paper has its roots in his powerful idea.

Lastly, this paper probably could not have been written were it not for all I have learned over the years about images, algorithms and true elegance of design from working with Josh Pines.

References

1. Cook, R., "Shade Trees," *Computer Graphics*, vol. 18, no. 3, July 1984.

2. Kernighan B., Ritchie D., *The C programming language*, Prentice Hall, Englewood Cliffs, 1978.

3. Gardner, G., "Simulation of natural scenes using textured quadric surfaces," *Computer Graphics*, vol. 18, no. 3, July 1984.

4. Marr, D., *Vision*, W. H. Freeman and Company, San Francisco, 1982.

5. Fournier, A., Fussel, D., and Carpenter, L., "Computer rendering of stochastic models," *Comm. ACM* 25, 6 (June 1982), 371-384.

6. Schacter, B., "Long-crested wave models," *Computer Graphics* and *Image Processing*, vol 12., 1980.

7. Blinn, J., "Simulation of wrinkled surfaces," *Computer Graphics*, vol. 12, no. 3, July 1978.

8. Max, N., "Vectorized procedure models for natural terrain: waves and islands in the sunset," *Computer Graphics*, vol. 15, no. 3, August 1981.

9. Sverdrup, Johnson & Fleming, *The Oceans*, Prentice Hall, Englewood Cliffs, 1942.

10. Porter, T., Duff, T., "Compositing digital images," *Computer Graphics*, vol. 18, no. 3, July 1984.

11. Reeves, W., "Particle systems, - A technique for modeling a class of fuzzy objects," *ACM Transactions on Graphics*, vol. 2, no. 2, April 1983.

12. Perlin, K., Author's unpublished Ph.D. dissertation - work in progress.

13. Mike Ferraro, personal communication.

14. Voss, R., *Fractal Lunar Mist*, Cover of SIGGRAPH '83 proceedings, July 1983.

15. Blinn, J., "A Generalization of Algebraic Surface Drawing." *ACM Transactions on Graphics*, vol. 1, pp 235., 1982.

16. Lance Williams, personal communication.

17. Suggested by Carl Ludwig, personal communication.

THE RENDERING EQUATION

James T. Kajiya
California Institute of Technology
Pasadena, Ca. 91125

ABSTRACT. We present an integral equation which generalizes a variety of known rendering algorithms. In the course of discussing a monte carlo solution we also present a new form of variance reduction, called Hierarchical sampling and give a number of elaborations shows that it may be an efficient new technique for a wide variety of monte carlo procedures. The resulting rendering algorithm extends the range of optical phenomena which can be effectively simulated.

KEYWORDS: computer graphics, raster graphics, ray tracing, radiosity, monte carlo, distributed ray tracing, variance reduction.

CR CATEGORIES: I.3.3, I.3.5, I.3.7

1. The rendering equation

The technique we present subsumes a wide variety of rendering algorithms and provides a unified context for viewing them as more or less accurate approximations to the solution of a single equation. That this should be so is not surprising once it is realized that all rendering methods attempt to model the same physical phenomenon, that of light scattering off various types of surfaces.

We mention that the idea behind the rendering equation is hardly new. A description of the phenomenon simulated by this equation has been well studied in the radiative heat transfer literature for years [Siegel and Howell 1981]. However, the form in which we present this equation is well suited for computer graphics, and we believe that this form has not appeared before.

The rendering equation is

$$I(x,x') = g(x,x')\left[\epsilon(x,x') + \int_S \rho(x,x',x'')I(x',x'')dx''\right]. \quad (1)$$

where:

$I(x,x')$ is the related to the intensity of light passing from point x' to point x
$g(x,x')$ is a "geometry" term
$\epsilon(x,x')$ is related to the intensity of emitted light from x' to x
$\rho(x,x'x'')$ is related to the intensity of light scattered from x'' to x by a patch of surface at x'

Permission to copy without fee all or part of this material is granted provided that the copies are not made or distributed for direct commercial advantage, the ACM copyright notice and the title of the publication and its date appear, and notice is given that copying is by permission of the Association for Computing Machinery. To copy otherwise, or to republish, requires a fee and/or specific permission.

© 1986 ACM 0-89791-196-2/86/008/0143 $00.75

The equation is very much in the spirit of the radiosity equation, simply balancing the energy flows from one point of a surface to another. The equation states that the transport intensity of light from one surface point to another is simply the sum of the emitted light and the total light intensity which is scattered toward x from all other surface points. Equation (1) differs from the radiosity equation of course because, unlike the latter, no assumptions are made about reflectance characteristics of the surfaces involved.

Each of the quantities in the equation are new quantities which we call *unoccluded multipoint transport* quantities. In section 2 we define each of these quantities and relate them to the more conventional quantities encountered in radiometry.

The integral is taken over $S = \bigcup S_i$, the union of all surfaces. Thus the points x, x', and x'' range over all the surfaces of all the objects in the scene. We also include a global background surface S_0, which is a hemisphere large enough to act as an enclosure for the entire scene. Note that the inclusion of a enclosure surface ensures that the total positive hemisphere for reflection and total negative hemisphere for transmission are accounted for.

As an approximation to Maxwell's equation for electromagneticseq. (1) does not attempt to model all interesting optical phenomena. It is essentially a geometrical optics approximation. We only model time averaged transport intensity, thus no account is taken of phase in this equation—ruling out any treatment of diffraction. We have also assumed that the media between surfaces is of homogeneous refractive index and does not itself participate in the scattering light. The latter two cases can be handled by a pair of generalizations of eq. (1). In the first case, simply by letting $g(x,x')$ take into account the eikonal handles media with nonhomogenous refractive index. For participating propagation media, a integro-differential equation is necessary. Extensions are again well known, see [Chandrasekar 1950], and for use in a computer graphics application [Kajiya and von Herzen 1984]. Elegant ways of viewing the eikonal equation have been available for at least a century with Hamilton-Jacobi theory [Goldstein 1950]. Treatments of participatory media and of phase and diffraction can be handled with path integral techniques. For a treatment of such generalizations concerned with various physical phenomena see [Feynman and Hibbs 1965]. Finally, no wavelength or polarization dependence is mentioned in eq. (1). Inclusion of wavelength and polarization is straightforward and to be understood.

2. Discussion of transport quantities

We discuss each of the quantities and terms of equation (1). This equation describes the intensity of photon transport for a simplified model. $I(x,x')$ measures the energy of radiation passing from point x' to point x. We shall name $I(x,x')$ the *unoccluded two point transport intensity* from x' to x, or more compactly the *transport intensity*. The transport intensity $I(x,x')$ is the energy of radiation per unit time per unit area of source dx' per unit area dx of target.

$$dE = I(x, x') \, dt \, dx \, dx'. \quad (2)$$

The units of I are joule/m^{4}sec,

The term $g(x, x')$ is a geometry term. This term encodes the occlusion of surface points by other surface points. If in the scene, x' and x are not in fact mutually visible then the geometry term is 0. On the other hand if they are visible from each other then the term is $1/r^2$ where r is the distance from x' to x. Note that an occluding perfectly transparent surface can make $g(x, x')$ to be equal 0. For, in fact, the transparent surface, intercepts the radiation and reradiates it on the other side.

The emittance term, $\epsilon(x, x')$ measures the energy emitted by a surface at point x' reaching a point x. We shall call it the *unoccluded two point transport emittance* from x' to x. It gives the energy per unit time per unit area of source and per unit area of target. That is,

$$dE = \frac{1}{r^2} \epsilon(x, x') dt \, dx \, dx'. \quad (3)$$

The units of $\epsilon(x, x')$ are joule/m^{2}sec,

Finally the scattering term $\rho(x, x', x'')$ is the intensity of energy scattered by a surface element at x' orginating from a surface element at x'' and terminating at a surface element at x. We shall call it the *unoccluded three point transport reflectance* from x'' to x through x'.†
The term ρ is a dimensionless quantity. So the energy reaching x is given by

$$dE = \frac{1}{r^2} \rho(x, x', x'') I(x', x'') \, dt \, dx \, dx' \, dx'' \quad (4)$$

We now relate the transport quantities to more conventional radiometric quantites. We shall do this by equating the energy transported by each quantity for the given geometric configuration.

Ordinary radiometric intensity is defined as energy per unit time per unit of projected area of source per unit of solid angle

$$dE = i(\theta', \phi') d\omega \, dx'_p \, dt. \quad (5)$$

To relate these quantities we look at the imaging geometry in figure 1.

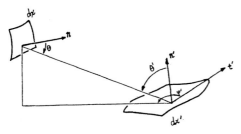

Figure 1. Two point imaging geometry. A frame is attached to each surface element giving a normal, tangent, and binormal vector.

From the figure we obtain

$$\begin{aligned} r &= \|x - x'\| \\ dx'_p &= dx' \cos \theta \\ \cos \theta &= \frac{1}{r} \langle \mathbf{n}, x - x' \rangle \\ \cos \theta' &= \frac{1}{r} \langle \mathbf{n}', x - x' \rangle \\ \cos \phi' &= \frac{1}{r} \langle \mathbf{t}', x - x' \rangle \end{aligned} \quad (6)$$

where:

---
† This term also covers the transmittance of light through surfaces as well. To simplify the ensuing discussion we will ignore transmission scattering altogether.

n is the normal to surface element dx
n' is the normal to surface element dx'
t' is the tangent vector to the element dx'
r is the distance from x' to x

The solid angle subtended by a surface element dx is the fractional area of a sphere of radius r taken up by the projected area dx_p of dx.

$$d\omega = \frac{dx_p}{r^2} = \frac{1}{r^2} \cos \theta \, dx. \quad (7)$$

Thus substituting eq. (7) in eq. (5) we get

$$dE = i(\theta', \phi') \frac{1}{r^2} \cos \theta \cos \theta' dt \, dx \, dx'. \quad (8)$$

Equating eq. (2) and eq. (5) gives the relationship between transport intensity and ordinary intensity

$$I(x, x') = i(\theta', \phi') \frac{1}{r^2} \cos \theta \cos \theta'. \quad (9)$$

The relation between transport emittance and ordinary emittance is derived likewise. Assuming that there are no occluding surfaces, the energy transmitted by emission from surface element dx' to dx is given by eq. (3). Using the definition of ordinary emittance we can follow exactly the same procedure as above to obtain

$$\epsilon(x, x') = \epsilon(\theta', \phi') \cos \theta \cos \theta' \quad (10)$$

Finally, we relate the transport reflectance to the ordinary radiometric total bidirectional reflectance function $\rho(\theta', \phi', \psi', \sigma')$ from the definition

$$i(\theta', \phi') = \rho(\theta', \phi', \psi', \sigma') i(\psi', \sigma') d\omega'' \cos \psi' \quad (11)$$

Where the imaging geometry appears in figure 2.

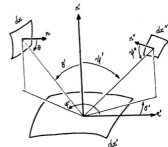

Figure 2. Three point imaging geometry.

From the diagram we obtain in addition to equations (6) and (7), the following

$$\begin{aligned} r'' &= \|x' - x''\| \\ dx''_p &= dx'' \cos \psi'' \\ \cos \psi' &= \frac{1}{r''} \langle \mathbf{n}', x' - x'' \rangle \\ \cos \psi'' &= \frac{1}{r''} \langle \mathbf{n}'', x' - x'' \rangle \\ \cos \sigma' &= \frac{1}{r''} \langle \mathbf{t}', x' - x'' \rangle \\ d\omega'' &= \frac{dx''_p}{r''^2} = \frac{1}{r''^2} \cos \psi'' dx'' \end{aligned} \quad (12)$$

where:
n'' is the normal to surface element dx''
r'' is the distance from x'' to x'
$d\omega''$ is the solid angle subtended by surface element dx''

Combining eqs. (2), (8), (9), (11), and (12) we obtain the relationship between the unoccluded three point transport reflectance and the ordinary total bidirectional reflectance

$$\rho(x, x', x'') = \rho(\theta', \phi', \psi', \sigma') \cos\theta \cos\theta' \qquad (13)$$

3. Methods for approximate solution

In this section we shall review approximations to the solution of the rendering equation. It appears that a wide variety of rendering algorithms can be viewed in a unified context provided by this equation. During the course of this discussion, many other untried approximations may occur to the reader. We welcome additional work on this area. This territory remains largely unexplored, since the bulk of the present effort has concentrated solely on the solution methods to be presented below.

Neumann series

One method of solving integral equations like eq.(1) comes from a well known formal manipulation, see [Courant and Hilbert 1953]. We rewrite it as:

$$I = g\epsilon + gMI$$

where M is the linear operator given by the integral in eq.(1). Now if we rewrite this equation as

$$(1 - gM)I = g\epsilon$$

where 1 is the identity operator, then we can formally invert the equation by

$$\begin{aligned}I &= (1 - gM)^{-1} g\epsilon \\ &= g\epsilon + gMg\epsilon + gMgMg\epsilon + g(Mg)^3\epsilon \cdots \end{aligned} \qquad (2)$$

A condition for the convergence of the infinite series is that the spectral radius of the operator M be less than one. (Which is met in the case of interest to us). A physical interpretation of the Neumann expansion is appealing. It gives the final intensity of radiation transfer between points x and x' as the sum of a direct term, a once scattered term, a twice scattered term, etc.

The Utah approximation

For lack of a better name, we shall call the classical method for rendering shaded surfaces the Utah approximation. In this approximation we approximate I with the two term sum:

$$I = g\epsilon + gM\epsilon_0$$

Thus the Utah approximation ignores all scattering except for the first. The geometry term is by far the most difficult to compute. The Utah approximation computes the g term only for the final scattering into the eye. This is, of course, the classical hidden surface problem studied by many early researchers at the University of Utah. Note that in the second term, the operator M does not operate on $g\epsilon$ but rather directly on ϵ_0. Thus this approximation ignores visibilty from emitting surfaces: it ignores shadows. The ϵ_0 term is meant to signify that only point radiators are allowed. No extended lighting surfaces were allowed. This simplification reduces the operator M to a small sum over light sources rather than an integration over x''.

Since that time many extensions have appeared, most notably shadow algorithms and extended light sources.

The Ray Tracing approximation

Whitted [1980], proposed a different approximation:

$$I = g\epsilon + gM_0 g\epsilon_0 + gM_0 gM_0 g\epsilon_0 + \cdots$$

In this famous approximation, M_0 is a scattering model which is the sum of two delta functions a cosine term. The two delta functions of course represent the reflection and refraction of his lighting model. The cosine term represents the diffuse component. Note that he gives $g\epsilon_0$: shadows but with point radiators. Whitted's ambient term translates directly to the ϵ term. Again the operator M can be approximated by a small sum.

The distributed ray tracing approximation

In 1984, Cook [Cook et al 1984], introduced distributed ray tracing. This approximation uses an extension of the three component Whitted model resulting in a more accurate scattering model. This extension necessitated the evaluation of an integral in computing the operator M. In this model M is approximated by a distribution around the reflection and refraction delta functions. The innovation that made this possible was the use of monte carlo like techniques for the evaluation. As is well known, the ability to evaluate integrals has widely extended the range of optical phenomena captured by this technique. A proper treatment of the ambient term, however, remained elusive to distributed ray tracing.

The radiosity approximation

In 1984, Goral, Torrance, and Greenburg [Goral et. al. 1984, Cohen and Greenburg 1985, Nishita and Nakamae 1985] introduced radiosity to the computer graphics world. This is a major new rendering technique which handles the energy balance equations for perfectly diffuse surfaces. That is, surfaces which have no angular dependence on the bidirectional reflectance function

$$\rho(\theta', \phi', \psi', \sigma') = \rho_0. \qquad (14)$$

The *radiosity* $B(x')$ of a surface element dx' is the energy flux over the total visible hemisphere. It is the energy per unit time per unit (unprojected) area, measured in watts per meter squared. It is defined by

$$\begin{aligned} dB(x') &= dx' \int_{hemi} i(\theta', \phi') \cos\theta' d\omega \\ &= dx' \int_{hemi} \frac{I(x, x') r^2}{\cos\theta} d\omega \\ &= dx' \int_S I(x, x') dx \end{aligned} \qquad (15)$$

Thus to calculate hemispherical quantities we may simply integrate over all the surfaces in the scene. So from eq.(1) and (15) we obtain

$$dB(x') = dx' \int \Big\{ g(x, x')\epsilon(x, x') \\ + g(x, x') \int \rho(x, x', x'') I(x', x'') dx'' \Big\} dx \qquad (16)$$

If there is an occlusion between x and x' then the contribution of the emmitance term is zero. Otherwise the contribution is

$$\begin{aligned} dB_e(x') &= dx' \int \frac{\epsilon(x, x')}{r^2} dx \\ &= dx' \int \epsilon(\theta', \phi') \cos\theta' \frac{\cos\theta dx}{r^2} \\ &= dx' \int \epsilon(\theta', \phi') \cos\theta' d\omega \\ &= dx' \pi \epsilon_0 \end{aligned} \qquad (17)$$

Where ϵ_0 is the hemispherical emittance of the surface element dx'.

Similarly for the reflectance term, the contribution to radiosity is again zero for an occluded surface. Otherwise we get

$$\begin{aligned}dB_r(x') &= dx' \int \frac{1}{r^2} \int \rho(x,x',x'')I(x',x'')dx''dx \\ &= dx' \int \frac{1}{r^2}\rho(\theta',\phi',\psi',\sigma')\cos\theta\cos\theta' dx \\ &\quad \times \int I(x',x'')dx'' \quad (18)\\ &= dx'\rho_0 \int \cos\theta\, d\omega \int I(x',x'')dx'' \\ &= dx'\rho_0 \pi H(x')\end{aligned}$$

Where H is the hemispherical incident energy per unit time and unit area. In this derivation we switched the order of integration and used identities (13),(12), and (14). Now using equations (17) and (18) in (16) we see that the rendering equation becomes

$$dB(x') = \pi[\epsilon_0 + \rho_0 H(x')]dx' \quad (19)$$

Which is equation (4) in Goral et. al. [1984].

Calculating the total integrated intensity H is essential to calculate the final $F_{i,j}$ matrix in radiosity. This requires a visibility calculation which may be quite expensive. Since the matrix equation is solved by a number of relaxation steps, it is essentially equivalent to summing the first few terms of the Neumann series: propagating the emitters across four or so scatterers. To use relaxation requires that the full matrix be calculated. Relaxation also gives all the intensities at all the surfaces in the scene. While in certain cases this may be an advantage, it is suggested that the monte carlo method outlined below may be quite superior.

4. Markov chains for solving integral equations

The use of Markov chains is perhaps the most popular numerical method for for solving integral equations. It is used in fields as diverse as queuing theory and neutron transport. In fact, the use of monte carlo Markov chain methods in radiative heat transfer has been in use for quite some time, [Siegel and Howell 1981]. In the heat transfer approach, a packet of radiation of specified wavelength is emitted, reflected, and absorbed from a configuration of surfaces in some enclosure. Counting the number of packets absorbed by each surface after a run gives an estimate of the geometric factors whose exact calculation would pose an intractible problem. This is similar to ray tracing a scene from the light sources to the eye. Rather than follow these methods, we will choose to solve eq.(1) more directly going back to an early monte carlo method first put forth by von Neumann and Ulam [Rubenstein 1981].

Finite dimensional version

By way of introduction we first present the method in a finite dimensional context. This simplifies the notation and makes obvious the essential ideas involved. Again we note that this example method may possibly hold many advantages over the currently used relaxation schemes popular in radiosity: intensities at only visible points need be computed, and calculation of the full radiosity matrix may be exchanged for a very much smaller set of selected matrix elements.

Suppose we wish to solve the vector equation:

$$x = a + Mx$$

where x and a are n-dimensional vectors, x an unknown, and $M = (m_{ij})$ is an $n \times n$ matrix.

Now from a Neumann expansion we see that for M a matrix with eigenvalues lying within the unit circle, the solution x is given by

$$x = a + \sum_{k=1}^{\infty} M^k a$$

The method evaluates this sum by averaging over paths through the matrix multiplies. That is, it follows a path through rows and columns that comprises an iterated matrix product. For each point in the path we get a row or column which can be indexed by an integer from 1 to n.

Construct a probability space Ω where each point ω is a path visiting one of n points at each discrete time, viz, $\omega = (n_0, n_1, \ldots, n_k)$ where each n_i is an integer from 1 to n. The length $k = l(\omega)$ of the path ω is finite but otherwise arbitrary and corresponds to an entry in the kth matrix power. Each path is assigned a probability $p(\omega)$.

If we wish to calculate the value of one coordinate of x, say x_1, then we calculate the quantity

$$\hat{x}_1 = \left(\prod_{i=0}^{l(\omega)} m_{n_{i-1}n_i}\right) a_{n_{l(\omega)}} \frac{1}{p(\omega)}$$

averaged over all paths $\omega \in \Omega$. Simply taking expected values verifies that this quantity gives the desired quantity.

The probability space of paths is most easily constructed using Markov chains. A (stationary) discrete Markov chain consists of a set of states X, and an assignment of a *transition probability* $p(x, x')$ from one state $x' \in X$ to another $x \in X$, and an initial probability density of states $p(x)$. Some subset of states may be designated as *absorbing* in that no transitions out of an absorbing state are permitted.

The probability of a path generated by a Markov chain is simply the the product of the initial state and all the transition probabilities until an absorbing state is reached. So for a path

$$\omega = (x_0, x_1, \ldots, x_{l(\omega)})$$

we have the probability is

$$p(\omega) = p(x_{l(\omega)}, x_{l(\omega)-1}) \cdots p(x_2, x_1) \cdot p(x_1, x_0) \cdot p(x_0)$$

In the finite dimensional case we let the state set of the Markov chain be the set of indices into the vector or matrix, $X = \{1, \ldots, n\}$. Note that although we are allowed wide lattitude in choosing the transition probabilities, they must be positive for the corresponding nonzero entries in the matrix. In the limit our estimate of the solution is quite independent of the probability distribution of the paths. But the rate of convergence to the limit is highly dependent on the manner of choosing the transition probabilities. Section 5 gives a set of new techniques for choosing the transition probabilities.

Infinite dimensional solution

Extending the monte carlo Markov chain method to infinite dimensional equations is straightforward. For the equation at hand, we note that it is a variant of a Fredholm equation of the second kind. The passivity of surfaces in reflecting and transmitting radiation assures the convergence of the Neumann series. We simply replace the state set by the set of points x on a surface. The procedure for calculating the points is thus:

1. Choose a point x' in the scene visible through the imaging aperture to a selected pixel x on the virtual screen.
2. Add in the radiated intensity.
3. For the length of a Markov path do
   3.1 Select the point x'' and calculate the geometrical factor $g(x, x')$.
   3.2 Calculate the reflectance function $\rho(x, x', x'')$ and multiply by $\epsilon(x', x'')$.
   3.3 Add this contribution to the pixel intensity.

Note that calculating the emittance and scattering factors is simply a matter of consulting texture maps and lighting models. Calculating the geometrical factor is, in fact, the ray-object intersection calculation of ray tracing. Note also, that by choosing the next point x'' on the Markov path by shooting a ray at an chosen angle and finding the closest intersection point, we in effect perform a powerful importance sampling optimization. That is, we do not bother to calculate the integral for points x', x'' which are occluded by another surface because we know the integral will be zero. This is in contrast to the relaxation procedure in radiosity which always takes energy contributions from all surfaces.

5. Hierarchical sampling

We now present a number of new variance reduction techniques invented for solving the rendering equation. We hasten to point out, however, that the variance reduction techniques exposed here are of much wider scope. Generally they will have utility in all manner of monte carlo integration problems in which the integrand is particularly difficult. In this situation, the increased overhead beyond previously known methods becomes negligible. We present five methods which take increasing advantage of precious samples of the integrand. All the techniques outlines below were inspired by stratified sampling.

Sequential uniform sampling

The first sampling technique stems from a common sequential sampling strategy. Often samples of the integrand are repeatedly collected until the sample variance of the integral estimate falls below a fixed threshold. This strategy has been shown to be of advantage in [Lee, Redner and Uselton 1985], where many samples were collected at interesting parts of the image while few were collected at uninteresting parts.

Unfortunately, this sequential strategy is incompatible with stratified sampling. In the stratified sampling technique, the domain of interest is divided into subcells. Lee, et. al. used a fixed subdivision of 8 cells per pixel and randomly collected samples within each cell. Ideally, better convergence is obtained when one sample per cell is collected, where the cells uniformly divide the domain—this is the so called jitter sampling method, where ordinarily we think of the centers of the cells as forming a lattice. The incompatibility between sequential and jitter sampling arises because a uniform subdivision of the domain is impossible until it is known precisely how many samples will be collected.

Sequential uniform sampling achieves this by keeping a tree of cells of varying sizes. Each time a sample is to be cast, a cell is first chosen and then divided into cells. The old sample of the original cell must lie in one of the new subcells. The new sample is chosen to lie in the opposite cell. A simple example will illustrate this technique.

Suppose we are sampling a unit interval and have already cast 5 samples. The cells chosen with sample points appear thus:

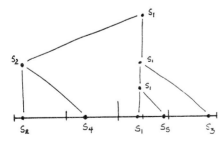

To cast a new sample point we traverse the tree until a leaf cell is encountered. We then split the leaf cell in half and cast the sample into the empty half cell.

REFINE A NODE
1. If the node is an internal node
   1.1 Choose a subnode
   1.2 Refine the chosen subnode
   1.3 Return
2. Else, split the leaf node
3. Propagate the old sample into the subleaf containing it.
4. Cast a new sample in the remaining empty subleaf

How can we assure that the most uniform possible subdivision is computed? One way would be to traverse the sampling tree in breadth first order. Splitting each leaf node at every level before splitting deeper nodes. This strategy produces highly nonrandom sample distributions, essentially scanning across the interval. A better method is to split nodes breadth first in random order. The following criteria effect this strategy

CHOOSE A SUBNODE
1. If either is a leaf choose it.
2. Choose left node if
   level(left)<level(right) and left is balanced
3. Choose right node if
   level(right)<level(left) and right is balanced
4. Choose randomly otherwise.

Note that this strategy will in effect perform a random search throughout the interval, without concentrating on any particular area.

The multidimensional case

The above algorithm is easily extended to higher dimensions simply by using a data structure known as a *k-d tree* due to Bentley [Bentley 1979]. In this data structure, the domain is successively divided into two halves by a hyperplane perpendicular to successive coordinate axes. Thus for say a unit square, the k-d tree subdivides first along a vertical line, then on the next level down along the horizontal. The uniform subnode choice rules above ensure a uniform subdivision without any modification. Generalization to path spaces is straightforward.

Hierarchical integration

The third version of the above technique takes advantage of the fact that the cells for each sample are recorded with each sample. In this way we may compute a Riemann sum using the volume of the cell and the value of the cast sample as integrand. Yakowitz [Yakowitz et al 1978] has proposed a variant of this method (using the samples themselves as boundary points with no stratification). He has reported a variance of $O(n^{-4})$ in the one dimensional case, and a variance of $O(n^{-2})$ in the two dimensional case. This is in vastly superior to the $O(n^{-1})$ of simple monte carlo. The analysis of our technique is still under investigation, and will appear in a companion paper. But due to the stratification of our samples, early evidence suggests that this is a superior technique for integration.

Each time a leaf cell is split, its contribution to the total integral is divided in half. The new integrand sample is multiplied by the volume of empty cell. After splitting and sampling has occurred, the path from the leaf to the root is traversed, updating the integral stored at each node to be the sum of the integrals of its subnodes. By keeping the integral of nonroot internal nodes we are able to automatically scale the by the density of the samples to maintain a constant measure.

Figure 3 shows the convergence of a two dimensional integral as compared to the conventional monte carlo technique. The value of the integral estimate is plotted versus number of samples cast. The conventional estimator is shown above and the hierarchical integrator is shown below. We are integrating a simple step function on a connected region of the plane.

Adaptive hierarchical integration

The fourth elaboration of this technique concerns other criteria besides uniformity of samples in the domain. In this variation, we seek to concentrate samples in interesting parts of the domain and to sparsely sample those areas in which the integrand is nearly constant.

We seek criteria for selecting interesting parts of the tree to undergo further refinement. How can these criteria be included in the algorithm? It is easy to think of the subnode selection rules of the uniform sequential sampler as a way of setting probability thresholds. Choose a uniform random number in the unit interval. The uniform rule calculates a threshold ϕ_u which is either 1 or 0 if the rule says to choose left or right subnode. If the rule says to choose randomly, the threshold is set to 0.5.

Now let us calculate a number of thresholds $\phi_1, \ldots, \phi_k$. To take all these threshold functions into account a effective scheme is to form the convex combination of them as the global threshold, that is the global threshold ϕ is given by

$$\phi = c_1\phi_1 + c_2\phi_2 + \cdots + c_k\phi_k$$
$$\sum_{i=1}^{k} c_i = 1$$

where $c_i \geq 0$ for every i. Each c_i provides a weight for its corresponding threshold function so that the total strategy can undergo tuning.

What are the useful threshold functions? We have found a few, but it is clear that the number of useful criteria left to be discovered is many. Among the threshold functions we have found useful are 1) the uniform sampling threshold; 2) The totally random threshold ($\phi = .5$); 3) The difference of integrals of the two subnodes; 4) A history of the activity of change in this subnode (which may be the variance, or some weighted time history of the integral); and 5) *A priori* functions that can predict where large illumination components will be.

So far our experiments in finding adaptive criteria have not been terribly successful. We have not used adaptation in computing the final images.

Again we note as in the last section, that recording the volumes of the cells in each node automatically provides the normalization that is needed when the sampling distribution is skewed. This is often problematical in adaptive sampling schemes.

Figure 4 shows the unit square subdivided according to criterion 1) and 3) in equal proportion. This is a snapshot of the subdivision when 165 samples have been cast.

Nonuniform sampling: Importance sampling analogs

Finally, the fifth technique takes into account importance sampling. Instead of dividing a leaf cell exactly in half, it is possible to divide it along a hyperplane that represents the median of some probability density function. The hyperplane chosen is given by the level of the k-d tree in the second technique. Representing the probability density as an integrated distribution function makes it easy to choose the median hyperplane by a quick binary search: to find the median of a probability density $f(x)$ we simply search for the point at which $F(x) = .5$.

Importance sampling is a very important variance reduction technique which can be used to great advantage in solving the rendering equation.

6. Application to the rendering equation

The monte carlo algorithms presented above can all be applied to a solution of the rendering algorithm. For example, sequential uniform sampling is used to sample the aperture for depth of field blur. Adaptive hierarchical integration is used to subsample the pixel. Importance sampling by splitting along the medians is used in choosing a direction to shoot the next ray. We store the lighting model as a summed area table [Crow 1985], giving a probability distribution function which can undergo binary search to find the median in a reflectance cell. Since we search for a median hyperplane of the lighting model, nonlinear transformations of the domain are not particularly important. We simply project the pair of input and output hemispheres onto the tangent plane.

It is interesting to compare the path solution to the conventional ray tracing algorithm. It is in fact quite easy to convert a conventional ray tracer to this algorithm. We essentially perform a conventional ray tracing algorithm, but instead of branching a tree of rays at each surface, we follow only one of the branches to give a path in the tree. We always shoot toward known light sources, which, of course, may be extended areas. Thus a schematic of ray tracing versus the integral equation method appears thus:

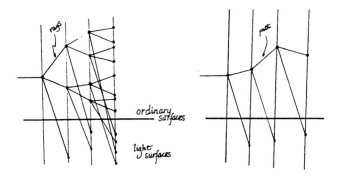

Now an important phenomenon is pointed out by this diagram. Due to the passivity of surfaces, it is widely known that the first generation rays as well as the light source rays are the most important to in terms of variance that they contribute to the pixel integral. Second and higher generation rays contribute much less to the variance. But conventional ray tracing expends the vast bulk of the work on precisely those rays which contribute least to the variance of the image, it shoots too many rays of higher generations. The integral equation method is not prone to this criticism. Because a path is a tree with branching ratio 1, there are as many different first generation rays as there are higher generation rays. This is very important for variance reduction for motion blur, depth of field, and other effects in distributed ray tracing.

This diagram also points out an alternative algorithm for conventional distributed ray tracing. Rather than shooting a branching tree, just shoot a path with the rays chosen probabilistically. For scenes with much reflection and refraction, this cuts down vastly on the number of ray object intersections to be computed for a given pixel and performs a remarkable speed up of ray tracing for very little programming work. However, for this new fast form of ray tracing—called *path tracing*—we have found that it is very important to maintain the correct proportion of reflection, refraction, and shadow ray types contributing to each pixel. Rather than choosing the ray type randomly, there are two alternatives. First, keep track of of the number of each type shot. Make sure the sample distribution of ray types closely matches the desired distribution by varying the the probability of each type so that it is more certain that the sample distribution matches. This is the approach we have actually implemented. A second approach is to let the ray types be chosen randomly but to scale the contribution of each ray type by the ratio of desired distribution to the resulting weighted sample distribution.

7. Results

Figures 5 and 6 show resulting images from the integral equation technique. At each surface element hit, a random variable was calculated from a distribution determined by the specular, diffuse, and transmission coefficients. This random variable was used to choose the shooting of one ray from the surface element. A random point was chosen on each light source to serve as a target for an illumination ray. The variance reduction methods actually used were multidimensional sequential sampling for choosing the diffuse direction, specular direction, and refracted direction of a new ray. Multidimensional sequential sampling was also used to choose points on the light sources and imaging aperture. Hierarchical integration was used for antialiasing the pixel values. No adaptive or nonuniform sampling was used for either of these images. It is clear that importance sampling would improve the variance of the image considerably. Although implementation of importance sampling is simple and straightforward it has not yet been done. Also, keeping track of the variance of each pixel and collecting sequential has shown to be a significant speed up. However, our program did not do this for these images, we shot a constant 40 paths per pixel.

Figure 5 shows a model rendered via two techniques. On the left side is the model rendered via the standard ray tracing technique (albeit with ambient coefficient set to 0 and the single branching ratio speedup mentioned above). The right image shows the result of rendering via the integral equation. Both images are 256 by 256 pixels with a fixed 40 paths per pixel. The images were computed on an IBM-4341. The first image took 401 minutes of CPU time, the second image took 533 minutes. Note that the area of the sphere in shadow is picking up ambient illumination missing in the ray tracing picture. Also light is bouncing off the bottom of the sphere and lighting up the base plane.

In figure 6 we show an image illustrating the power of the integral equation technique. All objects in the scene are a neutral grey except for the green glass balls and the base polygon (which is slightly reddish). Any color on the grey objects would be missing from a ray tracing image. Note that the green glass balls cast caustics on objects in the scene. There is color bleeding from the lightly colored base polygon onto the bottom of the oblate spheroid in the upper right. For simplicity and comparison purposes, the opaque surfaces in this scene are lambertian, but there is no restriction on the lighting models that can be used. Figure 6 is a 512 by 512 pixel image with 40 paths per pixel. It was computed on an IBM 3081 and consumed 1221 minutes of CPU time. Al Barr provided the model for this image.

ACKNOWLEDGMENTS Thanks to Al Barr, Tim Kay, Rob Cook, Jim Blinn, and the members of CS286 Computer Graphics Seminar, for technical discussions. I am grateful to IBM, Juan Rivero of the Los Angeles Science Center and Alan Norton of Yorktown Heights Research for donating large numbers of mainframe cycles to Caltech. I also wish to thank the reviewers for their many thoughtful comments.

References

J.L. BENTLEY, J.H. FRIEDMAN "Data structures for range searching", ACM Comp. Surv., 11,4, pp.397-409., 1979.

S. CHANDRASEKAR *Radiative Transfer*, Oxford University Press, 1950.

M.F. COHEN, D.P. GREENBURG "The Hemi-cube: a Radiosity solution for complex environments", Computer Graphics 19,3, pp.31-40, 1985.

R.L. COOK, T. PORTER, L CARPENTER "Distributed ray tracing", Computer Graphics 18,3, pp.137-146, 1984.

R.L. COOK, "Stochastic sampling in computer graphics", to appear in ACM Transactions of Graphics

R. COURANT AND D. HILBERT, *Methods of mathematical physics* 2 vols., Interscience, New York 1953, 1962.

F.C. CROW "Summed area tables for texture mapping", Computer Graphics 18,3, pp.207-212, 1984.

R.P. FEYNMAN AND A.P. HIBBS *Quantum Mechanics and Path Integrals*, McGraw-Hill, New York 1965.

H. GOLDSTEIN *Classical Mechanics* Addison-Wesley, Reading, Mass. 1950.

C.M. GORAL, K.E. TORRANCE, D.P. GREENBURG "Modeling the interaction of light between diffuse surfaces", Computer Graphics 18,3, pp.213-222, 1984.

I.H. HALTON "A retrospective and prospective survey of the monte carlo method", SIAM Rev. 12, pp.1-63, 1970.

J.T. KAJIYA, B. VON HERZEN "Ray tracing volume densitites", Computer Graphics 18,3, pp.165-174, 1984.

M.E. LEE, R.A. REDNER, S.P. USELTON "Statistically Optimized Sampling for distributed ray tracing" Computer graphics v.19,3 pp.61-67.

T. NISHITA, E. NAKAMAE "Continuous tone representation of three dimensional objects taking account of shadows and interreflection", Computer Graphics 19,3, pp.23-30, 1985.

R.Y. RUBENSTEIN *Simulation and the Monte Carlo Method*, J.Wiley, New York, 1981.

R. SIEGEL, J.R. HOWELL *Thermal Radiation Heat Transfer*, McGraw Hill, New York, 1981.

T. WHITTED "An improved illumination model for shaded display", Comm. ACM, 23,6, pp.343-349, June 1980.

S. YAKOWITZ, et. al. "Weighted monte carlo integration", SIAM J. Num. An. 15,6, pp.1289-1300, 1978.

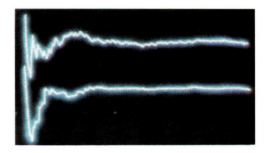

Figure 3. Convergence of naieve monte carlo vs. hierarchical integration. Shown are integral estimates as a function of number of samples cast. Naieve monte carlo is the top curve.

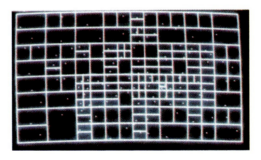

Figure 4. Subdivision of domain by adaptive hierarchical integration.

Figure 5. A comparison of ray tracing vs. integral equation technique. Note the presence of light on the base polygon scattered by the sphere from the light source.

Figure 6. A sample image. All objects are neutral grey. Color on the objects is due to caustics from the green glass balls and color bleeding from the base polygon.

Ray Tracing JELL-O® Brand Gelatin

Paul S. Heckbert

Dessert Foods Division
Pixar
San Rafael, CA

ABSTRACT

Ray tracing has established itself in recent years as the most general image synthesis algorithm. Researchers have investigated ray-surface intersection calculations for a number of surface primitives, including checkerboards, glass balls, green fractal hills, mandrills, abstract blue surfaces, more glass balls, robot arms, pool balls, low-resolution clouds, morphine molecules, aquatic blobby things making strange noises, fantastic cities, and running skeletons. Unfortunately, *nobody has ray traced any food*. The *Dessert Realism Project* here at Pixar is addressing this problem. This paper presents new technology for ray tracing Jell-O® brand gelatin. We believe the method may have application to other brands of gelatin and perhaps pudding as well.

CR Categories: C.1 [**Processor Architectures**]: Multiprocessors – *Array and vector processors;* I.3.7 [**Computer Graphics**]: Three-Dimensional Graphics and Realism – *color, shading, shadowing, and texture;* J.3 [**Life and Medical Sciences**]: Health.

General Terms: algorithms, theory, food.

Additional Key Words and Phrases: ray tracing, lattice algorithm, Jell-O®, gelatin.

Permission to copy without fee all or part of this material is granted provided that the copies are not made or distributed for direct commercial advantage, the ACM copyright notice and the title of the publication and its date appear, and notice is given that copying is by permission of the Association for Computing Machinery. To copy otherwise, or to republish, requires a fee and/or specific permission.

© 1987   ACM-0-89791-227-6/87/007/0073 $00.75

Introduction

Ray tracing has established itself in recent years as the most general image synthesis algorithm [Whitted, 1980]. Ray tracing food has remained an open problem, however. So far the most realistic foods were Blinn's classic orange and strawberry images, but these were created with a scanline algorithm [Blinn, 1978]. This paper presents new technology for ray tracing a restricted class of dessert foods, in particular Jell-O®† brand gelatin.

Our paper is divided into three parts: methods for modeling static Jell-O®, simulation of Jell-O® motion using impressive mathematics, and ray-Jell-O® intersection calculations.

Jell-O® Shape

To model static Jell-O® we employ a new synthesis technique wherein attributes are added one at a time using abstract object-oriented classes we call *ingredients*. Ingredient attributes are combined during a preprocessing pass to accumulate the desired set of material properties (consistency, taste, torsional strength, flame resistance, refractive index, etc.). We use the RLS orthogonal basis (raspberry, lime, and strawberry), from which any type of Jell-O® can be synthesized [Weller, 1985].

Ingredients are propagated through a large 3-D lattice using vectorized pipeline SIMD parallel processing in a systolic array architecture which we call the *Jell-O® Engine*. Furthermore, we can compute several lattice points simultaneously. Boundary conditions are imposed along free-form surfaces to control the Jell-O® shape, and the *ingredients* are mixed using *relaxation* and *annealing* lattice algorithms until the matrix is chilled and *ready-to-eat*.

Jell-O® Dynamics

Previous researchers have observed that, under certain conditions, Jell-O® *wiggles* [Sales, 1966]. We have been able to simulate these unique and complex Jell-O® dynamics using spatial deformations [Barr, 1986] and other hairy mathematics. From previous research with rendering systems we have learned that a good dose of gratuitous partial differential equations is needed to meet the paper quota for impressive formulas.

Therefore, we solve the Schrödinger wave equation for the Jell-O® field **J**:

$$\nabla^2 \mathbf{J} + \frac{2m}{\hbar}(E - V)\mathbf{J} = 0$$

Reprinted with permission from *Computer Graphics* Vol. 21, No. 4, July 1987, 73-74.

Transforming to a spherical coordinate system [Plastock, 1986]:

$$\nabla J = \xi_x \frac{\partial J}{\partial r} + \xi_y \frac{1}{r}\frac{\partial J}{\partial \theta} + \xi_z \frac{1}{r \sin\theta}\frac{\partial J}{\partial \phi}$$

$$\nabla^2 J = \frac{1}{r^2}\frac{\partial}{\partial r}\left[r^2 \frac{\partial J}{\partial r}\right] + \frac{1}{r^2 \sin\theta}\frac{\partial}{\partial \theta}\left[\sin\theta \frac{\partial J}{\partial \theta}\right] + \frac{1}{r^2 \sin^2\theta}\frac{\partial^2 J}{\partial \phi^2}$$

Fuller has given a concise and lucid explanation of the derivation from here [Fuller, 1975]:

> *The "begetted" eightness as the system-limit number of the nuclear uniqueness of self-regenerative symmetrical growth may well account for the fundamental octave of unique interpermutative integer effects identified as plus one, plus two, plus three, plus four, as the interpermuted effects of the integers one, two, three, and four, respectively; and as minus four, minus three, minus two, minus one, characterizing the integers five, six, seven, and eight, respectively.*

In other words, to a first approximation:

$$J = 0$$
The Jell-O® Equation

Ray-Jell-O® Intersection Calculation

The ray-Jell-O® intersection calculations fortunately require the solution of integral equations and the simulation of Markov chains [Kajiya, 1986], so they cannot be computed efficiently. In fact, we have proven that their solution is linear-time reducible to the traveling salesman problem, where *n* is the number of Jell-O® molecules, so we can be sure that ray tracing Jell-O® will be practical only on a supercomputer [Haeberli, 1872].

Implementation

A preliminary implementation has been completed on a VAX 11/780 running the UNIX‡ operating system. To create a picture using the full Jell-O® Engine simulation, we estimate that 1 cpu-eon of CRAY time and a lot of hard work would be required. We made several simplifying approximations, however, since the paper is due today. As a first approximation we have modeled a gelatin cube governed by the first order Jell-O® Equation with judiciously selected surface properties, i.e. color=(0,255,0). Figure 1 was created with this model.

Work is underway on a complete Jell-O® Engine implementation in lisp *flavors*. We will shortly begin computing a 100x100 image of a bowl of lime Jell-O® using a roomful of Amigas [Graham, 1987]. The picture should be ready in time for SIGGRAPH with hours to spare.

---

† JELL-O® is a trademark of General Foods. ‡ UNIX is a trademark of Bell Laboratories.

Conclusions

Jell-O® goes well with a number of other familiar objects, including mandrills, glass balls, and teapots. The composition and animation possibilities are limited only by your imagination [Williams, 1980]. The Dessert Foods Division is generalizing the methods described here to other brands of gelatin. Future research areas include the development of algorithms for ray tracing puddings and other dessert foods. Another outstanding problem is the suspension of fruit in Jell-O®, in particular fresh pineapple and kiwi fruit.

Acknowledgements

Thanks to Paul Haeberli for tipping back a few with me on this research and to H.B. Siegel for key observations. The SIGGRAPH technical committee also deserves thanks for recognizing that *There's always room for Jell-O®*.

References

[Barr, 1986] Barr, Alan H., "Ray Tracing Deformed Surfaces", *SIGGRAPH '86 Proceedings*, 20(4), Aug. 1986, pp. 287-296.

[Blinn, 1978] Blinn, James F., "Computer Display of Curved Surfaces", PhD thesis, CS Dept, U. of Utah, 1978.

[Fuller, 1975] Fuller, R. Buckminster, *Synergetics*, MacMillan Publishing Co., 1975, p. 125.

[Graham, 1987] Graham, Eric, "Graphic Scene Simulations", *Amiga World*, May/June 1987, pp. 18-95.

[Haeberli, 1872] Haeberli, Paul, and Paul Heckbert, "A Jell-O® Calculus", *ACM Transactions on Graphics*, special issue on ray tracing moist surfaces, 1872, to appear.

[Kajiya, 1986] Kajiya, James T., "The Rendering Equation", *SIGGRAPH '86 Proceedings*, 20(4), Aug. 1986, pp. 143-150.

[Plastock, 1986] Plastock, Roy A., and Gordon Kalley, *Schaum's Outline of Computer Graphics*, McGraw-Hill, New York, 1986.

[Sales, 1966] Sales, Soupy, *The Soupy Sales Show*, 1966.

[Weller, 1985] Weller, Tom, *Science Made Stupid*, Houghton Mifflin Co., Boston, 1985.

[Whitted, 1980] Whitted, Turner, "An Improved Illumination Model for Shaded Display", *Communications of the ACM*, 23(6), June 1980, pp. 343-349.

[Williams, 1980] Williams, Lance, personal communication, 1980.

fig. 1: lime Jell-O®

A Progressive Refinement Approach to Fast Radiosity Image Generation

Michael F. Cohen, Shenchang Eric Chen, John R. Wallace, Donald P. Greenberg

Program of Computer Graphics, Cornell University

Abstract

A reformulated radiosity algorithm is presented that produces initial images in time linear to the number of patches. The enormous memory costs of the radiosity algorithm are also eliminated by computing form-factors on-the-fly. The technique is based on the approach of rendering by progressive refinement. The algorithm provides a useful solution almost immediately which progresses gracefully and continuously to the complete radiosity solution. In this way the competing demands of realism and interactivity are accommodated. The technique brings the use of radiosity for interactive rendering within reach and has implications for the use and development of current and future graphics workstations.

CR Categories and Subject Descriptors: I.3.3 [Computer Graphics]: Picture/Image Generation - Display algorithms. I.3.7 [Computer Graphics]: Three-Dimensional Graphics and Realism

General Terms: Algorithms

Additional Key Words and Phrases: radiosity, progressive refinement, backward ray tracing, z-buffer, global illumination, adaptive subdivision.

1 Introduction

Two goals have largely shaped the field of image synthesis since its inception: visual realism and interactivity. The desire for realism has motivated the development of global illumination algorithms such as ray tracing [19], [5], [12] and radiosity [7], [13], [3], with often impressive results. However, the need for interactive manipulation of objects for geometric modeling and other computer aided design areas has generated another path of evolution. This path, dominated by speed, led from the work of early researchers [18], [8], [14] and others, to the development of current engineering workstations capable of drawing thousands of shaded polygons a second [16], [6]. In order to achieve this performance, much of what is central to the goal of realism has had to be sacrificed, including the effects of shadows and global illumination. On the other hand, algorithms like ray-tracing and radiosity are too expensive on current machines to be used as the basis of interactive rendering.

One approach to accommodating the competing demands of interactivity and image quality is offered by the method of rendering by adaptive refinement [2]. In this approach rendering begins with a simple, quickly rendered version of the image, and progresses through a sequence of increasing realism, until a change in the scene or view requires that the process start again. The aim is to provide the highest quality image possible within the time constraints imposed by the user's manipulation of the scene. It is crucial to this approach that the early images be of usable quality at interactive speeds and that the progression to greater realism be *graceful*, that is, automatic, continuous, and not distracting to the user. In the words of Bergman, what is needed is a *golden thread*, a single rendering operation that, with repeated application, will continually refine the quality of an image.

This paper presents a reformulation of the radiosity algorithm that provides such a *thread*. The radiosity approach is a particularly attractive basis for a progressive approach for two reasons. First, the process correctly simulates the global illumination of diffuse environments. Second, it provides a view-independent

Reprinted with permission from *Computer Graphics* Vol. 22, No. 4, August 1988, 137-145.

solution of the diffuse component of reflection. Thus the refinement process may continue uninterrupted as the user views the scene from different directions. Unfortunately, the conventional radiosity algorithm provides no usable results until after the solution is complete, a computation of order n^2, (where n is the number of discrete surface patches). The original algorithm has the additional disadvantage of using $O(n^2)$ storage.

In the revised radiosity algorithm presented here, an initial approximation of the global diffuse illumination provides a starting point for refinement. A reorganization of the iterative solution of the radiosity equations allows the illumination of all surfaces in the environment to be updated at each step and ensures that the correct solution is approached early in the process. In addition to providing a basis for graceful image refinement, the new algorithm requires only $O(n)$ storage.

2 The Cost of Realism for the Conventional Radiosity Algorithm

The radiosity algorithm is a method for evaluating the intensity or radiosity at discrete points and surface areas in an environment. The relationship between the radiosity of a given discrete surface area, or patch, and the radiosity of all other patches in the environment is given by:

$$B_i A_i = E_i A_i + \rho_i \sum_{j=1}^{n} B_j F_{ji} A_j \quad (1)$$

where
B_i = radiosity of patch i (energy/unit area/unit time),
E_i = emission of patch i (energy/unit area/unit time),
A_i = area of patch i, A_j = area of patch j,
F_{ji} = form-factor from j to i (fraction of energy leaving patch j which arrives at patch i),
ρ_i = reflectivity of patch i, and
n = number of discrete patches.

Using the reciprocity relationship for form-factors [15],

$$F_{ij} A_i = F_{ji} A_j \quad (2)$$

and dividing through by Ai, the more familiar radiosity equation is obtained:

$$B_i = E_i + \rho_i \sum_{j=1}^{n} B_j F_{ij} \quad (3)$$

or in matrix form:

$$\begin{bmatrix} 1 - \rho_1 F_{11} & -\rho_1 F_{12} & \cdots & -\rho_1 F_{1n} \\ -\rho_2 F_{21} & 1 - \rho_2 F_{22} & \cdots & -\rho_2 F_{2n} \\ \cdot & \cdot & \cdots & \cdot \\ \cdot & \cdot & \cdots & \cdot \\ -\rho_n F_{n1} & -\rho_n F_{n2} & \cdots & 1 - \rho_n F_{nn} \end{bmatrix} \begin{bmatrix} B_1 \\ B_2 \\ \cdot \\ \cdot \\ B_n \end{bmatrix} = \begin{bmatrix} E_1 \\ E_2 \\ \cdot \\ \cdot \\ E_n \end{bmatrix} \quad (4)$$

The computation involved in the conventional hemi-cube radiosity algorithm is divided into three major sections as follows:

1. Computing the form-factors (F_{ij}). This requires determining the patches visible to each patch over the entire hemisphere of directions above the patch. For each patch, all the other patches of the environment are projected onto the five faces of a *hemi-cube* placed over the patch and a z-buffer hidden-surface operation is performed for each face [3]. Using standard scan conversion and hidden surface routines, the cost of each hemi-cube is proportional to the number of discrete patches as well as the resolution of the hemi-cube. This results in an $O(n^2)$ computation for the whole environment.

2. Solving the radiosity matrix equation (4) using the Gauss-Siedel method. Due to the strict diagonal dominance of the matrix, the solution converges in a few iterations and its cost is thus proportional to square of the number of patches [10]. The solution is performed for each color band. Since the form-factors are dependent on geometry only, this does not have a significant impact on the cost of the radiosity algorithm.

3. Displaying the results. This involves selecting viewing parameters, determining hidden surfaces, and interpolating the radiosity values. Current workstations are capable of rapidly displaying high resolution radiosity images from any vantage point through the use of Gouraud shading and z-buffer hardware.

The overwhelming cost of the radiosity method lies in the computation of the form-factors. To reduce this cost, the form-factors are calculated once and stored for repeated use during the iterative matrix solution. The total number of form-factors to be stored is potentially the number of patches squared, although the matrix of coefficients is normally quite sparse since many patches cannot *see* each other. Even so, the n by n matrix of coefficients will quickly exceed a reasonable storage size. For example, assuming a matrix that is 90 percent sparse and four bytes of memory per form-factor, an environment of 50,000 patches will require a gigabyte of storage.

For rendering by progressive refinement, an important criterion is the time required to achieve a useful as opposed to complete solution. In the conventional radiosity algorithm, all the form-factors for the entire environment are pre-calculated before the solution begins at a cost of $O(n^2)$. Furthermore, using the Gauss-Siedel solution for the system of radiosity equations, an estimate of the radiosity of all patches is not available until after the first complete iteration cycle. This clearly cannot be implemented at interactive speeds and is not the graceful first step required for progressive refinement.

3 Progressive Refinement Methods for the Radiosity Algorithm

The radiosity algorithm can be restructured to achieve the goals of progressive refinement. In the restructured algorithm, form-factors are calculated on-the-fly to eliminate the $O(n^2)$ storage and startup costs. Although the basic Gauss-Siedel approach still remains, the order of operations of the iteration cycle has been modified so that a good approximation of the final results can be displayed early in the solution process.

The restructured algorithm differs from the previous ones primarily in two aspects. First, the radiosity of all patches is updated simultaneously. Second, patches are processed in sorted order according to their energy contribution to the environment.

To further improve the quality of the images generated during the earliest stages of the algorithm, an estimate of global illumination is determined directly from the known geometric and reflective characteristics of the environment. This estimate is gradually replaced by more exact information as the solution progresses, providing a graceful and continuous convergence to a realistic image.

3.1 Simultaneous Update of Patch Radiosities: Shooting vs. Gathering Light

In the conventional radiosity algorithm, the Gauss-Siedel method is used to obtain the solution to the simultaneous equations(4). This iterative approach converges to the solution by solving the system of equations one row at a time. The evaluation of the $i'th$ row of the equations provides an estimate of the radiosity of patch i based on the current estimates of the radiosities of all other patch radiosities:

$$B_i = E_i + \rho_i \sum_{j=1}^{n} B_j F_{ij} \qquad (5)$$

In a sense, the light leaving patch i is determined by *gathering* in the light from the rest of the environment (figure 1).

A single term from the summation in (5) determines the contribution to the radiosity of patch i from patch j:

$$B_i \ due \ to \ B_j = \rho_i B_j F_{ij} \qquad (6)$$

It is possible to reverse this process by determining the contribution made by patch i to the radiosity of all other patches. The reciprocity relationship (2) provides the basis for reversing this relationship. The contribution of the radiosity from patch i to the radiosity of patch j is:

$$B_j \ due \ to \ B_i = \rho_j B_i F_{ij} A_i / A_j \qquad (7)$$

This is true for all patches j. Thus the total contribution to the environment from the radiosity of patch i is given by:

$$For \ all \ patches \ j: B_j \ due \ to \ Bi = \rho_j B_i F_{ij} A_i / A_j \qquad (8)$$

It should be noted that while this equation adds radiosity to patches j, the form-factors used, F_{ij}, are still the form-factors calculated using the hemi-cube placed at patch i. Thus, each step of the solution now consists of performing a single hemi-cube over a patch and adding the contribution from the radiosity of that patch to the radiosities of all other patches, in effect, *shooting* light out from that patch into the environment.

During the course of the iterative solution this step may be repeated for patch i several times as the solution converges. Each time the estimate of the radiosity of patch i will be more accurate. However, the environment will already include the contribution of the previous estimate of B_i. Thus, only the difference, ΔB_i, between the previous and current estimates of B_i needs to be considered. ΔB_i represents the *unshot radiosity*.

The solution step may be restated as follows:

for each iteration, for each patch i:
  calculate the form-factors F_{ij} using a hemi-cube at patch i;
  for each patch j:
    $\Delta Rad = \rho_j \Delta B_i F_{ij} A_i / A_j$;
    $\Delta B_j = \Delta B_j + \Delta Rad$; /* update change since last time patch j shot light */
    $B_j = B_j + \Delta Rad$; /* update total radiosity of patch j */
  $\Delta B_i = 0$; /*reset unshot radiosity for patch i to zero*/

All radiosities, Bi and ΔB_i, are initialized to zero for all non-light sources and are set to the emission values for emitting patches.

The above step continues until the solution converges to within the desired tolerance. Each intermediate step simultaneously improves the solution for many patches, providing intermediate results which can be displayed as the algorithm proceeds.

This approach bears some relationship to backward ray-tracing solutions [1] which shot light out from light sources onto diffuse surfaces, but did not propagate the reflected light any further into the environment. A recursive extension of the Atherton-Weiler shadow algorithm was proposed and briefly described by Heckbert and Hanrahan [9] as a way of propagating light from light sources through the environment, but light reflected from diffuse surfaces was likewise not propagated further.

3.2 Solving in Sorted Order

In addition to converging gracefully, it is desirable for the solution to improve in accuracy as quickly as possible.

The final radiosity B_j of a given patch j consists of the sum of the contributions from all other patches. The final value of this sum will be approached earliest in the process if the

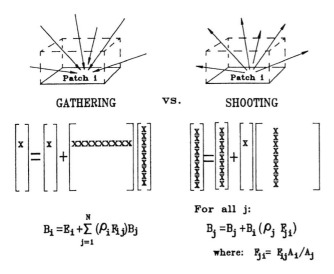

Figure 1: Gathering vs. Shooting

Gathering light through a hemi-cube allows one patch radiosity to be updated. In contrast, shooting light through a single hemi-cube allows the whole environment's radiosity values to be updated simultaneously.

largest contributions are added first. These will tend to come from those patches which radiate the most energy, i.e. have the largest product $B_i A_i$. Stated intuitively, those patches radiating the most light energy typically have the greatest effect on the illumination of the environment and should be treated first.

The algorithm is implemented by always shooting from the patch for which the difference, $\Delta B_i A_i$, between the previous and the current estimates of unshot radiant energy is greatest. Most light sources are automatically processed first by this rule, since initially all other patches will have a radiosity of zero. Since lights are typically the most significant source of illumination for many patches, following the initial processing of light sources much of the environment will already be well illuminated. The next set of patches processed according to this rule will be those patches that received the most light from the light sources, and so on.

When solving in sorted order, the solution tends to proceed in approximately the same order as light would propagate through the environment. A similar approach was taken by Immel [11] in order to increase the efficiency of the view-independent specular radiosity algorithm. The reordering of the patches generally provides an accurate solution in less than a single iteration, substantially reducing computation costs.

3.3 The Ambient Term

Using the procedures described above, intermediate images will progress from a dark environment, continuously brightening to a fully illuminated scene including all diffuse interreflection. The illumination of the scene during early stages of the solution process will be inadequate, particularly for regions which do not receive direct illumination, since global illumination is not yet accurately represented. In earlier lighting models, the effect of global illumination was approximated by adding an arbitrary ambient term. Similar use is made of an *ambient* term here, but its value at any given point during the solution is based on the current estimate of the radiosities of all patches and the reflectivity of the environment. The ambient term is added for display purposes only and is not taken into account by the solution itself. The contribution of the ambient term gracefully decreases as the solution continues, providing a useful image almost immediately which unobtrusively progresses to an accurate rendering.

3.3.1 Computation of the Ambient Term

A reasonable first approximation to the form-factors can be made without any knowledge of the visibility or the geometric relationships between patches. The form-factor from any patch i to patch j can be approximated as the fraction of the total area of the environment taken up by the area of patch j. As with the correct form-factors the total will sum to unity. Thus,

$$F_{*j} \approx \frac{A_j}{\sum_{j=1}^{n} A_j} \qquad (9)$$

An average reflectivity for the environment can be computed as an area weighted average of the patch reflectivities:

$$\rho_{ave} = \frac{\sum_{i=1}^{n} \rho_i A_i}{\sum_{i=1}^{n} A_i} \qquad (10)$$

For any unit energy sent into the environment, ρ_{ave} will on average be reflected, and some of that will be reflected, etc. Thus, an overall interreflection factor R is simply the geometric sum:

$$R = 1 + \rho_{ave} + \rho_{ave}^2 + \rho_{ave}^3 + \dots = \frac{1}{1 - \rho_{ave}} \qquad (11)$$

From these assumptions an *Ambient* radiosity term is derived. It is simply the area average of the radiosity which has not yet been *shot* via form-factor computation times the reflection factor R.

$$Ambient = R \sum_{j=1}^{n} (\Delta B_j F_{*j}) \qquad (12)$$

Thus at any point in the computation, the estimate of the radiosity of each patch can be improved by adding the contribution of the ambient radiosity. If B_i is the radiosity of patch i due to the radiosity received via shooting from other patches, an improved estimate is given by:

$$B'_i = B_i + \rho_i Ambient \qquad (13)$$

This estimate of B'_i is used for display purposes only since the ambient contribution is not added to ΔB_i and thus is not shot during the solution. As the solution progresses the average unshot energy decreases and thus the ambient term decreases along with it. The values of B_i and B'_i converge and the initial ambient image yields gracefully to the more accurate estimate of global illumination provided by the radiosity equations.

3.4 Adaptive Subdivision: Achieving an Appropriate Surface Discretization

There are competing influences on how fine the subdivision of the surfaces of the environment should be. A finer subdivision means more computation but results in a more accurate representation of the sharp radiosity gradients that can occur at shadow boundaries. The original hemi-cube algorithm solved this problem by using a two level subdivision in which patches are further subdivided into elements [4].

In the revised algorithm as in the original algorithm, patch subdivision is kept coarse since the specific distribution of radiosity is less important for the patches, which act as the illuminators of the environment. The patches are subdivided into smaller elements. It is the elements which act as the receivers of light from the patches. The elements are projected onto a single hemi-cube for each patch to determine patch-to-element form-factors, F_{ie}. The light is thus shot from the patch to all elements. The radiosity of a patch is determined as the area weighted average of its element radiosities.

The number of patches, and thus the number of hemi-cubes, generally will grow very little during the radiosity analysis. Large patches need to be subdivided only if the radiosity varies greatly across the surface causing illumination inaccuracies or if the ratio of the areas in equation (7) causes the form-factor term $(F_{ij} A_i / A_j)$ to grow larger than unity.

The elements are free to be adaptively subdivided based on radiosity gradients without changing the patch geometry and thus no additional hemi-cube computation is required. The number of elements projected onto the hemi-cubes will grow as high gradients such as shadow boundaries are discovered. Images are generated by rendering the elements themselves as Gouraud shaded polygons with the radiosity at the vertices interpolated from adjacent elements.

4 Implementation

The complete algorithm is summarized in the following pseudo-code description:

```
/* initialization */
determine reflection factor, R;
/* determine initial ambient from given emission */
Ambient = R ∑_{i=1}^{n}(E_i A_i) / ∑_{i=1}^{n} A_i;
/* initialize unshot radiosity to given emission */
for each patch: ΔB_i = E_i;
/* element e is a sub-unit of patch i */
for each element: B_e = E_i + ρ_i Ambient;
/* initialize change in ambient radiosity */
ΔAmbient = 0;

/* radiosity solution */
Until convergence {
   select patch i with greatest unshot energy, ΔB_i A_i;
 † project elements onto hemi-cube located at patch i
      to compute patch i to element form-factors, F_ie;
   for each element e {
     /* determine increase in radiosity of element e due to
        ΔB_i */
     ΔRad = ρ_e ΔB_i F_ie A_i / A_e;
     /* add area weighted portion of increased radiosity of
        element e to radiosity of the patch j which contains
        element e */
     B_e = B_e + ΔRad + ρ_e ΔAmbient;
     ΔB_j = ΔB_j + ΔRad A_e / A_j;
   }
   interpolate vertex radiosities from neighboring elements;
   if( gradient from neighboring vertices is too high )
      subdivide elements and reshoot patch i;
   ΔB_i = 0;
   determine ΔAmbient from new unshot radiosities, ΔB_j;
 † display environment as Gouraud shaded elements;
}
```

†Processes which can take advantage of current graphics hardware for scan conversion and hidden surface calculation.

The algorithms described above were implemented initially on a VAX 8700 and then on an HP 825 with an SRX graphics accelerator. The hemi-cube algorithm was performed in software and alternatively with the use of graphics hardware for the hidden surface determination and scan conversion portions of the form-factor routines. The ability to perform transformations, clipping and scan conversion on the HP workstation can potentially accelerate the hemi-cube computation and allows the intermediate results to be interactively displayed as a fully rendered image.

5 Results

The methods described above were compared experimentally in several combinations to determine the effect on the solution process. Tests included comparing the use of Gathering vs. Shooting, Sorted vs. Unsorted Patches, and With and Without Ambient effects. All the methods converged to the same final radiosity results in different amounts of time and with different intermediate results. The final converged results were used as a control with which to measure the error at stages in the image refinement. Individual errors were determined as the absolute differences between the converged and estimated radiosities of each element. (The average radiosity values of the color bands was used for the purposes of error measurement.) The square root of the area weighted mean of the square of individual errors (RMS) is used as a quantitative measure of overall radiosity inaccuracy.

$$RMS\ Error = \sqrt{\frac{\sum_{e=1}^{m}((B_e^* - B_e)^2 A_e)}{\sum_{e=1}^{m} A_e}} \quad (14)$$

where B_e^* is the converged radiosity and B_e is the intermediate radiosity of element e. m is the total number of elements.

The images themselves offer a qualitative basis for comparison.

5.1 A Test Environment

Test were performed on a model of two office cubicles subdivided into 500 patches and 7000 elements. Four iterative approaches to solving the radiosity equations were run. After each hemi-cube, images using the current radiosity estimates were displayed as hardware Gouraud shaded polygons on a Hewlett Packard 825SRX workstation.

The four approaches were:

1. Gathering Only: This is the *traditional* radiosity method using a Gauss-Siedel solution. One hemi-cube is placed at each element.

2. Shooting Only: This method consists of reversing the process by shooting light to each element through a hemi-cube placed at each patch.

3. Shooting with Sorting: The same as the second approach, but with the patch with the largest *unshot* energy being used at each step.

4. Shooting with Sorting and Ambient: This time the radiosity due to an estimated ambient term is included for display.

Figures 2 through 5 each contain eight images from methods 1 through 4 respectively. From top to bottom they show the results after 1, 2, 24, and 100 hemi-cubes. The right hand image is a pseudo-color version. Gray indicates an accurate solution when comparing each of these images to the converged result in figure 6. The blue intensity indicates under-estimated radiosity values and red indicates an over-estimate. The inclusion of the ambient term provides an immediately useful image as illustrated in figure 5, (repeated on the cover). Note that as the algorithm progresses, the over-estimates in the shadowed regions due to the ambient term are continuously redistributed

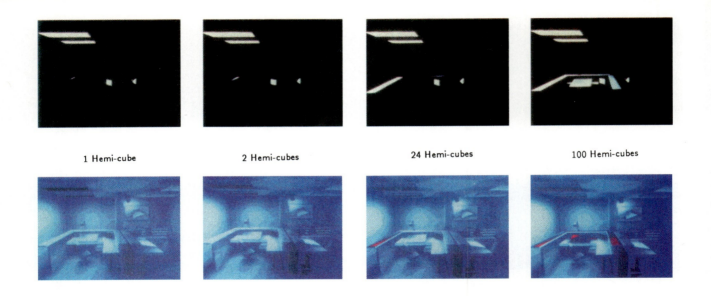

Figure 2: Gathering Only

Since the radiosity of only one patch is estimated for each hemi-cube performed, the gathering approach converges very slowly. Thus even after 100 hemi-cubes, the radiosity of very few surfaces in the environment have been estimated. The pseudo-color images on the right indicate underestimates of radiosity in blue and overestimates in red. (The small amounts of red are due to numerical differences between the hemi-cubes used for gathering and shooting.)

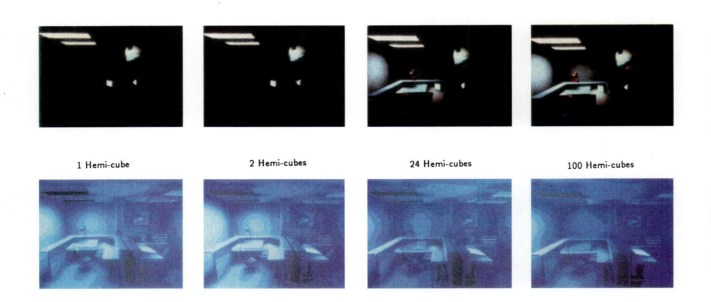

Figure 3: Shooting Only

By shooting light, more of the environment is illuminated for each hemi-cube. However, the order in which the patches shoot light is arbitrary, thus loosing potential efficiency. Note in the graph of figure 3, the jumps which occur when original light sources are processed.

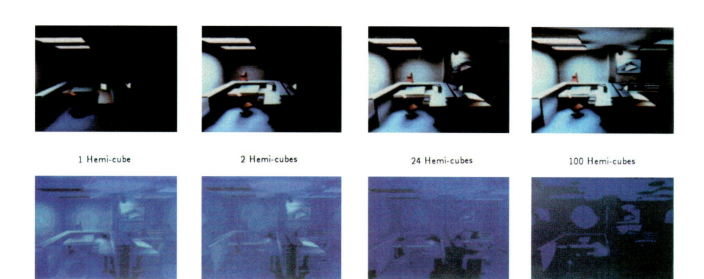

Figure 4: Shooting and Sorting

By sorting the patches according to "unshot" energy, a continuity and efficiency are achieved. Note the continual brightening of the environment as the interreflection between surfaces is accounted for. After only 100 hemi-cubes, a near complete radiosity solution has been found. Note that the under-illumination, indicated by the blueness of the pseudo-color images diminishes gradually after each step in the solution.

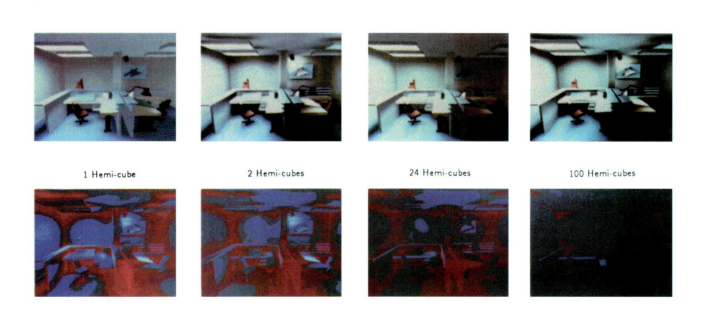

Figure 5: Shooting, Sorting and Ambient

The inclusion of the ambient radiosity provides an immediately useful image after only a single hemi-cube. Note that as the solution continues, the contrast is enhanced as the over-illumination in shadowed areas (indicated by the red pseudo-color) is transferred to the under-illuminated (blue) regions. The ambient term maintains a consistent overall illumination level allowing a more graceful transition to a final image.

to the brighter areas of the environment which were initially under-estimated.

Figure 6 contains an image produced after allowing the methods to run until convergence. The graph below, figure 7, follows the first 100 hemi-cubes and shows the RMS error of the radiosities of the elements. The graph clearly illustrates the improvements generated by the reformulation of the radiosity algorithm. In figure 8, all four methods are compared at the same point early in the solution process. At a cost of only two hemi-cubes, a radiosity image sufficient for many applications is rendered by the fourth method.

The computation of a single hemi-cube with resolution 150 by 150 for the test environment takes approximately ten seconds in the software implementation on the Hewlett Packard 825SRX workstation. The Hewlett Packard workstation was able to display each intermediate stage of the test environment in one to two seconds. Although these clearly cannot be termed interactive speeds at present, the next generation of workstation hardware should acheive near interactive speeds for an environment like the one shown. In addition, the ability to rotate or move through the environment does not depend on hemi-cube computation time. If the display of the environment and the hemi-cube calculations are performed in parallel on separate processors, walkthroughs can be performed during the iterative cycle without disturbing the radiosity computation.

Figure 6: Two Office Cubicles: The Converged Results

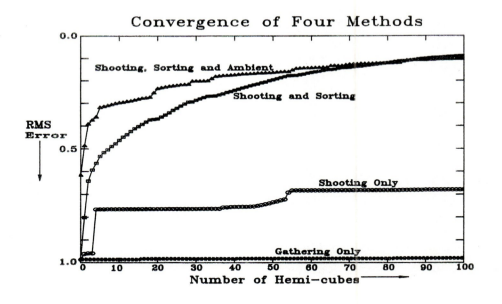

Figure 7: Plot of Normalized RMS Errors for the First 100 Hemi-Cubes

Note the initial improvement in accuracy of the fourth method due to the inclusion of the ambient term.

Gathering Only

Shooting Only

Shooting and Sorting

Shooting, Sorting, and Ambient

Figure 8: The Four Methods Compared After Two Hemi-cubes

These four images extracted from the same point in the previous four sequences illustrate the great advantage provided by the fourth method for displaying immediate results.

5.2 A Steel Mill

An early software version of the shooting and sorting algorithm described above was implemented on a VAX8700 and run on a highly complex scene to test its performance. A model of a steel mill was constructed containing 30,000 patches which were subdivided into 50,000 elements. The patch solution was run for only 2,000 of the patches in 5 hours providing a close approximation of the global diffuse illumination. This was followed by a view dependent post-process taking 190 hours in which the radiosity at the vertices of visible elements was computed by gathering light through a hemi-cube at each vertex. The results were then displayed by interpolating radiosity values across the elements. Figure 9 is the result of this process.

A traditional radiosity approach would have required the computation of 1.5×10^9 form-factors or 6 gigabytes worth of storage (sparcity would probably have reduced this by an order of magnitude). The iterative approach required the storage of only one row of form-factors or 0.12 Mbytes. In addition, the preprocess solution required only 2,000 hemi-cubes, or less than 5 percent of the 50,000 required for earlier implementations.

Figure 9: The Steel Mill

A radiosity solution for this complex environment containing 50000 elements would have been virtually impossible due to storage and computational requirements without the use of the reformulated radiosity approach described in this paper.

6 Conclusion and Future Directions

A reformulated version of the radiosity algorithm for image synthesis has been presented. Two major advantages over the traditional radiosity algorithm are evident: a useful image (although not the final image) is produced in time linear to the number of patches, and the $O(n^2)$ storage requirements for the form-factors have been eliminated. The reformulation allows the rapid generation of approximate solutions which gracefully, progressively refine themselves to accurate representation of global illumination in diffuse environments. This allows the method to be used in applications requiring interaction. It also provides a means to examine the progress of image development early in the rendering process thus providing a valuable previewing capability.

The results of the radiosity analysis make possible the display of high quality diffuse realistic images from any view point. This view independent solution provides a starting point for further adaptive refinement to add view dependent effects such as highlights and specular reflection. Such refinement might include pixel by pixel post processes as as the modified ray tracing algorithm as described in [17], or Monte Carlo methods which can take advantage of global illumination information for importance sampling.

A variety of issues arise when implementing the methods described above. How much and when should the patches and elements be subdivided? How high a hemi-cube resolution is necessary to eliminate form-factor aliasing? What is the interrelationship between patch size, element size, hemi-cube resolution, radiosity gradients, and image resolution. The answers are environment dependent and also clearly depend on the uses to which the images will be applied. Further research should be directed towards providing a body of heuristics tuned to environments, computational resources, and user needs.

Taking advantage of all information about environmental illumination at each stage in the solution process is a concept central to the ideas described in this paper. Future research should be able to apply similar ideas to the problem of rendering dynamic environments needed for geometric modeling and other applications.

Future research should also examine the possible impact of this approach on the design of graphics workstations. Hardware design can provide specialized frame buffers dedicated to hemi-cube computation or for complex reflectance computation. The goal is clear; to provide the best image possible in interactive times and to provide a continuity to a realistic image synthesis.

7 Acknowledgements

The research in this paper was carried out under a grant from the National Science Foundation #DCR8203979 with equipment generously donated by Digital Equipment Corporation and Hewlett Packard. The office model was originally created by Keith Howie and modified by Shenchang Eric Chen. The Steel Mill was modeled through a great effort by Stuart I. Feldman. The photography was done by Emil Ghinger. Special thanks to Holly Rushmeier for technical discussions and to Julie O'Brien and Helen Tahn for helping assemble the paper.

References

[1] Arvo, James, "Backward Ray Tracing," *Developments in Ray Tracing(SIGGRAPH '86 Course Notes)*, Vol.12, August 1986.

[2] Bergman, Larry, Henry Fuchs, Eric Grant, Susan Spach, "Image Rendering by Adaptive Refinement," *Computer Graphics(SIGGRAPH '86 Proceedings)*, Vol.20, No.4, August 1986, pp.29-38.

[3] Cohen, Michael F., Donald P. Greenberg, "A Radiosity Solution for Complex Environment," *Computer Graphics(SIGGRAPH '85 Proceedings)*, Vol.19, No.3, July 1985, pp.31-40.

[4] Cohen, Michael F., Donald P. Greenberg, David S. Immel, Philip J. Brock, "An Efficient Radiosity Approach for Realistic Image Synthesis," *IEEE Computer Graphics and Applications*, Vol.6, No.2, March 1986, pp.26-35.

[5] Cook, Robert L., Thomas Porter, Loren Carpenter, "Distributed Ray Tracing," *Computer Graphics(SIGGRAPH '84 Proceedings)*, Vol.18, No.3, July 1984, pp.137-145.

[6] Fuchs, Henry, et. al., "Fast Spheres, Shadows, Textures, Transparencies, and Image Enhancements in Pixel-Planes," *Computer Graphics(SIGGRAPH '85 Proceedings)*, Vol.19, No.3, July 1985, pp.111-120.

[7] Goral, Cindy M., Kenneth E. Torrance, Donald P. Greenberg, "Modeling the Interaction of Light Between Diffuse Surfaces," *Computer Graphics(SIGGRAPH '84 Proceedings)*, Vol.18, No.3, July 1984, pp.213-222.

[8] Gouraud, H., "Continuous Shading of Curved Surfaces," *IEEE Transactions on Computers*, Vol.20, No.6, June 1971, pp.623-628.

[9] Heckbert, Paul S. and Pat Hanrahan, "Beam Tracing Polygonal Objects," *Computer Graphics(SIGGRAPH '84 Proceedings)*, Vol.18, No.3, July 1984, pp.119-128.

[10] Hornbeck, Robert W., *Numerical Methods*, Quantum Publishers, New York, NY, 1974, pp.101-106.

[11] Immel, David S., Michael F. Cohen, Donald P. Greenberg, "A Radiosity Method for Non-Diffuse Environments," *Computer Graphics(SIGGRAPH '86 Proceedings)*, Vol. 20, No.4, August 1986, pp.133-142.

[12] Kajiya, James T., "The Rendering Equation," *Computer Graphics(SIGGRAPH '86 Proceedings)*, Vol.20, No.4 August 1986, pp.143-150.

[13] Nishita, Tomoyuki, Eihachiro Nakamae, "Continuous Tone Representation of Three-Dimensional Objects Taking Account of Shadows and Interreflection," *Computer Graphics(SIGGRAPH '85 Proceedings)*, Vol. 19, No.3, July 1985, pp.22-30.

[14] Phong, Bui Tuong, "Illumination for Computer Generated Pictures," *Communications of the ACM*, Vol.18, No.6, June 1975, pp.311-317.

[15] Siegel, Robert, John R. Howell, *Thermal Radiation Heat Transfer*, Hemisphere Publishing Corp., Washington DC., 1981.

[16] Swanson, Roger W. and Larry J. Thayer, "A Fast Shaded-Polygon Render," *Computer Graphics(SIGGRAPH '86 Proceedings)*, Vol.20, No.4, August 1986, pp.95-102.

[17] Wallace, John R., Michael F. Cohen, Donald P. Greenberg, "A Two-pass Solution to the Rendering Equation: A Synthesis of Ray Tracing and Radiosity Methods," *Computer Graphics(SIGGRAPH '87 Proceedings)*, Vol. 21, No.4, July 1986, pp.311-320.

[18] Watkins, G. S., "A Real-Time Visible Surface Algorithm," *University of Utah, UTECH-CSC-70-101*, 1970.

[19] Whitted, Turner, "An Improved Illumination Model for Shaded Display," *Communication of the ACM*, Vol.23, No.6, June 1980, pp.343-349.

Behaviour of recursive division surfaces near extraordinary points

D Doo and M Sabin[*]

The behaviour of the limit surface defined by a recursive division construction can be analysed in terms of the eigenvalues of a set of matrices. This analysis predicts effects actually observed, and leads to suggestions for the further improvement of the method.

A recursive division surface definition takes a polyhedron-like configuration of points, edges and faces (the faces need not be plane), and generates a surface as the limit of a 'chopping off the corners' process. There are many detailed variants of this process. All of them construct a new polyhedron at each step with more vertices and smaller faces than the original, the surface being the limit after many steps of division. They differ in the rules by which the new vertices are constructed.

After several steps, the bulk of the polyhedron consists of faces arranged in a regular lattice. There are, however, a finite number of extraordinary points at which the regularity of the lattice is disturbed. The properties of the regular parts of the surface are derived in terms of Cartesian product B-spline surfaces. This paper is concerned with the behaviour near the extraordinary points.

Because the number of extraordinary points does not increase with successive steps of the algorithm, the distance between them remains more or less constant. As the sizes of the faces shrink at every step, the number of faces between the extraordinary points has to grow, so they can be treated as being isolated from each other by regions of regular lattice.

CATMULL CLARK CUBIC FORMULATION

In this formulation[1,2], which is used as an example, the extraordinary points are vertices at which n edges join, when n is not 4. Such points are separated by regions of regular rectangular lattice. The region of an extraordinary point may be represented diagrammatically as in Figure 1.

Applying one step of their algorithm gives Figure 2. Note that the configuration round the extraordinary point is topologically similar to Figure 1. The points are deliberately labelled to stress this similarity. In the original formulation (which for illustration has simpler

Brunel University, Uxbridge, UK.
*Kongsberg Limited, Maidenhead, Berks., UK.

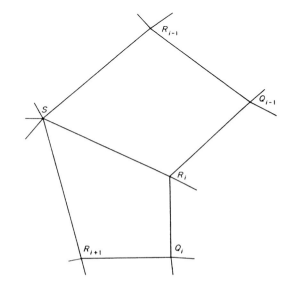

Figure 1. Region of an extraordinary point

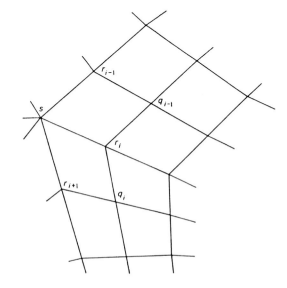

Figure 2. Applying one step of the Catmull–Clark algorithm to an extraordinary point

numbers than the most recent variant), the new points are computed from the old by the equations

$$q_i = (Q_i + R_i + R_{i+1} + S)/4 \quad i=1,n$$
$$r_i = (q_i + q_{i-1} + R_i + S)/4 \quad i=1,n \quad (1)$$
$$s = (\sum_i \frac{q_i}{n} + \sum_i \frac{R_i}{n} + 2S)/4$$

The notation used here is slightly modified from the original, but conveys the same information.

MATRIX FORM

These equations are linear in the points, and so may be expressed in matrix form

$$\begin{bmatrix} q_1 \\ \vdots \\ q_n \\ r_1 \\ \vdots \\ r_n \\ s \end{bmatrix} = M \begin{bmatrix} Q_1 \\ \vdots \\ Q_n \\ R_1 \\ \vdots \\ R_n \\ S \end{bmatrix}$$

At each step, the new surroundings of the extraordinary point are obtained by multipying the old by matrix M of constant elements.

It is a standard result in linear algebra that repeated multiplication of a vector by a constant matrix converges toward the eigenvector corresponding to the largest eigenvalue of the matrix. The behaviour of the limit surface is analysed, therefore, in terms of the eigenproperties of M.

FOURIER TRANSFORM

Although it is possible to evaluate eigenvalues and eigenvectors numerically, it provides considerably more insight to use the cyclic symmetry of Figure 1 to replace M by a number of smaller matrices for which algebraic manipulation is possible. The method used here applies a discrete Fourier transform to Q, R and S, and then separates the terms of different frequency.

Let
$$Q_i = \sum_{\omega=0}^{n/2} Q_\omega e^{2\pi ij\omega/n} \quad j = \sqrt{-1}$$

define the Fourier coefficients Q_ω, $\omega = 0 . n/2$. Similar equations for R_i, q_i, r_i define corresponding sets of coefficients R_ω q_ω and r_ω.

Because Q_ω are complex and Q_i are real (Q_ω is real if $\omega = 0$ or $2\omega = n$), there are always exactly n degrees of freedom to satisfy the n equations.

S and s can also be forced into this pattern by setting

$S_0 = S$

$S_\omega = 0, \omega \neq 0$

Note that
$$Q_{i+1} = \sum_{\omega=0}^{n/2} Q_\omega e^{2\pi(i+1)j\omega/n}$$
$$= \sum_{\omega=0}^{n/2} Q_\omega e^{2\pi ij\omega/n} e^{2\pi ij\omega/n}$$
$$= \sum_{\omega=0}^{n/2} Q_\omega e^{2\pi j\omega/n} e^{2\pi ij\omega/n}$$

and, writing a_ω for $e^{2\pi j\omega/n}$ and a_ω^* for $e^{-2\pi j\omega/n}$

$$Q_{i+1} = \sum_{\omega=0}^{n/2} a_\omega Q_\omega e^{2\pi ij\omega/n}$$

With this substitution made, equations (1) can be rewritten as a set of equations for each value of ω, and in each set we can cancel out the $e^{2\pi ij\omega/n}$. This procedure is closely analogous to the treatment of time series data in terms of components of different frequencies. In this case, the frequency ω may be thought of as the number of complete oscillations of, say, z per complete cycle through the Q_i.

This gives

$$q_\omega = (Q_\omega + (1+a_\omega)R_\omega + S_\omega)/4$$
$$r_\omega = ((1+a_\omega^*)q_\omega + R_\omega + S_\omega)/4 \quad \omega = 0, n/2$$
$$s_0 = (q_0 + R_0 + 2S_0)/4$$

which, by substituting the equations for q_ω into those for r_ω and s_0, gives

$$\begin{bmatrix} q_0 \\ r_0 \\ s_0 \end{bmatrix} = \begin{bmatrix} 4/16 & 8/16 & 4/16 \\ 2/16 & 8/16 & 6/16 \\ 1/16 & 6/16 & 9/16 \end{bmatrix} \begin{bmatrix} Q_0 \\ R_0 \\ S_0 \end{bmatrix} \quad \omega=0$$

$$\begin{bmatrix} q_\omega \\ r_\omega \end{bmatrix} = \begin{bmatrix} 4/15 & 4(1+a_\omega)/16 \\ (1+a_\omega^*)/16 & ((1+a_\omega^*)(1+a_\omega)+4)/16 \end{bmatrix} \begin{bmatrix} Q_\omega \\ R_\omega \end{bmatrix} \quad \omega \neq 0$$

The eigenvalues of these equations are readily determined to be 1, 1/4, 1/16 at $\omega = 0$ and, writing $(1 + a_\omega^*)(1 + a_\omega) = 2\phi_\omega \ (=2(1 + \cos 2\pi\omega/n))$

$$\frac{4 + \phi_\omega \pm \sqrt{[\phi_\omega(8 + \phi_\omega)]}}{16} \quad \text{at } \omega \neq 0$$

INTERPRETATION: $n = 4$

Consider first the situation where $n = 4$. This is an ordinary point of the surface, and so it is known, for example, that it has continuity of first and second derivatives.

The relevant values of ω are 0, 1 and 2 only

- at $\omega = 1$ $\phi_\omega = 1 + \cos\frac{2\pi}{4} = 1$
- at $\omega = 2$ $\phi_\omega = 1 + \cos\frac{4\pi}{4} = 0$

Thus the eigenvalues of interest are

- $\omega = 0$ 1, 1/4, 1/16
- $\omega = 1$ 1/2, 1/8
- $\omega = 2$ 1/4, 1/4

The largest eigenvalue is the value 1.0 at $\omega = 0$. This indicates that as the iterations proceed, the configuration as a whole stays in the same place. This unit eigenvalue must have this value because all rows of the $\omega = 0$ matrix sum to unity, which will always happen when the new points at each step are calculated as weighted means of the old points. The effect of this eigenvalue can be cancelled by taking as coordinate system origin the position to which the extraordinary point converges, and so this eigenvalue will be ignored in the rest of this analysis.

The next eigenvalue is the value 1/2 at $\omega = 1$. This indicates that, as iteration proceeds, both the Q_i and the R_i converge to affine-regular n-gons (affine projections of regular n-sided polygons[3]) which halve in size without rotation at each step. This behaviour has been observed.

Convergence occurs because the relative contribution from other terms in the series shrinks, their eigenvalues being smaller.

Affine-regular n-gons appear because $\omega = 1$ for the dominant eigenvalue. If the unit frequency were the only term present, which holds in the limit, the components of Q_i and R_i have the form

$$x = a_x \sin(\tfrac{2\pi i}{n} + b_x)$$
$$y = a_y \sin(\tfrac{2\pi i}{n} + b_y)$$
$$z = a_z \sin(\tfrac{2\pi i}{n} + b_z)$$

which generate the vertices of such an n-gon when i is given the integer values from 1 to n.

Halving takes place because the value of the eigenvalue is 1/2. Rotation is absent because the eigenvalue is real, so that the phase shifts (values of b) remain constant from iteration to iteration, while the values of a halve.

If that $X-Y$ plane is chosen towards which the plane of the n-gons converges, the behaviour of Z, on which the continuity of the limit surface then depends, is dominated by the third eigenvalue, in this case the values 1/4 at $\omega = 0$ and $\omega = 2$.

The $\omega = 0$ eigenvalue controls the behaviour of cup-shaped configurations; the $\omega = 2$ eigenvalue for saddle-shaped data. In both cases the out-of-plane components are divided by four every step.

CONTINUITY

Writing λ_ω for the dominant eigenvalue at frequency ω gives

$\lambda_0 = 1/4$ (excluding the unit eigenvalue)
$\lambda_1 = 1/2$
$\lambda_2 = 1/4$

The slope continuity may be investigated by setting up a one-sided estimate of the first derivative, and examining its limiting behaviour.

Such an estimate is kz/r $(r^2 = x^2 + y^2)$ for any point, such as Q_i.

Because of the choice of axes, r will be multiplied by λ_1 at each step and z by λ_ω, so that the limit of kz/r depends on $\lambda_\omega / \lambda_1$.

If this is less than unity, the estimate will shrink at every step, converging to zero, and since this limit is independent of the direction taken in the $X-Y$ plane, the surface is slope-continuous.

Having established this, z/r^2 can be used as an estimate of the second derivative. This estimate is multiplied by $\lambda_\omega / \lambda_1^2$ at every step. For $n = 4$ this ratio is 1.0 and so the curvature takes some finite nonzero value. (The continuity of curvature follows from the symmetry of the $\omega = 0$ and $\omega = 2$ configurations.)

INTERPRETATION: $n \neq 4$

The values of λ_ω, together with λ_ω/λ_1 and $\lambda_\omega/\lambda_1^2$ are tabulated for various values of n in Table 1.

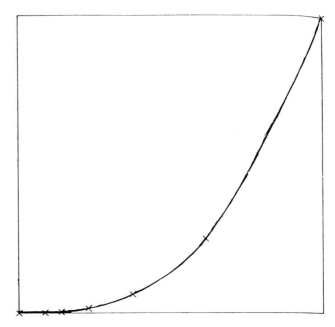

Figure 3. $\lambda_\omega/\lambda_1^2 < 1$

Table 1. Eigenvalues of original form

	$n = 3$	$n = 5$	$n = 6$	$n = 8$	$n \to \infty$
λ_0	0.250	0.250	0.250	0.250	0.250
λ_1	0.410	0.550	0.580	0.611	0.655
λ_2		0.340	0.410	0.500	0.655
λ_3			0.250	0.366	0.655
λ_4				0.250	0.655
λ_0/λ_1	0.609	0.455	0.431	0.409	0.381
λ_0/λ_1^2	1.487	0.826	0.744	0.670	0.584
λ_2/λ_1		0.618	0.707	0.818	1.000
λ_2/λ_1^2		1.124	1.220	1.339	1.528

It can be seen that λ_ω/λ_1 is less than unity for all n, and so slope continuity is achieved. $\lambda_\omega/\lambda_1^2$, however, is considerably greater than unity for $n = 3$, and so the estimate of curvature increases without limit as division proceeds, giving behaviour of the form

$z = r^p$ with $1 < p < 2$

This behaviour may be described loosely as a discontinuity of a fractional derivative.

For $n > 4$, λ_0/λ_1^2 is less than unity, so that the curvature tends to zero, giving a local flat spot on the surface.

These types of behaviour are illustrated by Figures 3–5 which show the effects of $\lambda_\omega/\lambda_1^2 < 1$, $=1$ and >1. The points plotted use $\lambda_0 = 0.250$, $\lambda_1 = 0.611$ and $\lambda_2 = 0.500$, which are the values for the original Catmull–Clark cubic when $n = 8$. Figure 5 is directly comparable with Figure 10 of the Catmull–Clark paper[2]. Figure 4 illustrates the desirable behaviour with $\lambda_\omega = \lambda_1^2 = 0.373$.

IMPROVEMENTS

The behaviour described above has been observed by Catmull and Clark[2], and they have produced a modified version, in which the equation for s is weighted by the connectivity of S.

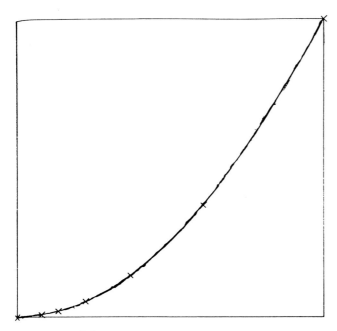

Figure 4. $\lambda_\omega/\lambda_1^2 = 1$

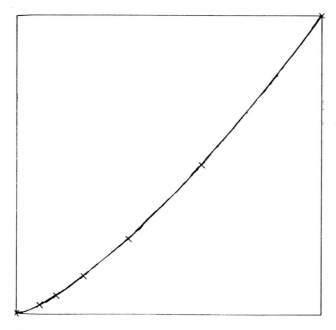

Figure 5. $\lambda_\omega/\lambda_1^2 > 1$

$$s = (\sum_i \frac{q_i}{n} + \sum_i \frac{R_i}{n} + (n-2)S)/n$$

This changes the $\omega = 0$ matrix and its eigenvalues, but does not alter the $\omega > 0$ properties (Table 2).

The value of λ_0/λ_1^2 for $n = 3$ is now much closer to unity, thus explaining the improvement seen on the tetrahedral data.

λ_0/λ_1^2 is also brought closer to unity for $n > 4$, but the value is now greater than unity instead of less. The local flat spots are replaced by local infinities of curvature.

It is clear that further improvement could be made by using as the equation for s

$$s = (\sum \frac{q_i}{n} + \sum \frac{R_i}{n} + (W-2)S)/W$$

where W is a precomputed function of n, chosen to give

$$\lambda_0/\lambda_1^2 = 1$$

The values of W could be stored as a table indexed by n for reasonable values of n, and as an asymptotic expression for very large values; so very little extra computing cost need be incurred.

Even this change would not affect the behaviour with data containing components of high ω value. A scheme of higher performance could use weighted means in all three equations, with precomputed weights chosen to give either

$$\lambda_0/\lambda_1^2 = 1 = \lambda_2/\lambda_1^2 = \lambda_3/\lambda_1^3$$

or $\lambda_0 = 1/4$ $\lambda_1 = 1/2$ $\lambda_2 = 1/4$

for all values of n

The nonlinear simultaneous equations need only be solved once for each n, because the values could again be stored in tables.

RELEVANCE

It may be asked whether such 'fine tuning' is important, when the only effect visible is a slight highlighting. The answer must be that for application in manufacturing, there are two reasons for avoiding fractional power derivative discontinuities.

The first is that concavities of zero radius cannot be machined, and so it is better if the numerical model does not include them.

The second is that many analysis procedures will function by using the closed-form equations rather than using the

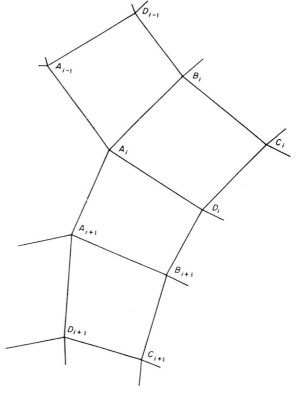

Figure 6. Quadratic form

Table 2. Eigenvalues of revised form

	$n = 3$	$n = 5$	$n = 6$	$n = 8$	$n \to \infty$
λ_0	0.167	0.322	0.375	0.443	0.655
λ_1	0.410	0.550	0.580	0.611	0.655
λ_0 / λ_1	0.406	0.586	0.647	0.725	1.000
λ_0 / λ_1^2	0.991	1.066	1.116	1.186	1.528

Table 3. Eigenvalues for quadratic formulations

	$n = 3$	$n = 4$	$n = 5$	$n = 6$	$n = 8$	$n \to \infty$
λ_0	0.250	0.250	0.250	0.250	0.250	0.250
λ_1	0.375	0.500	0.577	0.625	0.677	0.750
λ_2		0.250	0.298	0.375	0.500	0.750
λ_0 / λ_1	0.667	0.500	0.433	0.400	0.369	0.333
λ_0 / λ_1^2	1.778	1.000	0.750	0.640	0.546	0.444
λ_2 / λ_1		0.500	0.516	0.600	0.739	1.000
λ_2 / λ_1^2		1.000	0.894	0.960	1.092	1.333

subdivision process itself. In this case, the recursive division proceeds locally only until an approximation can be generated for the infinite sequence of patches round each extraordinary point. It is likely that fractional power behaviour will be much less easy to approximate, thus delaying the level at which approximation is possible.

QUADRATIC FORMULATIONS

Two quadratic forms have been analysed, in which the extraordinary points are at the centres of n-sided faces. During the division step, each face is replaced by a new face, which is connected across the old edges and across the old vertices by other new faces.

Applying this process to Figure 6 gives Figure 7.

In such methods the vertices of each new face are functions only of the vertices of the corresponding old face.

$$a_i = \sum_{j=1}^{n} W_{ij} A_j$$

By symmetry, W_{ij} is a function of $|i-j|$ only,

and so a vector of $n/2 + 1$ values of W for each value of n defines the variant completely.

The original Catmull quadratic[1] uses

$W_{ij} = (4n + 2)/8n$ $|i-j| = 0$
$W_{ij} = (n + 2)/8n$ $|i-j| = 1$
$W_{ij} = 2/8n$ $|i-j| > 1$

which results in the eigenvalues in Table 3.

This is considerably better than the original cubic.

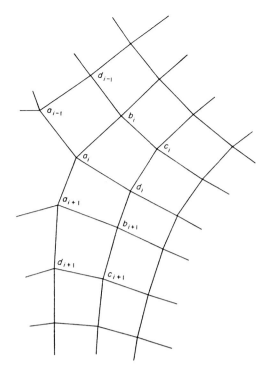

Figure 7. Quadratic form after division

The Doo–Sabin quadratic[4] uses

$W_{ij} = (n + 5)/4n$ $i = j$
$W_{ij} = (3 + 2\cos(2\pi(i-j)/n))/4n$ $i \neq j$

which gives dominant eigenvalues

$\lambda_0 = 1/4, \lambda_1 = 1/2, \lambda_\omega = 1/4 \; \omega > 1$

for all n, thus giving discontinuity of exactly the second derivative under all circumstances.

This ideal behaviour may not be significantly better than the Catmull quadratic in normal use, but that it can be achieved in the quadratic case encourages the search for an equally optimal cubic formulation.

REFERENCES

1 **Catmull, E and Clark, J** private communications (1978)

2 **Catmull, E and Clark, J** 'Recursively generated B-spline surfaces on arbitrary topological meshes' *Comput. Aided Des.* Vol 10 No 6 (November 1978) pp 000–000

3 **Bachmann, F and Schmidt, E** *n-gons* University of Toronto Press (1975)

4 **Doo, D** PhD thesis, Brunel University (to appear)

Recursively generated B-spline surfaces on arbitrary topological meshes

E Catmull and J Clark

This paper describes a method for recursively generating surfaces that approximate points lying on a mesh of arbitrary topology. The method is presented as a generalization of a recursive bicubic B-spline patch subdivision algorithm. For rectangular control-point meshes, the method generates a standard B-spline surface. For non-rectangular meshes, it generates surfaces that are shown to reduce to a standard B-spline surface except at a small number of points, called extraordinary points. Therefore, everywhere except at these points the surface is continuous in tangent and curvature. At the extraordinary points, the pictures of the surface indicate that the surface is at least continuous in tangent, but no proof of continuity is given. A similar algorithm for biquadratic B-splines is also presented.

Recursive patch subdivision algorithms have been used extensively in computer graphics since Catmull first devised them for rendering shaded pictures of curved surface patches[1]. The algorithm he devised recursively subdivides a surface patch into four subpatches until the resulting patch is roughly the size of a picture element (pixel) of the raster display on which it is to be rendered. At this point, the tests of its visibility and the respresentation of its shading properties are greatly simplified.

When Catmull's work was near completion, George Chaikin described in a seminar a method for generating smooth curves by recursively cutting the corners from a control polygon[2]. Motivated by this, Catmull invented a method for generating cubic surfaces for polyhedral nets of arbitrary topology. However, since he could not prove that the surface was well-behaved at all points on the surface, he did not implement it. Recently, Clark implemented the method to empirically determine if the surface is well behaved and generalized the rule for determining the new surface points. Presented in this paper is a set of subdivision rules that have been refined to the point where the pictures suggest that the generated surface is continuous in tangent and curvature. Doo and Sabin have analysed the behaviour of the surface in the neighbourhood of the extraordinary points[5], and the pictures presented here incorporate some tests of their predictions.

Computer Graphics Laboratory, New York Institute of Technology
P O Box 170, Old Westbury, New York 11568, USA

The algorithm described herein is very useful for the purposes of making smooth pictures of three dimensional objects. The task of defining smooth approximations to objects is much simpler if the points in terms of which the object is defined do not have to lie on a topologically rectangular grid.

The basis of the method results from considering a standard bicubic B-spline patch on a rectangular control-point mesh. The shape of such a patch is governed by 16 control-points, as shown in Figure 1. The original points are circled. In subdividing this patch into 4 subpatches, 25 *subcontrol* points are generated. These are indicated in the figure by Xs. Note that some of the Xs lie in the middles of the squares of the original mesh; these are called new face points. Likewise, some of the new points lie on the edges connecting original control points; these are called new edge points. The points corresponding to the old control points are called new vertex points. In splitting the original patch, it is found that each new control point of a given type is computed from its neighbouring points by the same form of algebraic expression. For example, new face points are computed as the average of the four old vertices that define the face.

This paper describes a method for generalizing these subdivision rules to arbitrary control-points meshes. The method applies the same expressions that are generated in the rectangular case to faces, edges and points of

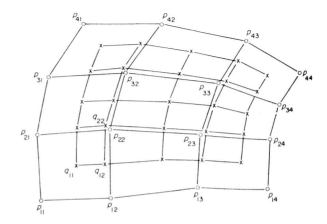

Figure 1. Standard bicubic B-spline patch on a rectangular control-point mesh

arbitrary meshes. That is, new face points are computed as the average of the old points defining the face, etc., and the new vertex points depend upon the number of edges incident on a vertex in such a way that the correct expressions result when this number is 4, as in the rectangular case.

RECTANGULAR B-SPLINE PATCH SPLITTING

The bicubic B-spline patch can be expressed in matrix form by

$$S(u,v) = U M G M^t V^t \quad (1)$$

where

$$M = \frac{1}{6}\begin{bmatrix} -1 & 3 & -3 & 1 \\ 3 & -6 & 3 & 0 \\ -3 & 0 & 3 & 0 \\ 1 & 4 & 1 & 0 \end{bmatrix}$$

is the B-spline basis matrix for cubics, and

$$G = \begin{bmatrix} P_{11} & P_{12} & P_{13} & P_{14} \\ P_{21} & P_{22} & P_{23} & P_{24} \\ P_{31} & P_{32} & P_{33} & P_{34} \\ P_{41} & P_{42} & P_{43} & P_{44} \end{bmatrix}$$

is the set of control points, which are arranged on a topologically rectangular mesh according to their subscripts, and

$$U = [\,u^3\,u^2\,u\,1\,] \quad \text{and} \quad V = [\,v^3\,v^2\,v\,1\,]$$

are the primitive basis vectors.

We will consider just the subpatch of this patch corresponding to $0 < u,v < \tfrac{1}{2}$. The other subpatches need not be considered due to the symmetry of the B-spline basis. This is the subpatch $S(u_1, v_1)$, where $u_1 = u/2$ and $v_1 = v/2$. Substituting these two expressions into (1)

$$S(u_1, v_1) = U S M G M^t S^t V^t \quad (2)$$

is obtained, where

$$S = \begin{bmatrix} \tfrac{1}{8} & 0 & 0 & 0 \\ 0 & \tfrac{1}{4} & 0 & 0 \\ 0 & 0 & \tfrac{1}{2} & 0 \\ 0 & 0 & 0 & 1 \end{bmatrix}$$

$$U = [\,u^3\,u^2\,u\,1\,]$$

and

$$V = [\,v^3\,v^2\,v\,1\,]$$

This patch must still be a bicubic B-spline with its own control-point mesh G_1, satisfying

$$S(u, v) = U M G_1 M^t V^t$$

Requiring that this expression be equal to (2), this will be true for arbitrary values of u and v if and only if

$$M G_1 M^t = S M G M^t S^t$$

Assuming that the basis matrix M is invertible, which is the case, it is found

$$G = [\,M^{-1} S M\,] G [\,M^t S M^{-t}\,]$$
$$= H_1 G H_1^t$$

where

$$H_1 = M^{-1} S M$$

is called the splitting matrix. Carrying out the matrix multiplications, it is found

$$H_1 = \begin{bmatrix} 4 & 4 & 0 & 0 \\ 1 & 6 & 1 & 0 \\ 0 & 4 & 4 & 0 \\ 0 & 1 & 6 & 1 \end{bmatrix}$$

Hence the control point mesh corresponding to the subpatch in question is related to the old control point mesh by the expression

$$G_1 = H_1 G H_1^t \quad (3)$$

Referring now to Figure 1, the new face point labelled q is the (1,1) element of G. Carrying out the algebra of (3) gives

$$q_{11} = \frac{(p_{11} + p_{12} + p_{21} + p_{22})}{4} \quad (4)$$

Likewise, the point q_{12}, a new edge point, is given by

$$q_{12} = \frac{\frac{(C + D)}{2} + \frac{(p_{12} + p_{22})}{2}}{2} \quad (5)$$

where

$$q_{11} = C = \frac{(p_{11} + p_{12} + p_{21} + p_{22})}{4}$$

and

$$q_{13} = D = \frac{(p_{12} + p_{13} + p_{22} + p_{23})}{4}$$

The new vertex point, q_{22}, is given by

$$q_{22} = \frac{Q}{4} + \frac{R}{2} + \frac{p_{22}}{4} \quad (6)$$

where

$$Q = \frac{(q_{11} + q_{13} + q_{31} + q_{33})}{4}$$

and

$$R = \tfrac{1}{4}\left[\frac{(p_{22} + p_{12})}{2} + \frac{(p_{22} + p_{21})}{2} + \frac{(p_{22} + p_{32})}{2} + \frac{(p_{22} + p_{23})}{2}\right]$$

It is easily verified that each of the elements of G satisfies an expression similar to one of (4, 5, 6). Since these expressions were deduced from the standard B-spline basis, they generate a bicubic B-spline surface.

ARBITRARY TOPOLOGY

For the purposes of generalizing the expressions (4, 5, 6) to arbitrary topologies, it is convenient to express them as a set of rules which are dependent on the number of points around a face and on the number of edges incident to a vertex. Of course the rules must yield the expressions (4, 5, 6) when that number is four. The rules are:

(A) New face points — the average of all of the old points defining the face.
(B) New edge points — the average of the midpoints of the old edge with the average of the two new face points of the faces sharing the edge.
(C) New vertex points — the average

$$\frac{Q}{n} + \frac{2R}{n} + \frac{S(n-3)}{n}$$

where

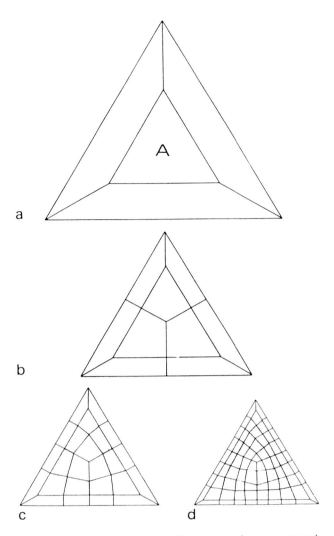

Figure 2. Result of applying rules to a simple nonrectangular topology

Q = the average of the new face points of all faces adjacent to the old vertex point.
R = the average of the midpoints of all old edges incident on the old vertex point.
S = old vertex point.

After these points have been computed, new edges are formed by

- connecting each new face point to the new edge points of the edges defining the old face
- connecting each new vertex point to the new edge points of all old edges incident on the old vertex point

New faces are then defined as those enclosed by new edges.

The results of applying these rules to a simple nonrectangular topology are shown in Figures 2(a,b,c,d). Figure 2a shows the original triangular region labelled A that will be approximated by a triangular surface *patch*. The other three regions around the perimeter of region A assist in defining the slope and curvature of the patch at its boundaries, as in a rectangular topology.

Figure 2b shows the result of applying the rules one time. Note that all new faces have four sides. However, now four vertex points have only 3 edges incident upon them. These are the three new vertex points corresponding to the original old vertices of the region A plus the new face point for the region. Following a suggestion by Coons, we refer to these points as *extraordinary* points because it is only at the final vertex points associated with these points that the resulting surface is not a standard B-spline surface.

Application of the rules once again yields Figure 2c. In this figure, six faces have emerged that have associated with them a set of 16 points that lie on a rectangular topology, as with the standard B-spline. Each of these faces has been shaded for clarity. Since the rules being applied generate a standard bicubic B-spline patch for points having this topology, these regions generate B-spline patches. Hence, a portion of the final triangular surface is now defined, and since bicubic B-splines that share vertices in this way are continuous in position, tangent and curvature, this portion of the surface is similarly continuous.

Applying the rules a third time results in further definition of B-spline surface patches near the extraordinary points, as shown in Figure 2d. The cross-hatched regions indicate where the new surface patches emerge with this application of the rules. Each of these new patches joins to the appropriate patches of Figure 2c with standard bicubic B-spline continuity. This is evident if we also subdivide the patches generated at that level; the points in common between patches dictate the continuity. However, since it is computationally more efficient to render standard patches by another algorithm, each time a standard B-spline patch is generated it is passed to a standard rendering algorithm.

It is clear that further application of the rules to the regions surrounding the extraordinary points will generate more standard patches near these points. In the limiting case, the entire triangular region, excluding the extraordinary points, is covered by a B-spline surface. Therefore, the triangular region is approximated by a surface that is continuous, except possibly at the extraordinary points. Since the rules hold for arbitrary topologies, the shape of the regions need not be simple triangles. Any number of sides will generate a B-spline surface except at the extraordinary points.

It should be noted that after one iteration all faces are four-sided, hence all new vertices created subsequently will have four incident edges. Therefore after one iteration the number of extraordinary points on the surface remains constant.

Figure 3. Surface generated from a tetrahedron

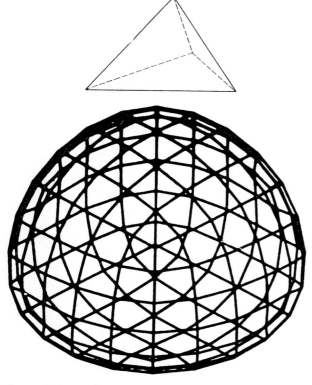

Figure 4. Original tetrahedron used to generate Figure 3 with line drawing of the generated surface

The authors would like to know the behaviour of the surface at the extraordinary points. At the present time they have not made an analytical proof of the continuity at these points. However, the pictures of the surfaces generated by these rules suggest that the surface is at least continuous in tangent everywhere.

Figure 3 shows a view of a surface generated using as a starting shape a tetrahedron, which is the smallest volume element that does not have a rectangular grid of control points. The surface is closed and has 8 extraordinary points, one for each original degree 3 vertex of the tetrahedron and one for each face, since each face yields a degree 3 vertex after the first application of the rules. The original tetrahedron used to generate Figure 3 is shown in Figure 4, along with a line drawing of the generated surface. It is evident from Figure 3 that the surface is continuous in tangent at the final vertex points corresponding to the original vertices of the tetrahedron.

Another grid of points is shown in Figure 5. This grid generates the closed volume shown in Figure 6.

The set of rules presented above is somewhat arbitrary. In fact initially a different rule was tried for (C). The new vertex point was

(C) (alternate) $\frac{Q}{4} + \frac{R}{2} + \frac{S}{4}$

The results using that rule were unsatisfactory in that the surface became too *pointy* for the tetrahedron. The pictures made using that rule motivated us to find a better set of rules, the best of which was presented above. A better set of rules, indeed, a better criterion for judging the rules than the qualitative appearance of a picture, is yet to be devised.

At the suggestion of M Sabin a net of points taken from the saddle $z = xy$ has been made. The centre polygon has eight sides. Figure 7 shows an orthogonal view along the z axis. After one iteration of the algorithm there is a vertex in the centre with 8 edges attached to it (Figures 8, 9). A shaded picture of the saddle shows that with a large number of edges around a saddle, the centre is not well behaved (Figure 10). The saddle demonstrates that the authors have not found the best set of rules.

BIQUADRATIC SURFACES

The method can also be applied to biquadratic B-splines. The subdivided net is generated by creating a new face for each face, edge, and vertex of the original net. In Figure 11 the heavy lines are the original net and the light lines are the new net. The rule for finding each new point is dependent on the corner it is near. After analysing the biquadratic subdivision in a manner similar to that described above it can be seen that in Figure 11

$$q_{11} = \frac{(9P_{11} + 3P_{12} + 3P_{21} + P_{22})}{16}$$

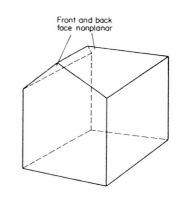

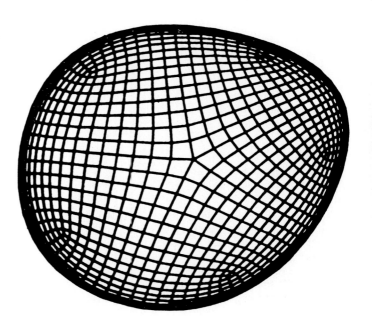

Figure 5. Grid of points

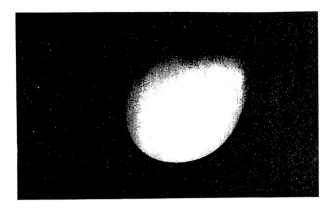

Figure 6. Closed volume generated from grid in Figure 5

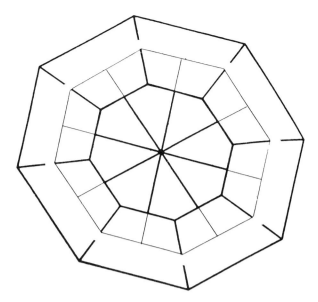

Figure 8. View of Figure 7 after one iteration

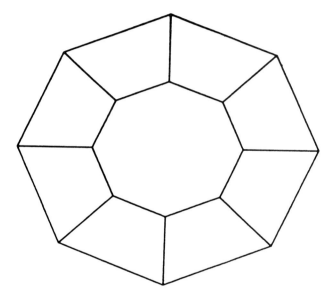

Figure 7. Orthogonal view along z axis of z=xy

This can be rewritten as a rule to find a new vertex q near an old vertex p

$$q = \frac{F}{n} + \frac{2E}{n} + \frac{P(n-3)}{n}$$

where

n = number of vertices in the face
F = the average of the vertices in the face
E = the average of the two edges incident on P

This rule can likewise be applied to any topology. In this case, after one iteration the number of non-four faces remains constant while all vertices have four incident-edges.

CONCLUSIONS

The methods presented in this paper generate B-spline surfaces on arbitrary meshes that are continuous except at a small number of *extraordinary* points. The pictures generated indicate that the surface is also continuous at these points, although no analytical proof of continuity is given.

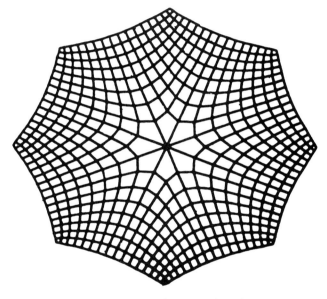

Figure 9. View of Figure 7 after many iterations

Figure 10. Shaded picture of the saddle

Other methods have been developed for approximating non-rectangular control-point meshes. For example, Lane and Riesenfeld[3] have presented an approach that is formulated in terms of a generalized basis function of two parametric variables. Also, Barnhill[4] describes a triangular patch approximation scheme. Neither of these approaches is the same as the method described in this paper.

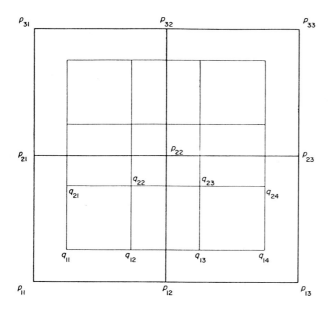

Figure 11. Biquadratic B-spline

In addition to the need for a proof of continuity at the extraordinary points of these surfaces, there is also a need for a coherent mathematical treatment of approximation schema on arbitrary topological meshes; such a treatment should encompass all of these approaches. It is hoped that this paper might stimulate such investigations.

REFERENCES

1 **Catmull, Edwin** 'A subdivision algorithm for computer display of curved surfaces' Technical Report UTEC-CSc-74-133, University of Utah, USA (1974)

2 **Riesenfeld, R F** 'On Chaikin's Algorithm' *Comput. Graph. Image Proc.* Vol 4 (1975) pp 304–310

3 **Lane, J M, Riesenfeld, R F** 'The application of total positivity to computer aided curve and surface design' Technical Report, Dept. of Computer Science, University of Utah, USA (1977)

4 **Barnhill, R E** 'Smooth interpolation over triangles' *Computer Adided Geometric Design* Academic Press (1974) pp 45–70

5 **Doo, D and Sabin, M** 'Analysis of the behaviour of recursive division surfaces' *Comput. Aided Des.* Vol 10 No 6 (November 1978) pp 356–360

Graphics and Image Processing

James Foley*
Editor

Computer Rendering of Stochastic Models

Alain Fournier
University of Toronto

Don Fussell
The University of Texas at Austin

Loren Carpenter
Lucasfilm

A recurrent problem in generating realistic pictures by computers is to represent natural irregular objects and phenomena without undue time or space overhead. We develop a new and powerful solution to this computer graphics problem by modeling objects as sample paths of stochastic processes. Of particular interest are those stochastic processes which previously have been found to be useful models of the natural phenomena to be represented. One such model applicable to the representation of terrains, known as "fractional Brownian motion," has been developed by Mandelbrot.

The value of a new approach to object modeling in computer graphics depends largely on the efficiency of the techniques used to implement the model. We introduce a new algorithm that computes a realistic, visually satisfactory approximation to fractional Brownian motion in faster time than with exact calculations. A major advantage of this technique is that it allows us to compute the surface to arbitrary levels of details without increasing the database. Thus objects with complex appearances can be displayed from a very small database. The character of the surface can be controlled by merely modifying a few parameters. A similar change allows complex motion to be created inexpensively.

CR Categories and Subject Descriptors: I.3.3. [**Computer Graphics**]: Picture/Image Generation—*display algorithms*; I.3.5. [**Computer Graphics**]: Computational Geometry and Object Modeling—*curve, surface, solid, and object representation*; I.3.7 [**Computer Graphics**]: Three Dimensional Graphics and Realism—*color, shading, shadowing, and texture.*

General Term: Algorithms

Additional Key Words and Phrases: fractals, terrain models, stochastic models

---

B. Mandelbrot, on whose work this paper is based, has raised certain objections which will be published in a subsequent issue.

This paper reports the results of two independent research efforts—one by Carpenter and the other by Fournier and Fussell. They both submitted papers to the 1980 SIGGRAPH conference, and through the conference to *CACM*. Both papers were accepted for *CACM* with the understanding that the authors would consolidate their work into a single integrated and definitive piece.—J. Foley.

* Former editor of Graphics and Image Processing. Robert Haralick is the current editor of this department, which has recently been renamed Image Processing and Computer Vision (see April '82 *Communications*, pp 311–312.)

Alain Fournier and Don Fussell's work was performed at The University of Texas at Dallas, and was partially supported by NSF Grant MCS-79-01168 and facilitated by the use of the Theory Net, NSF Grant MCS-78-01689. Loren Carpenter's work was performed while at Boeing Computer Services.

Authors' Present Addresses: A. Fournier, Computer Systems Research Group, 121 St Joseph St, University of Toronto, Toronto, Ontario M5S 1A1; D. Fussell, Department of Computer Science, The University of Texas at Austin, Austin, Texas 78712; L. Carpenter, Lucasfilm, P. O. Box 2009, San Rafael, California 94912.

Permission to copy without fee all or part of this material is granted provided that the copies are not made or distributed for direct commercial advantage, the ACM copyright notice and the title of the publication and its date appear, and notice is given that copying is by permission of the Association for Computing Machinery. To copy otherwise, or to republish, requires a fee and/or specific permission.
© 1982 ACM 0001-0782/82/0600-0371 $00.75.

1. Introduction

Traditional modeling techniques used in computer graphics have been based on the assumption that objects are essentially a collection of smooth surfaces which can be mathematically described by deterministic functions. The simplest such technique assumes that objects are collections of polygons whose surfaces are obviously described by linear functions. Greater flexibility is achieved by the use of surfaces which are described by higher-order polynomials, as with Bezier [1] or B-spline surface patches [12].

These techniques have been quite successful in rendering realistic images of artificial objects, with their relatively simple macroscopic characteristics and their regularly periodic surface features. Natural objects, such as stones, clouds, trees, terrain, etc. are characterized in general by no such regular features or simple macroscopic structures, and these methods have been less effective in modeling them.

Macroscopic features of natural objects are often represented explicitly using large amounts of data. In the case of terrain, the information is usually obtained from contour maps, and in some fashion transformed into a surface represented by a large number of polygons [11]. Similarly, smoke has been modeled as volumes containing very large numbers of points distributed according to certain theoretical functions used in the study of smoke formation [8]. In both cases, capturing the macroscopic features to be modeled involves significant time and/or space requirements and the use of specialized techniques that are not generally applicable to other types of natural features. The problem is that these conceptually simple objects require a large number of modeling primitives (points, polygons, or patches) because they are visually quite complex. On the other hand, a conceptually or technologically complex object, like an airplane, can be very effectively modeled with a smaller number of such primitives.

Using a completely different approach, small-scale textures of natural objects have generally been modeled by some single repetitive texture function mapped onto all patches comprising such an object. However, the regularity of the effect detracts considerably from a natural appearance.

A fundamental limitation of these approaches is that objects are modeled at a predetermined, fixed scale regardless of its suitability for any particular viewing distance. Thus, from sufficiently far away, all but the most large-scale changes in terrain modeled by a fixed set of polygons may be invisible, rendering a large portion of the database and the processing required to display it superfluous. Likewise, a view of such terrain from very close up may reveal no more than a flat, featureless portion of a polygon, lacking any cues that it does indeed represent terrain. The latter problem may be alleviated somewhat by texture mapping, but with the usual static texture definitions it is still possible to get too close for the resolution of the texture pattern.

In many applications in which natural phenomena are to be represented, one is primarily interested in achieving sufficient realism in the representation of the objects for their nature to be easily recognizable. The specific features of any such objects on all but the most macroscopic scale are of secondary importance. For example, in a computer-generated animated sequence we may wish to have a mountain range which is obviously a mountain range but which is not intended to correspond to any particular real-world mountains. In such a case, we are interested only in the general size, shape, and position of the mountain range as specific features to be modeled explicitly. In order to make such an "object" recognizable as a mountain range, we would like to generate the macroscopic features that any typical mountain range would have. It would be advantageous to have a technique that would allow us to do this without the use of a large database to represent the object. In applications where one wishes to display real-world data, the addition of suitable information at various scales may be used to enhance realism. For example, in flight simulators, various types of terrain are represented by a few large polygons whose color, shape, and position provide vague cues as to their nature. If a pseudo-random rocky texture could be added to surfaces representing mountainous terrain, much more realistic images could be generated. The use of an extremely large, detailed database for such purposes would be prohibitive, while the use of traditional, deterministic texture mapping techniques would not be fully satisfactory.

The representation of motion in computer graphics systems has suffered, less obviously, from a similar limitation. Previous attempts to represent turbulent motion have been limited by the apparent complexity of the task. An effective means of generating an irregular surface with an irregular motion in a flexible way will allow the solution of such problems as realistically modeling a waterfall, rapids, or ocean waves, all of which present serious challenges to computer graphics researchers [19], [24].

All of the drawbacks mentioned above result primarily because most traditional models of real-world phenomena in computer graphics are totally deterministic in philosophy. There have been some exceptions, however. Early work by Mezei et al. [20] generated textures and irregular shapes by random techniques, and Blinn [2] improved the realism of previous shading methods by using a model based on probabilistic assumptions. Also, research in image analysis and pattern recognition has produced a body of results on the statistical analysis of texture as well as some interesting examples of image synthesis using stochastic techniques [10], [23], [21].

We propose to extend the flexibility of the mathematical modeling techniques in computer graphics by generalizing the assumptions made about the characteristics of an object's surface and of its motion. Our basic approach is to model both primitives and their motion as a combination of both deterministic and stochastic features. Thus the surface of an object may be a polynomial function of a set of predetermined locations, or it may be a stochastic function of those locations, or both. Likewise, the motion of an object may be described as a smooth function interpolating its initial and final positions, or it may vary irregularly along the way. In this paper, we introduce simple and efficient techniques for rendering a large class of stochastic models which can be used to represent a variety of natural phenomena.

2. Stochastic Models

In a traditional graphics system, the modeling system is the part where the objects are defined in terms of the basic building blocks: the modeling primitives. The modeling primitives mainly used have been points, lines, polygons, and parametric patches. We define here a new kind of modeling primitive.

A stochastic model of an object (or more generally of a phenomenon, to extend the concept of an object to include possibly a time parameter), is defined to be a model where the object is represented by a sample path (a realization) of some stochastic process of one of more variables.

Stochastic objects can be made from several stochastic modeling primitives just as traditional deterministic objects are built from, for example, polygons or parametric patches. Also, since the class of stochastic processes properly includes the deterministic functions, the definition of stochastic models includes all previously used primitives.

Table I. Possible Applications of Stochastic Models.

Dimension of Primitive	Dimension of Stochastic Process (number of parameters)			
	One-D Process	Two-D Process	Three-D Process	Four-D Process
1	Intensity on a line, Intensity in time	Scalar field	Intensity in 3-D space	Intensity in 3-D space in time
2	Direction on a plane, Surface in time	2-D vector on a surface	Intensity and altitude on a surface	Intensity and altitude on a surface in time
3	Direction in space in time, Color in time	Normal to a surface, Color on a surface	Color in space, Vector field in 3-D space	Color in space in time, Moving vectors

At the level of resolution normally used, the natural objects to be modeled can be taken to be continuous and will need continuous stochastic processes to model them. Since ultimately the models will be used for display on discrete devices, it is very convenient to have a means of computing a discrete sample of the continuous model at the rate required by the resolution of the image. This would usually correspond to the Nyquist rate, but if anti-aliasing is needed the rate of sampling can be chosen to be higher.

It is now clear that the three elements required for stochastic modeling are: (1) an appropriate object (phenomenon) to be modeled; (2) a stochastic process to model it with; (3) an algorithm to compute the sample paths of this process.

Objects that have features with stochastic properties that are strong enough so that appreciable savings in both storage and processing are obtained by replacing the stored values for the stochastic features by the few parameters needed by the definition of the stochastic process are likely to be represented most effectively using stochastic models. To use signal processing terminology, an object which has a high noise/signal ratio is a good candidate. It should be noted, however, that the stochastic process might model what at first appears to be signal, as will be seen in the example given below.

The stochastic process to be used can have two kinds of origin.

—It can be a legitimate mathematical model of the phenomenon to be modeled. A model in computer graphics is not normally required to be a mathematical model, but, of course, it does not hurt if it is. The example given for terrain falls into this category.

—The stochastic process can be empirically chosen, with the parameters determined to fit a particular application. Techniques need to be developed which employ some sort of canonical stochastic processes, to be used in stochastic approximation the same way power functions, for example, are used in curve fitting.

Since the stochastic process used can be analytically defined, many traditional algorithmic techniques can be considered as means to compute the sample paths. One of the most effective for display purposes is the recursive subdivision technique, introduced by Catmull [5] for parametric patches, and most notably used by Clark [7] and Lane et al. [13]. The same technique can be used in the context of stochastic modeling, and the advantages are even more important here.

—The depth of the recursion will be controlled by the on-screen resolution, giving two important benefits. We never run out of details, since the process can always generate new data as we close in. We never produce more details than necessary, therefore the computational effort is always commensurate with the on-screen image complexity.

—The basic computational step in the recursive subdivision uses an interpolation formula. Interpolation formulas are in general much easier to compute than incremental ones, especially those for midpoint interpolation, therefore further lowering the computational cost.

Depending upon the phenomenon being modeled, the stochastic process will have dimensions from 1–4, and the computed sample path, or more exactly the stochastic element computed from the sample path will have dimensions from 1–3. The various possibilities are in Table I, and some of the applications are indicated. Since in addition the stochastic element can be composed with various deterministic modeling primitives, the development of a wide range of new modeling techniques will be required, and some new computational issues will be raised.

The following sections address these issues in the context of one particularly useful and interesting stochastic model.

3. Fractals: A Stochastic Terrain Model

Perhaps the most common natural phenomenon to be represented in current applications of computer graphics is terrain. Since terrain is generally characterized by randomly distributed features that are recognizable by their overall properties as opposed to specific macroscopic features (as in the case of the mountain range example), its strong stochastic properties make it a good choice for the application of a stochastic model.

As noted above, we require a stochastic process that is appropriate for modeling terrain and an algorithm for computing sample paths of the process. In the following section we describe a suitable process for modeling terrains as well as a variety of other natural phenomena. We will then proceed in the subsequent section to develop new techniques for rendering the sample paths and for the construction of stochastic primitives which are especially suited for use in computer graphics.

3.1 Fractional Brownian Motion

In 1968, Mandelbrot and van Ness introduced the term "fractional Brownian motion" (which will be abbreviated to fBm) to denote a family of one-dimensional Gaussian stochastic processes which provide useful models for many natural time series [14]. Since then, multidimensional extensions of fBm have been studied by Mandelbrot as models of a wide range of natural phenomena, including in particular terrains (in two dimensions) and the isosurfaces (positions in space at which some parameter has equal value) of turbulent fluids [16].

We give a brief description of fBm. Let u be a real parameter such that $-\infty < u < \infty$, and let w be the set of all values of a random function taken from a sample space W. Ordinary Brownian motion, $B(u, w)$ is a real random function with independent Gaussian increments such that $B(u + \Delta, w) - B(u, w)$ has mean zero and variance σ^2 and $B(u_2, w) - B(u_1, w)$ is independent of $B(u_4, w) - B(u_3, w)$ whenever the intervals (u_1, u_2) and (u_3, u_4) do not overlap. Let H be a real parameter such that $0 < H < 1$ and let b_0 be an arbitrary real number. The random function $B_H(u, w)$, called reduced fractional Brownian motion, is defined by

$$B_H(0, w) = b_0$$

$$B_H(u, w) - B_H(0, w) = [1/\Gamma(H + 0.5)]$$
$$\left\{ \int_{-\infty}^{0} [(u - s)^{H-0.5} - (-s)^{H-0.5}] \, dB(s, w) \right.$$
$$\left. + \int_{0}^{u} (u - s)^{H-0.5} \, dB(s, w) \right\}$$

Thus $B_H(u, w)$ is a moving average of $B(u, w)$ weighted by $(u - s)^{H-0.5}$. Note that $B_{0.5}(u, w) = B(u, w)$, so when $H = 0.5$ we obtain ordinary Brownian motion. Thus we have a family of random functions whose values at any value of u depend upon all past values of u.

As for ordinary Brownian motion, the increments of fBm are stationary. Typical sample paths for $H = 0.5$ (ordinary Brownian motion), $H = 0.3$, and $H = 0.7$ are given in Figs. 1, 2, and 3.

A Fourier analysis of samples of such functions shows no dominant frequency, but rather a range of frequencies at all orders of magnitude. Fractional Brownian motions are members of the class of "1:f noises" [14], that is, those signals in which the contribution of each frequency to the power spectrum is nearly inversely proportional to the frequency. Additionally, the increments of fBm are statistically self-similar. This means formally that $B_H(u + \Delta u, w) - B_H(u, w)$ and $h^{-H}[B_H(u + h\Delta u, w) - B_H(u, w)]$ have the same finite joint distribution functions. Intuitively these features of fBm indicate that we may observe a sample of one of these functions at any scale and perceive identical statistical features. A surface generated using fBm would thus possess macroscopic features up to the order of magnitude of the overall surface generated, corresponding to the lowest possible frequencies in the Fourier spectrum of the sample, as well as arbitrarily small surface detail, corresponding to the higher frequencies in the Fourier spectrum.

Fig. 1. Ordinary Brownian Motion ($H = 0.5$).

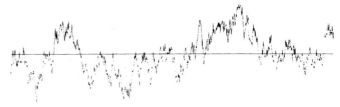

Fig. 2. Fractional Brownian Motion ($H = 0.3$).

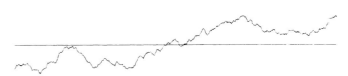

Fig. 3. Fractional Brownian Motion ($H = 0.7$).

3.2 Algorithms For Realizing Models Based On FBm

3.2.1 Algorithmic Requirements

In order for fractional Brownian motion to be generally useful for modeling in computer graphics, appropriate algorithms for computing its sample paths must be found. Since high quality images of complex scenes typically require that on the order of 10^6 sample points be generated, the efficiency of any such algorithm is obviously of critical importance. Not only should the asymptotic complexity of the algorithm be linear in the number of sample points generated, but the amount of computation involved in generating each sample point must also be as small as possible.

Although it is important, efficiency alone is not sufficient to make a sample path generating algorithm appropriate for use in graphics. In order to achieve the flexibility of deterministic models used in graphics, objects should be modeled piecewise as collections of stochastic primitives. Any modeling primitives in computer graphics must have two properties in order to be useful. The first of these, which we call *internal consistency*, is the reproducibility of the primitive at any position in an appropriate coordinate space and at any level of detail. That is, a modeling primitive should be rendered in such a way that its features do not depend on its position or orientation in space. In addition, the features visible when the primitive is rendered at high magnification should be consistent with those rendered at a coarser scale. For deterministic primitives of any type, scale consistency is easily maintained on smooth curves or surfaces. Likewise, positional consistency (modulo the aliasing problem) is easy to maintain for primitives such as points, lines, or polygons, and for higher-order curves and surfaces has been achieved through the use of parametric definitions. Internal consistency of either type is, however, more difficult to maintain for stochastic sample paths and requires more care in the design of generating algorithms.

The other crucial property of modeling primitives is what we term *external consistency*. This refers to the continuity properties of adjacent modeling primitives. If modeling primitives are intended to share a common boundary, it must be possible to ensure that they are indeed continuous across this boundary at any scale at which they may be rendered. Additional consistency constraints such as derivative or higher-order surface continuity may be required in some cases, and other properties such as color may be subject to consistency constraints across primitives. As with internal consistency, this property has been easily maintained in the rendering of first-order primitives, although it has presented a serious research concern in the design of efficient algorithms for rendering higher-order deterministic curves and surfaces [7], [13]. Again, the problem of maintaining external consistency promises to be an even more serious concern in the design of algorithms for rendering stochastic primitives.

Let us again note here that when rendering any continuous analytically defined curve or surface, we are actually calculating a discrete set of sample points from the surface. These points are generally only approximations to the surface since even for deterministic functions the limited word size of a computer allows only for approximate representation of arbitrary real numbers. In computing sample paths of stochastic functions, it is often the case that only approximations can be calculated efficiently or at all, even leaving aside the numerical problems just mentioned. Nevertheless, such approximations are acceptable provided they are sufficiently good, which in computer graphics means that they meet visual criteria of indistinguishability from the actual sample paths. Indeed, since the process we are applying is a good model of terrain only on the basis of empirical statistical tests and not because they are derived from a theoretical model of terrain formation, any approximation which is sufficiently good to pass our visual test may itself be likely to be an equally good model by these statistical tests. In any case, visual acceptability as opposed to statistical criteria will be the basis on which we judge the quality of an approximation algorithm for graphical use.

3.2.2 Previous Algorithms

Mandelbrot has published a number of methods for calculating discrete approximations to fBm in various dimensions. These involve three basic approaches: a shear displacement process, a modified Markov process, and an inverse Fourier transformation.

The first uses the fact that fBm is the limit of a fractional Poisson field [17]. A fractional Poisson field in n-dimensions is a scalar field where at each point $\mathbf{P}$ the value of $F(\mathbf{P})$ is the sum of an infinite collection of steps (in the case of terrain, these steps can be seen as straight faults) whose directions, locations, and amplitudes are three sequences of mutually independent random variables. This method was used by Mandelbrot to generate the first computer simulation of a fractional Brownian surface. While it has solid theoretical foundations and has been used to produce striking pictures, it is not suitable for our applications, both for its $O(N^3)$ time complexity for surfaces, and for the fact that it is not clear that it could be adapted to our boundary constraints.

The second method is based on an algorithm to compute an approximation to discrete fractional Gaussian noise, which is the increment of fBm [15]. The algorithm computes what Mandelbrot called fast fractional Gaussian noise (ffGn) as a sum of a low frequency term and a high frequency term. The high frequency term is a Markov–Gauss process. The low frequency term is a weighted sum of M Markov–Gauss processes, M being a number proportional to $\log(N)$. The fast fractional Gaussian noise algorithm represents a considerable improvement in the computation of linear fBm, since its time complexity is $O(N\log(N))$ and its parameters can be adjusted to suit the observed time series if it is to be used in statistical analysis. Although some objection to the use of a two-dimensional extension to this method may be made on the grounds that its time complexity is greater than linear, a much more serious objection is that it appears that there is no valid extension of the method to two dimensions. Also, there seems to be no obvious method to adjust the computation to the needed resolution while maintaining any consistency.

The third approach, which also gives an $O(N\log(N))$ time complexity involves the generation of Gaussian white noise, in which all frequencies are equally represented, and then filtering it using fast Fourier transform techniques in order to force the different frequencies to fall off as required by the value of the parameter H for the particular fractional Gaussian noise desired. Fourier techniques were used by R. Voss to illustrate [18].

Each of the methods discussed above has its own theoretical and practical advantages. However, they have in common the drawbacks that their time complexity is greater than linear and that the basic operations involved in their computation are costly (involving transcendental functions). We will now present our own method for computing an approximation to fBm which avoids these drawbacks.

3.2.3 A Recursive Subdivision Algorithm

We have noted above the three basic requirements that an approximation algorithm appropriate for stochastic modeling must meet, and we have discussed the advantages of the recursive subdivision algorithms for rendering models of any type in computer graphics. We now present such a recursive algorithm for generating approximations to the sample paths of one-dimensional fBm.

In order to be able to use this type of algorithm, the crucial requirement is that the distribution of the process for which samples are to be computed can be interpolated from the boundary points of the sample. Since one of the features of fBm is an infinite span of interdependence, it is not *a priori* obvious that such an approach would be successful. However, two facts help design an approximation algorithm.

—Fractional Brownian motion is self-similar. This means, as stated above, that the increments of $B_H(u)$ (for simplicity of notation, we will henceforth use $B_H(u)$ instead of $B_H(u, w)$) are such that $B_H(u + \Delta u) - B_H(u)$ and $B_H(u + h\Delta u) - B_H(u)$ have the same distribution if the latter is rescaled by a factor of h^{-H}, H being the self-similarity parameter.

—A formula exists [14] for the conditional expectation of $B_H(u)$, $0 \leq u \leq 1$, knowing $B_H(0) = 0$ and $B_H(1) = 1$: $E[B_H(u)|B_H(1)] = \frac{1}{2}(u^{2H} + 1 - |u - 1|^{2H})$. When $u = \frac{1}{2}$, the right-hand side becomes $\frac{1}{2}$ independently of H.

These two properties give an estimate of the expected value and the variance of the increment of the process, which is all that is needed, since the process is Gaussian.

An algorithm designed using these properties is given below in Pascal. The function GAUSS(seed, index) returns a Gaussian random variable with zero mean and unit variance. It uses the variable "seed" as its seed. Explicit control over this seed is given in order to allow for external consistency as discussed below.

Declarations in main program:
    type result = array [0..maxsize] of real;
    var maxlevel, seed, i:integer; scale, h:real; Fh:result;
Procedure called:
    procedure fractal (maxlevel, seed:integer; h, scale:real);
    var first, last:integer;
        ratio, std:real;
    procedure subdivide (f1, f2:integer; std:real);
        var fmid:integer; stmid:real;
    begin
        fmid := (f1 + f2) div 2;
        if (fmid <> f1) & (fmid <> f2) then
            begin
                Fh [fmid] := (Fh [f1] + Fh [f2])/2.0 + gauss (seed, fmid)*
                      std;
                stdmid := std * ratio;
                subdivide (f1, fmid, stdmid);
                subdivide (fmid, f2, stdmid);
            end
    end; /* subdivide */
begin
    first := 0;
    last := 2↑maxlevel;
    Fh [first] := gauss (seed, first) * scale;
    Fh [last] := gauss (seed, last) * scale;
    ratio := 2↑ − h;
    std := scale * ratio;
    subdivide (first, last, std)
end; /* fractal */

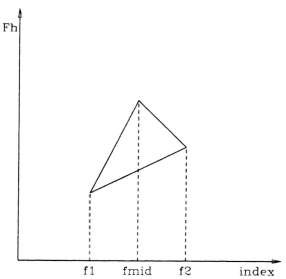

Fig. 4. Computation of a Scalar Value by Subdivision.

The algorithm recursively subdivides the interval [first, last] and generates a scalar value at the midpoint which is proportional to the current standard deviation times the scale or "roughness" factor (see Fig. 4). h is a parameter which determines the "fractal dimension" of the sequence output by the algorithms. (For a definition and discussion of fractal dimension, see [18].) It is equivalent to the H of fBm and can take on values between 0 and 1. Maxlevel determines the level of recursion needed. This algorithm is suitable for parametric applications since the recursion subdivides a parameter space into equal intervals. A similar algorithm which operates directly in a two-dimensional object space is given below. This algorithm is particularly suited for nonparametric subdivision.

    procedure fractal(t1, t2, epsilon, h, scale:real; seed:integer);
    var f1, f2, ratio, std:real;
    procedure subdivide (f1, f2, t1, t2, std:real);
        var tmid, fmid:real;
    begin
        if (t2 − t1) > epsilon then
            begin
                tmid := (t1 + t2)/2.0;
                fmid := (f1 + f2)/2.0
                      + std*gauss(seed, tmid);
                std := std*ratio;
                subdivide (f1, fmid, t1, tmid, std);
                subdivide(fmid, f1, tmid, t1, std)
            end
        else output (f1, t1, f2, t2)
    end /* subdivide */
begin
    f1 := gauss(seed, t1) scale;
    f2 := gauss(seed, t2) scale;
    ratio := 2↑ − h;
    std := scale*ratio;
    subdivide (f1, f2, t1, t2, std)
end; /* fractal */

The sequence of scalar displacements generated gives an approximate sample path of one-dimensional fBm of parameter R. Unlike fBm, this approximation is neither stationary, isotropic, nor self-similar, as pointed out by B. Mandelbrot. This sample path can be used to create

Fig. 5. Typical Curve Obtained at Two Resolutions. h = 0.8, 17, and 257 sample points.

Fig. 6. Using the Scalar Value to Compute a Curve in the Plane.

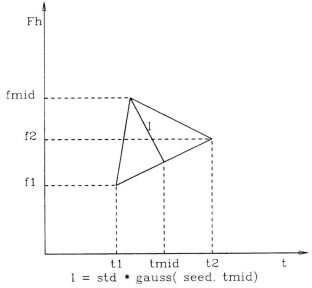

stochastic primitives as needed, as discussed in the following section. The graphs of Fig. 5 show typical samples at two resolutions for h = 0.6 and for 257 and 17 sample points. The two graphs are then from the same sample paths, but sampled by computation at different rates. This ability of the algorithm to generate discrete sample paths only at the rate needed makes it ideal for the purposes of stochastic modeling.

It is easy to see that the number of steps in the algorithm is a linear function of N, the number of sample points computed. Moreover, the amount of computation required to generate each sample point is small, requiring in the second case only 4 real additions, 1 subtraction, 3 real multiplications, and two divisions by 2 in addition to the generation of the pseudo-random variable. This makes it superior to the methods discussed above in terms of efficiency. By tying the random numbers generated at the endpoints to the values of t1 and t2, external consistency can be ensured since any adjacent sample paths generated with this algorithm would have the same endpoints. Internal consistency with respect to scale is assured by tying the seeds of the random number generator to the positions of the points calculated. Of course, internal consistency with respect to position is violated in this case unless t1 and t2 are assumed to be parametric variables and hence not subject to positional change. This can be avoided by using point-specific indices to compute the seed instead of the position, and using t1, t2 only for recursion control.

4. Applications of the Model

4.1 Creation of Stochastic Primitives

The most generally useful application of a stochastic model in graphics is in the construction of stochastic modeling primitives, which can be used for piecewise construction of objects with stochastic features. We describe in this section the construction of one and two-dimensional modeling primitives based on our recursive fBm sample path generator. We also discuss appropriate applications for these primitives and give examples.

4.1.1 One-Dimensional Primitives

The algorithm given in Sec. 3 for generating our approximations to fBm can be viewed as the construction of a "fractal polyline" primitive from an initial deterministic line segment. Of course, all displacements generated can either be viewed as offset vectors in the y direction of a two-dimensional coordinate system as indicated in Fig. 4 or simply as scalar displacements as mentioned above. In the former case, rather unsatisfactory primitives are generated since displacements are tied to the coordinate system rather than the line segment from which the displacement occurs. To eliminate this coordinate system dependency, it is better to take the scalar displacement of the midpoint at each step in the recursion, and use it as an offset from that midpoint along a vector normal to the original line segment. This construction is illustrated in Fig. 6. The only inherent directionality in the resulting curve is that imparted by the slope of the original line segment at the highest level of detail. Figure 7 shows a typical curve resulting from such a procedure, with h = 0.5, with 2, 5, and 257 points.

In order to construct continuous curves from these fractal polylines the displacements of the endpoints of

Fig. 7. Typical Curve Obtained. h = 0.5, 0, 3, and 255 interpolated points.

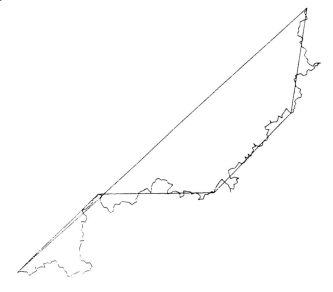

Fig. 8. Construction for a Parametric Curve.

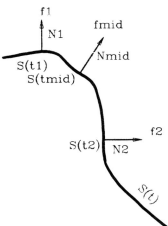

Fig. 9. Australia: 8 Sample Points.

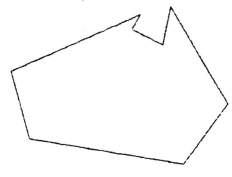

Fig. 10. Stochastic Interpolation. 8 original points and 8 × 127 interpolated points (h = 0.5).

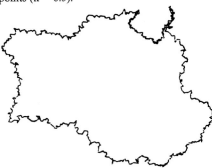

Fig. 11. Stochastic Interpolation. (h = 0.7).

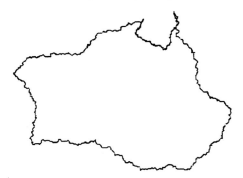

the initial line segment should be fixed at 0. This makes it trivial to guarantee the zero-order continuity of the curve produced. Higher orders of continuity of the fractal surface are meaningful only in a statistical sense since fBm has no derivative at any point [14]. It may be desirable to construct fractal curves based on smooth curves rather than the perimeters of polygons. In this case, the initial curve can be constructed piecewise, for instance, from either interpolating or approximating splines [12]. In this way, various statistical orders of continuity can be assured for this curve with derivative continuity being the most interesting. The scalar sequence generated by the subdivision process can be considered as displacements along vectors normal to the base curve at the appropriate midpoints in parameter space of the curve, as shown in Fig. 8. A more expensive alternative is to let the original spline curve be subdivided into two new spline curves with the original midpoint in parameter space becoming their common boundary and a new set of control points being generated. This common point is then displaced the generated random scalar distance along the common normal to the two curves at their boundary by displacing the adjacent end control points of the curves appropriately.

Any of the fractal polyline primitives constructed in these ways can be combined in arbitrary ways to construct representations of natural phenomena. For instance, the course of an imaginary river as it appears on a map could be generated using an appropriate value of h and level of scale. The instantaneous configuration of a bolt of lightning is also an appropriate candidate, as illustrated in the film *Vol Libre* [4]. An imaginary coastline on a map can also be created from fractal polylines like those of Fig. 7.

A more interesting application allows fractal primitives based on real data to be constructed using a technique we will call "stochastic interpolation." For instance, consider the polygon of Fig. 9 whose 8 vertices are sample points digitized from a map of Australia. The polygon is obtained as a linear interpolation of the positions of adjacent pairs of endpoints. However, it is well known that the coastline of Australia is very irregular when viewed at most any magnification, and so the regular polygon, although maybe recognizable as Australia by its overall shape, is not very realistic and looks nothing like the representation of the coastline presented on any reasonably accurate map. Moreover, empirical data suggests that the stochastic characteristics of Australia's coastline are nearly identical to those of one-dimensional fBm with $H = 0.87$ [18], [22]. Figures 10–13 show fractal polylines generated from the line segments of Fig. 9, with various values of h. All of them are much more realistic than Fig. 9, and Fig. 12 looks so real that those of us ignorant in geography would have difficulty arguing that this is not in fact the coastline of Australia traced from a map. Note that h in Fig. 12 is very close to the empirically measured value.

The visual evidence just cited provides a very strong argument that coastlines are best represented by curves

Fig. 12. Stochastic Interpolation. (h = 0.87).

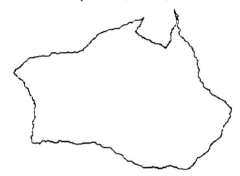

Fig. 13. Stochastic Interpolation (h = 1.0).

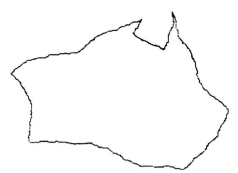

with matching stochastic properties. All the real data obtained by digitizing the map is present in all of Figs. 9–13 since the endpoints of the line segments are not displaced in any case, but the stochastic interpolated curves give a much truer picture of Australia's coastline than a polygon does. In general, for natural phenomena with random, irregular characteristics, it can be argued that the quality of an interpolation between real sample points obtained from that phenomenon should be judged by the correspondence of its stochastic properties with those of the real sample itself.

4.1.2 Two-Dimensional Primitives

One of the most useful applications of a stochastic model in a three-dimensional environment is the representation of irregular surfaces, in this case, terrains. As in one-dimensional modeling, we wish to define a surface which is stochastic rather than deterministic, which at the same time maintains all the nice properties of the surface models currently most useful in computer graphics. We present two somewhat different approaches to the construction of two-dimensional fractal surface primitives. The first is based on a subdivision of polygons to create "fractal polygons" similar to the fractal polylines described above. The second is to define a stochastic parametric surface.

4.1.2.1 Polygon Subdivision. Consider a scene in which all surfaces consist of triangles. This type of model is very commonly used to represent real-world data which has been acquired automatically [11]. Each triangle can be subdivided into four smaller triangles by connecting the midpoints of the sides of the triangles. If the positions in three-space of these midpoints is obtained by a fractal polyline subdivision step given above, a single step in the rendering of a "fractal triangle" is obtained. These subdivisions can be continued until a level of scale is reached in which no triangle has a side exceeding a specified length. The original triangle is now a fractal triangle whose irregular surface consists of many small triangular facets.

A quadrilateral can be subdivided in a slightly more complex way. Generate the midpoint of each of the four sides using fractal polyline subdivision. For each of the two pairs of opposed midpoints, displace the midpoint of the line connecting them using the same procedure. The midpoint of the line connecting these two "midpoints" becomes the center point of the quadrilateral subdivision and four smaller quadrilaterals are generated. This process is continued as with triangles until the desired resolution is obtained, resulting in a fractal quadrilateral whose surface is composed of many quadrilateral facets.

If a scene is modeled by a mesh of triangles or quadrilaterals which are to be rendered as stochastic primitives using polygon subdivision, some care must be taken to ensure internal and external consistency. Internal consistency with respect to position requires that the seeds of the random number generator be indexed by some sort of invariant point identifiers rather than by functions dependent on the positions of the points. Internal consistency with respect to scale requires that the same random numbers be generated in the same order at each level of the subdivision, as before. External consistency is a bit trickier. Since adjacent polygons share a common boundary which must be subdivided, this subdivision must generate the same points on that boundary for both polygons. An obvious requirement is that the same random displacements must be generated on each boundary, which can be accomplished again by tying the seeds of the random number generator to identifers of points on the boundary, making certain that the same identifiers are assigned to the corresponding points in the representation of each polygon's boundary. However, if these displacements are allowed to be in a direction normal to the surface of the original polygon, problems arise when the adjacent polygons are not coplanar, as is generally the case. This is illustrated in Fig. 14. A solution is to calculate the normal of each point in the mesh as the average of the normals of the polygons containing it. Points randomly displaced along these normals will coincide when calculated for adjacent polygons, as desired. Of course, a similar problem exists for every new point calculated in the subdivision, even those completely internal to an original polygon. This can either be solved the same way, calculating the normals during the subdivision, or, less expensively, by letting all displacements be in a direction normal to the original polygon instead of averaging the normals of adjacent polygons created by subdivision.

Fig. 14. Gap Created by Tangent Discontinuity at the Boundary Between Two Polygons (0 original points, × interpolated points).

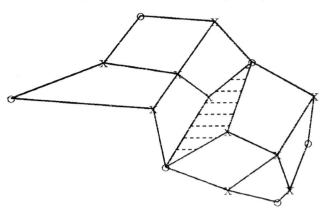

Fig. 15. Surface Produced Using the Stochastically Interpolated Points as Control Points for a B-spline Surface.

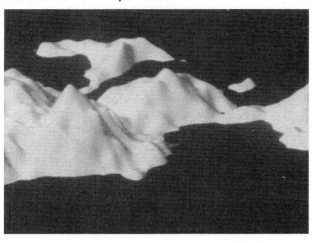

The primary advantage to this approach is the speed with which calculations can be done since only linear functions need be used. It does generate a surface which is self-similar within the range of scale covered by the subdivision and which does have a fractal dimension when carried to the limit. Thus its statistical properties are similar to those of two-dimensional fBm [14], although a better method for approximating fBm is given below. One important difference is that the surface generated in the limit is Markovian (for two-dimensional continuous processes, this means the values of opposite sides of an arbitrary boundary are independent given the boundary), while fBm, in which all sample points are correlated with all others, is not Markovian. As we have stated, however, our primary criterion is visual, and these methods can produce striking pictures of many terrains. The foreground of the cover picture, for instance, was produced using triangle subdivision. The most serious pitfall in using this method to produce good pictures is that derivative discontinuities across adjacent polygons can be annoyingly obvious in pictures that are not smooth shaded if the roughness factor used in the subdivision is not carefully chosen. (Note that smooth shading pictures of rugged terrain has a tendency to destroy the character of the surface.) The Markovian nature of the process, with no correlation between non-neighboring points, also tends to lead to the occasional generation of new polygons with radically divergent normals relative to other neighboring polygons during the subdivision process unless the random number generator is carefully constrained. Another way to obtain smooth surfaces is to use the computed stochastic points as control points of parametric patches, as was done to produce Fig. 15.

4.1.2.2 Stochastic Parametric Surfaces. Stochastic surface primitives can be created by extending deterministic parametric primitives as well as by polygon subdivision. In this case, we wish to define a surface description which is stochastic in nature rather than deterministic, which at the same time maintains the nice properties of the models currently most useful to represent complex objects in computer graphics. It is natural then, to consider functions of the form $\mathbf{X}(u, v) = \mathbf{P}(u, v) + \mathbf{R}(u, v, w)$,
where $\mathbf{P}(u, v)$ is a vector-valued polynomial in u and v and $\mathbf{R}(u, v, w)$ is a vector-valued random function on the sample space space $\mathbf{W}$, $w \varepsilon \mathbf{W}$. Thus $\mathbf{X}(u, v)$ is a two-dimensional stochastic process which we call *a stochastic surface function*. Intuitively, $\mathbf{P}(u, v)$ provides a way of defining the overall position of the surface while $\mathbf{R}(u, v, w)$ causes a stochastic variation in that position over the range of the parameters u and v.

$\mathbf{P}(u, v)$ can be any deterministic parametric function of two dimensions such as a bicubic or bilinear patch. $\mathbf{R}(u, v, w)$ is a vector normal to $\mathbf{P}(u, v)$ whose length is a random scalar $r(u, v, w)$. The calculation of $\mathbf{P}(u, v)$ and its normal are well-understood procedures for many surfaces which are useful in graphics [1], [5], [12]. We are interested in methods for generating $\mathbf{R}(u, v, w)$ as a two-dimensional extension of our fBm approximation algorithm.

The most straightforward approach is to use a method identical to the quadrilateral subdivision given above. This retains the drawbacks of that method, with the exception that normal averaging is unnecessary for those deterministic functions that assure derivative continuity across patch boundaries. If we compute the vector normal along with each subdivision, what is really needed is a non-Markovian approach which provides a better approximation to fBm across the surface of a patch. Of course, since we compute each patch separately, the overall surface cannot be strictly a fBm surface. If the parametric surface definition of the object has the proper stochastic properties globally, however, the approximation of the stochastic surface to fBm will be reasonable. An alternative would be to generate the entire stochastic surface at once, but this is impractical in most situations. Note that this difficulty, caused by the nonlocal character of fBm, does not arise in other stochastic processes of interest, making such computations easier.

To introduce the needed interdependence between points in the two-dimensional approximations to fBm, we will use the following scheme. First we compute the

Fig. 16. Order of Computation for Grid in Two Dimensions. (Order is 0, 1a, 1b, 2a, 2b, ···) * indicates points interpolated from boundary values only.

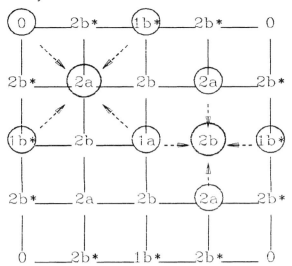

boundary of the patch, using the one-dimensional version of the algorithm to the level desired. We then fill the square for each level, computing the centers, then the sides, using at each step the four neighbors (diagonally for the centers, horizontally and vertically for the sides). At each step the new point is computed as a Gaussian pseudo-random variable, whose expected value is the mean of the four neighbors at this level, and whose standard deviation is $c^{-\ell H}$, with ℓ the level, H the self-similarity parameter, and c a constant to be adjusted to fit the application (see illustration in Fig. 16).

Figures 17–19 show a planet that has been generated with this technique using 10 bicubic Bezier patches. The "land" is made of patches with stochastic surfaces and the "sea" is made of the same patches with no stochastic component. The "coastlines" are then the zerosets of the two-dimensional fBm generated. Note that we used a depth-buffer algorithm to compute these intersections, but we could just as well have added the texture only

Fig. 18. Planets at Different World Space Resolutions but Similar Screen Space Resolutions.

Fig. 17. Planets at Different Resolutions (coastlines are from depth-buffer computations).

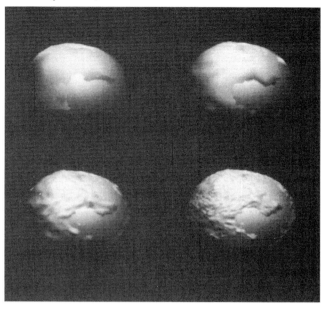

where the displacement is positive and obtained the same "coastlines." The value of h has been chosen to be 0.6 since it is close to the empirical value obtained from actual measurements of geographic features [22]. The altitude has been exaggerated to give a more dramatic effect (the altitude of the highest peaks is about 10 percent of the radius of the planet). The subdivision has been stopped at a fairly low resolution, to illustrate the properties of the method, and the patches are actually processed as polygons (triangles to be specific) by the display system.

Figure 17 shows different resolutions for the planet at the same screen coordinate size, with the level of recursion being 2, 3, 4, and 5. At this on-screen size, though the overall appearance is similar, details, espe-

Fig. 19. Zooming in to the Planet.

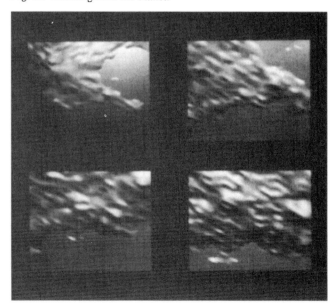

cially for coastlines, are obviously different. This is due to the fact that the screen coordinate distance between computed points on the surface is much more than one pixel (about 20 pixels for the first planet of Fig. 17), and at the next level of computation the midpoint can be above or below sea level, changing locally the appearance of the coast. Features whose size is about the distance between points (in screen coordinates) can be significantly altered. For this reason in normal practice this distance should be kept at or below the size of a pixel.

Figure 18 shows the four objects together at sizes such that the on-screen resolution is the same. Observe that even though we are still above the pixel level (the average distance between computed points is about 2 pixels), the quality of the picture is satisfactory, and there are no noticeable differences in the appearance of the four planets. Considering that the whole database for the planet consists of only 90 three-dimensional points (defining the 10 Bezier patches), the comparison with a picture produced from a real terrain database which could require several 10,000 triangles for a comparable visual complexity is highly favorable. Of course, if the reproduction of a specific set of surface features obtained from cartographic data, for example, were required, it would still be necessary to model these features deterministically to the level of detail desired, and the database would grow accordingly.

Figure 19 illustrates how the process can be continued to zoom in to the surface to any desired level of detail, while keeping the same on-screen resolution. On the upper left is an easily recognizable part (the lower left corner) of the planet. On each of the other views, the central area is enlarged about twice. The main features of each view carry over to the next one, while new details appear. Here the average distance between computed points is about 6 pixels. This process can be continued further, still *with no modification* of the database, until we are arbitrarily close to the surface. Care has to be taken, however, because as the differences between two neighboring points become very small, the computation of the surface normals and the comparisons of the depth values in the Z-buffer can become inaccurate. The zooming in and out process can be repeated as often as desired since the particular stochastic surface generated is fixed and reproducible.

Parametric techniques will generally require somewhat more computation than polygon subdivision since the nonlinear deterministic functions involved require more computation for the rendering of points. In addition, since the recursive subdivision is done in parameter space, it is difficult to tie the depth of the recursion to the final distances apart in world or screen coordinates of the sample points generated. On the other hand, most of the difficulties cited for polygon subdivision are solved using this method. In particular, a surface is generated which has non-Markovian properties very close to those of fBm, and thus provides a much closer approximation. As a result, the value of h in the subdivision corresponds closely to H of fBm, so that empirical determinations of this value can be directly employed to generate terrain representations with characteristics similar to the measured surface, alleviating much experimental "twiddling" of parameters. Also, the higher correlations between points on the patch eliminate the need for tight control of the random number generator to avoid the glitches mentioned above.

The cost of the computation of the surface is a linear function of the number of points *displayed*. The cost of computation of the stochastic variables can be lowered using table lookup techniques (note that the numbers used do not need to pass very stringent tests for randomness). This indicates that the increase in computational cost will be small relative to the cost of the usual transformations and shading algorithms.

These algorithms share the general advantages of subdivision algorithms. They allow continuing the computation of the texture down to the pixel level, or even the subpixel level if some anti-aliasing is needed, while at the same time keeping the level of surface details constant as the object gets larger or smaller in screen space.

At the other end of the range in screen space, if the object is much larger than the screen size, the texture should be computed to the highest level of detail only for the portion of the patch or polygon that is not clipped out. Since such a subpatch or subpolygon cannot be computed solely on the basis of local information, some points outside of the displayed area are needed. It can be shown [9] that the total number of sample points to be computed is bounded by a linear function of the number of points to be displayed. So this algorithm allows "zooming" in and out on the surface, keeping the same displayed level of complexity (within one binary order of magnitude), while the time and space complexity grows only linearly as a function of the number of points actually displayed. This is then an implementation of a truly hierarchical approach to surface modeling, the importance of which was pointed out by Clark [6].

Another interesting feature of the algorithm for practical applications is that it is easy to change the value of the parameter h at any level of the computation. Therefore a terrain that looks very rugged from a distance (a low value of h), can become rather smooth at a higher scale (a high value of h). This models what happens if valleys are filled with sediments, for instance. This is a particular example of a general technique, namely changing the characteristic of the stochastic process, or even the stochastic process itself, according to the recursion level.

In our planet example, the nonstochastic components of the stochastic surface are the patches defining a close approximation of the sphere. As a result, the macroscopic features of the land masses are not predetermined. In most applications, however, the macroscopic features would be known, and some points of the surface would have the actual measured coordinates. In this case, it is better (and easy) to force the stochastic component to be zero at these points. Thus the stochastic surface will interpolate these points, and we have a method for stochastic interpolation in two dimensions. Of course, the polygon subdivision methods generate no displacements at the original vertices and thus always produce stochastic interpolations of these vertices.

5. Further Applications of the Model

5.1 Other Stochastic Surface Properties

We have thus far only considered the application of fBm and other stochastic models to the creation of primitives whose surface position has stochastic characteristics. Other properties of a surface, such as its color, might also be allowed to vary stochastically. For instance, another instance of two-dimensional fBm with a high value of H and a low roughness factor could be used to determine the color of the surface of the planet. Of course, this property should also be continuous across patch boundaries. Another technique for color variation which can be used with polygon subdivision requires that a color be initially assigned to each vertex of the polygon to be subdivided. When a midpoint is computed for a side of the polygon, its color becomes that of one of the endpoints of the side. Which endpoint is chosen is decided according to a Boolean random function. When the subdivision is complete, the color of each facet's surface can simply be taken as the average of the colors of its vertices. This technique was used in generating the color variations and snow cap on the mountain range in the foreground of the cover picture.

5.2 Motion

Although various effective techniques have been developed for creating a series of images of a scene in which smooth, continuous motions of objects in the scene are depicted, these tend not to be very effective in handling complex irregular motions such as the path of a lightning bolt or the motion of a leaf in the wind. Stochastic techniques can provide powerful means of modeling motion which would have been difficult or impossible to represent otherwise. Consider, for instance, the action of unfolding a crumpled piece of paper. Figure 20 is four frames from a sequence representing such an action. These frames were generated using Bezier patches mapped with approximations to fBm with varying values of h. As h is changed from 0.3 to 0.9, the patch is rescaled to keep its surface area constant.[1] Thus a complex motion that would have been very expensive to generate previously is modeled very easily with stochastic

---

[1] Note that a real fBm surface has infinite area, although our discrete approximations to it are, of course, finite. See [18].

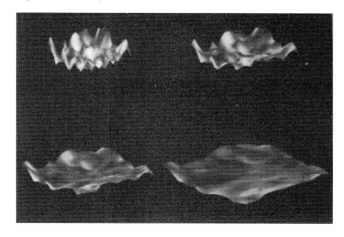

Fig. 20. Motion by Variation of h (h = 0.3, 0.5, 0.7, 0.9).

techniques. Another example is the motion of a simple lightning bolt. The path of the lightning bolt can be represented as a fBm function from one dimension into three, like Brownian motion of a molecule in three-space. By simply changing the random numbers generated, while keeping the endpoint displacements fixed at 0, a sequence of instantaneous positions of the lightning bolt is created. Generating the same number of sample points in each instance, and allowing the motion of each sample point to interpolate the positions of that point in each of the "key frames" generated above, the motion of the lightning can be generated. Note that the interpolated path of each sample point can be created using either a deterministic or a stochastic technique. The lightning in the film *Vol Libre* [4] was generated in this way.

6. Conclusion

We suggest that recognition of the importance of the stochastic properties of the real world will lead to greatly increased flexibility in the modeling techniques used in computer graphics, just as probabilistic models have contributed significantly to the development of several related disciplines. We have applied Mandelbrot's fBm model for terrain and other natural phenomena and have developed efficient and appropriate sample path generating algorithms. We have shown several methods for creating stochastic modeling primitives of one and two-dimensions based on these algorithms and have demonstrated the use of stochastic interpolation of real sampled data points to create realistic representations of sampled phenomena. These methods constitute very natural and compact hierarchical object descriptions which are applicable to the modeling of various natural phenomena at a small fraction of the cost of deterministic methods of comparable quality, when these exist at all.

The techniques presented here barely scratch the surface of the possibilities of the stochastic approach to modeling. The most immediate extensions of this work are to use the same techniques to modify surface characteristics other than position, for example, to create stochastic color patterns as has subsequently been done in the movie *Peak* by Mark Snilily, or to render small scale texture by stochastic variation of surface normals analogous to Blinn's method [3]. In contrast to these one and two-dimensional stochastic methods, the study of three and four-dimensional stochastic models should lead to interesting techniques for the representation of complex volumes and motions.

As indicated above, there are two general sources of stochastic models that may be of use in graphics. Although in this paper we have illustrated a mathematical model useful in representing terrain, there might be many natural objects for which it is unlikely that one will find a suitable mathematical model. Techniques which allow the empirical determination of parameters of a flexible canonical stochastic model which fit specific natural objects would be very useful in this regard. Research in the development of such techniques holds the promise of rich rewards for computer graphics.

Acknowledgments. The first two authors would like to thank Zvi Kedem for his many helpful suggestions and overall support, and Henry Fuchs, who taught them how to make pictures with computers. We thank Benoit Mandelbrot for providing inspiration through his book, and for his kindness and encouragement. We also thank Martin Tuori and Martin Taylor of DCIEM in Toronto, who helped in producing Figures 17 to 20.

Received 3/80; revised 12/81; accepted 2/82.

References
1. Bezier, P. Mathematical and practical possibilities of UNISURF. In Barnhill, R.E. and Riesenfeld, R.F. (Eds.). *Computer Aided Geometric Design*, Academic, (1974).
2. Blinn, J.F. Models of light reflection for computer synthesized pictures. In *Proceedings of SIGGRAPH '77*. Also published as *Comput. Graphics*, 11, 2, (Aug. 1977), 192–198.
3. Blinn, J.F. Simulation of wrinkled surfaces. In *Proceedings of SIGGRAPH '77*. Also published as *Comput. Graphics*, 12, 3, (Aug. 1978), 286–292.
4. Carpenter, L.C. *Vol Libre*. Computer generated animated movie. First Showing at SIGGRAPH '80 (July 1980).
5. Catmull, E. Computer display of curved surfaces. In *Proc. IEEE Conference on Computer Graphics, Pattern Recognition and Data Structure*. (May 1975).
6. Clark, J.H. Hierarchical geometric models for visible surface algorithms. *Comm. ACM*, 19, 10, (Oct. 1976), 547–554.
7. Clark, J.H. A fast algorithm for rendering parametric surfaces. In *Proceedings of SIGGRAPH '79*. Also published as *Computer Graphics*, 13, 2 (Aug. 1979), 174.
8. Csuri, C., Hackathorn, R., Parent, R., Carlson, W., and Howard, M. Toward an interactive high visual complexity animation system. In *Proceedings of SIGGRAPH '79*. Also published as *Comput. Graphics*, 13, 2, (Aug. 1979), 289–299.
9. Fournier, A. *Stochastic Modeling in Computer Graphics*. Ph.D. Dissertation, University of Texas at Dallas, (1980).
10. Fu, K.S. Syntactic image modeling using stochastic tree grammars. *Computer Graphics and Image Processing*, 12, (1980), 136–152.
11. Fuchs, H., Kedem, Z.M., and Uselton, S.P. Optimal surface reconstruction from planar contours. *Comm. ACM*, 20, 10, (Oct. 1977), 693–702.
12. Gordon, W.J. and Riesenfeld, R.F. B-spline curves and surfaces. In Barnhill, R.E. and Riesenfeld, R.F. (Eds.), *Computer Aided Geometric Design*, Academic, (1974).
13. Lane, J.M., Carpenter, L.C., Whitted, T., and Blinn, J. Scan-line methods for displaying parametrically defined surfaces. *Comm. ACM*, 23, 1, (Jan. 1980), 23–34.
14. Mandelbrot, B.B. and Van Ness, J.W. Fractional Brownian motions, fractional noises and applications. *SIAM Review*, 10, 4, (Oct. 1968), 422–437.
15. Mandelbrot, B.B.. A fast fractional Gaussian noise generator. *Water Resources Research*, 7, 3, (June 1971), 543–553.
16. Mandelbrot, B.B. On the geometry of homogeneous turbulence, with stress on the fractal dimension of iso-surfaces of scalars. *J. Fluid Mechanics*, 72, 2, (1975), 401–416.
17. Mandelbrot, B.B. Stochastic models for the earth's relief, the shape and fractal dimension of coastlines, and the number area rule for islands. *Proc. Nat. Acad. Sci. USA*, 72, 10, (Oct. 1975), 2825–2828.
18. Mandelbrot, B.B. *Fractals: Form, Chance and Dimension*. Freeman, San Francisco, (1977).
19. Max, N. Vectorized procedural models for natural terrains: Waves and islands in the sunset. In *Proceedings of SIGGRAPH '81*. Also published as *Comput. Graphics*, 15, 3, (Aug. 1981), 317–324.
20. Mezei, L., Puzin, M., and Conroy, P. Simulation of patterns of nature by computer graphics. *Information Processing* 74, 52–56.
21. Modestino, J.W., Fries, R.W., and Vickers, A.L. Stochastic image models generated by random tessellations in the plane. *Computer Graphics and Image Processing*, 12, (1980), 74–98.
22. Richardson, L.F. The problem of statistics of deadly quarrels. *General Systems Yearbook*, 6, (1961), 139–187.
23. Schachter, B. and Ahuja, N. Random pattern generation process. *Computer Graphics and Image Processing*, 10, (1979), 95–114.
24. Schachter, B. Long crested wave models. *Computer Graphics and Image Processing*, 12, (1980), 187–201.

Particle Systems—A Technique for Modeling a Class of Fuzzy Objects

WILLIAM T. REEVES
Lucasfilm Ltd

This paper introduces particle systems—a method for modeling fuzzy objects such as fire, clouds, and water. Particle systems model an object as a cloud of primitive particles that define its volume. Over a period of time, particles are generated into the system, move and change form within the system, and die from the system. The resulting model is able to represent motion, changes of form, and dynamics that are not possible with classical surface-based representations. The particles can easily be motion blurred, and therefore do not exhibit temporal aliasing or strobing. Stochastic processes are used to generate and control the many particles within a particle system. The application of particle systems to the wall of fire element from the Genesis Demo sequence of the film *Star Trek II: The Wrath of Khan* [10] is presented.

Categories and Subject Descriptors: I.3.3 [**Computer Graphics**]: Picture/Image Generation; I.3.5 [**Computer Graphics**]: Computational Geometry and Object Modeling; I.3.7 [**Computer Graphics**]: Three-Dimensional Graphics and Realism

General Terms: Algorithms, Design

Additional Key Words and Phrases: Motion blur, stochastic modeling, temporal aliasing, dynamic objects

---

1. INTRODUCTION

Modeling phenomena such as clouds, smoke, water, and fire has proved difficult with the existing techniques of computer image synthesis. These "fuzzy" objects do not have smooth, well-defined, and shiny surfaces; instead their surfaces are irregular, complex, and ill defined. We are interested in their dynamic and fluid changes in shape and appearance. They are not rigid objects nor can their motions be described by the simple affine transformations that are common in computer graphics.

This paper presents a method for the modeling of fuzzy objects that we call particle systems. The representation of particle systems differs in three basic ways from representations normally used in image synthesis. First, an object is represented not by a set of primitive surface elements, such as polygons or patches, that define its boundary, but as clouds of primitive particles that define its volume. Second, a particle system is not a static entity. Its particles change form and move with the passage of time. New particles are "born" and old

---

Author's address: William T. Reeves, Lucasfilm Ltd, P.O. Box 2009, San Rafael, CA 94912.
Permission to copy without fee all or part of this material is granted provided that the copies are not made or distributed for direct commercial advantage, the ACM copyright notice and the title of the publication and its date appear, and notice is given that copying is by permission of the Association for Computing Machinery. To copy otherwise, or to republish, requires a fee and/or specific permission.
© ACM 0-89791-109-1/83/007/0359 $00.75

particles "die." Third, an object represented by a particle system is not deterministic, since its shape and form are not completely specified. Instead, stochastic processes are used to create and change an object's shape and appearance.

In modeling fuzzy objects, the particle system approach has several important advantages over classical surface-oriented techniques. First, a particle (for now, think of a particle as a point in three-dimensional space) is a much simpler primitive than a polygon, the simplest of the surface representations. Therefore, in the same amount of computation time one can process more of the basic primitives and produce a more complex image. Because a particle is simple, it is also easy to motion-blur. Motion-blurring of fast-moving objects for the removal of temporal aliasing effects has been largely ignored in computer image synthesis to date. A second advantage is that the model definition is procedural and is controlled by random numbers. Therefore, obtaining a highly detailed model does not necessarily require a great deal of human design time as is often the case with existing surface-based systems. Because it is procedural, a particle system can adjust its level of detail to suit a specific set of viewing parameters. As with fractal surfaces [5], zooming in on a particle system can reveal more and more detail. Third, particle systems model objects that are "alive," that is, they change form over a period of time. It is difficult to represent complex dynamics of this form with surface-based modeling techniques.

Modeling objects as collections of particles is not a new idea. Fifteen years ago, the earliest computer video games depicted exploding spaceships with many little glowing dots that filled the screen. Point sources have been used as a graphics data type in many three-dimensional modeling systems (e.g., the early Evans and Sutherland flight simulators), although there are few real references to them in the literature. Roger Wilson at Ohio State [4] used particles to model smoke emerging from a smokestack. There were neither stochastic controls nor dynamics in his model. Alvy Ray Smith and Jim Blinn used particles to model star creation and death in galaxies for the Cosmos series [11]. Alan Norton [9] used particles to generate and display three-dimensional fractal shapes. Jim Blinn [3] discussed light reflection functions for simulating light passing through and being reflected by layers of particles. His technique was used to produce images of the rings of Saturn. Blinn did not address the fuzzy object modeling problem which is the topic of this paper. Volumetric representations have also been proposed as viable alternatives to surface representations. Solid modeling [13] is a form of volumetric representation, as is the work of Norm Badler and Joe O'Rourke on "bubbleman" [2]. The use of stochastic modeling relates our work to the recent advances in fractal modeling [5].

Section 2 decribes the basic framework of particle systems in more detail. Section 3 examines how particle systems were used to produce the fire element in the Genesis Demo sequence from the movie *Star Trek II: The Wrath of Khan* [10]. Section 4 presents several other applications of particle systems, and Section 5 discusses ongoing and future research in this area.

2. BASIC MODEL OF PARTICLE SYSTEMS

A particle system is a collection of many minute particles that together represent a fuzzy object. Over a period of time, particles are generated into a system, move and change from within the system, and die from the system.

To compute each frame in a motion sequence, the following sequence of steps is performed: (1) new particles are generated into the system, (2) each new particle is assigned its individual attributes, (3) any particles that have existed within the system past their prescribed lifetime are extinguished, (4) the remaining particles are moved and transformed according to their dynamic attributes, and finally (5) an image of the living particles is rendered in a frame buffer. The particle system can be programmed to execute any set of instructions at each step. Because it is procedural, this approach can incorporate any computational model that describes the appearance or dynamics of the object. For example, the motions and transformations of particles could be tied to the solution of a system of partial differential equations, or particle attributes could be assigned on the basis of statistical mechanics. We can, therefore, take advantage of models which have been developed in other scientific or engineering disciplines.

In the research presented here, we use simple stochastic processes as the procedural elements of each step in the generation of a frame. To control the shape, appearance, and dynamics of the particles within a particle system, the model designer has access to a set of parameters. Stochastic processes that randomly select each particle's appearance and movement are constrained by these parameters. In general, each parameter specifies a range in which a particle's value must lie. Normally, a range is specified by providing its mean value and its maximum variance.

The following subsections describe in more detail the basic model for particle systems, and how they are controlled and specified within the software we have written.

2.1 Particle Generation

Particles are generated into a particle system by means of controlled stochastic processes. One process determines the number of particles entering the system during each interval of time, that is, at a given frame. The number of particles generated is important because it strongly influences the density of the fuzzy object.

The model designer can choose to control the number of new particles in one of two ways. In the first method, the designer controls the mean number of particles generated at a frame and its variance. The actual number of particles generated at frame f is

$$NParts_f = MeanParts_f + Rand() \times VarParts_f,$$

where $Rand$ is a procedure returning a uniformly distributed random number between -1.0 and $+1.0$, $MeanParts_f$ the mean number of particles, and $VarParts_f$ its variance.

In the second method, the number of new particles depends on the screen size of the object. The model designer controls the mean number of particles generated per unit of screen area and its variance. The procedural particle system can determine the view parameters at a particular frame, calculate the approximate screen area that it covers, and set the number of new particles accordingly. The corresponding equation is

$$NParts_f = (MeanParts_{sa_f} + Rand() \times VarParts_{sa_f}) \times ScreenArea,$$

where $MeanParts_{sa}$ is the mean per screen area, $VarParts_{sa_f}$ its variance, and $ScreenArea$ the particle system's screen area. This method controls the level of detail of the particle system and, therefore, the time required to render its image. For example, there is no need to generate 100,000 particles in an object that covers 4 pixels on the screen.

To enable a particle system to grow or shrink in intensity, the designer is able to vary over time the mean number of particles generated per frame (i.e., $MeanParts_f$ and $MeanParts_{sa_f}$ are, as used above, functions of frame number). Currently, we use a simple linear function

$$MeanParts_f = InitialMeanParts + DeltaMeanParts \times (f - f_0)$$

or

$$MeanParts_{sa_f} = InitialMeanParts_{sa} + DeltaMeanParts_{sa} \times (f - f_0),$$

where f is the current frame, f_0 the first frame during which the particle system is alive, $InitialMeanParts$ the mean number of particles at this first frame, and $DeltaMeanParts$ its rate of change. The variance controls, $VarParts_f$ and $VarParts_{sa_f}$, are currently constant over all frames. More sophisticated quadratic, cubic, or perhaps even stochastic variations in both the mean and variance parameters would be easy to add.

To control the particle generation of a particle system, therefore, the designer specifies f_0 and either the parameters $InitialMeanParts$, $DeltaMeanParts$, and $VarParts$, or the parameters $InitialMeanParts_{sa}$, $DeltaMeanParts_{sa}$, and $VarParts_{sa}$.

2.2 Particle Attributes

For each new particle generated, the particle system must determine values for the following attributes:

(1) initial position,
(2) initial velocity (both speed and direction),
(3) initial size,
(4) initial color,
(5) initial transparency,
(6) shape,
(7) lifetime.

Several parameters of a particle system control the initial position of its particles. A particle system has a position in three-dimensional space that defines its origin. Two angles of rotation about a coordinate system through this origin give it an orientation. A particle system also has a *generation shape* which defines a region about its origin into which newly born particles are randomly placed. Among the generation shapes we have implemented are: a sphere of radius r, a circle of radius r in the x-y plane of its coordinate system, and a rectangle of length l and width w in the x-y plane of its coordinate system. Figure 1 shows a typical particle system with a spherical generation shape. More complicated generation shapes based on the laws of nature or on chaotic attractors [1] have been envisioned but not yet implemented.

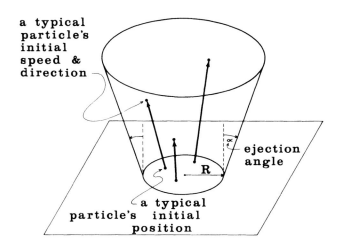

Fig. 3. Form of an explosion-like particle system.

parameters, but varied stochastically. Varying the mean velocity parameter caused the explosions to be of different heights.

All particles generated by the second-level particle systems were predominately red in color with a touch of green. Recall from Section 2.5 that particles are treated as point light sources and that colors are added, not matted, into a pixel. When many particles covered a pixel, as was the case near the center and base of each explosion, the red component was quickly clamped at full intensity and the green component increased to a point where the resulting color was orange and even yellow. Thus, the heart of the explosion had a hot yellow-orange glow which faded off to shades of red elsewhere. Actually, a small blue component caused pixels covered by very many particles to appear white. The rate at which a particle's color changed simulated the cooling of a glowing piece of some hypothetical material. The green and blue components dropped off quickly, and the red followed at a slower rate. Particles were killed when their lifetime expired, when their intensity fell below the minimum intensity parameter, or if they happened to fall below the surface of the planet.

A quickly moving object leaves a blurred image on the retina of the human eye. When a motion picture camera is used to film live action at 24 frames per second, the camera shutter typically remains open for 1/50 of a second. The image captured on a frame is actually an integration of approximately half the motion that occurred between successive frames. An object moving quickly appears blurred in the individual still frames. Computer animation has traditionally imaged scenes as individual instants in time and has ignored motion blur. The resulting motion often exhibits temporal aliasing and strobing effects that are disconcerting to the human eye. Motion blur is a complex topic that is beginning to appear in the literature [7, 12].

The particles in our wall-of-fire element are motion-blurred. Three-dimensional positions are calculated for a particle at the beginning of a frame and about halfway through the frame, and an antialiased straight line is drawn between the corresponding screen coordinate positions in the frame buffer.[4] Antialiased lines are used to prevent staircasing (moving jaggies) and strobing (popping on and off) effects. To be perfectly correct, screen motion due to movement of the camera should be considered when calculating where to blur a particle. One can also argue that simulating the imperfect temporal sampling of a movie camera is not ideal and that motion blur should really simulate what happens in the human eye. This is a good area for future research.

In the finished sequence, the wall of fire spread over the surface of the planet both in front of and behind the planet's limb (outer edge). The rendering algorithm generated two images per frame—one for all particles between the camera's position and the silhouette plane of the planet, and one for all particles on the other side of this clipping plane. These two elements were composited with the barren moonlike planet element and the stars element in back-to-front order—stars, background fires, planet, and foreground fires.

Because the wall of fire was modeled using many small light-emitting particles, light from the fire should have reflected off the planet's surface. Our current implementation of particle systems does not handle light reflection on surface-based objects. To achieve this effect, Lucasfilm team member Tom Duff added an additional strong local light source above the center of the rings of fire when he rendered the planet's surface. This produced the glow that circles the ring of fire on the planet's surface. (This glow is visible in Figure 5.)

Figure 4 is a frame showing the initial impact of the Genesis bomb. It was generated from one very large particle system and about 20 smaller ones about its base. About 25,000 particles exist in this image. Figure 5 occurs partway through the first half of the sequence. It contains about 200 particle systems and 75,000 particles. Figure 6 shows the ring of fire extending over and beyond the limb of the planet. It is formed from about 200 explosions and 85,000 particles. Figure 7 shows the wall of fire just before it engulfs the camera; in Figure 8 the camera is completely engulfed. Both employ about 400 particle systems and contain over 750,000 particles. The textures in Figure 8 are completely synthetic and yet have a "natural" and highly detailed appearance that is uncommon in most computer graphics images. These images are interesting statically, but they only really come alive on the movie screen. It is interesting to note that this is also the case for many of the best traditional (i.e., non-computer-generated) special effects shots where motion blur is an important factor.

A few points concerning random numbers are of interest from a production point of view. The random number routine we use is based on [6], and generates numbers uniformly in the range [0.0, 1.0]. It is an incremental algorithm based on updating a table of seed values. To checkpoint a production, all that need be saved is this random number table—we do not save all the parameters of 750,000 particles. To restart a computation at frame n, the closest preceding frame p is found that cannot contribute particles to frame n (this is determined from the lifetime parameters of all the active particle systems). Frame $p + 1$'s random number table is then read, and particle generation can begin from there. No

---

[4] A particle's trajectory is actually parabolic, but the straight-line approximation has so far proved sufficient.

Fig. 4. Initial explosion.

Fig. 5. Expanding wall of fire.

Reprinted From **acm Transactions On Graphics**—April 1983—Vol. 2, No. 2

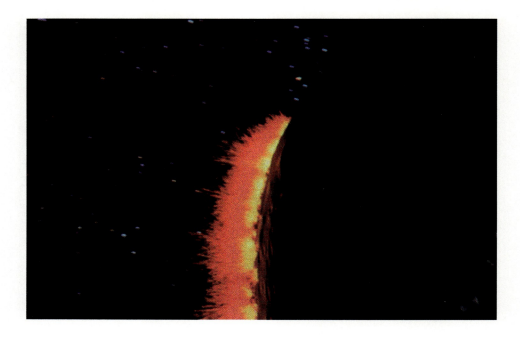

Fig. 6. Wall of fire over limb of planet.

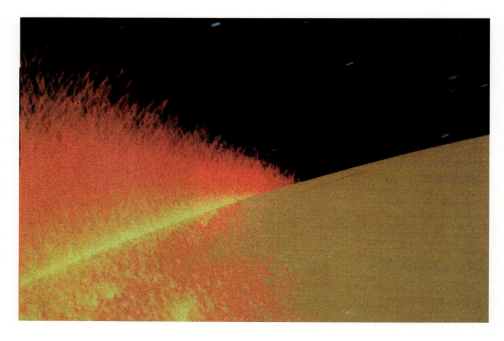

Fig. 7. Wall of fire about to engulf camera.

Reprinted From **acm Transactions On Graphics**—April 1983—Vol. 2, No. 2

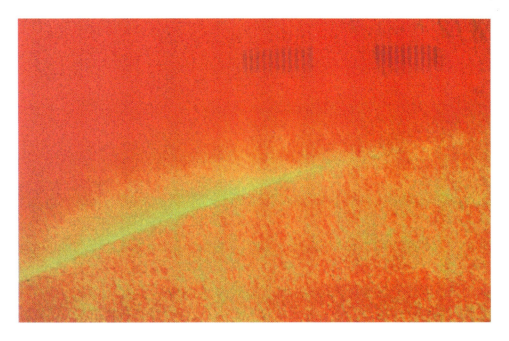

Fig. 8. Wall of fire completely engulfing camera.

particles are drawn until the simulation reaches frame *n*, so this backing up and restarting usually takes only a few minutes.

Particles moving off screen or being extinguished for any reason do not affect the randomness of other particles. This is because all stochastic decisions concerning a particle are performed when it is generated. After that, its motion is deterministic. If stochastic elements were to be used to perturbate the dynamics of a particle (e.g., to simulate turbulence), more care would have to be taken when checkpointing a frame and killing particles. In that case, it would probably be better to use a more deterministic and reproducible random number generator.

4. OTHER APPLICATIONS OF PARTICLE SYSTEMS

4.1 Fireworks

We are currently using particle systems to model fireworks. The fireworks differ from the Genesis Demo in that the control parameters of the particle systems vary more widely, and streaking is more predominate. Figure 9 shows two red explosions superimposed. One explosion is tall, thin, and near the end of its lifetime, and the other is short, fat, and building up to full steam. Figure 10 shows several green explosions dying off and blue spherical explosion starting up. Figure 11 contains overlapping, multicolored explosions formed with different generation shapes and ejection angles. Again, these images only really come alive when projected at 24 frames per second.

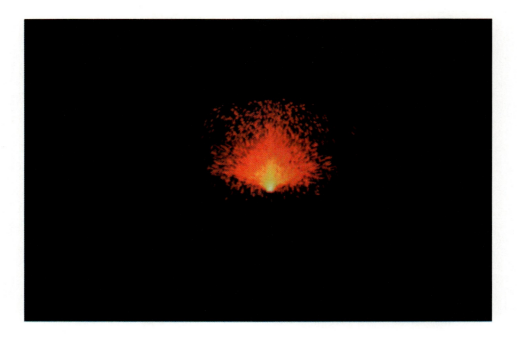

Fig. 9. Two red fireworks.

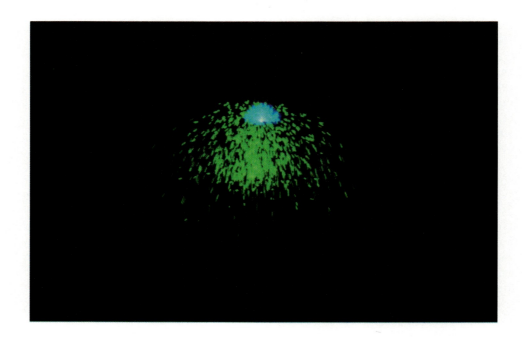

Fig. 10. Green and blue fireworks.

Reprinted From **acm Transactions On Graphics**—April 1983—Vol. 2, No. 2

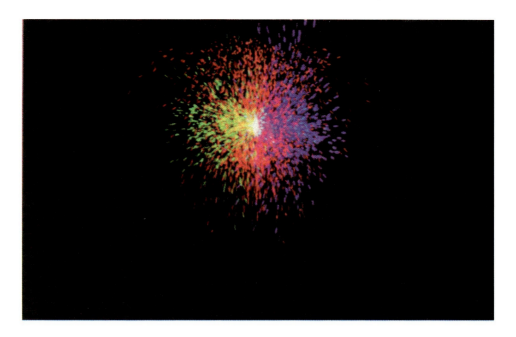

Fig. 11. Multicolored fireworks.

4.2 Line Drawing Explosions

Particle systems are being used to model exploding objects in a computer-simulated tactical display for a scene from the movie *Return of the Jedi* [8]. In this case, the particle systems are implemented on a line-drawing display. In order to simulate motion blur, the particles are drawn as very small straight lines instead of as points. The texturing effects that are evident in the previous examples are lost on a line-drawing display, and yet the motion still looks real and the sequence gives the viewer the impression that something is exploding. This is because the model is dynamic—it moves well.

4.3 Grass

To model grass, we use an explosive type of particle system, similar to that used in the Genesis Effect. Instead of drawing particles as little streaks, the parabolic trajectory of each particle over its entire lifetime is drawn. Thus, the time-domain motion of the particle is used to make a static shape. Grasslike green and dark green colors are assigned to the particles which are shaded on the basis of the scene's light sources. Each particle becomes a simple representation of a blade of grass and the particle system as a whole becomes a clump of grass. Particle systems randomly placed on a surface and overlapping one another are used to model a bed or patch of grass.

Figure 12 is a picture entitled *white.sand* by Alvy Ray Smith of Lucasfilm. The grass elements of this image were generated as described above. The plant

Fig. 12. *white.sand*.

elements were generated using a partially stochastic technique similar to particle systems.

5. ONGOING RESEARCH IN PARTICLE SYSTEMS

A logical extension of this research will be to use particle systems to model fuzzy objects in which the individual particles can not be rendered as point light sources, but must be rendered as individual light-reflecting objects.

To this end, we have begun to investigate the modeling of clouds. Clouds are difficult for several reasons. First, the shape and form of clouds are complex, depending on many factors such as wind direction, temperature, terrain, and humidity. The atmospheric literature abounds with cloud models that are simple in concept but computationally difficult, since most are based on partial differential equations. Second, clouds are difficult because they can throw shadows on themselves. This property is very important in making a cloud look like a cloud. Third, the number of particles needed to model a cloud will be very large. This will require an efficient rendering algorithm.

8. CONCLUSIONS

We have presented particle systems, a method for the modeling of a class of fuzzy objects, and have shown how they were used in making the fire element of the Genesis Demo sequence for the movie *Star Trek II: The Wrath of Khan*. Particle systems have been used as a modeling tool for other effects and appear promising for the modeling of phenomena like clouds and smoke.

Particles, especially when modeled as point light sources or as streaks of light, have proved efficient to render—they are merely antialiased lines. Because they are so simple, they lend themselves to a hardware or firmware implementation. With a hardware antialiased line-drawing routine, the computation of our wall-of-fire element would have been two to three times faster.

Particle systems are procedural stochastic representations controlled by several global parameters. Stochastic representations are capable of producing minute detail without requiring substantial user design time. The textures in the fire sequence could not have been modeled with other existing methods. Fire images, scanned in from a photograph or painted, could have been texture mapped, but they would still have been static. Another advantage of a procedural representation is its ability to adapt to several different viewing environments. For example, procedural representations can generate only as much detail as is needed in a frame, potentially saving significant amounts of computation time.

Having finally come to grips with spatial aliasing, it is now time for computer image synthesis to being to investigate and solve temporal aliasing problems. The Genesis Demo is the first "big screen" computer-synthesized sequence to include three-dimensional dynamic motion blur. The particles in a particle system can easily be motion-blurred because they are so simple. A great deal of work remains to be done in this area—blurring particles is much easier than blurring curved surface patches.

Particle systems can model objects that explode, flow, splatter, puff up, and billow. These kinds of dynamics have not been produced with surface-based representations. The most important aspect of particle systems is that they move: good dynamics are quite often the key to making objects look real.

7. ACKNOWLEDGMENTS

The author gratefully acknowledges the suggestions and encouragement of all members of the graphics project at Lucasfilm Ltd, especially those who worked on the Genesis Demo sequence: Loren Carpenter, Ed Catmull, Pat Cole, Rob Cook, David DiFrancesco, Tom Duff, Rob Poor, Tom Porter, and Alvy Ray Smith. The crusade for motion blur and antialiasing in computer image synthesis is a goal of the entire graphics project and Lucasfilm as a whole. One of the referees deserves credit for pointing out several extensions and improvements to the motion blurring discussion. Finally, thanks to Ricki Blau for editorial and photographic assistance.

REFERENCES

1. ABRAHAM, R., AND SHAW, C. *DYNAMICS—The Geometry of Behavior*. City on the Hill Press, Santa Cruz, Calif., 1981.
2. BADLER, N. I., O'ROURKE, J., AND TOLTZIS, H. A spherical human body model for visualizing movement. *Proc. IEEE 67*, 10 (Oct. 1979).
3. BLINN, J. F. Light reflection functions for simulation of clouds and dusty surfaces. Proc. SIGGRAPH '82. In *Comput. Gr. 16*, 3, (July 1982), 21–29.
4. CSURI, C., HACKATHORN, R., PARENT, R., CARLSON, W., AND HOWARD, M. Towards an interactive high visual complexity animation system. Proc. SIGGRAPH 79. In *Comput. Gr. 13*, 2 (Aug. 1979), 289–299.
5. FOURNIER, A., FUSSEL, D., AND CARPENTER, L. Computer rendering of stochastic models. *Commun. ACM 25*, 6, (June 1982), 371–384.

6. KNUTH, D. E. *The Art of Computer Programming*, vol. 2. Addison-Wesley, Reading, Mass., (1969), p. 464.
7. KOREIN, J., AND BADLER, N. I. Temporal anti-aliasing in computer generated animation. To appear in Proc. SIGGRAPH '83 (July 1983).
8. LUCASFILM. *Return of the Jedi* (film), May 1983.
9. NORTON, A. Generation and display of geometric fractals in 3-D. Proc. SIGGRAPH '82. In *Comput. Gr. 16*, 3 (July 1982), 61–67.
10. PARAMOUNT. *Star Trek II: The Wrath of Khan* (film), June 1982.
11. PBS. *Carl Sagan's Cosmos Series.* (television series), Public Broadcasting System, 1980.
12. POTMESIL, M., AND CHAKRAVARTY, I. Modeling motion blur in computer-generated images. To appear in Proc. SIGGRAPH '83 (July 1983).
13. REQUICHA, A. A. G., AND VOELCKER, H. B. Solid modelling: A historical summary and contemporary assessment. *IEEE Comput. Gr. Appl.* (March 1982).
14. SMITH, A. R., CARPENTER, L., CATMULL, E., COLE, P., COOK, R., POOR, T., PORTER, T. AND REEVES, W. *Genesis Demo Documentary* (film), June 1982, Lucasfilm Ltd.

Received February 1983; revised April 1983; accepted April 1983

GLOBAL AND LOCAL DEFORMATIONS OF SOLID PRIMITIVES

Alan H. Barr
Computer Science Department †
California Institute of Technology
Pasadena, California

Abstract

New hierarchical solid modeling operations are developed, which simulate twisting, bending, tapering, or similar transformations of geometric objects. The chief result is that the normal vector of an arbitrarily deformed smooth surface can be calculated directly from the surface normal vector of the undeformed surface and a transformation matrix. Deformations are easily combined in a hierarchical structure, creating complex objects from simpler ones. The position vectors and normal vectors in the simpler objects are used to calculate the position and normal vectors in the more complex forms; each level in the deformation hierarchy requires an additional matrix multiply for the normal vector calculation. Deformations are important and highly intuitive operations which ease the control and rendering of large families of three-dimensional geometric shapes.

KEYWORDS: Computational Geometry, Solid Modeling, Deformation

Introduction

Modeling hierarchies are a convenient and efficient way to represent geometric objects, allowing users to combine simpler graphical primitives and operators into more complex forms. The leaf-nodes in the hierarchy are the hardware/firmware commands on the equipment which draws the vectors, changes the colors of individual pixels, and operates on lists of line segments or polygons. With the appropriate algorithms and interfaces, users can develop a strong intuitive feeling for the results of a manipulation, can think in terms of each operation, and are able to create the objects and scenes which they desire.

In this paper, we introduce globally and locally defined deformations as new hierarchical operations for use in solid modeling. These operations extend the conventional operations of rotation, translation, Boolean union, intersection and difference. In section one, the transformation rules for tangent vectors and for normal vectors are shown. In section two, several examples of deformation functions are listed. A method is shown in section three to convert arbitrary local representations of deformations to global representations, for space curves and surfaces. Finally, in section four, applications of the methods to the rendering process are described, opening future research directions in ray-tracing algorithms. Appendix A contains a derivation of the normal vector transformation rule.

Deformations allow the user to treat a solid as if it were constructed from a special type of topological putty or clay, which may be bent, twisted, tapered, compressed, expanded, and otherwise transformed repeatedly into a final shape. They are highly intuitive and easily visualized operations which simulate some important manufacturing processes for fabricating objects, such as the bending of bar stock and sheet metal. Deformations can be incorporated into traditional CAD/CAM solid modeling and surface patch methods, reducing the data storage requirements for simulating flexible geometric objects, such as objects made of metal, fabric or rubber.

† Previous address, Raster Technologies Inc., N. Billerica, Mass.

Although it is possible to use these techniques to accurately model the physical properties of different elastic materials with the partial differential equations of elasticity and plasticity theory, simpler mathematical deformation methods exist. These simpler methods have reduced computational needs, are widely applicable in modeling, and are described in the examples section. It is beyond the scope of this paper to formulate the mathematical details of exact mechanical descriptions of physical deformation properties of materials.

1.0 Background and Derivations.

A globally specified deformation of a three dimensional solid is a mathematical function $\underline{F}$ which explicitly modifies the global coordinates of points in space. Points in the undeformed solid are called (small) $\underline{x}$, while points in the deformed solid are called (capital) $\underline{X}$. Mathematically, this is represented by the equation

$$\underline{X} = \underline{F}(\underline{x}). \qquad [Equation\ 1.1a]$$

The x, y, and z components of the three dimensional vector $\underline{x}$ are designated x_1, x_2, and x_3. (For notational convenience, x_1, x_2, and x_3 and x, y, and z are used interchangably. A similar convention holds for the upper case forms.)

A locally specified deformation modifies the tangent space of the solid. Differential vectors in the substance of the solid are rotated and/or skewed; these vectors are integrated to obtain the global position. The differential vectors can be thought of as separate chain-links which can rotate and stretch; the local specification of the deformation is the rotation and skewing matrix function. The position of the end-link in the chain is the vector sum of the previous links, as shown in section three.

Tangent vectors and normal vectors are the two most important vectors used in modeling — the former for delineating and constructing the local geometry, and the latter for obtaining surface orientation and lighting information. Tangent and normal vectors on the undeformed surface may be transformed into the tangent and normal vectors on the deformed surface; the algebraic manipulations for the transformation rules involve a single multiplication by the Jacobian matrix $\underline{\underline{J}}$ of the transformation function $\underline{F}$. In this paper, the term "tangent transformation" substitutes for "contravariant transformation" and is the transformation rule for the tangent vectors. The term "normal transformation" substitutes for "covariant transformation" and is the transformation rule for the normal vectors.

The Jacobian matrix $\underline{\underline{J}}$ for the transformation function $\underline{X} = \underline{F}(\underline{x})$ is a function of $\underline{x}$, and is calculated by taking partial derivatives of $\underline{F}$ with respect to the coordinates x_1, x_2, and x_3:

$$\underline{J}_i(\underline{x}) = \frac{\partial \underline{F}(\underline{x})}{\partial x_i} \qquad [Equation\ 1.1b]$$

In other words, the ith column of $\underline{\underline{J}}$ is obtained by the partial derivative of $\underline{F}(\underline{x})$ with respect to x_i.

When the surface of an object is given by a parametric function of two variables u and v,

$$\underline{x} = \underline{x}(u, v), \qquad [Equation\ 1.1c]$$

any tangent vector to the surface may be obtained from linear combinations of partial derivatives of $\underline{x}$ with respect to u and v. The normal vector direction may be obtained from the cross product of two linearly independent surface tangent vectors.

The **tangent vector transformation rule** is a restatement of the chain rule in multidimensional calculus. The new vector derivative is equal to the Jacobian matrix times the old derivative.

In matrix form, this is expressed as:

$$\frac{\partial \underline{X}}{\partial u} = \underline{\underline{J}} \frac{\partial \underline{x}}{\partial u} \qquad [Equation\ 1.2a]$$

This is equivalent in component form to:

$$X_{i,u} = \sum_{j=1}^{3} J_{ij} x_{j,u} \qquad [Equations\ 1.2b]$$

In other words, the new tangent vector $\partial \underline{X}/\partial u$ is equal to the Jacobian matrix $\underline{\underline{J}}$ times the old tangent vector $\partial \underline{x}/\partial u$

The **normal vector transformation rule** involves the inverse transpose of the Jacobian matrix. A derivation of this result is found in Appendix A.

$$[Equation\ 1.3]$$

$$\underline{n}^{(X)} = \det \underline{\underline{J}}\, \underline{\underline{J}}^{-1T} \underline{n}^{(x)}$$

Of course, since only the direction of the normal vector is important, it is not necessary to compute the value of the determinant in practice, although it sometimes is implicitly calculated as shown in Appendix A. As is well known from calculus, the determinant of the Jacobian is the local volume ratio at each point in the transformation, between the deformed region and the undeformed region.

2.0 Examples of Deformations.

Example 2.1: Scaling. One of the simplest deformations is a change in the length of the three global components parallel to the coordinate axes. This produces an orthogonal scaling operation :

$$X = a_1 x$$
$$Y = a_2 y \qquad [Equation \quad 2.1a]$$
$$Z = a_3 z$$

The components of the Jacobian matrix are given by

$$J_{ij} = \frac{\partial X_i}{\partial x_j},$$

so

$$\underline{\underline{J}} = \begin{pmatrix} a_1 & 0 & 0 \\ 0 & a_2 & 0 \\ 0 & 0 & a_3 \end{pmatrix} \qquad [Equation \quad 2.1b]$$

The volume change of a region scaled by this transformation is obtained from the Jacobian determinant, which is $a_1 a_2 a_3$. The normal transformation matrix is the inverse transpose of the Jacobian matrix (optionally times the determinant of the Jacobian matrix), and is given by:

$$\det J \quad \underline{\underline{J}}^{-1T} = \begin{pmatrix} a_2 a_3 & 0 & 0 \\ 0 & a_1 a_3 & 0 \\ 0 & 0 & a_1 a_2 \end{pmatrix}$$

Without the factor of the determinant, the normal transformation matrix is:

$$\underline{\underline{J}}^{-1T} = \begin{pmatrix} 1/a_1 & 0 & 0 \\ 0 & 1/a_2 & 0 \\ 0 & 0 & 1/a_3 \end{pmatrix}$$

To obtain the new normal vector at any point on the surface of an object subjected to this deformation, we multiply the original normal vector by either of the above normal transformation matrices. The new **unit** normal vector is easily obtained by dividing the output components by the magnitude of the vector.

For instance, consider converting a point $[x_1, x_2, x_3]^T$ lying on a roughly spherical surface centered at the origin, with normal vector $[n_1, n_2, n_3]^T$. The transformed surface point on the resulting ellipsoidal shape is $[a_1 x_1, a_2 x_2, a_3 x_3]^T$ and the transformed normal vector is parallel to $[n_1/a_1, n_2/a_2, n_3/a_3]^T$. The volume ratio between the shapes is $a_1 a_2 a_3$.

The scaling transformation is a special case of general affine transformations, in which the Jacobian matrix is a constant matrix. Affine transformations include skewing, rotation, and scaling transformations. When the transformation consists of pure rotation, it is interesting to note that the inverse of the matrix is equal to its transpose. For pure rotation, this means that the tangent vector and the normal vector are transformed by a single matrix. For more general affine transformations, pairs of constant matrices are required.

Example 2.2: Global Tapering along the Z Axis. Tapering is similar to scaling, by differentially changing the length of two global components without changing the length of the third. In figure 2.2, the function $f(z)$ is a piecewise linear function which decreases as z increases (from page bottom to the top). The magnitude of the tapering rate progressively increases from figure 2.2 a through figure 2.2 d. When the tapering function $f(z) = 1$, the portion of the deformed object is unchanged; the object increases in size as a function of z when $f'(z) > 0$, and decreases in size when $f'(z) < 0$. The object passes through a singularity at $f(z) = 0$ and becomes everted when $f(z) < 0$.

$$r = f(z),$$
$$X = rx,$$
$$Y = ry, \qquad [Equation \quad 2.2a]$$
$$Z = z$$

The tangent transformation matrix is given by:

$$\underline{\underline{J}} = \begin{pmatrix} r & 0 & f'(z)x \\ 0 & r & f'(z)y \\ 0 & 0 & 1 \end{pmatrix} \qquad [Equation \quad 2.2b]$$

The local volumetric rate of expansion, from the determinant, is r^2.

The normal transformation matrix is given by:

$$r^2 \underline{\underline{J}}^{-1T} = \begin{pmatrix} r & 0 & 0 \\ 0 & r & 0 \\ -rf'(z)x & -rf'(z)y & r^2 \end{pmatrix}$$

The inverse transformation is given by:

$$r(Z) = f(Z),$$
$$x = X/r,$$
$$y = Y/r, \qquad [Equation \quad 2.2c]$$
$$z = Z$$

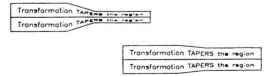

Figure 2.2 Progressive Tapering of a Ribbon

Example 2.3: Global Axial Twists. For some applications, it is useful to simulate global twisting of an object. A twist can be approximated as differential rotation, just as tapering is a differential scaling of the global basis vectors. We rotate one pair of global basis vectors as a function of height, without altering the third global basis vector. The deformation can be demonstrated by twisting a deck of cards, in which each card is rotated somewhat more than the card beneath it.

The global twist around the z axis is produced by the following equations:

$$\theta = f(z)$$
$$C_\theta = cos(\theta)$$
$$S_\theta = sin(\theta)$$

$$X = xC_\theta - yS_\theta,$$
$$Y = xS_\theta + yC_\theta, \qquad [Equation \quad 2.3a]$$
$$Z = z.$$

The twist proceeds along the z axis at a rate of $f'(z)$ radians per unit length in the z direction.

The tangent transformation matrix is given by

$$\underline{\underline{J}} = \begin{pmatrix} C_\theta & -S_\theta & -xS_\theta f'(z) - yC_\theta f'(z) \\ S_\theta & C_\theta & xC_\theta f'(z) - yS_\theta f'(z) \\ 0 & 0 & 1 \end{pmatrix}$$

Note that the determinant of the Jacobian matrix is unity, so that the twisting transformation preserves the volume of the original solid. This is consistent with our "card-deck" model of twisting, since each individual card retains its original volume.

The normal transformation matrix is given by:

$$\underline{\underline{J}}^{-1T} = \begin{pmatrix} C_\theta & -S_\theta & 0 \\ S_\theta & C_\theta & 0 \\ yf'(z) & -xf'(z) & 1 \end{pmatrix}$$

Our original deck of cards is a rectangular solid, with orthogonal normal vectors. We can see from the above transformation matrix that the normal vectors to the twisted deck will generally tilt out of the x-y plane.

Figures 2.3.1 a–d show the effect of a progressively increasing twist. In these line drawings of solids, vectors are hidden by the normal vector criterion—if the normal vector (as calculated by the above transformation matrix) faces the viewer, the line is drawn, otherwise, the line segment is not drawn. Figure 2.3.3 shows an object which has been twisted and tapered, while figures 2.3.4 and 2.3.2 show the results from twisting an object around an axis not within the object itself.

The inverse transformation is given by:

$$[Equation \quad 2.3b]$$

$$\theta = f(Z),$$
$$x = XC_\theta + YS_\theta,$$
$$y = -XS_\theta + YC_\theta,$$
$$z = Z$$

which is basically a twist in the opposite direction.

Figure 2.3.1 Progressive Twisting of a Ribbon

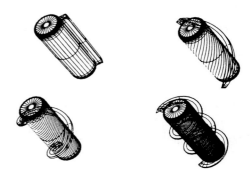

Figure 2.3.2 Progressive Twisting of Two Primitives

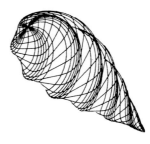

Figure 2.3.3 Twisting of a Tapered Primitive

Figure 2.3.4 Tapering of a Twisted offset Primitive

Example 2.4: Global Linear Bends along the Y-Axis. For other applications, it is useful to have a simple simulation of bending.

The following equations represent an isotropic bend along a centerline parallel to the y-axis: the length of the centerline does not change during the bending process. The bending angle θ, is constant at the extremities, but changes linearly in the central region. In the bent region, the bending rate k, measured in radians per unit length, is constant, and the differential basis vectors are simultaneously rotated and translated around the third local basis vector. Outside the bent region, the deformation consists of a rigid body rotation and translation. The range of the bending deformation is controlled by y_{min}, and y_{max}, with the bent region corresponding to values of y such that $y_{min} \leq y \leq y_{max}$. The axis of the bend is located along $[s, y_0, 1/k]^T$, where s is the parameter of the line. The center of the bend occurs at $y = y_0$—i.e., where one would "put one's thumbs" to create the bend. The radius of curvature of the bend is $1/k$.

The bending angle θ is given by:

$$\theta = k(\hat{y} - y_0),$$
$$C_\theta = cos(\theta),$$
$$S_\theta = sin(\theta),$$

where

$$\hat{y} = \begin{cases} y_{min}, & \text{if } y \leq y_{min} \\ y, & \text{if } y_{min} < y < y_{max} \\ y_{max}, & \text{if } y \geq y_{max} \end{cases}$$

The formula for this type of bending along the y axis centerline is given by the following relations:

[*Equation* 2.4a]

$$X = x$$

$$Y = \begin{cases} -S_\theta(z - \frac{1}{k}) + y_0, & y_{min} \leq y \leq y_{max}, \\ -S_\theta(z - \frac{1}{k}) + y_0 + C_\theta(y - y_{min}), & y < y_{min} \\ -S_\theta(z - \frac{1}{k}) + y_0 + C_\theta(y - y_{max}), & y > y_{max} \end{cases}$$

$$Z = \begin{cases} C_\theta(z - \frac{1}{k}) + \frac{1}{k}, & y_{min} \leq y \leq y_{max}, \\ C_\theta(z - \frac{1}{k}) + \frac{1}{k} + S_\theta(y - y_{min}), & y < y_{min} \\ C_\theta(z - \frac{1}{k}) + \frac{1}{k} + S_\theta(y - y_{max}), & y > y_{max} \end{cases}$$

These functions have continuous values at the boundaries of each of the three regions for y, and in the limit, for $k = 0$. However, there is a jump in the derivative of the bending angle θ at the $y = y_{min}$ and $y = y_{max}$ boundaries. The discontinuities may be eliminated by using a smooth function for θ as a function of y, but the transformation matrices would need to be re-derived.

The tangent transformation matrix is given by:

$$\underline{\underline{J}} = \begin{pmatrix} 1 & 0 & 0 \\ 0 & C_\theta(1 - \hat{k}z) & -S_\theta \\ 0 & S_\theta(1 - \hat{k}z) & C_\theta \end{pmatrix}$$

where

$$\hat{k} = \begin{cases} k, & \text{if } \hat{y} = y \\ 0, & \text{if } \hat{y} \neq y. \end{cases}$$

The local rate of expansion, as obtained from the determinant, is $1 - \hat{k}z$.

The normal transformation matrix is given by:

$$(1 - \hat{k}z)\underline{\underline{J}}^{-1T} = \begin{pmatrix} 1 - \hat{k}z & 0 & 0 \\ 0 & C_\theta & -S_\theta(1 - \hat{k}z) \\ 0 & S_\theta & C_\theta(1 - \hat{k}z) \end{pmatrix}$$

The inverse transformation is given by:

[*Equation* 2.4b]

$$\theta_{min} = k(y_{min} - y_0)$$
$$\theta_{max} = k(y_{max} - y_0)$$
$$\hat{\theta} = -tan^{-1}\left(\frac{Y - y_0}{Z - \frac{1}{k}}\right)$$

$$\theta = \begin{cases} \theta_{min}, & \text{if } \hat{\theta} < \hat{\theta}_{min} \\ \hat{\theta}, & \text{if } \theta_{min} \leq \hat{\theta} \leq \theta_{max} \\ \theta_{max}, & \text{if } \hat{\theta} > \theta_{max} \end{cases}$$

$$x = X$$

$$\hat{y} = \frac{\theta}{k} + y_0$$

$$y = \begin{cases} \hat{y}, & y_{min} < \hat{y} < y_{max} \\ (Y - y_0)C_\theta + (z - \frac{1}{k})S_\theta + \hat{y}, & \hat{y} = y_{min} \text{ or } y_{max} \end{cases}$$

$$z = \begin{cases} \frac{1}{k} + ((Y - y_0)^2 + (Z - \frac{1}{k})^2)^{1/2}, & y_{min} < \hat{y} < y_{max} \\ -(Y - y_0)S_\theta + (z - \frac{1}{k})C_\theta + \hat{y}, & \hat{y} = y_{min} \text{ or } y_{max} \end{cases}$$

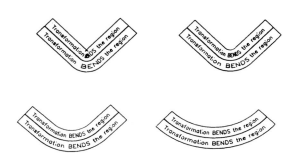

Figure 2.4.2 Progressive Change in Bending Range of a Region

In figure 2.4.2, a constant 90° bend is produced by varying the range and the bend rate. In other words, $k(y_{max} - y_{min}) = \pi/2$ in each of the examples. In figure 2.4.3, a twisted object is subjected to a progressive bend to produce a Moebius band. Figures 2.4.4 a and b show a hierarchy of tapering, twisting, and bending, by superimposing a bend on the objects in figures 2.3.2 and 2.3.3. In figure 2.4.5, a chair is made from six primitives using seven bends. The details of the crimp in the coordinate systems is shown in figures 2.4.6 a - b.

However, the type of bending shown in the figures does not retain all of the generality that true bending requires. Some materials are anisotropic and have an intrinsic "grain" or directionality in them. Although this is beyond the scope of this paper, it is interesting to note that the tangent and normal transformation rules may still be utilized.

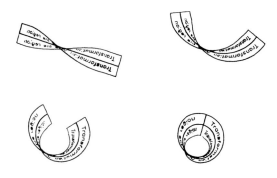

Figure 2.4.3 Moebius band is produced with a twist and a bend

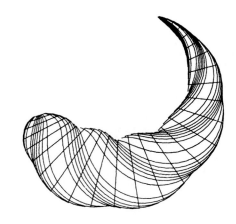

Figure 2.4.4 a Bent, Twisted, Tapered Primitive

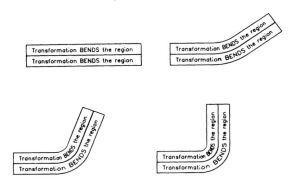

Figure 2.4.1 Progressive Bending of a Region

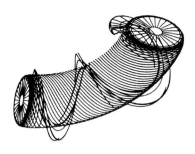

Figure 2.4.4 b Bent, Twisted Primitive

Figure 2.4.5 Chair Model, with six primitives and seven bends.

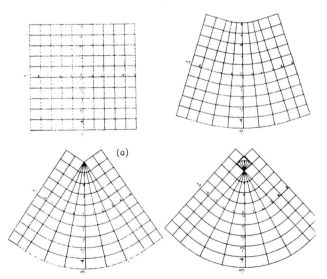

Figure 2.4.6 Details of the Bend near the Crimp

3.0 Converting Local Representations to Global Representations.

In this section, a method for generating more general shapes is addressed. The Jacobian matrix $\underline{J}(\underline{x})$ is assumed to be known as a function of x_1, x_2, and x_3, but a closed form expression for the corresponding coordinate deformation function $\underline{X} = \underline{F}(\underline{x})$ is not known (i.e., in terms of standard mathematical functions). The basic method involves

(1) the conversion of the undeformed input shape into its tangent vectors by differentiation,

(2) transforming the tangent vectors via the tangent transformation rule into the tangent vectors of the deformed object, and then

(3) integrating the new tangent vectors to obtain the new position vectors of the deformed space curve, surface, or solid.

This "local-to-global" operation converts the local tangent vectors and Jacobian matrix into the global position vectors. The absolute position in space of the deformed object is defined within an arbitrary integration constant vector .

The above method provides a completely general description of deformation, and may be directly coupled to the output from the elasticity equations, finite element analysis, or other advanced mathematical models of deformable entities describing a profoundly general collection of shapes. The integrations outlined above need not be calculated explicitly in a ray-tracing environment: a multidimensional Newton's method can use the Jacobian matrix directly.

3.1 Transformations of Space Curves. Given a space curve, parameterized by a single variable s,

$$\underline{x} = \underline{x}(s), \quad s_0 \leq s \leq s_1$$

a new curve $\underline{X}(s)$ is desired which is the deformed version of $\underline{x}(s)$. The Jacobian matrix $\underline{J}(s)$ or $\underline{J}(\underline{x}(s))$ is assumed to be known, but the coordinate transformation function $\underline{X} = \underline{F}(\underline{x})$ is assumed to be unavailable. As stated above, the equation for $\underline{X}(s)$ may be derived from the fact that,

(1) by definition, the position $\underline{X}(s)$ is a constant vector plus the integral of the derivative of the position, i.e.,

[*Equation* 3.1a]

$$\underline{X}(s) = \int_0^s \underline{X}'(\tilde{s})d\tilde{s} + \underline{x}_0,$$

(2) the derivative of the position is obtained via the tangent transformation rule, Equation 1.2 a, so

[Equation 3.1b]
$$\underline{X}(s) = \int_0^s \underline{\underline{J}}(\underline{x}(\tilde{s}))\underline{x}'(\tilde{s})d\tilde{s} + \underline{x}_0$$

where $\underline{\underline{J}}(\underline{x}(s))$ is the Jacobian matrix which depends upon the value of s, and $\underline{x}'(s)$ is the arclength derivative (a tangent vector) of the input curve $\underline{x}(s)$. At each point in the untransformed curve, $\underline{x}(s)$, the tangent vectors $\underline{x}'(s)$ are rotated and skewed to a new orientation in the transformed curve: the curve can be bent and twisted with or without being being stretched. For this case, any matrix function which allows the integral to be evaluated may serve as a Jacobian, since there is only one path along which to integrate.

For inextensible bending and twisting transformations of the space curve, with no stretching at any point of the curve, the Jacobian matrix $\underline{\underline{J}}(s)$ must be a varying rotation matrix function. (Even though this is not a constant affine rotation, the matrix function for the tangent vector transformation rule is identical to that used for the normal vector transformation rule.)

3.2 Transformations of 3-D surfaces and solids.
The representation of a transformed surface or solid can be obtained much in the same manner as a space curve. First, an origin O is chosen in the object to be deformed. For each point $\underline{x}$ in the surface of the object, a piecewise smooth space curve is chosen, which connects the origin O to the input point $\underline{x}$. The space curve is then subjected to the deformation as in section 3.1. If $\underline{\underline{J}}(\underline{x})$ is in fact the Jacobian of some (unspecified) deformation function $\underline{X} = \underline{F}(\underline{x})$, the transformation from $\underline{x}$ to $\underline{X}$ is unique: all smooth paths connecting O and $\underline{x}$ will be equivalent. Since the equation of the surface is given by $\underline{x} = \underline{x}(u,v)$, the space curve in the surface may be obtained by selecting two functions of a single variable, say s, for u and for v. i.e.,

$$u = u(s)$$

$$v = v(s)$$

so that the space curve in the surface $\hat{\underline{x}}(s)$ is obtained by substituting the values of u and v into the equation for $\underline{x}$.

$$\hat{\underline{x}}(s) = \underline{x}(u(s), v(s))$$

This space curve is then transformed as shown above, in Equation 3.1 b. The space curve should be piecewise differentiable, so that the derivatives can be evaluated and integrated. The equation for the deformed curve is

[Equation 3.2.1]
$$\underline{X}(u(s), v(s)) =$$
$$\int_0^s \underline{\underline{J}}(\underline{x}(u(\hat{s}), v(\hat{s})))\underline{x}'(u(\hat{s}), v(\hat{s}))d\hat{s} + \underline{x}_0$$

Expanding the above equation, using the fact that the symbol $'$ means d/ds, and using the multidimensional chain rule, we obtain

$$\underline{X}(u(s), v(s)) =$$
$$\int_0^s \underline{\underline{J}}(\underline{x}(u(\hat{s}), v(\hat{s})))(\frac{\partial \underline{x}}{\partial u}u'(\hat{s}) + \frac{\partial \underline{x}}{\partial v}v'(\hat{s}))d\hat{s} + \underline{x}_0$$

As stated before, for consistency, $\underline{\underline{J}}$ must be the Jacobian matrix of some global function $\underline{F}(\underline{x})$, so that the results are independent of the path connecting O and $\underline{x}$, and so that the tangent and normal vector transformation rules apply. The test for the "Jacobian-ness" of the matrix, (in the absence of a prespecified deformation function $\underline{F}(\underline{x})$) depends on the partial derivatives of the columns of $\underline{\underline{J}}(\underline{x})$

The columns must satisfy

$$\underline{\underline{J}}_{i,j} = \underline{\underline{J}}_{j,i} \qquad [Equation\ 3.2.2]$$

In other words, the partial derivative of the ith column of $\underline{\underline{J}}$ with respect to x_j must be equal to the partial derivative of the jth column of $\underline{\underline{J}}$ with respect to x_i. (The underlying principle to prove this result is a multiple-integration path consistency requirement. The integrand must be an exact differential.) The values of the Jacobian may be directly related to the material properties of the substance to be modeled, and may utilize the plasticity and elasticity equations.

4.0 Applications to Rendering

To obtain a set of control points and normal vectors with which to create surface patches like polygons or spline patches, we sample the deformed surface parametrically, With the appropriate sampling, the patches can faithfully tesselate the desired object, with more detail where the surface is highly curved, and less detail where the surface is flat.

First, the object is sampled with a raw grid of parametric u-v values. This raw parametric sampling of the surface is then refined using normal vector criteria, as calculated by the transformation rule: the surface is recursively subdivided when the adjacent normal vectors diverge too greatly. Dot products which are far enough from unity indicate that more recursive detail is necessary in that region.

In this way, patch-oriented methods like depth-buffer and scan-line encoding schemes are effective. These algorithms are linear in terms of the total surface area and total number of patches. The direct subdivison approach is not as well-suited to ray tracing, since the total number of operations is quadratic in the number of ray comparisons and objects.

The incident ray can be intersected with the deformed primitive analytically, to reduce the number of objects. In addition, it is possible to use the inverse deformation to undeform the primitives and trace along the deformed rays. (See figures 4.1 and 4.2). This reduces the dimensionality of the parameter search from three to one, indicating a tremendous saving in numerical complexity.

The Jacobian techniques in this paper aid the traditional solution methods to find roots of nonlinear ray equations (in the context of ray-tracing deformed objects), including the multidimensional Newton-Raphson method, the method of regula falsi, and the one-dimensional Newton's methods in N-space. (See [ACTON].) The analysis of rendering deformed primitives using these techniques is left to a future study.

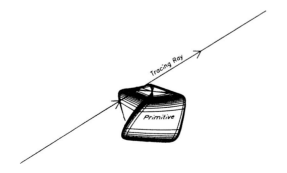

Figure 4.1 Deformed primitive, in undeformed space.

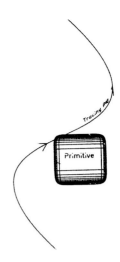

Figure 4.2 Undeformed primitive, in its undeformed coordinate system, showing path of ray

Appendix A:
Proof of the normal vector transformation rule.

A short derivation in cross product and dot product style demonstrates the normal vector transformation rule.

The surface of an undeformed object is given by a parametric function of two variables u and v, $\underline{x} = \underline{x}(u,v)$. The goal is to discover an expression for the normal vector to the surface after it has been subjected to the deformation $\underline{X} = F(\underline{x})$.

We note that the inverse of an arbitrary three by three matrix $\underline{M}$ may be obtained from the cross-products of pairs of its columns via:

$$[\underline{M}_1, \underline{M}_2, \underline{M}_3]^{-1} = \frac{[\underline{M}_2 \wedge \underline{M}_3, \underline{M}_3 \wedge \underline{M}_1, \underline{M}_1 \wedge \underline{M}_2]^T}{\underline{M}_1 \cdot (\underline{M}_2 \wedge \underline{M}_3)}.$$

We start the derivation using the fact that the normal vector is the cross product of independent surface tangent vectors:

$$\underline{n}^{(X)} = \frac{\partial \underline{X}}{\partial u} \wedge \frac{\partial \underline{X}}{\partial v} \qquad [Equation\ \ B.1d]$$

The tangent vectors for $\underline{X}(u,v)$ are expanded in terms of $\underline{x}(s,t)$.

$$\underline{n}^{(X)} = \left(\underline{\underline{J}} \frac{\partial \underline{x}}{\partial u}\right) \wedge \left(\underline{\underline{J}} \frac{\partial \underline{x}}{\partial v}\right)$$

Matrix multiplication is expanded, yielding

$$\underline{n}^{(X)} = \left(\sum_{i=1}^{3} \underline{J}_i x_{i,u}\right) \wedge \left(\sum_{j=1}^{3} \underline{J}_j x_{j,v}\right)$$

The summations are combined together:

$$= \sum_{i=1}^{3} \sum_{j=1}^{3} \left(\underline{J}_i \wedge \underline{J}_j \right) x_{i,s} x_{j,t}$$

Since the cross product of a vector with itself is the zero vector, and since for any vectors $\underline{b}$ and $\underline{c}$, $\underline{b} \wedge \underline{c} = -\underline{c} \wedge \underline{b}$, this expands to:

$$\underline{n}^{(X)} = \left(\underline{J}_2 \wedge \underline{J}_3, \underline{J}_3 \wedge \underline{J}_1, \underline{J}_1 \wedge \underline{J}_2 \right) \begin{pmatrix} x_{2,u} x_{3,v} - x_{3,u} x_{2,v} \\ x_{3,u} x_{1,v} - x_{1,u} x_{3,v} \\ x_{1,s} x_{2,v} - x_{2,u} x_{1,v} \end{pmatrix}$$

Thus,

$$\underline{n}^{(X)} = [\underline{J}_2 \wedge \underline{J}_3, \underline{J}_3 \wedge \underline{J}_1, \underline{J}_1 \wedge \underline{J}_2] \underline{n}^{(x)}$$

Since $\det \underline{\underline{M}} = \underline{M}_1 \cdot (\underline{M}_2 \wedge \underline{M}_3)$ for an arbitrary matrix $\underline{\underline{M}}$,

$$\underline{n}^{(X)} = \det \underline{\underline{J}} \, \underline{\underline{J}}^{-1T} \underline{n}^{(x)}$$

In other words, the new normal vector $\underline{n}^{(X)}$ is expressed as a multiplication of matrix $\underline{\underline{J}}^{-1T}$ and the old normal vector $\underline{n}^{(x)}$.

Since only the direction of the normal vector is important, it is not necessary to compute the value of the determinant in practice, unless one needs the local volume ratio between corresponding points in the deformed and undeformed objects.

The fact that the normal vector follows this type of transformation rule makes it less expensive to calculate, increasing its applicability in a variety of modeling circumstances.

Acknowledgements

I would like to thank Dan Whelan, of the California Institute of Technology, and Olin Lathrop, of Raster Technologies Inc., for technical help with the typography and the illustrations.

Bibliography

1. Acton, F.S., Numerical Methods that Work, Harper and Row, 1970.
2. Barr, A.H., "Superquadrics and Angle-Preserving Transformations," IEEE Computer Graphics and Applications, Volume 1 number 1 1981.
3. Buck, R. C., Advanced Calculus, McGraw-Hill, 2nd edition, 1965
4. Faux, I.D., and M.J. Pratt, Computational Geometry for Design and Manufacture, Ellis Horwood Ltd., Wiley and Sons, 1979.
5. Franklin, W.R., and A.H. Barr, "Faster Calculation of Superquadric Shapes," IEEE Computer Graphics and Applications, Volume 1 number 3, 1981.
6. Kajiya, J.T., "Ray Tracing Parametric Patches," SigGraph 82 Conference Proceedings, Computer Graphics, Volume 16, Number 3, 1982.
7. Segel, L.A., Mathematics Applied to Continuum Mechanics, Macmillan Publishing Co., 1977.
8. Solkolnikoff, I.S., Mathematical Theory of Elasticity, McGraw Hill, 1956.

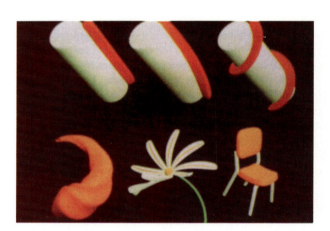

A System for Computer Generated Movies

Edwin Catmull, University of Utah

With the recent developments in fast hidden surface algorithms and a method for smooth shading of half-tone pictures, it has become feasible to generate useful movies with the computer. This paper describes a system used to make computer generated movies. It also explains the methods used to attempt to solve the problems of object representation, object manipulation, concurrent motion, and ease of specifying motion. The system was first used to make a movie of a hand that lasts for little more than a minute.

KEY WORDS AND PHRASES: half-tone computer graphics, hidden surface, polygonal surface structure presentations, animation, graphic language, movie
CR CATEGORIES: 3.41, 4.29, 8.2

INTRODUCTION

Computer generated pictures and movies have been made by artists and computer scientists for several years now, and have recently caught the public eye. Most of the computer movies, however, have consisted of line drawings. The state of the art in half-tone pictures was not advanced enough to make it reasonable to produce half-tone movies. Half-tone pictures are displayed on a screen much as a TV picture is presented: surfaces are painted with differing shades on scan lines. The most basic problem with half-tone pictures was deciding which surface was in front and therefore should be painted on the scope. Several algorithms have been developed for different classes of surfaces. Most were quite time consuming. Recently there have been fast hidden surface algorithms for surfaces made up of polygons (1,2,3). This research uses Watkins (3) algorithm since it has been implemented in hardware and is remarkably fast. One of the objections to these algorithms is that all surfaces must be made up of polygons. This is a severe restriction for curved surfaces such as spheres or skin. Fortunately, Henri Gouraud (4) has developed a method, called smooth shading, for making polygonal surfaces appear curved.

With these developments, it has become feasible to generate useful half-tone movies with the computer. This paper describes a system used to generate movies. It explains the methods used to solve the problems of object representation, object manipulation, concurrent motion, and ease of specifying motion.

THE SYSTEM

Figure 1 shows a block diagram of a system for making movies. The high precision scope is a raster scope similar to a TV but with higher resolution and quality. The hidden surface removal is done by a routine developed by Gary Watkins (3) which operates on polygons. The smooth shading was developed by Henri Gouraud (4). It is necessary to send these routines the points of a polygon, the normals at each point for shading, and the whiteness or colour for each polygon. All objects displayed by this system must be made up of polygons. This is usually not a serious limitation because of the smooth shading.

DATA DESCRIPTION

For the purpose of this paper, an "object" or "part" is a group of polygons that will transform together and a "body" is an organized group of objects. For example, the body of a hand is made up of several smaller objects: the palm, the bottom of the thumb, the middle of the thumb, the top of the thumb, etc. The objects are organized in a tree structure. By using a tree structure, any transformation applied to an object at a node also applies to its children.

---

*This research was supported in part by the University of Utah Computer Science Division and the Advanced Research Projects Agency of the Department of Defense monitored by the Rome Air Development Center, Griffiss Air Force Base, New York, under contract number F-30602-70-C-0300.

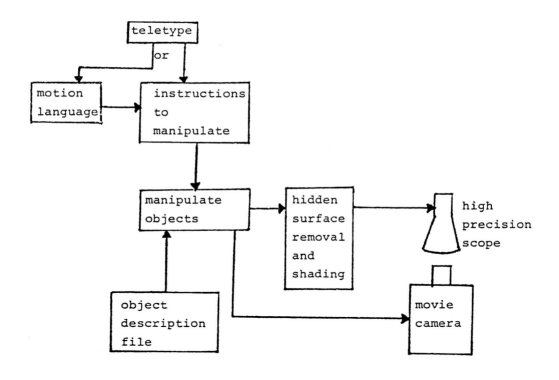

Figure 1.

If one rotates the bottom of the thumb, the other two parts of the thumb follow automatically. Each object is described as follows:

father brother
points
polygons
axes named positions

The points are a numbered list of x, y, and z coordinates. Polygons are described by a list of numbers where each number refers to the correspondingly numbered point. If the number is preceded by a "↑" the point is in the object named as father. If the number is preceded by a "←" then the point is in the object named as brother. This way objects can be connected together by having polygons with points in different objects to allow for flexible surfaces. Each object can be assigned a color.

One can define an axis of rotation for an object relative to its parent object. The axis of rotation is defined by three points where the axis passes through the second point and is perpendicular to the plane defined by the three points. A positive rotation is taken from the first to the third point. One can name different degrees of rotation. For example, in a forearm, we might call zero degrees OPEN and 170 degrees CLOSED. Then when one wants the arm to go straight, regardless of the position it is in, it is only necessary to give an instruction that the forearm go to position OPEN, rather than having to keep track of the position. This can prevent losing track of where one is at after making many changes.

For example, to describe a body consisting of two objects where each object consists of one polygon.

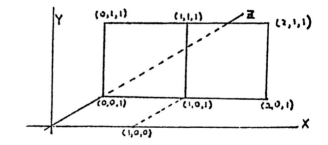

```
NAME=FLAP1
POINTS
1   0.   0.   1.
2   1.   0.   1.
3   1.   1.   1.
4   0.   1.   1.
5   1.   0.   0.
POLYGONS
1  2  3  4
END FLAP1
NAME=FLAP2
FATHER=FLAP1
POINTS
1   2.   0.   1.
2   2.   1.   1.
POLYGONS
1  2  ↑3  ↑2
AXIS 1  ↑1  ↑2  ↑5
FLAT=0
CLOSE=90
END FLAP2
```

This method of data representation is fairly convenient to use but still does not solve some of the more difficult problems of flexible surfaces. Careful inspection of the hand (figure 2) when the hand is closed will show that the joints become somewhat distorted. This is not just a matter of choosing wrong axes of rotation. Two possible solutions to this particular problem are:

1. Interpolation between two states taking into account rotation. Unfortunately, it would be extremely difficult to get the coordinate definition of a closed hand.
2. Generating the polygons of a flexible part using some curve fitting or B-spline technique. This has yet to be fully worked out.

MOTION - THE OBJECT MANIPULATION ROUTINE

The routine MOTION accepts instructions to manipulate objects, prepares the data for sending to the hidden surface algorithm, and controls the camera. The instructions to MOTION can come from either a teletype or a file. The most commonly used instructions are:

ROTATE <object name><axis number><degrees>
MOVE <object name><dx><dy><dz>
DISPLAY

There are other instructions to control resolution, background, intensity, camera, the instruction file, etc. There are instructions to return the current state of an object. For example, a controlling program may request the degrees of rotation that the top of the thumb has made or how many degrees the thumb must rotate to reach a given named position. This makes it usually unnecessary to keep track of the changes made to an object.

For a movie of a hand, each frame may require as many as 14 instructions, i.e. the fingers close while the hand rotates. In order to make a movie of only one minute (1440 frames), about 13,000 instructions must be executed. It is immediately apparent that it is unreasonable to specify frame by frame a complex behavior that lasts for more than a few frames. The problem is compounded by the fact that objects may move independently in time, thereby making normal looping techniques inadequate to generate the instructions needed.

MOP - A MOTION PICTURE LANGUAGE

Typical programming languages are much too sequential in nature for specifying easily the kinds of simultaneous and overlapping action we expect in a movie. There have been some animation systems that have tried to solve this problem (5,6,7,8). The language MOP is designed to allow concurrency from the point of view of the user. It generates instructions for MOTION which changes and displays the objects.

Figure 2 shows a sequence of 11 frames where a hand first closes and then opens in a fanout way. Notice that the motion starts slowly, speeds up, and then slows before stopping. The rate at which an object moves or changes can be specified by either some mathematical formulation (in this case a sine curve) or a table of empirical data. The program then integrates the area under some portion of the curve to determine the movement for each frame.

For example, if one wanted an object to accelerate (animators refer to it as a slow-in), a table could be created as follows:

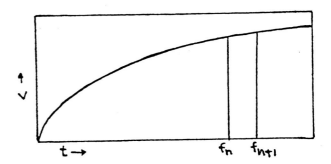

The user would have to specify the table either by guesswork or from empirical data. The table can be used for any frame period. The number of frames in the period is the number of divisions along the time axis. The movement in each frame can then be easily calculated.

Most statements in MOP are of the following form: <label> <frame period> <instruction> <parameters>. The label is an alphanumeric name followed by a colon. It is optional and is used to name a statement. It is not used for transfer of control since control is not sequential.

Figure 2. A sequence of 11 frames showing the hand close and open. Notice the rate of change is not constant.

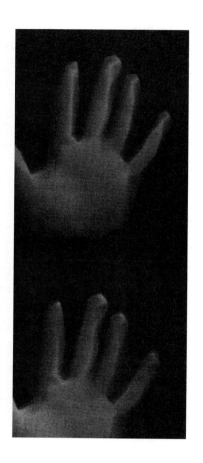

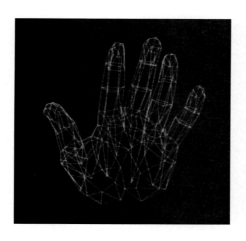

Figure 3. A line drawing of the hand as it was input.

Figure 4. The hand as displayed using hidden surface and smooth shading algorithms.

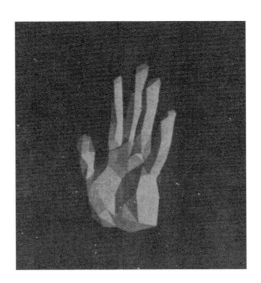

Figure 5. The hand as displayed using hidden surface algorithm but no smooth shading. The individual polygons can be seen.

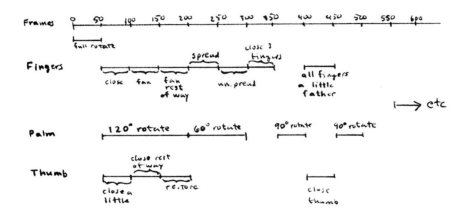

Figure 6.

The frame period is used to specify over what frames the statement is executed and at what rate changes occur. It is of the form:

<arith. expr.>,<arith. expr.>,<table name>

The first expression is the starting frame, the second is the last frame, and the third indicates which table or arithmetic formula is to be used to dictate the rate of change.

The instruction is either a reserved instruction or the name of another statement.

The parameters are arithmetic expressions or strings, the value of which may either be passed to another statement or passed to a reserved function for output.

When the program is read in, the frame sequence is either known or unknown. For example:

76,175,B ROTATE "PALM",1,30

has a known frame sequence 76-175 and will cause the palm to be rotated 30 degrees about axis 1 during that 100 frames. The amount rotated each frame is determined by the table or formula named "B". On the other hand:

LAB: FIRST,FIRST+50,B ROTATE "PALM",1,30

has an unknown frame sequence as long as FIRST does not have a value. Each statement is initially put into one of two lists: one for instructions where the frame sequence is known, the other for the unknown.

One of the reserved instructions is "BEGIN" which means that all of the following statements until an "END" will be grouped under the same label. However, the execution of each statement in the group is still determined by its own frame period specification.

A frame counter is started that is incremented for each frame. During each frame, every statement in the "known" list is checked to see if the frame counter is within its frame specification. If so, the statement is executed with appropriate modifications made depending on how far into the frame sequence the frame counter is. A statement may call by label a statement or group of statements from the "unknown" list to be in the "known" list by giving values to its undefined variables via the parameters. The new statements may take on the frame specification of the caller. This way routines of motion may be written.

The output is a file of instructions for the MOTION routine. A page and a half of coding in MOP to manipulate a hand to various positions for a minute movie will generate the some 13,000 changes that are made to the hand.

The statements to MOP may be in any order. This feature makes a considerable difference in programming ease.

THE MAKING OF A MOVIE

As an illustration of the capabilities of this system, a movie of a hand was made. A hand was chosen because it was difficult enough to show some of the possibilities and weaknesses of the system. The hand has a flexible surface and parts that move relative to other parts. The following steps were taken.

Data Acquisition

Although outside the scope of this paper, it should be noted that this is still a formidable task. For the hand, a plaster of paris mold was made. (A word of caution to anyone wishing to make a similar mold: it is more comfortable to shave the back of the hand before making the mold than to have the hairs pulled out by the mold.) Next, a plaster model was made from the mold and covered with a thin layer of latex material. Polygons were drawn on the latex. It was necessary to extract the three dimensional coordinates of some 270 corner points defining the surface of the hand, organize them into about 350 polygons, and organize the polygons into the parts of the hand. This was followed by determining the axes about which each part rotated. Figures 3, 4, and 5 show the polygons drawn as lines, polygon surfaces, and the smooth shaded version.

Mapping Out the Action

This consists of deciding what actions are to take place and when they are to occur. See figure 6. Some of this work can be done interactively. Baecker (7) has developed a scheme in two dimensions for specifying motion, however, this has not yet been worked out satisfactorily in three dimensions. Traditionally, the creation of an animated film begins with a story board. The system described in this paper is meant to be used with a storyboard format. However, the way one lays out the sequence of events is a matter of personal style.

Programming

The first step is to write routines of motion. As an example, the fingers move often enough that one might like to be able to type:

N,N+50 ROTFIN 45,45,50,60;

where the parameters specify how much the parts of the respective fingers would rotate. Once the routines of Motion have been written (in MOP) it is relatively trivial to program the movie using the plan specified in the previous step. Each bar segment in figure 6 can usually be taken care of by a single statement. Again, the order of statements is inconsequential.

Filming

The instructions created by MOP are given to the MOTION program which gets the objects, makes changes on them, sends necessary information to the picture processors, and advances the camera. For debugging purposes, the half tone processor may be replaced by processors that paint the polygon edges on a vector or storage scope (figure 3).

Computers and Animation

The kinds of control needed for a film making language are:
 1. that it must be set in a context of frames and concurrent actions.
 2. the creation and manipulation in general of shapes and relations.
 3. how motion occurs - specified by mathematical equations or empirical data.
 4. to prevent conflict of objects because of accident or data error, i.e. one would not like to see an elbow bent the wrong way or a car driving through a tree.
 5. keep track of where objects are at.
 6. create routines of motion, i.e. a walking routine that could be applied to a person for an arbitrary number of frames.
 7. naturalness in describing action, i.e.

IN FRAMES T TO T+400 WALK CHARLIE TO
  TABLE;

The system described in this paper gives most of the above controls to some extent. MOP is convenient for specifying concurrent actions in frames. It allows for rotation of objects in three dimensions in a very natural way. However, in general, there are many kinds of flexible surfaces, i.e. cloth and water, that are difficult to model. The best that this animation system can do is interpolate between extreme configurations of a surface. A great deal of research still needs to be done on the creation and manipulation of three dimensional objects.

For the kinds of motion allowed, the method of specifying action is very general. The problem still remains with the animator to dictate the rate of change of motion. This is a non-trivial problem if a nice-looking action is desired.

Conflict of objects is only partially taken care of. There is no check to keep one object from passing through another. This problem is partially taken care of because it is very easy to keep track of the location and amount of rotation of any object.

MOP allows for the writing of routines of motion, but does not have a very natural syntax. It has been used for making several small movies, none of which had a story theme. The next step is to create a language with a better syntax.

CONCLUSION

A movie of the hand lasting more than a minute was made using the above system. The making of a movie is trivial compared to the acquisition of data at this time. Data is currently being gathered for the surface definition of a whole human body. At the time of this writing, a hardware implementation of Watkins algorithm has been completed, which is capable of displaying the picture data at a rate of 30 frames per second. At present it takes three to ten seconds to transform the object description to a format acceptable for the Watkins processor, but with the addition of a hardware clipper and matrix multiplier, the real time display of computer generated half-tone animated objects is a real possibility.

The system described in this paper has the kind of control needed to make movies that look good. For making movies, it is more desirable to be a director than a programmer, recognizing, of course, that being a good director is still a lot of work.

ACKNOWLEDGMENT

I would like to thank R. E. Stephenson, Ivan Sutherland, Fred Parke, and Barry Wessler for ideas, cooperation, and encouragement.

REFERENCES

1. Warnock, J., "A Hidden Surface Algorithm for Computer Generated Halftone Pictures," Technical Report 4-15, Computer Science, University of Utah, Salt Lake City, Utah, June 1969.

2. Bouknight, W. J., "An Improved Procedure for Generation of Half-tone Computer Graphics Presentations," Report R-432, Coordinated Science Laboratory, University of Illinois, Urbana, Illinois, September 1969.

3. Watkins, G. S., "A Real-time Visible Surface Algorithm," UTEC-CSc-70-101, Computer Science, University of Utah, Salt Lake City, Utah, June 1970.

4. Gouraud, H., "Computer Display of Curved Surfaces," UTEC-CSc-71-113, Computer Science, University of Utah, Salt Lake City, Utah, June 1971.

5. Citron, J. and Whitney, J. H., "CAMP-Computer Assisted Movie Production,"

Proceedings of FJCC, 1968, vol. 2.

6. Weiner, D. D. and Anderson, S. E., "A Computer Animation Movie Language for Educational Motion Pictures," *Proceedings of FJCC*, 1968, vol. 2.

7. Baecker, R. M., "Picture-Driven Animation," *Proceedings of SJCC*, 1969.

8. Gracer, F. and Blasgen, M.W., "Karma- A System for Storyboard Animation," *Computer Graphics*, Vol. 5, No. 1, p. 26, 1971.

Computer Generated Animation of Faces

Frederick I. Parke, University of Utah

This paper describes the representation, animation and data collection techniques that have been used to produce "realistic" computer generated half-tone animated sequences of a human face changing expression. It was determined that approximating the surface of a face with a polygonal skin containing approximately 250 polygons defined by about 400 vertices is sufficient to achieve a realistic face. Animation was accomplished using a cosine interpolation scheme to fill in the intermediate frames between expressions. This approach is good enough to produce realistic facial motion. The three-dimensional data used to describe the expressions of the face was obtained photogrammetrically using pairs of photographs.

KEY WORDS AND PHRASES: computer graphics, half-tone rendering, smooth shading, computer animation, flexible surfaces, polygonal surfaces, facial topology, cosine interpolation, three-dimensional data acquisition.
CR CATEGORIES: 8.2, 3.41, 4.41, 6.35

INTRODUCTION

The human face is a challenge for computer animation for at least two reasons. First the face is not a rigid structure but is a complex flexible surface. How is the motion of such a surface specified? Secondly faces are very familiar to us, we have a well developed sense of what expressions and motions are natural for a face. We notice small deviations from our concept of how a face should appear.

This paper describes a fairly simple way of representing the face and an animation technique that allows the production of realistic half-tone animated sequences of the face changing expression. The paper also describes the method used to collect the data for the faces. These techniques could be used to animate other flexible surfaces.

REPRESENTATION OF THE FACE

The face is a very complex three-dimensional surface. This surface is flexible. It usually contains creases, and it has color variation. What is the best way to represent such a surface that allows both animation and half-tone rendering? One possibility would be to find an analytic surface or collection of analytic surface patches (1) to approximate the surface of the face. Assuming this were feasible, there remains the problem of animating this surface or collection of patches. Again assuming that appropriate animation techniques were available for such surfaces, there still remains the problem of producing half-tone renderings of the surfaces. Hidden surface and half-tone algorithms exist for quadric surfaces (2,3) but they tend to be quite expensive. One can imagine similar algorithms for surfaces of higher degree, but would expect them to increase rapidly in expense as the degree of the surface increased. For this reason, when half-tone renderings are desired, surfaces of high degree are usually approximated by a skin of polygons.

In order to approximate the face with analytic patches, one would expect these patches to be at least quadric, and probably of higher degree. The approach of approximating the face with analytic surfaces leads to approximating the approximate surfaces with polygons. This seems a rather complex and roundabout approach.

The approach taken in this paper is one first used by Henri Gouraud (4). His approach was to directly approximate the surface of the face with a non-analytic skin of polygons. This skin was constructed by sampling the surface of the face at a number of points and connecting these points to form a skin of polygons.

In order to produce a half-tone rendering of objects in a three-dimensional space several problems must be solved.

---

*This research was supported in part by the University of Utah Computer Science Division and by the Advanced Research Projects Agency of the Department of Defense, monitored by Rome Air Development Center, Griffis Air Force Base, New York 13440, under contract F30602-70-C-0300.

The first of these problems is usually referred to as clipping. This is the problem of determining if all or part of an object is within a viewing space. The viewing space is a pyramid defined by the position of the view, the direction the viewer is looking and his viewing angle. An example of a viewing space would be that part of the universe visible through a window, assuming that all objects except the window frame were transparent and could not occlude other objects. The second problem is the detection of hidden surfaces. In other words, which surfaces are in front of other surfaces when seen from a given position. The last problem is one of determining the shading of the visible surfaces and producing the shaded image on some output device, normally a CRT. The shading usually depends on the orientation of the surface with respect to the viewer and the light source.

Approximation with polygons has several advantages. For polygonal surfaces, the problems listed above have been solved by a number of algorithms (5-11). These algorithms are fast and inexpensive when compared to algorithms for surfaces of higher degree. At least one of these algorithms (9) is implemented in hardware and another (11) is currently being implemented in hardware. Also, the development by Gouraud (4) of a smooth shading algorithm for polygonal surfaces makes it possible to give a continuously curved appearance to a surface made up of polygons.

For polygonal shading the shade of each polygon is constant across the polygon. This shade is a function of the angle between the normal to the polygon and a line from the light source to the polygon. For Gouraud's smooth shading, however, the shade is not constant across the polygon. It is a function of the angle between the normal at each vertex of the polygon and a line from the light source to the polygon, and the position within in the polygon. The normal at a vertex is the average of the normals of the polygons that have this vertex in common.

In smooth shaded renderings a special procedure is necessary if creases are to be visible. Creases can be made visible by "doubling" vertices. Since creases can occur only along the boundary between adjoining polygons, each vertex along the crease is doubled. One vertex of the pair belongs to polygons on one side of the crease and the other vertex of the pair belongs to polygons on the other side of the crease. This causes separate normals to be computed. When the polygons are shaded, there will be a shading discontinuity along the boundary and the crease will be visible.

Figure 1 shows a face rendered with polygonal shading and a different expression of the same face rendered using the smooth shading algorithm.

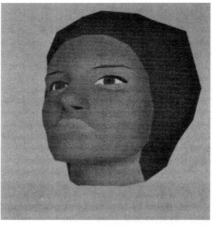

Figure 1
Two expressions of the same face. The top one was rendered using polygonal shading. The bottom one was rendered using Gouraud's smooth shading algorithm.

Having decided to use a polygonal representation, how does one go about approximating a face with polygons? There are several things to keep in mind.

1. To get good smooth shading, the density of polygons should be highest in the areas of highest curvature (the nose, mouth, around the eyes and the edge of the chin) and lowest in the areas of lowest curvature (the forehead, cheeks and neck).

2. Where creases occur on a face (under the eyes, the side of the nose, the edge of the lips and the corner of the mouth), edges of polygons must coincide with the creases. A polygon may not span a crease.

3. Use the smallest number of polygons consistent with good results. The reasons for this are obvious: a smaller amount of data, faster picture generation and minimization of the data acquisition problem.

4. If animation is desired, the polygons must be layed out in a way that allows the face to flex naturally. The polygons should remain approximately planar as the face flexes.

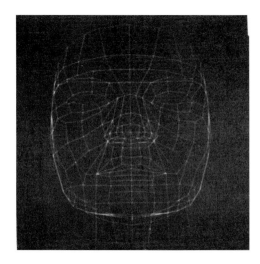

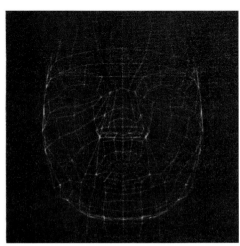

Figure 2
Two pictures showing the skin of polygons used to represent the face. Note that the polygons of the skin change shape and position as the face changes expression.

5. Since the face is approximately symmetric, we need worry only about one side of the face. The other side is obtained by "mirroring" or reflecting about the plane of symmetry.

6. Each polygon will have associated with it a color. Where color boundaries occur on the face, the lips and eyebrows for example, polygon edges must coincide with these boundaries. A polygon may not span a color boundary.

Keeping these things in mind the next step is to find a cooperative assistant who will allow you to draw or paint a set of polygons on his or her face. After drawing the polygon skin on one half of the face, ask the assistant to assume a number of different expressions. For each expression observe how well these polygons approximate the face. After modifying the polygon set several times you should arrive at a reasonable set of polygons to represent the face. Figure 2 shows the skin of polygons used to produce the faces shown in figures 1,3 and 4. One-half of this skin contains 124 polygons defined by 202 vertices.

A unique point number is assigned to each vertex of the skin. The skin is then specified by going around each polygon in a clockwise direction and recording the point numbers of its vertices.

The details of the face are very important in achieving realistic results. Figure 3 shows the effect details, such as the eyes, eyebrows, eyelashes and teeth have on the realism of the face. The eyebrows and teeth were included simply by adding polygons of the appropriate color. The illusion of eyelashes was achieved by changing the color of existing polygons directly above the eyes. The face by itself is not very realistic. It was necessary to complete the head in order to be convincing. Figure 3 shows how a "bonnet" of hair was used to complete the head.

Color is an important feature of the face. Each polygon has a color associated with it. This color is made up of three components; red, green and blue. By

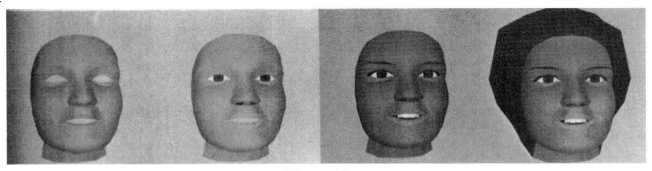

Figure 3
Four pictures that illustrate the effect of details on the realism of a face. The first picture shows the face alone. The next picture shows the face with eyes and nostrils. In the next picture, teeth, eyelashes, eyebrows and the inside of the mouth were added. The last picture shows the complete head.

specifying the value of each component it is possible to achieve the desired colors. Color half-tone renderings are produced by scanning out the picture three times, once for each of the primary colors. The appropriate color filter is placed in front of the camera lens before each scan.

After some experimentation the component values for flesh-tone and the other colors of the face were determined. These component values depend on a number of variables, including: the phosphor of the CRT, the type of filters used, the type of film used, the intensity setting of the CRT, and the compensation function used to overcome the non-linear characteristics of the CRT.

ANIMATION

Assuming that we have a satisfactory skin of polygons for the face, how do we animate it? We would like to specify the motion of the surface in the simplest way consistent with natural motion.

The approach taken in this research is somewhat similar to the approach taken by the conventional animator. The animator specifies the desired motion by blocking it out with a series of key drawings. He then gives these key drawings to the assistant animators who generate the required intermediate frames. For the computer animation, the key drawings are replaced by data files describing the face for each of a number of different expressions. The data for each expression or "phase" of the face consists of the three-dimensional position of each point defining the polygon skin used to represent the face. Figure 4 shows two phases of a face.

The animation program takes the place of the assistant animators and generates the required intermediate frames between the phases as the face changes expression.

To change the face from one expression to another is a matter of moving each point a small distance in successive frames. The position of each point of the skin in each frame is determined by interpolating between the previous phase position and the next phase position. Figure 2 shows how the polygons of the skin change shape and position as the face changes expression.

Since the face is governed by physical laws, its motion is not linear but tends to accelerate and decelerate. A cosine interpolation scheme was used to approximate the acceleration and deceleration of the facial motions. Each frame has associated with it a phase number. This phase number is a real number whose integer part refers to the previous phase and whose fractional part indicates the position of this frame between the previous phase and the next phase. For example, if phase 2 is a smile and phase 3 is a frown then the phase number 2.5 means an expression halfway between a smile and a frown. Each component of a point's position is computed using the following algorithm.

current position = position in the previous phase + C * difference

where

difference = position in next phase - position in previous phase

$C = (1.0 - \cos(\Phi))/2.0$

and

Φ = phase fraction * 3.14159

DATA ACQUISITION

Measuring the three-dimensional position of points on the surface of a face or any other complex object is a significant problem.

If we still have our assistant whose face is painted with polygons, we ask the assistant to assume a number of different expressions. We "freeze" each expression photographically. For each expression a

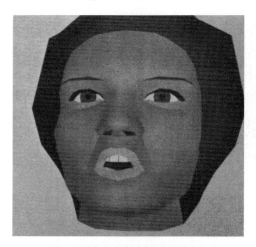

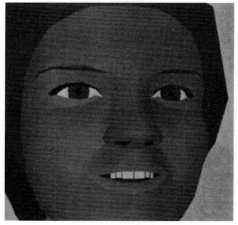

Figure 4
Two phases of a face.

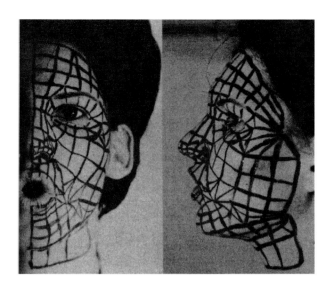

Figure 5
A typical pair of data photographs.

pair of orthogonal views of the face is taken, one from directly in front and one from the side. Figure 5 shows a typical pair of these photographs. Using these pairs of photographs we establish an origin and a coordinate system. The three-dimensional position of each point is measured directly from the photographs.

Note that the coordinate system should be chosen such that two of the coordinate axes define the symmetry plane of the face. This facilitates the mirroring or reflection operation necessary to obtain the data for the other half of the face.

This data collection method has some shortcomings. Photographs are not orthographic projections but are perspective projections. Therefore, the images on the photographs are somewhat distorted. This distortion can be reduced by using long focal length lenses when the pictures are taken. Some adjustment of the data may be necessary due to this distortion. Another shortcoming is that some points on the face may not be visible in both views. A best guess must be made for at least one of the coordinates of these occluded points.

THE ANIMATION PROGRAM

The animation program contains arrays to store the topology and phase data for the face. Up to three phases may be stored in the program. The topology and phase data is read in from data files. The user of the program interacts with it to specify which data files he wants read in.

The phase data files consist of the data for a sequence of points. For each point there is a point number and a three-dimensional position. The topology data consists of a specification for each polygon of the face. The polygon specification is made up of the point numbers of the vertices of the polygon and its color.

After the desired data is read in, the data for the other half of the face is constructed by mirroring or reflecting the data for the first half of the face.

For each frame of a sequence a number of tasks must be accomplished in order to compute the data needed to pass on to the hidden surface and shading algorithms.

Using the phase number associated with each frame, the program interpolates the phase data to get the position of each vertex of the skin for this frame.

These point positions are specified in a coordinate system centered near the center of the head. The hidden surface algorithm requires the data to be specified in a different coordinate system. The new coordinate system, refered to as the viewing system, has its origin at the position we wish to look from. The Z axis of the viewing system must be pointing in the direction we wish to look. The position data must be transformed (12, 13) into this new coordinate system. The animation program first translates the data so the origin moves from the center of the head to the position we wish to look from. It then rotates the coordinate system so that the Z axis of the viewing system is pointing toward the position we wish to look at.

After the data is transformed into the viewing system, the normal to each polygon is computed. Using these normals, the normal at each vertex of the skin is computed. This is done for each vertex by averaging the normals of the polygons that have the vertex in common.

For each frame of a sequence the following parameters are passed on to the hidden surface and shading algorithms:

1. The viewing angle (this is used to determine the viewing space and is also used in the perspective transformation (12,13)).
2. The color of each polygon.
3. The position of the beginning and ending points of each edge of each polygon and the normals at these points.
4. The desired resolution.

The animation program was written in SAIL (14), an extended algol for the PDP-10.

IMPLEMENTATION

The system used to produce animated sequences, and the half-tone renderings included in this paper is shown in Figure 6. This system uses two PDP-10 computers. One of these is a dedicated machine that allows only one user at any given time.

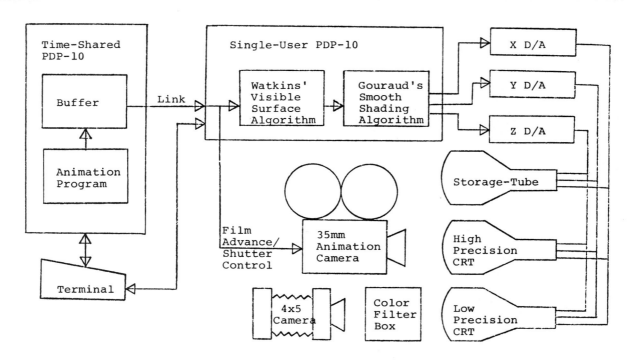

Figure 6
System configuration.

This processor is interfaced to the special equipment needed to produce half-tone pictures. The other PDP-10 is time-shared, and runs under the TENEX operating system. There is a link between the machines that allows data to be transfered between them.

This system allows us to take advantage of the TENEX operating system, particularly the file system, on one machine and the special half-tone display equipment on the other machine.

When one wishes to use this system, he connects the terminal to the single-user PDP-10 and loads a program which contains; a software version of Watkin's visible surface algorithm, Gouraud's smooth shading algorithm, a procedure to calibrate the half-tone displays and procedures to handle the single-user side of the data transfers across the link. When this program begins execution, it first allows the user to calibrate the display equipment. It then initializes the receiving side of the data link and goes to sleep. At this point the user switches the terminal to the time-shared machine. After logging in, the user loads and starts the execution of the animation program. This program asks the user a number of questions, including: which phase data files he wants read in, the desired number of frames between phases, the resolution to use, where he wants to look, where he wants to look from, and whether he wants smooth or polygonal shading. After receiving this information, the program begins processing the first frame of the sequence.

Data to be passed to the hidden surface and shading algorithms is stored into one of two buffers. When a buffer is full, a flag is set. This causes the animation program to transfer to the other buffer and wakes up the single-user program. When the single-user program wakes up, it transfers the data out of the full buffer into its memory, resets the flag and goes back to sleep. Resetting the buffer flag allows the animation program to reuse the buffer.

When all the data for a single frame has been transfered, the single-user program begins working on it to generate the half-tone image. The animation program goes on to the next frame of the sequence. While the single-user program is in the process of generating the half-tone image, it ignores the buffer flags set by the animation program. This means that as soon as the animation program fills both buffers it must wait until the single-user program completes the picture and empties a buffer.

The output of the single-user program goes to three digital-to-analog converters which in turn drive any combination of the display devices shown in Figure 6.

This system works well if the time-shared system is not heavily loaded. If the time-shared system is heavily loaded the single-user is idle much of the time waiting for data.

All of the half-tone renderings shown in this report were produced with the high precision display using a resolution of 1024x1024. At this resolution it takes about 2½ minutes to scan out a single black-and-white picture.

Animated sequences are recorded using a 35 mm animation camera. Film advance and shutter are under program control. Animated sequences of the face are produced at the rate of about 20 frames per hour.

ACKNOWLEDGMENTS

I am grateful to Professors R. E. Stephenson and I. E. Sutherland and to Barry Wessler and Ed Catmull for their help and encouragement, also to Mike Milochik for his photographic assistance.

REFERENCES

1. Coons, S. A., "Surfaces for Computer Aided Design of Space Forms", M.I.T., Cambridge, Mass., Project MAC Report MAC-TR-41, June 1967.

2. Mahl, R., "Visible Surface Algorithm for Quadric Patches", Computer Science, University of Utah, Technical Report UTEC-CSc-70-111, December 1970.

3. Weiss, R. A., "Be Vision, A Package of IBM 7090 Fortran Programs to Draw Orthographic Views of Combinations of Plane and Quadric Surfaces", JACM, vol. 13, April 1966, pp. 194-204.

4. Gouraud, H., "Computer Display of Curved Surfaces", Computer Science, University of Utah, Technical Report UTEC-CSc-71-113, June 1971.

5. Wylie, C., Romney, G., Evans, D., and Erdahl, A., "Half-tone Perspective Drawing by Computer", Proc FJCC, vol. 31, pp. 49-58, 1967.

6. Appel, A., "The Notion of Quantitative Invisibility and the Machine Rendering of Solids", Proc ACM, vol. 14, pp. 387-393, 1967.

7. Kelley, K. C., "A Computer Program for the Generation of Half-Tone Images with Shadows", Coordinated Science Laboratory, University of Illinois, Report R-444, November 1969.

8. Romeny, G. W., "Computer Assisted Assembly and Rendering of Solids", Rome Air Development Center, Griffiss Air Force Base, New York, Technical Report RADC-TR-69-365, September 1969.

9. Rougelot, R. S. and Shoemaker, R., "G. E. Real Time Display", General Electric Co., Syracuse N. Y., NASA Report NAS 9-3916.

10. Warnock, J. E., "A Hidden Surface Algorithm for Computer Generated Halftone Pictures", Computer Science, University of Utah, Technical Report 4-15, June 1969.

11. Watkins, G. S., "A Real-Time Visible Surface Algorithm", Computer Science, University of Utah, Technical Report UTECH-CSc-70-101, June 1970.

12. Coons, S. A., "Transformations and Matrices", Notes for the 1967 Summer School on Computer Graphics for Designers, University of Michigan, June 5-16, 1967.

13. Ahuja, D. V. and Coons, S. A., "Geometry for Construction and Display", IBM Systems Journal, vol. 7, pp. 188-205, 1968.

14. Swinehart, D. and Sproull B., "SAIL", Stanford Artificial Intelligence Project Operating Note No. 57.1, April 1970.

Graphics and
Image Processing

Interactive Skeleton Techniques for Enhancing Motion Dynamics in Key Frame Animation

N. Burtnyk and M. Wein
National Research Council of Canada

A significant increase in the capability for controlling motion dynamics in key frame animation is achieved through skeleton control. This technique allows an animator to develop a complex motion sequence by animating a stick figure representation of an image. This control sequence is then used to drive an image sequence through the same movement. The simplicity of the stick figure image encourages a high level of interaction during the design stage. Its compatibility with the basic key frame animation technique permits skeleton control to be applied selectively to only those components of a composite image sequence that require enhancement.

Key Words and Phrases: interactive graphics, computer generated animation, key frame animation, interactive skeleton, skeleton control, stick figure animation

CR Categories: 3.41, 3.49, 4.9, 8.2

Copyright © 1976, Association for Computing Machinery, Inc. General permission to republish, but not for profit, all or part of this material is granted provided that ACM's copyright notice is given and that reference is made to the publication, to its date of issue, and to the fact that reprinting privileges were granted by permission of the Association for Computing Machinery.
A version of this paper was presented at SIGGRAPH '76: The Third Annual Conference on Computer Graphics, Interactive Techniques, and Image Processing, The Wharton School, University of Pennsylvania, July 14–16, 1976.
Author's address: National Research Council of Canada, Division of Electrical Engineering, Ottawa, Canada K1A OR8.
[1] Cel has been derived from celluloids, the material on which drawings are prepared in conventional cel animation. Component images that move separately are usually drawn on separate cels and stacked into a cel sandwich for filming.

Introduction

Previous work has demonstrated that key frame animation techniques constitute a successful approach to animation of free-form images [1–3]. Using this technique, the artist draws key images at selected intervals in an animation sequence and the playback program computes the in-between images by interpolation. Interpolation between related key images allows the animation of change of shape or distortion. It permits a direct and intuitive method for specifying the action, whereas mathematically defined distortion requires trial and error experimentation. One strength of key frame animation techniques is the analogy to conventional hand animation techniques, simplifying the transition when a classically trained animator adapts to using computers.

Figure 1 illustrates a typical image sequence generated using key frame animation. The first and last images were drawn by the artist, while the six intermediate images were selected from the 240 frames in the actual film sequence.

The animation package is implemented on a minicomputer based interactive graphics system. This package supports the four major phases of a production: (1) the drawing phase, (2) the assembly of drawings into key frame sequences, (3) the preview/modification phase, and (4) the final processing and recording of the sequences on film.

The drawing phase is carried out in two stages. The first stage is off-line at the drawing board. Analysis of the action depicted by the story board establishes key positions from which drawings are prepared. The second stage involves tracing these drawings on a graphic tablet at the display console. During this stage, the order in which strokes are traced to describe an image is important. Since the interpolation process is based on stroke to stroke mapping, this ordering of strokes between related images controls the form of the intermediate image.

The second phase consists of the interactive assembly of individual drawings or cels[1] into key frames, including a specification of the interpolation law for each cel and a key to key time interval. Concatenated key frames form a sequence. This process is repeated for all concurrent sequences that make up a composite sequence.

During the preview phase, playback of any individual sequence or concurrent sequences on the interactive display permits an assessment of the resulting animation. Modification involves returning to the interactive assembly phase to edit the sequences. In practice, direct playback assures only that the form of the interpolated images can be assessed, since it is difficult to achieve playback at the cine rate with complex images. Proper assessment of motion and timing requires further conversion to a raster format which maintains display at the cine rate independent of the image content.

This technique of animating free-form images has been directed mainly towards drawn images and hence two-dimensional. The image, material, of course, attempts to represent a 3-D space much as in conventional cel animation. The basic capability includes a simplified solution to the problem of hidden surfaces by treating the image as a hierarchy of parallel planes. The simplification lies in the fact that the animator-specified order of planes establishes the order of visibility computation, thus eliminating any programmed sorting of data by depth. The composite playback facility produces separately a composite line image with hidden lines removed and a composite surface sequence.

Consideration of Motion Dynamics

The greatest shortcoming in key frame animation results from incomplete control of motion dynamics, both in complexity and in smoothness or continuity. It is relatively simple to have good control over the dynamics in time. The amount of change from one frame to the next is determined by a weighting factor which is a single-valued function of time. Thus one can easily compute, or store precomputed, various functions representing different "tapers." However, the same value of weighting function is applied to an entire picture component. There is no "spatial weighting."

The shortcomings manifest themselves in the following ways: (a) the motion of each point in the image is along a straight line and the relative change from one frame to the next is the same for all points belonging to one picture element, and (b) there is a discontinuity at key frames in both the amount of frame to frame change and in the direction of apparent motion. Therefore it is difficult to synthesize smooth continuous motion spanning several key positions. There is a dilemma in that smoothness is achieved by having as few key images as possible (and therefore widely spaced in time), while close control requires many closely spaced keys. In addition, a large number of closely spaced drawings negates much of the economic advantage of using computers.

Various techniques have been examined for overcoming these problems. One technique provides an ability to include a rotational component as part of the image change, which in effect superimposes rotation on the interpolation process [2]. This permits some variation in the spatial dynamics but its application is limited and discontinuities at key frames remain.

Synthesis of complex motion could be achieved by using additional intermediate keys, but preparation of additional drawings by the animator is uneconomical. Skeleton techniques were developed to derive variations of existing key drawings to be used as intermediate keys [2]. This involves representation of a drawing by a simple skeleton and then extracting a distorted form of the image by modifying only the skeleton. Even when such additional keys are used, discontinuity in motion is difficult to avoid.

Another technique involves the use of smooth drawn paths to control the interpolation process. Motion along a path, as a method distinct from key frame animation, has been used extensively in computer animation [4–7]. A single path to control interpolation between key images offers a limited solution somewhat equivalent to the use of rotation—it tends to be satisfactory only when the distortion of the image is minimal. For a distorting image, different portions must follow entirely different paths. This immediately leads to a problem if several paths are to be drawn for different portions of the image. It is difficult to establish points of simultaneity on several paths such that one could easily perceive the shape of the image at any instant.

An examination of the methods used in conventional animation has led to a solution to this problem.

Fig. 1. Selected frames from a key frame animation sequence. The first and last images are drawn, the intermediate images are interpolated. Multilayer visibility is included in computing the composite image. From "Visage," a film by Peter Foldes

To visualize a complex movement, the animator often sketches stick figure representations at equal-time intervals between key positions. He may use smooth curves through related skeletal points as a further guide. This set of stick figures achieves both objectives: the frame to frame spacing conveys the rate of movement and the shape of each skeleton represents the shape of the object at that instant. Thus the problem reduces to animating a stick figure representation of the image which will in turn impart the movement to the actual image sequence.

The system described in this paper incorporates the use of skeletons into the key frame technique to provide overall control in the playback process. As in the basic key frame animation system, the process of producing a sequence involves two steps. The first is the interactive stage at which the animator prepares the key images and establishes the stick figure representations at as many intermediate positions as desired. The intermediate skeletons define intermediate control keys. During playback the program selects those image components that are skeleton driven and applies the necessary deformation.

There are two significant aspects of the skeleton driven technique. First, the skeletons are simple images composed of only a few points, so that it is possible to provide a high level of interaction. The second aspect of this technique is its compatibility with basic key frame animation. Skeleton sequences are prepared only where necessary and the playback system identifies those image components that are skeleton driven and those that are not.

It should be noted that the concept of skeletons used in the context of this paper differs from that used by Blum [8]. Blum's skeletons are used for image representation in a compressed form and are derived automatically from the coordinate data. Our skeleton representation of an image provides a definition of some coordinate space within which the image, described in relative coordinates, is distributed.

Skeleton Coordinate System

The nature of the coordinate space that is used to define relative skeleton coordinates may be thought of as a network of polygons that form a mesh (Figure 2).

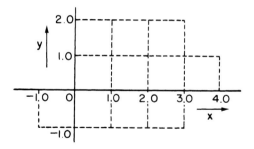

Each polygon has a relative coordinate range of 0 to 1.0 along each axis. Now the nodes in this mesh may be displaced relative to one another to change its geometry. However, because the relative coordinate system within each polygon is based on its geometry, coordinate values remain continuous across common edges between adjacent polygons. Thus any image whose coordinates are defined within this system will take on the overall distortion exhibited by the coordinate space (Figure 3).

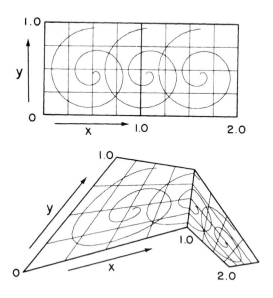

Geometric transformation of contours from one coordinate space to another is, of course, well known in conformal mapping.

The notion of skeleton control implies a central core of connected "bones" with a surrounding image distribution. In order to restrict the transverse distance away from the core over which skeleton control will be active, delimiting boundaries must be specified. Consequently, the practical form of skeleton coordinate space spans two units in width, but may extend in length as desired (Figure 4).

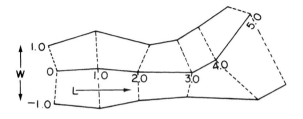

For convenience, the central core always represents the L axis, which is also the $W = 0$ coordinate reference; the delimiting boundary which is specified first is the positive or $W = 1.0$ boundary, the other is the $W = -1.0$ boundary. The L coordinate range starts at $L = 0$

and is incremented by one for each node on the central core. If desired, the L coordinate space may be separated at any coordinate boundary by providing a redefinition of that coordinate boundary before continuing the coordinate space. Of course, the related image will not normally continue through such a separation. In addition, ambiguities can occur if separated coordinate spaces overlap. In general, it is preferable to treat these as separate skeletons so that no restrictions are imposed. On the other hand, any given image need not fall entirely within the coordinate space of a skeleton. Those points which lie outside the skeleton space will remain unaffected by the distortion of the skeleton coordinate space.

Relative coordinates, denoted by (l, w), may be defined as the fractional distance along each axis which is occupied by a line passing through the point while intersecting the two opposing edges of the polygon at this fractional distance. In Figure 5(a), the coordinates of point P are (0.75, 0.5) by this definition. In order to minimize the computation involved in coordinate conversion, the simpler definition of Figure 5(b) is used.

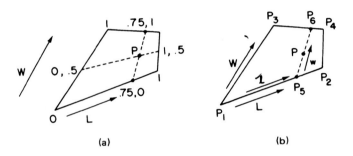

(a)   (b)

Given the absolute vertex coordinates of the polygon and an image point P, the fractional distance of points P_5 and P_6 along lines P_1P_2 and P_3P_4 is expressed by l, giving

$$x_5 = l(x_2 - x_1) + x_1, \quad y_5 = l(y_2 - y_1) + y_1,$$
$$x_6 = l(x_4 - x_3) + x_3, \quad y_6 = l(y_4 - y_3) + y_3,$$

These expressions are substituted into $(x - x_6)/(y - y_6) = (x_5 - x)/(y_5 - y)$, the equation of the line P_5P_6 passing through point P, giving

$$[x - x_3 - l(x_4 - x_3)]/[y - y_3 - l(y_4 - y_3)]$$
$$= [x - x_1 - l(x_2 - x_1)]/[y - y_1 - l(y_2 - y_1)].$$

This reduces to

$$(BH - DF)l^2 + (CF - DE - AH - BG)l + (AG - CE) = 0$$

where

$$A = x - x_1, \quad E = x - x_3,$$
$$B = x_2 - x_1, \quad F = x_4 - x_3,$$
$$C = y - y_1, \quad G = y - y_3,$$
$$D = y_2 - y_1, \quad H = y_4 - y_3,$$

The desired root for l has a value between 0 and 1, the other root will be negative or greater than 1. The w-coordinate, expressing the fractional distance of point P along line P_5P_6, is given by

$$w = (x - x_5)/(x_6 - x_5)$$
$$= (A - Bl)/[A - E - (B - F)l].$$

To convert relative coordinates back to display coordinates, the l-coordinate is applied to the vertex coordinates to determine the coordinates of P_5 and P_6 from which P is found.

The effect of skeleton control is to take any specified area of the display plane and distort it into another area of the display plane as if it were made up of rubber sheet patches. In that sense, it is similar to the distorted raster scan technique used in Caesar [9], and equivalent to the mapping of images into curved surfaces described by Catmull [10]. While the skeleton coordinate space is distorting, however, the relative coordinates of the image itself may be undergoing a change. Relative coordinates may be treated in the same way as absolute coordinates, as if the reference coordinate space was always uniform and orthogonal, its particular shape being important only for display purposes (Figure 6). Therefore the key frame interpolation process may still be carried out even if key images are represented in relative coordinates. It is this compatibility with key frame animation that makes the skeleton control technique so powerful and attractive. No other practical techniques have been developed that offer a comparable degree of image control in computer generated animation.

Implementation within Key Frame Animation

The benefits that may be derived in practice from skeleton control are closely related to the method of implementation. While there is little doubt that any capability for enriching motion is useful, it is equally clear that the compulsory use of skeleton control for all parts of an animation sequence would be a great hindrance. The full advantage in the use of this technique is realized only if the animator can apply it selectively. In fact, it is most attractive if it can be used to improve motion dynamics of sequences which were previously created. This is the form in which it has been implemented in our system.

Component sequences are first assembled in the usual form and displayed as a composite image sequence for previewing. If, after assessment, the animator wants to modify or improve parts of it, he does so by adding skeleton control to those components only. This is accomplished by attaching a reference skeleton, which he has drawn, to each image which will be controlled. These image components, which are referenced to skeletons, are converted to relative coordinates and tagged during assembly of the sequence.

Now the composite sequence is regenerated in this modified form. During playback, all coordinate data pass through the interpolation process, but those identified as being relative must be mapped to a particular skeleton reference for display. A skeleton reference defines a display space in absolute coordinates. These skeleton coordinate references for each frame are provided by assembling stick figure control sequences which are also played back as part of the composite sequence.

The design of the skeleton control sequence itself is developed interactively in a separate package. Stick figure representations of key images provide the starting point (Figure 7(a)). Two such skeletons are used to define a start and end frame. When the INBETWEEN display mode is active, intermediate frames are interpolated and presented on the screen as a superposition of many frames (Figure 7(b)). For convenience, the delimiting boundaries about the skeleton core are eliminated from display to prevent excessive clutter. Any frame may now be selected and modified using tablet interaction. In this mode, the modified coordinates of the selected frame are stored as a control frame within the sequence. The interpolated intermediate frames adjust accordingly in response to tablet interaction (Figure 7(c)). Additional frames may be modified in a similar manner (Figure 7(d)).

Frame to frame change is easily related to the spacing between stick figures. This interaction continues, giving the animator control over motion dynamics down to the frame level as in conventional animation, if desired. The user-modified control frames are preserved, whereas all other intermediate stick figures are recomputed when needed. Display of the final sequence of control frames is shown in Figure 7(e). The skeleton boundaries have been adjusted where required through similar tablet interaction to maintain their desired form. Alternatively skeleton keys which have been drawn in these desired positions may be brought in from the picture library and assembled as control frames in the same way.

In practice, the number of control frames that are used to generate a motion sequence will be kept to a minimum. Because of this, simple linear interpolation between specified control frames may not adequately reproduce a smooth continuous movement. This result is illustrated in Figure 7(f), where the dynamics of the movement suffer from excessive discontinuities in rate at two of the control frames. Additional intermediate frames have been interpolated and plotted for clarity.

This deficiency is removed if a smoothing function is applied during computation of intermediate frames (Figure 7(g)). This process maintains continuity of movement of corresponding points through successive control frames. The parametric method of curve fitting is adapted from the work of Akima [11]. Not only does it produce a smooth path for each point, but progression

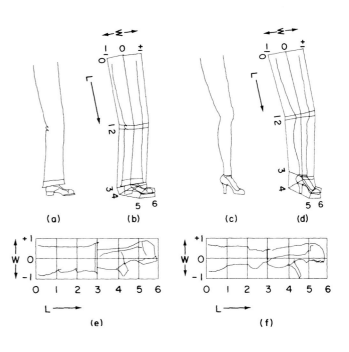

Fig. 6. (a), (c) two drawn images in absolute coordinates; (b), (d) same images with reference skeletons; (e), (f) the relative coordinates presented on an orthogonal coordinate system.

Fig. 7. Development of a skeleton control sequence: (a) start and end frames; (b) interpolated inbetweens presented for interaction; (c), (d) frames 5 and 9 modified in turn by the animator (control frames); (e) final sequence of control frames, shown with boundaries; (f) linearly interpolated inbetweens; (g), (h) with curve smoothing; (i), (j) images driven by the motion sequence.

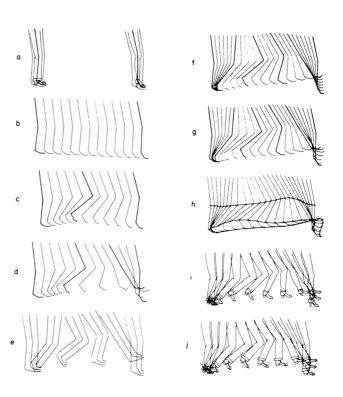

along each path is tapered to accommodate changes in rate in a complex movement. Successive positions of several points have been joined in Figure 7(h) to emphasize the effect. This process has all the characteristics of drawing smooth paths to control interpolation between images without any of its limitations.

Now the skeleton control information is complete for driving the original image sequence through the desired movement (Figure 7(i)). It may equally well be applied to drive any other compatible image sequence through the same motion. In Figure 7(j), although the image sequence itself specifies a HOLD during that interval, the skeleton sequence drives it through the same motion cycle. The relationship between a start/end frame skeleton pair and the number of key images in that interval is arbitrary. It should also be clear that the interpolation rate between key images is independent of the progression of its skeleton through a movement. Because of this, the smoothing process may span as many key images as required to complete a continuous movement.

Various program features assist the animator in developing a skeleton control sequence. Direct viewing of skeleton movement is obtained by requesting the ANIMATE display mode at any time. This causes the sequence of intermediate frames from the start to the end frame to be continuously cycled at the cine rate instead of being presented as a static ensemble. Companion skeletons that have been developed for several cels may be previewed together in this mode as well as during interaction. If the INBETWEEN display presentation contains confusing frame to frame overlap (e.g. walking on the spot), a positional offset may be introduced into successive control frames to remove the ambiguity. Similarly any number of intermediate frames may be skipped to simplify the overall display during interactive modification.

Proposed Extensions to the System

Because final processing of skeleton control sequences is performed in the composite playback program, the same camera control commands that apply pan, tilt, and zoom to an image sequence can be applied to the control sequence. With an extension of the system, more complex processing functions could be applied to the control skeleton. This approach may be useful for superimposing complex forms of movement control on the skeleton. It may also significantly reduce the processing time for rotation since only the skeleton coordinate references need to be rotated.

Another useful extension deals with the capability for creating a library of common movements. If sequences of control frames are saved in a normalized form, they can be retrieved and superimposed on any particular skeleton as a starting point for developing variations of that movement. Since the details of the image itself are not contained in the skeleton, this necessitates only that the form of this skeleton match the standard normalized form (i.e. it consists of the same connection of bones). All the physical characteristics of the particular skeleton being used (such as relative length and width of each section) will be retained while only the stored motion characteristics will be transferred. Although this capability has not been implemented in the present system, it does indeed offer an important potential reduction in animation production costs.

References
1. Burtnyk, N., and Wein, M. Computer generated key frame animation. *J. Soc. Motion Picture and Television Engineers 80*, 3 (1971), 149–153.
2. Burtnyk, N., and Wein, M. Towards a computer animating production tool. Proc. Eurocomp Conf., Brunel U., 1974, Online Pub. Co., 172–185.
3. Burtnyk, N., and Wein, M. Computer animation of free form images. Computer Graphics 9, 1 (1975), 78–80 (Issue of Proc. Second Ann. Conf. Computer Graphics and Interactive Techniques).
4. Baecker, R.M. Picture-driven animation. Proc. AFIPS 1969 SJCC, Vol. 34, AFIPS Press, Montvale, N.J., pp. 273–288.
5. Csuri, C. Real-time animation. Proc. Ninth Ann. Meeting UAIDE (Users of Automatic Inform. Display Equipment), Miami, 1970, pp. 289–305.
6. Burtnyk, N., et al. Computer graphics and film animation. *Canadian J. Operational Res. and Inform. Processing (INFOR) 9*, 1 (1971), 1–11.
7. Burtnyk, N., and Wein, M. A computer animation system for the animator. Proc. Tenth Ann. Meeting UAIDE (Users of Automatic Inform. Display Equipment), Los Angeles, 1971, pp. 3.5–3.24.
8. Blum, H. A transformation for extracting new descriptors of shape. In *Models of Speech and Visual Form*, MIT Press, Cambridge, Mass., 1967, pp. 362–380.
9. Honey, F.J. Computer animated episodes by single axis rotations—CAESAR. Proc. Tenth Ann. Meeting UAIDE (Users of Automatic Inform. Display Equipment), Los Angeles, 1971, pp. 3–210 to 3–226.
10. Catmull, E. Computer display of curved surfaces. Proc. Conf. Computer Graphics, Pattern Recognition and Data Structure, May 1975, pp. 11–17 (IEEE Cat. No. 75CH0981-IC).
11. Akima, H. A new method of interpolation and smooth curve fitting based on local procedures. *J. ACM 17*, 4 (1970), 589–602.

Computational Modeling for the Computer Animation of Legged Figures

Michael Girard
and
A. A. Maciejewski

Computer Graphics Research Group
The Ohio State University

OSU CGRG /Cranston Center
1501 Neil Avenue
Columbus OH 43201

Abstract

Modeling techniques for animating legged figures are described which are used in the PODA animation system. PODA utilizes pseudoinverse control in order to solve the problems associated with manipulating kinematically redundant limbs. PODA builds on this capability to synthesize a kinematic model of legged locomotion which allows animators to control the complex relationships between the motion of the body of a figure and the coordination of its legs. Finally, PODA provides for the integration of a simple model of legged locomotion dynamics which insures that the accelerations of a figure's body are synchronized with the timing of the forces applied by its legs.

CR Categories and Subject Descriptors: 1.3.7 [Computer Graphics]: Graphics and Realism: Animation. Additional Key Words and Phrases: motion control, computational modeling, manipulators, legged locomotion

Introduction

The problems of animating articulated figures with multiple legs have long been a source of difficulty in the computer animation field. Joint angle interpolation between "key" joint positions is the most widely used method of animating jointed animals. This method fails to work, however, for cases in which the end of a limb must be constrained to move along a particular path – the interpolated joint positions of two "key" leg positions planted on the ground will not, in general, remain on the ground (fig. 1).

Another difficulty is the sheer tedium of positioning "keys" for limbs containing many degrees of freedom. The animal shown in figure 2 possesses 9 degrees of freedom in each leg, 9 degrees of freedom in the neck, and 18 degrees of freedom in the "spine." An animator using a key joint system would have to manage positioning a total of 63 joints.

A further problem is that a walking or running figure is more than an assemblage of moving limbs – the coordination of legs, body and feet are functionally related in a complex fashion. The motion of the body of a figure and the timing and placement of legs are both kinematically and dynamically coupled.[20-36]

The approach taken in the design of the PODA system is to provide the animator with a computational model which facilitates the integration and direct control of the functional dependencies between different parts of a figure. An interactive menu-driven interface is used for both the incremental construction and behavioral control of animals possessing any number of legs composed of any number of joints. A strategy is implemented in which the figure's motion may be designed and manipulated at different levels of control. At the lowest level the animator may define and adjust the character of the movement of the legs and feet. At a higher level the animator may direct the coordination of the legs and control the overall motion dynamics and path of the body.

The primary goal of our efforts is to build a framework in which the synthesis of legged figure motion may be artistically conceived and controlled at increasingly higher levels of complexity and abstraction. In this regard, our initial efforts have been focussed on developing a general model for legged locomotion due to its importance to the execution of more complex motor skills, such as those which are required for dance and gymnastics[27].

In this first section we will outline the solution taken in PODA for the control of single limbs. This will set the stage for the discussion of the legged locomotion model which utilizes the limb control methods described.

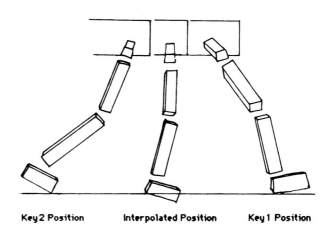

Figure 1

The research described in this paper was supported, in part, by National Science Foundation grant DCR-8304185, and in part, by a National Science Foundation Fellowship.

Permission to copy without fee all or part of this material is granted provided that the copies are not made or distributed for direct commercial advantage, the ACM copyright notice and the title of the publication and its date appear, and notice is given that copying is by permission of the Association for Computing Machinery. To copy otherwise, or to republish, requires a fee and/or specific permission.

© 1985 ACM 0-89791-166-0/85/007/0263 $00.75

THE CONTROL OF LIMBS

Representing articulated limbs

In order to define the functionality of an arbitrary articulated figure, PODA has adopted the kinematic notation presented by Denavit and Hartenberg [3]. This specifies a unique coordinate system for every individual degree of freedom present in the figure. These degrees of freedom, whether rotary or prismatic, will be referred to as joints and the fixed interconnecting bodies as links. The four parameters used to define the transformation between adjacent coordinate systems are the length of the link a, the twist of the link α, the distance between links d, and the angle between links θ. The single variable associated with the transformation depends on the type of joint represented, that is θ for rotary or d for prismatic joints (fig. 3).

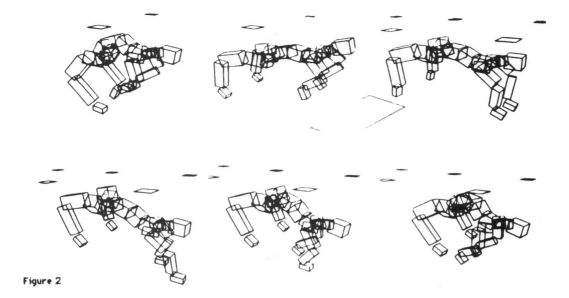

Figure 2

Given the above definitions, it can be shown [12] that the transformation between adjacent coordinate frames $i-1$ and i denoted by $^{i-1}T_i$ is given by the homogeneous transformation:

$$^{i-1}T_i = \begin{bmatrix} \vec{n} & \vec{o} & \vec{a} & \vec{p} \\ 0 & 0 & 0 & 1 \end{bmatrix}$$

where

$$\begin{aligned} p_x &= a_i \cos\theta_i & n_x &= \cos\theta_i \\ p_y &= a_i \sin\theta_i & n_y &= \sin\theta_i \\ p_z &= d_i & n_z &= 0 \\ o_x &= -\cos\alpha_i \sin\theta_i & a_x &= \sin\alpha_i \sin\theta_i \\ o_y &= \cos\alpha_i \cos\theta_i & a_y &= -\sin\alpha_i \cos\theta_i \\ o_z &= \sin\alpha_i & a_z &= \cos\alpha_i \end{aligned}$$

By repeatedly applying adjacent link transformations the relationship between any two coordinate systems i and j is easily obtained using

$$^iT_j = {}^iT_{i+1}\, {}^{i+1}T_{i+2} \cdots {}^{j-1}T_j$$

The above equation permits any link of the figure, defined in its own coordinate frame, to be represented in any arbitrary reference or world coordinate frame. More importantly, it can be used to determine the number and characteristics of the degrees of freedom available for simulating coordinated movement.

The Jacobian Matrix

Given the above framework, one can easily see that, given the state of the joint angle variables, we can compute the position of all of the links and arrive at the position of the end of the limb. This is called the *forward kinematics* problem. The reverse situation, that of computing the joint angles from the position of the end of the limb, is necessary if we wish to place a foot or hand in some desired place–what Korein and Badler have called "goal directed motion" [32]. This is called the *inverse kinematics* problem. The legged locomotion models in PODA rely heavily on the need for goal-directed motion: feet must be moved along trajectories, placed exactly at desired footholds and held in place as the body passes over them.

The solution of the inverse kinematics problem is the source of much of the difficulty in dealing with controlling articulated figures. A general solution for arbitrary articulated chains does not exist and even those that lend themselves to an analytic solution result in nonlinear equations [12]. Additional complications are incurred when redundant degrees of freedom are present.

The solution adopted by PODA is to linearize the equations about the current operating point. The six-dimensional vector representing an incremental change in position and orientation in three space of an arbitrary link is linearly related to the vector $\Delta\vec{\theta}$ by the Jacobian matrix J through the equation

$$\Delta\vec{x} = J(\vec{\theta})\Delta\vec{\theta} \qquad (1)$$

for changes which are sufficiently small. Thus by updating the Jacobian each cycle time, the advantages of a linear system are obtained. This allows the application of all of the techniques of solving linear equations to obtain the desired result (to be discussed in the next section). The use of Jacobians has long been a common practice in nonlinear control system theory and has been successfully applied in the field of robotics [18,19].

Due to its central nature in the animation of articulated figures, an efficient implementation for generating the Jacobian is essential to a viable system. While there are may different techniques available, a particularly elegant method has been formulated with the use of screw motor variables [17]. A screw motor is characterized by the variables $\vec{\omega}$, the angular velocity of the screw axis, and $\vec{\mu}$, the velocity of a point attached to the screw axis which coincides with the origin of the world coordinate frame. In terms of these variables, the desired displacement of the foot may be expressed as

$$\begin{aligned} \vec{\omega} &= R\vec{\omega}_f \\ \vec{\mu} &= R\vec{v}_f - \vec{\omega} \times \vec{p} \end{aligned} \qquad (2)$$

with the original foot displacement $\Delta\vec{x}$ given by

$$\Delta\vec{x} = \begin{bmatrix} \vec{v}_f \\ \vec{\omega}_f \end{bmatrix}$$

where R is the upper 3×3 rotation partition of the homogeneous transformation describing the desired point whose velocity is being specified and $\vec{p}$ is the position of this point given by the fourth column of its homogeneous transformation. It can be shown [16] that the Jacobian is given by

$$J = \begin{bmatrix} p_1 \times a_1 & p_2 \times a_2 & \ldots & p_n \times a_n \\ a_1 & a_2 & \ldots & a_n \end{bmatrix} \qquad (3)$$

where a_i and p_i are the third and fourth columns, respectively, of the homogeneous transformation matrix $^0T_{i-1}$. The first column of the Jacobian is given by

$$p_1 = [0\ 0\ 0]^T \qquad a_1 = [0\ 0\ 1]^T.$$

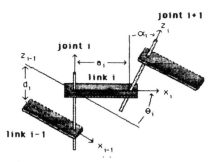

Link Parameters Associated With Link i

This formulation of the Jacobian allows a minimal amount of extra computation since the majority of the work has already been done in generating the homogeneous transformations required to display the object. This is in contrast with other techniques which do not express the Jacobian in the world coordinate frame [37].

Inverting the Jacobian

Given a linear system by virtue of the Jacobian, we now need to invert the relationship represented by equation (1) in order to determine the required $\Delta\vec{\theta}$ to achieve a desired $\Delta\vec{x}$. Since we are dealing with arbitrary articulated figures, the Jacobian is in general not square and therefore its inverse is not defined. To obtain a useful solution regardless of the rank of J, the pseudoinverse is applied. The pseudoinverse will be denoted by J^+ and is the unique [13] matrix which satisfies the four properties:

$$J J^+ J = J$$
$$J^+ J J^+ = J^+$$
$$(J^+ J)^\top = J^+ J$$
$$(J J^+)^\top = J J^+ \quad (4)$$

The advantages of using the pseudoinverse lie in that it returns the least squares minimum norm solution to equation (1). Thus it provides useful results in both the under and over determined cases. Other generalized inverses may also be applied [1,2]. An excellent overview concerning the pseudoinverse control of redundant manipulators as well as a geometric interpretation of the pseudoinverse using singular value decomposition is presented in [7].

A number of different methods for calculating pseudoinverses have been discussed in the literature [6,14]. A discussion of the some of the numerical considerations involved in computing the pseudoinverse is presented by Noble [11]. The simplest expressions for a pseudoinverse appear for matrices known to be of full rank. For an $m \times n$ matrix A of rank r, the expression for the pseudoinverse is given by

$$A^+ = \begin{cases} (A^\top A)^{-1} A^\top & \text{if } m > n = r \text{ and} \\ A^\top (A A^\top)^{-1} & \text{if } r = m < n \end{cases} \quad (5).$$

The use of Gaussian elimination with pivoting removes the need for an explicit inverse calculation and results in a stable and efficient technique for computing the pseudoinverses under these conditions.

For matrices of unknown rank a recursive procedure for computing the pseudoinverse presented by Greville [4] may be used, the details of which are beyond the scope of this paper.

Controlling Redundant Limbs in PODA

While the above section illustrates how the pseudoinverse can be used to obtain a useful solution to equation (1), for cases where redundant degrees of freedom exist, it is only one of an infinite number of solutions. The manner in which the animator is given the flexibility to determine which of the available solutions is most desirable is through a projection operator. It can be shown that shown [5] that the general solution of equation (1) is given by

$$\Delta\vec{\theta} = J^+ \Delta\vec{x} + (I - J^+ J)\vec{z} \quad (6)$$

where I is an $n \times n$ unity matrix and z is an arbitrary vector in $\Delta\theta$-space. Thus the homogeneous portion of this solution is described by a projection operator $(I - J^+ J)$ that maps the arbitrary vector $\vec{z}$ into the null space of the transformation. The physical interpretation of the homogeneous solution is illustrated in figure 4.

Thus by different choices for the vector $\vec{z}$, various desirable properties described in θ-space can be achieved under the constraint imposed by exact achievement of the specified $\Delta\vec{x}$. One particularly useful property is to keep joints as close as possible to some particular angles chosen by the animator. This is done [8] by specifying the vector $\vec{z}$ in equation (6) to be

$$\vec{z} = \nabla H$$

with

$$H = \sum_{i=1}^{n} \alpha_i (\theta_i - \theta_{c_i})^2$$

where θ_i is the ith joint angle, θ_{c_i} is the center angle of the ith joint angle, and α_i is a center angle gain value between zero and one. The equation may also be generalized for H equal to any smooth function one wishes to minimize.

The center angles define the desired joint angle positions and their associated gains define their relative importance of satisfaction. From the animators point of view, the gains may be thought of as "springs" which define the stiffness of the joint about some desired center position. PODA provides interactive specification of center angles and gains as a means of controlling redundant degrees of freedom in the legs.

The implementation of this formulation can be included in the gaussian elimination procedure for computing the pseudoinverse if it is properly decomposed [7].

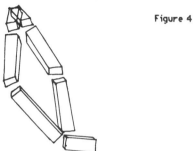

Figure 4

Homogeneous solution to the Jacobian equation is the set of joint velocities which cause no end effector motion.

MODELING THE KINEMATICS OF LEGGED LOCOMOTION

The task of a kinematic model for legged locomotion is to coordinate the motion of the legs, feet and body in terms of their respective positions and velocities (Newtonian mechanical properties such as force and mass are not considered). The kinematic model must enable the animator to design the timing relationships between the legs and the character of the steps taken by each leg in accordance with the design of the body's trajectory, orientation and speed. Ideally, it should be easily adaptable to any extensions made in the dynamics domain.

Gait Design in PODA

The model of locomotion implemented in PODA utilizes a number of parameters which are convenient for describing the gait of a figure-the terms and relations are derived from robotics research on walking machines [22-26].

A *gait pattern* describes the sequence of lifting and placing of the feet. The pattern repeats itself as the figure moves: each repetition of the sequence is called the *gait cycle*.

The time (or number of frames) taken to complete a single gait cycle is the *period P* of the cycle.

The *relative phase of leg i*, R_i, describes the fraction of the gait cycle period which transpires before leg i is lifted. The relative phases of the legs may be used to classify the well known gaits of quadrupedal animals (fig. 5).

During each gait cycle period any given leg will spend a percentage of that time on the ground—this fraction is called the *duty factor of leg i*. For example, the duty factor may be used to distinguish between the walking and running gaits of bipeds. Walking requires that the duty factor of the each of the legs exceed 0.5 since, by definition, the feet must be on the ground simultaneously for a percentage of the gait cycle period. Lower duty factors (less than 0.5) result in ballistic motion identified with running, wherein the entire body leaves the ground for some duration.

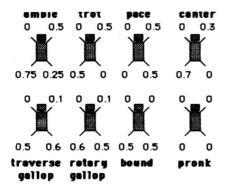

Figure 5

We will call the time a leg spends on the ground its *support duration*. The time spent in the air is the leg's *transfer duration*.

The *stroke* is defined as the distance traveled by the body during a leg's support duration. If we acknowledge that the foot must traverse the stroke during the transfer phase in order to "keep up" with the body, the stroke may alternatively be regarded as the length of the step taken by the leg over the ground (fig. 6a). The body may move over the ground plane in PODA, so the stroke in this context becomes the diameter of a circle in that plane (fig. 6b).

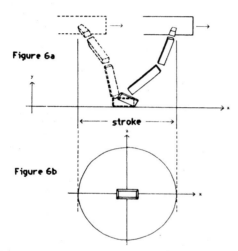

Figure 6a

Figure 6b

Leg Coordination

The following relationship holds between the legs and the body:

$$\text{supportDuration} = \frac{\text{stroke}}{\text{bodySpeed}} \quad (7)$$

The above equation solves for the time (or number of frames) that each leg must spend on the ground. By definition we also have

$$\text{dutyFactor} = \frac{\text{supportDuration}}{P}$$

The amount of time which a leg spends in the air depends on both the leg speed and the arclength of the transfer phase trajectory. That is:

$$\text{transferDuration} = \frac{\textbf{arcLength}(\text{transferTrajectory})}{\text{legSpeed}}$$

During the gait cycle period P, a single leg will move through one cycle of support and transfer, hence we have:

$$P = \text{supportDuration} + \text{transferDuration} \quad (8)$$

for any leg k. In fact, one may imagine the period as a duration subdivided into support and transfer durations (fig. 7). The *leg state* at time t may be determined as

$$\text{legState} = (\text{legState}_0 + t) \bmod P \quad (9)$$

where

$$\text{legState}_0 = (R_i)(P)$$

If the leg state is less than the support duration then the leg is in its support phase, otherwise the leg is in its transfer phase. Moreover, the time of foot placement occurs when the leg state equals zero and the foot liftoff occurs when the leg state is equal to the support duration (fig. 7).

An animator using PODA may design gaits for figures having any number of legs by instantiating the parameters given above. The model makes sure that all the variables are updated according to functional dependencies, thereby freeing the animator to experiment with the variables of interest such as relative phase without worrying about the integrity of the other related variables.

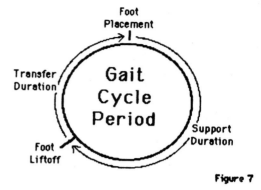

Figure 7

Leg Support and Transfer Trajectories

Aside from the problem of coordinating the timing of the legs, one must design the motion of the step taken during the transfer phase and insure that the feet will remain planted on the ground during the support phase.

A step is specified in PODA by the desired trajectory of the feet and the center angles and gains on the joints (which may change dynamically). The curve which defines the foot trajectory is defined by a Catmull-Rom (interpolating) spline. Because the desired shape of the curve depends on the geometry of the leg, the control points of the spline are set by moving the foot of the leg. The animator may conceptualize the design of the step as the specification of "key leg positions," in the spirit of a key-framing system. In PODA, a key position records the position of the foot (as a control point in the spline) and the center angles and gains that are associated with that position. The animator manipulates the foot into each position using PODA's inverse kinematic procedures, and then, once the foot is in place, the joint angles may be adjusted using the center angle and gain parameters.

This approach is distinguished from key-framing or joint angle interpolation systems in that the goal of achieving the desired foot position in Cartesian space is primary–the foot will travel precisely along the smooth Catmull-Rom spline from foothold to foothold. By contrast, if we interpolate the the leg positions in joint space, there is no general means of either moving the foot along a curve or placing the foot at a particular place on the ground.

The problem of keeping the legs on the ground as the body translates and rotates is simplified due to PODA's inverse kinematic capability. The problem reduces to solving for the position of the foot in the leg's moving coordinate system so that it is identical to the placement of the foot in the previous frame's world coordinate system (thereby keeping the foot stationary in the world). We we solve for this position using:

$$^{\text{World}}\overrightarrow{\text{prevFrameFoot}}_{t-1} = {}^{\text{World}}T_{\text{Hip}_{t-1}}\left(^{\text{Hip}}\overrightarrow{\text{Foot}}_{t-1}\right) \quad (10)$$

$$^{\text{Hip}}\overrightarrow{\text{prevFrameFoot}}_{t} = {}^{\text{Hip}}T_{\text{World}_t}\left(^{\text{World}}\overrightarrow{\text{prevFrameFoot}}_{t-1}\right)$$

Directional Control of the Body

If the animator is to have supervisory control over the legged figure, a means for directing the body's full translational and rotational degree's of freedom must be available. Given that all the legs are on the ground, the problem may be solved using equation (10). The fundamental problem is to calculate footholds and plan the foot transfer trajectories between them so as to adapt to the desired body motion.

Foothold and Transfer Trajectory Planning

An important concept of foothold planning is the notion of a *reference leg position*[22]. This is the desired position of the leg in midstance or half way though the leg's support duration (fig. 10). The posture of an animal when all of its legs are in their reference positions may be regarded as the "standing" position of the animal (fig. 11).

The other key ingredient for the foothold calculation is the ability to predict the body's future positions. In PODA, the body's trajectory may be computed as a function of the desired body trajectory over the ground plane (a cubic spline designed by the animator) and dynamic constraints due the timing and force limitations of legs (to be discussed) before the precise footholds are chosen. Since the body's position is known in advance, it is possible to plan ahead in order step toward the next stable position

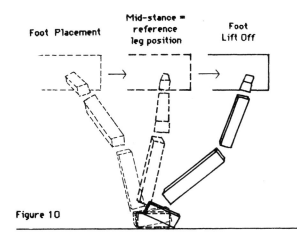

Figure 10

At the beginning of the leg transfer phase of leg i, say at frame t, we must compute the reference leg position in world space at frame f_1 as follows:

$$^{\text{World}}T_{\text{Hip}_{f_1}} = {}^{\text{World}}T_{\text{Body}_{f_1}} {}^{\text{Body}}T_{\text{Hip}}$$

$$^{\text{World}}\overrightarrow{\text{refLegPos}}_{f_1} = {}^{\text{World}}T_{\text{Hip}_{f_1}} \left({}^{\text{Hip}}\overrightarrow{\text{refLegPos}}\right) \quad (11)$$

where

$$f_1 = t + \text{transferDuration} + 0.5(\text{supportDuration})$$

This foothold will insure that that leg i comes to its "mid-stance" position half way through its support phase. We must still determine the position of the foot in the body's coordinate system at the time the foot is placed down. This knowledge is required in order to facilitate moving the foot horizontally with respect to the body during the transfer. This may be accomplished by:

$$^{\text{Body}}\overrightarrow{\text{refLegPos}}_{f_2} = {}^{\text{Body}}T_{\text{World}_{f_2}} \left({}^{\text{World}}\overrightarrow{\text{refLegPos}}_{f_1}\right)$$

where

$$f_2 = t + \text{transferDuration}$$

The generic transfer trajectory designed by the animator may then be adapted to move between the current foot position and the calculated foothold so that the height in the world and proportional distance moved next to the body are preserved.

Robotics research on walking vehicles has provided a rich source of computational models for the solution of body motion planning and leg coordination[22-26]. However, their design criteria is somewhat different the requirements of animation.

The primary design concerns of the robotics algorithms are to maintain dynamic stability of the walking vehicle, to avoid leg intersections, to optimize the load balancing and energy consumption, and to insure that the feet never stray beyond their kinematic limits. Because the algorithms must actually work for real walking machines (rather than simulated figures), their scope is conservative. Restrictions are placed on the types of gait patterns and relative phase relationships between the legs, thereby drastically limiting the repertoire of behaviors.

The design philosophy of PODA is to give the animator absolute control over the entire set of of available gaits in order to exploit the coupling between rhythm and dynamics (to be discussed) since these matters are of extreme importance in artistic design. Moreover, since PODA's current implementation on the Ridge 32C minicomputer provides for realtime computation of a figure possessing four 9-degree of freedom legs at 2 frames per second, leg interference and unnatural leg stretching may be detected immediately, leaving the range of many reasonable solutions to these problems up to the artist rather than hard-wiring a single solution into the motion model.

MODELING THE DYNAMICS OF LEGGED LOCOMOTION

The simulation of the dynamics of motion control in legged animals is an extremely complex modeling problem. Models for single limbs (industrial robots) which compute the relationships between the torques applied at the joints, the masses and moments of inertia of each of the links, and the position of the joints and their associated time derivatives, are well understood [38]. Work has also been published in the biomechanics field on the the relationship between muscular forces and motion parameters of simplified "ideal" models of animals[33,34]. Although these models may produce interesting animation, their appropriateness for artistic design and control must be considered as well as their (usually substantial) computational costs.

Simulation vs. Animation

In contrast to industrial robots and biomechanical simulations, animation does not necessarily require the computation of actual forces. The application of dynamics to animation is simplified by the fact that we are interested only in what can be seen.

The essential concern is to make the motion look as if forces were being applied. In other words, we are primarily interested in solving for the acceleration in dynamics models - the computation of parameters such as forces, torques and moments of inertia is only relevant if it can help us easily manipulate accelerations to produce coherent dynamic realism.

The necessity for modeling dynamics in PODA was apparent as soon as the kinematic model was completed. In a purely kinematic model the motion of the body is quickly seen to be independent from the coordination of the legs, and it appears as though the body is suspended from strings, pulling its legs behind it.

The development of dynamics for PODA is an ongoing research project. The initial goal was to see whether very simple dynamic models of legged locomotion could be developed which were both amenable to artistic control and as fully general as the kinematic model (applicable to any figure constructed by the animator). At the time of this writing, PODA is capable of modeling the translational acceleration of the center of mass of body in the vertical direction and ground plane, and the rotational acceleration of the body that is required to insure that it is facing in the direction of movement (if turning is desired). At all stages, the body's motion is constrained and propelled by the simulated forces applied by the legs.

Decomposition of Dynamic Control in PODA

The simple model used in PODA was inspired by Raibert's work on legged hopping machines. He and his coworkers have built a one-legged hopping machine which is able to balance and move in three dimensions. His control algorithms are based on a decomposition into hopping height, forward velocity, and attitude control[31,28].

The model used in PODA decomposes the dynamic coupling between the legs and the body along two lines: decomposition by leg and decomposition by body direction.

Vertical Control

Dynamics in the vertical direction must take into account the effects of gravity and the gait cycle period of each leg. Since PODA's decomposition scheme is based on decomposition by leg, it will be helpful to consider a one-legged figure.

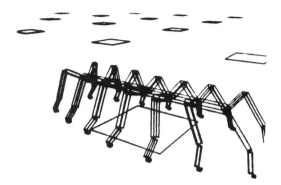

A 14 legged insect shown in its standing position.

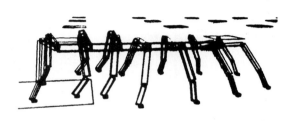

Moving in a wave gait, the legs near the rear advance toward their next footholds.

Figure 11

The current model makes the simplifying assumption that the upward force applied by the leg on the body is constant during its support phase. The animator supplies PODA with both the value of this force, the mass of the body, and the downward acceleration due to gravity. Net upward acceleration of the center of mass is then given by:

$$\vec{a}_{y_i} = \left(\frac{\vec{F}_{y_i}}{\text{mass}_{body}} - g \right) \text{ for leg } i \qquad (12)$$

The gait cycle period may be subdivided into three dynamic stages of the leg's motion: pushing the body up, free falling, and then restoring the body to its original position (as long as the application of upward leg forces are symmetrical about the mid-stance position, the body will stabilize to zero velocity at that position). We will call these the *push duration, fall duration,* and *restore duration* respectively (fig. 12).

The leg support duration is a function of the body speed in the horizontal plane and the stroke (equation 7). Since the leg's traversal of the transfer trajectory must coincide with the body's ballistic motion, we have:

$$\text{transferDuration} = \left(\frac{\vec{a}_{y_i}}{g} \right) (\text{supportDuration}) \qquad (13)$$

The vertical position of figures with multiple legs is determined in PODA by the superposition of the ballistic motion of the body due of each of its legs considered independently. This extremely simple model produces remarkably realistic motion for both walking and running in multiple leg figures: if the magnitude of vertical acceleration is low and the phase relationships of the legs are in opposition, the upward accelerations will cancel, resulting in a smooth walking oscillation. High accelerations resulting from strong single leg forces (e.g. running in a trot) or the sum of forces of many legs pushing from the ground together (e.g. hopping) propel the body into the air.

The trajectory taken by the body due to the summation of vertical leg accelerations and downward gravitational accelerations taken from each of the legs is automatically synchronized with rhythm of the phase relationships in the legs. For example, convincing cantors, trots, and bounding motion may be animated simply by altering the figure's gait.

Another advantage to PODA's leg decomposition of vertical dynamics is that changes in the figure's motion parameters which evolve over gait cycle periods, such as body speed or upward leg force may be easily accommodated by adjusting the related dynamic parameters for each leg's contribution independently at the beginning of its upward pushing phase. The stability of each leg's contribution guarantees the vertical stability of the body as a whole. A gait shifting algorithm has been developed by one of the authors which exploits the ability for legs to undergo phase shifts by varying the distribution of vertical pushing forces among them.

Horizontal Control

The desired horizontal path taken by the figure is specified in PODA by the animator with a cubic spline (Catmull-Rom or B-spline). Given the desired body speed along different parts of the curve, PODA may calculate the desired positions and velocities along it using a numerical arclength calculation.

However, a legged figure's acceleration toward a desired direction and speed must be coherent with its leg support duration pattern and it must also simulate the effects of momentum in a given direction in order to give the body a sense of weight.

In PODA, the body's ability to turn and speed up is consistent with the number of feet on the ground and the magnitude of the maximum achievable force $\|\vec{F}_{max_i}\|$ assigned by the animator to each supporting leg. The maximum achievable acceleration of the body is governed by the sum of their forces:

$$\|\vec{a}_{xz_{max}}\| = \sum_{i=1}^{n} \frac{\|\vec{F}_{max_i}\|}{\text{mass}_{body}} \qquad (14)$$

where n is the number of feet on the ground.

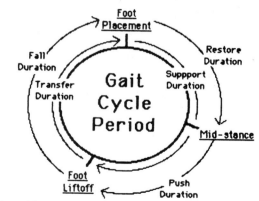

Figure 12

At each frame PODA computes the next desired velocity along the desired body path. Then PODA determines the desired acceleration at a given frame through velocity error feedback, that is, by subtracting the desired velocity from the current velocity at that frame. The horizontal acceleration of the body at frame t is then computed as:

$$\vec{a}_{xz} = \|\vec{a}_{xz}\| \frac{\vec{a}_{xz_{desired}}}{\|\vec{a}_{xz_{desired}}\|} \qquad (15)$$

where

$$\|\vec{a}_{xz}\| = \min(\|\vec{a}_{xz_{desired}}\|, \|\vec{a}_{xz_{max}}\|)$$

$$\vec{a}_{xz_{desired}} = \left(\vec{Vel}_{desired} - \vec{Vel} \right)$$

An additional backward acceleration during the restore duration and forward acceleration during the push duration is necessary in order to simulate the effects foot position with respect to the body at foot placement and foot liftoff [28].

Rotational Control

The foothold and leg transfer calculations described adapt to allow for full rotational control of the body. At the time of this writing, however, only the dynamics of accelerations about the yaw axis have been implemented (the pitch axis rotation apparent in figure 2 is due to the separation of the application of vertical acceleration between the front and rear sections of the body). Yaw axis accelerations are necessary if we wish the body to realistically turn so that it is facing in the direction of movement.

The simple frame to frame strategy applied for horizontal control is not sufficient for coordinated turning, especially for running gaits wherein the legs are off the ground. In such cases one must know where the body is going in order to effectively anticipate the rotational accelerations required to keep the body properly oriented before its feet leave the ground.

The solution adopted by PODA for rotational control takes advantage of its ability to know the translational coordinates of the body in advance. The order of calculation for body dynamics plays an important role in this matter (fig. 13). The direction of body motion may be derived from the sequence of actual velocities taken by the body.

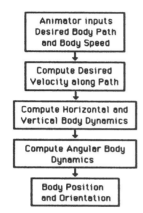

Figure 13

Once the desired body orientations are known, PODA is able to exploit the leg decomposition strategy employed for vertical control. Each leg applies a positive acceleration during its pushing phase and a negative restoring acceleration during its restoring phase in order to bring the body exactly to the desired angle computed at its mid-stance reference leg position. If we solve Newton's equations of motion with the constraint that we wish the final mid-stance rotational velocity to be zero, we have:

$$\ddot{\sigma} = \frac{(\sigma_{\text{midStance}+P} - \sigma_{\text{midStance}})}{(\text{pushDuration})(\text{pushDuration} + \text{fallDuration})}$$

where σ is angle about the yaw axis.

Conclusion

The described formulations have proven to be successful models for the synthesis of legged locomotion. However, many interesting problems remain to be solved. We will refine the legged locomotion model in PODA as more is learned from each simpler model. The addition of rotational dynamics for body pitch and, more generally, the modeling of body dynamics due to the motion of non-supporting limbs are obvious choices for extension.

Other problems of interest include the development of control techniques for maintaining postural balance, the inclusion of obstacle avoidance and collision detection, and a means of designing motor skills above and beyond the requirements of walking and running.

Acknowledgements

The authors wish to thank John Renner and Susan Amkraut for the preparation of this document, and Charles Csuri and Thomas Linehan for their maintenance of the stimulating environment at CGRG.

REFERENCES

[1] Ben-Israel, Adi and Thomas N. E. Greville, "Generalized Inverses: Theory and Applications," *Wiley-Interscience*, New York, 1974.

[2] Boullion, T. L. and P. L. Odell, "Generalized Inverse Matrices," *Wiley-Interscience*, New York, 1971.

[3] Denavit, J. and R. S. Hartenberg, "A Kinematic Notation for Lower-Pair Mechanisms Based on Matrices," *ASME Journal of Applied Mechanics*, Vol. 23, pp. 215-221, June, 1955.

[4] Greville, T. N. E., "Some Applications of the Pseudoinverse of a Matrix," *SIAM Review*, Vol. 2, No. 1, January, 1960.

[5] Greville, T. N. E., "The Pseudoinverse of a Rectangular or Singular Matrix and its Applications to the Solutions of Systems of Linear Equations," *SIAM Review*, Vol. 1, No. 1, January, 1959.

[6] Hanson, R. J. and C. L. Lawson, "Extensions and Applications of the Householder Algorithm for Solving Linear Least Squares Problems," *Mathematics of Computation*, Vol. 23, pp. 787-812, 1969.

[7] Klein, C. A. and Huang, C. H., "Review of Pseudoinverse Control for Use with Kinematically Redundant Manipulators," *IEEE Transactions on Systems, Man, and Cybernetics*, Vol. SMC-13, No. 2, pp. 245-250, March/April, 1983.

[8] Liegeois, A., "Automatic Supervisory Control of the Configuration and Behavior of Multibody Mechanisms," *IEEE Transactions on Systems, Man and Cybernetics*, Vol. SMC-7, No. 12, December, 1977.

[9] Maciejewski, A. A., and Klein, C. A., "Obstacle Avoidance for Kinematically Redundant Manipulators in Dynamically Varying Environments," to appear in *International Journal of Robotics Research*.

[10] Maciejewski, A. A., and Klein, C. A., "SAM - Animation Software for Simulating Articulated Motion," submitted to *IEEE Computer Graphics and Applications*.

[11] Noble, B., "Methods for Computing the Moore-Penrose Generalized Inverses, and Related Matters," pp. 245-301, in *Generalized Inverses and Applications*, ed. by M. A. Nashed, Academic Press, New York, 1975.

[12] Paul, R., *Robot Manipulators*, MIT Press, Cambridge, Mass., 1981.

[13] Penrose, R., "On Best Approximate Solutions of Linear Matrix Equations," *Proc. Cambridge Philos. Soc.*, Vol. 52, pp. 17-19, 1956.

[14] Peters, G. and J. H. Wilkinson, "The Least Squares Problem and Pseudo-Inverses," *The Computer Journal*, Vol. 13, No. 3, August, 1970.

[15] Ribble, E. A., "Synthesis of Human Skeletal Motion and the Design of a Special-Purpose Processor for Real-Time Animation of Human and Animal Figure Motion," Master's Thesis, The Ohio State University, June, 1982.

[16] Waldron, K. J., "Geometrically Based Manipulator Rate Control Algorithms", *Seventh Applied Mechanics Conference*, Kansas City, December, 1981.

[17] Waldron, K. J., "The Use of Motors in Spatial Kinematics," *Proceedings of the IFToMM Conference on Linkages and Computer Design Methods*, Bucharest, June, 1973, Vol. B., pp. 535-545.

[18] Whitney, D. E., "Resolved Motion Rate Control of Manipulators and Human Prostheses," *IEEE Transactions on Man-Machine systems*, Vol. MMS-10, No. 2, pp. 47-53, June, 1969.

[19] Whitney, D. E., "The Mathematics of Coordinated Control of Prostheses and Manipulators," *Journal of Dynamic Systems, Measurement, and Control, Transactions ASME*, Vol. 94, Series G, pp. 303-309, December, 1972, pp. 49-58.

[20] Alexander, R., "The Gaits of Bipedal and Quadrupedal Animals," *The International Journal of Robotics Research*, Vol. 3. No. 2, Summer 1984.

[21] McGhee, R.B., and Iswandhi, G.I., "Adaptive Locomotion of a Multilegged Robot over Rough Terrain", *IEEE Transactions on Systems, Man, and Cybernetics*, Vol. SMC-9, No. 4, April, 1979, pp. 176–182.

[22] Orin, D.E., "Supervisory Control of a Multilegged Robot", *International Journal of Robotics Research*, Vol. 1. No. 1, Spring, 1982, pp. 79–91.

[23] Klein, C.A., Olson, K.W., and Pugh, D.R., "Use of Force and Attitude Sensors for Locomotion of a Legged Vehicle over Irregular Terrain," *International Journal of Robotics*, Vol. 2, No. 2, Summer, 1983, pp. 3–17.

[24] Ozguner, F., Tsai, L.J., and McGhee, R.B., "Rough Terrain Locomotion by a Hexapod Robot Using a Binocular Ranging System," *Proceedings of First International Symposium of Robotics Research*, Bretton Woods, N.H., August 28, 1983.

[25] Lee, Wha-Joon, "A Computer Simulation Study of Omnidirectional Supervisory Control for Rough–Terrain Locomotion by a Multilegged Robot Vehicle," Ph.D. Dissertation, The Ohio State University, Columbus, Ohio, March, 1984.

[26] Yeh, S. "Locomotion of a Three–Legged Robot Over Structural Beams," Masters Thesis, The Ohio State University, Columbus, Ohio, March, 1984.

[27] Zeltzer, D.L., "Representation and Control of Three Dimensional Computer–Animated Figures," Ph.D Dissertation, The Ohio State University, Columbus, Ohio, March, 1984.

[28] Murphy, K.N., and Raibert, M.H., "Trotting and Bounding in a Planar Two-Legged Model," *Fifth CISM-IFTOMM Symposium on Theory and Practice of Robots and Manipulators*, June 26–29, 1984, Udine, Italy.

[29] Miura, H. and Shimoyama, I. "Dynamic Walk of a Biped," *The International Journal of Robotics Research*, Vol. 3, No. 2., Summer 1984, pp 60–74.

[30] Pearson, K.G., and Franklin, R., "Characteristics of Leg Movements and Patterns of Coordination in Locusts Walking on Rough Terrain," *The International Journal of Robotics Research*, Vol. 3, No. 2., Summer 1984, pp 101–107.

[31] Raibert, M.H., Brown, H.B.Jr, and Chepponis, M., "Experiments in Balance with a 3D One–Legged hopping Machine," *The International Journal of Robotics Research*, Vol. 3, No. 2., Summer 1984, pp 75–82.

[32] Korein, J.U., and Badler, N.I., "Techniques for Generating the Goal–Directed Motion of Articulated Structures," *IEEE Computer Graphics and Applications*, November 1982, pp. 71–81.

[33] Hemami, H. and Zheng, Y., "Dynamics and Control of Motion on the Ground and in the Air with Application to Biped Robots," *Journal of Robotic Systems*, Vol 1. No. 1, 1984, pp. 101–116.

[34] Hemami, H. and Chen, B. "Stability Analysis and Input Design of a Two–Link Planar Biped, *The International Journal of Robotics Research*, Vol. 3, No. 2., Summer 1984, pp. 93–100.

[35] McMahon, T.A., "Mechanics of Locomotion," *The International Journal of Robotics Research*, Vol. 3, No. 2., Summer 1984, pp 4–18.

[36] Lundin, R.V. "Motion Simulation," *Nicograph Proceedings 1984*, pp. 2–10.

[37] Orin, D. E., and Schrader, W. W., "Efficient Jacobian Determination for Robot Manipulators," *Sixth IFToMM Congress*, New Dehli, India, December 15–20, 1983.

[38] Orin, D.E., McGhee, R.B., Vukobratovic, M.,and Hartoch, G., "Kinematic and Kinetic Analysis of Open-Chain Linkages Utilizing Newton–Euler Methods," *Mathematical Biosciences*, Vol. 43, pp. 107–130, 1979.

PRINCIPLES OF TRADITIONAL ANIMATION APPLIED TO 3D COMPUTER ANIMATION

John Lasseter
Pixar
San Rafael
California

"There is no particular mystery in animation... it's really very simple, and like anything that is simple, it is about the hardest thing in the world to do." Bill Tytla at the Walt Disney Studio, June 28, 1937. [14]

ABSTRACT

This paper describes the basic principles of traditional 2D hand drawn animation and their application to 3D computer animation. After describing how these principles evolved, the individual principles are detailed, addressing their meanings in 2D hand drawn animation and their application to 3D computer animation. This should demonstrate the importance of these principles to quality 3D computer animation.

CR Categories and Subject Descriptors:

I.3.6 *Computer Graphics* : Methodology and Techniques - Interaction techniques;

I.3.7 *Computer Graphics* : Three-dimensional Graphics and Realism - Animation;

J.5 *Computer Applications* : Arts and Humanities - Arts, fine and performing.

General Terms: Design, Human Factors.

Additional Keywords and Phrases: Animation Principles, Keyframe Animation, Squash and Stretch, Luxo Jr.

1. INTRODUCTION

Early research in computer animation developed 2D animation techniques based on traditional animation. [7] Techniques such as storyboarding [11], keyframe animation, [4,5] inbetweening [16,22] scan/paint, and multiplane backgrounds [17] attempted to apply the cel animation process to the computer. As 3D computer animation research matured, more resources were devoted to image rendering than to animation. Because 3D computer animation uses 3D models instead of 2D drawings, fewer techniques from traditional animation were applied. Early 3D animation systems were script based [6], followed by a few spline-interpolated keyframe systems. [22] But these systems were developed by companies for internal use, and so very few traditionally trained animators found their way into 3D computer animation.

"Luxo" is a trademark of Jac Jacobsen Industries AS.

Permission to copy without fee all or part of this material is granted provided that the copies are not made or distributed for direct commercial advantage, the ACM copyright notice and the title of the publication and its date appear, and notice is given that copying is by permission of the Association for Computing Machinery. To copy otherwise, or to republish, requires a fee and/or specific permission.

© 1987   ACM-0-89791-227-6/87/007/0035 $00.75

The last two years have seen the appearance of reliable, user friendly, keyframe animation systems from such companies as Wavefront Technologies Inc., [29] Alias Research Inc., [2] Abel Image Research (RIP), [1] Vertigo Systems Inc., [28] Symbolics Inc., [25] and others. These systems will enable people to produce more high quality computer animation. Unfortunately, these systems will also enable people to produce more **bad** computer animation.

Much of this bad animation will be due to unfamiliarity with the fundamental principles that have been used for hand drawn character animation for over 50 years. Understanding these principles of traditional animation is essential to producing good computer animation. Such an understanding should also be important to the designers of the systems used by these animators.

In this paper, I will explain the fundamental principles of traditional animation and how they apply to 3D keyframe computer animation.

2. PRINCIPLES OF ANIMATION

Between the late 1920's and the late 1930's animation grew from a novelty to an art form at the Walt Disney Studio. With every picture, actions became more convincing, and characters were emerging as true personalities. Audiences were enthusiastic and many of the animators were satisfied, however it was clear to Walt Disney that the level of animation and existing characters were not adequate to pursue new story lines-- characters were limited to certain types of action and, audience acceptance notwithstanding, they were not appealing to the eye. It was apparent to Walt Disney that no one could successfully animate a humanized figure or a life-like animal; a new drawing approach was necessary to improve the level of animation exemplified by the *Three Little Pigs* . [10]

FIGURE 1. Luxo Jr.'s hop with overlapping action on cord. Flip pages from last page of paper to front. The top figures are frames 1-5, the bottom are frames 6-10.

Disney set up drawing classes for his animators at the Chouinard Art Institute in Los Angeles under instructor Don Graham. When the classes were started, most of the animators were drawing using the old cartoon formula of standardized shapes, sizes, actions, and gestures, with little or no reference to nature. [12] Out of these classes grew a way of drawing moving human figures and animals. The students studied models in motion [20] as well as live action film, playing certain actions over and over. [13] The analysis of action became important to the development of animation.

Some of the animators began to apply the lessons of these classes to production animation, which became more sophisticated and realistic. The animators continually searched for better ways to communicate to one another the ideas learned from these lessons. Gradually, procedures were isolated and named, analyzed and perfected, and new artists were taught these practices as rules of the trade. [26] They became the fundamental principles of traditional animation:

1. *Squash and Stretch* -- Defining the rigidity and mass of an object by distorting its shape during an action.

2. *Timing* -- Spacing actions to define the weight and size of objects and the personality of characters.

3. *Anticipation* -- The preparation for an action.

4. *Staging* -- Presentating an idea so that it is unmistakably clear.

5. *Follow Through and Overlapping Action* -- The termination of an action and establishing its relationship to the next action.

6. *Straight Ahead Action and Pose-To-Pose Action* -- The two contrasting approaches to the creation of movement.

7. *Slow In and Out* -- The spacing of the inbetween frames to achieve subtlety of timing and movement.

8. *Arcs* -- The visual path of action for natural movement.

9. *Exaggeration* -- Accentuating the essence of an idea via the design and the action.

10. *Secondary Action* -- The action of an object resulting from another action.

11. *Appeal* -- Creating a design or an action that the audience enjoys watching.

The application of some of these principles mean the same regardless of the medium of animation. 2D hand drawn animation deals with a sequence of two dimensional drawings that simulate motion. 3D computer animation involves creating a three dimensional model in the computer. Motion is achieved by setting keyframe poses and having the computer generate the inbetween frames. Timing, anticipation, staging, follow through, overlap, exaggeration, and secondary action apply in the same way for both types of animation. While the meanings of squash and stretch, slow in and out, arcs, appeal, straight ahead action, and pose-to-pose action remain the same, their application changes due to the difference in medium.

2.1 SQUASH AND STRETCH

The most important principle is called *squash and stretch*. When an object is moved, the movement emphasizes any rigidity in the object. In real life, only the most rigid shapes (such as chairs, dishes and pans) remain so during motion. Anything composed of living flesh, no matter how bony, will show considerable movement in its shape during an action. For example, when a bent arm with swelling biceps straightens out, only the long sinews are apparent. A face, whether chewing, smiling, talking, or just showing a change of expression, is alive with changing shapes in the cheeks, the lips, and the eyes. [26]

The squashed position depicts the form either flattened out by an external pressure or constricted by its own power. The stretched position always shows the same form in a very extended condition. [26]

The most important rule to squash and stretch is that, no matter how squashed or stretched out a particular object gets, its volume remains constant. If an object squashed down without its sides stretching, it would appear to shrink; if it stretched up without its sides squeezing in it would appear to grow. Consider the shape and volume of a half filled flour sack: when dropped on the floor, it squashed out to its fullest shape. If picked up by the top corners, it stretched out to its longest shape. It never changes volume. [26]

The standard animation test for all beginners is drawing a bouncing ball. The assignment is to represent the ball by a simple circle, and then have it drop, hit the ground, and bounce back into the air. A simple test, but it teaches the basic mechanics of animating a scene, introducing timing as well as squash and stretch. If the bottom drawing is flattened, it gives the appearance of bouncing. Elongating the drawings before and after the bounce increases the sense of speed, makes it easier to follow and gives more snap to the action. [26,3] (figure 2)

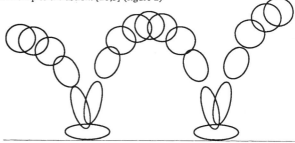

FIGURE 2. Squash & stretch in bouncing ball.

Squash and stretch also defines the rigidity of the material making up an object. When an object is squashed flat and stretches out drastically, it gives the sense that the object is made out of a soft, pliable material and vice versa. When the parts of an object are of different materials, they should respond differently: flexible parts should squash more and rigid parts less.

An object need not deform in order to squash and stretch. For instance, a hinged object like Luxo Jr. (from the film, *Luxo Jr.* [21]), squashes by folding over on itself, and stretches by extending out fully. (figure 3)

FIGURE 3. Squash & stretch in Luxo Jr.'s hop.

Squash and stretch is very important in facial animation, not only for showing the flexibility of the flesh and muscle, but also for showing the relationship of between the parts of the face. When a face smiles broadly, the corners of the mouth push up into the cheeks. The cheeks squash and push up into the eyes, making the eyes squint , which brings down the eyebrows and stretches the forehead. When the face adopts a surprised expression, the mouth opens, stretching down the cheeks. The wide open eyes push the eyebrows up, squashing and wrinkling the forehead.

Another use of squash and stretch is to help relieve the disturbing effect of strobing that happens with very fast motion because sequencial positions of an object become spaced far apart. When the action is slow enough, the object's positions overlap, and the eye smooths the motion out. (figure 4a) However, as the speed of the action increases, so does the distance between positions. When the distance becomes far enough that the object does not overlap from frame to frame, the eye then begins to perceive separate images. (figure 4b) Accurate motion blur is the most realistic solution to this problem of strobing, [8,9] but when motion blur is not available, squash and stretch is an alternative: the object should be stretched enough so that its positions do overlap from frame to frame (or nearly so), and the eye will smooth the action out again. (figure 4c)

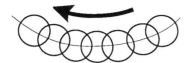

FIGURE 4a. In slow action, an object's position overlaps from frame to frame which gives the action a smooth appearance to the eye.

FIGURE 4b. Strobing occurs in a faster action when the object's positions do not overlap and the eye perceives seperate images.

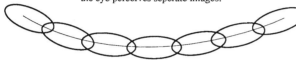

FIGURE 4c. Stretching the object so that it's positions overlap again will relieve the strobing effect.

In 3D keyframe computer animation, the scale transformation can be used for squash and stretch. When scaling up in Z, the object should be scaled down in X and Y to keep the volume the same. Since the direction of the stretch should be along the path of action, a rotational transformation may be required to align the object along an appropriate axis.

2.2 TIMING

Timing, or the speed of an action, is an important principle because it gives meaning to movement-- the speed of an action defines how well the idea behind the action will read to an audience. It reflects the weight and size of an object, and can even carry emotional meaning.

Proper timing is critical to making ideas readable. It is important to spend enough time (but no more) preparing the audience for: the anticipation of an action; the action itself; and the reaction to the action. If too much time is spent on any of these, the audience's attention will wander. If too little time is spent, the movement may be finished before the audience notices it, thus wasting the idea. [30]

The faster the movement, the more important it is to make sure the audience can follow what is happening. The action must not be so fast that the audience cannot read it and understand the meaning of it. [30]

More than any other principle, timing defines the weight of an object. Two objects, identical in size and shape, can appear to be two vastly different weights by manipulating timing alone. The heavier an object is, the greater its mass, and the more force is required to change its motion. A heavy body is slower to accelerate and decelerate than a light one. It takes a large force to get a cannonball moving, but once moving, it tends to keep moving at the same speed and requires some force to stop it. When dealing with heavy objects, one must allow plenty of time and force to start, stop or change their movements, in order to make their weight look convincing. [30]

Light objects have much less resistance to change of movement and so need much less time to start moving. The flick of a finger is enough to make a balloon accelerate quickly away. When moving, it has little momentum and even the friction of the air quickly slows it up. [30]

Timing can also contribute greatly to the feeling of size or scale of an object or character. A giant has much more weight, more mass, more inertia than a normal man; therefore he moves more slowly. Like the cannonball, he takes more time to get started and, once moving, takes more time to stop. Any changes of movement take place more slowly. Conversely, a tiny character has less inertia than normal, so his movements tend to be quicker. [30]

The way an object behaves on the screen, the effect of weight that it gives, depend entirely on the spacing of the poses and not on the poses themselves. No matter how well rendered a cannonball may be, it does not look like a cannonball if it does not behave like one when animated. The same applies to any object or character. [30]

The emotional state of a character can also be defined more by its movement than by its appearance, and the varying speed of those movements indicates whether the character is lethargic, excited, nervous or relaxed. Thomas and Johnston [26] describe how changing the timing of an action gives it new meaning:

Just two drawings of a head, the first showing it leaning toward the right shoulder and the second with it over on the left and its chin slightly raised, can be made to communicate a multitude of ideas, depending entirely on the Timing used. Each inbetween drawing added between these two "extremes" gives a new meaning to the action.

NO inbetweens........... The Character has been hit by a tremendous force. His head is nearly snapped off.

ONE inbetweens......... The Character has been hit by a brick, rolling pin, frying pan.

TWO inbetweens......... The Character has a nervous tic, a muscle spasm, an uncontrollable twitch.

THREE inbetweens..... The Character is dodging a brick, rolling pin, frying pan.

FOUR inbetweens........... The Character is giving a crisp order, "Get going!" "Move it!"

FIVE inbetweens........... The Character is more friendly, "Over here." "Come on-hurry!"

SIX inbetweens........... The Character sees a good looking girl, or the sports car he has always wanted.

SEVEN inbetweens........... The Character tries to get a better look at something.

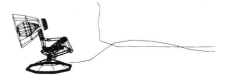

EIGHT inbetweens............ The Character searches for the peanut butter on the kitchen shelf.

NINE inbetweens............The Character appraises, considering thoughtfully.

TEN inbetweens............ The Character stretches a sore muscle.

FIGURE 5. Wally B.'s zip off shows use of squash and stretch, anticipation, follow through, overlapping action, and secondary action.

2.3 ANTICIPATION

An action occurs in three parts: the preparation for the action, the action proper, and the termination of the action. *Anticipation* is the preparation for the action; the latter two are discussed in the next sections.

There are several facets to Anticipation. In one sense, it is the anatomical provision for an action. Since muscles in the body function through contraction, each must be first be extended before it can contract. A foot must be pulled back before it can be swung forward to kick a ball. [12] Without anticipation many actions are abrupt, stiff and unnatural.

Anticipation is also a device to catch the audience's eye, to prepare them for the next movement and lead them to expect it before it actually occurs. Anticipation is often used to explain what the following action is going to be. Before a character reaches to grab an object, he first raises his arms as he stares at the article, broadcasting the fact that he is going to do something with that particular object. The anticipatory moves may not show **why** he is doing something, but there is no question about **what** he is going to do next. [26]

Anticipation is also used to direct the attention of the audience to the right part of the screen at the right moment. This is essential for preventing the audience from missing some vital action. In the very beginning of *Luxo Jr.*, Dad is on screen alone looking offstage. He then reacts, anticipating something happening there. When Jr. does hop in, the audience is prepared for the action.

The amount of anticipation used considerably affects the speed of the action which follows it. If the audience expects something to happen, then it can be much faster without losing them. If they are not properly prepared for a very fast action, they may miss it completely; the anticipation must be made larger or the action slower. [30] In a slow action the anticipation is often minimized and the meaning carried in the action proper. [12] In one shot in *The Adventures of Andre and Wally B.*, Wally B. zips off to the right. The actual action of the zip off is only 3 or 4 frames long, but he anticipates the zip long enough for the audience to know exactly what is coming next. (figure 5)

Anticipation can also emphasize heavy weight, as for a character picking up an object that is very heavy. An exaggerated anticipation, like bending way down before picking up the object, helps the momentum of the character to lift the heavy weight. Likewise for a fat character standing up from a seated position: he will bend his upper body forward, with his hands on the armrests of the chair, before pushing up with his arms and using the momentum of his body. [31]

2.4 STAGING

Staging is the presentation of an idea so it is completely and unmistakably clear; this principle translates directly from 2-D hand drawn animation. An action is staged so that it is understood; a personality is staged so that it is recognizable; an expression so that it can be seen; a mood so that it will affect the audience. [26]

To stage an idea clearly, the audience's eye must be led to exactly where it needs to be at the right moment, so that they will not miss the idea. Staging, anticipation and timing are all integral to directing the eye. A well-timed anticipation will be wasted if it is not staged clearly.

It is important, when staging an action, that only one idea be seen by the audience at a time. If a lot of action is happening at once, the eye does not know where to look and the main idea of the action will be "upstaged" and overlooked. The object of interest should contrast from the rest of the scene. In a still scene, the eye will be attracted to movement. In a very busy scene, the eye will be attracted to something that is still. Each idea or action must be staged in the strongest and the simplest way before going on to the next idea or action. The animator is saying, in effect, "Look at this, now look at this, and now look at this." [26]

In *Luxo Jr.*, it was very important that the audience was looking in the right place at the right time, because the story, acting and emotion was being put across with movement alone, in pantomime, and sometimes the movement was very subtle. If the audience missed an action, an emotion would be missed, and the story would suffer. So the action had to be paced so that **only** Dad **or** Jr. was doing an important action at any one time, never both. In the beginning of the film, Dad is on screen alone your eye was on him. But as soon as Jr. hops on-screen, he is moving faster than Dad, therefore the audience's eyes immediately goes to him and stays there.

Most of the time Jr. was on-screen, Dad's actions were very subtle, so the attention of the audience was always on Jr. where most of the story was being told. If Dad's actions were important, Jr.'s actions were toned down and Dad's movements were emphasized and the attention of the audience would transfer to Dad. For example, when Jr. looks up to Dad after he's popped the ball and Dad shakes his head, all eyes are on him.

Another idea developed in the early days at Disney was the importance of staging an action in silhouette. In those days, all the characters were black and white, with no gray values to soften the contrast or delineate a form. Bodies, arms and hands were all black, so there was no way to stage an action clearly except in silhouette. A hand in front of a chest would simply disappear. Out of this limitation, the animators realized that it is always better to show an action in silhouette. Charlie Chaplin maintained that if an actor knew his emotion thoroughly, he could show it silhouette. [26]

In *The Adventures of Andre and Wally B.*, Andre awakes and sits up, then scratches his side. If he were to scratch his stomach instead of his side, the action would happen in front of his body and would be unclear what was happening. (figure 6)

FIGURE 6. Andre's scratch was staged to the side (in "silhouette") for clarity and because that is where his itch was.

In *Luxo Jr.*, all the action was animated with silhouette in mind. When Dad and Jr. come face to face for the first time, it is easy to see what is happening because it is staged to the side. If Jr. was in front of Dad looking up at him, it would be difficult to read. (figure 7) Jr. hopping on the ball would be confusing if the action was to happen with Jr. facing the camera. Viewed from the side it is perfectly clear. (figure 8)

2.5 FOLLOW THROUGH AND OVERLAPPING ACTION

Just as the anticipation is the preparation of an action, *follow through* is the termination of an action. Actions very rarely come to a sudden and complete stop, but are generally carried past their termination point. For example, a hand, after releasing a thrown ball, continues past the actual point of release.

In the movement of any object or figure, the actions of the parts are not simultaneous: some part must initiate the move, like the engine of a train. This is called the *lead*. In walking, the action starts with the hips. As the hip swings forward, it sets a leg in motion. The hip "leads", the leg

FIGURES 7-8. In *Luxo Jr.*, all action was staged to the side for clarity.

"follows." As the hip twists, the torso follows, then the shoulder, the arm, the wrist, and finally the fingers. Although most large body actions start in the hips, the wrist will lead the fingers in a hand gesture, and the eyes will usually lead the head in an action. [12]

Appendages or loose parts of a character or object will move at a slower speed and "drag" behind the leading part of the figure. Then as the leading part of the figure slows to a stop, these appendages will continue to move and will take longer to settle down. As with squash and stretch, the object's mass is shown in the way the object slows down. The degree that the appendages drag behind and the time it takes for them to stop is directly proportional to their weight. The heavier they are the farther behind they drag and the longer they take to settle to a stop. Conversely, if they are lighter, they will drag less and stop more quickly.

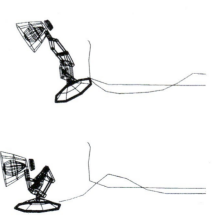

In *The Adventures of Andre and Wally B.*, this principle was used extensively on Wally B.'s feet, antennae and stinger. They all dragged behind his head and body, and continued to move well after the body had stopped. To convey that these loose appendages were made of different materials and different masses, the rate of the follow through was different for each type. His antennae were fairly light, so they dragged behind just slightly. His stinger was like stainless steel, so it dragged behind the action more than the antennae. And his feet were heavy and very flexible, as though they were water balloons; therefore, they always followed far behind the main action with a lot of squash and stretch. In the zip off illustrated above (figure 5), the action of Wally B.'s body was so fast and the feet weighed so much that they dragged far behind. They were even left on screen frames after the body had disappeared.

Often, slight variations are added to the timing and speed of the loose parts of objects. This *overlapping action* makes the object seem natural, the action more interesting. In Wally's zip off (figure 5), his feet zipped off, one after the other, about one or two frames apart. The action was so fast that it was difficult to see each foot going off separately, but It made the action as a whole more interesting.

Perhaps more important, overlapping is critical to conveying main ideas of the story. An action should never be brought to a complete stop before starting another action, and the second action should overlap the first. Overlapping maintains a continual flow and continuity between whole phrases of actions.

Walt Disney once explained overlapping this way, *"It is not necessary for an animator to take a character to one point, complete that action completely, and then turn to the following action as if he had never given it a thought until after completing the first action. When a character knows what his is going to do he doesn't have to stop before each individual action and think to do it. He has it planned in advance in his mind. For example, the mind thinks, ' I'll close the door - lock it - then I'm going to undress and go to bed.' Well, you walk over to the door - before the walk is finished you're reaching for the door - before the door is closed you reach for the key - before the door is locked you're turning away - while you're walking away you undo your tie - and before you reach the bureau you have your tie off. In other words, before you know it you're undressed - and you've done it in one thought, ' I'm going to bed.' "* [12]

2.6 STRAIGHT AHEAD ACTION AND POSE-TO-POSE ACTION (KEYFRAMES)

There are two main approaches to hand drawn animation. The first is known as *straight ahead action* because the animator literally works straight ahead from his first drawing in the scene. He knows where the scene fits in the story and the business it has to include. He does one drawing after another, getting new ideas as he goes along, until he reaches the end of the scene. This process usually produces drawings and action that have a fresh and slightly zany look, because the whole process was kept very creative. Straight ahead action is used for wild, scrambling actions where spontaneity is important.

The second approach is called *pose-to-pose.* Here the animator plans his actions, figures out just what drawings will be needed to animate the business, makes the drawings concentrating on the poses, relates them to each other in size and action, and then draws the inbetweens. Pose-to-pose is used for animation that requires good acting, where the poses and timing are all important.

The pose-to-pose technique applies to keyframe computer animation with timing and pose control of extremes and inbetweens. The difficulty in controlling the inbetweens makes it incorrect to approach keyframe computer animation exactly as one would pose-to-pose hand drawn animation. In working with a complex model, creating a complete pose at a time would make the inbetweens too unpredictable. The path of action will in general be incorrect and objects will intersect one another. The result is much time-consuming reworking of inbetweens.

There is a much better approach in the context of a hierarchical modelling system, which works "layer by layer" down the hierarchy. Instead of animating one complete pose to another, one transformation is animated at a time, starting with the trunk of the hierarchical tree structure, working transformation by transformation down the branches to the end. Fewer extremes are used. Not all translates, rotates and scales have extremes on the same frames; some have many extremes and others very few. With fewer extremes, the importance of the inbetweens increases. Tension and direction controls on the interpolating splines are helpful in controlling the spacing of the inbetween and to achieve slow in and out. [16] (See Slow In and Out)

This layer approach to animation shares many important elements with the pose-to-pose technique in hand drawn animation. Planning the animation out in advance, as in pose-to-pose, becomes even more important. The action must be well thought out, the timing and poses planned so that even in the early layers, the poses and actions are clear.

The Aventures of Andre and Wally B. and *Luxo Jr.* were both animated using a keyframe animation system called Md (Motion Doctor). [19] *Luxo Jr.* was animated using this layered approach to the keyframes. Jr.'s hop (figure 1) was animated by first setting the keyframes for his forward movement only: two keyframes were set for the X translation, the first where the hop starts and the second where he lands. This defined the timing of his hop. The height of his hop was then defined by setting a keyframe in the Z translation (Z being up in this case). The next step, animating the rotation of Jr.'s arms, was important because the arms define the anticipation, squash and stretch, and follow through of the action. Keyframes were set for just about every frame, rotating the arms together before the hop for the anticipation, then immediately far apart for the stretch of the jump. The arms were rotated together again at the top of the arc where the action slows slightly, then rotated far apart, stretching to anticipate the landing. To indicate the shock of the landing, the arms were rotated quickly together two frames after the base lands on the floor. This is the follow through of the action. His base and shade were animated in the next two steps. Like the arms, many keyframes were set to define the rotation of the base and shade because their movement was important for anticipation and follow through.

2.7 SLOW IN AND OUT

Slow in and slow out deals with the spacing of the inbetween drawings between the extreme poses. Mathematically, the term refers to second- and third-order continuity of motion.

In early animation, the action was limited to mainly fast and slow moves, the spacing from one drawing to the next fairly even. But when the poses of pose-to-pose animation became more expressive, animators wanted the audience to see them. They found that by grouping the inbetweens closer to each extreme, with only one fleeting drawing halfway between, they could achieve a very spirited result, with the character zipping from one attitude to another. "Slowing out" of one pose, then "slowing in" to the next pose simply refers to the timing of the inbetweens.

The animator indicates the placement of the inbetweens, the slow in or slow out, with a "timing chart" drawn on the side of the drawing. This tells himself, or his assistant who will be doing the inbetweens later, how he wanted the timing to be and where he wanted the inbetween drawings placed. (figure 9)

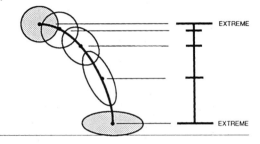

FIGURE 9. Timing chart for ball bounce.

In most 3D keyframe computer animation systems, the inbetweening is done automatically using spline interpolation. Slow in and slow out is achieved by adjusting the tension, direction or bias, and continuity of the splines. [16] This works well to give the affect of slow in and out, but a graphical representation of the spline is required to see the effect of tension, direction, and continuity have on its shape.

With this type of spline interpolation, a common problem is the spline overshooting at extremes when there is a large change in value between them, especially over a small number of frames. This also happens when the direction control of an extreme is adjusted. The danger is that, depending on the variable the spline controls (translate, rotate, or scale), the value will shoot in the wrong direction just before (or just after) the large change in value. Sometimes this effect works out well when it occurs just before a large movement, it may appear to be an anticipation. However, more often than not, it gives an undesirable effect.

In *Luxo Jr.*, there was an example of this problem of overshooting splines. Jr.'s base was very heavy and when he hopped, we wanted the base to start stationary, then pop up in the air from the momentum of his jump, arc over, then land with a thud, suddenly stationary again. For the up translation, there were three keyframes, the two stationary positions and the highest point of his jump. The spline software forced continuity, so that his base would move down under the surface of the floor just before and after the jump. (figure 10a) The solution was to put two new extremes, equal to the two stationary extremes, on the frames just before and just after the extremes. This "locked" down the spline, so that the up translation stayed the same value, popped up in the air, landed and then stayed the same value again. This gave the desired feeling of weight to his little base. (figure 10b)

The same solution can be achieved by breaking the spline using its continuity parameter [16] at the two stationary extremes. This solution requires a graphical display of the spline so that the correct shape can be achieved.

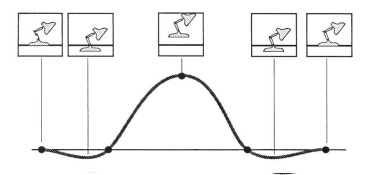

FIGURE 10a. This spline controls the Z (up) translation of Luxo Jr. Dips in the spline cause him to intersect the floor.

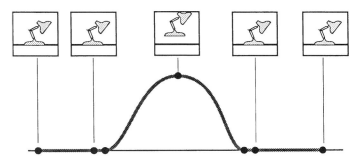

FIGURE 10b. Two extra extremes are added to the spline which removes the dips and prevents Jr. from going into the basement.

2.8 ARCS

The visual path of action from one extreme to another is always described by an *arc*. Arcs in nature are the most economical routes by which a form can move from one position to another. In animation, such arcs are used extensively, for they make animation much smoother and less stiff than a straight line for the path of action. In certain cases, an arc may resolve itself into a straight path, as for a falling object, but usually, even in a straight line action, the object rotates. [12]

In most 3D keyframe computer animation systems, the path of action from one extreme to another is controlled by the same spline that controls the timing (slow in and out) of the inbetween values. This may simplify computating the inbetweens but it has unfortunate effects. When a motion is slow, with many inbetweens, the arc of the path of action is curved, as desired. But when the action is fast, the arc flattens out: the faster the action, the flatter the arc. Sometimes this is desirable, but more often, the path of even a fast motion should be curved or arced. Straight inbetweens can completely kill the essence of an action.

The spline that defines the path of action should be separate from the spline that defines the timing or spacing of the inbetweens for several reasons: so that the arc of a fast action doesn't flatten out; so that you can adjust the timing of the inbetweens without effecting the path of action; so that you can use different splines to define the path of action (where a B-spline is appropriate for its smoothness) and the timing (a Catmull - Rom spline so you can adjust it's tension and direction controls to get slow in and out). This technique is not common, but research is being done in this area. [15]

2.9 EXAGGERATION

The meaning of exaggeration is, in general, obvious. However, the principle of *exaggeration* in animation does not mean arbitrarily distorting shapes or objects or making an action more violent or unrealistic. The animator must go to the heart of anything or any idea and develop its essence, understanding the reason for it , so that the audience will also understand it. If a character is sad, make him sadder; if he is bright, make him shine; worried, make him fret; wild, make him frantic.

A scene has many components to it: the design, the shape of the objects, the action, the emotion, the color, the sound. Exaggeration can work with any component, but not in isolation. The exaggeration of the various components should be balanced. If just one thing is exaggerated in an otherwise lifelike scene, it will stick out and seem unrealistic.

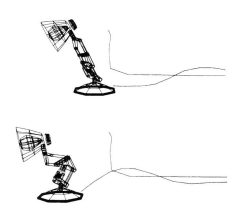

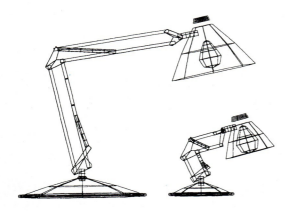

FIGURE 11. Varying the scale of different parts of Dad created the child-like proportions of Luxo Jr.

FIGURE 12. Andre's yawn was made more interesting by not duplicating the poses and the action from one side of his body to the other.

However, exaggerating everything in a scene can be equally unrealistic to an audience. Some elements must be based in nature, with others exaggerated unnaturally. If there is an element that the audience can recognize, something that seems natural to them, that becomes the ground for comparison of the exaggeration of the other elements, and the whole scene remains very realistic to them.

In *Luxo Jr.*, all the components of the scene, some naturalistic, some exaggerated, worked together to make it believable and realistic. The design of the lamps was based on the real Luxo lamp, but certain parts were exaggerated. Jr.'s proportions were exaggerated to give the feeling of a child (See Appeal).

The movement had the sense of natural physics, yet almost every motion and action was exaggerated to accentuate it: when Jr. he hit the ball, he really whacked it. When he jumped up for a hop, his whole body movement was exaggerated to give the feeling of realistic weight to his base. When he landed after a hop, the impact was shown in the exaggeration of his body movements. On the soundtrack, the lamp sounds were recorded from a real Luxo lamp, then exaggerated sounds were added to accent certain actions. [23] The ironic effect of all this exaggeration was to make the film more realistic, while making it entertaining.

2.10 SECONDARY ACTION

A *secondary action* is an action that results directly from another action. Secondary actions are important in heightening interest and adding a realistic complexity to the animation. A secondary actions is always kept subordinate to the primary action. If it conflicts, becomes more interesting, or dominates in any way, it is either the wrong choice or is staged improperly. [26]

Wally B.'s feet dragging behind the main action of his body is a secondary action because the movement of the feet is a direct result of the movement of the body. (figure 5) The rippling movement of Luxo Jr.'s cord results directly from the hopping action of his base. (figure 1)

The facial expression of a character will sometimes be a secondary action. When the main idea of an action is being told in the movement of the body, the facial expression become subordinate to the main idea. If this expression is going to animate or change, the danger is **not** that the expression will dominate the scene, but that it will never be seen. The change must come before, or after, the move. A change in the middle of a major move will go unnoticed, and value intended will be lost. It must also be staged to be obvious, though secondary. [26]

2.11 APPEAL

The word *appeal* is often misrepresented to suggest cuddly bunnies and soft kittens. It doesn't; it means anything that a person likes to see: a quality of charm, pleasing design, simplicity, communication, or magnetism. Your eye is drawn to the figure or object that has appeal, and, once there, it is held while you appreciate the object. A weak drawing or design lacks appeal. A design that is complicated or hard to read lacks appeal. Clumsy shapes and awkward moves all have low appeal. Where the live action actor has charisma, the animated character has appeal. [26]

The appeal in *Luxo Jr.* was achieved in different ways. In designing the characters, the feeling of a baby lamp and a grown up lamp was very important. The effect was achieved using exaggeration in proportion, in the same way a puppy is proportioned very differently than an adult dog, or a human baby is different from an adult. The light bulb is the same size on Jr., while the shade is smaller. The springs and support rods are the same diameter as Dad's, yet they are much shorter. (figure 11)

In creating an appealing pose for a character, one thing to avoid is called "twins", where both arms and both legs are in the same position, doing the same thing. This gives the pose a stiff, wooden, unappealling quality. If each part of the body varies in some way from its corresponding part, the character will look more natural and more appealing. Likewise one side of a face should never mirror the other.

In *The Aventures of Andre and Wally B.* , Andre wakes up and yawns. The yawn is more appealing because the poses and actions are not duplicated from one side of his body to the other. His feet rotate with a slight difference, the head rotates to one side, the upper part of his body rotates to the right and tilts, which raises his right arm higher than his left. When he stretches his arms, the right arm moves out first, followed by the left, and the actions overlap. (figure 12)

3. PERSONALITY

This final section discusses the underlying goal of all the principles discussed earlier. *Personality* in character animation is not a principle unto itself, but the intelligent application of all of the principles of animation.

When character animation is successful and the audience is thoroughly entertained, it is because the characters and the story have become more important and apparent than the technique that went into the animation. Whether drawn by hand or computer, the success of character animation lies in the **personality** of the characters

In character animation, all actions and movements of a character are the result of its thought processes. "The thinking animation character *becomes* a character." [12] Without a thought process, the actions of a character are just a series of unrelated motions. With a thought process to connect them, the actions bring a character to life.

In order to get a thought process into an animation, it is critical to have the personality of a character clearly in mind at the outset, so that it makes sense to ask at any moment, "What mood is the character in. How would he do this action?"

One character would not do a particular action the same way in two different emotional states. An example of this, in *Luxo Jr.*, is the action of Jr. hopping. When he is chasing the ball, he is very excited, happy, all his thoughts on the ball. His hops are fast, his head up looking at the ball, with very little time on the ground between hops because he can't wait to get to the ball. After he pops the ball, however, his hop changes drastically, reflecting his sadness that the object of all of his thoughts and energy just a moment ago is now dead. As he hops off, each hop is slower, with much more time on the ground between hops, his head down. Before, he had a direction and purpose to his hop. Now he is just hopping off to nowhere.

No two characters would do the same action in the same way. For example, in *Luxo Jr.*, both Dad and Jr. bat the ball with their heads. Yet Dad, who is larger and older, leans over the ball and uses only his shade to bat it. Jr., however, who is smaller, younger, and full of excited energy, whacks the ball with his shade, putting his whole body into it.

When defining the character, it is important to make the personality distinct, and at the same time have characteristics that are familiar to the audience. If the actions of a character ring true, the audience will be able to relate to the character, and he will be believable to them.

4. CONCLUSION

Whether it is generated by hand or by computer, the first goal of the animator is to entertain. The animator must have two things: a clear concept of exactly what will entertain the audience; and the tools and skills to put those ideas across clearly and unambiguously. Tools, in the sense of hardware and software, are simply not enough. The principles discussed in this paper, so useful in producing 50 years of rich entertainment, are tools as well... tools which are just as important as the computers we work with.

5. ACKNOWLEDGMENTS

The author would like to express sincere thanks to Bill Reeves and Eben Ostby for their unending support, education and creativity with the technical aspects of computer animation. Steve Upstill for making it sound like I know English. Nancy Tague for her ruthless editing even on my birthday. Kate Smith and Michael Shantzis for their assistance in editing this paper even when they could have been watching Willie Wonka on video tape. Craig Good for helping with the video tape portion of this paper. Joey Tague for being pals and for telling us what happened in Willie Wonka. And especially to Frank Thomas and Ollie Johnston for their instruction in animation when the author was at the Disney Studio, and for their continued inspiration with their book. [26]

6. REFERENCES

1. Abel Image Research, 953 N. Highland Ave., Los Angeles, CA 90038-2481

2. Alias Research Inc., 110 Richmond St. East, Suite 500, Toronto, Ontario, Canada m5c-1p1

3. Blair, Preston, *Animation* , Walter T. Foster, Santa Ana CA, 1949.

4. Burtnyk, Nester and Wein, Marceli, "Computer Generated Keyframe Animation," Journal of the SMPTE 80, pp.149-153, March 1971.

5. Burtnyk, Nester and Wein, Marceli, "Interactive Skeleton Techniques for Enhanced Motion Dynamics in Key Frame Animation," Communications of the ACM 19 (10), pp 564-569, October, 1976.

6. Catmull, Edwin, "A System for Computer Generated Movies," Proceedings ACM Annual Conference, pp. 422-431, August 1972.

7. Catmull, Edwin, "The problems of Computer- Assisted Animation," SIGGRAPH '78, Computer Graphics, Vol. 12, No. 3, pp. 348-353, August 1978.

8. Cook, Robert L., "Stochastic Sampling in Computer Graphics," ACM Transactions on Graphics, Vol. 5, No. 1, pp. 51-72, January 1986.

9. Cook, Robert L., Porter, Thomas, and Carpenter, Loren, "Distributed Ray Tracing," SIGGRAPH '84, Computer Graphics, Vol. 18, No. 3, pp.137-145, July, 1984.

10. Walt Disney Productions, *Three Little Pigs* , (film), 1933.

11. Gracer, F., and Blagen, M. W., "Karma: A System for Storyboard Animation," Proceeding Ninth Annual UAIDE Meeting, pp. 210-255, 1970.

12. Graham, Don, *The Art of Animation* , unpublished.

13. Graham, Don, transcripts of action analysis class at the Walt Disney Studio, June 21, 1937.

14. Graham, Don, transcripts of action analysis class with Bill Tytla at the Walt Disney Studio, June 28, 1937.

15. Hardtke, Ines, and Bartels, Richard, "Kinetics for Key-Frame Interpolation," unpublished.

16. Kochanek, Doris, and Bartels, Richard, "Interpolating Splines with Local Tension, Continuity, and Bias Control," SIGGRAPH '84, Computer Graphics, Vol. 18, No. 3, pp. 33-41, July, 1984.

17. Levoy, Marc, "A Color Animation System Based on the Multi-Plane Technique," SIGGRAPH '77, Computer Graphics, Vol. 11, No. 2, pp. 64-71, July, 1977.

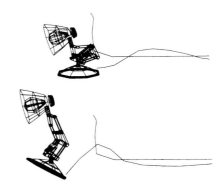

18. Lucasfilm Ltd. Computer Graphics Div., *The Adventures of Andre and Wally B.*, (film), 1984.

19. Ostby, Eben, Duff, Tom, and Reeves, William, Md (motion doctor), animation program, Lucasfilm Ltd., 1982-1986.

20. Perine, Robert, *Chouinard, An Art Vision Betrayed*, Artra Publishing, Encinitas CA, 1985.

21. Pixar, *Luxo Jr.*, (film), 1986.

22. Reeves, William, "Inbetweening for Computer Animation Utilizing Moving Point Constraints," SIGGRAPH '81, Computer Graphics, Vol. 15, No. 3, pp. 263-270, August 1981.

23. Rydstrom, Gary, Soundtrack for *Luxo Jr.*, Sprocket Systems Div., Lucasfilm Ltd., July, 1986.

24. Stern, Garland, "Bboop--A System for 3D Keyframe Figure Animation," Tutorial Notes: Introduction to Computer Animation, SIGGRAPH '83, July 1983.

25. Symbolics Inc., 1401 Westwood Blvd., Los Angeles, CA 90024

26. Thomas, Frank and Johnston, Ollie, *Disney Animation-- The Illusion of Life*, Abbeville Press, New York, 1981.

27. Thomas, Frank, "Can Classic Disney Animation Be Duplicated On The Computer?" Computer Pictures, Vol. 2, Issue 4, pp. 20-26, July/August 1984.

28. Vertigo Systems International Inc., 119 W. Pender St., Suite 221, Vancouver, BC, Canada v6b 1s5

29. Wavefront Technologies, 530 East Montecito, Santa Barbara, CA 93101

30. Whitaker, Harold and Halas, John, *Timing for Animation*, Focal Press, London, 1981.

31. White, Tony, *The Animator's Workbook*, Watson-Guptill, New York, 1986.

Flocks, Herds, and Schools: A Distributed Behavioral Model

Craig W. Reynolds
Symbolics Graphics Division

1401 Westwood Boulevard
Los Angeles, California 90024

(Electronic mail: cwr@Symbolics.COM)

Abstract

The aggregate motion of a flock of birds, a herd of land animals, or a school of fish is a beautiful and familiar part of the natural world. But this type of complex motion is rarely seen in computer animation. This paper explores an approach based on simulation as an alternative to scripting the paths of each bird individually. The simulated flock is an elaboration of a particle system, with the simulated birds being the particles. The aggregate motion of the simulated flock is created by a distributed behavioral model much like that at work in a natural flock; the birds choose their own course. Each simulated bird is implemented as an independent actor that navigates according to its local perception of the dynamic environment, the laws of simulated physics that rule its motion, and a set of behaviors programmed into it by the "animator." The aggregate motion of the simulated flock is the result of the dense interaction of the relatively simple behaviors of the individual simulated birds.

Categories and Subject Descriptors: I.2.10 [Artificial Intelligence]: Vision and Scene Understanding; I.3.5 [Computer Graphics]: Computational Geometry and Object Modeling; I.3.7 [Computer Graphics]: Three-Dimensional Graphics and Realism—*Animation*; I.6.3 [Simulation and Modeling]: Applications.

General Terms: Algorithms, design.

Additional Key Words, and Phrases: flock, herd, school, bird, fish, aggregate motion, particle system, actor, flight, behavioral animation, constraints, path planning.

Introduction

The motion of a flock of birds is one of nature's delights. Flocks and related synchronized group behaviors such as schools of fish or herds of land animals are both beautiful to watch and intriguing to contemplate. A flock* exhibits many contrasts. It is made up of discrete birds yet overall motion seems fluid; it is simple in concept yet is so visually complex, it seems randomly arrayed and yet is magnificently synchronized. Perhaps most puzzling is the strong impression of intentional, centralized control. Yet all evidence indicates that flock motion must be merely the aggregate result of the actions of individual animals, each acting solely on the basis of its own local perception of the world.

One area of interest within computer animation is the description and control of all types of motion. Computer animators seek both to invent wholly new types of abstract motion and to duplicate (or make variations on) the motions found in the real world. At first glance, producing an animated, computer graphic portrayal of a flock of birds presents significant difficulties. Scripting the path of a large number of individual objects using traditional computer animation techniques would be tedious. Given the complex paths that birds follow, it is doubtful this specification could be made without error. Even if a reasonable number of suitable paths could be described, it is unlikely that the constraints of flock motion could be maintained (for example, preventing collisions between all birds at each frame). Finally, a flock scripted in this manner would be hard to edit (for example, to alter the course of all birds for a portion of the animation). It is not impossible to script flock motion, but a better approach is needed for efficient, robust, and believable animation of flocks and related group motions.

This paper describes one such approach. This approach assumes a flock is simply the result of the interaction between the behaviors of individual birds. To simulate a flock we simulate the behavior of an individual bird (or at least that portion of the bird's behavior that allows it to participate in a flock). To support this behavioral "control structure," we must also simulate portions of the bird's perceptual mechanisms and aspects of the physics of aerodynamic flight. If this simulated bird model has the correct flock-member behavior, all that should be required to create a simulated flock is to create some instances of the simulated bird model and allow them to interact.**

Some experiments with this sort of simulated flock are described in more detail in the remainder of this paper. The suc-

---

*In this paper *flock* refers generically to a group of objects that exhibit this general class of *polarized, noncolliding, aggregate motion*. The term *polarization* is from zoology, meaning alignment of animal groups. English is rich with terms for groups of animals; for a charming and literate discussion of such words see *An Exultation of Larks*. [16]

**This paper refers to these simulated bird-like, "bird-oid" objects generically as "boids" even when they represent other sorts of creatures such as schooling fish.

cess and validity of these simulations is difficult to measure objectively. They do seem to agree well with certain criteria [25] and some statistical properties [23] of natural flocks and schools which have been reported by the zoological and behavioral sciences. Perhaps more significantly, many people who view these animated flocks immediately recognize them as a representation of a natural flock, and find them similarly delightful to watch.

Our Foreflocks

The computer graphics community has seen simulated bird flocks before. The Electronic Theater at SIGGRAPH '85 presented a piece labeled "motion studies for a work in progress entitled 'Eurythmy'" [4] by Susan Amkraut, Michael Girard, and George Karl from the Computer Graphics Research Group of Ohio State University. In the film, a flock of birds flies up out of a minaret and, passing between a series of columns, flies down into a lazy spiral around a courtyard. All the while the birds slowly flap their wings and avoid collision with their flockmates.

That animation was produced using a technique completely unlike the one described in this paper and apparently not specifically intended for flock modeling. But the underlying concept is useful and interesting in its own right. The following overview is based on unpublished communications [3]. The software is informally called "the force field animation system." Force fields are defined by a 3 x 3 matrix operator that transform from a point in space (where an object is located) to an acceleration vector; the birds trace paths along the "phase portrait" of the force field. There are "rejection forces" around each bird and around static objects. The force field associated with each object has a bounding box, so object interactions can be culled according to bounding box tests. An incremental, linear time algorithm finds bounding box intersections. The "animator" defines the space field(s) and sets the initial positions, orientations, and velocities of objects. The rest of the simulation is automatic.

Karl Sims of MIT's Media Lab has constructed some behaviorally controlled animation of groups of moving objects (spaceships, inchworms, and quadrupeds), but they are not organized as flocks [35]. Another author kept suggesting [28, 29, 30] implementing a flock simulation based on a distributed behavioral model.

Particle Systems

The simulated flock described here is closely related to *particle systems* [27], which are used to represent dynamic "fuzzy objects" having irregular and complex shapes. Particle systems have been used to model fire, smoke, clouds, and more recently, the spray and foam of ocean waves [27]. Particle systems are collections of large numbers of individual particles, each having its own behavior. Particles are created, age, and die off. During their life they have certain behaviors that can alter the particle's own state, which consists of *color*, *opacity*, *location*, and *velocity*.

Underlying the boid flock model is a slight generalization of particle systems. In what might be called a "subobject system," Reeves's dot-like particles are replaced by an entire geometrical object consisting of a full local coordinate system and a reference to a geometrical shape model. The use of shapes instead of dots is visually significant, but the more fundamental difference is that individual subobjects have a more complex geometrical state: they now have orientation.

Another difference between boid flocks and particle systems is not as well defined. The behavior of boids is generally more complex than the behaviors for particles as described in the literature. The present boid behavior model might be about one or two orders of magnitude more complex than typical particle behavior. However this is a difference of degree, not of kind. And neither simulated behavior is nearly as complex as that of a real bird.

Also, as presented, particles in particle systems do not interact with one another, although this is not ruled out by definition. But birds and hence boids must interact strongly in order to flock correctly. Boid behavior is dependent not only on *internal state* but also on *external state*.

Actors and Distributed Systems

The behavioral model that controls the boid's flight and flocking is complicated enough that rather than use an *ad hoc* approach, it is worthwhile to pursue the most appropriate formal computational model. The behaviors will be represented as rules or programs in some sense, and the internal state of each boid must be held in some sort of data structure. It is convenient to encapsulate these behaviors and state as an *object*, in the sense of object-oriented programming systems [10, 11, 21]. Each *instance* of these objects needs a computational *process* to apply the behavioral programs to the internal data. The computational abstraction that combines process, procedure, and state is called an *actor* [12, 26, 2]. An actor is essentially a virtual computer that communicates with other virtual computers by *passing messages*. The actor model has been proposed as a natural structure for animation control by several authors [28, 13, 29, 18]. It seems particularly apt for situations involving interacting characters and behavior simulation. In the literature of parallel and distributed computer systems, flocks and schools are given as examples of robust self-organizing distributed systems [15].

Behavioral Animation

Traditional hand-drawn cel animation was produced with a medium that was completely inert. Traditional computer animation uses an active medium (computers running graphics software), but most animation systems do not make much use of the computer's ability to automate motion design. Using different tools, contemporary computer animators work at almost the same low level of abstraction as do cel animators. They tell their story by directly describing the motion of their characters. Shortcuts exist in both media; it is common for computer animators and cel animators to use helpers to interpolate between specified keyframes. But little progress has been made in automating motion description; it is up to the animator to translate the nuances of emotion and characterization into the motions that the character performs. The animator cannot simply tell the character to "act happy" but must tediously specify the motion that conveys happiness.

Typical computer animation models only the shape and physical properties of the characters, whereas *behavioral* or *character-based* animation seeks to model the behavior of the character. The goal is for such simulated characters to handle many of the details of their actions, and hence their motions. These *behaviors* include a whole range of activities from simple path planning to complex "emotional" interactions between characters. The construction of behavioral animation characters has attracted many researchers [19, 21, 13, 14, 29,

30, 41, 40], but it is still a young field in which more work is needed.

Because of the detached nature of the control, the person who creates animation with character simulation might not strictly be an *animator*. Traditionally, the animator is directly responsible for all motion in animation production [40]. It might be more proper to call the person who directs animation via simulated characters a *meta-animator*, since the animator is less a designer of motion and more a designer of behavior. These behaviors, when acted out by the simulated characters, lead indirectly to the final action. Thus the animator's job becomes somewhat like that of a theatrical director: the character's performance is the indirect result of the director's instructions to the actor. One of the charming aspects of the work reported here is not knowing how a simulation is going to proceed from the specified behaviors and initial conditions; there are many unexpected, pleasant surprises. On the other hand, this charm starts to wear thin as deadlines approach and the unexpected annoyances pop up. This author has spent a lot of time recently trying to get uncooperative flocks to move as intended ("these darn boids seem to have a mind of their own!").

Geometric Flight

A fundamental part of the boid model is the geometric ability to *fly*. The motion of the members of a simulated school or herd can be considered a type of "flying" by glossing over the considerable intricacies of wing, fin, and leg motion (and in the case of herds, by restricting freedom of motion in the third dimension). In this paper the term *geometric flight* refers to a certain type of motion along a path: a dynamic, incremental, rigid geometrical transformation of an object, moving along and tangent to a 3D curve. While the motion is rigid, the object's underlying geometric model is free to articulate or change shape within this "flying coordinate system." Unlike more typical animated motion along predefined spline curves, the shape of a flight path is not specified in advance.

Geometric flight is based on incremental translations along the object's "forward direction," its local positive Z axis. These translations are intermixed with *steering*—rotations about the local X and Y axes (*pitch* and *yaw*), which realign the global orientation of the local Z axis. In real flight, turning and moving happen continuously and simultaneously. Incremental geometric flight is a discrete approximation of this; small linear motions model a continuous curved path. In animation the motion must increment at least once per frame. Running the simulation at a higher rate can reduce the discrete sampling error of the flight model and refine the shape of motion blur patterns.

Flight modeling makes extensive use of the object's own coordinate system. Local space represents the "boid's eye view;" it implies measuring things relative to the boid's own position and orientation. In Cartesian terms, the left/right axis is X, up/down is Y, and forward/back is Z. The conversion of geometric data between the local and global reference frames is handled by the geometric operators *localize* and *globalize*. It is convenient to use a local scale so that the unit of length of the coordinate system is one *body length*. Biologists routinely specify flock and school statistics in terms of body lengths.

Geometric flight models conservation of momentum. An object in flight tends to stay in flight. There is a simple model of viscous speed damping, so even if the boid continually accelerates in one direction, it will not exceed a certain *maximum speed*. A *minimum speed* can also be specified but defaults to zero. A *maximum acceleration*, expressed as a fraction of the maximum speed, is used to truncate over-anxious requests for acceleration, hence providing for smooth changes of speed and heading. This is a simple model of a creature with a finite amount of available energy.

Many physical forces are not supported in the current boid model. *Gravity* is modeled but used only to define banking behavior. It is defined procedurally to allow the construction of arbitrarily shaped fields. If each boid was accelerated by gravity each frame, it would tend to fall unless gravity was countered by *lift* or *buoyancy*. Buoyancy is aligned against gravity, but aerodynamic lift is aligned with the boid's local "up" direction and related to velocity. This level of modeling leads to effects like normally level flight, going faster when flying down (or slower up), and the "stall" maneuver. The speed limit parameter could be more realistically modeled as a frictional *drag*, a backward pointing force related to velocity. In the current model steering is done by directing the available *thrust* in the appropriate direction. It would be more realistic to separately model the *tangential* thrusting forces and the *lateral* steering forces, since they normally have different magnitudes.

Banking

Geometric flight relates translation, pitch, and yaw, but does not constrain *roll*, the rotation about the local Z axis. This degree of freedom is used for *banking*—rolling the object to align the local Y axis with the (local XY component of the total) acceleration acting upon it. Normally banking is based on the lateral component of the acceleration, but the tangential component can be used for certain applications. The lateral components are from steering and gravity. In straight flight there is no radial force, so the gravitational term dominates and banking aligns the object's -Y axis with "gravitational down" direction. When turning, the radial component grows larger and the "accelerational down" direction swings outward, like a pendulum hanging from the flying object. The magnitude of the turning acceleration varies directly with the object's velocity and with the curvature of its path (so inversely with the radius of its turn). The limiting case of infinite velocity resembles banking behavior in the absence of gravity. In these cases the local +Y (up) direction points directly at the center of curvature defined by the current turn.

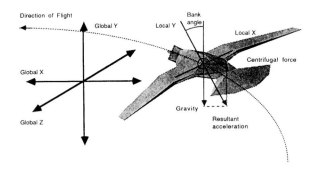

Figure 1.

With correct banking (what pilots call a *coordinated turn*) the object's local space remains aligned with the "perceptual" or "accelerational" coordinate system. This has several advantages: it simplifies the bird's (or pilot's) orientation task, it keeps the lift from the airfoils of the wings pointed in the most efficient direction ("accelerational up"), it keeps the passengers' coffee in their cups, and most importantly for animation, it makes the flying boid fit the viewer's expectation of how flying objects should move and orient themselves. On the other hand, realism is not always the goal in animation. By simply reversing the angle of bank we obtain a cartoony motion that looks like the object is being flung outward by the centrifugal force of the turn.

Boids and Turtles

The incremental mixing of forward translations and local rotations that underlies geometric flight is the basis of "turtle graphics" in the programming language *Logo* [5]. Logo was first used as an educational tool to allow children to learn experimentally about geometry, arithmetic, and programming [22]. The Logo *turtle* was originally a little mechanical robot that crawled around on large sheets of paper laid on the classroom floor, drawing graphic figures by dragging a felt tip marker along the paper as it moved. Abstract *turtle geometry* is a system based on the frame of reference of the turtle, an object that unites position and heading. Under program control the Logo turtle could move forward or back from its current position, turn left or right from its current heading, or put the pen up or down on the paper. The turtle geometry has been extended from the plane onto arbitrary manifolds and into 3D space [1]. These "3d turtles" and their paths are exactly equivalent to the boid objects and their flight paths.

Natural Flocks, Herds, and Schools

"... and the thousands of fishes moved as a huge beast, piercing the water. They appeared united, inexorably bound to a common fate. How comes this unity?"
—Anonymous, 17th century (from Shaw)

For a bird to participate in a flock, it must have behaviors that allow it to coordinate its movements with those of its flockmates. These behaviors are not particularly unique; all creatures have them to some degree. Natural flocks seem to consist of two balanced, opposing behaviors: a desire to stay close to the flock and a desire to avoid collisions within the flock [34]. It is clear why an individual bird wants to avoid collisions with its flockmates. But why do birds seem to seek out the airborne equivalent of a nasty traffic jam? The basic urge to join a flock seems to be the result of evolutionary pressure from several factors: protection from predators, statistically improving survival of the (shared) gene pool from attacks from predators, profiting from a larger effective search pattern in the quest for food, and advantages for social and mating activities [33].

There is no evidence that the complexity of natural flocks is bounded in any way. Flocks do not become "full" or "overloaded" as new birds join. When herring migrate toward their spawning grounds, they run in schools extending as long as 17 miles and containing millions of fish [32]. Natural flocks seem to operate in exactly the same fashion over a huge range of flock populations. It does not seem that an individual bird can be paying much attention to each and every one of its flockmates. But in a huge flock spread over vast distances, an individual bird must have a localized and filtered perception of the rest of the flock. A bird might be aware of three categories itself, its two or three nearest neighbors, and the rest of the flock [23].

These speculations about the "computational complexity" of flocking are meant to suggest that birds can flock with any number of flockmates because they are using what would be called in formal computer science a *constant time algorithm*. That is, the amount of "thinking" that a bird has to do in order to flock must be largely independent of the number of birds in the flock. Otherwise we would expect to see a sharp upper bound on the size of natural flocks when the individual birds became overloaded by the complexity of their navigation task. This has not been observed in nature.

Contrast the insensitivity to complexity of real flocks with the situation for the simulated flocks described below. The complexity of the flocking algorithm described is basically $O(N^2)$. That is, the work required to run the algorithm grows as the *square* of the flock's population. We definitely **do** see an upper bound on the size of simulated flocks implemented as described here. Some techniques to address this performance issue are discussed in the section Algorithmic Considerations.

Simulated Flocks

To build a simulated flock, we start with a boid model that supports geometric flight. We add behaviors that correspond to the opposing forces of collision avoidance and the urge to join the flock. Stated briefly as rules, and in order of decreasing precedence, the behaviors that lead to simulated flocking are:
1. Collision Avoidance: avoid collisions with nearby flockmates
2. Velocity Matching: attempt to match velocity with nearby flockmates
3. Flock Centering: attempt to stay close to nearby flockmates

Velocity is a vector quantity, referring to the combination of *heading* and *speed*. The manner in which the results from each of these behaviors is reconciled and combined is significant and is discussed in more detail later. Similarly, the meaning *nearby* in these rules is key to the flocking process. This is also discussed in more detail later, but generally one boid's awareness of another is based on the distance and direction of the offset vector between them.

Static *collision avoidance* and dynamic *velocity matching* are complementary. Together they ensure that the members of a simulated flock are free to fly within the crowded skies of the flock's interior without running into one another. Collision avoidance is the urge to steer away from an imminent impact. *Static* collision avoidance is based on the relative position of the flockmates and ignores their velocity. Conversely, velocity matching is based only on velocity and ignores position. It is a *predictive* version of collision avoidance: if the boid does a good job of matching velocity with its neighbors, it is unlikely that it will collide with any of them any time soon. With velocity matching, separations between boids remains *approximately invariant* with respect to ongoing geometric flight. Static collision avoidance serves to establish the minimum required separation distance; velocity matching tends to maintain it.

Flock centering makes a boid want to be near the center of the flock. Because each boid has a localized perception of the world, "center of the flock" actually means the center of the nearby flockmates. Flock centering causes the boid to fly in a direction that moves it closer to the centroid of the nearby boids. If a boid is deep inside a flock, the population density in its neighborhood is roughly homogeneous; the boid density is approximately the same in all directions. In this case, the centroid of the neighborhood boids is approximately at the center of the neighborhood, so the flock centering urge is small. But if a boid is on the boundary of the flock, its neighboring boids are on one side. The centroid of the neighborhood boids is displaced from the center of the neighborhood toward the body of the flock. Here the flock centering urge is stronger and the flight path will be deflected somewhat toward the local flock center.

Real flocks sometimes split apart to go around an obstacle. To be realistic, the simulated flock model must also have this ability. Flock centering correctly allows simulated flocks to bifurcate. As long as an individual boid can stay close to its nearby neighbors, it does not care if the rest of the flock turns away. More simplistic models proposed for flock organization (such as a *central force* model or a *follow the designated leader* model) do not allow splits.

The flock model presented here is actually a better model of a school or a herd than a flock. Fish in murky water (and land animals with their inability to see past their herdmates) have a limited, short-range perception of their environment. Birds, especially those on the outside of a flock, have excellent long-range "visual perception." Presumably this allows widely separated flocks to join together. If the flock centering urge was completely localized, when two flocks got a certain distance apart they would ignore each other. Long-range vision seems to play a part in the incredibly rapid propagation of a "maneuver wave" through a flock of birds. It has been shown that the speed of propagation of this wavefront reaches three times the speed implied by the measured startle reaction time of the individual birds. The explanation advanced by Wayne Potts is that the birds perceive the motion of the oncoming "maneuver wave" and time their own turn to match it [25]. Potts refers to this as the "chorus line" hypothesis.

Arbitrating Independent Behaviors

The three behavioral urges associated with flocking (and others to be discussed below) each produce an isolated suggestion about which way to steer the boid. These are expressed as *acceleration requests*. Each behavior says: "if **I** were in charge, **I** would accelerate in *that* direction." The acceleration request is in terms of a 3D vector that, by system convention, is truncated to unit magnitude or less. Each behavior has several parameters that control its function; one is a "strength," a fractional value between zero and one that can further attenuate the acceleration request. It is up to the *navigation module* of the boid brain to collect all relevant acceleration requests and then determine a single behaviorally desired acceleration. It must combine, prioritize, and arbitrate between potentially conflicting urges. The *pilot module* takes the acceleration desired by the navigation module and passes it to the *flight module*, which attempts to fly in that direction.

The easiest way to combine acceleration requests is to average them. Because of the included "strength" factors, this is actually a weighted average. The relative strength of one behavior to another can be defined this way, but it is a precarious interrelationship that is difficult to adjust. An early version of the boid model showed that navigation by simple weighted averaging of acceleration requests works "pretty well." A boid that chooses its course this way will fly a reasonable course under typical conditions. But in critical situations, such as potential collision with obstacles, conflicts must be resolved in a timely manner. During high-speed flight, hesitation or indecision is the wrong response to a brick wall dead ahead.

The main cause of indecision is that each behavior might be shouting advice about which way to turn to avoid disaster, but if those acceleration requests happen to lie in approximately opposite directions, they will largely cancel out under a simple weighted averaging scheme. The boid would make a very small turn and so continue in the same direction, perhaps to crash into the obstacle. Even when the urges do not cancel out, averaging leads to other problems. Consider flying over a gridwork of city streets between the skyscrapers; while "fly north" or "fly east" might be good ideas, it would be a bad idea to combine them as "fly northeast."

Techniques from artificial intelligence, such as expert systems, can be used to arbitrate conflicting opinions. However, a less complex approach is taken in the current implementation. *Prioritized acceleration allocation* is based on a strict priority ordering of all component behaviors, hence of the consideration of their acceleration requests. (This ordering can change to suit dynamic conditions.) The acceleration requests are considered in priority order and added into an accumulator. The *magnitude* of each request is measured and added into another accumulator. This process continues until the sum of the accumulated magnitudes gets larger than the *maximum acceleration* value, which is a parameter of each boid. The last acceleration request is trimmed back to compensate for the excess of accumulated magnitude. The point is that a fixed amount of acceleration is under the control of the navigation module; this acceleration is parceled out to satisfy the acceleration request of the various behaviors in order of priority. In an emergency the acceleration would be allocated to satisfy the most pressing needs first; if all available acceleration is "used up," the less pressing behaviors might be temporarily unsatisfied. For example, the flock centering urge could be correctly ignored temporarily in favor of a maneuver to avoid a static obstacle.

Simulated Perception

The boid model does not directly simulate the senses used by real animals during flocking (vision and hearing) or schooling (vision and fishes' unique "lateral line" structure that provides a certain amount of pressure imaging ability [23, 24]). Rather the perception model tries to make available to the behavior model approximately the same information that is available to a real animal as the end result of its perceptual and cognitive processes.

This is primarily a matter of filtering out the surplus information that is available to the software that implements the boid's behavior. Simulated boids have direct access to the geometric database that describes the exact position, orientation, and velocity of all objects in the environment. The real bird's information about the world is severely limited because it perceives through imperfect senses and because its nearby flockmates hide those farther away. This is even more pronounced in herding animals because they are all constrained to be in the same plane. In fish schools, visual perception of neighboring fish is further limited by the scattering and absorption of light by the sometimes murky water between them. These factors combine to strongly localize the information available to each animal.

Not only is it unrealistic to give each simulated boid perfect and complete information about the world, it is just plain wrong and leads to obvious failures of the behavior model. Before the current implementation of localized *flock centering* behavior was implemented, the flocks used a central force model. This leads to unusual effects such as causing all members of a widely scattered flock to simultaneously converge toward the flock's centroid. An interesting result of the experiments reported in this paper is that the aggregate motion that we intuitively recognize as "flocking" (or schooling or herding) **depends** upon a limited, localized view of the world.

The behaviors that make up the flocking model are stated in terms of "nearby flockmates." In the current implementation, the neighborhood is defined as a spherical zone of sensitivity centered at the boid's local origin. The magnitude of the sensitivity is defined as an inverse exponential of distance. Hence the neighborhood is defined by two parameters: a radius and exponent. There is reason to believe that this field of sensitivity should realistically be exaggerated in the forward direction and probably by an amount proportional to the boid's speed. Being in motion requires an increased awareness of what lies ahead, and this requirement increases with speed. A forward-weighted sensitivity zone would probably also improve the behavior in the current implementation of boids at the leading edge of a flock, who tend to get distracted by the flock behind them. Because of the way their heads and eyes are arranged, real birds have a wide field of view (about 300 degrees), but the zone of overlap from both eyes is small (10 to 15 degrees). Hence the bird has stereo depth perception only in a very small, forward-oriented cone. Research is currently under way on models of forward-weighted perception for boids.

In an early version of the flock model, the metrics of attraction and repulsion were weighted linearly by distance. This spring-like model produced a bouncy flock action, fine perhaps for a cartoony characterization, but not very realistic. The model was changed to use an inverse square of the distance. This more gravity-like model produced what appeared to be a more natural, better damped flock model. This correlated well with the carefully controlled quantitative studies that Brian Partridge made of the spatial relationships of schooling fish [23]; he found that "a fish is much more strongly influenced by its near neighbors than it is by the distant members of the school. The contribution of each fish to the [influence] is inversely proportional to the square or the cube of the distance." In previous work he and colleagues [23, 24] demonstrated that fishes school based on information from both their visual system and from their "lateral line" organ which senses pressure waves. The area of a perspective image of the silhouette of an object (its "visual angle") varies inversely with the square of its distance, and that pressure waves traveling through a 3D medium like water fall off inversely with the cube of the distance.

The boid perception model is quite *ad hoc* and avoids actually simulating vision. Artificial vision is an extremely complex problem [38] and is far beyond the scope of this work. But if boids could "see" their environment, they would be better at path planning than the current model. It is possible to construct simple maze-like shapes that would confuse the current boid model but would be easily solved by a boid with vision.

Impromptu Flocking

The flocking model described above gives boids an eagerness to participate in an acceptable approximation of flock-like motion. Boids released near one another begin to flock together, cavorting and jostling for position. The boids stay near one another (*flock centering*) but always maintain prudent separation from their neighbors (*collision avoidance*), and the flock quickly becomes "polarized"—its members heading in approximately the same direction at approximately the same speed (*velocity matching*); when they change direction they do it in synchronization. Solitary boids and smaller flocks join to become larger flocks, and in the presence of external obstacles (discussed below), larger flocks can split into smaller flocks.

For each simulation run, the initial position (within a specified ellipsoid), heading, velocity, and various other parameters of the boid model are initialized to values randomized within specified distributions. A restartable random-number generator is used to allow repeatability. This randomization is not required; the boids could just as well start out arranged in a regular pattern, all other aspects of the flock model are completely deterministic and repeatable.

When the simulation is run, the flock's first action is a reaction to the initial conditions. If the boids started out too closely crowded together, there is an initial "flash expansion" where the mutual desire to avoid collision drives the boids radially away from the site of the initial over-pressure. If released in a spherical shell with a radius smaller than the "neighborhood" radius, the boids contract toward the sphere's center; otherwise they begin to coalesce into small flockettes that might themselves begin to join together. If the boids are confined within a certain region, the smaller flocks eventually conglomerate into a single flock if left to wander long enough.

Scripted Flocking

The behaviors discussed so far provide for the ability of individual birds to fly and participate in happy aimless flocking. But to combine flock simulations with other animated action, we need more direct control over the flock. We would like to direct specific action at specific times (for example, "the flock enters from the left at :02.3 seconds into the sequence, turns to fly directly upward at :03.5, and is out of the frame at :04.0").

The current implementation of the boid model has several facilities to direct the motion and timing of the flock action. First, the simulations are run under the control of a general-purpose animation scripting system [36]. The details of that scripting system are not relevant here except that, in addition to the typical interactive motion control facilities, it provides the ability to schedule the invocation of user-supplied software (such as the flock model) on a frame-by-frame basis. This scripting facility is the basic tool used to describe the timing of various flock actions. It also allows flexible control over the time-varying values of parameters, which can be passed down to the simulation software. Finally the script is used to set up and animate all nonbehavioral aspects of the scene, such as backgrounds, lighting, camera motion, and other visible objects.

The primary tool for scripting the flock's path is the *migratory urge* built into the boid model. In the current model this urge is specified in terms of a global target, either as a global direction (as in "going Z for the winter") or as a global position—a target point toward which all birds fly. The model computes a bounded acceleration that incrementally turns the boid toward its migratory target.

With the scripting system, we can *animate* a dynamic parameter whose value is a global position vector or a global direction vector. This parameter can be passed to the flock, which can in turn pass it along to all boids, each of which sets its own "migratory goal register." Hence the global migratory behavior of all birds can be directly controlled from the script. (Of course, it is not necessary to alter all boids at the same time, for example, the delay could be a function of their present position in space. Real flocks do not change direction simultaneously [25], but rather the turn starts with a single bird and spreads quickly across the flock like a shock wave.)

We can lead the flock around by animating the goal point along the desired path, somewhat ahead of the flock. Even if the migratory goal point is changed abruptly the path of each boid still is relatively smooth because of the flight model's simulated conservation of momentum. This means that the boid's own flight dynamics implement a form of smoothing interpolation between "control points."

Avoiding Environmental Obstacles

The most interesting motion of a simulated flock comes from interaction with other objects in the environment. The isolated behavior of a flock tends to reach a steady state and becomes rather sterile. The flock can be seen as a *relaxation* solution to the constraints implied by its behaviors. For example, the conflicting urges of *flock centering* and *collision avoidance* do not lead to constant back and forth motion, but rather the boids eventually strike a balance between the two urges (the degree of damping controls how soon this balance is reached). Environmental obstacles and the boid's attempts to navigate around them increase the apparent complexity of the behavior of the flock. (In fact the complexity of real flocks might be due largely to the complexity of the natural environment.)

Environmental obstacles are also important from the standpoint of modeling the scene in which we wish to place the flock. If the flock is scripted to fly under a bridge and around a tree, we must be able to represent the geometric shape and dimension of these obstacles. The approach taken here is to independently model the "shape for rendering" and the "shape for collision avoidance." The types of shapes currently used for environmental obstacles are much less complicated than the models used for rendering of computer graphic models. The current work implements two types of shapes of environmental collision avoidance. One is based on the *force field* concept, which works in undemanding situations but has some shortcomings. The other model called *steer-to-avoid* is more robust and seems closer in spirit to the natural mechanism.

The force field model postulates a field of repulsion force emanating from the obstacle out into space; the boids are increasingly repulsed as they get closer to the obstacle. This scheme is easy to model; the geometry of the field is usually fairly simple and so an avoidance acceleration can be directly calculated from the field equation. These models can produce good results, such as in "Eurythmy" [4], but they also have drawbacks that are apparent on close examination. If a boid approaches an obstacle surrounded by a force field at an angle such that it is exactly opposite to the direction of the force field, the boid will not turn away. In this case the force field serves only to slow the boid by accelerating it backwards and provides no side thrust at all. The worst reaction to an impending collision is to fail to turn. Force fields also cause problems with "peripheral vision." The boid should notice and turn away from a wall as it flies toward it, but the wall should be ignored if the boid is flying alongside it. Finally, force fields tend to be too strong close up and too weak far away; avoiding an obstacle should involve long-range planning rather than panicky corrections at the last minute.

Steer-to-avoid is a better simulation of a natural bird guided by vision. The boid considers only obstacles directly in front of it. (It finds the intersection, if any, of its local Z axis with the obstacle.) Working in local perspective space, it finds the silhouette edge of the obstacle closest to the point of eventual impact. A radial vector is computed which will aim the boid at a point one body length beyond that silhouette edge (see figure 2). Currently steer-to-avoid has been implemented for several obstacle shapes: spheres, cylinders, planes, and boxes. Collision avoidance for arbitrary convex polyhedral obstacles is being developed.

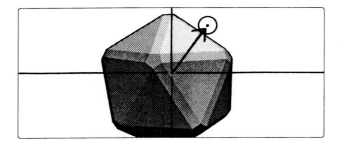

Figure 2.

Obstacles are not necessarily fixed in space; they can be animated around by the script during the animation. Or more interestingly, the obstacles can be behavioral characters. Sparrows might flock around a group of obstacles that is in fact a herd of elephants. Similarly, behavioral obstacles might not merely be in the way; they might be objects of fear such as predators. It has been noted [25] that natural flocking instincts seem to be sharpened by predators.

Other Applications of the Flock Model

The model of polarized noncolliding aggregate motion has many applications, visual simulation of bird flocks in computer animation being one. Certain modifications yield a fish school model. Further modifications, such as limitation to a 2D surface and the ability to follow the terrain, lead to a herd model. Imagine a herd of PODA-style legged creatures [9], using Karl Sims' techniques for locomotion over uneven, complex terrain [35]. Other applications are less obvious. Traffic patterns, such as the flow of cars on a freeway, is a flock-like motion. There are specialized behaviors, such as being constrained to drive within the lanes, but the basic principles that keep boids from colliding are just as applicable on the freeway. We could imagine creating crowds of "extras" (human or otherwise) for feature films. However the most fun are the offbeat combinations possible in computer graphics by mixing and matching: a herd of pogo sticks, a flock of Pegasus-like winged horses, or a traffic jam of spaceships on a 3D interplanetary highway.

One serious application would be to aid in the scientific investigation of flocks, herds, and schools. These scientists must work almost exclusively in the observational mode; experiments with natural flocks and schools are difficult to perform and are likely to disturb the behaviors under study. It might be possible, using a more carefully crafted model of the realistic behavior of a certain species of bird, to perform controlled and repeatable experiments with "simulated natural flocks." A theory of flock organization can be unambiguously tested by implementing a distributed behavioral model and simply comparing the aggregate motion of the simulated flock with the natural one.

Algorithmic Considerations

A naive implementation of the basic flocking algorithm would grow in complexity as the order of the square of the flock's population ("$O(N^2)$"). Basically this is because each boid must reason about each of the other boids, even if only to decide to ignore it. This does not say the algorithm is slow or fast, merely that as the size of the problem (total population of the flock) increases, the complexity increases even faster. Doubling the number of boids quadruples the amount of time taken.

However, as stated before, real birds are probably not as sensitive to the total flock population. This gives hope that the simulated boid could be taught to navigate independently of the total population. Certainly part of the problem is that we are trying to run the simulation of the whole flock on a single computer. The natural solution is to use distributed processing, as the real flock does. If we used a separate processor for each boid, then even the naive implementation of the flocking algorithm would be $O(N)$, or *linear* with respect to the population. But even that is not good enough. It still means that as more boids are added to the flock, the complexity of the problem increases.

What we desire is a *constant time algorithm*, one that is insensitive to the total population. Another way to say this is that an N^2 algorithm would be OK if there was an efficient way to keep N very small. Two approaches to this goal are currently under investigation. One is dynamic spatial partitioning of the flock; the boids are sorted into a lattice of "bins" based on their position in space. A boid trying to navigate inside the flock could get quick access to the flockmates that are physically nearby by examining the "bins" near its current position. Another approach is to do incremental collision detection ("nearness testing"). General collision detection is another N^2 algorithm, but if one does collision detection incrementally, based on a partial solution that described the situation just a moment before, then the algorithm need worry only about the changes and so can run much faster, assuming that the incremental changes are small. The incremental collision detection algorithm used in Girard's PODA system [9] apparently achieves constant time performance in the typical case.

Computing Environment

The boids software was written in Symbolics Common Lisp. The code and animation were produced on a Symbolics 3600 Lisp Machine, a high-performance personal computer. The flock software is implemented in Flavors, the object-oriented programming extensions to Symbolics Common Lisp. The geometric aspects of the system are layered upon S-Geometry, an interactive geometric modeler [37]. Boids are based on the flavor 3D:OBJECT, which provides their geometric abilities. The flock simulations are invoked from scripts created and animated with the S-Dynamics [36] animation system, which also provided the real-time playback facility used to view the motion tests. The availability of this graphical toolkit allowed the author to focus immediately on the issues unique to this project. One example of the value of this substrate is that the initial version of the flock model, including implementation, testing, debugging, and the production of seven short motion tests was accomplished in the ten days before the SIGGRAPH '86 conference.

The boid software has not been optimized for speed. But this report would be incomplete without a rough estimate of the actual performance of the system. With a flock of 80 boids, using the naive $O(N^2)$ algorithm (and so 6400 individual boid-to-boid comparisons), on a single Lisp Machine without any special hardware accelerators, the simulation ran for about 95 seconds per frame. A ten-second (300 frame) motion test took about eight hours of real time to produce.

Future Work

This paper has largely ignored the internal animation of the geometrical model that provides the visual representation of the boid. The original motion tests produced with these models all show flocks of little abstract rigid shapes that might be paper airplanes. There was no flapping of wings nor turning of heads, and there was certainly no character animation. These topics are all important and pertinent to believable animation of simulated flocks. But the underlying abstract nature of flocking as polarized, noncolliding aggregate motion is largely independent of these issues of internal shape change and articulation. This notion is supported by the fact that most viewers of these simulations identify the motion of these abstract objects as "flocking" even in the absence of any internal animation.

But doing a believable job of melding these two aspects of the motion is more than a matter of concatenating the action of an internal animation cycle for the character with the motion defined by geometrical flight. There are important issues of synchronization between the current state of the flight dynamics model, and the amplitude and frequency of the wing motion cycle. Topics of current development include internal animation, synchronization, and interfaces between the simulation-based flock model and other more traditional, interactive animation scripting systems. We would like to allow a skilled computer animator to design a bird character and define its "wing flap cycle" using standard interactive modeling and scripting techniques, and then be able to take this cyclic motion and "plug it in" to the flock simulation model causing the boids in the flock to fly according to the scripted cycle.

The behaviors that have been discussed in this paper are all simplistic, isolated behaviors of low complexity. The boids have a geometric and kinematic state, but they have no significant *mental state*. Real animals have more elaborate, abstract behaviors than a simple desire to avoid a painful collision; they have more complex motivations than a simple desire to fly to a certain point in space. More interesting behavior models would take into account hunger, finding food, fear of predators, a periodic need to sleep, and so on. Behavior models of this type have been created by other investigators [6, 19, 21], but they have not yet been implemented for the boid model described here.

Conclusion

This paper has presented a model of polarized, noncolliding aggregate motion, such as that of flocks, herds, and schools. The model is based on simulating the behavior of each bird independently. Working independently, the birds try both to stick together and avoid collisions with one another and with other objects in their environment. The animations showing simulated flocks built from this model seem to correspond to the observer's intuitive notion of what constitutes "flock-like motion." However it is difficult to objectively measure how valid these simulations are. By comparing behavioral aspects of the simulated flock with those of natural flocks, we are able to improve and refine the model. But having approached a certain level of realism in the model, the parameters of the simulated flock can be altered at will by the animator to achieve many variations on flock-like behavior.

Acknowledgments

I would like to thank flocks, herds, and schools for existing; nature is the ultimate source of inspiration for computer graphics and animation. I would also like to acknowledge the contributions to this research provided by workers in a wonderfully diverse collection of pursuits:

To the natural sciences of behavior, evolution, and zoology: for doing the hard work, the Real Science, on which this computer graphics approximation is based. To the Logo group who invented the appropriate geometry, and so put us in the driver's seat. To the Actor semantics people who invented the appropriate control structure, and so gave the boid a brain. To the many developers of modern Lisp who invented the appropriate programming language. To my past and present colleagues at MIT, III, and Symbolics who have patiently listened to my speculations about flocks for years and years before I made my first boid fly. To the Graphics Division of Symbolics, Inc., who employ me, put up with my nasty disposition, provide me with fantastic computing and graphics facilities, and have generously supported the development of the work described here. And to the field of computer graphics, for giving professional respectability to advanced forms of play such as reported in this paper.

References

1. Abelson, H., and diSessa, A., "Maneuvering a Three Dimensional Turtle" in *Turtle Geometry: The Computer as a Medium for Exploring Mathematics*, The MIT Press, Cambridge, Massachusetts, 1981, pp. 140–159.

2. Agha, G., *Actors: A Model of Concurrent Computation in Distributed Systems*, The MIT Press, Cambridge, Massachusetts, 1986.

3. Amkraut, S., personal communication, January 8, 1987.

4. Amkraut, S., Girard, M., Karl, G., "motion studies for a work in progress entitled 'Eurythmy'" in *SIGGRAPH Video Review*, Issue 21 (second item, time code 3:58 to 7:35), 1985, produced at the Computer Graphics Research Group, Ohio State University, Columbus, Ohio.

5. Austin, H., "The Logo Primer," MIT A.I. Lab, Logo Working Paper 19, 1974.

6. Braitenberg, V., *Vehicles: Experiments in Synthetic Psychology*, The MIT Press, Cambridge, Massachusetts, 1984.

7. Burton, R., *Bird Behavior*, Alfred A. Knopf, Inc., 1985.

8. Davis, J. R., Kay, A., Marion, A., unpublished research on behavioral simulation and animation, Atari Research, 1983.

9. Girard, M., Maciejewski, A. A., "Computational Modeling for the Computer Animation of Legged Figures," in *Computer Graphics* V19 #3, 1985, (proceedings of acm SIGGRAPH '85), pp. 263–270.

10. Goldberg, A., Robson, D., *SMALLTALK-80, The Language and its Implementation*, Addison-Wesley Publishing Company, Reading Massachusetts, 1983.

11. Goldberg, A., Kay, A., *SMALLTALK-72 Instruction Manual*, Learning research group, Xerox Palo Alto Research Center, 1976.

12. Hewitt, C., Atkinson, R., "Parallelism and Synchronization in Actor Systems," *acm Symposium on Principles of Programming Languages 4*, January 1977, Los Angeles, California.

13. Kahn, K. M., *Creation of Computer Animation from Story Descriptions*, MIT Artificial Intelligence Laboratory, Technical Report 540 (doctoral dissertation), August 1979.

14. Kahn, K. M., Hewitt, C., *Dynamic Graphics using Quasi Parallelism*, May 1978, proceedings of ACM SIGGRAPH, 1978.

15. Kleinrock, L., "Distributed Systems," in *Communications of the ACM*, V28 #11, November 1985, pp. 1200–1213.

16. Lipton, J., *An Exaltation of Larks (or, The Venereal Game)*, Grossman Publishers, 1977. Reprinted by Penguin Books 1977, 1980, 1982, 1983, 1984, 1985.

17. Maciejewski, A. A., Klein, C.A., "Obstacle Avoidance for Kinematically Redundant Manipulators in Dynamically Varying Environments," to appear in *International Journal of Robotic Research*.

18. Magnenat-Thalmann, N., Thalmann, D., *Computer Animation: Theory and Practice*, Springer-Verlag, Toyko, 1985.

19. Marion, A., "Artificially Motivated Objects," [installation piece], ACM SIGGRAPH art show, 1985.

20. Moon, D. A., "Object-oriented Programming with Flavors," in *Proceedings of the First Annual Conference on Object-Oriented Programming Systems, Languages, and Applications*, ACM, 1986

21. Myers, R., Broadwell, P., Schaufler, R., "Plasm: Fish Sample," [installation piece], ACM SIGGRAPH art show, 1985.

22. Papert, S., "Teaching Children to be Mathematicians vs. Teaching Them About Mathematics," *International Journal of Mathematical Education and Sciences*, V3, pp. 249–262, 1972.

23. Partridge, B. L., "The Structure and Function of Fish Schools," *Scientific American*, June 1982, pp. 114–123.

24. Pitcher, T. J., Partridge, B. L., Wardle, C. S., "Blind Fish Can School," *Science* 194, #4268 (1976), p. 964.

25. Potts, W. K., "The Chorus-Line Hypothesis of Manoeuver Coordination in Avian Flocks," letter in *Nature*, Vol 309, May 24, 1984, pp. 344–345.

26. Pugh, J., "Actors—The Stage is Set," acm SIGPLAN Notices, V19 #3, March 1984, pp. 61–65.

27. Reeves, W., T., "Particle Systems—A Technique for Modeling a Class of Fuzzy Objects," acm *Transactions on Graphics*, V2 #2, April 1983, and reprinted in *Computer Graphics*, V17 #3, July 1983, (acm SIGGRAPH '83 Proceedings), pp. 359–376.

28. Reynolds, C. W., *Computer Animation in the World of Actors and Scripts*, SM thesis, MIT (the Architecture Machine Group), May 1978.

29. Reynolds, C. W., "Computer Animation with Scripts and Actors," *Computer Graphics*, V16 #3, July 1982, (acm SIGGRAPH '82 Proceedings), pp. 289–296.

30. Reynolds, C. W., "Description and Control of Time and Dynamics in Computer Animation" in the notes for the course on Advanced Computer Animation at acm SIGGRAPH '85, and reprinted for the notes of the same course in 1986.

31. Selous, E., *Thought-transference (or what?) in Birds*, Constable, London, 1931.

32. Scheffer, V. B., *Spires of Form: Glimpses of Evolution*, Harcourt Brace Jovanovich, San Diego, 1983 (reprinted 1985 by Harvest/HBJ), p. 64.

33. Shaw, E., "Schooling in Fishes: Critique and Review" in *Development and Evolution of Behavior*. W. H. Freeman and Company, San Francisco, 1970, pp. 452–480.

34. Shaw, E., "Fish in Schools," *Natural History* 84, no. 8 (1975), pp. 40–46.

35. Sims, K., *Locomotion of Jointed Figures Over Complex Terrain*, SM thesis, MIT Media Lab, currently in preparation, April 1987.

36. Symbolics Graphics Division, *S-Dynamics* (user's manual), Symbolics Inc., November 1986.

37. Symbolics Graphics Division, *S-Geometry* (user's manual), Symbolics Inc., October 1986.

38. Pinker, S. (editor), *Visual Cognition*, The MIT Press, Cambridge, Massachusetts, 1985.

39. Thomas, F., Johnson, O., *Disney Animation: The Illusion of Life*, Abbeville Press, New York, 1981, pp. 47–69.

40. Wilhelms, J., "Toward Automatic Motion Control," *IEEE Computer Graphics and Applications*, V7 #4, April 1987, pp. 11–22.

41. Zeltzer, D., "Toward an Integrated View of 3-D Computer Animation," *The Visual Computer*, V1 #4, 1985, pp. 249–259.

REAL-TIME DISPLAY OF COMPUTER GENERATED HALF-TONE PERSPECTIVE PICTURES

GORDON W. ROMNEY, GARY S. WATKINS and DAVID C. EVANS

Computer Science Department, University of Utah,
Salt Lake City, Utah, USA

This paper deals with the problem of attaining real-time generation and display of half-tone perspective pictures. The FORTRAN IV program which produces the picture generation simplifies the input required of the user to obtain a given view of an object. Freedom in specifying both the orientation of the object and the view point allows complete control over the perspective. The hidden line algorithm utilizes the order in which triangles enter from one scan line to the next and greatly reduces the amount of scan line computations. With this algorithm, real-time picture generation becomes more of a possibility and real-time display a near-future reality.

1. ALGORITHM

The feasibility of producing half-tone pictures of computer described objects and eliminating all hidden lines has previously been shown [1, 2]. This paper deals with the problem of attaining real-time generation and display of half-tone perspective pictures. Generation is the computation necessary to describe an entire picture (sections 2 to 4). Display, on the other hand, entails the technique used in the conversion of the digital description of the generation to analog form capable of producing the picture (section 5).

2. INPUT DATA

The hidden line algorithm confines the user to work with planar surfaces only, or curved surfaces so approximated (figs. 4 and 5). Furthermore, the object description must be in terms of triangles. The object description (set of vectors $\{X'\}$) is not constrained to lie within any limiting physical confines of three-space, and it may be described relative to any orthogonal coordinate system in Euclidean space (the case of usual real-world application). The user must also specify the particular view of the object he desires. This consists of two parts, 1) the orientation of the object (section 3.1) and 2) the particular perspective desired.

Now, consider a coordinate system in which the observer is seated (fig. 1). The view-plane is constrained to lie in the $z = 0$ plane, parallel to the x and y-axes, and has a 512×512 point

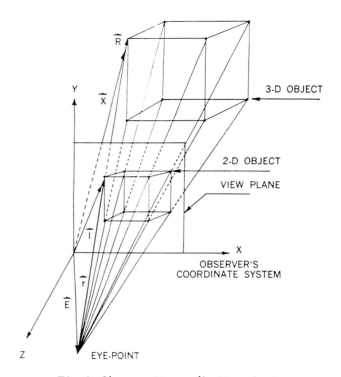

Fig. 1. Observer's coordinate system.

resolution. If one desires the association, the display device screen may be thought of as the view-plane with the object being transformed (section 3.1) in front of the viewer. The user specifies an eye-point E such that $E_z \geq 0$. For orthogonal perspectives, however, E_x and E_y correspond respectively to the x and y coordinates of the centroid of the object $\{X'\}$. The flexibility in the choice of both the object location and eye-point relative to the view-plane allows both orthogonal (fig. 6) and non-orthogonal (artistic) perspectives [3].

3. PRE-SCAN COMPUTATION

3.1. *Data transformation*

It is at this stage that the previously specified orientation of the object is executed. The object description $\{X'\}$, relative to the object coordinate system is transformed to the observer's (fig. 1) coordinate system.

$$X = S \cdot X' \qquad (1)$$

where S is a linear transformation and $\{X\}$ are the transformed vectors. The linear transformation S may be either rotations, translations or stretchings about the three axes. Since rotations are not commutative [4] the user must also select the particular rotation matrix he desires.

3.2. *Projection onto the view-plane*

The vectors $\{X\}$ describe the three vertices of each triangle. Thus, with N triangles, $\{X\}$ consists of $3N$ vertices, and each vertex will be mapped onto the view-plane (fig. 1).

$$I = E - r$$
$$I = E - R \cdot w \qquad r = w \cdot R$$
$$I = E - (X - E) \cdot w \qquad R = X - E$$
$$\qquad w = r / R$$
$$\qquad = E_z / E_z$$
$$I = E + (X - E) \cdot E_z / R_z$$

The above equations describe the two-dimensional mapping. Also, during the mapping, the projected object image is centered on the view-plane if so specified by the user, and is now completely described by the two-dimensional image vectors $\{I\}$. The image vectors are sorted with respect to y and the vertices corresponding to the y-max and y-min values for each triangle are respectively called vertices one and three. Using the sorted $\{I\}$, an array LISTY is created which will be used to tell when a scan line (section 4) enters and exits from a triangle.

3.3. *Hidden line interpolation parameters*

In order to minimize the computation of the hidden line stage of the algorithm, the distance $|R|$ to each triangle (in reality this need only be computed for each planar surface) is determined as a function of the corresponding vectors of $\{I\}$ and linear interpolation parameters a_1, a_2 and a_3. The linear relationship was chosen in order to simplify the distance evaluation which is the most frequent computation of the hidden line algorithm.

The evaluation of the hidden line interpolation parameters previously described [1] is not adequate to compare the distance to various surfaces in three-space. The distance from the eye-point to any given vertex in three-space is

$$|R| = \sqrt{[(X_x - E_x)^2 + (X_y - E_y)^2 + (X_z - E_z)^2]} \qquad (2)$$

and an attempt was made to describe this distance $|R|$ as a linear function of the two-space coordinates I_x and I_y. Clearly $|R|$ is not a linear function. However, one can describe R_z, its z-component, as a linear function of I_x and I_y. For the hidden line computation, the image point (I_x, I_y) is known, but the distance $|R|$ or alternatively R_z to a point on the surface of the triangle needs to be determined. A plane may be described by

$$a_1 X_x + a_2 X_y + a_3 X_z = 1 \qquad (3)$$

where $X = (X_x, X_y, X_z)$ is a point on the plane. Using the three vertices of each triangle, a set of three equations in three unknowns is obtained.

$$1/R_z^i = a_1 I_x^i + a_2 I_y^i + a_3 \qquad (i = 1, 2, 3). \qquad (4)$$

Using Cramer's Rule, a_1, a_2 and a_3 are found for each triangle, and

$$1/R_z = a_1 I_x + a_2 I_y + a_3. \qquad (5)$$

To this stage, all of the computation necessary to assist in the hidden line evaluation and produce a frame has been accomplished. A frame is considered to be a picture of the object from a particular eye-point and orientation. If any of the input data is changed (such as a new eye-point or orientation) a new frame must be calculated.

4. SCAN LINE COMPUTATION

A fictitious "raster" scan is generated across the view-plane for $y = 1$ to $y = 512$. For each scan line y, LISTY (section 3.2) is checked to see which triangles are intersected.

4.1. *Intercepts*

The intercepts of the present scan line y and two sides of each intersected triangle are evaluated and LISTX created in a similar manner to LISTY (section 3.2). LISTX tells when a given scan ray enters and exits a triangle with respect to x. In fig. 2 the scan line intersects eight tri-

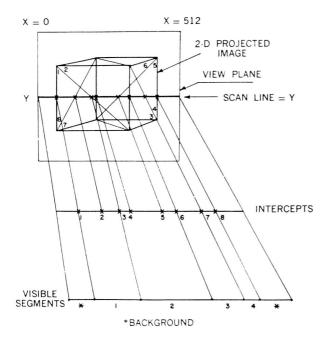

Fig. 2. Visible segments.

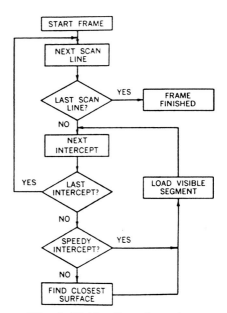

Fig. 3. Hidden line algorithm.

angles and eight distinct intercept points are found.

4.2. Hidden line computation

Only at the eight intercept points in fig. 2 will hidden line computations need be made. Intercept one illustrates the case where the relative distance to triangles one and eight in three-space must be determined using eq. (5). The hidden line interpolation parameters for each of the two triangles are used in the computation. The triangle yielding the minimum R_z is considered the visible triangle.

4.3. Visible segments

Each intercept in turn is checked and if the present visible triangle either exits (e.g. triangle 1 exits at intercept 3) or is suddenly hidden (case of overlapping triangles) the visible triangle is loaded into a visible list along with the x-end of its segment and where

$$x\text{-begin}_j = x\text{-end}_{j-1} + 1, j \geq 1. \quad (6)$$

Thus, a scan line results in being a sequence of visible segments (e.g. six visible segments in fig. 2). Fig. 3 is a simplified flow chart of the scan line computation.

4.4. Incremental intensity list

The intensity L of light incident upon a triangle surface due to a point source of illumination at the eye-point is proportional to $\cos^2\theta/|R|^2$, where θ is the angle between R and the normal N to the triangle plane. The normal N is found by taking the absolute value of the cross product between any two adjacent sides of the triangle.

$$L = L_0 \cos^2\theta/|R|^2. \quad (7)$$

The intensity L' actually detected at the eye due to reflection from the surface is a function of L. As a first approximation, L' was made proportional to L^2.

Concerning the intensity evaluation, the user must once again specify certain parameters - namely a base intensity level and the spread desired above this base level. Although the display device (section 5) is not capable of differentiating the number of levels used (64 up to 1024), nevertheless, a large range of values is used in the computation and the truncation which occurs is in the display device itself.

As a triangle is determined to be visible, intensity interpolation parameters are evaluated in a similar manner to the hidden line interpolation parameters (section 3.3). Using the intensity L^i evaluated at each of the three vertices, L at an image point (I_x, I_y) is found to be

$$L = b_1 I_x + b_2 I_y + b_3. \quad (8)$$

Once again, a linear approximation was used in order to minimize the computation time required to determine the intensity at any point on the surface of a visible triangle. Eq. (7) is definitely non-linear and consequently eq. (8) is merely an

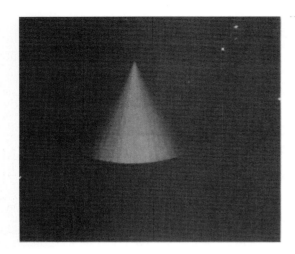

Fig. 4. Cone.

Fig. 5. Sphere.

Fig. 6. "Graphics".

Fig. 7. Letter "G".

Fig. 8. Sculpture "4-Head".

Fig. 9. Gondola building.

approximation, but it does yield rather appealing results (figs. 4 to 9).

Subsequent to its first entry as a visible triangle, each triangle's interpolation parameters and eq. (8) are used to evaluate the intensity at the segment's x-begin point. The result is each visible segment described as a list of 1) intensity L at x-begin, 2) the $\Delta L = b_1$ of eq. (8) which is needed to be added to L at each x as x is incremented to x-end, and 3) the x-end value. This is a very compact representation which can be stored quite economically until an entire frame is generated.

4.5. "Speedy" visible segment load

One advantageous result occurs from the manner in which the lists are created - namely the order in which the triangles fall for a given scan line. For example, in fig. 2, considering both entry and exit intercepts, the triangle list 1, 8, 8, 7, 1, 2, 7, 6, 6, 5, 2, 3, 3, 4, 4, 5 is obtained. Now, for all or a portion of the next scan line (y incremented by 1) where the order of the triangles remains the same, hidden line computations are unnecessary and a "speedy" visible segment load occurs. The latter consists of using the visible triangles in the last scan line in the same order, but with their new x-begin and x-end values. This simple check on ordering and the utilization of the "speedy" segment load has speeded up the algorithm phenomenally (fig. 3).

In a frame of resolution 512×512, a considerable portion of the frame is background. The algorithm is only concerned with that portion of the frame which contains the object. The number of scan lines which describe an object are those which actually intersect the two-space triangle images that describe the object. A cube such as that shown in fig. 1 was described by 280 scan lines. Of these, only 27 scan line computations (involving complete or partial hidden line computations) were needed; the other 253 were complete scan line "speedy" loads. The cube, of course, is a simple object of only twelve triangles, but consider one of the objects shown in fig. 8. This object is describes by 136 triangles and of the 263 scan lines involved, only 145 were complete or partial scan line computations.

5. DISPLAY

The incremental intensity information (section 4.4) is presently being used after a complete frame is generated to produce the intensity at each point of the frame ($512 \times 512 = 262,144$ points). The point information consisting of intensity values is then transmitted from a Univac 1108 (36-bit word) to a PDP-8 (12-bit word). A program in the PDP-8 increments x and y and produces the raster scan. The point information then passes through a DAC (Digital to Analog Converter) to a Tektronix 453 oscilloscope, where a time exposure is taken of the raster generated picture. The entire frame transmission and display takes 35 seconds.

6. RESULTS

A FORTRAN IV program of the algorithm is operational. Portions of the program are coded in Univac 1108 assembly language to minimize core requirements. The program occupies approximately 51K 36-bit words of core, of which 6K are instructions and 45K are data. The latter storage requirement allows a picture of 1000 triangle complexity.

The execution time is most dependent on the number and complexity of scan lines that intersect the two-space image of the object due to the many hidden line computations (section 4.2) involved (table 1). The "speedy" load (section 4.5) which has been developed, drastically reduces these computations.

Fig. 4 of the cone illustrates the phenomenon known as "Mach bands". Each triangle is, by and large, a constant intensity level, but, a scalloped effect results which is an optical illusion. The sphere in fig. 5 also illustrates the approximation of a curved surface by triangles. The dark areas were intentionally colored to illustrate the capability of specifying a given intensity to a surface. The "4-HEADS" in fig. 8 emphasize the capability of rotating objects in relation to one another as desired. Also, several triangles of the front "4-HEAD" were tagged as invisible, allowing the viewer to actually look inside of an object.

Table 1
A comparison of the number of triangles, segments and computation time for various objects

Figure number	Figure	Number triangles	Number segments	Hidden line computation time (sec)
4	CONE	100	6560	8.0
5	SPHERE	256	5706	7.0
6	GRAPHICS	360	5450	7.5
7	"G"	60	3690	3.0
8	4-HEAD	272	8894	13.0
9	GONDOLA	166	3327	5.5

7. CONCLUSION

The ultimate goal of computer graphics is to portray three-dimensional objects in such a manner that their dimensionality is unambiguous. The following techniques assist in making this portrayal more true-to-life: 1) Elimination of hidden lines, 2) Half-tone shading, 3) Perspective, 4) Stereo, and 5) Motion. The present algorithm has the capability of using the first four techniques. Stereo views of half-tone pictures are most impressive. Due to the time needed for both generation and display, real-time motion is nor presently possible, but without any doubt will be in the very near future for limited complexity objects.

Also, the algorithm is not dependent upon a full frame production prior to display. Using the "speedy" test, a given scan line is dependent only on the previous scan line. Individual scan lines may be sent to the display while computation is proceeding on subsequent scan lines.

The logical design of a hardware display system that will allow real-time display is near completion. The device will receive segment information from the Univac 1108 and generate the intensity data for each point which will be stored in digital form on a DATA DISK. The output of the DATA DISK will in turn be converted to analog voltages and refresh a TV monitor at video rates. This compatibility with TV systems is one of the reasons the raster or scan line approach was used in the algorithm [1, 2, 5].

Additional copies of any of the ARPA reports [2, 5] or this paper and photographs may be obtained upon request.

ACKNOWLEDGEMENTS

This research was sponsored by the Advanced Research Projects Agency, Department of Defense, and was monitored by AFSC, Research and Technology Division, Rome Air Development Center, Griffiss Air Force Base, New York 13440, under Contract AF30(602)-4277, at the University of Utah.

REFERENCES

[1] C. Wylie, G. Romney, D. Evans and A. Erdahl, Half-Tone Perspective Drawings by Computer, AFIPS Proc. FJCC 31 (1967) p. 49.
[2] C. Wylie, G. Romney, D. Evans and A. Erdahl, Half-Tone Perspective Drawings by Computer, ARPA Technical Report 4-2, University of Utah, 1968.
[3] E. W. Watson, How to Use Creative Perspective (Reinhold Publishing Co., New York, 1955).
[4] H. Goldstein, Classical Mechanics (Addison-Wesley Publ. Co., Inc., Reading, Massachusetts, 1959) p. 124.
[5] G. W. Romney, G. S. Watkins and D. C. Evans, Computer Generated Half-Tone Perspective Pictures, ARPA Technical Report 4-3, University of Utah, 1968.

DISCUSSION

Question
Your algorithm is not analytically correct. Is this not a drawback?

Answer
The scan line computation can be done using parallel hardware which makes possible simultaneous scan lines. This overcomes the difficulty.

Question
Does the user provide details of the triangulation for his application?

Answer
Yes. We are trying to build up a library of useful surfaces, e.g. doughnut and Möbius strip. We use the triangulation scheme at present. We are trying to develop other means, but this is still in the development stage.

Question
Do you actually have a graphic input system?

Answer
Yes, it has just become operational.

Question by R. Krutar
You mentioned Warnock's hidden-line program. Would you compare your program and his in a little more detail?

Answer
The other program allows intersecting triangles. It is based on a binary search of a square by successive division, and is readily adaptable to machine hardware, but takes considerably longer, e.g. one minute as compared with 10 seconds.

On the Design of Display Processors

T. H. MYER
Bolt Beranek and Newman Inc, Cambridge, Mass.
AND
I. E. SUTHERLAND[*]
Harvard University, Cambridge, Mass.

The flexibility and power needed in the data channel for a computer display are considered. To work efficiently, such a channel must have a sufficient number of instructions that it is best understood as a small processor rather than a powerful channel. As it was found that successive improvements to the display processor design lie on a circular path, by making improvements one can return to the original simple design plus one new general purpose computer for each trip around. The degree of physical separation between display and parent computer is a key factor in display processor design.

KEY WORDS AND PHRASES: display processor design, display system, computer graphics, graphic terminal, displays, graphics, display generator, display channel, display programming, graphical interaction, remote displays

CR CATEGORIES: 2.44, 6.22, 6.29, 6.35

1. Introduction

In mid-1967 we specified a research display system. This paper describes some of the problems we encountered and some conclusions we have drawn. The display will be an adjunct to an SDS-940 time-shared computer system. The chief purpose for the display and the parent computer is programming research.

When we first approached the task, we assumed we had merely to select one of the several available commercial displays. This proved possible with the analog equipment that constitutes a *display generator*; we found several display generators that combined good accuracy, resolution, and speed. However, the control part of the display, which we have come to call the *display processor*, was another story. We were not completely happy with the command repertoire of any of the commercial systems we saw; we were not sure just how to couple the display to our computer, and above all, we had serious doubts about what a display processor should *be*.

This work was sponsored by the Advanced Research Projects Agency under ARPA Order No. 627, Amendment No. 2, and conducted under Contract No. AF19(628)-5965, Air Force Cambridge Research Laboratories, Office of Aerospace Research, United States Air Force, Bedford, Massachusetts 01730.
* And Bolt Beranek and Newman Inc, Cambridge, Mass.

Reprinted with permission from *Communications of the ACM* Vol. 11, No. 6, June 1968, 410-414.

Finally we decided to design the processor ourselves, because only in this way, we thought, could we obtain a truly complete display processor. We approached the task by starting with a simple scheme and adding commands and features that we felt would enhance the power of the machine. Gradually the processor became more complex. We were not disturbed by this because computer graphics, after all, *are* complex. Finally the display processor came to resemble a full-fledged computer with some special graphics features. And then a strange thing happened. We felt compelled to add to the processor a second, subsidiary processor, which, itself, began to grow in complexity. It was then that we discovered a disturbing truth. Designing a display processor can become a never-ending cyclical process. In fact, we found the process so frustrating that we have come to call it the "wheel of reincarnation." We spent a long time trapped on that wheel before we finally broke free. In the remainder of this paper we describe our experiences. We have written it in the hope that it may speed others on toward "Nirvana."

2. The Wheel of Reincarnation

The simplest displays merely plot points from coordinate information. The TX-0 display at MIT (circa 1957) or the PDP-1 with DEC Type 30 (circa 1960) are of this type. Such a display has no processor; it is tied to the central registers of the parent computer. To display a point, its coordinates are first loaded into the central registers of the computer. For example, with a DEC Type 30 and a PDP-1 the accumulator is loaded with x and the input-output register with y. A display command is then executed which results in a point flashed on the screen.

One problem with this scheme is that the processor is tied up in generating display. If an attempt is made to compute concurrently with display, the display may develop an objectionable flicker. The situation seems even worse when one considers that refreshing a static display is a repetitive operation that need not occupy an entire processor full time.

For just a little more money one can buy a data channel for the display. The data channel has a display address register and a word counter. The channel takes successive data words from a display file in core until the word count goes zero, at which point the central processor restarts the channel at the beginning of the display file. Now the processor is freed for other work and the display can operate as fast as its analog circuits permit.

Point-by-point display is, of course, expensive of time and memory, even with a data channel. Any modern display should be able to draw lines and plot characters automatically. For such a display delta x and y information and characters will appear in the display file, as well as position values. In addition, there must be codes to set intensity and to tell whether beam movement is to generate a line or a point. These codes are regarded as new kinds of data for the display.

Now someone points out that a special code to stop the channel—a channel halt—could be used to end the display file. The word counter could be eliminated, thus saving money. At this time one realizes something one had begun to suspect earlier—that a display is inherently unlike other input/output devices. A magnetic tape unit, for example, must be able to transmit arbitrary combinations of bits onto tape. The display, on the other hand, may interpret some combinations of bits in its data as special commands, since its only function is to post a picture on the screen.

For just a little more money one can add some other commands to the display data channel. One is a jump command. This allows the channel to display a file repetitively—to refresh the display without intervention from the central processor. It also provides more flexibility in handling display data, since the channel can now handle noncontiguous display files.

In many engineering applications the pictures which will be displayed have repeated subpictures such as circuit symbols or small parts. So, for just a little more money, one adds a subroutine feature to the display's data channel. Repetitive circuit symbols can now be drawn by successive calls to appropriate channel subroutines.

The subroutine feature requires two new commands and means adding a new register to the display channel. A subroutine jump command saves the return address in a special register. In early implementations of the subroutine feature a store-exit command, usually the first command in the subroutine, deposits the saved address as a jump command at the end of the subroutine. This scheme not only allows for subpictures, but also permit nested subpictures to an indefinite depth.

Now this marks a kind of cardinal point in the wheel of reincarnation. The DEC 340-347 reached this point in design and was still thought to be a display channel. At this level of increasing complexity, however, one should realize and admit that the display data channel is not a mere data channel at all; it is a processor. From here on out one's thinking about the display changes radically.

First of all, one admits that the display's x and y registers form an accumulator and that the display address register is a program counter. What one has is a special purpose computer with a limited and somewhat unusual command repertorire:

    Load Immediate and Flash   (point)
    Add Immediate and Flash   (line)
    Halt
    Jump
    Subroutine Jump
    Store Subroutine Exit

Taking a broader view, one also realizes that one has a multiprocessor system, with the central processor (the parent computer) and the display processor sharing the same memory. From this viewpoint the Store Subroutine Exit command is a problem since it can change the shared memory and lead to painful debugging. Another problem is that the subroutine mechanism, useful as it is, does not make it particularly easy to trace one's path back through a multilevel subroutine structure after a light-pen hit.

To solve both these problems, one indulges in a bit more incremental funding and adds a pushdown stack system to the display processor. A subroutine jump stores the return address in the stack and increments the stack pointer. A subroutine return causes a jump to the location stored at the top of the stack and decrements the pointer. All return addresses are stored in one part of memory and one's only concern is to keep the stack from overflowing. Moreover, the contents of the stack give the main processor immediate access in one compact part of memory to the display processor's path through a subroutine hierarchy. As far as we know, the DEC-338 was the first commercial display to include a pushdown stack, and as this is written, the only domestic one[1] with stack hardware.[2]

While all this was going on, one has been adding pushbuttons and keyboards to the display, and has included appropriate registers and flags in the display processor to deal with these, to indicate light-pen hits, to scope edge violations, and the like. All of this information is available to the main processor, but the display processor, which is a rather passive device as we have described it so far, has no way of reacting to button pushes, edge violations, etc. So, for just a little more money, one adds some conditional branch commands that let the display processor test for button pushes, light-pen hits, and so forth. Conditional branch instructions give the display processor the power to do more than merely post complex pictures on the screen. Now it can interact with the user without recourse to the main processor. In fact, with some cleverness, one can write very involved interactive programs for a display processor with conditional branch instructions.

Even with conditionals, the display processor still has a few flaws. For one thing, one would like to make a subroutine transparent to all conditions that may have existed in the calling routine. Transparency is possible for beam position, since subroutines using relative vectors can always return the beam to its initial location, but it is not yet possible for display parameters, such as intensity, character size, and the like, nor for subroutines that use absolute beam positions. So, for a little more money, one makes the stack system a little more elaborate by adding instructions to push the current x and y beam position and the display parameters into the stack, and pop them back.

Now the issue of transparency brings to mind the idea of passing parameters to a subroutine. Parameter passing might be quite useful in display subroutines, and since one can load and store in the pushdown stack, one already has the basic machinery for passing parameters. All that is needed is some way of getting free access to the stack, and all this takes is a means for changing the contents of the stack pointer. So, for very little more money, one adds a command to add to or subtract from the stack pointer.

Thinking about parameters, of course, makes one realize one has been considering local parameters, and it would be nice to have global parameters as well. That is, it would be nice if all parts of a display program could be affected by changing one key word. The convenient way to do this would be to have addressable load and store commands. So, since it won't cost much, why not?

The processor has acquired the following command repertoire:

Load Immediate and Flash	(point)
Add Immediate and Flash	(line)
Halt	
Jump	
Push-Jump	(subroutine)
Conditional Skip	(possibly more than one of these)
Push Parameters	(into stack)
Push X, Y Position	(into stack)
Pop	(restore top item from stack)
Add Immediate to Stack Pointer	
Load	(addressable: C (address) → X, Y)
Store	(addressable: X, Y → C (address))

Many of these commands would be included in a general purpose processor. In fact, to make the display processor general, for just a little more money, one can add:

Execute	(addressable)
Complement	(for subtraction, and logic)
Shift	
Mask	(logical AND, OR, etc.)

And these probably won't add much to the price.

With all these commands, it occurs to one that the display processor could do things like track the light-pen, create "rubber band lines," and handle many other interactive functions that heretofore have been relegated to the main processor. To do these things conveniently, the display processor should have its own interrupt system, and, considering what one has spent so far, that should not cost much to add.

Now where are we? We have built up the display channel until it is itself a general purpose processor with a display. The display is tied directly to its processor; to generate a picture the display processor's central registers are used. In short, we have come exactly once around the wheel of reincarnation.

---

[1] The British NCR-ELLIOT 4100 is another example.
[2] Graphic II at Bell Telephone Laboratories uses a software approach.

However, we have made some very significant progress during the trip. We have given the processor Load Immediate and Add Immediate commands for displaying points and lines. These operations now take one, rather than three, memory cycles. We have added a pushdown stack system, a mechanism uniquely suited to display subroutining and tracing light-pen hits. In short, we have specially adapted the processor to the task of running a display.

Should we continue around the wheel? We might argue that much of the display processor's power is idle most of the time and that it is wasteful to tie up a general purpose processor merely to refresh a static display. Therefore (for just a little more money) we might consider adding a *channel* to the display processor. We might then consider adding some special commands to the channel to let it follow more complex data structures. If we did so we could move into a second turn around the wheel.

Throughout this discussion we have been assuming that the display processor will operate directly from the memory of the parent computer. The reader should note that we might just as well have started with a display having its own local memory. In either case the wheel of reincarnation works in much the same way. The display processor starts simple and grows until it has become a full computer. Then it gives birth to a second processor which in turn begins to grow.

Looking at some commercial displays, one can find examples at various points around the wheel. As we have said, the DEC Type 30 represents a starting point, while the DEC 340-347 represents about a half-turn. The IDI 10000 series, I.I.I. 1050, Tasker 9000 and the CDC-250 also represent positions less than once around. The IDIIOM represents a full revolution and a quarter, while the DEC 338 represents a revolution and a half. We have found no examples exactly once around the wheel, but we submit this as an interesting design problem: a small general purpose computer with an integrated display system and a single program counter.

3. General Conclusions

It was not until we had traveled around the wheel several times that we realized what was happening. Once we did, we tried to view the whole problem from a broader perspective. We found that some questions had fairly clear answers, but others remained in doubt. The remainder of this paper outlines our conclusions and sets forth the questions we could not answer.

The problem breaks down into two general questions: How closely should the display system be tied to the parent computer? How much computing power should be included in the display processor?

The first question seems simpler to answer than the second. If the display must be located far from the main computer, then the problems of data transmission dictate that it have at least a local memory. Likewise, there are arguments for detaching the display from a parent computer that is running a time-shared system. If the display is too closely coupled to the main machine, competition over memory access and demands from the display for interactive service may degrade the display's or the system's performance. Moreover, if the display processor can change information in memory, there is the danger that it may destroy the time-sharing software.

While a remote display with its own memory seems a good choice for some situations, we feel it has unjustifiable disadvantages unless communication bandwidths force it. We feel a better approach is to locate the display close enough to the main computer so that both can access the same core directly. This approach allows display files to be used in the core where they are prepared; there is no need to ship display data, at a cost of two memory cycles per word, to a remote memory. In interactive situations, this approach makes it easy for the main computer to find out what went on between the display processor, the user, and the display file. Most importantly, particularly in a research system, this approach gives the user the ability to experiment with approaches in which the picture data is merged with other data in his program system. Consequently one of our conclusions has been that the display processor should be closely coupled with the parent computer, that it should take its data from the main computer's core, and that the user should have complete, bit-by-bit control over that data. We recognize that this poses problems in a time-shared system, but we feel the advantages to be gained make it worthwhile to solve them.

If, for geographic or other reasons, one has decided on a tenuous connection between display and main computer, the question of how much power to give the display processor can be answered in terms of how one wishes to use the display. If one plans to display relatively static pictures and can tolerate fairly long delays on interactive services, such as light-pen hits, and button pushes, then there is little point to including general computing power in the display processor. On the other hand, to save memory space, one would probably want to include jump and subroutine commands.

If, by contrast, one wishes to produce more dynamic displays and handle highly interactive situations, then one must at least include general computing power remotely with the display. The question is then whether to integrate the general purpose capability in the display processor itself or to include a separate display channel in the remote device, i.e. whether to go around the wheel of reincarnation exactly once or more than once. Many interactive situations, such as light-pen handling, require that the main display loop be halted, at least while the initial servicing is performed. One could handle these by interrupting the display processor itself. Other functions, such as responding to push buttons, adding to the display file, and interpreting commands from the main computer, can be performed without halting the display. This fact argues for a display channel combined with a small general purpose computer.

As we have said, we know of no remote display in which the computer and display channel are integrated into one machine, i.e. exactly one turn around the wheel. However, this approach seems to offer some advantages. Having one processor would be cheaper and would eliminate problems arising from the need for communication between two separate processors. By careful interrupt programming the execution time of the slower graphic commands could be utilized for other processing.

Most existing remote displays are based on the second approach, i.e. more than one turn around the wheel. The DEC 338 incorporates a powerful channel with jump, subroutine, and conditional commands in addition to a complete local computer. The Bell Telephone Laboratories Graphic II display[3] represents a different variation of the same approach. Its premise is that in a remote display system, consisting of computer plus display channel, the computer will be idle most of the time and might just as well perform the functions that would otherwise be wired into the channel. The Graphic II channel has a command that interrupts the computer (a PDP-9). The address field of this command indicates what function to perform. Subroutining, conditionals, etc., are done for the display through programs executed by the main computer.

The Graphic II scheme allows great flexibility in building display data structures since the PDP-9 can be programmed to follow almost any structure. However, this flexibility is achieved at a sacrifice in speed. It takes considerably longer to perform jumps, subroutine jumps, etc., by program than by hardware. This time burden could be quite serious, since a single picture may contain many subroutine calls, and all must be repeated each time the picture is refreshed. However, the designer of Graphic II points out that the time burden can be largely eliminated by programs that allow the PDP-9 to follow structure while the display is simultaneously executing graphic commands embedded in the structure.

If it is possible to locate the display processor near to the main computer, we feel, as we have pointed out, that they should share the same memory. In this case, the question of how much display processor to buy becomes rather complicated. No longer is a minimum general purpose capability required. One can choose a design anywhere from a primitive channel to a dedicated general purpose processor plus channel. One way of deciding how much display processor to buy is to look at the jobs the display processor might reasonably be expected to do. There are four.

(1) The display processor must generate pictures from some form of internal representation, which may include multiple calls on display subroutines.

(2) The display processor might generate pictures or picture elements by computation rather than from a static representation in memory. Such pictures as the light-pen tracking cross, point rasters, random points, and arrays of objects are more compactly specified by generation procedures than by listing their elements.

(3) The display processor might provide immediate feedback to the user or handle simple interactive functions such as editing, and light-pen tracking.

(4) The display processor might compile displayable picture representations from higher level data in the user's program system. This would include handling the routine computations required for rotation, scaling, curve generation, and the like, when these are not handled by the display hardware.

As for Job 1, the display processor must certainly follow data structures in core. In our view, a desirable goal is to eliminate the secondary display file that must usually be generated from some higher level structure. The more complex the structures the display processor can follow directly, the more closely, we feel, that goal will be approached. However, in the interest of speed, the display processor must follow structures by executing display commands embedded within the data. It would not be useful, in our view, to give the display processor general computing power merely so that it could *interpret* such structures.

As for Jobs 2 and 3, we feel it does not much matter where the computing power comes from, provided it can be had immediately on demand. One can either provide high level interrupt routines in the main system at risk of degrading the system's performance, or spend the extra money to include the necessary computing power, and possibly an interrupt system in the display processor.

Job 4 does not seem to belong to the display processor at all. As far as generating pictures from data is concerned, we feel the display processor should be a specialized device, capable only of generating pictures from read-only representations in core. A data structure, useful for high level manipulation, represents objects abstractly, and includes, as parameters, the numerical information necessary to generate any particular view. The display processor should be able to follow such structures directly but not generate secondary display files from the information contained in them. Generation of secondary display files is properly the job of the central computer.

The view suggested by Daniel Bobrow that the display processor need not, indeed should not, contain mere general purpose computing power, largely determined the design of our display processor. The design reflects that view most directly in its lack of an addressable store command and in the limitations imposed on access to the stack. For example, information put into the stack can only be returned to the register from whence it came. General computing power, whatever its purpose, should come from the central resources of the system. If these resources should prove inadequate, then it is the system, not the display, that needs more computing power. This decision let us finally escape from the wheel of reincarnation.

---

[3] Ninke, William. Bell Telephone Laboratories, telephone conversation, 11 August 1967.

RECEIVED AUGUST, 1967; REVISED NOVEMBER, 1967

A head-mounted three dimensional display*

by IVAN E. SUTHERLAND**

The University of Utah
Salt Lake City, Utah

INTRODUCTION

The fundamental idea behind the three-dimensional display is to present the user with a perspective image which changes as he moves. The retinal image of the real objects which we see is, after all, only two-dimensional. Thus if we can place suitable two-dimensional images on the observer's retinas, we can create the illusion that he is seeing a three-dimensional object. Although stereo presentation is important to the three-dimensional illusion, it is less important than the change that takes place in the image when the observer moves his head. The image presented by the three-dimensional display must change in exactly the way that the image of a real object would change for similar motions of the user's head. Psychologists have long known that moving perspective images appear strikingly three-dimensional even without stereo presentation; the three-dimensional display described in this paper depends heavily on this "kinetic depth effect."[1]

In this project we are not making any effort to measure rotation of the eyeball. Because it is very difficult to measure eye rotation, we are fortunate that the perspective picture presented need not be changed as the user moves his eyes to concentrate on whatever part of the picture he chooses. The perspective picture presented need only be changed when he moves his head. In fact, we measure only the position and orientation of the optical system fastened to the user's head. Because the optical system determines the virtual screen position and the user's point of view, the position and orientation of the optical system define which perspective view is appropriate.

Our objective in this project has been to surround the user with displayed three-dimensional information. Because we use a homogeneous coordinate representation,[2,3] we can display objects which appear to be close to the user or which appear to be infinitely far away. We can display objects beside the user or behind him which will become visible to him if he turns around. The user is able to move his head three feet off axis in any direction to get a better view of nearby objects. He can turn completely around and can tilt his head up or down thirty or forty degrees. The objects displayed appear to hang in the space all around the user.

The desire to surround a user with information has forced us to solve the "windowing" problem. The "clipping divider" hardware we have built eliminates those portions of lines behind the observer or outside of his field of view. It also performs the division necessary to obtain a true perspective view. The clipping divider can perform the clipping computations for any line in about 10 microseconds, or about as fast as a modern high-performance display can paint lines on a CRT. The clipping divider is described in detail in a separate paper[4] in this issue. Because the clipping divider permits dynamic perspective display of three-dimensional drawings and arbitrary magnification of two-dimensional drawings, we feel that it is the most significant result of this research to date.

In order to make truly realistic pictures of solid three-dimensional objects, it is necessary to solve the "hidden line problem." Although it is easy to compute the perspective positions of all parts of a complex object, it is difficult to compute which portions of one object are hidden by another object. Of the software solutions now available,[2,5–10] only the MAGI[9] and the Warnock[10] approaches seem to have potential as eventual real-time solutions for reasonably com-

---

*The work reported in this paper was performed at Harvard University, supported in part by the Advanced Research Projects Agency (ARPA) of the Department of Defense under contract SD 265, in part by the Office of Naval Research under contract ONR 1866(16), and in part by a long standing agreement between Bell Telephone Laboratories and the Harvard Computation Laboratory. The early work at the MIT Lincoln Laboratory was also supported by ARPA.

**Formerly of Harvard University

plex situations; the time required by the other methods appears to grow with the square of situation complexity. The only existing real-time solution to the hidden line problem is a very expensive special-purpose computer at NASA Houston[11] which can display only relatively simple objects. We have concluded that showing "opaque" objects with hidden lines removed is beyond our present capability. The three-dimensional objects shown by our equipment are transparent "wire frame" line drawings.

Operation of the display system

In order to present changing perspective images to the user as he moves his head, we have assembled a wide variety of equipment shown in the diagram of Figure 1. Special spectacles containing two miniature cathode ray tubes are attached to the user's head. A fast, two-dimensional, analog line generator provides deflection signals to the miniature cathode ray tubes through transistorized deflection amplifiers. Either of two head position sensors, one mechanical and the other ultrasonic, is used to measure the position of the user's head.

As the observer moves his head, his point of view moves and rotates with respect to the room coordinate system. In order to convert from room coordinates to a coordinate system based on his point of view, a translation and a rotation are required. A computer uses the measured head position information to compute the elements of a rotation and translation matrix appropriate to each particular viewing position. Rather than changing the information in the computer memory as the user moves his head, we transform information from room coordinates to eye coordinates dynamically as it is displayed. A new rotation and translation matrix is loaded into the digital matrix multiplier once at the start of each picture repetition. As a part of the display process the endpoints of lines in the room coordinate system are fetched from memory and are individually transformed to the eye coordinate system by the matrix multiplier. These translated and rotated endpoints are passed via an intermediate buffer to the digital clipping divider. The clipping divider eliminates any information outside the user's field of view and computes the appropriate perspective image for the remaining data. The final outputs of the clipping divider are endpoints of two-dimensional lines specified in scope coordinates. The two-dimensional line specifications are passed to a buffered display interface which drives the analog line-drawing display.

We built the special-purpose digital matrix multiplier and clipping divider to compute the appropriate perspective image dynamically because no available general-purpose computer is fast enough to provide a flicker-free dynamic picture. Our equipment can provide for display of 3000 lines at 30 frames per second which amounts to a little over 10 microseconds per line. Sequences of vectors which form "chains" in which the start of one vector is the same as the end of the previous one can be processed somewhat more efficiently than isolated lines. Assuming, however, two endpoints for every line, the matrix multiplier must provide coordinate transformation in about 5 microseconds per endpoint. Each matrix multiplication requires 16 accumulating multiplications; and therefore a throughput of about 3,000,000 multiplications per second. The clipping divider, which is separate and asynchronous, operates at about the same speed, processing two endpoints in slightly over 10 microseconds. Unlike the fixed time required for a matrix multiplication, however, the processing time required by the clipping divider depends on the data being processed. The time required by the analog line generator depends on the length of the line being drawn, the shortest requiring about 3 microseconds, the longest requiring about 36 microseconds and an average of about 10 microseconds.

The matrix multiplier, clipping divider, and line-generator are connected in a "pipe-line" arrangement. Data "stream" through the system in a carefully interlocked way. Each unit is an independently timed digital device which provides for its own input and output synchronization. Each unit examines an input flag which signals the arrival of data for it. This data are held until the unit is ready to accept them. As the unit accepts a datum, it also reads a "directive" which tells it what to do with the datum. When the unit has accepted

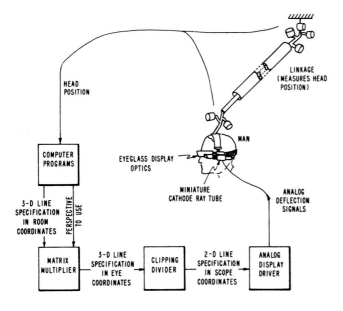

FIGURE 1—The parts of the three-dimensional display system

a datum, it clears its input flag. When it has completed its operation, it presents the answer on output lines and sets an output flag to signal that data is ready. In some cases the unit will commence the next task before its output datum has been taken. If so, it will pause in the new computation if it would have to destroy its output datum in order to proceed. Orderly flow of information through the system is ensured because the output flag of each unit serves as the input flag of the next. The average rate of the full system is approximately the average rate of the slowest unit. Which unit is slowest depends on the data being processed. The design average rate is about 10 microseconds per line.

The computer in this system is used only to process the head-position sensor information once per frame, and to contain and manipulate the three-dimensional drawing. No available general-purpose computer would be fast enough to become intimately involved in the perspective computations required for dynamic perspective display. A display channel processor serves to fetch from memory the drawing data required to recompute and refresh the CRT picture. The channel processor can be "configured" in many ways so that it is also possible to use the matrix multiplier and clipping divider independently. For example, the matrix multiplier can be used in a direct memory-to-memory mode which adds appreciably to the arithmetic capability of the computer to which it is attached. For two-dimensional presentations it is also possible to bypass the matrix multiplier and provide direct input to the clipping divider and display. These facilities were essential for debugging the various units independently.

Presenting images to the user

The special headset which the user of the three-dimensional display wears is shown in Figure 2. The optical system in this headset magnifies the pictures on each of two tiny cathode ray tubes to present a virtual image about eighteen inches in front of each of the user's eyes. Each virtual image is roughly the size of a conventional CRT display. The user has a 40 degree field of view of the synthetic information displayed on the miniature cathode ray tubes. Half-silvered mirrors in the prisms through which the user looks allow him to see both the images from the cathode ray tubes and objects in the room simultaneously. Thus displayed material can be made either to hang disembodied in space or to coincide with maps, desk tops, walls, or the keys of a typewriter.

The miniature cathode ray tubes mounted on the optical system form a picture about one half of an inch square. Because they have a nominal six tenths mil spot size, the resolution of the virtual image seen by the user is about equivalent to that available in standard

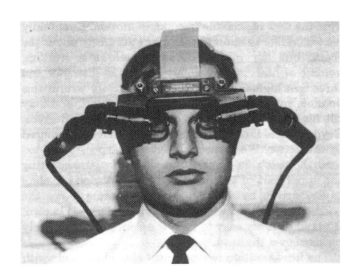

FIGURE 2—The head-mounted display optics with miniature CRT's

large-tube displays. Each cathode ray tube is mounted in a metal can which is carefully grounded to protect the user from shorts in the high voltage system. Additional protection is provided by enclosing the high voltage wiring in a grounded shield.

The miniature cathode ray tubes have proven easy to drive. They use electrostatic deflection and focussing. Because their deflection plates require signals on the order of only 300 volts, the transistorized deflection amplifiers are of a relatively straightforward design. Complementary-symmetry emitter followers are used to drive four small coaxial cables from the amplifier to each cathode ray tube. Deflection and intensification signals for the miniature cathode ray tubes are derived from a commercial analog line-drawing display which can draw long lines in 36 microseconds (nominal) and short lines as fast as three microseconds (nominal).

The analog line generator accepts picture information in the coordinate system of the miniature cathode ray tubes. It is given two-dimensional scope coordinates for the endpoints of each line segment to be shown. It connects these endpoints with smooth, straight lines on the two-dimensional scope face. Thus the analog line-drawing display, transistorized deflection amplifiers, miniature cathode ray tubes, and head-mounted optical system together provide the ability to present the user with any two-dimensional line drawing.

Head position sensor

The job of the head position sensor is to measure and report to the computer the position and orientation of the user's head. The head position sensor should provide the user reasonable freedom of motion. Eventually we would like to allow the user to walk freely about the room, but our initial equipment allows a working volume of head motion about six feet in diameter and three feet high. The user may move freely within this volume, may turn himself completely about, and may tilt his head up or down approximately forty degrees. Beyond these limits, head position cannot be measured by the sensor. We suspect that it will be possible to extend the user's field of motion simply by transporting the upper part of the head position sensor on a ceiling trolley driven by servo or stepping motors. Since the position of the head with respect to the sensor is known, it would be fairly easy to keep the sensor approximately centered over the head.

The head position measurement should be made with good resolution. Our target is a resolution of 1/100 of an inch and one part in 10,000 of rotation. Resolution finer than that is not useful because the digital-to-analog conversion in the display system itself results in a digital "grain" of about that size.

The accuracy requirement of the head position sensor is harder to determine. Because the miniature cathode ray tubes and the head-mounted optical system together have a pin-cushion distortion of about three per-

FIGURE 4—The ultrasonic head position sensor in use

cent, information displayed to the user may appear to be as much as three tenths of an inch out of place. Our head position sensor, then, should have an accuracy on the order of one tenth of an inch, although useful performance may be obtained even with less accurate head-position information.

We have tried two methods of sensing head position. The first of these involves a mechanical arm hanging from the ceiling as shown in Figure 3. This arm is free to rotate about a vertical pivot in its ceiling mount. It has two universal joints, one at the top and one at the bottom, and a sliding center section to provide the six motions required to measure both translation and rotation. The position of each joint is measured and presented to the computer by a digital shaft position encoder.

The mechanical head position sensor is rather heavy and uncomfortable to use. The information derived from it, however, is easily converted into the form needed to generate the perspective transformation. We built it to have a sure method of measuring head position.

We have also constructed a continuous wave ultrasonic head position sensor shown in Figure 4. Three transmitters which transmit ultrasound at 37, 38.6, and

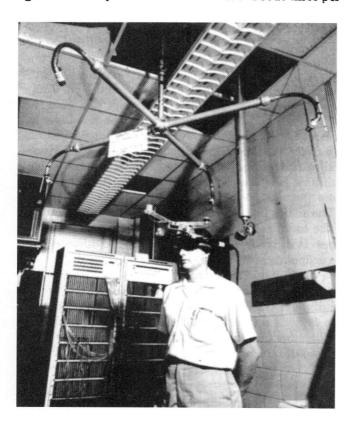

FIGURE 3—The mechanical head position sensor in use

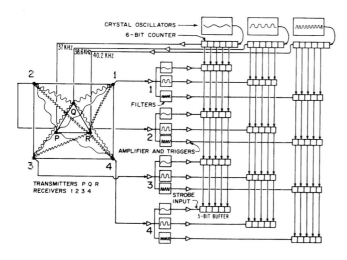

FIGURE 5—The ultrasonic head position sensor logic

40.2 kHz are attached to the head-mounted optical system. Four receivers are mounted in a square array in the ceiling. Each receiver is connected to an amplifier and three filters as shown in Figure 5, so that phase changes in sound transmitted over twelve paths can be measured. The measured phase shift for each ultrasonic path can be read by the computer as a separate five-bit number. The computer counts major changes in phase to keep track of motions of more than one wavelength.

Unlike the Lincoln Wand[12] which is a pulsed ultrasonic system, our ultrasonic head position sensor is a continuous wave system. We chose to use continuous wave ultrasound rather than pulses because inexpensive narrow-band transducers are available and to avoid confusion from pulsed noise (such as typewriters produce) which had caused difficulty for the Lincoln Wand. The choice of continuous wave ultrasound, however, introduces ambiguity into the measurements. Although the ultrasonic head position sensor makes twelve measurements from which head-position information can be derived, there is a wave length ambiguity in each of the measurements. The measurements are made quite precisely within a wave, but do not tell which wave is being measured. Because the wavelength of sound at 40 kHz in air is about 1/3 of an inch, each of the twelve measurements is ambiguous at 1/3 inch intervals. Because the computer keeps track of complete changes in phase, the ambiguity in the measurements shows up as a constant error in the measured distance. This error can be thought of as the "initialization error" of the system. It is the difference between the computer's original guess of the initial path length and the true initial path length.

We believe that the initialization errors can be resolved by using the geometric redundancy inherent in making twelve measurements. We have gone to considerable effort to write programs for the ultrasonic head position sensor. These programs embody several techniques to resolve the measurement ambiguities. Although we have had some encouraging results, a full report on the ultrasonic head position sensor is not yet possible.

The perspective transformation

Generating a perspective image of three dimensional information is relatively easy. Let us suppose that the information is represented in a coordinate system based on the observer's eye as shown in Figure 6. If the two-dimensional scope coordinates, X_s and Y_s, are thought of as extending from -1 to $+1$, simple geometric reasoning will show that the position at which a particular point should be displayed on the screen is related to its position in three-dimensional space by the simple relations:

$$X_s = \frac{x'}{z'} \cotan \frac{\alpha}{2}$$

$$Y_s = \frac{y'}{z'} \cotan \frac{\alpha}{2}$$

If an orthogonal projection is desired, it can be obtained by making the value of z' constant. Because the perspective (or orthogonal) projection of a straight line in three-dimensional space is a straight line, division by the z' coordinate need be performed only for the endpoints of the line. The two-dimensional analog line-

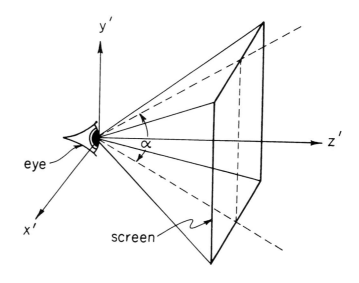

FIGURE 6—The x', y', z' coordinates system based on the observer's eye position

generating equipment can fill in the center portion of a three-dimensional line by drawing a two-dimensional line. The digital perspective generator computes values only for the endpoint coordinates of a line.

The three-dimensional information to be presented by the three-dimensional display is stored in the computer in a fixed three-dimensional coordinate system. Because this coordinate system is based on the room around the user, we have chosen to call it the "room" coordinate system. The drawing data in the room coordinate system is represented in homogeneous coordinates. This means that each three-dimensional point or end of a three-dimensional line is stored as four separate numbers. The first three correspond to the ordinary X Y and Z coordinates of three-dimensional space. The fourth coordinate, usually called W, is a scale factor which tells how big a value of X Y or Z represents a unit distance. Far distant material may thus easily be represented by making the scale factor, W, small. Infinitely distant points are represented by setting the scale factor, W, to zero, in which case the first three coordinates represent only the direction to the point. Nearby points are usually represented by setting the scale factor, W, to its largest possible value, in which case the other three coordinates are just the familiar fixed-point representations of X Y and Z.

The matrix multiplier

We have designed and built a digital matrix multiplier to convert information dynamically from the fixed "room" coordinate system to the moving "eye" coordinate system. The matrix multiplier stores a four-by-four matrix of 18 bit fixed-point numbers. Because the drawing data are represented in homogeneous coordinates, the single four-by-four matrix multiplication provides for both translation and rotation.[2] The matrix multiplier accepts the four 18 bit numbers which represent an endpoint, treating them as a four-component vector which it multiplies by the four-by-four matrix. The result is a four-component vector, each component of which is truncated to 20 bits. The matrix multiplier delivers this 80 bit answer to the clipping divider in approximately 5 microseconds. It therefore performs about three million scalar multiplications per second.

The matrix multiplier uses a separate multiplier module for each column. Each module contains an accumulator, a partial product register, storage for the four matrix elements in that column, and the multiplication logic. The entries of a row of the matrix serve simultaneously as four separate multiplicands. An individual component of the incoming vector serves as the common multiplier. The four multiplications for a single row are thus performed simultaneously. For additional speed, the bits of the multiplier are examined four at a time rather than individually to control multiple-input adding arrays.

The clipping or windowing task

The job of the clipping divider is to accept three-dimensional information in the eye coordinate system and convert it to appropriate two-dimensional endpoints for display. If both ends of the line are visible, the clipping divider needs merely to perform four divisions, one for each two-dimensional coordinate of each end of the line. Enough equipment has been provided in the clipping divider to perform these four divisions simultaneously.

If the endpoints of a line are not within the observer's field of view, the clipping divider must decide whether any portion of the line is within the field of view. If so it must compute appropriate endpoints for that portion as illustrated in Figure 7. Lines outside the field of view or behind the user must be eliminated. Operation of the clipping divider is described in a separate paper[4] in this issue.

Like the matrix multiplier, the clipping divider is an independently-timed digital device which provides for its own input and output synchronization. It has an input and an output flag which provide for orderly flow of information through the clipping divider. If a line lies entirely outside the field of view, the clipping divider will accept a new input without ever raising its output flag. Thus only the visible portions of lines that are all or partly visible get through the clipping divider.

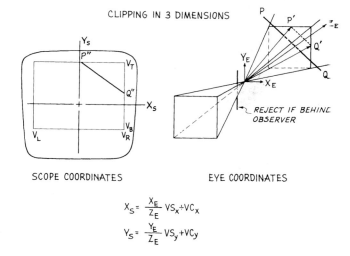

$$X_S = \frac{X_E}{Z_E} VS_x + VC_x$$

$$Y_S = \frac{Y_E}{Z_E} VS_y + VC_y$$

FIGURE 7—Clipping and perspective projection in three dimensions

Results

I did some preliminary three-dimensional display experiments during late 1966 and early 1967 at the MIT Lincoln Laboratory. We had a relatively crude optical system which presented information to only one of the observer's eyes. The ultrasonic head position sensor operated well enough to measure head position for a few minutes before cumulative errors were objectionable. The coordinate transformations and perspective computations were performed by software in the TX-2. The clipping operation was not provided: if any portion of a line was off the screen, the entire line disappeared.

Even with this relatively crude system, the three dimensional illusion was real. Users naturally moved to positions appropriate for the particular views they desired. For instance, the "size" of a displayed cube could be measured by noting how far the observer must move to line himself up with the left face or the right face of the cube.

Two peculiar and as yet unexplained phenomena occurred in the preliminary experiment. First, because the displayed information consisted of transparent "wire-frame" images, ambiguous interpretations were still possible. In one picture a small cube was placed above a larger one giving the appearance of a chimney on a house. From viewpoints below the roof where the "chimney" was seen from inside, some concentration was required to remember that the chimney was in fact further away than the building. Experience with physical objects insisted that if it was to be seen, the chimney must be in front.

A second peculiar phenomenon occurred during the display of the bond structure of cyclo-hexane as shown in Figure 8. Observers not familiar with the rippling hexagonal shape of this molecule misinterpreted its shape. Because their view of the object was limited to certain directions, they could not get the top view of the molecule, the view in which the hexagonal shape is most clearly presented. Observers familiar with molecular shapes, however, recognized the object as cyclo-hexane.

In more recent experiments with the improved optical system and vastly improved computation capability, two kinds of objects have been displayed. In one test, a "room" surrounding the user is displayed. The room is shown in Figure 9 as it would look from outside. The room has four walls marked N, S, E, and W, a ceiling marked C and a floor marked F. An observer fairly quickly accommodates to the idea of being inside the displayed room and can view whatever portion of the room he wishes by turning his head. In another test a small cube was displayed in the center of the user's operating area. The user can examine it from whatever side he desires.

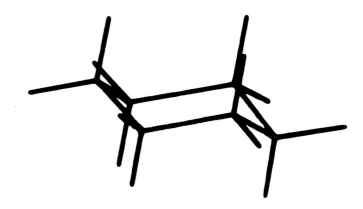

FIGURE 8—A computer-displayed perspective view of the cyclo-hexane molecule

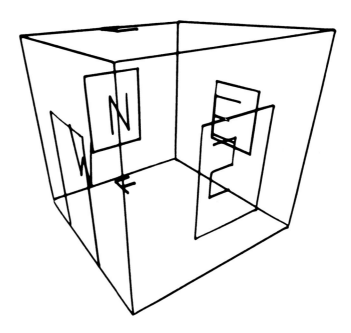

FIGURE 9—A computer-displayed perspective view of the "room" as seen from outside

The biggest surprise we have had to date is the favorable response of users to good stereo. The two-tube optical system presents independent images to each eye. A mechanical adjustment is available to accommodate to the different pupil separations of different users. Software adjustments in our test programs also permit us to adjust the virtual eye separation used for the stereo computations. With these two adjustments it is quite easy to get very good stereo presentations. Observers capable of stereo vision uniformly remark on the realism of the resulting images.

ACKNOWLEDGMENT

When I started work on the head-mounted display I had no idea how much effort would be involved. The project would have died many times but for the spirit of the many people who have become involved. The ultrasonic head-position sensor was designed and built at the MIT Lincoln Laboratory by Charles Seitz and Stylianos Pezaris and is available for our continued use through the cooperation of Lincoln Group 23. Seitz, as a Harvard employee, later designed the matrix multiplier. Robert Sproull, a most exceptionally capable Harvard Senior, simulated, designed most of, built parts of, and debugged the clipping divider. Two graduate students, Ted Lee and Dan Cohen have been an essential part of the project throughout. Our many arguments about perspective presentation, clipping, hidden-line algorithms, and other subjects form one of the most exciting educational experiences I have had. Ted Lee's programs to display curved surfaces in stereo have been the basis for many experiments. Cohen's programs to exercise the entire system form the basis of the demonstrations we can make. I would also like to thank Quintin Foster who supervised construction and debugging of the equipment. And finally, Stewart Ogden, so called "project engineer," actually chief administrator, who defended us all from the pressures of paperwork so that something could be accomplished.

REFERENCES

1. B F GREEN Jr
   Figure coherence in the kinetic depth effect
   Journal of Experimental Psychology Vol 62 No 3 272-282 1961
2. L G ROBERTS
   Machine perception of three-dimensional solids
   MIT Lincoln Laboratory Technical Report No 315 May 22 1963
3. L G ROBERTS
   Homogeneous matrix representation and manipulation of N-dimensional constructs
   The Computer Display Review Adams Associates May 1965
4. R F SPROULL I E SUTHERLAND
   A clipping divider
   Proceedings of the Fall Joint Computer Conference 1968 this issue
5. D COHEN
   A program for drawing bodies with the hidden lines removed
   A term-project for course 6.539 MIT Fall 1965
6. H T HAYNES
   A computer method for perspective drawing
   Master's Thesis Texas A&M University Aug 1966
7. P LOUTREL
   A solution to the hidden-line problem for computer-drawn polyhedra
   New York University Technical Report 400-167 (Thesis) Bronx New York September 1967
8. A APPEL
   The notion of quantitative invisibility and the machine rendering of solids
   Proceedings of 22nd National Conference ACM
   ACM Publication p 67 Thompson Book Company Washington DC 1967
9. Mathematical Spplications Group Inc (MAGI)
   3-D simulated graphics
   Datamation February 1968
10. J E WARNOCK
    A hidden line algorithm for halftone picture representation
    University of Utah Technical Report 4-5 May 1968
11. Equipment installed at the Manned Space Craft Center at Houston Texas. The project is under the direction of the General Electric Company Electronics Laboratory under NASA Contract No NAS 9-3916
12. L G ROBERTS
    The Lincoln wand
    MIT Lincoln Laboratory Report June 1966
13. A C TRAUB
    Stereoscopic display using rapid varifocal mirror oscillations
    Applied Optics Vol 6 number 6 June 1967
14. P VLAHOS
    The three-dimensional display: Its cues and techniques
    Journal of the Society for Information Display Vol 2 Number 6 Nov/Dec 1965
15. R LAND I E SUTHERLAND
    Real time color stereo computer displays
    To be published in Applied Optics

Scientific Applications
C.L. Lawson, Editor

Scanned-Display Computer Graphics

A. Michael Noll
Bell Telephone Laboratories, Inc.
Murray Hill, New Jersey

A television-like scanned-display system has been successfully implemented on a Honeywell DDP-224 computer installation. The scanned image is stored in the core memory of the computer, and software scan conversion is used to convert the rectangular coordinates of a point to the appropriate word and bit in an output display array in core storage. Results thus far indicate that flicker-free displays of large amounts of data are possible with reasonably fast graphical interaction. A scanned image of size 240 × 254 points is displayed at a 30 frame-per-second rate.

Key Words and Phrases: computer graphics, scanned-display, scan conversion, raster displays
CR Categories: 4.41, 6.35

Prologue. The search for the simple inexpensive graphics terminal for interactive man-machine communication has continued for many years. Various terminals have been proposed, developed, implemented, used, and found to be lacking in either simplicity, inexpensiveness, or effectiveness of interaction.

Introduction

For many years now, a simple dot-plotting cathode-ray tube has been used for graphical output from a Honeywell DDP-224 computer used for speech research and man-machine communication research at Bell Telephone Laboratories [1]. Since experience demonstrated that most hardware line and character generators were relatively expensive or a continuing source of trouble, lines and characters were drawn as a series of closely-spaced dots. Unfortunately only about 4000 dots could be displayed before flicker became intolerable because sufficient time had to be allowed for the transient response of the electron beam deflection for the display applications using the DDP-224. Also, considerable amounts of core storage were required for the x-axis and y-axis coordinate pairs for each dot. One solution to these two problems was to output the data points from a single large output buffer of fixed length in a uniform manner so that the electron beam could be uniformly swept or scanned across the face of the screen. Hence, a scanned-display system was implemented for use with the Honeywell DDP-224 computer installation.

The idea of a scanned display is not new [2]. However, scanned output for general purpose fast-interaction computer graphics is presently somewhat novel even though one such system is already in active use at the Brookhaven National Laboratory [3]. There are, however, some unique problems associated with scanned displays for general purpose fast-interaction computer graphics, and the particular solutions strongly differentiate actual implementations and their flexibility. This paper explores these problems and describes in detail one particular implementation. The actual implemented system is described first and this is followed by a discussion of the various compromises, problems, and alternatives which affected the design of the actual implementation.

Implementation

General Description

The scanned-display system as presently implemented on a Honeywell DDP-224 computer installation is shown in block diagram form in Figure 1. A given pair of (x, y) coordinates of a point to be displayed is converted by suitable software to a corresponding word and bit in an output array in the computer's core storage.

A single-bit code or a two-bit code can be used so that either two-brightness or four-brightness levels are available, respectively. The image size is 240 × 254

Reprinted with permission from Communications of the ACM Vol. 14, No. 3, March 1971, 143-150.

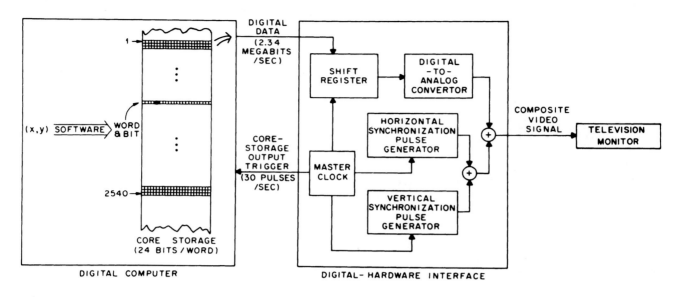

Fig. 1. Block diagram of scanned-display system as presently implemented on a Honeywell DDP-224 computer installation. Software scan conversion is used to convert (x, y) coordinates to their appropriate word-bits in an output array in core storage. A digital hardware interface converts the information stored in this output array into an analog video signal which is used as input to a television monitor. The television monitor has been modified to run at a rate slower than conventional television.

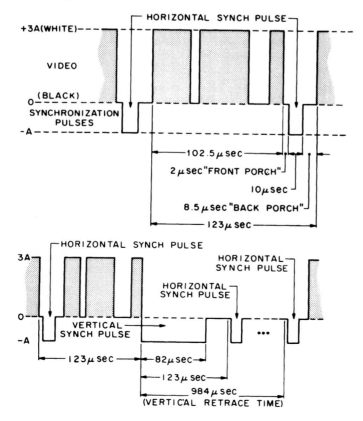

Fig. 2. Waveform timing specifications for the horizontal and vertical synchronization pulses for compatibility with the PICTUREPHONE® Mod II

points, and the output array containing the scanned image consists of 2540 words for the single-bit code or 5080 words for the two-bit code for the 24-bit word length of the DDP-224.

The actual final display is produced on a Conrac television monitor which has been modified to operate at a faster rate of 8130 lines per second, approximately half the rate of American commercial television. The modified monitor requires an input signal consisting of negative horizontal and vertical synchronization pulses and positive pulses for the potentially visible portions of each scan across the face of the television picture tube. The potentially visible scan signal is commonly called the video signal; the video signal together with the synchronization pulses is called the composite video signal.

A digital hardware interface is used for generating the required video signal and synchronization pulses. All of this hardware is controlled by a single oscillator from which the appropriate pulses are derived for sequentially outputting each word in the computer's display array into a single-word buffer, for shifting the bits of this single word, for converting these shifted bits to an analog video signal, and for producing the vertical and horizontal synchronization pulses. The video signal and synchronization pulses are added together to produce the composite video signal which is finally used as input to the television monitor. Standard Honeywell digital circuit cards were used to construct the digital hardware interface.

This scanned display offers the advantages of low cost and simplicity since the scan technology borrows strongly from conventional television while the scanned image is stored in excess core storage in the DDP-224 computer. The faster specifications are reasonably close to the PICTUREPHONE® specifications so that the PICTUREPHONE® switching network and terminal become applicable to interactive computer graphics.

The following subsections describe the implementation in more detail.

Display Specifications

The PICTUREPHONE® Mod II B raster specifications require 102.5 μsec for the potentially visible portion of each horizontal scan and 255 potentially visible horizontal scan lines. To be compatible with this vertical resolution, each horizontal line is sampled at 240 points or ten 24-bit words for the DDP-224 computer. This horizontal sampling means that the DDP-224 must output in 102.5 μsec a number of words equal to ten (240 points/24 bits per word) times the number of bits per point. The implementation using only one bit per point thereby results in a maximum output rate from the DDP-224 computer of 240 bits in 102.5 μsec or approximately 2.3 megabits per second (98,000 words per second). Similarly, the master clock must run at approximately 2.3 MHz so that the final composite video signal meets the proper raster specifications.

The display uses a 2-to-1 interlace with a complete picture every 1/30 second. However, 8130 lines per second ($\pm 1.0\%$), approximately half that of conventional commercial television, are used with 271 lines per picture of which 255 lines are potentially visible image and 16 lines are vertical blanking and synchronization. Each half picture consists of 127.5 lines (984 μsec) vertical blanking and synchronization. The wave form timings are shown in Figure 2.

Figure 3 depicts the odd and even scan lines. A half line occurs at the top and bottom of a complete picture. Since these two half lines would complicate programming somewhat, they have been made invisible, and no data is stored in the computer for them. The result is a 240 × 254 image. The odd interlace lines occupy the first half of the display array in the computer; the even interlace lines occupy the second half.

Software

The operation of changing the (x, y) coordinates of some point to the corresponding word and bit in the scan-display output array is called scan conversion. Software scan conversion is accomplished by performing the following relatively simple calculations for the single-bit code.

The first half of the output array consists of the odd interlace lines, and hence odd y-axis coordinates must be placed in the first half of the output array. This is determined by simply examining the least significant bit of the y-axis coordinate. The determination of the word and bit in the appropriate half of the output array is accomplished by dividing the y-axis coordinate by two. The quotient is multiplied by the bit length of the x-axis scan (here 240), the x-axis coordinate is added to this product, and finally this sum is divided by the bit length of a word in the memory buffer (24 bits for the DDP-224 computer). The quotient indicates the word in memory while the remainder indicates which bit in memory should be set to either 0 or 1 for the appropriate brightness level. A subroutine requiring approximately 200 μsec of computer time for each coordinate pair was written for performing these calculations.

A graphics software package was already available for drawing lines and dots on a conventional cathode-ray-tube display. Since the lines were drawn as a series of closely spaced dots, this graphics package was easily modified for scan output by using the (x, y) coordinates of the dots as input to the scan conversion subroutine which performed the scan conversion and changed the appropriate bit in the scan-display array. The subroutine for displaying dots was similarly modified. Characters are produced from a 5 × 7 matrix of dots. Subroutines for stereoscopic projections are also included in the scan-display graphics package. The stereoscopic projection subroutine package requires about 160 (decimal) locations while the scan graphics subroutine package requires a little less than 700 (decimal) locations including the character table required by the character subroutine.

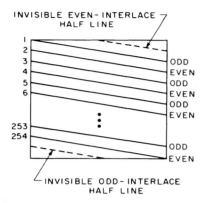

Fig. 3. Odd and even interlace scan lines. The half lines at the top and bottom have been made invisible to simplify programming somewhat.

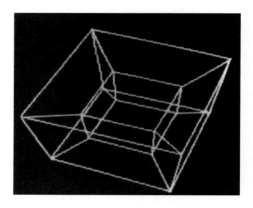

Fig. 4. Photograph of the scanned-display television screen showing the perspective projection of a four-dimensional hypercube which can be rotated in real-time

Examples

Figure 4 is a photograph of the television screen showing the perspective projection of a four-dimensional hypercube which can be rotated in real-time [4]. The available character set and their corresponding octal codes are shown in Figure 5 as photographed directly from the display screen; a 5 × 7 dot matrix is used to form each character. A full page of text of a program listing is shown in Figure 6. Speech spectrograms have been displayed, as shown in Figure 7, by equalizing and quantizing the spectrum to two levels [5].

All of the programs and applications thus far investigated indicate that real-time interaction with flicker-free displays of large quantities of data is possible with suitable, careful programming. All of the main programs of the preceding examples were written in FORTRAN once again affirming FORTRAN's usefulness and appropriateness for interactive-display programming.

Discussion

Television

In general, the deflection speed of conventional cathode-ray tube displays limits the amount of data which can be displayed flicker-free. The output from the computer could be organized in such a way as to minimize the distance between each point to be displayed so that the beam could be moved at a faster rate. Alternatively, or in conjunction with output data organization, incremental displays in which the changes in (x, y) positions of the electron beam are specified rather than the actual (x, y) positions themselves could be used. However, as one outputs more and more data from the computer, these techniques, when optimized, all approach a uniform scan across the face of the display tube. The voltages for controlling the x-axis and y-axis movements of the electron beam become completely periodic, and the computer need only control the beam intensity to produce an image.

The deflection circuitry would only be a duplication of much of the circuitry of a conventional television set, since conventional television already utilizes a uniform scanning scheme, and the required circuits for vertical and horizontal deflection are already built into the television set. It is indeed tempting to use a conventional television set as a computer graphics display terminal.

Although the deflection circuits are built into a conventional television set, the set requires synchronization pulses for synchronizing the horizontal and vertical deflection of the beam with the corresponding changes in the electron beam intensity. Hence, some form of electronic equipment or interface between the computer and television set is required to generate both the synchronization pulses and the beam intensity or video signal, or alternatively, the computer might calculate the complete composite video signal. Since the synchronization information is always the same, it is easier for this information to be generated externally and for the computer to specify only the changing video signal.

Storage of the Scanned Image

Once the computer has calculated the scanned image, this information must be stored and repetitively used to determine the composite video signal. This repetitive cyclic nature of the scanned image immediately suggests a rotating magnetic drum or disk as an appropriate storage medium [3, 6]. However, refreshing the data stored on the drum or disk becomes a problem, since new information cannot be written by the computer until the appropriate location on the drum or disk passes the write head. This means that any data to be changed must be prepared to be in the same sequence as the information stored on the disk or drum. Otherwise, the computer would have to wait one drum or disk cycle until the appropriate location came around again. In other words, drums and disks are not randomly addressable, and this leads to software complications.

Fig. 5. (*Top*) Photograph of the television screen showing the available character set and corresponding octal codes. A 5 × 7 dot matrix is used to form each character.

Fig. 6 (*Bottom*) Photograph of the television screen showing a page of text of a program listing. Twenty-one lines of 40 characters each are easily readable.

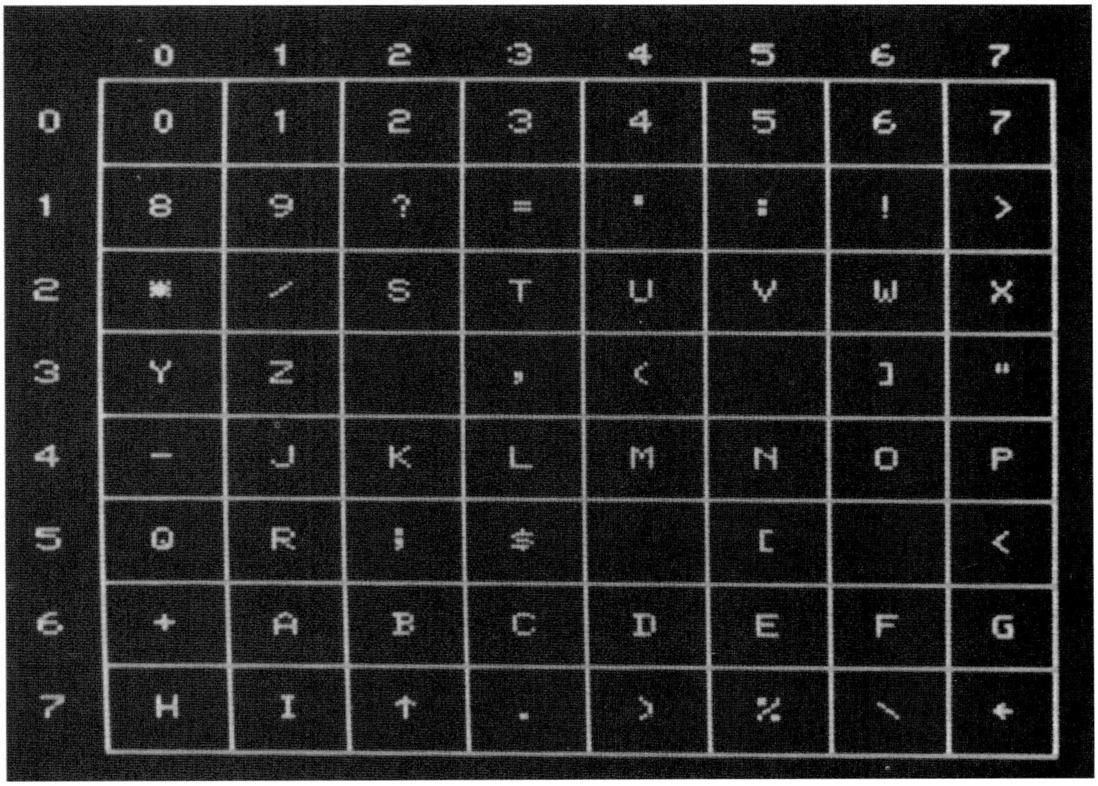

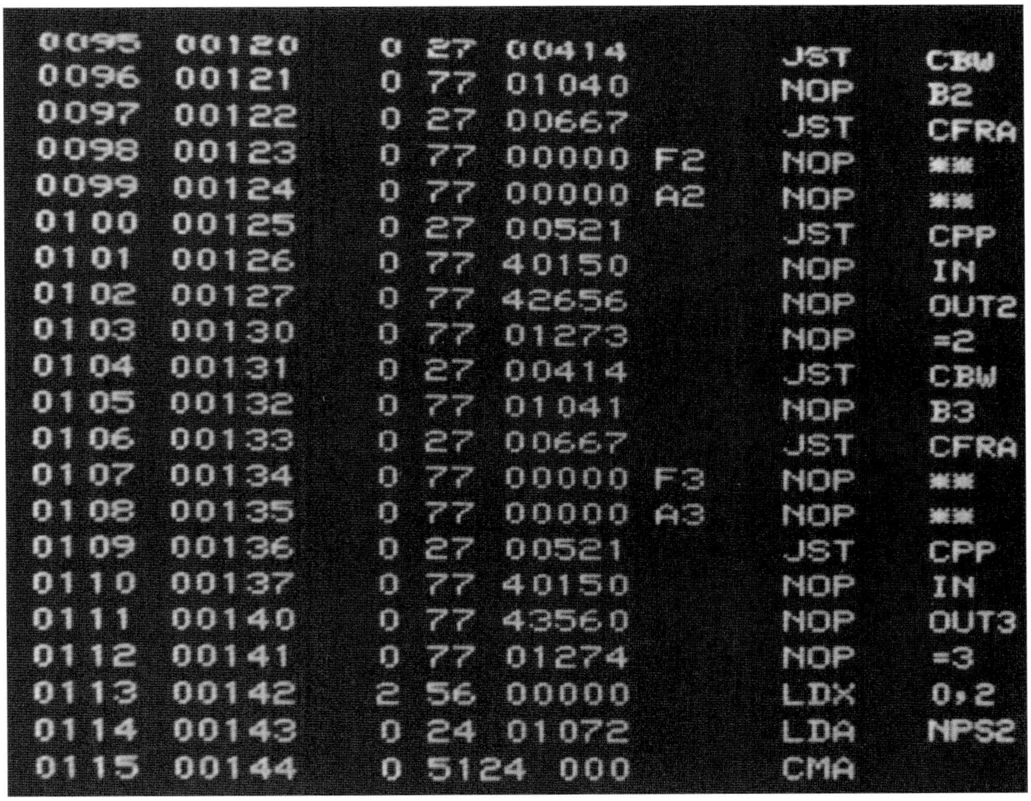

Also, since drums and disks are pieces of rotating machinery, they are mechanically complicated and expensive and must be carefully maintained.

A separate addressable digital core storage eliminates the disadvantages of drums and disks. However, if the complete image must be changed quickly, then the data transfer from the computer to the separate core storage must occur in one picture cycle or at the maximum data transfer rate. Hence, the separate core storage is superfluous if the computer itself has a sufficiently large core storage and if the complete image must be changed often. An external, addressable digital core storage would be applicable if only small portions of the complete image were to be changed infrequently. However, the output from this external core storage to the television interface would have to be at the maximum date rate, although the data channel between the computer and the external core storage could operate at a much slower rate.

If two bits were used to determine the intensity of each point of scanned image of size 240×254 on a computer with a word size of 24 bits, then a total of 5080 words $(2 \times 240 \times 254/24)$ would be required to store the scanned image in the computer's memory. Suppose some time-sharing application were envisioned using a large number of scanned displays, then each separate display would require something in the vicinity of 5080 words. Quite obviously core storage space would disappear quickly for such an application, but the recent advances in technology would imply that low-cost, small-sized, low-power digital memories are only a few years away. Thus, allocation of 5080 words, or some similar order of magnitude of the computer's core storage, does not seem unreasonable in terms of foreseeable technological advances.

Scan Conversion

The scanned image is stored in the computer's core storage as an array of successive locations with individual groups of bits determining the voltage level of the video signal. However, most calculations performed within the computer are in terms of (x, y) coordinates. Hence, each (x, y) coordinate pair for graphic output must be converted to the appropriate bit or bits in the appropriate word in the display array. Such conversion from (x, y) coordinates to word-bits is called scan conversion, and can be done either by analog hardware or software.

In analog hardware scan conversion, the scan conversion is performed externally to the computer. A conventional cathode-ray tube being driven by (x, y) coordinates from the computer might be used as an intermediate output. The face of this cathode-ray tube would be scanned electronically by an image orthicon tube, thereby resulting in the desired scan conversion. Alternatively, a vidicon or a direct image converter might be used. The scanned signal might then be stored either in analog form or in digital form after sampling and quantization. However, these forms of analog hardware scan conversion involve devices which are subject to all the wear and tear, cost, and reliability problems usually associated with fairly complicated analog equipment.

In software scan conversion, the computer calculates the appropriate word and bits from the (x, y) coordinates. This calculation is fairly straightforward and consists of a few simple arithmetic operations. Unfortunately, these simple operations must be performed for each (x, y) coordinate pair, so that the computer calculation time rapidly adds up. The net result is that a small portion of an image can be changed in real-time, but a few seconds of calculation time might be required to change an appreciable portion of an image. However, considerable savings in calculation time are sometimes possible by major changes in programming philosophy as will be described later in this paper. The major advantages of programming flexibility and digital hardware reliability obtained with software scan conversion are strong enough to outweigh any presently available analog hardware scan-conversion schemes.

Programming Philosophy

As was just mentioned, software scan conversion seems to be a reasonably good solution to the incompatibility between the scanned-display storage requirement of word-bits and the computing flexibility of (x, y) coordinates. Including bookkeeping and setup time, software scan conversion takes nearly 200 μsec on the DDP-224 computer for each pair of (x, y) coordinates. This time might not seem too long, but if one were to change a complete 240×254 one-bit picture this way, then 12 seconds would be required! This is certainly not real-time, but then again, only a small portion of the picture is usually changed. This helps the time situation, but with a scanned display one must also remove the old portion of the picture in addition to putting the new portion into the display array. All of this makes for some intriguing programming problems. The following example shows one unique pitfall of scanned displays.

Suppose one has a scanned display showing a line and a single dot. The dot can be moved around the display screen by turning two knobs. As either knob changes, the new (x, y) coordinate pair is given by (IXX, IYY). The required FORTRAN programming must display the dot in the new position (IXX, IYY) and remove the old position (IX, IY). If the background were initially made black by placing all 0's in the output array, then a 0 must be placed in the array position corresponding to (IX, IY), and a 1 must be placed in the array position corresponding to (IXX, IYY). If this dot crosses the line, a problem occurs. The program does not know the line from the background, and placing a 0 in the array position corresponding to (IX, IY) removes the old position of the dot, but since this old position was on the line, one dot making up the line disappears!

This destruction problem can be eliminated by observing the bit in the array position corresponding to (IX, IY) before any change was made. If this bit were a 1, then it is not set to 0 when the dot moves off the line. Although this approach works well for dots, it does not

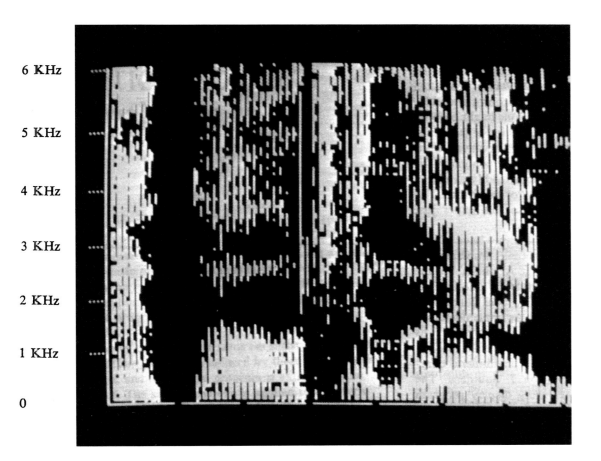

Fig. 7. Photograph of the television screen showing a speech spectrogram. Frequency is plotted along the y-axis, and time is plotted along the x-axis.

work at all for lines, since lines are constructed from interpolated dots, and one does not know in advance the number of dots which might be used.

The experience thus far gained from programming for the scanned-display indicates that completely different graphic capabilities and limitations exist as compared with a conventional (x, y) display. For example, the background of the image can be changed simply by flipping all the bits in the output buffer. However, there are severe problems when one moves one area over a background and formerly hidden portions of the background must be restored, although techniques analogous to video mixing are quite applicable [7]. Also, simple shifts of portions of the picture are most efficiently handled on the word-bit level. All of this leads to bit manipulating software, perhaps referenced to (x, y) coordinates when appropriate. The software would require some hierarchical structure and would perhaps be something like a FORTRAN-callable movie language [8]. Unfortunately, such a software package is not yet available for the scanned-display, but it is nevertheless an absolute necessity if the unique and real-time capabilities of scanned displays are to be exploited fully.

Some Future Predictions and Their Implications

As mentioned before, the DDP-224 computer could output two bits for each point in the scanned image. Although these two bits could be used to give four intensity levels in a black and white display, they could almost as easily be decoded to give four different colors in a color display. The design of such a scanned color display is presently in progress. A conventional color television set is being modified to work at the slower raster rate while the interface need only decode the two bits and set corresponding voltages for the red, blue, and green video signals. The programmer would assign different color mixtures for the four two-bit configurations at the beginning of the program by a call to a color-code assignment subroutine. These color assignments could be changed later as many times as desired, and the color display would change appropriately.

The implementation described in this paper using a PICTUREPHONE®-raster modified television monitor strongly demonstrates the future applicability of PICTUREPHONE® terminals and switching networks for general purpose fast-interaction computer graphics. A somewhat limited computer graphics display capability for the PICTUREPHONE® for displaying text in a slow interactive mode has already been implemented for commercial PICTUREPHONE® service [9]. However, the experience gained in using the implementation described in this paper emphasizes the applicability and, in some cases, the absolute necessity of a scanned-display for presenting large amounts of graphical data in an interactive man-machine environment. Computer graphics might easily become a prime application with graphical data readily switched and transmitted from computer to computer and to man as PICTUREPHONE® service becomes available. The present PICTUREPHONE® specifications might become more flexible to meet possible demands for higher resolution for computer applications. The PICTUREPHONE® in some form might thus emerge as a strong contender for the role of the extremely effective and readily available man-machine communication facility of the future. The search mentioned in the Prologue to this paper just might be finally over

Acknowledgments. Scanned-displays have been talked about for many years and actually implemented in a nontelevision format. Mr. George A. Michael of the Lawrence Radiation Laboratory strongly affected me with his verbal proposals, while Dr. Bela Julesz was responsible for an early scanned-display implementation at Bell Labs. The hardware described in this paper was designed by Mr. John J. Dubnowski, while the general purpose subroutine for generating alphanumeric characters was written by Miss Martha J. Southern. The spectrogram program and the listing display program were written by Mrs. Ellen S. Kippel and Mrs. Barbara E. Caspers, respectively. The continual encouragement and innumerable discussions with Dr. Peter B. Denes contributed greatly to the ideas and their implementation as described in this paper.

Received March 1970; revised October 1970

References

1. Denes, P. B., and Mathews, M. V. The laboratory computer: its power and how to make it work for you. *Proc. IEEE 58*, 4 (Apr. 1970), 520–530.
2. Gelernter, H. L., Birnbaum, J., Mikelsons, M., Russell, J. D., Cochrane, F., Groff, D., Schofield, J. F., and Bromley, D. A. An advanced computer-based nuclear physics data acquisition system. *Nucl. Instr. Meth. 54*, 1 (Sept. 1967), 77–90.
3. Ophir, D., Rankowitz, S., Shepherd, B. J., and Spinrad, R. J. BRAD: the Brookhaven raster display. *Comm. ACM 11*, 6 (June 1968), 415–416.
4. Noll, A. Michael. A computer technique for displaying n-dimensional hyperobjects. *Comm. ACM 10* (Aug. 1967), 469–473.
5. Mermelstein, P. Spectrogram displays from computers. *IEEE Trans. Audio & Electroacoustics* (Mar. 1971), 19.
6. McDonald, H. S., Ninke, W. H., and Weller, D. R. A direct-view CRT console for remote computing. 1967 Intern. Solid-State Circuits Conf. Digest of Papers, pp. 68–69.
7. Rougelot, Rodney S. The General Electric computed color TV display. In *Pertinent Concepts in Computer Graphics*, M. Faiman and J. Nievergelt, Eds., U. of Illinois Press, Urbana, Ill., 1969, pp. 261–281.
8. Knowlton, Kenneth C. A computer technique for producing animated movies. Proc. AFIPS 1964 SJCC, Vol. 25, Spartan Books, New York, pp. 67–87.
9. *Bell Laboratories Record 47*, 5 (May-June 1969).

DISTRIBUTING A VISIBLE SURFACE ALGORITHM OVER MULTIPLE PROCESSORS*

Henry Fuchs
The University of Texas at Dallas
Richardson, Texas

ABSTRACT

Described is a procedure for executing a visible surface algorithm in a new multi-microprocessor system which utilizes distributed image and depth ("Z") buffers. It is shown that despite image distribution over a large number of processing and memory units, object coherence can still be maintained and used to reduce the number of calculations needed to generate a continuous-tone visible surface image.

Key words and phrases: Visible surface algorithms, multi-processing, microprocessors, three-dimensional computer graphics

CR Categories: 8.2, 6.22, 6.35, 4.32

INTRODUCTION

Visible surface algorithms which generate continuous-tone, most often video, images have always been computationally expensive. It is easy to see why this is so. Such an algorithm has to calculate an appropriate intensity value for each picture element ("pixel") in the image array.

In order to do this, it first has to determine which object in the scene is closest to the viewer of all the objects which cover that particular pixel. (It is this closest object which will be visible and will obscure any objects behind it.) Once this closest object is found, the intensity of the pixel is calculated, based on 1) the shade assigned to that closest object surface, 2) the angle of the surface to the viewer, and 3) the illumination to the object surface. (This procedure is most lucidly explained in Blinn (1976).)

To find the object which is closest to the viewer at a particular picture element, all the object definition components -- usually planar tiles ("polygons") -- are sorted, in order, along all three axes: X and Y, the horizontal and vertical directions in the image, and Z, the distance away from the image. Sutherland (1973) has classified many of the major visible surface algorithms based largely on the order of the axes in which this sorting is performed. The classic algorithm by Watkins (1970), for example, uses a Y, X, Z sort, first sorting all the object polygons along Y -- from top to bottom of the image, according to the tops of each polygon, then for all the polygons which intersect a particular Y value (a scan line) it sorts along X, left to right, by the position at which each polygon first "appears." Then, for a particular X value of interest along the scan line, it sorts by Z all polygons which appear there, from front to back. The polygon at the head of this list is the one visible at the particular pixel at this X,Y location.

Sutherland (1973) notes that the major efficiency gained by these algorithms is the reliance on a high degree of picture coherence; that is, the structure and appearance of the image at a given pixel or line is almost always very similar to its structure and appearance at an adjacent pixel or line. This fact, together with the ease of updating the sorted list values at the previous pixel or line, allows the closest-object sort to be executed not from the beginning at each pixel, but simply as a modification of the sort's result at a previously calculated adjacent pixel or line. In general, for a Watkins-type algorithm (as well as for the one to be described below) this update consists of 1) updating all the polygon elements in the sorted list from the previous pixel to obtain each element's Z value at the new pixel location, 2) culling this sorted list to remove all those polygons for which a terminal edge has been encountered and which thus do not appear in the current pixel, and 3) merging this culled, but still sorted list with the sorted list of all those object polygons which have an entering edge here and thus begin to appear at this current pixel. Minimizing the number of steps in this update process is crucial to the effectiveness of the resulting algorithm. It will be shown that the new distributed algorithm can also perform such efficient updating, and in fact needs to update only a single polygon at any one time.

---

*This work was supported in part by NSF Grant MCS-77-03905

Reprinted with permission from *Proceedings of the ACM National Conference* 1977, 449-451.

The algorithm for the new distributed system is most similar to a "Z buffer" algorithm, as described by Catmull (1974). Such an algorithm uses two buffers, each containing a cell for each pixel in the image: the "image" or "frame" buffer contains the intensity of the image at each pixel, the other, the "Z" buffer contains at each pixel the distance from the viewer of the closest object surface which has so far been encountered for that particular pixel. The "image" buffer is initialized to some arbitrary background intensity — usually white or black. (Generalizations to color images are not included in this discussion, but they are straightforward.) The Z buffer elements are each initialized to the maximum possible value. In this algorithm no sorting is necessary; rather, the polygons can be treated individually, in any order. For each polygon, each pixel which is covered by the polygon is considered. The Z value of the polygone at this pixel is calculated. It is compared with that pixel's current value in the Z buffer. If the new polygon's value if greater, then there must have been a previous polygon which covered this pixel which was closer to the viewer; so processing of the current polygon at this pixel is aborted and processing continues with the calculation of the polygon's Z value at the next pixel. If, however, the new polygon's Z value is smaller than the value in the Z buffer, then this new polygon is closer than the closest previously encountered one; thus, 1) the new polygon's value is stored in the Z buffer, and 2) an intensity for this polygon's surface at this pixel is calculated and stored in this pixel's image buffer. After all the pixels covered by the current polygon are considered, another polygon is processed. After all the polygons have been processed, the Z buffer contains, at each pixel, the distance of the closest polygonal surface at that pixel, and the image buffer contains the intensity of this closest — and thus visible — surface.

SYSTEM ARCHITECTURE AND ALGORITHM STRUCTURE

The multi-processor system on which the algorithm is to be implemented is based on a variable number of processing elements and a variable number of memory units over which the image and Z buffers are distributed. The system architecture and implementation are described in detail in Fuchs and Johnson (1977). In this paper only those details necessary to understand the algorithm will be described.

The system (see Figure 1) consists of a number of processing elements — usually a power of 2 — and a number of memory units, usually some power of 2 multiple of the number of processing elements, some of which make up the image buffer, and others which make up the Z buffer. The spatial resolution desired for the image determines the number of memory units which are needed. The image buffer memory units are dual ported with alternate accesses allocated to the video scan generator which constantly displays onto a video monitor the current contents of the distributed image buffer. The remaining memory cycles can be utilized by the processing element connected to the memory unit.

Each processing element contains a CPU, local program and data store and is connected to some number of memory units. All the processing elements simultaneously receive data, in the form of polygon vertices, from the central broadcast controller which is the system's sole interface with the host computer. Upon receiving a polygon's definition, each processing element performs a Z buffer-like algorithm on the parts of the image which are covered by this polygon and are under the processing element's control. When a processing element has completed its calculations for the current polygon, it signals the central broadcaster by raising the value on a one-bit output "done" line. This line, controlled by an open-collector gate at each processing element, will only go high after all the processing elements have signalled "done." Since a polygon will generally occupy a slightly different number of pixels in the various processing elements' buffers, the processing completion times will be staggered. When the broadcast controller detects that the "done" line has gone positive, it will begin to transmit the vertices of the next polygon to all the processing elements. This over-all sequence is repeated until all the polygons have been processed and the entire image generated. (Slightly less overall waiting may occur between transmission periods if more than one polygon description is transmitted at one time. The polygons are then stored by each processing element in its local memory and processed in sequence, with the processing element signalling "done" only after completing all the polygons.)

Clearly the execution time of this system is dependent on the number of steps needed by the most burdened processing element for a particular polygon. Therefore the processing elements and their associated buffers have been interlaced according to the lowest bits of the X and Y image addresses. Figure 2 gives a sample organization of an 8-processor, 16-image-memory system and its image interlacing scheme. Since no two adjacent pixels are located in the same buffer and since no two buffers with adjacent pixels are assigned to the same processing element, it is easy to see that all polygons greater than one pixel in size will be processed by more than one processing element. In general, if a polygon encloses a square region of some modest size — whose area is approximately the number of processing elements — then all the processing elements will be guaranteed to participate in the polygon's pixel calculations.

The regularity of the interleaving pattern allows the system to retain the advantages of picture coherence discussed in the introduction. Thus a processing element can calculate its own next candidate pixel by simply updating its current pixel's X, Y and Z values with increments which are standard for the entire system.

This kind of system has the additional advantage that it doesn't fall into the usual rigid dichotomy of real-time or non-real-time implementations. Current systems tend to fall into one of these two categories because software implementations are usually much too slow for real-time (1/30 second) image generation and thus only very specialized hardware systems can perform image generation "on the fly." Even these systems, however, can only perform with such speed for scenes under a certain level of complexity. Once the particular threshold is exceeded, the hardware cannot keep up with the video scan, and the resulting image degrades rather rapidly.

This distributed algorithm, since it generates the image into a buffer, never suffers from image degradation, it may simply take longer to complete a more complex scene than a less-complicated one. Further, if high speed image generation is desired, with the last completed image in one half of each memory unit constantly being accessed by the video scan generator, while the new image is created in the other half of the memory unit. A single system line could be utilized to switch between the two halves whenever the entire scene -- i.e., all the polygons -- were completed.

If the scene complexity were found to cause execution time to be longer than desired, the system could be reconfigured with additional processing elements. The new configuration, with fewer memory units attached to each processing element, would execute precisely the same algorithm, but taking less time to process each polygon, thus less time to process the entire scene. Alternately less expensive configurations could be constructed with fewer memory processing modules, with a resulting sacrifice in speed of execution and/or spacial resolution. Thus it may now be possible to have the same basic architecture, as well as identical software, and thus basic compatibility between the large, fast real-time systems and the desk-top terminals in offices and laboratories.

ACKNOWLEDGEMENTS

The author wishes to thank Brian Johnson for many helpful discussions, and David Rowe for implementing the initial designs of the memory and processing units.

REFERENCES

[1] Blinn, J. F., and Newell, M. E. Texture and reflection in computer generated images. Comm. ACM 19, 10 (October 1976), 542-546.

[2] Catmull, E. A. Computer display of curved surfaces. Proc. Conf. on Comptr. Graphics, Pattern Recognition, and Data Structure, May 1975, pp. 11-17 (IEEE Cat. No. 75CHO981-1C).

[3] Fuchs, H and Johnson, B. W. A multi-microprocessor system for video graphics. Tech. Rep. MMS-31, Mathematical Sciences, U. of Texas at Dallas, Richardson, Texas, September 1977.

[4] Sutherland, I. E., Sproull, R. F., and Schumaker, R. A. A characterization of ten hidden-surface algorithms. Computing Surveys 6, 1 (March 1974), 1-55.

[5] Watkins, G. S. A real-time visible surface algorithm. Tech. Rep. UTEC-CSC-70-101, Dep. Comptr. Sci., U. of Utah, Salt Lake City, Utah, June 1970.

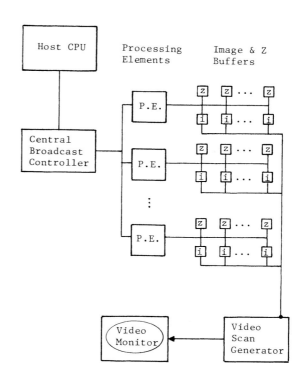

Figure 1: Distributed System Architecture

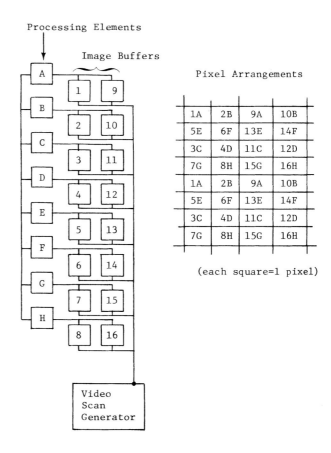

Figure 2: Image Interlacing

A RANDOM-ACCESS VIDEO FRAME BUFFER

James T. Kajiya
Evans & Sutherland Computer Corporation
3 Research Road
Salt Lake City, Utah 84112

Ivan E. Sutherland
The Rand Corporation
1700 Main Street
Santa Monica, California 90406

Edward C. Cheadle
Evans & Sutherland Computer Corporation
3 Research Road
Salt Lake City, Utah 84112

Abstract

This paper described a random-access semiconductor memory designed to drive a shaded-picture television display. The memory provides eight bits per picture element to store a shaded grey-scale picture. The memory has four ports, one for the host computer, one for the TV display, and two which can service an external picture-processing device. A color map, 256 words of 36 bits each, provides for conversion of the eight bit codes into red, green, and blue components of 12 bits each. A flexible addressing and synchronizing system is included to provide for variable picture format and to simplify memory management. Analog deflection signals for precision CRT recording are generated in addition to the RTMA standard TV synchronizing signals. This paper discusses the central design considerations of this type of display system.

INTRODUCTION

Computer processing of photographic images and computer production of synthetic pictures have been topical in recent years [1,2,3]. Considerable success has been achieved in processing digitized pictures in various ways to remove blurring, improve contrast, compensate for geometric distortions, and in other ways to enhance the appearance of the picture. Success has been achieved in producing entirely synthetic pictures from descriptions of the objects to be depicted, the viewing position, and the locations and magnitudes of light sources. Both of these research endeavors have required raster-scan picture output equipment of some kind. This paper describes a random access frame buffer memory and associated display intended to provide flexibility in the presentation and processing of such computer pictures.

The pictures we are interested in are grey scale or "half tone" pictures. For each picture element an eight bit number is used to represent one of 256 levels of intensity to be portrayed at that picture element. When these intensity levels are distributed logarithmically, the 256 levels provide adequate intensity resolution to conceal any intensity quantization effects which might otherwise be visible. In the system described here, enough memory for a 512 by 512 raster is provided. We would have liked to have 24 bits per picture element, eight for each of three colors, but until the cost of memory comes down further, we have contented ourselves with a single grey scale. Colored pictures can be produced by the system using a programmable "color map" which is provided.

We elected to use random access semiconductor memory as the picture memory of the video frame buffer. The random access memory is interfaced to the host computer as a part of its main memory, thus not only providing a degree of accessibility to the picture data not available with shift register or rotating mechanical memory, but also ensuring that any computer to which the video frame buffer is connected with have enough random access memory to store an entire picture. The cost differential for using random access memory seemed in mid-1974, to be small enough that considering its convenience, its secondary role as ordinary computer memory, and the simplicity of design it permits, random access memory was the cost effective choice. We anticipated, and so far quite correctly, that further cost reductions in semiconductor random access memory would be forthcoming.

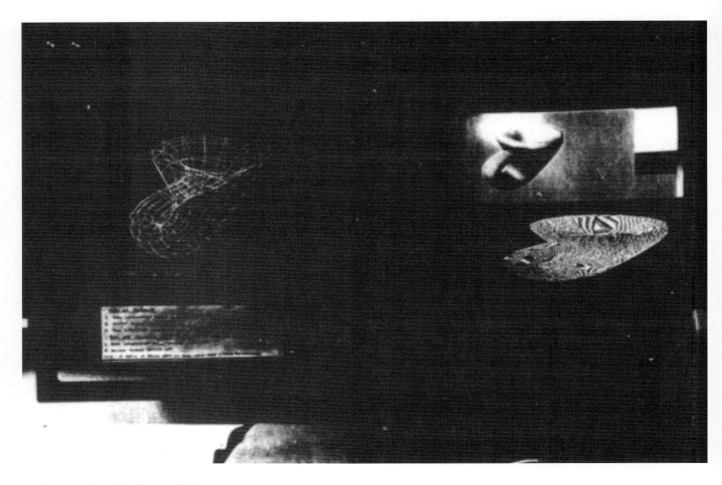

Fig. 1 – The video frame buffer (right) and an E&S PICTURE SYSTEM (left) being used to display a Klein bottle. In this application the lower half of the video frame buffer is being used as ordinary memory to store the range to the nearest surface behind each picture element. The resulting hidden-surface picture is seen in the upper part of the screen. Picture courtesy of Frank Crow, University of Utah.

Moreover, the random accessibility of the memory can itself play an important role in the generation of synthetic pictures. A large part of the task of creating a synthetic hidden-surface picture is the sorting and comparison of individual surfaces. [3] The surfaces must be compared to see which ones hide others; these comparisons can be speeded up substantially if the surfaces are properly sorted first. Because the output picture is of finite resolution, it is often possible to accomplish the sorting task in a single pass provided enough random access memory is available in which to place the sorted data. Priority algorithms such as that of Schumacker [4,5] and Newell et al. [6] can profit greatly from direct random access to the picture data. Figure 1 by Frank Crow of the University of Utah, is a picture produced by such an algorithm as displayed using the frame buffer memory.

The Memory

The random access memory of the frame buffer is a multi-port design. One port serves to deliver data via the color map and the D/A converters to the color TV monitor. A second port provides read and write access for the host computer. A third and fourth port provide, respectively, input and output channels for future connection to the memory of special high-speed picture processing devices.

The task we have undertaken in the frame buffer memory design is simultaneously to maximize bandwidth while minimizing the number of signal wires required. High bandwidth is required of the memory because it can be called on simultaneously to refresh the TV display and to accept new data for the next frame from a picture generation device (future) or computer program. It is important to minimize the number of signal paths because the cost of the system is influenced heavily by the number of paths, not only because of the cost of the interconnection wires and requisite gates, but also because of the cost of testing each such path to see that it is working. Although the bandwidth requirements can be met only by organizing the memory into words which are effectively 128 bits wide, all signal paths outside the memory printed circuit cards are only 8 or 16 bits wide. The integral memory buffer registers provided in the design serve not only to buffer the data independently for each channel but also to accommodate the narrower format to the memory's wide word. The high speed ports are buffered by two ranks of flip flops as shown in Fig. 2 so that data from one port may be used during a period of time also used for accessing data for another port.

On the input side the integral memory buffers can be thought of as belonging to the writing device. The writing device assembles as many 8 or 16 bit segments as are required in the input memory buffer. Parity is computed. In addition a single bit is recorded for each 8-bit byte of input to indicate whether valid data are stored there or not. When as many bytes are assembled as can be put into a single word of the video frame memory, the writing device indicates that a write cycle should take place. The 128 data bits plus the byte parity bits and the validity bits are transferred in parallel into another level of buffer within the memory, thus freeing the input buffer to accept more data. When a memory cycle is available, only those bytes marked as valid data are overwritten into a 128 bit word in the memory. A high-speed input device can continuously fill the first-rank input buffer with successive 8 or 16 bit data elements at a rate of over 10 MHz without interruption because transfer to the second rank need not wait for a memory cycle.

The output buffers operate in a similar fashion. The first rank of the TV output channel buffers, for example, is used to capture a 128 bit word from the memory chips at the time in a memory cycle when the data are available at the memory output. The second stage of buffering is used to sequentially gate 8 bits at a time onto a high-speed output bus. Because transfer between ranks need not wait for a memory cycle, continuous output is assured. For TV refresh it takes about 1.6 μsec to empty the sixteen bytes of eight bits each in the second rank of buffering. The memory operates in such a way as to devote a memory cycle to the TV refresh function whenever the first rank of buffering can accept such data. Thus from the time the first rank becomes empty until it must have received new data is 1.6 μsec, adequate time for nearly three memory cycles.

Mechanically, the memory chips and buffers for multi-port operation are all mounted together on printed circuit cards. Each card, 5 by 7 inches in size, contains sixteen thousand bytes arranged as 8 bits of the 128 bit memory width. Sixteen such cards make up the total memory. By mounting all of the multi-port buffers on the cards and using three state output switching, a minimum of back panel wiring is required. Ordinary two-layer printed circuits are used, but careful attention has been paid to routing of ground and critical signal wires.

We have used the MOSTEK 4096 bit MOS memory chips in the memory. We have experienced some difficulty with "stuck" bits on some of the chips purchased from early batches produced by MOSTEK, and substantial difficulty in getting adequate deliveries. We anticipated these difficulties and fully expect them to pass with time and experience. We do not yet have adequate operating experience to report on in-use failures. The MOSTEK memory chip will be second sourced by both Fairchild and Intel sometime in 1975.

Analog Output

Signals from the video frame buffer memory are delivered 8 bits at a time on a high-speed bus to the color map memory. The color map is buffered in such a way that it results in a net delay of several picture elements but operates at the full video rate. The color map consists of 256 words of high-speed flip flop memory, each word containing three 12 bit-intensity numbers, one for each primary color. Twelve bit intensity numbers are stored in the color map to provide for the very fine gradations of shade which are required, particularly in the dark parts of the picture, to produce a picture free of visible intensity quantization steps. The color map is ordinarily used to convert from 8 bits per picture element logarithmic coding to 12 bits per picture element linear coding.

The output of the color map goes to three digital to analog converters, one for each of the three primaries. These digital to analog converters are specially designed to be free of transition glitches as well as operating at the 10 MHz sample rate of the system. It is essential that, when changing from one shade of grey to another, the D/A converter not introduce a transition spike in-between.

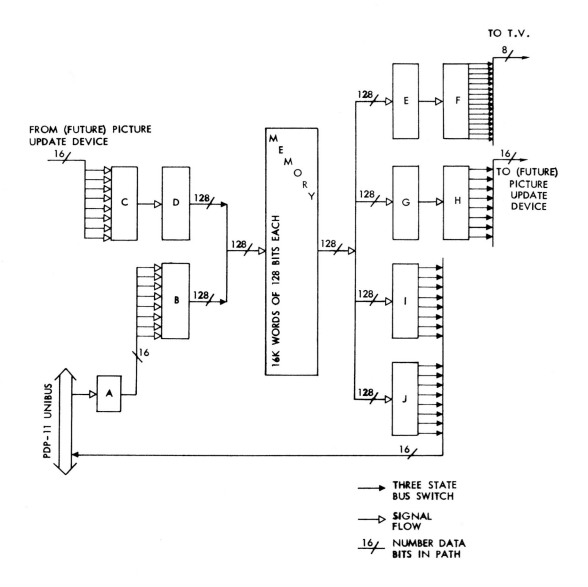

Fig. 2 – Video frame buffer memory organization. The memory consists of 512 MOSTEK integrated circuits storing 4096 bits each mounted on 16 printed circuit cards 5 by 7 inches in size. The same cards also hold the flip flop registers B through J, 128 bits each, plus memory circuits and register extensions for byte parity. The 16 bit buffer "A" permits quick release of the UNIBUS during PDP-11 write cycles; the two output registers "I" and "J" serve as a 16 word "Cache" memory for PDP-11 read cycles. High speed transfer to the TV and the picture update device (future) are provided by rapid switching of the three state output switches of registers "F" and "H".

The availability of high-speed integrated D/A converters and suitable high frequency amplifiers has made the design of this part of the circuit straightforward. The three color outputs are delivered to the monitor in RGB format with separate horizontal and vertical synchronizing signals. No attempt to generate NTSC encoded color has been made.

Picture Format Control

A micro-programmed picture format control has been assembled to control the operation of all parts of the system. This micro-programmed device executes each micro-instruction in 400 μsec. Conditional and branching instructions are provided in the micro-control as well as commands suitable for controlling the various operations involved in vertical and horizontal retrace calling for memory cycles, etc. The micro-instructions are stored in a read/write flip flop memory which can be loaded by the host computer. Micro-programs for externally synchronized TV, internally synchronized precision recording at lower speed, and free running TV have been written. Thirty two micro-instruction locations are provided.

The micro-controller controls a simple arithmetic machine designed to be particularly good at incrementing and counting. The increment values and counts shown in Table 1 are stored in flip flop registers

---

Table 1

Programmable Increments and Counts
Which Control Picture Format

Number picture elements per line (multiple of 16).
Number of scan lines per field.
Number of fields in a frame for current interlace scheme.
Initial memory address for picture data.
Address change per memory access (16 picture elements).
Address change during horizontal retrace.
Time duration of horizontal sync pulse.
The separation of horizontal sync pulse.
Number horizontal sync pulses during vertical retrace.
Interlace delay time.

---

also accessible to the host computer. Thus, for example, the user can vary the number of picture elements per line, the duration of horizontal retrace, the number of lines per field and the form of interlace desired by changing the values of the constants stored in these registers. Similarly, by adding a constant to the previously established address for each access, the controller computes the addresses from which data are to be fetched in the main video frame buffer memory. By changing the size of this address step or the initial value of the given address, the user can accommodate a variety of data storage schemes within the memory or obtain the effect of "waterfall" display. By sacrificing resolution t save memory, more than one picture can be stored in the frame buffer memory and accessed in sequence for comparison or to study some changing detail of the picture.

Precision CRT Output

The frame buffer memory can also be used to drive a precision CRT picture recorder. This makes it possible to record the pictures seen on the TV output device with substantially higher quality than is possible on a shadow mask TV monitor.

Deflection in signals for the precision CRT recorder are generated in the frame buffer system. The horizontal deflection is generated by an analog sweep circuit consisting of a D/A converter followed by an integrator. The integration rate is variable over a wide range, as (indirectly through the controller's counting activity) is the integration time. DC offset is also under computer control. Thus the program has the ability to change the horizontal picture format over a wide range.

The vertical deflection signal is produced by a very high precision D/A converter. Fortunately, this 16 bit conversion system does not have to operate at high speed, since the entire horizontal retrace time is available for establishing the new output value. However, precision in this conversion is essential. Let us suppose, for example, that 1000 scan lines are to be placed on the face of the precision CRT. Each line must be placed on the face of the precision CRT. Each line must be placed correctly within about 3% of its own width, or a visible defect will occur in the picture where one line overlaps its neighbor. Thus for a nominal 1000-line system, a conversion accuracy of one part of 30,000 is required. Again, this kind of digital to analog conversion accuracy is easy to achieve using standard high resolution D/A converters now readily available.

A variety of precision recording devices could be used with the system. In the University of Utah installation, an existing Beta Instruments Company precision CRT is used. An animation camera mounted so as to face the precision CRT is used for recording the images on 35 mm film. Colored filters are placed between the CRT phosphor and the film. Film advance and selection of color filters are all under computer control.

When recording on the precision CRT, the color map is used to compensate for the difference in response of the CRT phosphor in the pass bands of the three color filters and for the differences in efficiency of the filters as well as for the color sensitivity of the film itself. These factors can, of course, be multiplied together to provide one compensation table stored in the map. The programmer can select whether the contents of the red, green, or blue map is to be used in driving the precision CRT device.

Applications

A variety of research applications are contemplated for the unit now installed at the University of Utah. Frank Crow has already used the frame buffer memory to implement a straightforward hidden-surface algorithm. This program uses half of the available memory to store a 16 bit number indicative of the range from viewer to nearest object at each picture element in a 256 by 256 square picture raster. The program also uses one quarter of the memory to display the resulting picture; the remainder of the memory is unused. New picture elements are entered into the memory simply by comparing their depth on a point by point basis with the depth already recorded in the memory. Objects further from the viewer than already-entered objects are discarded. As the process proceeds the display shows not only the picture being produced but also a colored representation of the depth data.

Efforts to understand the use of grey scale control to minimize the effects of lateral quantization are also underway. A line drawn on the 512 by 512 display raster, for example, if represented merely as all black or all white elements will look jagged. If on the other hand, points adjacent to the line are shaded partly in the color of the line and partly in background color, the "jaggies" can be substantially reduced. Experiments indicate that substantial care must be exercised in the algorithms which accomplish this if Moire patterns are to be avoided in pictures which contains parallel structures of lines.

These applications are typical of the need for display capability which will enable a researcher to look at the pictures which his program is processing. We are confident that the random access memory which we have provided will serve well in this quick-look function. We also believe that the convenient access to the picture data provided by the use of random access memory will be of substantial value to quickly seeing changes caused by different processing steps and thus will provide not only for more rapid picture processing but also for better understanding of the implications of processes being tested.

Bibliography

1. *Proceedings of IEEE, Special Issue on Digital Picture Processing*, Vol. 60, No. 1, July 1972.
2. *Proceedings of IEEE, Special Issue on Two-Dimensional Spectral Analysis*, Vol. 62, No. 10, October 1974.
3. Sutherland, Ivan E., Robert F. Sproul, and Robert A. Schumacker, "A Characterization of Ten Hidden-Surface Algorithms," *Computing Surveys*, Vol. 6, No. 1, March 1974.
4. Schumacker, R.A., B. Branc, M. Gilliland, and W. Sharp, "Study for Applying Computer-Generated Images to Visual Simulation," *AFHRL-TR-69-14*, U.S. Air Force Human Resources Laboratory, September 1969.
5. Wild, E., R.S. Rougelot, and R.A. Schumacker, "Computing Full Color Perspective Images, paper presented at XDS Users Group, 20 May 1972. Also published in General Electric Technical Information Series, *R71els-26,* May 1971.
6. Newell, M. E., R. G. Newell, and T. L. Sancha, "A New Approach to the Shaded Picture Problem," *Proceedings of ACM National Conference,* 1972.

The Geometry Engine:
A VLSI Geometry System for Graphics

by

James H. Clark

Computer Systems Laboratory
Stanford University
and
Silicon Graphics, Inc.
Palo Alto, California

Abstract

The *Geometry Engine* [1] is a special-purpose VLSI processor for computer graphics. It is a four-component vector, floating-point processor for accomplishing three basic operations in computer graphics: matrix transformations, clipping and mapping to output device coordinates. This paper desribes the Geometry Engine and the Geometric Graphics System it composes. It presents the instruction set of the system, its design motivations and the Geometry System architecture.

Keywords: VLSI, Geometric processing, real-time graphics, arithmetic processing

CR Categories: 3.3, 3.4, 3.7

Geometry System Overview

The *Geometry System* is a floating-point, geometric computing system for computer graphics constructed from a basic building block, the *Geometry Engine*. Twelve copies of the Geometry Engine arranged in a pipeline compose the complete system in its most general form. In its present form, the Geometry Engine occupies a single, 40-pin IC package.

The notable characteristics of the system are:

- **General Instruction Set** - It executes a very general 2D and 3D instruction set of utility in all engineering graphics applications. This instruction set includes operations for matrix transformations, windowing (clipping), perspective and orthographic projections, stereo pair production and arbitrary output device coordinate scaling.

- **Curve Generation** - The system will generate quadratic and cubic curves and all of the conic sections, i.e. circles, parabolas, hyperbolas, etc.

- **Device Independent** - The system is independent of the output device used and works equally well in either vector-based or raster-based systems. It allows color or black and white polygons, lines and characters.

- **Flexible Input Format** - The system accepts input coordinates in either integer or floating point format.

Permission to copy without fee all or part of this material is granted provided that the copies are not made or distributed for direct commercial advantage, the ACM copyright notice and the title of the publication and its date appear, and notice is given that copying is by permission of the Association for Computing Machinery. To copy otherwise, or to republish, requires a fee and/or specific permission.

© 1982 ACM 0-89791-076-1/82/007/0127 $00.75

- **High Performance Floating Point** - Its effective computation rate is equivalent to 5 million floating-point operations per second, corresponding to a fully transformed, clipped, scaled coordinate each 15 microseconds.

- **Reconfigurable** - Each Geometry Engine is "softly" configured; that is, one device with a single configuration register serves in twelve different capacities.

- **Selection/Hit-Testing Mechanism** - The Geometry Engine has a "hit-testing" mechanism to assist in "pointing" functions, such as are required for a fast, interactive graphics system with a tablet, mouse or other input devices.

- **Scales to a Single Chip** - The system can be put in a smaller number of IC packages as soon as the technology for fabrication reduces the size of the Geometry Engine design. Ultimately, the entire 12 Engine system will fit on in one IC package, be a factor of 4 faster and be correspondingly reduced in cost.

The Geometry Engine is a four-component vector function unit whose architecture is best illustrated by the chip photograph shown in Figures 1 and 2. Each of the four function units along the bottom two-thirds of the photo consists of two copies of a computing unit, a mantissa and characteristic. The chip also has an internal clock generator, at the top left corner, and a microprogram counter with push-down subroutine stack, shown at the top right. The upper third of the chip is the control store, which holds the equivalent of 40k bits of control store. This control store contains all of the microcode that implements the instructions and floating-point computations described below.

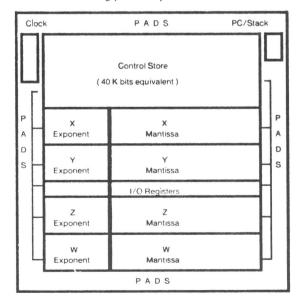

Figure 1: A Block Diagram of the Geometry Engine corresponding to the photo in Figure 2.

Reprinted with permission from *Computer Graphics* Vol. 16, No. 3, July 1982, 127-133.

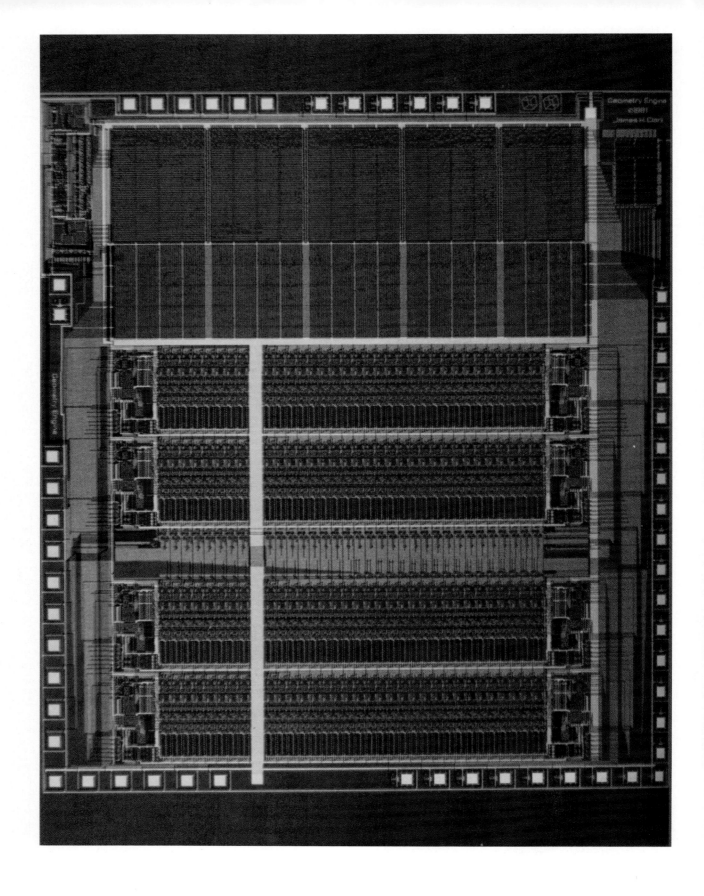

Figure 2: Photograph of the Geometry Engine.

Geometry System Functions

The Geometry System [2] is designed for high-performance, low-cost, floating-point geometric computation in computer graphics applications. It is composed of three subsystems, each of which is composed of Geometry Engines. These subsystems are illustrated in Figure 3. The particular position of a Geometry Engine in the pipeline determines its particuar function in the whole system. Each Engine has a configuration register that is loaded when the system is powered on, after a Reset command is issued. Until the system is reset again, the Engine behaves according to the configuration code.

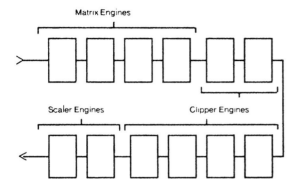

Figure 3: Geometry System; each block is a Geometry Engine.

The subsystems are:
- **Matrix Subsystem** - A stack of 4x4 floating-point matrices for completely general, 2D or 3D floating-point coordinate transformation of graphical data.
- **Clipping Subsystem** - A windowing, or clipping, capability for clipping 2D or 3D graphical data to a window into the user's virtual drawing space. In 3D, this window is a volume of the user's virtual, floating-point space, corresponding to a truncated viewing pyramid with "near" and "far" clipping.
- **Scaling Subsystem** Scaling of 2D and 3D coordinates to the coordinate system of the particular output device of the user. In 3D, this scaling phase also includes either orthographic or perspective projection onto the viewer's virtual window. Stereo coordinates are computed and optionally supplied as the output of the system.

The characteristics of each of these subsystems follows.

Matrix Subsystem

The matrix subsystem provides arbitrary 2D and 3D transformation ability, including object rotations, translations, scaling, perspective and orthographic projection. Using this matrix, it is possible to define a completely arbitrary 2D or 3D viewing window and accomplish all affine transformations.

The matrix transformation subsystem is the first four Geometry Engines in the pipeline. Distributed over these Engines is a 4x4 matrix and an eight-deep, 4x4 matrix stack to accommodate picture subroutine structure. The top element of the stack is the *current* matrix that is used to multiply all incoming coordinates. Full, floating-point transformation of all incoming coordinates is done by this subsystem in 15 microseconds. Transformed points are supplied by this subsystem to the clipping subsystem.

The matrix stack allows the use of picture subroutines. All incoming matrix multiplication commands cause the *current* matrix (top-of-stack) to be multiplied by the incoming matrix. This allows a graphic object to be attached to a "parent" graphic object, thereby providing for a hierarchical drawing. This is done in the same way that a push-down stack is used in a general-purpose computer for storing arguments to subroutines. The **LoadMM** command causes a new matrix to be loaded onto the top of the stack, while a **MultMM** command causes the current top of the stack to be multiplied by the supplied matrix.

The matrix stack can be manipulated by user instructions. In addition to the normal **Push** and **Pop** commands, there is also a **StoreMM** command to provide for overflow handling of the stack if picture structure depth exceeds the eight levels allowed by the depth of the stack.

This subsystem also generates cubic and rational cubic curves [3]. An incremental difference matrix for forward difference curves can be loaded onto the top of the stack, and a special **Iterate** command causes the forward differences of this matrix to be computed, with the result that a new coordinate on the curve is output to the clipping subsystem. Conic curves are generated using rational cubics. New points on the curve are generated in 10 microseconds.

Clipping Subsystem

The four to six Geometry Engines following the Matrix Subsystem comprise the Clipping Subsystem. Each Geometry Engine in the clipping subsystem clips the objects to a single boundary (plane) of the viewing window. Thus, if there is no need or desire to clip objects to the *near* or *far* clipping boundaries, either or both of the corresponding Engines may be eliminated, with no undesired side effects. This might be done to decrease the cost of the system.

The clipping subsystem gets all input data after it has passed through the matrix subsystem, so that only transformed coordinates are supplied to it. It has no explicit registers that the user may manipulate. It always clips transformed coordinates to specific boundaries. The boundaries are made to correspond to particular boundaries of the user's drawing space by altering the transformation matrix so that the desired portion of the environment to be within the window is scaled to be within the standard clipping boundaries.

As an assistance in testing objects for intersection with the viewer's window, a special *hit-testing* mode is included in the clipping subsystem. This mode disables output of certain data from the Geometry System. For example, to *select* an object on the screen that is being pointed to by the input device *cursor*, *hit-testing* is enabled and a special hit-testing matrix is loaded into the *current* matrix. This matrix is computed from the screen coordinates of the cursor; it might correspond to a tiny window centered at the pointing device's screen coordinates. If anything comes out of the geometry system in this mode, it signifies that an object has passed within the tiny window near the cursor position. Of course, the hit-testing window may be of any size, so that this feature can be useful in area-select functions, as well.

To provide further information useful in identifying *how* objects pass through the *hit-window*, each drawing instruction gets from one to six bits set in it to signify which of the one to six clipping boundaries were intersected by the line-segment drawn. To assist in identifying the object, a special object naming convention is used, thereby providing a completely general selection and hit-testing mechanism.

Scaling Subsystem

The last two Geometry Engines in the pipeline are the Scaling Subsystem. This subsystem converts output from the Clipping Subsystem to the coordinate system of the output device. This process causes the *window* on the user's drawing space, which is specified by loading the appropriate matrix into the Matrix Subsystem, to be mapped onto a *viewport* of the output device, which is specified by loading the scaling subsystem's *viewport* registers. The viewport registers allow up to 24-bit integer values, depending upon the coordinate system of the output device; they are the only device-dependent part of the system. In 3D, the mapping process includes an orthographic or perspective projection and stereo pair production.

Because the Geometry System is a homogeneous system that treats all three coordinates (x,y,z) the same, the Scaling Subsystem also maps the z coordinate. Thus, by loading the z viewport registers with appropriate values, either perspective depth values or intensity depth-cue values will be supplied by the Geometry System, according to the manner in which the output device interprets the z values. Of course, if no depth values are needed in the particular application, they may be discarded.

Either two or four integer values are output by the Scaling Subsystem for each coordinate point that comes out of the system. When two values come out, they are X and Y, in screen coordinates. If the Scaler Engines are configured properly, these four values are:

- X right - the x screen coordinate for the right eye.
- X left - the x screen coordinate for the left eye.
- Y - the y screen coordinate for both eyes.
- Z - the perspective depth value for both eyes.

Geometry System Computations

The matrix system does the computation:

$$[x'\ y'\ z'\ w'] = [x\ y\ z\ w]\ M,$$

where M is the top of the matrix stack and [x y z w] is the input vector to be transformed. The coordinates [x' y' z' w'] are supplied to the clipping subsystem, which clips them so that they satisfy

$$-w' < x' < w',$$
$$-w' < y' < w',$$
$$\text{and } -w' < z' < w'.$$

Note that these clipping boundaries are somewhat different from those used in most homogeneous clipping systems [4], in that the z coordinate is treated identically to the x and y coordinates. This simplifies the system, and is equivalent to all other homogeneous clipping systems if the correct matrix is used and the proper viewport scale factors are used.

After clipping, since all points coming out of the clipper satisfy these inequalities, the scaler does the final mapping to output device coordinates with the following computations:

$$D = (z'/w')*Ss + Cs,$$
$$Z = (z'/w')*Sz + Cz,$$
$$X = (x'/w')*Sx + Cx,$$
$$\text{and } Y = (y'/w')*Sy + Cy.$$

The coefficients Sx and Cx are the X half-size and X center of the viewport in the coordinate system of the output device. Similarly for the Y and Z values. The Ss and Cs values are explained in the next section.

Stereo Computation

The Geometry Engine can be used to obtain stereo pair pictures at no extra computational cost. Consider first the ordinary monographic case.

Monographic Case

In a system where the origin is the perspective projection point, the ordinary projection for 3 dimensional scenes [4] is to divide both x and y by z. That is, the screen coordinates of the point are given by

$$X = (x/z)*Sx + Cx$$
$$\text{and } Y = (y/z)*Sy + Cy,$$

where (Cx,Cy) is the center of the "viewport" and (Sx,Sy) is its half-size.

If homogeneous coordinates are used, these equations are modified to compute perspective depth. The transformation on [x,y,z] is modified to compute homogeneous coordinates as follows:

$$[x'\ y'\ z'\ w'] = [x\ y\ z\ 1]\ M.$$

M is chosen to yield

$$[x',\ y',\ z',\ w'] = [x,\ y,\ az+b,\ z],$$
$$\text{where } a = (1+N/F)/(1-N/F)$$
$$\text{and } b = -2N/(1-N/F).$$

N and F are the respective distances of the Near and Far clipping planes from the projection point. With these definitions, the projected coordinates are computed from

$$X = (x'/w')*Sx + Cx, \quad (1)$$
$$Y = (x'/w')*Sy + Cy,$$
$$\text{and } Z = (z'/w')*Sz + Cz = (a+b/z)*Sz + Cz,$$

where we have substituted the values of z' = az+b and w' = z from above.

This yields the same values for X and Y as before. In addition, however, it computes perspective depth, which can be useful in hidden-surface computations. With this computation, points at the Near clipping plane will be mapped into Cz-Sz and points at the Far clipping plane will be mapped into Cz+Sz.

Stereographic Case

For proper stereo, we wish to compute two different views, one for the left eye and one for the right eye. In other words, there are two different projection points that differ in a displacement in the x direction only:

$$\text{Xright} = ((x'+dx)/w')*Sx + Cx.\text{right},$$
$$\text{and Xleft} = ((y'-dx)/w')*Sx + Cx.\text{left},$$

where dx is half the distance between the two projection points (distance from the center of the head to each of the eyes). Cx.left is the center of the left projection viewport and Cx.right is the center of the right projection viewport. The Y and Z coordinates are unaffected.

Defining Cx.offset to be the offset of the right and left viewports from a "center" viewport, Cx, we have

$$\text{Cx.left} = \text{Cx} - \text{Cx.offset}$$

and Cx.right = Cx + Cx.offset.

The foregoing equations then become

Xright = (x'/w')*Sx + Cx + { (dx/w')*Sx + Cx.offset }
and Xleft = (x'/w')*Sx + Cx - { (dx/w')*Sx + Cx.offset },

or

Xleft = X + D,
and Xright = X - D,

where X is the "normal" X computation in Equation 1 and D is the quantity in brackets.

Note that D is a computation like that of X,Y and Z in Equation 1. In other words, it involves a division, a multiplication and an add. Inspection of the third of Equation 1 suggests that we define "stereo viewport" parameters as follows:

Ss = dx*Sx/b,
and Cs = Cx.offset - a*(dx*Sx/b).

Then the quantity D is computed to be

D = (z'/w')*Ss + Cs,

giving the required result for D when these substitutions are made.

The Geometry Engine has four floating-point function units; two are required to accomplish one computation of the sort

A = (B/C) * E + F.

Therefore, one Engine will perform two of these computations, for example for the X and Y coordinates. Since another Engine is required to compute Z, it has two free units that can be computing D as well, using the Ss and Cs values defined above. If the Engine computing D and Z is put in the pipeline before the X and Y Engine, the X-Y Engine's microcode can compute X+D and X-D, outputting the four values [X+D,X-D,Y,Z]. Of course, if no stereo is desired, but Z is still needed, the coefficients Ss and Cs can be zero. The Geometry Engine implements this stereo computation, and when properly configured, will output these four quantities.

Programming the Geometry System

The Geometry System is a slave processor. It has no instruction fetch unit: it must be given every instruction and data value by a controlling processor. Likewise, the display controller must take each value that comes out of the Geometry System.

The instruction/data stream supplied to the system is a high-level graphics instruction set mixed with coordinate data. Instructions and data are supplied to the system via its input port, which is the set of input pins of the first Matrix Subsystem Engine, and output data and instructions are taken from its output port, which is the set of output pins of the last Scaling Engine. A convenient view of the system is as a hardware subroutine; in fact, this is precisely the first way it will be used, as a hardware subroutine to the IRIS processor/memory system, which is based on the Motorola 68000 and IEEE Multi-bus.

Input data must always be in user's virtual-drawing (integer or floating-point) coordinate system, and except in special non-display circumstances such as hit-testing, output data is always in the coordinate system of the user's output device.

Instruction Set Summary

The instruction set for the geometry engine partitions into three types:

- **Register Manipulation** - These instructions alter the matrix, matrix stack, or viewport registers. They are used to set the *window* for a particular view of the virtual drawing, load the *viewport* registers, change the matrix or matrix stack to draw a different object, orient a particular object (rotate, translate, etc.) or save the state of the matrix stack for later restoration. Instructions in this category are:
  - **LoadMM** - Load the following 16 floating-point data values onto the top of the stack, destroying the current matrix. The 16 floating-point numbers are the 4x4 matrix.
  - **MultMM** - Multiply the *current* matrix on the top of the stack with the following 4x4 matrix.
  - **PushMM** - Push all matrices on the stack down one position, leaving the current top of stack unaltered. (After this operation the second stack position is a copy of the top of the stack.)
  - **PopMM** - Pop all matrices in the stack up one position.
  - **StoreMM** - Store the top of the matrix stack. This instruction input to the geometry system causes the StoreMM instruction, followed by the 4x4 matrix (16 floating-point numbers) to come out of the Geometry System at its output port. It can be used to save the complete state of the matrix stack.
  - **LoadVP** - Load the viewport registers. Following this instruction, eight 32-bit numbers describing the viewport parameters must be supplied.

- **Drawing Instructions** - These instructions actually cause graphic objects to be drawn. All drawing instructions are followed by four 32-bit floating-point numbers, representing the (x,y,z,w) coordinates of the point being supplied to the Matrix Subsystem for transformation. Each drawing command assumes that there is a current point in the drawing, for example the current pen position in a virtual-space plotter. Certain instructions update that position, while others cause things to be drawn from that point. We refer to this position as the Current Point. Assuming clipping does not eliminate them, each of the following instructions except **Curve** comes out of the Geometry System at its output port, followed by the device coordinates.
  - **Move** - Move the Current Point to the position specified by the floating-point vector that follows.
  - **MoveI** - Same as Move, but integer data is supplied.
  - **Draw** - Draw from the Current Point to the position specified by the following data. Update the Current Point with this value after drawing the line segment.
  - **DrawI** - Same as Draw, except that integer data is supplied.
  - **Point and PointI** - Cause a dot to appear at the point specified in the following data. Update the Current Point with this value after drawing the point.
  - **Curve** - Iterate the forward differences of the matrix on the top of the matrix stack; issue from the Matrix Subsystem to the Clipping Subsystem a **Draw** command followed by the computed coordinates of the point on the curve. The Current Point is updated just as with the Draw command. This command should *not* be followed by data as with the other drawing commands.
  - **MovePoly and MovePolyI** - In Polygon mode, move

the Current Point to the position supplied by the following data. This command must be used rather than **Move** if a closed polygon is to be drawn.
- o **DrawPoly** and **DrawPolyI** - In polygon mode, same as **Draw** command.
- o **ClosePoly** - Close the currently open polygon, flushing the polygon from the clipping subsystem.

• **Miscellaneous Commands** -
- o **SetHit** - Set Hit Mode. This causes the state of the Clipping Subsystem to change so that only commands, and not data, are output. Refer to the "Selection and Hit-testing" section for a complete description.
- o **ClearHit** - Clear Hit Mode. This restores the state of the Clipping Subsystem to normal. Refer to the "Selection and Hit-testing" section for a complete description.
- o **PassThru** - This instruction allows the passing of a variable number of 16-bit words through the geometry system unaltered and uninterpreted. It is useful for passing instructions and data that are unique to the display controller and that have no meaninng to the Geometry System. The number of words to be passed through is specified by a 7-bit field in the instruction.

Selecting and Hit-testing

In an interactive computer graphics environment it is frequently necessary to select certain objects that appear in the display for special attention. This is usually done with the aid of some type of input device, such as a light-pen, mouse, tablet or joy-stick.

If the input device being used is a light-pen, the common selection mechanism varies, but involves detecting in hardware when the "beam" of the CRT is under the field of view of the light-pen. This approach is good for pointing at objects on the screen but poor for entering new objects into the drawing, because a tracking mechanism must be drawing some type of tracking object that the light-pen must be sensing. Because of the extra expense of the light-pen tracking mechanism and because many people no longer believe it necessary to actually point to objects directly on the screen, the light-pen is not feasible in low-cost systems.

The alternatives to the light-pen, the tablet and mouse (we chose to ignore the joy-stick) are useful for entering new data into drawings, but without an extra mechanism, they are poor for pointing at existing objects in a drawing. The hit-testing mechanism in the Geometry System solves this problem.

The common software mechanism for doing this selection task is to check each object to see if it is in the selection area. This selection area might be an area specified by identifying some portion of the drawing space to check objects against or it might be a small neighborhood around the cursor, which is tracking the position of the mouse or tablet. Intelligent operations can be done to reduce the amount of time spent in checking. For example, the bounding box around an object can be tested to see if any portion of the object is in the selection area; if it is not, then none of the object is in the selection area and therefore need not be further tested. This selection task is basically a clipping task, and the Geometry System has a special mode for handling it.

The Hit-testing mode disables all data from coming out of the Geometry System. However, specific drawing instructions still come out of the system, missing their corresponding data. Thus, in hit-testing mode, if anything comes out of the output port of the system, this means that there was a "hit." In other words, something was in the selection area established by loading the selection matrix into the Matrix Subsystem.

For a completely general selection mechanism, one might not only like to know whether an object passes through the selection window, but also which boundaries it intersects, or whether it is completely contained within the selection area, or perhaps completely surrounds the area. To accommodate these needs, the Geometry System provides information in the form of "hit-bits" that tell which of the six clipping boundaries are intersected by each drawing command. In this way, the device that is receiving Geometry System output may assemble the necessary information by "integrating" the various "hit-bits" from successive drawing commands used in drawing the object.

Hit-testing is useful only when combined with a naming mechanism for identifying the objects being drawn. This can be done by loading a *name* register in the display controller before drawing each object that is to be identified with a hit. This can be done using the **PassThru** instruction.

Character Handling

Characters provide a special problem for any geometric transformation subsystem. Of course, characters may be defined as strokes, or vectors, and supplied just as all other data to the Geometry System, but since the number of strokes to make up a character might be quite large, we ordinarily do not wish to draw characters in this way. On the other hand, any other approach will not provide for complete, general rotations, etc. of 3D characters. As a result, most systems must make a compromise and provide characters as a special case.

The usual problem with characters is that if they are a special case, then clipping them is a special case. The Geometry System clips characters only if they are defined as strokes, just like all other data. However, since it must make possible the clipping of special-case characters and character generation in the display controller, the **LoadVP** instruction and corresponding data is always passed on to the output port of the system. The reason for this is that this data defines the boundaries of the *character* clipping window in the display controller.

Mixing special-case characters and graphics presents another problem. There are two cases:

- Putting characters in a drawing - this is handled by combining special sentinels to the display controller via the **PassThru** command with the **Point** command. The **Point** command is used to position the beginning of the character string. The Raster Subsystem, which is designed as a companion to the Geometry Subsystem, does the actual character clipping. Completely general character clipping is accomplished by proper use of these subsystems together.
- Putting a drawing with characters - This case is straightforwardly handled by properly modifying the tranformation matrix to reflect the character clipping window position. Then drawing can proceed as usual. The particular modifications for each case are handled by the software package mentioned above.

The IRIS Graphics System

The Geometry System is being implemented on the a system called the Integrated Raster Imaging System, IRIS, which consists of the following components:

- A processor/memory board with the Motorola 68000 and 256k bytes of RAM: the memory can be expanded to 2M bytes. The 68000 microprocessor executes instructions in the on-board memory at 8 MHz. This memory is fully mapped and segmented for 16 processes. Additional memory is accessed over the Multibus at normal Multibus rates.

- A Geometry Subsystem, with a multibus interface, FIFO's at the input and output of the Geometry System and from ten to twelve copies of the Geometry Engine.
- A custom 1024x1024 Color Raster Subsystem, with high-performance hardware for polygon fill, vector drawing and arbitrary, variable-pitch characters. The hardware and firmware provide for color and textured lines and polygons, character clipping, color mapping of up to 256 colors and selectable double or single-buffered image planes.
- A 10 Megabit EtherNet interface board.

Summary

The Geometry System is a powerful computing system for graphics applications. It combines a number of useful geometric computing primitives in a custom VLSI system that has a future because of its scalable nature. It is quite likely that within 5 years the system will be implemented on one, 1/2-million transistor, integrated-circuit chip, with a correspondingly reduced cost and increased speed.

Acknowledgements

Many people provided advice and suggestions during the two years over which this project has been done. Marc Hannah's masterful ability with VLSI Design Tools and UNIX and his graphics understanding were indispensible. Professor John Hennessy provided an indispensible microcode development tool in SLIM, and his willingness to help us when in need is appreciated. Lynn Conway of Xerox PARC made resources available during the formative stages of the project, and without them, it probably would not have been carried out; we are indebted to her for this. Forest Baskett of Stanford made it possible by supporting us in the early stages. Dick Lyon was an important first advisor on IC design. Martin Haeberli was very helpful in the testing phase. Valuable conversations were had with Chuck Thacker, Bob Sproull, Alan Bell, Martin Newell, Ed Chang, Danny Cohen, Doug Fairbairn, John Warnock, Chuck Seitz, Carver Mead, and Lance Williams. Hewlett-Packard Corporation fabricated the first copy of the first part of the datapath, and Bob Spencer and Bill Meuli of Xerox PARC's Integrated Circuits Laboratory fabricated the first fully functional copy of the entire chip.

We are especially grateful for the enthusiasm and support of Xerox Corporation's Palo Alto Research Center; this project could not have been done without the support of the insightful people there.

The research was supported by the Advanced Research Projects Agency of the Department of Defense, DARPA, under contract number MDA 903-79-C-0680.

References

1. Clark, J.H. "A VLSI Geometry Processor for Graphics." *Computer 13*, 7 (July 1980), 59-68.

2. Clark, J. H. Graphic Display Processing System and Processor. Patent Pending.

3. Clark, J. H. Parametric Curves, Surfaces and Volumes in Computer Graphics and Computer-Aided Geometric Design. Tech. Rept. 221, Computer Systems Laboratory, Stanford University, November, 1981.

4. Newman, W. and Sproull, R. F., *Principles of Interactive Computer Graphics*. Addison-Weseley, Reading, Mass., 1980.

Graphics and
Image Processing

Texture and Reflection in Computer Generated Images

James F. Blinn and Martin E. Newell
University of Utah

In 1974 Catmull developed a new algorithm for rendering images of bivariate surface patches. This paper describes extensions of this algorithm in the areas of texture simulation and lighting models. The parametrization of a patch defines a coordinate system which is used as a key for mapping patterns onto the surface. The intensity of the pattern at each picture element is computed as a weighted average of regions of the pattern definition function. The shape and size of this weighting function are chosen using digital signal processing theory. The patch rendering algorithm allows accurate computation of the surface normal to the patch at each picture element, permitting the simulation of mirror reflections. The amount of light coming from a given direction is modeled in a similar manner to the texture mapping and then added to the intensity obtained from the texture mapping. Several examples of images synthesized using these new techniques are included.

Key Words and Phrases: computer graphics, graphic display, shading, hidden surface removal
CR Categories: 3.41, 5.12, 5.15, 8.2

Copyright © 1976, Association for Computing Machinery, Inc. General permission to republish, but not for profit, all or part of this material is granted provided that ACM's copyright notice is given and that reference is made to the publication, to its date of issue, and to the fact that reprinting privileges were granted by permission of the Association for Computing Machinery.
A version of this paper was presented at SIGGRAPH '76: The Third Annual Conference on Computer Graphics, Interactive Techniques, and Image Processing, The Wharton School, University of Pennsylvania, July 14–16, 1976.
This work was supported in part by ARPA under Contract DAH15-73-C-0363. Author's address: Computer Science Department, University of Utah, Salt Lake City, UT 84112.

Introduction

In 1974 Edwin Catmull [2] developed an algorithm for rendering continuous tone images of objects modeled with bivariate parametric surface patches. Unlike most earlier algorithms [6, 8, 9, 10], which require that objects be approximated by collections of planar polygons, Catmull's algorithm works directly from the mathematical definition of the surface patches. The algorithm functions by recursively subdividing each patch into smaller patches until the image of each fragment covers only one picture element. At this stage, visibility and intensity calculations are performed for that picture element. Since the subdivision process will generate picture elements in a somewhat scattered fashion, the image must be built in a memory called a depth buffer or Z-buffer. This is a large, random access memory which, for each picture element, stores the intensity of the image and the depth of the surface visible at that element. As each patch fragment is generated, its depth is compared with that of the fragment currently occupying the relevant picture element. If greater, the new fragment is ignored, otherwise the picture element is updated.

This paper describes extensions of Catmull's algorithm in the areas of texture and reflection. The developments make use of digital signal processing theory and curved surface mathematics to improve image quality.

Texture Mapping

Catmull recognized the capability of his algorithm for simulating variously textured surfaces. Since the bivariate patch used is a mapping of the unit square in the parameter space, the coordinates of the square can be used as a curvilinear coordinate system for the patch. It is a simple matter for the subdivision process to keep track of the parameter limits of each patch fragment, thereby yielding the parameter values at each picture element. These parameter values may then be used as a key for mapping patterns onto the surface. As each picture element is generated, the parametric values of the patch within that picture element are used as input to a pattern definition function. The value of this function then scales the intensity of that picture element. By suitably defining the pattern function, various surface textures can be simulated.

As Catmull pointed out, simply sampling the texture pattern at the center of each picture element is not sufficient to generate the desired picture, since two adjacent picture elements in the image can correspond to two widely separated points in the patch parameter space, and hence to widely separated locations in the texture pattern. Intermediate regions, which should somehow influence the intensity pattern, would be skipped over entirely. This is a special case of a phenomenon known as "aliasing" in the theory of digital signal processing. This theory [7] treats the image as a continuous signal which is sampled at intervals corresponding to the distance between picture elements. The well-known "sampling theorem" states that the sampled picture cannot represent spatial frequencies greater than 1 cycle/2 picture elements. "Aliasing" refers to the result of sampling a signal containing frequencies higher than this limit. The high spatial frequencies (as occur in fine detail or sharp edges) reappear under the alias of low spatial frequencies. This problem is most familiar as staircase edges or "jaggies." In the process of texture mapping, the aliasing can be extreme, owing to the potentially low sampling rate across the texture pattern.

To alleviate this problem we must filter out the high spatial frequency components of the image (in this case the texture pattern) before sampling. This filtering has the effect of applying a controlled blur to the pattern. This can be implemented by taking a weighted average of values in the pattern immediately surrounding the sampled point. Digital image processing theory provides a quantitative measure of the effectiveness of such weighting functions in terms of how well they attenuate high frequencies and leave low frequencies intact.

Catmull achieved the effect of filtering by maintaining an additional floating-point word for each picture element. This word contained the fraction of the picture element covered by patch fragments. For each new fragment added to the picture element, the texture pattern was sampled and the intensity was averaged proportionally to the amount of the picture element covered by the patch fragment. Examination of the spatial frequency filter effectively implemented by this technique shows that it is much better than point sampling but is not optimal.

The method discussed here does not require the extra storage and uses a better anti-aliasing filter. This filter is implemented by a weighting function originally used by Crow [3] to minimize aliasing at polygon edges ("jaggies"). It takes the form of a square pyramid with a base width of 2×2 picture elements. In the texture mapping case, the 2×2 region surrounding the given picture element is inverse mapped to the corresponding quadrilateral in the u,v parameter space (which is the same as the texture pattern space), see Figure 1. The values in the texture pattern within the quadrilateral are weighted by a pyramid distorted to fit the quadrilateral and summed.

The derivation of the quadrilateral on the texture pattern makes use of an approximation that the parametric lines within one picture element are linear and equally spaced. The X,Y position within a picture element can then be related to the u,v parameters on the patch by a simple affine transformation. This transformation is constructed from the u,v and X,Y values which are known exactly at the four corners of the patch fragment.

Given this algorithm, we now investigate the effects of various texture definition methods. We will use, as our sample object, a plain teapot constructed of 26 bicubic patches. First, the pattern may be some simple function of the u,v parametric values. A useful example of this is a simple gridwork of lines. The result is as though parametric lines of the component patches are painted on the surface, Figure 2. Note that the edges of the pattern lines show very little evidence of aliasing in the form of staircases. Second, the pattern may come from a digitized hand drawn picture, Figure 3. Third, the pattern may come from a scanned-in photograph of a real scene, as in Figure 4. Incidentally, this picture makes the individual patches very clear. This type of pattern definition enables the computer production of "anamorphic" pictures. These are pictures which are distorted in such a way that when viewed in a curved mirror the original picture is regenerated Figure 5. The patch itself is defined so that the parametric lines are stretched in approximately the correct fashion and a real photograph is mapped onto the patch. Figure 5 should be viewed in a cylindrical mirror (e.g. a metal pen cap) with the axis perpendicular to the page. The fourth source of texture patterns shown here is Fourier synthesis. A two-dimensional frequency spectrum is specified and the inverse Fourier transform generates the texture pattern. This is a simple way of generating wavy or bumpy patterns. Certain restrictions on the form of the input spectrum must be followed to ensure that the pattern has an even distribution of intensities and is continuous across the boundaries. An example of this type of texture is shown in Figure 6. The texture patterns used here were generated before picture synthesis began and stored as 256×256 element pictures in an array in random access memory.

Reflection in Curved Surfaces

The second topic discussed in this paper concerns lighting models. Typically, visible surface algorithms

Fig. 1. Region of texture pattern corresponding to picture element: left-hand side shows texture; right-hand side shows image.

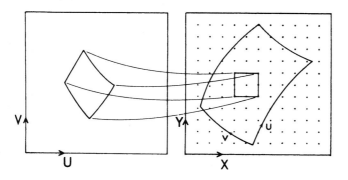

Fig. 2. Simple gridwork texture pattern: left-hand side shows texture pattern; right-hand side shows textured object.

Fig. 3. Hand sketched texture pattern: left-hand side shows texture pattern; right-hand side shows textured object.

Fig. 4. Photographic texture pattern: left-hand side shows texture pattern; right-hand side shows textured object.

determine intensities within an image by using Lambert's (cosine) law: $i = s(L \cdot N)$, where i = intensity, s = surface shade, L = light direction vector, N = surface normal vector, and "$\cdot$" denotes vector inner product.

Variants on this function, such as

$$i = s(L \cdot N)**n, \quad \text{for} \quad n > 1$$

have been used to give the impression of shiny surfaces, but there is little physical justification for such functions, and the range of effects is limited. The modeling of more realistic lighting was first investigated by Bui-Tuong Phong [1]. His model of reflection incorporated a term which produced a highlight over portions of the surface where the normal falls midway between the light source direction and the viewing direction. This is motivated by the fact that real surfaces tend to reflect more light in a direction which forms equal angles of incidence and reflectance with the surface normal. This can be easily implemented by simulating a virtual light source in a direction halfway between the light source and viewing directions, and raising the result to some high power to make the highlights more distinct:

$$i = s(L \cdot N) + g(L' \cdot N)**n$$

where L' = virtual light source direction, g = glossiness of surface (0 to 1). Figure 7 shows an image generated using the above function with $n = 60$. These techniques work well for satin type surfaces but images of highly polished surfaces still lack realism. This is largely due to the absence of true reflections of surrounding objects and distributed light sources.

The simulation of reflections in curved surfaces requires an accurate model of the properties of the surface and access to accurate normal vectors at all points on the surface. The approximation of curved surfaces by collections of planar polygons is inadequate for this purpose, so extensions of the techniques of Gouraud [5] and Bui-Tuong Phong [1] hold little promise.

The subdivision algorithm, however, provides accurate information about surface position and can be made to give accurate surface normals at every picture element. This is the first algorithm that provides the appropriate information for the simulation of mirror reflections from curved surfaces. For each picture element, the vector from the object to the observer and the normal vector to the surface are combined to determine what part of the environment is reflected in that surface neighborhood. It can be shown that, for surface normal vector (Xn, Yn, Zn) and viewing position $(1, 0, 0)$, the direction reflected, (Xr, Yr, Zr), is

$$Xr = 2*Xn*Zn, \quad Yr = 2*Yn*Zn, \quad Zr = 2*Zn*Zn - 1,$$

Having established the direction of the ray which is reflected to the eye, it remains to find what part of the environment generated that ray. For this, a model of the environment is needed which represents surrounding objects and light sources. Clearly, the view of the environment as seen from different points on the surface will vary. However, if it is assumed that the environment is composed of objects and light sources which are greatly distant from the object being drawn, and that occlusions of the environment by parts of the object itself are ignored, then the environment can be modeled as a two-dimensional projection surrounding the drawn object. Stated another way, the object is positioned at the center of a large sphere on the inside of which a picture of the environment has been painted. These simplifications allow the environment to be modeled as a two-dimensional intensity map indexed by the polar coordinate angles of the ray reflected

Fig. 5. Anamorphic image.

Fig. 6. Fourier synthesis of texture: top shows texture pattern; bottom, texture object.

Fig. 7. Plain teapot with highlights.

source direction and the viewing direction. This is motivated by the fact that real surfaces tend to reflect more light in a direction which forms equal angles of incidence and reflectance with the surface normal. This can be easily implemented by simulating a virtual light source in a direction halfway between the light source and viewing directions, and raising the result to some high power to make the highlights more distinct:

$$i = s(L \cdot N) + g(L' \cdot N)**n$$

where L' = virtual light source direction, g = glossiness of surface (0 to 1). Figure 7 shows an image generated using the above function with $n = 60$. These techniques work well for satin type surfaces but images of highly polished surfaces still lack realism. This is largely due to the absence of true reflections of surrounding objects and distributed light sources.

The simulation of reflections in curved surfaces requires an accurate model of the properties of the surface and access to accurate normal vectors at all points on the surface. The approximation of curved surfaces by collections of planar polygons is inadequate for this purpose, so extensions of the techniques of Gouraud [5] and Bui-Tuong Phong [1] hold little promise.

The subdivision algorithm, however, provides accurate information about surface position and can be made to give accurate surface normals at every picture element. This is the first algorithm that provides the appropriate information for the simulation of mirror reflections from curved surfaces. For each picture element, the vector from the object to the observer and the normal vector to the surface are combined to determine what part of the environment is reflected in that surface neighborhood. It can be shown that, for surface normal vector (Xn, Yn, Zn) and viewing position $(1, 0, 0)$, the direction reflected, (Xr, Yr, Zr), is

$$Xr = 2*Xn*Zn, \quad Yr = 2*Yn*Zn, \quad Zr = 2*Zn*Zn - 1,$$

Having established the direction of the ray which is reflected to the eye, it remains to find what part of the environment generated that ray. For this, a model of the environment is needed which represents surrounding objects and light sources. Clearly, the view of the environment as seen from different points on the surface will vary. However, if it is assumed that the environment is composed of objects and light sources which are greatly distant from the object being drawn, and that occlusions of the environment by parts of the object itself are ignored, then the environment can be modeled as a two-dimensional projection surrounding the drawn object. Stated another way, the object is positioned at the center of a large sphere on the inside of which a picture of the environment has been painted. These simplifications allow the environment to be modeled as a two-dimensional intensity map indexed by the polar coordinate angles of the ray reflected

Fig. 5. Anamorphic image.

Fig. 6. Fourier synthesis of texture: top shows texture pattern; bottom, texture object.

Fig. 7. Plain teapot with highlights.

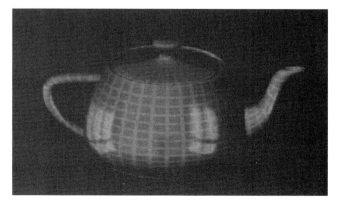

COLOR IMAGE QUANTIZATION FOR FRAME BUFFER DISPLAY

Paul Heckbert
Computer Graphics Lab
New York Institute of Technology

ABSTRACT

Algorithms for adaptive, tapered quantization of color images are described. The research is motivated by the desire to display high-quality reproductions of color images with small frame buffers. It is demonstrated that many color images which would normally require a frame buffer having 15 bits per pixel can be quantized to 8 or fewer bits per pixel with little subjective degradation. In most cases, the resulting images look significantly better than those made with uniform quantization.

The color image quantization task is broken into four phases:
1) Sampling the original image for color statistics
2) Choosing a colormap based on the color statistics
3) Mapping original colors to their nearest neighbors in the colormap
4) Quantizing and redrawing the original image (with optional dither).

Several algorithms for each of phases 2-4 are described, and images created by each given.

CR CATEGORIES: H.3.3 (Information Storage and Retrieval): Information Search and Retrieval - clustering; search process; I.3.3 (Computer Graphics): Picture/Image Generation - digitization and scanning; display algorithms; I.4.1 (Image Processing): Digitization - quantization.

General Terms: Algorithms.

Additional Key Words and Phrases: dither.

Permission to copy without fee all or part of this material is granted provided that the copies are not made or distributed for direct commercial advantage, the ACM copyright notice and the title of the publication and its date appear, and notice is given that copying is by permission of the Association for Computing Machinery. To copy otherwise, or to republish, requires a fee and/or specific permission.

© 1982 ACM 0-89791-076-1/82/007/0297 $00.75

INTRODUCTION

The power and versatility of frame buffers has created an increasing demand for them in industry, education, and the home. Most of these frame buffers are capable of displaying a static color image, yet many of them do not contain the amount of memory necessary to match the spatial and color resolution of the human eye. The eye is capable of distinguishing at least fifty thousand colors [15]. Therefore, it would take a frame buffer with at least 15 bits per pixel to reproduce and display a color image with no noticeable contouring. On smaller frame buffers, contouring effects can become objectionable. One way to eliminate some of this quantization error is to employ the method of tapered quantization.

The purpose of this paper is to explore techniques for color image quantization with the goal of high-quality image display on frame buffers.

The Original Image

Our input data are the red, green, and blue separations of a digitized color image. A typical form for the input image is a rectangular array of pixels each having 24 bits (8 bits per component). The color components are usually represented by numbers in the range [0,255]. If the original image is in this form, then strictly speaking it has already been quantized (when it was digitized from a video signal, for instance). We will assume that this initial quantization does not cause perceptible quantization errors. This will be the case if (a) the full gamut of RGB space is used, that is, if the digitization equipment is set up so that black is quantized to $(r,g,b)=(0,0,0)$, white to $(255,255,255)$, red to $(255,0,0)$, etc. and (b) the 256 levels are approximately equally spaced perceptually. Given these conditions, we can regard the 24-bit original image as the "true" image. We will try to approximate it as closely as possible when we quantize.

Frame Buffers and Colormaps

It is useful to distinguish between two types of frame buffer architectures: let's call them "segregated" and "integrated". In segregated frame buffers, there are three independent memories for the red, green, and blue components of an image. Typically 8 bits are used per pixel. An integrated frame buffer, on the other hand, stores a single color number for each pixel rather than three separate components. These color numbers (pixel values) are used as addresses into a single color lookup table (colormap). The colormap provides a level of indirection between the data in the picture memory and the actual displayed image. For a more thorough discussion of frame buffer hardware, see Newman and Sproull [18].

The algorithms we will discuss are intended for integrated frame buffers having a colormap.

Introduction to Quantization

Definitions:
   Quantization is the process of assigning representation values to ranges of input values. In image processing, the value being quantized can be an analog or digital signal.

   Color image quantization is the process of selecting a set of colors to represent the color gamut of an image, and computing the mapping from color space to representative colors.

   There are two general classes of quantization methods: uniform and tapered. In uniform quantization, the range of the input variable is divided into intervals of equal length. The choice of intervals in tapered quantization is usually based on the statistical distribution of the input variable. To compare the quality of different quantizations, a distortion measure, or error metric, is often introduced. With this formalism, one can search for the "optimal" tapered quantization of a variable (or image).

Notation:
   In the following, let x be an M-dimensional input point (a 3-D color for our purposes). A quantizer consists of:
   (a) a set of K representative or output points: $Y = \{y_i, i=1,2,\ldots,K\}$,
   (b) a partition of the input space into regions (quantization cells): $R = \{r_i, i=1,2,\ldots,K\}$,
   (c) a mapping from input points to representative indices:
       $p(x) = i$ if $x \in r_i$, and
   (d) the quantization function which maps input points into output points:
       $q(x) = y[p(x)]$.
In color image quantization, Y is the colormap into which we will quantize, K is the number of colors in the colormap (usually 1024 or less), and p is a mapping from colors in the original image to pixel values in the quantized image.

The images are notated as follows:
   Let $c_{i,j}$ be the color of the pixel in the original image at row i, column j, where $0 \leq i < NI$ and $0 \leq j < NJ$. Denote the pixel value at row i, column j of the final (quantized) image by $f_{i,j}$. Note that c is a vector matrix and f a scalar matrix. We assume the original and final images have the same resolution.

COLOR IMAGE QUANTIZATION

Uniform quantization, though computationally much faster than adaptive, tapered quantization, leaves much room for improvement. Compare the 24-bit original image in fig. 2 with the uniform 8-bit quantization in fig. 3. The contouring here is quite serious. It results because many of the colors in the colormap are not used in the final picture; they are wasted. By adapting a colormap to the color gamut of the original image, we are assured of using every color in the colormap, and thereby reproducing the original image more closely. That is the intuitive concept behind tapered color image quantization. We will now develop these ideas formally.

When an image is quantized, each of the 3-dimensional colors in the original image must be encoded into a single pixel value. To do this we compute the mapping:
   $f_{i,j} = p(c_{i,j})$ for $0 \leq i < NI$, $0 \leq j < NJ$.

The display processor in the frame buffer displaying our final picture passes the pixel values through the colormap Y:
   $y_{p(c_{i,j})} = q(c_{i,j})$.
This will display a picture closely resembling the original if we have quantized well.

Measuring Quantization Error

To measure the difference between the original and quantized images (the total quantization error), we use the following formula:

$$D = \sum_{i,j} d(c_{i,j}, q(c_{i,j}))$$

where $d(x,y)$ is a distortion function or color metric which measures the "difference" between corresponding colors in the original and final images [7]. We will use a very simple color metric, distance squared in RGB space:

$$d(x,y) = (x_r - y_r)^2 + (x_g - y_g)^2 + (x_b - y_b)^2$$

where $x = (x_r, x_g, x_b)$ and $y = (y_r, y_g, y_b)$.

This formula is chosen for its computational speed and simplicity. Ideally, the color metric should be perceptually-based, since the human eye is final judge of quantization quality. The use of YIQ or Lab color space for the color metric would probably improve our quantizers somewhat [15].

We define the "optimal" quantizer (for a given image and number of colors K) as the one which minimizes D.

Quantization Literature

One-dimensional quantization has an extensive literature [4],[9],[17],[19]. It is possible to find optimal 1-dimensional quantizers efficiently. Algorithms which make use of dynamic programming [1] to find an optimal quantizer for an N-level input in $O(N^2K)$ time are given in [3] and [8]. These can be used to quantize a monochrome picture in a matter of seconds at today's computer speeds.

Color image quantization has received little attention in the literature until recently. It is usually done by treating the three color components independently. Independent quantization in spaces such as YIQ and Lab (see [15] and [20]) is inefficient because much of their space lies outside the RGB color cube [11]. Subjective experiments were used by In der Smitten to subdivide RGB space into 125 volumes [10]. Some contouring is visible with his quantizer. Stenger has also done some tests of tapered color quantization [22]. Koontz, Narendra, and Fukunaga [14] have published an algorithm for finding the optimal quantization (they call them "clusterings") for small input and output sets. Their program required 28 seconds to find the optimal classification of 120 points into 8 classes. They do not analyze the speed of their algorithm, so it is difficult to predict the computation time for larger quantization jobs such as ours. Assuming a linear-time algorithm (a conservative guess), quantizing several hundred thousand colors would take half a day. Clearly this is not practical.

Multidimensional quantization is much more difficult than 1-dimensional quantization. The reason for this is the increased interdependency of quantization cells. While in the one-dimensional case all intervals are determined by the two thresholds at either end, in the multidimensional case the quantization cells can be polytopes with any number of sides. The complex topology of multidimensional tapered quantization cells is suggested by the shapes in fig. 18.

Optimal multidimensional quantization has no known fast solution [7]. The methods we will describe use heuristic approaches to approximate the optimal.

ALGORITHMS FOR COLOR IMAGE QUANTIZATION

The algorithms for color quantization described below use the following four phases:
1) sample image to determine color distribution
2) select colormap based on the distribution
3) compute quantization mapping from 24-bit colors to representative colors (ie. colors in the colormap)
4) redraw the image, quantizing each pixel.

Choosing the colormap is the most challenging task. Once this is done, computing the mapping table from colors to pixel values is straightforward.

PHASE 1: SAMPLING THE ORIGINAL IMAGE

The information needed by the colormap selection algorithms of phase 2 is a histogram of the colors in the original image. This is collected in one pass over the input image. To conserve memory, a prequantization from 24 bits to 15 bits (5 bits red, 5 bits green, 5 bits blue) is suggested. In this case the color frequency histogram will be a table of length 32768. This clumping of the colors has the effect of reducing the number of different colors and increasing the frequency of each color. These properties are important to the algorithms described below.

PHASE 2: CHOOSING A COLORMAP

We discuss two algorithms for choosing a set of representatives (colormap) based on the input distribution, and a process which can be used to perturb the choice of representatives to improve a quantizer.

The Popularity Algorithm

The popularity algorithm was developed independently by two groups in 1978: Tom Boyle and Andy Lippman at MIT's Architecture Machine Group and Ephraim Cohen at the New York Institute of Technology. Boyle & Lippman's ideas were implemented by the author at MIT [8]; the latter is unpublished.

The assumption of this algorithm is that the colormap can be made by finding the densest regions in the color distribution of the original image. The popularity algorithm simply chooses the K colors from the histogram with the highest frequencies, and uses these for the colormap. This can be done with a simple selection sort [13]. This will take time $O(NK)$, where N is the number of colors in the histogram.

The popularity algorithm functions well for many images (fig. 4), but performs poorly on ones with a wide range of colors (fig. 15), or when asked to quantize to a small number of colors (say < 50). It often neglects colors in sparse regions of the color space.

The Median Cut Algorithm

The median cut algorithm was proposed by the author in [8], and is reprinted here with minor changes. Kenneth Sloan has pointed out that the database used in this algorithm is nearly identical to Bentley's k-d trees [2].

The concept behind the median cut algorithm is to use each of the colors in the synthesized colormap to represent an equal number of pixels in the original image. This algorithm repeatedly subdivides color space into smaller and smaller rectangular boxes. We start with one box which tightly encloses the colors of all NI×NJ pixels from the original image. The number of different colors in this first box is dependent on the color resolution used. Experimental results show that 15 bits per color (the resolution of the histogram) is sufficient in most cases.

Iteration step: split a box.
The box is "shrunk" to fit tightly around the points (colors) it encloses, by finding the minimum and maximum values of each of the color coordinates. Next we use "adaptive partitioning" (Bentley's terminology) to decide which way to split the box. The enclosed points are sorted along the longest dimension of the box, and segregated into two halves at the median point. Approximately equal numbers of points will fall on each side of the cutting plane.

The above step is recursively applied until K boxes are generated. If, at some point in the subdivision, we attempt to split a box containing only one point (repeated many times, perhaps), the spare box (which would have gone unused) can be reassigned to split the largest box we can find.

After K boxes are generated, the representative for each box is computed by averaging the colors contained in each. The list of representatives is the colormap Y.

The sorting used in the iteration step can be done efficiently with a radix list sort [13], since the color coordinates are small integers, generally within the range [0,255]. Splitting each box will therefore take time proportional to the number of different colors enclosed. Generating the colormap will take O(NlogK) time, where N is the number of different colors in the first box.

Images quantized by the median cut technique are shown in figures 5 and 11. Subjective tests have shown that the median cut algorithm produces better quantizers than the popularity algorithm. In some cases the difference is striking (compare figures 15 and 16).

Other criteria could be used to decide which coordinate to bisect. Instead of choosing the coordinate with the largest range, one might use the one with the largest variance. Likewise, one could choose the split plane so that the sum of variances for the two new boxes is minimized. This would tend to minimize the mean squared error better than the median criterion.

A Fixed Point Algorithm for Improving A Quantizer

Gray, Kieffer, and Linde [7], have described an algorithm for finding a locally optimal multidimensional quantizer. It is an extension of a method first proposed by Lloyd [16]. A quantizer is called locally optimal if small perturbations in Y, the set of representative points, cannot decrease the total distortion D.

Given a set of representatives Y, the optimal partition R'(Y) is:

$$r'_k = \{x : d(x,y_k) \leq d(x,y_j), j \neq k\}$$

which is the locus of points whose nearest neighbor is y_k. Given a partition R, the optimal set of representatives Y'(R) is the set of y'_k such that y'_k is the centroid of all input points $c_{i,j}$ which lie inside r_k. These can be combined to define a mapping T which perturbs Y so that D never increases:

$$TY = Y'(R'(Y)).$$

To paraphrase the equations, for each representative point y_k, one finds the centroid of all input points whose nearest neighbor in Y is y_k.

Lloyd's algorithm applies this mapping repeatedly in order to improve a quantizer, and hopefully converge on a fixed point of the mapping T (a point where TY=Y). Linde et al. have proven that the algorithm converges in a finite number of iterations if the input distribution is finite (as ours is). The fixed point will be a local minimum of D, but not necessarily a global one [7].

This fixed point algorithm can be used to improve quantizers generated by the popularity or median cut algorithms. Experimental results show that the improvement is slight for the latter. The iteration will help more when the first guess is crude, such as a uniform lattice of points, as seen in fig. 13.

To make this algorithm practical, one must be able to find nearest neighbors quickly. That is our next topic.

PHASE 3: MAPPING COLORS TO NEAREST NEIGHBORS IN COLORMAP

Given an input distribution c and a set of representatives Y, D is minimized when q maps a point to its nearest representative:

$$p(x) = i$$
$$q(x) = y_i$$ if $d(x,y_i) \leq d(x,y_j)$, $j \neq i$

This operation is sometimes called a "nearest neighbor query" [2]. In our application it could also be thought of as an "inverse colormap", since it maps colors into pixel values.

By evaluating this function for each color in the original image, and saving this information in a table, one can speed up phase 4 significantly. The alternative is to evaluate p once per pixel. The former will be faster if the number of different colors in the original image is smaller than the number of pixels in the image. If one uses a prequantization to 15 bits, as suggested for phase 1, the number of colors will be under 32768. For all but low-resolution frame buffers, this is smaller than the number of pixels. Note that the quantization mapping table will fit conveniently in the same array that was used for the histogram.

There are several methods for computing the function p:

Exhaustive Search

The straightforward way to compute p(x) is to test all K representatives and choose the one which minimizes $d(x,y_i)$. Unfortunately, this method is slow. Much time is wasted considering distant points which couldn't possibly be the nearest neighbor. It would be shrewder to do some preprocessing on Y to set up a database which enables faster queries.

Locally Sorted Search

We create a database consisting of an N×N×N lattice of cubical cells each containing a sorted list of representatives. Each cell's list should include all representatives which are the nearest neighbors of some point in that cell. Each list entry contains two variables: a representative's number (rep_no) and its distance (dist) from the nearest point in the cell. Dist is defined to be zero for representatives inside the cell. To create the list, we compute each representative's distance from the cell, put these in a list, and then sort the list by the distance key. Note that a given representative can occur in several lists.

A simple way to limit the length of the lists is to eliminate representatives which could not possibly be the nearest neighbors of any point inside the cell. As shown in fig. 1, one finds the representative point nearest the center of the cell and computes its distance from the farthest corner of the cell. This gives us an upper bound on the distance from any point in the cell to its nearest representative. All representatives whose distance to the cell is greater than this can be left out of the list, thereby speeding the list sorting operation and conserving memory.

To compute the function p(x) with this database, we first find the cell which encloses x, and then execute the following procedure:

```
min = infinity;
i = 0;
while (min > entry[i].dist) begin
   distance = d(x,y[entry[i].rep_no]);
   if (distance < min) then begin
      nearest = i;
      min = distance;
   end
   i = i+1;
end
return(nearest);
```

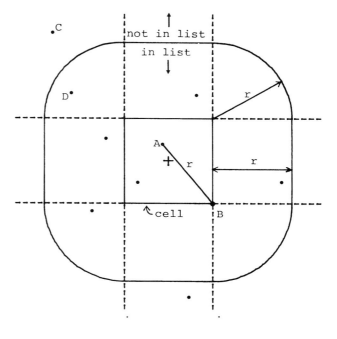

fig. 1: Point A is representative closest to cell center. The distance from A to the corner of the cell most distant from it (B) is r. Since all points in the cell are less than r units away from A, any representative more than r units away from the cell can be eliminated from the cell list. Thus C will be excluded, but D included.

How much memory and computation is involved in the creation of these lists? This is dependent on the size and number of cells. If we use a lattice of N^3 cells, and the average list length is L entries, the memory required by the database is $O(N^3L)$. Computing distances from each representative to a cubical cell takes $O(K)$ time, and the list sort takes $O(L\log L)$, so the preparation time is therefore $O(N^3K + N^3L\log L)$.

In practice, one should avoid computing the representative lists for unused cells. Only the most colorful images will contain colors in all N^3 cells. One way to compute only the needed cells is to create them dynamically, the first time they are used. When the function p is asked for the nearest neighbor of a point in an "uncharted" cell, it creates the representative list for that cell, processes the query, and marks the cell as "charted".

When choosing N one must compromise between fast search times and fast preprocessing times. A fine lattice (large N) will lead to short cell lists and hence low search times, but high preprocessing cost. An extremely coarse lattice, such as N=1, will function much like exhaustive search: the long lists will result in high search times, but the preprocessing time will be negligible. The best compromise will depend on the number and distribution of queries.

Experimental Results for Locally Sorted Search

The average list length L is dependent on the number and distribution of representatives and the number of cells. Empirical tests on the colormaps generated by the median cut algorithm for a sample set of 17 images had an average list length of 35 when K=256 and N=8. With exhaustive search, each call to the function p requires inspection of K representatives. Using locally sorted search, the average number of representatives tested was only 11 (also for the case K=256, N=8). This is 23 times smaller than the number of tests the exhaustive method would make.

Locally sorted search shows the greatest advantage over exhaustive search when K is large and when the colors in the input image have a wide distribution. In these cases the preprocessing time to create the database is overshadowed by the savings in search time. In the tests mentioned above, locally sorted search was never slower than the exhaustive method. For the image in fig. 11, it was three times faster than the exhaustive method.

K-D Tree Search

Another algorithm for nearest neighbor queries, which came to the attention of the author only recently, has been proposed by Friedman, Bentley, and Finkel [6]. Using a k-d tree database to structure the K representative points, they achieved a search time of $O(\log K)$. Their algorithm has not yet been tested for the application of color image quantization.

PHASE 4: QUANTIZING AND REDRAWING THE IMAGE

To quantize the image, we simply pass each pixel of the original image through the quantization mapping table created during phase 3, and write the pixel values into a frame buffer. This will redraw the image (quantized of course) using only K colors.

Depending on the image, the quantization errors may be obvious or invisible. Images with high spatial frequencies (such as hair or grass) will show quantization errors much less than pictures with large, smoothly shaded areas (such as faces). This is because the high-frequency contour edges introduced by the quantization are masked by the high frequencies in the original image.

When quantizing to very few colors, or to a poorly-chosen colormap, the contouring can be visually distracting (see fig. 6). Images which suffer from severe contouring when quantized can be improved with the technique of dithering.

Dithering

The basic strategy of dithering is to trade intensity resolution for spatial resolution. By averaging the intensities of several neighboring pixels one can get colors not represented by the colormap. If the resolution of the frame buffer is high enough, the eye will do the spatial blending for us. Taking advantage of this, it is possible to reproduce many color images using only four colors, as is done in color halftoning.

One simple way to dither is to modulate the original image with a high frequency signal, such as random noise, before quantization [21]. A survey of various dithering techniques can be found in [12].

The dithering technique we recommend is due to Floyd and Steinberg [5]. Their algorithm compensates for the quantization error introduced at each pixel by propagating it to its neighbors. If the propagation is directed only to pixels below or to the right of the "current pixel", we can do both quantization and propagation in one top-to-bottom pass over the image.

A program to quantize and dither a color image using their algorithm would look something like:

```
for i=0 to NI-1 do
   for j=0 to NJ-1 do begin
      x = c_{i,j};        (read a color)
      k = p(x);           (find nearest rep.)
      f_{i,j} = k;        (draw quantized image)
      e = x-y_k;          (quantization error)
                          (distrib. in 3 directions)
      c_{i,j+1}   = c_{i,j+1}   + e*3/8;    →
      c_{i+1,j}   = c_{i+1,j}   + e*3/8;    ↓
      c_{i+1,j+1} = c_{i+1,j+1} + e/4;      ↘
   end
```

In the above, x and e are vectors; i, j, and k are scalars.

The improvement that dithering makes for an image quantized by the median cut method is shown in figures 12 and 17. If the colors are carefully chosen, the Floyd-Steinberg scheme can do surprisingly well with only 4 colors (fig. 7).

Using dither in the last phase of our quantizers raises several unanswered questions. Should our algorithms for colormap selection be altered because we are dithering? If so, how? One would like to guarantee that all colors in the original image can be generated by blending (taking a linear combination of) colors in the colormap. This will be true only if the input colors lie inside the convex hull of the representative colors. Methods to guarantee this deserve further research.

CONCLUSIONS

We found that the architecture of integrated frame buffers forces certain restrictions on any attempt to display color images. One is naturally led to the non-separable multidimensional quantization problem. Although the optimal solution of this problem seems computationally intractable, there are approximate techniques which allow high-quality color quantization to be done efficiently. Using one of the algorithms described, it is possible to display a full-color image using only 256 colors, thus tripling memory efficiency.

To put together a color image quantizer with the algorithms described here, the author would recommend the following. The median cut algorithm is suggested for phase 2 because its sensitivity to the color distribution of the original image is much better than that of the popularity algorithm. To map colors to their nearest neighbors in the colormap, locally sorted search has proven fastest. Dithering is a nice option which is often worth the extra computation required. The author's implementation of the above ensemble on a VAX 11/780 can quantize a 512x480x24-bit image to 256 colors in under one minute.

The quantization techniques presented here could be improved in several ways. By changing the color metric to be more perceptually-based, better-looking quantization would result. Also, it would be nice to find a single database which functions for all phases of the quantization process, to replace the hodgepodge used here. Perhaps the k-d tree created by the median cut algorithm could be used for nearest neighbor search as well.

ACKNOWLEDGEMENTS

Much of the research reported here was done while I was an undergraduate at MIT, working part-time at the Architecture Machine Group. I would like to thank Professors Nicholas Negroponte and Andrew Lippman for their support. Thanks to Tom Boyle for introducing me to this fascinating topic, and to Paul Trevithick and Professor Gilbert Strang of the Math Department for assisting with the theoretical formulation of the problem. Dan Franzblau, Walter Bender, and Professor Ron MacNeil were my principal image critics. Kenneth Sloan, now at MIT, was partially responsible for re-sparking my interest in color image quantization.

At NYIT, Lance Williams lent a critical eye, and Becky Allen assisted with preparation of the paper.

REFERENCES

[1] Bellman, R. *Dynamic Programming*. Princeton University Press, Princeton, 1957.

[2] Bentley, J. L., Friedman, J. H. Data structures for range searching. *Computing Surveys* 11, 4 (Dec. 1979), 397-409.

[3] Bruce, J. D. *Optimum Quantization*. MIT R.L.E. Technical Report #429, (1965).

[4] Elias, P. Bounds on performance of optimum quantizers. *IEEE Trans. on Information Theory* IT-16, 2 (Mar. 1970) 172-184.

[5] Floyd, R. W., Steinberg, L. An adaptive algorithm for spatial gray scale. *SID 75, Int. Symp. Dig. Tech. Papers* (1975), 36.

[6] Friedman, J. J., Bentley, J. L., and Finkel, R. A. An algorithm for finding best matches in logarithmic expected time. *ACM Trans. Math. Software* 3, (Sept. 1977), 209-226.

[7] Gray, R. M., Kieffer, J. C., and Linde, Y. Locally optimal block quantizer design. *Information and Control* 45 (1980) 178-198.

[8] Heckbert, P. *Color Image Quantization for Frame Buffer Display.* B.S. thesis Architecture Machine Group, MIT, Cambridge, Mass., 1980.

[9] Huang, T. S., Tretiak, O. J., Prasada, B. T., and Yamaguchi, Y. Design considerations in PCM transmission of low-resolution monochrome still pictures. *Proc. IEEE* 55, 3 (Mar. 1967), 331.

[10] In der Smitten, F. J. Data-reducing source encoding of color picture signals based on chromaticity classes. *Nachrichtentech. Z.* 27, (1974), 176.

[11] Jain, A. K., and Pratt, W. K. Color image quantization. *National Telecommunications Conference 1972 Record*, IEEE Pub. No. 72, CHO 601-5-NTC, (Dec. 1972).

[12] Jarvis, J. F., Judice, N., and Ninke, W. H. A survey of techniques for the display of continuous tone pictures on bilevel displays. *Computer Graphics and Image Processing* 5, 1 (Mar. 1976), 13-40.

[13] Knuth, D. E. *The Art of Computer Programming*, vol. 3, Sorting and Searching. Addison-Wesley, Reading, Mass., 1973.

[14] Koontz, W. L. G., Narendra, P. M., and Fukunaga, K. A branch and bound clustering algorithm. *IEEE Trans. Comput.* C-24, 9 (Sept. 1975), 908-915.

[15] Limb, J. O., Rubinstein, C. B., and Thompson, J. E. Digital coding of color video signals - a review. *IEEE Trans. Commun.* COM-25, 11 (Nov. 1977), 1349-1385.

[16] Lloyd, S. P. *Least squares quantization in PCM's.* Bell Telephone Labs Memo, Murray Hill, N.J., 1957.

[17] Max, J. Quantizing for minimum distortion. *IRE Trans. Information Theory* IT-6, (Mar. 1960), 7.

[18] Newman, W. M., and Sproull, R. F. *Principles of Interactive Computer Graphics.* MacGraw-Hill, New York, 1979.

[19] Panter, P. F., and Dite, W. Quantization distortion in pulse-count modulation with nonuniform spacing of levels. *Proc. IRE* 39, 1 (Jan. 1951), 44.

[20] Pratt, W. K. *Digital Image Processing.* John Wiley and Sons, New York, 1978.

[21] Roberts, L. G. Picture coding using pseudo-random noise. *IRE Trans. Information Theory* IT-8, (Feb. 1962), 145.

[22] Stenger, L. Quantization of TV chrominance signals considering the visibility of small color differences. *IEEE Trans. Communications* COM-25, 11 (Nov. 1977), 1393.

fig. 2: 24 bit original image of "Pamela". All images 512x486 resolution.

fig. 3: uniform quantization to 8 bits (3 red, 3 green, 2 blue).

fig. 4: quantized by popularity algorithm (256 colors).

fig. 5: median cut, 256 colors

fig. 6: median cut, 4 colors. (no dither)

fig. 7: median cut, 4 colors. (with Floyd-Steinberg dither)

fig. 8: 24 bit original image of "Marc".

fig. 9: uniform quantization to 8 bits (3 red, 3 green, 2 blue).

fig. 10: popularity algorithm, 256 colors.

fig. 11: median cut, 256 colors

fig. 12: median cut, with dither, 256 colors.

fig. 13: colormap for fig. 9 after 3 iterations of Lloyd's fixed point algorithm (256 colors).

fig. 14: 24 bit original image of "Surface" (the surface of the RGB color cube unrolled).

fig. 15: popularity algorithm, 256 colors.

fig. 16: median cut, 256 colors.

fig. 17: median cut with dither, 256 colors.

fig. 18: exploded view of 16 tapered quantization cells in the RGB cube.

MARCHING CUBES: A HIGH RESOLUTION 3D SURFACE CONSTRUCTION ALGORITHM

William E. Lorensen
Harvey E. Cline

General Electric Company
Corporate Research and Development
Schenectady, New York 12301

Abstract

We present a new algorithm, called *marching cubes*, that creates triangle models of constant density surfaces from 3D medical data. Using a divide-and-conquer approach to generate inter-slice connectivity, we create a case table that defines triangle topology. The algorithm processes the 3D medical data in scan-line order and calculates triangle vertices using linear interpolation. We find the gradient of the original data, normalize it, and use it as a basis for shading the models. The detail in images produced from the generated surface models is the result of maintaining the inter-slice connectivity, surface data, and gradient information present in the original 3D data. Results from computed tomography (CT), magnetic resonance (MR), and single-photon emission computed tomography (SPECT) illustrate the quality and functionality of *marching cubes*. We also discuss improvements that decrease processing time and add solid modeling capabilities.

CR Categories: 3.3, 3.5

Additional Keywords: computer graphics, medical imaging, surface reconstruction

1. INTRODUCTION.

Three-dimensional surfaces of the anatomy offer a valuable medical tool. Images of these surfaces, constructed from multiple 2D slices of computed tomography (CT), magnetic resonance (MR), and single-photon emission computed tomography (SPECT), help physicians to understand the complex anatomy present in the slices. Interpretation of 2D medical images requires special training, and although radiologists have these skills, they must often communicate their interpretations to the referring physicians, who sometimes have difficulty visualizing the 3D anatomy.

Researchers have reported the application of 3D medical images in a variety of areas. The visualization of complex acetabular fractures [6], craniofacial abnormalities [17,18], and intracranial structure [13] illustrate 3D's potential for the study of complex bone structures. Applications in radiation therapy [27,11] and surgical planning [4,5,31] show interactive 3D techniques combined with 3D surface images. Cardiac applications include artery visualization [2,16] and nongraphic modeling applications to calculate surface area and volume [21].

Existing 3D algorithms lack detail and sometimes introduce artifacts. We present a new, high-resolution 3D surface construction algorithm that produces models with unprecedented detail. This new algorithm, called *marching cubes*, creates a polygonal representation of constant density surfaces from a 3D array of data. The resulting model can be displayed with conventional graphics-rendering algorithms implemented in software or hardware.

After describing the information flow for 3D medical applications, we describe related work and discuss the drawbacks of that work. Then we describe the algorithm as well as efficiency and functional enhancements, followed by case studies using three different medical imaging techniques to illustrate the new algorithm's capabilities.

2. INFORMATION FLOW FOR 3D MEDICAL ALGORITHMS.

Medical applications of 3D consist of four steps (Figure 1). Although one can combine the last three steps into one algorithm, we logically decompose the process as follows:

1. *Data acquisition.*
   This first step, performed by the medical imaging hardware, samples some property in a patient and produces multiple 2D slices of information. The data sampled depends on the data acquisition technique.

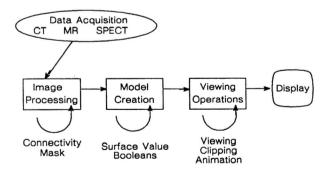

Figure 1. 3D Medical Information Flow.

X-ray computed tomography (CT) measures the spatially varying X-ray attenuation coefficient [3]. CT images show internal structure. For 3D applications, CT is frequently used to look at bone structure, although we have had success visualizing soft tissue.

Magnetic resonance (MR) measures three physical properties [20]. One property is the distribution of "mobile" hydrogen nuclei and shows overall structure within the slices. The other two properties measure relaxation times of the nuclei. MR, a recent technique, shows excellent contrast between a variety of soft tissues. However, the variety of surfaces presents a challenge to 3D surface construction and requires techniques for selective surface extraction and display.

A third acquisition technique, single-photon emission computed tomography (SPECT) measures the emission of gamma rays [24]. The source of these rays is a radioisotope distributed within the body. In addition to structure, SPECT can show the presence of blood in structures with a much lower dose than that required by CT.

2. *Image processing.*
Some algorithms use image processing techniques to find structures within the 3D data [1,32,30,29] or to filter the original data. MR data, in particular, needs image processing to select appropriate structure.

3. *Surface construction.*
Surface construction, the topic of this paper, involves the creation of a surface model from the 3D data. The model usually consists of 3D volume elements (voxels) or polygons. Users select the desired surface by specifying a density value. This step can also include the creation of cut or capped surfaces.

4. *Display.*
Having created the surface, the final step displays that surface using display techniques that include ray casting, depth shading, and color shading.

3. RELATED WORK.

There are several approaches to the 3D surface generation problem. An early technique [23] starts with contours of the surface to be constructed and connects contours on consecutive slices with triangles. Unfortunately, if more than one contour of surface exists on a slice, ambiguities arise when determining which contours to connect [14]. Interactive intervention by the user can overcome some of these ambiguities [8]; however, in a clinical environment, user interaction should be kept to a minimum.

Another approach, developed by G. Herman and colleagues [19] creates surfaces from cuberilles. A cuberille is "dissection of space into equal cubes (called voxels) by three orthogonal sets of parallel planes [7]." Although there are many ways to display a cuberille model, the most realistic images result when the gradient, calculated from cuberilles in a neighborhood, is used to find the shade of a point on the model [15]. Meagher [25] uses an octree representation to compress the storage of the 3D data, allowing rapid manipulation and display of voxels.

Farrell [12] uses ray casting to find the 3D surface, but rather than shade the image with a gray scale, uses hue lightness to display the surface. In another ray casting method, Hohne [22], after locating the surface along a ray, calculates the gradient along the surface and uses this gradient, scaled by an "appropriate" value, to generate gray scales for the image.

A different approach, used at the Mayo Clinic [26], displays the density volume rather than the surface. This method produces, in effect, a conventional shadow graph that can be viewed from arbitrary angles. Motion enhances the three-dimensional effect obtained using the volume model.

Each of these techniques for surface construction and display suffer shortcomings because they throw away useful information in the original data. The connected contour algorithms throw away the inter-slice connectivity that exists in the original data. The cuberille approach, using thresholding to represent the surface as blocks in 3D space, attempts to recover shading information from the blocks. The ray casting methods either use depth shading alone, or try to approximate shading with an unnormalized gradient. Since they display all values and not just those visible from a given point of view, volume models rely on motion to produce a three-dimensional sensation.

Our approach uses information from the original 3D data to derive inter-slice connectivity, surface location, and surface gradient. The resulting triangle model can be displayed on conventional graphics display systems using standard rendering algorithms.

4. MARCHING CUBES ALGORITHM.

There are two primary steps in our approach to the surface construction problem. First, we locate the surface corresponding to a user-specified value and create triangles. Then, to ensure a quality image of the surface, we calculate the normals to the surface at each vertex of each triangle.

Marching cubes uses a divide-and-conquer approach to locate the surface in a logical *cube* created from eight pixels: four each from two adjacent slices (Figure 2).

The algorithm determines how the surface intersects this cube, then moves (or *marchs*) to the next cube. To find the surface intersection in a cube, we assign a one to a cube's vertex if the data value at that vertex exceeds (or equals) the value of the surface we are constructing. These vertices are inside (or on) the surface. Cube vertices with values below the surface receive a zero and are outside the surface. The surface intersects those cube edges where one vertex is outside the surface (one) and the other is inside the surface (zero). With this assumption, we determine the topology of the surface within a cube, finding the location of the intersection later.

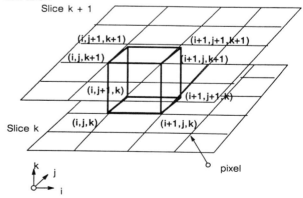

Figure 2. Marching Cube.

Since there are eight vertices in each cube and two states, inside and outside, there are only $2^8 = 256$ ways a surface can intersect the cube. By enumerating these 256 cases, we create a table to look up surface-edge intersections, given the labeling of a cubes vertices. The table contains the edges intersected for each case.

Triangulating the 256 cases is possible but tedious and error-prone. Two different symmetries of the cube reduce the problem from 256 cases to 14 patterns. First, the topology of the triangulated surface is unchanged if the relationship of the surface values to the cubes is reversed. Complementary cases, where vertices greater than the surface value are interchanged with those less than the value, are equivalent. Thus, only cases with zero to four vertices greater than the surface value need be considered, reducing the number of cases to 128. Using the second symmetry property, rotational symmetry, we reduced the problem to 14 patterns by inspection. Figure 3 shows the triangulation for the 14 patterns.

The simplest pattern, 0, occurs if all vertex values are above (or below) the selected value and produces no triangles. The next pattern, 1, occurs if the surface separates on vertex from the other seven, resulting in one triangle defined by the three edge intersections. Other patterns produce multiple triangles. Permutation of these 14 basic patterns using complementary and rotational symmetry produces the 256 cases.

We create an index for each case, based on the state of the vertex. Using the vertex numbering in Figure 4, the eight bit index contains one bit for each vertex.

This index serves as a pointer into an edge table that gives all edge intersections for a given cube configuration.

Using the index to tell which edge the surface intersects, we can interpolate the surface intersection along the edge. We use linear interpolation, but have experimented with higher degree interpolations. Since the algorithm produces at least one and as many as four triangles per cube, the higher degree surfaces show little improvement over linear interpolation.

The final step in *marching cubes* calculates a unit normal for each triangle vertex. The rendering algorithms use this normal to produce Gouraud-shaded images. A surface of constant density has a zero gradient component along the surface tangential direction; consequently, the direction of the gradient vector, $\vec{g}$, is normal to the surface. We can use this fact to determine surface normal vector, $\vec{n}$, if the magnitude of the gradient, $|\vec{g}|$, is nonzero. Fortunately, at the surface of interest between two tissue types of different densities, the gradient vector is nonzero. The gradient vector, $\vec{g}$, is the derivative of the density function

$$\vec{g}(x,y,z) = \nabla \vec{f}(x,y,z). \quad (1)$$

To estimate the gradient vector at the surface of interest, we first estimate the gradient vectors at the cube vertices and linearly interpolate the gradient at the point of intersection. The gradient at cube vertex (i, j, k), is estimated using central differences along the three coordinate axes by:

$$G_x(i,j,k) = \frac{D(i+1,j,k) - D(i-1,j,k)}{\Delta x} \quad (2)$$

$$G_y(i,j,k) = \frac{D(i,j+1,k) - D(i,j-1,k)}{\Delta y} \quad (3)$$

$$G_z(i,j,k) = \frac{D(i,j,k+1) - D(i,j,k-1)}{\Delta z} \quad (4)$$

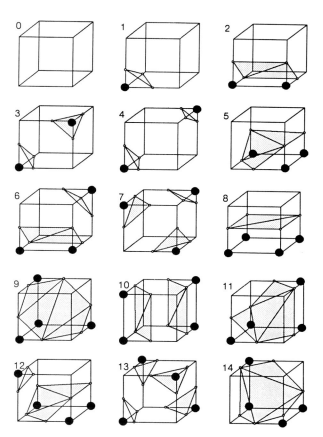

Figure 3. Triangulated Cubes.

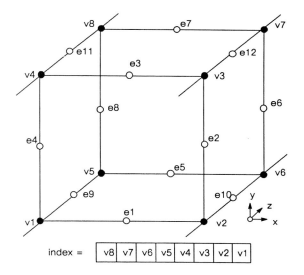

Figure 4. Cube Numbering.

where $D(i,j,k)$ is the density at pixel (i,j) in slice k and $\Delta x, \Delta y, \Delta z$ are the lengths of the cube edges. Dividing the gradient by its length produces the unit normal at the vertex required for rendering. We linearly interpolate this normal to the point of intersection. Note that to calculate the gradient at all vertices of the cube, we keep four slices in memory at once.

In summary, *marching cubes* creates a surface from a three-dimensional set of data as follows:

1. Read four slices into memory.
2. Scan two slices and create a cube from four neighbors on one slice and four neighbors on the next slice.
3. Calculate an index for the cube by comparing the eight density values at the cube vertices with the surface constant.
4. Using the index, look up the list of edges from a precalculated table.
5. Using the densities at each edge vertex, find the surface-edge intersection via linear interpolation.
6. Calculate a unit normal at each cube vertex using central differences. Interpolate the normal to each triangle vertex.
7. Output the triangle vertices and vertex normals.

5. ENHANCEMENTS TO THE BASIC ALGORITHM.

We have made several improvements to the original *marching cubes* that make the algorithm run faster and that add solid modeling capabilities.

5.1 Efficiency Enhancements.

The efficiency enhancements allow the algorithm to take advantage of pixel-to-pixel, line-to-line, and slice-to-slice coherence. For cubes interior to the original data limits (those not including slice 0, line 0, or pixel 0), only three new edges need to be interpolated for each cube. We can obtain the other nine edges from previous slices, lines, or pixels. In Figure 5, the shaded circles represent values available from prior calculations; only edges 6, 7, and 12 have to be calculated for the new cube.

Special cases are present along the boundaries of the data, but, by enumerating these cases, we can limit vertex calculations to once per vertex. In practice, we only save the previous pixel and line intersections because the memory required to save the previous slice's intersections is large. Using the coherence speeds up the algorithm by a factor of three.

Reducing the slice resolution, by averaging four pixels into one, decreases the number of triangles, improves the surface construction efficiency and smooths the image. Although there is some loss of detail in the averaged slices, the averaging makes the number of triangles more manageable for high-resolution slices.

5.2 Functional Enhancements.

We have added a solid modeling capability to the algorithm. Boolean operations permit cutting and capping of solid models, as well as the extraction of multiple surfaces. In a medical application, cutting is analogous to performing surgery and capping (and texture mapping) is analogous to the medical imaging technique of reformatting.

We use the cube index described earlier to do Boolean operations on the surfaces. Here, just consider three values of the index:

index = 0 for cubes outside the surface.
index = 255 for cubes inside the surface.
0 < index < 255 for cubes on the surface.

Solid modeling uses these notions of *inside*, *outside*, and *on* to create a surface. Analytic functions also provide the same information; so, for example the equation of a plane, $ax + by + cz - d$, tells where a given point lies with respect to the plane. Let ~**S**, δ**S**, and **S** represent sets of points that are outside, on, and inside a surface, respectively. Referring to Figure 6, we build a truth table, shown in Figure 7, for the Boolean intersection operation.

Nine entries in the truth table describe what to do when two surfaces have a given index. With **x**'s representing no operation, the entry for (**S**, ~**P**) shows that the cube in question is inside one surface but outside the other, resulting in no triangles. The (δ**S**, **P**) entry produces triangles from the *S* surface, while the (**S**, δ**P**) entry produces triangles from the *P* surface. The (δ**S**, δ**P**) entry, created when a cube is on both surfaces, requires special processing. We clip

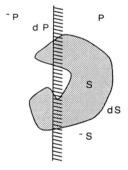

Figure 6. Point/Surface Relations.

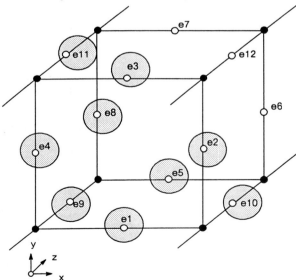

Figure 5. Coherence.

	P	~P	dP
S	x	x	P
~S	x	x	x
dS	S	x	*

Figure 7. Truth Table.

each triangle from one surface against each triangle from the other, using the Sutherland-Hodgman clipping algorithm [28].

This technique applies to any surfaces that have inside/outside functions. We have used it with planes and with connectivity masks generated by separate image processing algorithms [9]. Application of a "logical or" truth table provides the capability for multiple surface extraction.

We implement texture mapping by finding the triangles on a plane's surface and attenuating the normal's length using the original slice data.

6. IMPLEMENTATION.

Marching cubes, written in C, runs on Sun Workstations[1] under Unix[2], VAX's under VMS[3], and an IBM 3081 under IX/370[4]. We display the models using an in-house z-buffer program or a General Electric Graphicon 700[5]. For our models, the Graphicon displays at a rate of 10,000 triangles per second. In addition to surfaces of constant density, the software allows any number of planes that can be transparent, capped with triangles, or textured with interpolated density data. Medical practitioners refer to this texture mapping as reformatting. Execution times depend on the number of surfaces and resolution of the original data. Model creation times on a VAX 11/780 vary from 100 seconds for 64 by 64 by 48 SPECT data to 30 minutes for 260 by 260 by 93 CT studies. Times for the same studies on the IBM 3081 are twelve times faster. The number of triangles in a surface model is proportional to the area of the surface. This number can get large (over 500,000 in some cases), so we reduce it using cut planes and surface connectivity. Also, sometimes we reduce the resolution of the original data by filtering, producing a somewhat smoother surface with some loss of resolution.

7. RESULTS.

We have applied *marching cubes* to data obtained from CT, MR, and SPECT, as well as data generated from analytic functions. We present three case studies that illustrate the quality of the constructed surfaces and some modeling options. Each image was rendered at 512 by 512 resolution without antialiasing.

7.1 Computed Tomography.

The first case is a CT study of the head of a twelve year old male with a hole in the skull near the left side of the nose. The 93 axial slices are 1.5 mm thick, with pixel dimensions of 0.8 mm. This study by D.C. Hemmy, MD, of the Medical College of Wisconsin, illustrates the detail present in surfaces constructed by *marching cubes*. Figures 8 and 9 show the bone and soft tissue surfaces respectively. The tube in the patient's mouth is present to administer anesthetic during the scanning process. The soft tissue image shows fine detail that includes the patient's pierced ear and the impression of adhesive tape on the face. Although these details are not clinically significant, they do show the resolution present in the constructed surface. Figure 10 is a tilted view of the soft tissue surface that shows nasal and ear passages. In Figure 11, a sagittal cut, texture mapped with the original

---
1 Sun Workstation is a trademark of Sun Microsystems.
2 Unix is a trademark of Bell Laboratories.
3 VAX and VMS are trademarks of Digital Equipment Corporation
4 IX/370 is a trademark of IBM.
5 Graphicon is a trademark of General Electric Company.

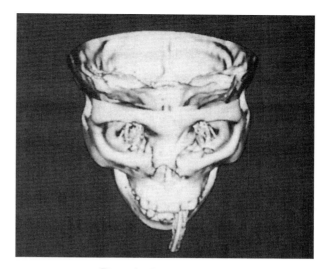

Figure 8. Bone Surface.

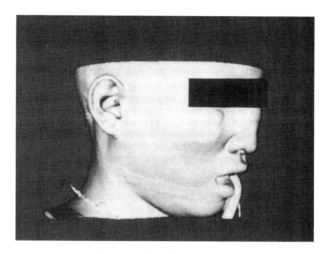

Figure 9. Soft Tissue Surface.

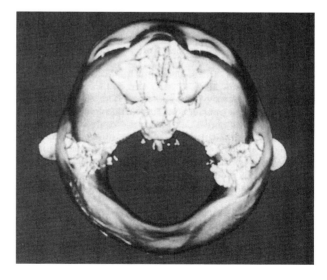

Figure 10. Soft Tissue, Top View.

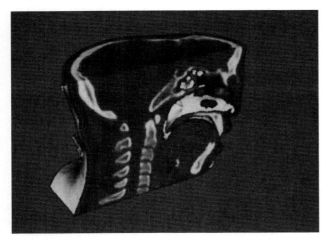

Figure 11. Sagittal Cut with Texture Mapping.

CT data, shows the slice data in relation to the constructed surface. The bone surface contains 550,000 triangles while the soft tissue surface has 375,000.

7.2 Magnetic Resonance.

The MR case of an adult male volunteer consists of 128 1.9 mm coronal slices. A 3D FT, flow compensated, fast sequence acquired the 128 slices in only 9 minutes. This pulse sequence, contrasting the unsaturated spins of the fresh blood flowing into the excited region of saturated spins, was produced by G. Glover of GE Medical Systems Group. Because of the complex anatomy present in the MR slices, we show, in Figure 12, the texture mapped cut surfaces intersected with the surface of the skin. Although the original slices are coronal, we show sagittal cuts to illustrate the algorithm's ability to interpolate texture on a cut plane. The largest surface model in the sequence contains 330,000 triangles, including triangles on the cut surface.

7.3 Single-Photon Emission Computed Tomography.

The SPECT study consisting of 29 coronal slices of the heart shows the algorithm's performance on low resolution data. D. Nowak from GE Medical Systems provided the 64 by 64 pixel data. Figure 13, showing the surface of the blood pool in the diastolic heart, contains 5,000 triangles. The descending aorta is the large vessel in the left of the picture.

8. CONCLUSIONS.

Marching cubes, a new algorithm for 3D surface construction, complements 2D CT, MR, and SPECT data by giving physicians 3D views of the anatomy. The algorithm uses a case table of edge intersections to describe how a surface cuts through each *cube* in a 3D data set. Additional realism is achieved by the calculation, from the original data, of the normalized gradient. The resulting polygonal structure can be displayed on conventional graphics display systems. Although these models often contain large numbers of triangles, surface cutting and connectivity can reduce this number. As CAD hardware increases in speed and capacity, we expect that *marching cubes* will receive increased use in practical, clinical environments.

Recently we developed another high-resolution surface construction algorithm called *dividing cubes* that generates points rather than triangles [10]. As the resolution of the 3D medical data increases, the number of triangles approaches

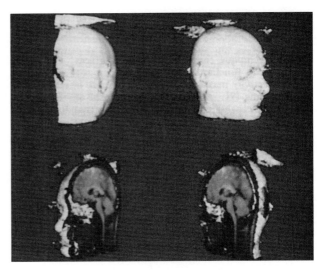

Figure 12. Rotated Sequence of Cut MR Brain

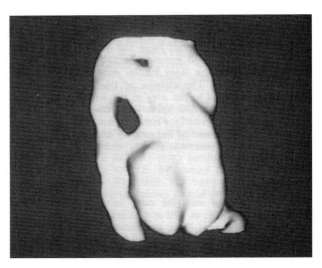

Figure 13. Blood Pool in the Diastolic Heart.

the number of pixels in the displayed image. The density of surface points is chosen to cover the raster display. Both algorithms produce the same quality images, since the shading governs the perceived quality of the image.

9. ACKNOWLEDGMENT.

We thank C. Crawford from General Electric's Medical Systems for stimulating our work in this area. Throughout the project, he has provided us with data and encouragement to improve the algorithm. R. Redington from our laboratory's Medical Diagnostics Branch provided a stable research environment and insight into the practical applications of 3D in medicine. W. Leue assisted us in converting between the different medical data formats and provided interfaces to our MR equipment.

10. REFERENCES

[1] Artzy, E., Frieder, G., and Herman, G. T. The Theory, Design, Implementation and Evaluation of a Three-Dimensional Surface Detection Algorithm. *Computer Graphics and Image Processing 15*, 1 (January 1981), 1-24.

[2] Barillot, C., Gibaud, B., Scarabin, J., and Coatrieux, J. 3D Reconstruction of Cerebral Blood Vessels. *IEEE Computer Graphics and Applications 5*, 12 (December 1985), 13-19.

[3] Bates, R. H., Garden, K. L., and Peters, T. M. Overview of Computerized Tomography with Emphasis on Future Developments. *Proc. of the IEEE 71*, 3 (March 1983), 356-372.

[4] Bloch, P. and Udupa, J. K. Application of Computerized Tomography to Radiation Therapy and Surgical Planning. *Proc. of the IEEE 71*, 3 (March 1983), 351-355.

[5] Brewster, L. J., Trivedi, S. S., Tut, H. K., and Udupa, J. K. Interactive Surgical Planning. *IEEE Computer Graphics and Applications 4*, 3 (March 1984), 31-40.

[6] Burk, D. L., Mears, D. C., Kennedy, W. H., Cooperstein, L. A., and Herbert, D. L. Three-Dimensional Computed Tomography of Acetabula Fractures. *Radiology 155*, 1 (1985), 183-186.

[7] Chen, L., Herman, G. T., Reynolds, R. A., and Udupa, J. K. Surface Shading in the Cuberille Environment. *IEEE Computer Graphics and Applications 5*, 12 (December 1985), 33-43.

[8] Christiansen, H. N. and Sederberg, T. W. Conversion of Complex Contour Line Definitions into Polygonal Element Meshes. *Computer Graphics 12*, 3 (August 1978), 187-192.

[9] Cline, H. E., Dumoulin, C. L., Lorensen, W. E., Hart, H. R., and Ludke, S. 3D Reconstruction of the Brain from Magnetic Resonance Images. *Magnetic Resonance Imaging* (1987, to appear).

[10] Cline, H. E., Lorensen, W. E., Ludke, S., Crawford, C. R., and Teeter, B. C. High-Resolution Three-Dimensional Reconstruction of Tomograms. *Medical Physics* (1987, to appear).

[11] Cook, L. T., Dwyer, S. J., Batnitzky, S., and Lee, K. R. A Three-Dimensional Display System for Diagnostic Imaging Applications. *IEEE Computer Graphics and Applications 3*, 5 (August 1983), 13-19.

[12] Farrell, E. J. Color Display and Interactive Interpretation of Three-Dimensional Data. *IBM J. Res. Develop 27*, 4 (July 1983), 356-366.

[13] Farrell, E. J., Zappulla, R., and Yang, W. C. Color 3D Imaging of Normal and Pathologic Intracranial Structures. *IEEE Computer Graphics and Applications 4*, 9 (September 1984), 5-17.

[14] Fuchs, H., Kedem, Z. M., and Uselton, S. P. Optimal Surface Reconstruction from Planar Contours. *Comm. of the ACM 20*, 10 (October 1977), 693-702.

[15] Gordon, D. and Reynolds, R. A. Image Space Shading of 3-Dimensional Objects. *Computer Graphics and Image Processing 29*, 3 (March 1985), 361-376.

[16] Hale, J. D., Valk, P. E., and Watts, J. C. MR Imaging of Blood Vessels Using Three-Dimensional Reconstruction: Methodology. *Radiology 157*, 3 (December 1985), 727-733.

[17] Hemmy, D. C., David, D. J., and Herman, G. T. Three-Dimensional Reconstruction of Craniofacial Deformity Using Computed Tomography. *Neurosurgery 13*, 5 (November 1983), 534-541.

[18] Hemmy, D. C. and Tessier, P. L. CT of Dry Skulls with Craniofacial Deformities: Accuracy of Three-Dimensional Reconstruction. *Radiology 157*, 1 (October 1985), 113-116.

[19] Herman, G. T. and Udupa, J. K. Display of 3D Digital Images: Computational Foundations and Medical Applications. *IEEE Computer Graphics and Applications 3*, 5 (August 1983), 39-46.

[20] Hinshaw, W. S. and Lent, A. H. An Introduction to NMR Imaging: From the Bloch Equation to the Imaging Equation. *Proc. of the IEEE 71*, 3 (March 1983), 338-350.

[21] Hoffman, E. A. and Ritman, E. L. Shape and Dimensions of Cardiac Chambers: Importance of CT Section Thickness and Orientation. *Radiology 155*, 3 (June 1985), 739-744.

[22] Hohne, K. H. and Bernstein, R. Shading 3D-Images from CT Using Gray-Level Gradients. *IEEE Trans. on Medical Imaging MI-5*, 1 (March 1986), 45-47.

[23] Keppel, E. Approximating Complex Surfaces by Triangulation of Contour Lines. *IBM J. Res. Develop 19*, 1 (January 1975), 2-11.

[24] Knoll, G. F. Single-Photon Emission Computed Tomography. *Proc. of the IEEE 71*, 3 (March 1983), 320-329.

[25] Meagher, D. J. Geometric Modeling Using Octree Encoding. *Computer Graphics and Image Processing 19*, 2 (June 1982), 129-147.

[26] Robb, R. A., Hoffman, E. A., Sinak, L. J., Harris, L. D., and Ritman, E. L. High-Speed Three-Dimensional X-Ray Computed Tomography: The Dynamic Spatial Reconstructor. *Proc. of the IEEE 71*, 3 (March 1983), 308-319.

[27] Sunguroff, A. and Greenberg, D. Computer Generated Images for Medical Application. *Computer Graphics 12*, 3 (August 1978), 196-202.

[28] Sutherland, I. E. and Hodgman, G. W. Reentrant Polygon Clipping. *Comm. of the ACM 17*, 1 (January 1974), 32-42.

[29] Trivedi, S. S., Herman, G. T., and Udupa, J. K. Segmentation Into Three Classes Using Gradients. *IEEE Trans. on Medical Imaging MI-5*, 2 (June 1986), 116-119.

[30] Udupa, J. K. Interactive Segmentation and Boundary Surface Formation for 3-D Digital Images. *Computer Graphics and Image Processing 18*, 3 (March 1982), 213-235.

[31] Vannier, M. W., Marsh, J. L., and Warren, J. O. Three Dimensional CT Reconstruction Images for Craniofacial Surgical Planning and Evaluation. *Radiology 150*, 1 (January 1984), 179-184.

[32] Zucker, S. W. and Hummel, R. A. A Three-Dimensional Edge Operator. *IEEE Trans. on Pattern Analysis and Machine Intelligence PAMI-3*, 3 (May 1981), 324-331.

Compositing Digital Images

Thomas Porter
Tom Duff †

Computer Graphics Project
Lucasfilm Ltd.

ABSTRACT

Most computer graphics pictures have been computed all at once, so that the rendering program takes care of all computations relating to the overlap of objects. There are several applications. however, where elements must be rendered separately, relying on compositing techniques for the anti-aliased accumulation of the full image. This paper presents the case for four-channel pictures, demonstrating that a matte component can be computed similarly to the color channels. The paper discusses guidelines for the generation of elements and the arithmetic for their arbitrary compositing.

CR Categories and Subject Descriptors: I.3.3 [**Computer Graphics**]: Picture/Image Generations — Display algorithms; I.3.4 [**Computer Graphics**]: Graphics Utilities — Software support; I.4.1 [**Image Processing**]: Digitization — Sampling.

General Terms: Algorithms

Additional Key Words and Phrases: compositing, matte channel, matte algebra, visible surface algorithms, graphics systems

---

† Author's current address: AT&T Bell Laboratories, Murray Hill, NJ 07974, Room 2C465

Permission to copy without fee all or part of this material is granted provided that the copies are not made or distributed for direct commercial advantage, the ACM copyright notice and the title of the publication and its date appear, and notice is given that copying is by permission of the Association for Computing Machinery. To copy otherwise, or to republish, requires a fee and/or specific permission.

© 1984 ACM 0-89791-138-5/84/007/0253 $00.75

1. Introduction

Increasingly, we find that a complex three dimensional scene cannot be fully rendered by a single program. The wealth of literature on rendering polygons and curved surfaces, handling the special cases of fractals and spheres and quadrics and triangles, implementing refinements for texture mapping and bump mapping, noting speed-ups on the basis of coherence or depth complexity in the scene, suggests that multiple programs are necessary.

In fact, reliance on a single program for rendering an entire scene is a poor strategy for minimizing the cost of small modeling errors. Experience has taught us to break down large bodies of source code into separate modules in order to save compilation time. An error in one routine forces only the recompilation of its module and the relatively quick reloading of the entire program. Similarly, small errors in coloration or design in one object should not force the "recompilation" of an entire image.

Separating the image into *elements* which can be independently rendered saves enormous time. Each element has an associated *matte,* coverage information which designates the shape of the element. The *compositing* of those elements makes use of the mattes to accumulate the final image.

The compositing methodology must not induce aliasing in the image; soft edges of the elements must be honored in computing the final image. Features should be provided to exploit the full associativity of the compositing process; this affords flexibility, for example, for the accumulation of several foreground elements into an aggregate foreground which can be examined over different backgrounds. The compositor should provide facilities for arbitrary dissolves and fades of elements during an animated sequence.

Several highly successful rendering algorithms have worked by reducing their environments to pieces that can be combined in a 2 1/2 dimensional manner, and then overlaying them either front-to-back or back-to-front [3]. Whitted and Weimar's graphics test-bed [6] and Crow's image generation environment [2] are both designed to deal with heterogenously rendered elements. Whitted and Weimar's system reduces all objects to horizontal spans which are composited using a Warnock-like algorithm. In Crow's system a supervisory process decides the order in which to combine images created by independent special-purpose rendering processes. The imaging system of Warnock and Wyatt [5] incorporates 1-bit mattes. The Hanna-Barbera cartoon animation system [4] incorporates soft-edge mattes, representing the opacity information in a less convenient manner than that proposed here. The present paper presents guidelines for rendering elements and introduces the algebra for compositing.

2. The Alpha Channel

A separate component is needed to retain the matte information, the extent of coverage of an element at a pixel. In a full color rendering of an element, the RGB components retain only the color. In order to place the element over an arbitrary background, a mixing factor is required at every pixel to control the linear interpolation of foreground and background colors. In general, there is no way to encode this component as part of the color information. For anti-aliasing purposes, this mixing factor needs to be of comparable resolution to the color channels. Let us call this an *alpha* channel, and let us treat an alpha of 0 to indicate no coverage, 1 to mean full coverage, with fractions corresponding to partial coverage.

In an environment where the compositing of elements is required, we see the need for an alpha channel as an integral part of all pictures. Because mattes are naturally computed along with the picture, a separate alpha component in the frame buffer is appropriate. Off-line storage of alpha information along with color works conveniently into run-length encoding schemes because the alpha information tends to abide by the same runs.

What is the meaning of the quadruple (r,g,b,α) at a pixel? How do we express that a pixel is half covered by a full red object? One obvious suggestion is to assign $(1,0,0,.5)$ to that pixel: the .5 indicates the coverage and the $(1,0,0)$ is the color. There are a few reasons to dismiss this proposal, the most severe being that all compositing operations will involve multiplying the 1 in the red channel by the .5 in the alpha channel to compute the red contribution of this object at this pixel. The desire to avoid this multiplication points up a better solution, storing the *pre-multiplied* value in the color component, so that $(.5,0,0,.5)$ will indicate a full red object half covering a pixel.

The quadruple (r,g,b,α) indicates that the pixel is α covered by the color $(r/\alpha, g/\alpha, b/\alpha)$. A quadruple where the alpha component is less than a color component indicates a color outside the [0,1] interval, which is somewhat unusual. We will see later that luminescent objects can be usefully represented in this way. For the representation of normal objects, an alpha of 0 at a pixel generally forces the color components to be 0. Thus the RGB channels record the true colors where alpha is 1, linearly darkened colors for fractional alphas along edges, and black where alpha is 0. Silhouette edges of RGBA elements thus exhibit their anti-aliased nature when viewed on an RGB monitor.

It is important to distinguish between two key pixel representations:
$black = (0,0,0,1);$
$clear = (0,0,0,0).$
The former pixel is an opaque black; the latter pixel is transparent.

3. RGBA Pictures

If we survey the variety of elements which contribute to a complex animation, we find many complete background images which have an alpha of 1 everywhere. Among foreground elements, we find that the color components roll off in step with the alpha channel, leaving large areas of transparency. Mattes, colorless stencils used for controlling the compositing of other elements, have 0 in their RGB components. Off-line storage of RGBA pictures should therefore provide the natural data compression for handling the RGB pixels of backgrounds, RGBA pixels of foregrounds, and A pixels of mattes.

There are some objections to computing with these RGBA pictures. Storage of the color components premultiplied by the alpha would seem to unduly quantize the color resolution, especially as alpha approaches 0. However, because any compositing of the picture will require that multiplication anyway, storage of the product forces only a very minor loss of precision in this regard. Color extraction, to compute in a different color space for example, becomes more difficult. We must recover $(r/\alpha, g/\alpha, b/\alpha)$, and once again, as alpha approaches 0, the precision falls off sharply. For our applications, this has yet to affect us.

4. The Algebra of Compositing

Given this standard of RGBA pictures, let us examine how compositing works. We shall do this by enumerating the complete set of binary compositing operations. For each of these, we shall present a formula for computing the contribution of each of two input pictures to the output composite at each pixel. We shall pay particular attention to the output pixels, to see that they remain pre-multiplied by their alpha.

4.1. Assumptions

When blending pictures together, we do not have information about overlap of coverage information within a pixel; all we have is an alpha value. When we consider the mixing of two pictures at a pixel, we must make some assumption about the interplay of the two alpha values. In order to examine that interplay, let us first consider the overlap of two semi-transparent elements like haze, then consider the overlap of two opaque, hard-edged elements.

If α_A and α_B represent the opaqueness of semi-transparent objects which fully cover the pixel, the computation is well known. Each object lets $(1-\alpha)$ of the background through, so that the background shows through only $(1-\alpha_A)(1-\alpha_B)$ of the pixel. $\alpha_A(1-\alpha_B)$ of the background is blocked by object A and passed by object B; $(1-\alpha_A)\alpha_B$ of the background is passed by A and blocked by B. This leaves $\alpha_A\alpha_B$ of the pixel which we can consider to be blocked by both.

If α_A and α_B represent subpixel areas covered by opaque geometric objects, the overlap of objects within the pixel is quite arbitrary. We know that object A divides the pixel into two subpixel areas of ratio $\alpha_A:1-\alpha_A$. We know that object B divides the pixel into two subpixel areas of ratio $\alpha_B:1-\alpha_B$. Lacking further information, we make the following assumption: *there is nothing special about the shape of the pixel; we expect that object B will divide each of the subpixel areas inside and outside of object A into the same ratio* $\alpha_B:1-\alpha_B$. The result of the assumption is the same arithmetic as with semi-transparent objects and is summarized in the following table:

description	area
$\bar{A} \cap \bar{B}$	$(1-\alpha_A)(1-\alpha_B)$
$A \cap \bar{B}$	$\alpha_A(1-\alpha_B)$
$\bar{A} \cap B$	$(1-\alpha_A)\alpha_B$
$A \cap B$	$\alpha_A\alpha_B$

The assumption is quite good for most mattes, though it can be improved if we know that the coverage seldom overlaps (adjacent segments of a continuous line) or always overlaps (repeated application of a picture). For ease in presentation throughout this paper, let us make this assumption and consider the alpha values as representing subpixel coverage of opaque objects.

4.2. Compositing Operators

Consider two pictures A and B. They divide each pixel into the 4 subpixel areas

B	A	name	description	choices
0	0	0	$\bar{A} \cap \bar{B}$	0
0	1	A	$A \cap \bar{B}$	0, A
1	0	B	$\bar{A} \cap B$	0, B
1	1	AB	$A \cap B$	0, A, B

listed in this table along with the choices in each area for contributing to the composite. In the last area, for example, because both input pictures exist there, either could survive to the composite. Alternatively, the composite could be clear in that area.

A particular binary compositing operation can be identified as a quadruple indicating the input picture which contributes to the composite in each of the four subpixel areas 0, A, B, AB of the table above. With three choices where the pictures intersect, two where only one picture exists and one outside the two pictures, there are $3 \times 2 \times 2 \times 1 = 12$ distinct compositing operations listed in the table below. Note that pictures A and B are diagrammed as covering the pixel with triangular wedges whose overlap conforms to the assumption above.

operation	quadruple	diagram	F_A	F_B
clear	(0,0,0,0)		0	0
A	(0,A,0,A)		1	0
B	(0,0,B,B)		0	1
A **over** *B*	(0,A,B,A)		1	$1-\alpha_A$
B **over** *A*	(0,A,B,B)		$1-\alpha_B$	1
A **in** *B*	(0,0,0,A)		α_B	0
B **in** *A*	(0,0,0,B)		0	α_A
A **out** *B*	(0,A,0,0)		$1-\alpha_B$	0
B **out** *A*	(0,0,B,0)		0	$1-\alpha_A$
A **atop** *B*	(0,0,B,A)		α_B	$1-\alpha_A$
B **atop** *A*	(0,A,0,B)		$1-\alpha_B$	α_A
A **xor** *B*	(0,A,B,0)		$1-\alpha_B$	$1-\alpha_A$

Useful operators include *A* **over** *B*, *A* **in** *B*, and *A* **held out by** *B*. *A* **over** *B* is the placement of foreground A in front of background B. *A* **in** *B* refers only to that part of A inside picture B. *A* **held out by** *B*, normally shortened to *A* **out** *B*, refers only to that part of A outside picture B. For completeness, we include the less useful operators *A* **atop** *B* and *A* **xor** *B*. *A* **atop** *B* is the union of *A* **in** *B* and *B* **out** *A*. Thus, *paper* **atop** *table* includes *paper* where it is on top of *table*, and *table* otherwise; area beyond the edge of the table is out of the picture. *A* **xor** *B* is the union of *A* **out** *B* and *B* **out** *A*.

4.3. Compositing Arithmetic

For each of the compositing operations, we would like to compute the contribution of each input picture at each pixel. This is quite easily solved by recognizing that each input picture survives in the composite pixel only within its own matte. For each input picture, we are looking for that fraction of its own matte which prevails in the output. By definition then, the alpha value of the composite, the total area of the pixel covered, can be computed by adding α_A times its fraction F_A to α_B times its fraction F_B.

The color of the composite can be computed on a component basis by adding the color of the picture A times its fraction to the color of picture B times its fraction. To see this, let c_A, c_B, and c_O be some color component of pictures A, B and the composite, and let C_A, C_B, and C_O be the true color component before pre-multiplication by alpha. Then we have

$$c_O = \alpha_O C_O$$

Now C_O can be computed by averaging contributions made by C_A and C_B, so

$$c_O = \alpha_O \frac{\alpha_A F_A C_A + \alpha_B F_B C_B}{\alpha_A F_A + \alpha_B F_B}$$

but the denominator is just α_O, so

$$\begin{aligned} c_O &= \alpha_A F_A C_A + \alpha_B F_B C_B \\ &= \alpha_A F_A \frac{c_A}{\alpha_A} + \alpha_B F_B \frac{c_B}{\alpha_B} \\ &= c_A F_A + c_B F_B \end{aligned} \quad (1)$$

Because each of the input colors is pre-multiplied by its alpha, and we are adding contributions from non-overlapping areas, the sum will be effectively pre-multiplied by the alpha value of the composite just computed. The pleasant result that the color channels are handled with the same computation as alpha can be traced back to our decision to store pre-multiplied RGBA quadruples. Thus the problem is reduced to finding a table of fractions F_A and F_B which indicate the extent of contribution of A and B, plugging these values into equation 1 for both the color and the alpha components.

By our assumptions above, the fractions are quickly determined by examining the pixel diagram included in the table of operations. Those fractions are listed in the F_A and F_B columns of the table. For example, in the A **over** B case, picture A survives everywhere while picture B survives only outside picture A, so the corresponding fractions are 1 and $(1-\alpha_A)$. Substituting into equation 1, we find

$$c_O = c_A \times 1 + c_B \times (1-\alpha_A).$$

This is almost the well used linear interpolation of foreground F with background B

$$B' = F \times \alpha + B \times (1-\alpha),$$

except that our foreground is pre-multiplied by alpha.

4.4. Unary operators

To assist us in dissolving and in balancing color brightness of elements contributing to a composite, it is useful to introduce a darken factor ϕ and a dissolve factor δ:

darken$(A,\phi) \equiv (\phi r_A, \phi g_A, \phi b_A, \alpha_A)$
dissolve$(A,\delta) \equiv (\delta r_A, \delta g_A, \delta b_A, \delta \alpha_A)$.

Normally, $0 \leq \phi, \delta \leq 1$ although none of the theory requires it.

As ϕ varies from 1 to 0, the element will change from normal to complete blackness. If $\phi > 1$ the element will be brightened. As δ goes from 1 to 0 the element will gradually fade from view.

Luminescent objects, which add color information without obscuring the background, can be handled with the introduction of a opaqueness factor ω, $0 \leq \omega \leq 1$:

opaque$(A,\omega) \equiv (r_A, g_A, b_A, \omega \alpha_A)$.

As ω varies from 1 to 0, the element will change from normal coverage over the background to no obscuration. This scaling of the alpha channel alone will cause pixel quadruples where α is less than a color component, indicating a representation of a color outside of the normal range. This possibility forces us to clip the output composite to the [0,1] range.

An ω of 0 will produce quadruples $(r,g,b,0)$ which do have meaning. The color channels, pre-multiplied by the original alpha, can be plugged into equation 1 as always. The alpha channel of 0 indicates that this pixel will obscure nothing. In terms of our methodology for examining subpixel areas, we should understand that using the **opaque** operator corresponds to shrinking the matte coverage with regard to the color coverage.

4.5. The PLUS operator

We find it useful to include one further binary compositing operator **plus**. The expression A **plus** B holds no notion of precedence in any area covered by both pictures; the components are simply added. This allows us to dissolve from one picture to another by specifying

dissolve(A,α) **plus dissolve**$(B,1-\alpha)$.

In terms of the binary operators above, **plus** allows both pictures to survive in the subpixel area AB. The operator table above should be appended:

operation	diagram	F_A	F_B
(0,A,B,AB)		1	1
A **plus** B			

5. Examples

The operations on one and two pictures are presented as a basis for handling compositing expressions involving several pictures. A normal case involving three pictures is the compositing of a foreground picture A over a background picture B, with regard to an independent matte C. The expression for this compositing operation is

$$(A \text{ in } C) \text{ over } B.$$

Using equation 1 twice, we find that the composite in this case is computed at each pixel by

$$c_O = c_A \alpha_C + c_B(1 - \alpha_A \alpha_C).$$

As an example of a complex compositing expression, let us consider a subwindow of Rob Cook's picture *Road to Point Reyes* [1]. This still frame was assembled from many elements according to the following rules:

$Foreground = FrgdGrass$ **over** $Rock$ **over** $Fence$
    over $Shadow$ **over** $BkgdGrass;$

$GlossyRoad = Puddle$ **over** ($PostReflection$ **atop**
    ($PlantReflection$ **atop** $Road$));

$Hillside = Plant$ **over** $GlossyRoad$ **over** $Hill;$

$Background = Rainbow$ **plus** $Darkbow$ **over**
    $Mountains$ **over** $Sky;$

$Pt.Reyes = Foreground$ **over** $Hillside$ **over** $Background.$

Figure 1 shows three intermediate composites and the final picture.

$Foreground = FrgdGrass$ **over** $Rock$ **over** $Fence$
    over $Shadow$ **over** $BkgdGrass;$

$Hillside = Plant$ **over** $GlossyRoad$ **over** $Hill;$

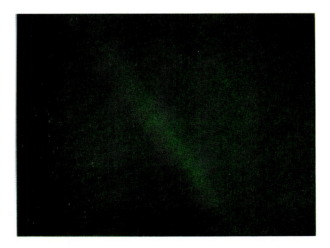

$Background = Rainbow$ **plus** $Darkbow$ **over**
    $Mountains$ **over** $Sky;$

$Pt.Reyes = Foreground$ **over** $Hillside$ **over** $Background.$

Figure 1

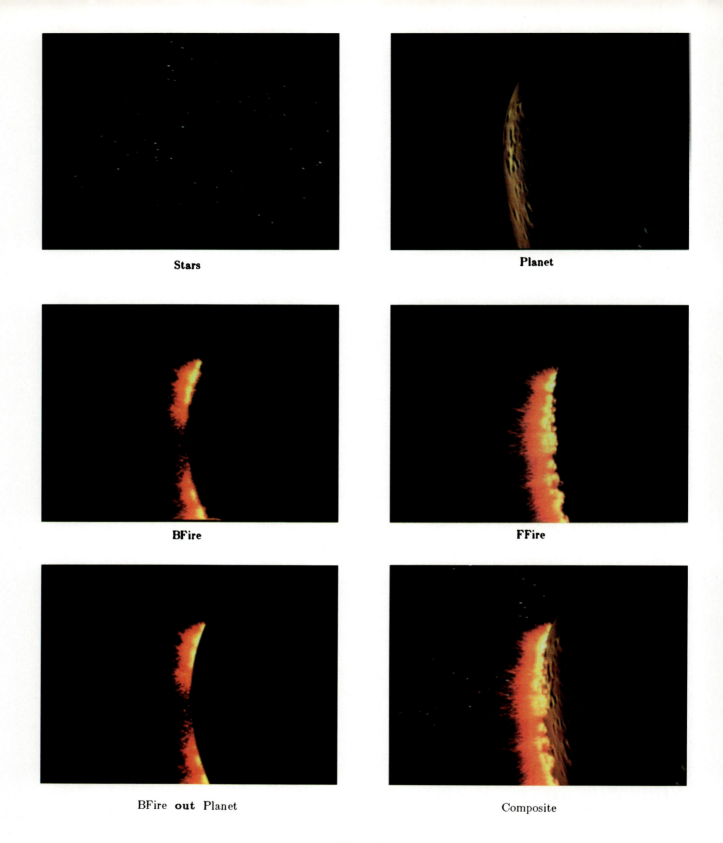

Figure 2

A further example demonstrates the problem of *correlated mattes*. In Figure 2, we have a star field background, a planet element, fiery particles behind the planet, and fiery particles in front of the planet. We wish to add the luminous fires, obscure the planet, darkened for proper balance, with the aggregate fire matte, and place that over the star field. An expression for this compositing is

(FFire **plus** (BFire **out** *Planet*))
  over darken(*Planet*,.8) **over** *Stars* .

We must remember that our basic assumption about the division of subpixel areas by geometric objects breaks down in the face of input pictures with correlated mattes. When one picture appears twice in a compositing expression, we must take care with our computations of F_A and F_B. Those listed in the table are correct only for uncorrelated pictures.

To solve the problem of correlated mattes, we must extend our methodology to handle n pictures: we must examine all 2^n subareas of the pixel, deciding which of the pictures survives in each area, and adding up all contributions. Multiple instances of a single picture or pictures with correlated mattes are resolved by aligning their pixel coverage. Example 2 can be computed by building a table of survivors (shown below) to accumulate the extent to which each input picture survives in the composite.

FFire	BFire	Planet	Stars	Survivor
			•	Stars
		•	•	Planet
	•		•	Planet
	•		•	BFire
	•	•	•	BFire
	•	•	•	Planet
	•	•	•	Planet
•				FFire
•			•	FFire
•		•		FFire
•		•	•	FFire
•	•			FFire,BFire
•	•		•	FFire,BFire
•	•	•		FFire
•	•	•	•	FFire

6. Conclusion

We have pointed out the need for matte channels in synthetic pictures, suggesting that frame buffer hardware should offer this facility. We have seen the convenience of the RGBA scheme for integrating the matte channel. A language of operators has been presented for conveying a full range of compositing expressions. We have discussed a methodology for deciding compositing questions at the subpixel level, deriving a simple equation for handling all composites of two pictures. The methodology is extended to multiple pictures, and the language is embellished to handle darkening, attenuation, and opaqueness.

There are several problems to be resolved in related areas, which are open for future research. We are interested in methods for breaking arbitrary three dimensional scenes into elements separated in depth. Such elements are equivalent to clusters, which have been a subject of discussion since the earliest attempts at hidden surface elimination. We are interested in applying the compositing notions to Z-buffer algorithms, where depth information is retained at each pixel.

7. References

1. Cook, R. Road to Point Reyes. *Computer Graphics* Vol 17, No. 3 (1983), Title Page Picture.
2. Crow, F. C. A More Flexible Image Generation Environment. *Computer Graphics* Vol. 16, No. 3 (1982), pp. 9-18.
3. Newell, M. G., Newell, R. G., and Sancha, T. L.. A Solution to the Hidden Surface Problem, pp. 443-448. *Proceedings of the 1972 ACM National Conference.*
4. Wallace, Bruce. Merging and Transformation of Raster Images for Cartoon Animation. *Computer Graphics* Vol. 15, No. 3 (1981), pp. 253-262.
5. Warnock, John, and Wyatt, Douglas. A Device Independent Graphics Imaging Model for Use with Raster Devices. *Computer Graphics* Vol. 16, No. 3 (1982), pp. 313-319.
6. Whitted, Turner, and Weimer, David. A Software Test-Bed for the Development of 3-D Raster Graphics Systems. *Computer Graphics* Vol. 15, No. 3 (1981), pp. 271-277.

8. Acknowledgments

The use of mattes to control the compositing of pictures is not new. The graphics group at the New York Institute of Technology has been using this for years. NYIT color maps were designed to encode both color and matte information; that idea was extended in the Ampex AVA system for storing mattes with pictures. Credit should be given to Ed Catmull, Alvy Ray Smith, and Ikonas Graphics Systems for the existence of an alpha channel as an integral part of a frame buffer, which has paved the way for the developments presented in this paper.

The graphics group at Lucasfilm should be credited with providing a fine test bed for working out these ideas. Furthermore, certain ideas incorporated as part of this work have their origins as idle comments within this group. Thanks are also given to Rodney Stock for comments on an early draft which forced the authors to clarify the major assumptions.

Volume Rendering

Robert A. Drebin, Loren Carpenter, Pat Hanrahan

Pixar
San Rafael, CA

Abstract

A technique for rendering images of volumes containing mixtures of materials is presented. The shading model allows both the interior of a material and the boundary between materials to be colored. Image projection is performed by simulating the absorption of light along the ray path to the eye. The algorithms used are designed to avoid artifacts caused by aliasing and quantization and can be efficiently implemented on an image computer. Images from a variety of applications are shown.

CR Categories: I.3.3 [Computer Graphics] Computational Geometry and Object Modeling - Curve, surface, solid, and object representations. I.3.5 [Computer Graphics] Three-Dimensional Graphics and Realism - Color, shading, shadowing and texture; Visible line/surface algorithms.

Additional Keywords and Phrases: Medical imaging, computed tomography (CT), magnetic resonance imaging (MRI), non-destructive evaluation (NDE), scientific visualization, image processing.

Introduction

Three-dimensional arrays of digital data representing spatial volumes arise in many scientific applications. Computed tomography (CT) and magnetic resonance (MR) scanners can be used to create a volume by imaging a series of cross sections. These techniques have found extensive use in medicine, and more recently, in non-destructive evaluation (NDE). Astrophysical, meteorological and geophysical measurements, and computer simulations using finite element models of stress, fluid flow, etc., also quite naturally generate a volume data set. Given the current advances in imaging devices and computer processing power, more and more applications will generate volumetric data in the future. Unfortunately, it is difficult to see the three-dimensional structure of the interior of volumes by viewing individual slices. To effectively visualize volumes, it is important to be able to image them from different viewpoints, and to shade them in a manner which brings out surfaces and subtle variations in density or opacity.

Most previous approaches to visualizing volumes capitalize on computer graphics techniques that have been developed to display surfaces by reducing the volume array to only the boundaries between materials. Two-dimensional contours from individual slices can be manually traced (Mazziotta, 1976) or automatically extracted (Vannier, 1983) and connected to contours in adjacent slices to form triangle strips (Keppel, 1975, Fuchs, 1977, Christianson, 1978, Ganapathy, 1982) or higher order surface patches (Sunguruff, 1978). These techniques have problems with branching structures, particularly if the distance between serial sections is large relative to the size of the volume elements or *voxels*. Other surface techniques output polygons at every voxel. The *cuberille* technique first sets a threshold representing the transition between two materials and then creates a binary volume indicating where a particular material is present. Each solid voxel is then treated as a small cube and the faces of this cube are output as small square polygons (Herman, 1979). Adjacent cubes can be merged to form an oct-tree; this representation compresses the original voxel array and reduces the subsequent processing requirements (Meagher, 1982). The *marching cubes* technique places the sample values at the vertices of the cube and estimates where the surface cuts through the cube (Lorensen, 1987). A variation of this technique, called the *dividing cubes* algorithm, approximates the polygon with points (Cline, 1988). These techniques are analogous to algorithms used to extract surfaces from implicit functions (Norton, 1982, Bloomenthal, 1987, Wyvill, 1986), or to produce three-dimensional contour maps (Wright, 1979).

Several researchers have developed methods which directly image the volume of data. The *additive reprojection* technique computes an image by averaging the intensities of voxels along parallel rays from the rotated volume to the image plane (Harris, 1978, Hoehne, 1987). This has the effect of simulating an x-ray image. The *source-attenuation reprojection* technique assigns a source strength and attenuation coefficient to each voxel which allows for object obscuration (Jaffey, 1982, Schlusselberg, 1986). Attenuation coefficients are often referred to as *opacities*. Depth shading algorithms trace rays through the volume array until they hit a surface and then assign an intensity inversely proportional to the distance to the eye (Vannier, 1983). This is usually referred to as *depth cueing* in the computer graphics literature. Radiation transport equations have been used to simulate transmission of light through volumes (Kajiya, 1984). The *low-albedo* or *single scattering* approximation has also been applied to model reflectance functions from layered volumes (Blinn, 1982). Several of these algorithms require the ability to trace rays in any direction through a volume array. Various algorithms for ray tracing volumes are described in (Fujimoto, 1986, Tuy, 1984, Levoy, 1988, Schlusselberg, 1986)

An implicit assumption in surface rendering algorithms is that a model consisting of thin surfaces suspended in an environment of transparent air accurately represents the original volume. Often the data is from the interior of a fluid-like substance containing mixtures of several different materials. Subtle surfaces that occur at the interface between materials, and local variations in volumetric properties, such as light absorption or emission, are lost if the volume is reduced to just surfaces. Also, since a voxel represents a point sample, information about the exact position and orientation of microsurfaces may be lost in the sampling process, and it is not reasonable to expect to be able to recover that information.

The technique presented in this paper deals with volumes directly. The volume array is assumed to be sampled above the Nyquist frequency, or if this is not possible, it is assumed that the continuous signal is low-pass filtered to remove high frequencies that cause aliasing. If this criterion is met, the original continuous representation of the volume can be reconstructed from the samples. The sampled volume will look smooth and realistic, and artifacts such as jagged edges will not be present. Each stage in the volume rendering algorithm is designed to preserve the continuity of the data. Thresholding and other highly non-linear operations are avoided, and when geometric transformations are applied to the data, the result is resampled carefully. The goal is to avoid introducing computational artifacts such as aliasing and quantization, since these interfere with the viewer's ability to interpret the data.

Overview of the Algorithm

Figure 1 shows a process diagram of the volume rendering algorithm. Associated with each stage is a slice from a volume corresponding to the stage. The first step in using the volume rendering algorithm is to convert the *input data volume* to a set of *material percentage volumes*. The values in each voxel of the material percentage volumes are the percentage of that material present in that region of space. These material percentage volumes either can be input directly, or can be determined from the input data volumes using probabilistic classification techniques. Many different classification techniques are possible and the one of choice depends on the type of input data. The classification of a CT volume data set is shown in Figure 1.

Given any material property and the material percentage volumes, a composite volume corresponding to that property can be calculated by multiplying the percentage of each material times the property assigned to that material. For example, a composite *color volume* is formed by summing the product of the percentage of each material times its color. An *opacity volume* is computed by assigning each material an opacity value. In Figure 1, the color volume shown is actually the product of the color and the opacity volume.

Boundaries between materials are detected by applying a three-dimensional gradient to a *density* or ρ *volume*. The ρ volume is computed from the material percentage volumes by assigning a ρ value to each material. The gradient is largest where there are sharp transitions between materials with different ρ's. The magnitude of the gradient is stored in a *surface strength volume* and is used to estimate the amount of surface present. The direction of the gradient is stored in the *surface normal volume* and is used in shading computations.

The *shaded color volume* represents the sum of the light emitted by the volume and scattered by the surfaces. The relative contributions of volume emission and surface scattering can be varied depending on the application. The reflected component is computed using a surface reflectance function whose inputs are the position and color of the light sources, the position of the eye, the surface normal volume, the surface strength volume, and the color volume. The amount of emitted light is proportional to the percentage of luminous material in the voxel.

To form an image, the shaded volume is first transformed and resampled so that it lies in the viewing coordinate system. In many cases the transform is just a rotation. Figure 1 shows the result as the *transformed volume*. In this coordinate system the eye is at infinity, so all rays are parallel to an axis of the volume. An image of the rotated volume can be formed by projecting the volume onto the image plane taking into account the emission and attenuation of light through each voxel. This projection may be calculated using a simple compositing scheme modeled after an optical film printer (Porter, 1984).

Voxel Mixtures and Classification

The volume rendering algorithm presented in this paper operates on volumes which are modeled as a composition of one or more materials. Examples include: a set of physical substances, such as bone, soft tissue, and fat in the musculoskeletal system; a set of simulated measurements, such as stress and strain in a finite element model; or a set of signals, such as the individual spin echoes of magnetic resonance. A voxel's composition is described by the percentage of each material present in the voxel.

When the material composition at each voxel is not provided, classification is used to estimate the percentages of each material from the original data. It is very important when classifying the data not to make *all-or-none* decisions about which material is present, but rather to compute the best estimate of how much is present within each voxel. Making material decisions by thresholding introduces artifacts in the material percentages which are easily visible in the final images (Drebin, 1987). Probabilistic classifiers work particularly well, because the probability that a material is present can be used as an estimate of the percentage of the material present in the voxel.

The first probabilistic classifier developed for this volume rendering technique was a maximum-likelihood classifier for musculoskeletal CT volumes. In this case the intensities in the input volume represent x-ray radiation absorption. The classification yields volumes containing the percentages of air, bone, soft-tissue, and fat. A histogram of the x-ray absorption of the input volume is the sum of three overlapping distributions, corresponding, in increasing order of intensity, to fat, soft-tissue, and bone. In the general case, the probability that any voxel has value (intensity) I is given by

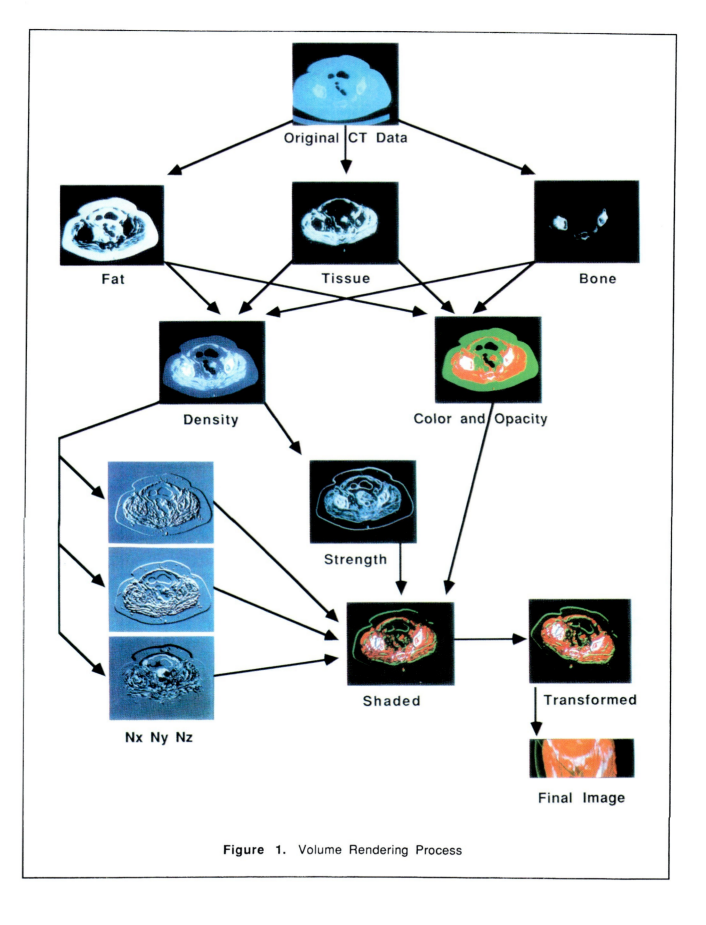

Figure 1. Volume Rendering Process

$$P(I) = \sum_{i=1}^{n} p_i P_i(I)$$

where n is the number of materials present in the volume, p_i is the percentage of material i in a given voxel, and $P_i(I)$ is the probability that material i has value I. In the case of musculoskeletal CT, the distribution functions $P_i(I)$ represent the x-ray absorption of each material, and are known *a-priori*. Once the individual distribution functions are known, the Bayesian estimate of the percentage of each material contained within a voxel of value I is given by:

$$p_i(I) = \frac{P_i(I)}{\sum_{j=1}^{n} P_j(I)}$$

Note that when the classification is a function of only a single intensity volume, as in this case, the classification can be performed by using table lookup on the input values. Furthermore, if no more then two material distributions overlap, the percentage of each material varies linearly between their peaks. This is roughly the case with musculoskeletal CT, because bone and fat intensity distributions rarely overlap, so voxels are either linear combinations of fat and soft-tissue or soft-tissue and bone. Figure 2 shows a hypothetical histogram, material distributions, and resulting classification functions. The first step in Figure 1 shows an actual classification of a CT data set.

Maximum likelihood classifiers can be built that handle more than one input data volume; these are like the multispectral classification algorithms commonly employed in remote sensing and statistical pattern recognition. However, maximum likelihood methods will not always work well. In performing the musculoskeletal classification described above, voxels are never classified as being a mixture of air and bone since the soft-tissue distribution lies between the air and bone distributions. However, within nasal passages mixtures of air and bone are common. Using knowledge about what combinations of materials may potentially mix will improve the classification and hence the estimates of the material percentages. Adaptive classification algorithms which take advantage of local neighborhood characteristics (Tom, 1985), multi-spectral mixture analysis (Adams, 1986), or probabilistic relaxation algorithms (Zucker, 1976) can all be used with the volume rendering algorithm. However, it should be stressed again, that only probabilistic classification algorithms should be used, since binary classification algorithms will introduce artifacts in the subsequent renderings.

Once material percentage volumes are available, volumes corresponding to other properties can be easily computed. As an example, consider creating a RGBα color-opacity volume. In this paper, a piece of colored material is modeled with four coordinates: R, G, B are the intensities of red, green and blue light, and α is the opacity. An α=1 implies that the material is completely opaque, and α=0 implies that it is completely transparent. (A more accurate model of transparency would use three color components because a real material will filter red, green and blue light differently.) The color of a mixture of materials is given by

$$C = \sum_{i=1}^{n} p_i C_i$$

where $C_i = (\alpha_i R_i, \alpha_i G_i, \alpha_i B_i, \alpha_i)$ is the color associated with material i. Note that in this representation, the colors are

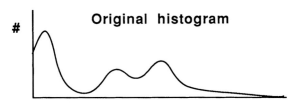

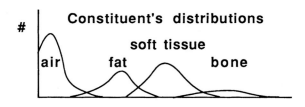

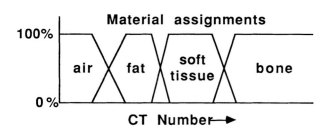

Figure 2. CT Classification

premultiplied by their opacities. This representation of colors and the advantages of premultiplying colors by opacity are is discussed in (Porter, 1984).

Matting

After the volume is classified, it is often helpful to remove sections or lessen the presence of certain regions or materials. *Matte volumes* are created for these operations. Each voxel of a matte is a scalar fraction, which defines the percentage of the voxel contained by the matte. Matte volumes can be simple geometric shapes, such as wedges or halfplanes, or regions computed from other volumes, such as an *air* matte volume which is the region not contained in any material percentage volumes.

Matting operations correspond roughly to fuzzy set operations. This allows *spatial set operations* to be performed on volumes. An example of this is merging multiple volumes into a single volume using union. Another example is to carve a shape out of a solid. One of the most common uses of matte volumes is to perform cut-aways; another is to remove regions where the data is unreliable or uninteresting. Finally, since matte values are fractional, they can be used to lower the percentage of material in a region, or to change the material properties in different regions. Depth cueing is done by matting a ramp in z with the final shaded color volume before projection. This has the effect of making near colors brighter than the far colors.

Each voxel of a matte volume M contains a value between 0 and 1 which indicates the presence or absence of the matte. A volume, V, is combined with a matte, M, with the following operations:

$$V \text{ in } M = MV$$

$$V \text{ out } M = (1-M)V$$

The **in** operator yields the portion of V inside of M. Set intersection is accomplished by multiplying the two volumes. The **out** operator returns the portion of V outside of M. This is done by complementing M and then forming the set intersection. Complementing M is performed by subtracting M from 1. By making mattes fractional instead of binary, the boundaries between inside and outside are smooth and continuous. This is important if the continuity of the data is to be preserved. Binary mattes will lead to artifacts in the final images.

Surface Extraction

The shading model described below requires information about surfaces within each voxel, including their normal and "strength." The strength of a surface is a combination of the percentage of surface within the voxel and the reflection coefficient of that surface. In this paper, the surface physics is approximated by assigning to each material a density characteristic ρ. A surface occurs when two or more materials of different ρ's meet. The strength of the surface is set equal to the magnitude of the difference in ρ.

A ρ volume is computed by summing the products of the percentage of each material in the voxel times the material's assigned ρ, such that:

$$D = \sum_{i=1}^{n} p_i \rho_i$$

where D is the total ρ of a voxel and ρ_i is the density assigned to material i. The material ρ assignments can be arbitrary; they do not have to be related to the actual mass of the materials or the imaged intensities. By assigning two materials the same ρ's they are effectively coalesced into a single material and the surface between them will not be detectable. The surface normal and strength volumes are derived from the ρ volume's gradient. The strength of a surface is proportional both to the magnitude of the difference in ρ and to the sharpness of the transition from one material to the other. The surface strength volume is used to indicate the presence of surfaces.

The surface normal, $\vec{N}$, is defined as:

$$N_x = \nabla_x D = D_{x+1} - D_x$$
$$N_y = \nabla_y D = D_{y+1} - D_y$$
$$N_z = \nabla_z D = D_{z+1} - D_z$$

This vector is normalized to have unit length and stored in a *surface normal volume*. The magnitude of the gradient is stored in a *surface strength volume*.

$$S = |\vec{N}|$$

Since a derivative is a high-pass filter, noisy volumes will have very noisy derivatives. When this is a problem, more accurate estimates of the derivatives can be computed by first blurring or running a low-pass filter over the material volume. This is directly analogous to the two-dimensional problem of

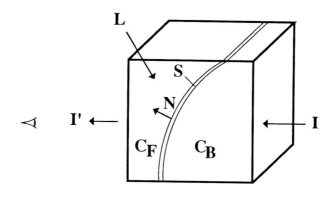

Figure 3. Voxel shading model

detecting edges in the presence of noise.

Figure 1 shows a ρ volume and the resulting surface normal and strength volumes. Note that surfaces are represented by a surface strength and not a binary value indicating whether surfaces are present or not. This allows diffuse transitions between material to be represented, and positions of surfaces in the final image often appear to lie between voxel boundaries.

Lighting Model

Figure 3 shows the lighting model used in each voxel. A light ray traveling towards the eye enters the voxel from behind with incoming intensity I, and exits from the front with outgoing intensity I'. The light intensity changes due to the following effects: i) materials may act as translucent filters, absorbing the incoming light, ii) they may be luminous and emit outgoing light, and iii) they may contain surfaces or particle scatterers which both attenuate the incoming light and also reflect light from light sources towards the eye. Light transmission through a volume can be modeled as a radiation transport problem (Kajiya, 1984). However, in this paper only a single scattering of radiation from a light source to the eye is assumed. Light rays from the light source are also not attenuated as they travel through the volume. These assumptions make the lighting model very easy to implement.

If a light ray travels through a colored translucent voxel, the resulting color is

$$I' = C \text{ over } I = C + (1-\alpha_C)I$$

where α_C is the alpha component of C. The first term models the emitted light and the second term the absorption of incoming light. In order to include surface shading, the voxel is subdivided into two regions: the region in front and behind a thin surface region. Each of these regions is assigned an RGBα color so that it can both emit and absorb light. The outgoing intensity is then

$$I' = (C_F \text{ over } (C_S \text{ over } (C_B \text{ over } I))) = C \text{ over } I$$

Since the **over** operator is associative, the three color volumes corresponding to front C_F, back C_B and surface C_S can be combined into a single volume $C = C_F \text{ over } C_S \text{ over } C_B$ before the integration is performed.

The reflected surface color, C_S, is a function of the surface normal, the strength of the surface, the diffuse color of the surface C_D, the direction $\vec{L}$ and color C_L of the light source, and the eye position $\vec{E}$. The color of the reflected light has two components, a diffuse component whose color is given by the color of the surface, and a specular component whose color is given by the color of the light. The formula is

$$C_S = (f(\vec{N},\vec{L})C_D + g(\vec{E},\vec{N},\vec{L})C_L) \text{ in } S$$

where f and g are diffuse and specular shading functions, and C_D is the diffuse color of the surface. Appropriate functions for f and g are discussed in (Phong, 1975, Blinn, 1982, Cook, 1982). Note that the amount of surface shading is proportional to the strength of the surface. No reflected light will appear in the interior of a homogeneous material.

The simplest approach is to set the surface diffuse color equal to $C_D = C_F + C_B$; that is, treat the color of the surface as the color of the mixture, and to just add it into the mixture. C is then set equal to C_S over C_D. The problem with this approach is that color from neighboring materials bleed into the surface. For example, if white bones are next to red muscle tissue, the bleeding will cause the surfaces of the bones to appear pink. The best choice for C_D is C_B, but this is technically difficult because it is not known which of the materials in the mixture is the back material and which is the front. One solution to this problem is to examine the sign of the density gradient in the direction of view. If it is positive, the front of the voxel has a lower ρ than the back; otherwise the front has a higher ρ. Once the materials are ordered from front to back, the colors can be assigned accordingly.

Viewing and Projection

An image is computed by projecting the volume onto the image plane. One common method used to perform this projection is to cast rays through the volume array. The problem with this approach is that sampling artifacts may occur and it is computationally expensive since it requires random access to the volume data. The approach used in this algorithm is to first transform the volume so that the final image lies along the front face of the viewing pyramid, and so that rays through the vantage point are all parallel and perpendicular to the image plane. The transformation of the volume can be done efficiently in scanline order which also allows it to be properly resampled. Modeling light transmission during projection is also particularly convenient in this coordinate system.

After the shading calculation, there exists a RGBα volume C. As the projection occurs, the intensity of light is modeled according to the equations described in the previous section. Each colored plane of the volume is overlaid on top of the planes behind it from back to front using the **over** operator. The orthographic projection through the $z'th$ plane of the volume can be expressed as:

$$I_z = C_z \text{ over } I_{z+1}$$

where I is the accumulated image, C_z is the color-opacity of plane z. The initial image I_n is set to black and the final image is I_0. This algorithm need not store the I volume, just the final image. This multi-plane merge could just as easily be done from front to back using the **under** operator (A **under** $B \equiv B$ **over** A).

It is important to be able to view the volume with an arbitrary viewing transformation, which includes translation, rotation, scaling, and perspective. In order to preserve the simplicity of the parallel merge projection, the viewing coordinate system is fixed, and the volume is geometrically transformed and resampled to lie in that coordinate system. This is done as a sequence of 4 transformations,

$$T = P_z(z_e) R_z(\psi) R_y(\phi) R_z(\theta)$$

where R_z and R_y are rotations about the z and y axes, respectively, and P_z is the perspective transformation. The transformations are parameterized by the Euler angles, (θ, ϕ, ψ), and z_e, the z coordinate of the eye point. In many applications, a sequence of orthographic views corresponding to a rotation about only single axis is required, so that only one of the rotates is required, and the viewing transformation can be done in 1/4 the time. Since each rotation is perpendicular to an axis of the volume, the volume rotation can be performed by extracting individual slices along the axis perpendicular to the rotation axis, rotating them individually as images, and then placing them into the result volume. Performing a three-dimensional rotation using a sequence of three rotates requires the ability to extract planes perpendicular to at least two axes (y and z). This requires either an intermediate transposition of the volume, or a storage scheme which allows fast access along two perpendicular directions. P_z is a perspective transformation with the eye point on the z-axis. This can be efficiently implemented by scanning sequentially through slices in z, and resizing the x-y images by $1/(z_e - z)$ — that is, magnifying images near the eye relative to images far from the eye. Rotations and scalings are both special cases of an affine transformation. Two-dimensional affine transformations can be performed using the two-pass scanline algorithms discussed in (Catmull, 1980). For the viewing transformation outlined above, this requires as many as 8 resampling operations. It should be possible to generalize the two-pass image transformation to a three-pass volume transformation and reduce the number of resampling operations. It is important when performing these geometric manipulations that the images be reconstructed and resampled using either triangular or bicubic filters to preserve the continuity of the data. Poor reconstruction and resampling will introduce artifacts in the final images.

Results

Figures 4-12 show images of various volumes rendered with the above techniques. Figures 4-6 are medical images based on CT data sets. Figure 4 shows four images rendered with different material properties and variations of the algorithms presented in this paper. Figure 5 illustrates an application of a matte volume to cut-away a wedge from the child's head. Figure 6 shows a whole body reconstruction of an adult male with different colors and opacities on the left and right halves. The volume rendering technique has been shown to be valuable in clinical applications (Fishman, 1987, Scott, 1987). A biological application of the volume rendering algorithm is shown in Figure 7: a whole body image of a sea otter. This image lead to the discovery that adult sea otters have an extra wrist bone not present in young otters (Discover, 1988). Figure 8 shows a physical sciences application of volume rendering. Figure 8 is a rendered image of a smoke puff. The original input data set was acquired as a sequence of images from a CCD camera. Each image was a cross section of the smoke

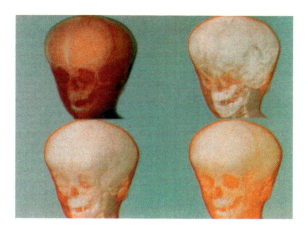

Figure 4(a-d). Rendered images from a 124 slice 256x256 CT study of a child. **4a** is a self-illuminated rendering with depth shading. **4b** and **4c** are surface-only renderings shaded with a directional light source. Cf+Cb is used as the surface color in **4b**, while a computed Cb is used to color the surface in **4c**. **4d** is rendered with both self-illumination and surface shading with a directional light source. The CT study is courtesy of Franz Zonnefeld, Ph.D., N.V. Philips.

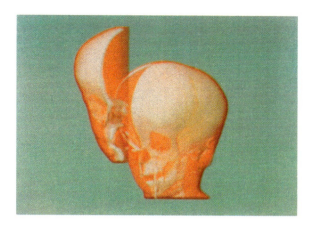

Figure 5. A matte volume is used to extract a section of the child's head.

puff illuminated by a plane of laser light. Figures 9-11 are images computed from the results of computer simulations. Figure 9 is an image of the results of the simulation of the containment of a plasma in a magnetic fusion reactor. Figure 10 is a simulation of the energy surrounding a "broom handle" moving at Mach 1.9. Figure 11 shows a comparison of volume rendering vs. standard surface rendering. In the image created by the volume rendering technique, the stress throughout the volume is visible. Regions of high stress are both more opaque and a "hotter" color. Showing the stress on just the surface doesn't convey nearly as much information. Finally, Figure 12 is an example of the NDE (non-destructive evaluation) of air flow through a turbine blade. An obstruction in the air flow inside the turbine blade is detected in the volume rendering. Since this obstruction is internal, it cannot be seen by direct visual inspection. The original input data set was a CT volume.

The volumetric qualities of these images are much more apparent when viewed in motion. The algorithm presented above can be efficiently adapted for this purpose, because only the stages of the calculation that change from frame to frame need to be recomputed.

Summary and Discussion

A method has been described for imaging volume arrays. This method produces significantly better images than conventional computer graphics renderings of extracted surfaces primarily because both volumetric color and opacity, and surface color and opacity are modeled and a great deal of attention was paid to maintaining a continuous representation of the image.

The distinguishing feature of volume rendering algorithms is that surface geometry is never explicitly represented as polygons or patches (even if a surface model alone would be sufficient). For a volume which contains fine detail, this approach makes more sense because the size of the polygons would be on the order of the size of a pixel. Rendering millions of small polygons is inefficient because it takes more information to represent a voxel-sized polygon than just a voxel, and because it is very difficult to produce high-quality antialiased renderings of subpixel-sized polygons.

Each stage in the algorithm inputs a volume and outputs another volume. Care is taken at all stages to not introduce any digital artifacts. Each input volume is interpreted as a sampled continuous signal, and each operation preserves the continuity of the input. All quantities are stored as fixed point fractional values with 11 bits to the right of the decimal point. Intermediate calculations typically use 16 bits, although when computing normals 32 bits are used. This appears to be enough precision to avoid quantization artifacts and numerical problems.

All the volume operations described in this paper can be performed on slices or small sets of adjacent slices – thus reducing volume computation to image computation. This is desirable since there is a large body of information about image computing. Many of the two-dimensional algorithms mentioned in this paper – table lookup, affine transformation, compositing, etc. – are typically available in standard image computing libraries. Special purpose processors exist to quickly execute image computations, making these techniques practical. Almost all two-dimensional image processing algorithms have analogous three-dimensional versions. Developing three-dimensional volume processing algorithms is a good area of research.

The viewing transformation and projection stages of the volume rendering algorithm can also be done using ray tracing. The technique for computing the attenuation of light along parallel rays as done in this paper can be generalized to

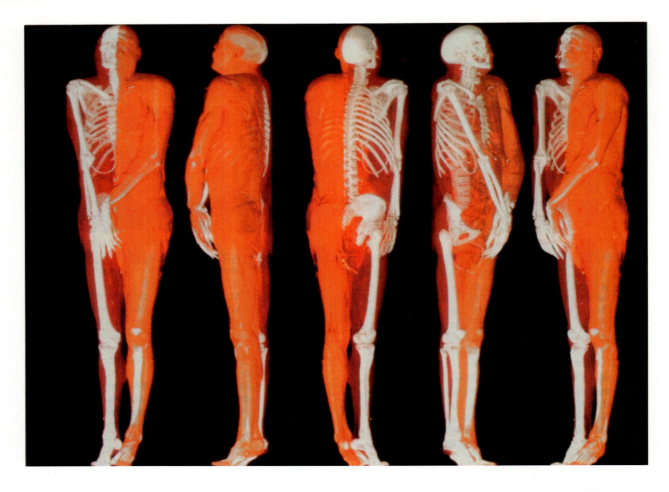

Figure 6. Rendered images from a 650 slice 256x256 CT study of a man. A matte volume was used to apply different levels of translucency to the tissue on the left and right halves. The CT study is courtesy of Elliot Fishman, M.D., and H.R. Hruban, M.D., Johns Hopkins Medical Institution.

attenuate light along a ray in any direction. One potential advantage of a ray tracer is that if a ray immediately intersects an opaque material, voxels behind that material need not be processed since they are hidden; however, in many situations a volume is easier to visualize if materials are not completely opaque. The major disadvantage of ray tracing is that it is very difficult to avoid artifacts due to point sampling. When rays diverge they may not sample adjacent pixels. Although rays can be jittered to avoid some of these problems, this requires a larger number of additional rays to be cast. Ray tracers also require random access (or access along an arbitrary line) to a voxel array. The algorithm described in this paper always accesses images by scanlines, and thus in many cases is much more efficient.

Future research should attempt to incorporate other visual effects into volume rendering. Examples of these include: complex lighting and shading, motion blur, depth-of-field, etc. Finding practical methods of solving the radiation transport equation to include multiple scattering would be useful. Tracing rays from light sources to form an illumination or shadow volume can already be done using the techniques described in the paper.

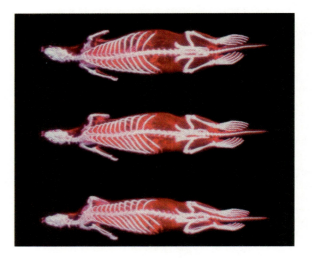

Figure 7. Rendered images from a 400 slice CT study of a sea otter. Data courtesy of Michael Stoskopf, M.D., and Elliot Fishman, M.D., The Johns Hopkins Hospital.

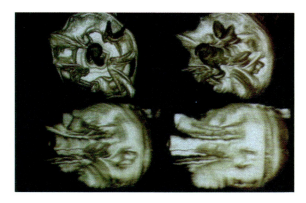

Figure 8. Rendered images of a smoke puff volume. Data courtesy of Juan Agui, Ph.D., and Lambertus Hesselink, Ph.D., Department of Aeronautics and Astronautics, Stanford University.

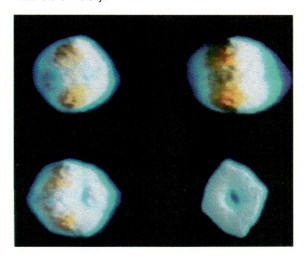

Figure 9. Magnetic fusion simulation. Data courtesy of Dan Shumaker, Ph.D., Lawrence Livermore National Laboratory.

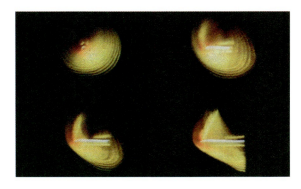

Figure 10. Rendered images showing the simulated energy near a cylinder moving at Mach 1.9. Data courtesy of University of Illinois, CSRD.

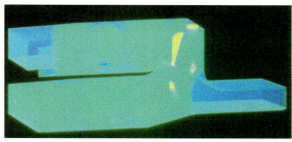

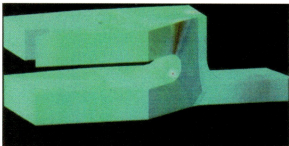

Figure 11. Comparison of volume and conventional surface rendering techniques depicting the stresses through the material of a simulated mechanical part. Figure **11a** is volume rendered, and **11b** is constructed from Gouraud-shaded polygons. Data courtesy of Mr. Harris Hunt, PDA Engineering.

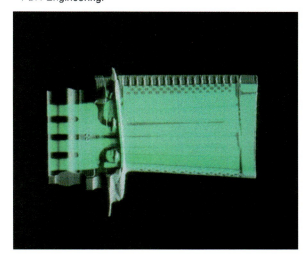

Figure 12. Turbine blade CT study. Air cooling passages are blue. Notice the obstruction in the lower left. Data courtesy of General Electric Aircraft Division Industrial CT.

Acknowledgements

Dana Batali and Malcolm Blanchard made many of the pictures shown in this paper; they also enthusiastically tried different techniques on different data sets. Dr. Elliot Fishman provided the original hip data set that motivated this work and later verified its clinical applications. Ed Catmull, Rob Cook, Tom Porter, and Alvy Ray Smith provided many ideas during frequent discussions which we have incorporated into the algorithm presented. Walter Karshat and Flip Phillips helped with the current implementation on the Pixar Image Computer.

References

"Why Abalones Don't Find Otters Cute," *Discover*, p. 10 (April 1988).

ADAMS, JOHN B., MILTON O. SMITH, AND PAUL E. JOHNSON, "Spectral Mixture Modeling: A New Analysis of Rock and Soil Types at the Viking 1 Lander Site," *Journal of Geophysical Research* **91**(B8) pp. 8098-8112 (July 1986).

BLINN, JAMES F., "Light Reflection Functions for Simulation of Clouds and Dusty Surfaces," *Computer Graphics (SIGGRAPH '82 Proceedings)* **16**(3) pp. 21-29 (July 1982).

BLOOMENTHAL, JULES, "Polygonization of Implicit Surfaces," Report CSL-87-2, Xerox PARC (May 1987).

CATMULL, EDWIN AND ALVY RAY SMITH, "3-D Transformations of Images in Scanline Order," *Computer Graphics (SIGGRAPH '80 Proceedings)* **14**(3) pp. 279-285 (July 1980).

CHRISTIANSON, H. N. AND T. W. SEDERBERG, "Conversion of Complex Contour Line Definitions into Polygonal Element Mosaics," *Computer Graphics (SIGGRAPH '78 Proceedings)* **12** pp. 187-192 (1978).

CLINE, HARVEY E., WILLIAM E. LORENSEN, SIGWALT LUDKE, CARL R. CRAWFORD, AND BRUCE C. TEETER, "Two Algorithms for the Reconstruction of Surfaces from Tomograms," *Medical Physics*, (June, 1988).

COOK, ROBERT L. AND KENNETH E. TORRANCE, "A Reflection Model for Computer Graphics," *ACM Transactions on Graphics* **1**(1) pp. 7-24 (1982).

DREBIN, ROBERT A., ELLIOT K. FISHMAN, AND DONNA MAGID, "Volumetric Three-dimensional Image Rendering: Thresholding vs. Non-thresholding Techniques," *Radiology* **165** p. 131 (1987).

FISHMAN, E. K., R. A. DREBIN, D. MAGID, AND ET. AL., "Volumetric Rendering Techniques: Applications for 3-Dimensional Imaging of the Hip," *Radiology* **163** pp. 737-738 (1987).

FUCHS, H., Z. M. KEDEM, AND S. P. USELTON, "Optimal Surface Reconstruction for Planar Contours," *CACM* **20**(1977).

FUJIMOTO, AKIRA, TAKAYUKI TANAKA, AND KANSEI IWATA, "ARTS: Accelerated Ray-Tracing System," *IEEE Computer Graphics and Applications*, pp. 16-26 (Apr. 1986).

GANAPATHY, S. AND T. G. DENNEHY, "A New General Triangulation Method for Planar Contours," *Computer Graphics (SIGGRAPH '82 Proceedings)* **16** pp. 69-75 (1982).

HARRIS, LOWELL D., R. A. ROBB, T. S. YUEN, AND E. L. RITMAN, "Non-invasive numerical dissection and display of anatomic structure using computerized x-ray tomography," *Proceedings SPIE* **152** pp. 10-18 (1978).

HERMAN, GABOR T. AND H. K. LIU, "Three-Dimensional Display of Organs from Computed Tomograms," *Computer Graphics and Image Processing* **9**(1) pp. 1-21 (January 1979).

HOEHNE, KARL HEINZ, ROBERT L. DELAPAZ, RALPH BERNSTEIN, AND ROBERT C. TAYLOR, "Combined Surface Display and Reformatting for the Three-Dimensional Analysis of Tomographic Data," *Investigative Radiology* **22**(7) pp. 658-664 (July 1987).

JAFFEY, STEPHEN M. AND KALYAN DUTTA, "Digital Perspective Correction for Cylindrical Holographic Stereograms," *Proceedings of SPIE* **367**(August 1982).

KAJIYA, JAMES T. AND BRIAN P. VON HERZEN, "Ray Tracing Volume Densities," *Computer Graphics (SIGGRAPH '84 Proceedings)* **18**(3)(July 1984).

KEPPEL, E., "Approximation of Complex Surfaces by Triangulation of Contour Lines," *IBM Journal of Research and Development* **19** pp. 2-11 (1975).

LEVOY, MARC, "Display of Surfaces from Volume Data," *IEEE Computer Graphics and Applications*, (May, 1988).

LORENSEN, WILLIAM E. AND HARVEY E. CLINE, "Marching Cubes: A High Resolution 3D Surface Construction Algorithm," *Computer Graphics (SIGGRAPH '87 Proceedings)*, (July 1987).

MAZZIOTTA, J. C. AND K. H. HUANG, "THREAD (Three-Dimensional Reconstruction and Display) with Biomedical Applications in Neuron Ultrastructure and Display," *American Federation of Information Processing Society* **45** pp. 241-250 (1976).

MEAGHER, DONALD J., "Efficient Synthetic Image Generation of Arbitrary 3-D Objects," *Proceedings of the IEEE Computer Society Conference on Pattern Recognition and Image Processing*, pp. 473-478 (June 1982).

NORTON, ALAN, "Generation and Display of Geometric Fractals in 3-D," *Computer Graphics (SIGGRAPH '82 Proceedings)* **16**(3) pp. 61-67 (July 1982).

PHONG, BUI-THONG, "Illumination for Computer Generated Images," *CACM* **18**(6) pp. 311-317 (June 1975).

PORTER, THOMAS AND TOM DUFF, "Compositing Digital Images," *Computer Graphics (SIGGRAPH '84 Proceedings)* **18**(3) pp. 253-260 (July 1984).

SCHLUSSELBERG, DANIEL S., WADE K. SMITH, AND DONALD J. WOODWARD, "Three-Dimensional Display of Medical Image Volumes," *Proceedings of NCGA*, (March 1986).

SCOTT, W. W. JR., E. K. FISHMAN, AND D. MAGID, "Acetabular Fractures: Optimal Imaging," *Radiology*, pp. 537-538 (1987).

SUNGURUFF, A AND D. GREENBERG, "Computer Generated Images for Medical Applications," *Computer Graphics (SIGGRAPH '78 Proceedings)* **12** pp. 196-202 (1978).

TOM, VICTOR T., "Adaptive Filter Techniques of Digital Image Enhancement," *SPIE Digital Image Processing: Critical Review of Technology* **528**(1985).

TUY, HEANG K. AND LEE TAN TUY, "Direct 2-D Display of 3-D Objects," *IEEE Computer Graphics and Applications* **4**(10) pp. 29-34 (October 1984).

VANNIER, MICHAEL W., JEFFREY L. MARSH, AND JAMES O. WARREN, "Three Dimensional Computer Graphics for Craniofacial Surgical Planning and Evaluation," *Computer Graphics (SIGGRAPH '83 Proceedings)* **17**(3) pp. 263-273 (July 1983).

WRIGHT, THOMAS AND JOHN HUMBRECHT, "ISOSURF - An Algorithm for Plotting Iso-Valued Surfaces of a Function of Three Variables," *Computer Graphics (SIGGRAPH '79 Proceedings)* **13**(2) pp. 182-189 (August 1979).

WYVILL, BRIAN, CRAIG MCPHEETERS, AND GEOFF WYVILL, "Data Structure for Soft Objects," *The Visual Computer* **2**(4) pp. 227-234 (1986).

ZUCKER, STEVEN W., "Relaxation Labelling and the Reduction of Local Ambiguities," *Proceedings 3rd International Conference on Pattern Recognition*, pp. 852-861 (November 1976).

Feature-Based Image Metamorphosis

Thaddeus Beier

Silicon Graphics Computer Systems
2011 Shoreline Blvd, Mountain View CA 94043

Shawn Neely

Pacific Data Images
1111 Karlstad Drive, Sunnyvale CA 94089

1 Abstract

A new technique is presented for the metamorphosis of one digital image into another. The approach gives the animator high-level control of the visual effect by providing natural feature-based specification and interaction. When used effectively, this technique can give the illusion that the photographed or computer generated subjects are transforming in a fluid, surrealistic, and often dramatic way. Comparisons with existing methods are drawn, and the advantages and disadvantages of each are examined. The new method is then extended to accommodate keyframed transformations between image sequences for motion image work. Several examples are illustrated with resulting images.

Keywords: Computer Animation, Interpolation, Image Processing, Shape Transformation.

2 Introduction

2.1 Conventional Metamorphosis Techniques

Metamorphosis between two or more images over time is a useful visual technique, often used for educational or entertainment purposes. Traditional filmmaking techniques for this effect include clever cuts (such as a character exhibiting changes while running through a forest and passing behind several trees) and optical cross-dissolve, in which one image is faded out while another is simultaneously faded in (with makeup change, appliances, or object substitution). Several classic horror films illustrate the process; who could forget the hair-raising transformation of the Wolfman, or the dramatic metamorphosis from Dr. Jekyll to Mr. Hyde? This paper presents a contemporary solution to the visual transformation problem.

Taking the cutting approach to the limit gives us the technique of stop-motion animation, in which the subject is progressively transformed and photographed one frame at a time. This process can give the powerful illusion of continuous metamorphosis, but it requires much skill and is very tedious work. Moreover, stop-motion usually suffers from the problem of visual strobing by not providing the motion blur normally associated with moving film subjects. A motion-controlled variant called go-motion (in which the frame-by-frame subjects are photographed while moving) can provide the proper motion blur to create a more natural effect, but the complexity of the models, motion hardware, and required skills becomes even greater.

2.2 3D Computer Graphics Techniques

We can use technology in other ways to help build a metamorphosis tool. For example, we can use computer graphics to model and render images which transform over time.

One approach involves the representation of a pair of three-dimensional objects as a collection of polygons. The vertices of the first object are then displaced over time to coincide in position with corresponding vertices of the second object, with color and other attributes similarly interpolated. The chief problem with this technique is the difficulty in establishing a desirable vertex correspondence; this often imposes inconvenient constraints on the geometric representation of the objects, such as requiring the same number of polygons in each model. Even if these conditions are met, problems still arise when the topologies of the two objects differ (such as when one object has a hole through it), or when the features must move in a complex way (such as sliding along the object surface from back to front). This direct point-interpolation technique can be effective, however, for transformations in which the data correspondence and interpolation paths are simple. For example, the technique was successfully used for the interpolation of a regular grid of 3D scanned data in "Star Trek IV: The Voyage Home" [13]. Methods for automatically generating corresponding vertices or polygons for interpolation have been developed. [5][6]

Other computer graphics techniques which can be used for object metamorphosis include solid deformations [1] [12] and particle systems [10]. In each case the 3D model of the first object is transformed to have the shape and surface properties of the second model, and the resulting animation is rendered and recorded.

2.3 2D Computer Graphics Techniques

While three-dimensional object metamorphosis is a natural solution when both objects are easily modeled for the computer, often the complexity of the subjects makes this approach impractical. For example, many applications of the effect require transformations between complex objects such as animals. In this case it is often easier to manipulate scanned photographs of the scene using two-dimensional image processing techniques than to attempt to model and render the details of the animal's appearance for the computer.

The simplest method for changing one digital image into another is simply to cross-dissolve between them. The color of each pixel is interpolated over time from the first image value to the corresponding second image value. While this method is more flexible than the traditional optical approach (simplifying, for example, different dissolve rates in different image areas), it is still often ineffective for suggesting the actual metamorphosis from one subject to another. This may be partially due to the fact that we are accustomed to seeing this visual device used for another purpose: the linking of two shots, usually signifying a lapse of time and a change in place [7].

Another method for transforming one image into another is to use a two-dimensional "particle system" to map pixels from one image onto pixels from the second image. As the pixel tiles move over time the first image appears to disintegrate and then restructure itself into the second image. This technique is used in several video effects systems (such as the Quantel Mirage) [11].

Another transformation method involves image warping so that the original image appears to be mapped onto a regular shape such as a plane or cylinder. This technique has limited application towards the general transformations under consideration in this paper, but has the advantage of several real-time implementations for video (such as the Ampex ADO) [11]. Extensions include mapping the image onto a free-form surface; one system has even been used for real-time animation of facial images [8].

Other interesting image warps have been described by Holzmann [3] [4], Smith [14], and Wolberg[16].

2.4 Morphing

We use the term "morphing" to describe the combination of generalized image warping with a cross-dissolve between image elements. The term is derived from "image metamorphosis" and should not be confused with morphological image processing operators which detect image features. Morphing is an image processing technique typically used as an animation tool for the metamorphosis from one image to another. The idea is to specify a warp that distorts the first image into the second. Its inverse will distort the second image into the first. As the metamorphosis proceeds, the first image is gradually distorted and is faded out, while the second image starts out totally distorted toward the first and is faded in. Thus, the early images in the sequence are much like the first source image. The middle image of the sequence is the average of the first source image distorted halfway toward the second one and the second source image distorted halfway back toward the first one. The last images in the sequence are similar to the second source image. The middle image is key; if it looks good then probably the entire animated sequence will look good. For morphs between faces, the middle image often looks strikingly life-like, like a real person, but clearly it is neither the person in the first nor second source images.

The morph process consists of warping two images so that they have the same "shape", and then cross dissolving the resulting images. Cross-dissolving is simple; the major problem is how to warp an image.

Morphing has been used as a computer graphics technique for at least a decade. Tom Brigham used a form of morphing in experimental art at NYIT in the early 1980's. Industrial Light and Magic used morphing for cinematic special effects in *Willow* and *Indiana Jones and the Last Crusade*. All of these examples are given in Wolberg's excellent treatise on the subject[15].

Wolberg's book effectively covers the fundamentals of digital image warping, culminating in a mesh warping technique which uses spline mapping in two dimensions. This technique is both fast and intuitive; efficient algorithms exist for computing the mapping of each pixel from the control grid, and a rubber-sheet mental model works effectively for predicting the distortion behavior. It will be compared to our technique in detail below.

2.5 Field Morphing

We now introduce a new technique for morphing based upon fields of influence surrounding two-dimensional control primitives. We call this approach "field morphing" but will often simply abbreviate to "morphing" for the remainder of this paper.

3 Mathematics of Field Morphing

3.1 Distortion of a Single Image

There are two ways to warp an image [15]. The first, called forward mapping, scans through the source image pixel by pixel, and copies them to the appropriate place in the destination image. The second, reverse mapping, goes through the destination image pixel by pixel, and samples the correct pixel from the source image. The most important feature of inverse mapping is that every pixel in the destination image gets set to something appropriate. In the forward mapping case, some pixels in the destination might not get painted, and would have to be interpolated. We calculate the image deformation as a reverse mapping. The problem can be stated "Which pixel coordinate in the source image do we sample for each pixel in the destination image?"

3.2 Transformation with One Pair of Lines

A pair of lines (one defined relative to the source image, the other defined relative to the destination image) defines a mapping from one image to the other. (In this and all other algorithms and equations, pixel coordinates are **BOLD UPPERCASE ITALICS**, lines are specified by pairs of pixel coordinates(*PQ*), scalars are **bold lowercase italics**, and primed variables (*X'*, *u'*) are values defined relative to the source image. We use the term *line* to mean a directed line segment.)

A pair of corresponding lines in the source and destination images defines a coordinate mapping from the destination image pixel coordinate *X* to the source image pixel coordinate *X'* such that for a line *PQ* in the destination image and *P'Q'* in the source image.

$$u = \frac{(X-P) \cdot (Q-P)}{\|Q-P\|^2} \quad (1)$$

$$v = \frac{(X-P) \cdot Perpendicular(Q-P)}{\|Q-P\|} \quad (2)$$

$$X' = P' + u \cdot (Q'-P') + \frac{v \cdot Perpendicular(Q'-P')}{\|Q'-P'\|} \quad (3)$$

where *Perpendicular( )* returns the vector perpendicular to, and the same length as, the input vector. (There are two perpendicular vectors; either the left or right one can be used, as long as it is consistently used throughout.)

The value *u* is the position along the line, and *v* is the distance from the line. The value *u* goes from 0 to 1 as the pixel moves from *P* to *Q*, and is less than 0 or greater than 1 outside that range. The value for *v* is the perpendicular distance in pixels from the line. If there is just one line pair, the transformation of the image proceeds as follows:

For each pixel X in the destination image
    find the corresponding u,v
    find the X' in the source image for that u,v
    destinationImage(X) = sourceImage(X')

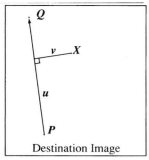 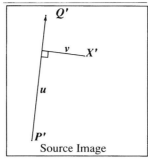

Figure 1: Single line pair

In Figure 1, X' is the location to sample the source image for the pixel at X in the destination image. The location is at a distance v (the distance from the line to the pixel in the source image) from the line $P'Q'$, and at a proportion u along that line.

The algorithm transforms each pixel coordinate by a rotation, translation, and/or a scale, thereby transforming the whole image. All of the pixels along the line in the source image are copied on top of the line in the destination image. Because the u coordinate is normalized by the length of the line, and the v coordinate is not (it is always distance in pixels), the images is scaled along the direction of the lines by the ratio of the lengths of the lines. The scale is only along the direction of the line. We have tried scaling the v coordinate by the length of the line, so that the scaling is always uniform, but found that the given formulation is more useful.

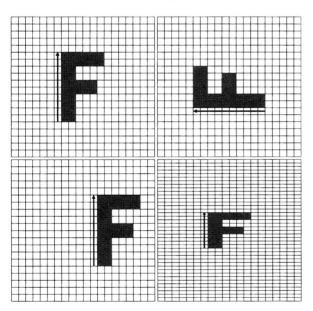

Figure 2: Single line pair examples

The figure on the upper left is the original image. The line is rotated in the upper right image, translated in the lower left image, and scaled in the lower right image, performing the corresponding transformations to the image.

It is possible to get a pure rotation of an image if the two lines are the same length. A pair of lines that are the same length and orientation but different positions specifies a translation of an image. All transformations based on a single line pair are affine, but not all affine transformations are possible. In particular, uniform scales and shears are not possible to specify.

3.3 Transformation with Multiple Pairs of Lines

Multiple pairs of lines specify more complex transformations. A weighting of the coordinate transformations for each line is performed. A position X_i' is calculated for each pair of lines. The displacement $D_i = X_i' - X$ is the difference between the pixel location in the source and destination images, and a weighted average of those displacements is calculated. The weight is determined by the distance from X to the line. This average displacement is added to the current pixel location X to determine the position X' to sample in the source image. The single line case falls out as a special case of the multiple line case, assuming the weight never goes to zero anywhere in the image. The weight assigned to each line should be strongest when the pixel is exactly on the line, and weaker the further the pixel is from it. The equation we use is

$$weight = \left(\frac{length^p}{(a + dist)} \right)^b \quad (4)$$

where *length* is the length of a line, *dist* is the distance[†] from the pixel to the line, and *a*, *b*, and *p* are constants that can be used to change the relative effect of the lines.

If *a* is barely greater than zero, then if the distance from the line to the pixel is zero, the strength is nearly infinite. With this value for *a*, the user knows that pixels on the line will go exactly where he wants them. Values larger than that will yield a more smooth warping, but with less precise control. The variable *b* determines how the relative strength of different lines falls off with distance. If it is large, then every pixel will be affected only by the line nearest it. If *b* is zero, then each pixel will be affected by all lines equally. Values of *b* in the range [0.5, 2] are the most useful. The value of *p* is typically in the range [0, 1]; if it is zero, then all lines have the same weight, if it is one, then longer lines have a greater relative weight than shorter lines.

The multiple line algorithm is as follows:

For each pixel X in the destination
    $DSUM$ = (0,0)
    $weightsum$ = 0
    For each line $P_i Q_i$
        calculate u,v based on $P_i Q_i$
        calculate X'_i based on u,v and $P_i'Q_i'$
        calculate displacement $D_i = X_i' - X_i$ for this line
        $dist$ = shortest distance from X to $P_i Q_i$
        $weight = (length^p / (a + dist))^b$
        $DSUM$ += D_i * $weight$
        $weightsum$ += $weight$
    $X' = X + DSUM / weightsum$
    destinationImage(X) = sourceImage(X')

[†] Note that because these "lines" are directed line segments, the distance from a line to a point is abs(v) if $0 < u < 1$, the distance from P to the point if $u < 0$, and the distance from Q to the point if $u > 1$.

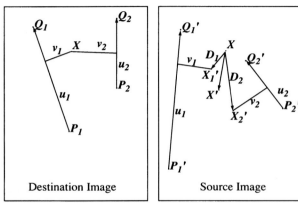

Figure 3: Multiple line pairs

In the above figure, X' is the location to sample the source image for the pixel at X in the destination image. That location is a weighted average of the two pixel locations X_1' and X_2', computed with respect to the first and second line pair, respectively.

If the value a is set to zero there is an undefined result if two lines cross. Each line will have an infinite weight at the intersection point. We quote the line from *Ghostbusters*: "Don't cross the streams. Why? It would be bad." This gets the point across, and in practice does not seem to be too much of a limitation. The animator's mental model when working with the program is that each line has a field of influence around it, and will force pixels near the line to stay in the corresponding position relative to the line as the line animates. The closer the pixels are to a line, the more closely they follow the motion of that line, regardless of the motion of other lines. This mental model gives the animator a good intuitive feel for what will happen as he designs a metamorphosis.

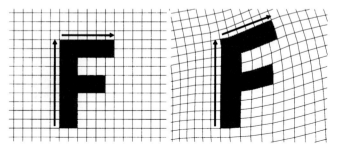

Figure 4: Multiple line pair example

With two or more lines, the transformation is not simple. The figure on the left is the original image, it is distorted by rotating the line above the F around its first point. The whole image is distorted by this transformation. It is still not possible to do a uniform scale or a shear with multiple lines. Almost any pair of lines results in a non-affine transformation. Still, it is fairly obvious to the user what happens when lines are added and moved. Pixels near the lines are moved along with the lines, pixels equally far away from two lines are influenced by both of them.

3.4 Morphing Between Two Images

A morph operation blends between two images, $I0$ and $I1$. To do this, we define corresponding lines in $I0$ and $I1$. Each intermediate frame I of the metamorphosis is defined by creating a new set of line segments by interpolating the lines from their positions in $I0$ to the positions in $I1$. Both images $I0$ and $I1$ are distorted toward the position of the lines in I. These two resulting images are cross-dissolved throughout the metamorphosis, so that at the beginning, the image is completely $I0$ (undistorted because we have not yet begun to interpolate away from the line positions associated with $I0$). Halfway through the metamorphosis it is halfway between $I0$ and $I1$, and finally at the end it is completely $I1$. Note that there is a chance that in some of the intermediate frames, two lines may cross even if they did not cross in the source images.

We have used two different ways of interpolating the lines. The first way is just to interpolate the endpoints of each line. The second way is to interpolate the center position and orientation of each line, and interpolate the length of each line. In the first case, a rotating line would shrink in the middle of the metamorphosis. On the other hand, the second case is not very obvious to the user, who might be surprised by how the lines interpolate. In any case, letting the user see the interpolated position helps him design a good set of beginning and end positions.

3.5 Performance

For video-resolution images (720x486 pixels) with 100 line pairs, this algorithm takes about 2 minutes per frame on a SGI 4D25. The runtime is proportional to the number of lines times the number of pixels in the image. For interactive placement of the lines, low resolution images are typically used. As is usually the case with any computer animation, the interactive design time is the dominant time; it often takes 10 times as long to design a metamorphosis than to compute the final frames.

4 Advantages and Disadvantages of this Technique

This technique has one big advantage over the mesh warping technique described in Wolberg's book[15]: it is much more expressive. The only positions that are used in the algorithm are ones the animator explicitly created. For example, when morphing two faces, the animator might draw line segments down the middle of the nose, across the eyes, along the eyebrows, down the edges of the cheeks, and along the hairline. Everything that is specified is moved exactly as the animator wants them moved, and everything else is blended smoothly based on those positions. Adding new line segments increases control in that area without affecting things too much everywhere else.

This feature-based approach contrasts with the mesh warping technique. In the simplest version of that algorithm, the animator must specify in advance how many control points to use to control the image. The animator must then take those given points and move them to the correct locations. Points left unmodified by mistake or points for which the animator could not find an associating feature are still used by the warping algorithm. Often the animator will find that he does not have enough control in some places and too much in others. Every point exerts the same amount of influence as each of the other points. Often the features that the animator is trying to match are diagonal, whereas the mesh vertices start out vertical and horizontal, and it is difficult for the animator to decide which mesh vertices should be put along the diagonal line.

We have found that trying to position dozens of mesh points around is like trying to push a rope; something is always forced where you don't want it to go. With our technique the control of the line segments is very natural. Moving a line around has a very predictable effect. Extensions of the mesh warping technique to allow refinement of the mesh would make that technique much more expressive and useful[2].

Another problem with the spline mesh technique is that the two-pass algorithm breaks down for large rotational distortions (bottleneck problem)[14][15]. The intermediate image in the two pass algorithm might be distorted to such an extent that information is lost. It is possible do mesh warping with a one-pass algorithm that would avoid this problem.

The two biggest disadvantages of our feature-based technique are speed and control. Because it is global, all line segments need to be referenced for every pixel. This contrasts with the spline mesh, which can have local control (usually the 16 spline points nearest the pixel need be considered).

Between the lines, sometimes unexpected interpolations are generated. The algorithm tries to guess what should happen far away from the line segments; sometimes it makes a mistake. This problem usually manifests itself as a "ghost" of a part of the image showing up in some unrelated part of the interpolated image, caused by some unforeseen combination of the specified line segments. A debugging tool can be useful in this case, in which the user can point to a pixel in the interpolated image and the source pixel is displayed, showing where that pixel originated. Using this information, the animator can usually move a line or add a new one to fix the problem.

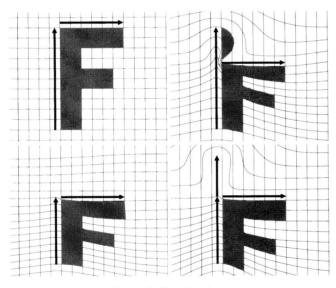

Figure 6: Ghostbusting

In Figure 6, the top left image is the original. Moving the horizontal line down creates a ghost above the line, that is made from pixels copied from the top edge of the F. The bottom left image shows one fix, shrinking the vertical line to match the horizontal one. If the vertical line must maintain its length for some other reason, then the ghost can be eliminated by breaking the vertical line into two parts, as shown on the lower right.

5 Animated Sequences

It is often useful to morph between two sequences of live action, rather than just two still images. The morph technique can easily be extended to apply to this problem. Instead of just marking corresponding features in the two images, there needs to be a set of line segments at key frames for each sequence of images. These sets of segments are interpolated to get the two sets for a particular frame, and then the above two-image metamorphosis is performed on the two frames, one from each strip of live action. This creates much more work for the animator, because instead of marking features in just two images he will need to mark features in many key frames in two sequences of live action. For example, in a transition between two moving faces, the animator might have to draw a line down the nose in each of 10 keyframes in both sequences, requiring 20 individual line segments. However, the increase in realism of metamorphosis of live action compared to still images is dramatic, and worth the effort. The sequences in the Michael Jackson video, *Black or White*, were done this way.

6 Results

We have been using this algorithm at Pacific Data Images for the last two years. The first projects involved interpolation of still images. Now, almost all of the projects involve morphing of live-action sequences.

While the program is straightforward and fun to use, it still requires a lot of work from the animator. The first project using the tool, (the *Plymouth Voyager* metamorphosis), involved morphs between nine pairs of still images. It took three animator-weeks to complete the project. While it was very quick to get a good initial approximation of a transition, the final tweaking took the majority of the time. Of course, it was the first experience any of us had with the tool, so there was some learning time in those three animator-weeks. Also, a large amount of time was spent doing traditional special effects work on top of the morph feature matching. For example, the images had to be extracted from the background (using a digital paint program), some color balancing needed to be done, and the foreground elements had to be separated form each other (more painting). These elements were morphed separately, then matted together. On current morph production jobs at PDI, we estimate that about 20-40 percent of the time is spent doing the actual metamorphosis design, while the rest of the time is used doing traditional special effects.

7 Acknowledgments

Tom Brigham of the New York Institute of Technology deserves credit for introducing us to the concept of morph. The magicians at Industrial Light and Magic took the idea to a new level of quality in several feature films, and provided inspiration for this work. Jamie Dixon at PDI was a driving force behind the creation of the tools, and the rest of the animators at PDI have been the best users that we can imagine. The great animation created with this program is mostly their work, not ours. Finally, Carl Rosendahl, Glenn Entis, and Richard Chuang deserve credit for making Pacific Data Images the creative, fun environment where great new things can happen, and for allowing us to publish details of a very profitable algorithm.

Figure 7

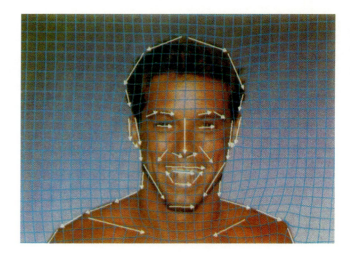

Figure 10

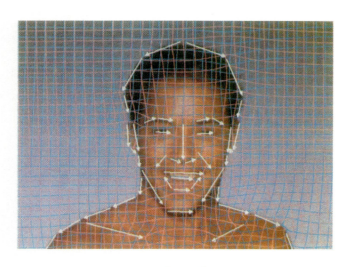

Figure 8

Figure 7 shows the lines drawn over the a face. figure 9 shows the lines drawn over a second face. Figure 8 shows the morphed image. with the interpolated lines drawn over it.

Figure 10 shows the first face with the lines and a grid. showing how it is distorted to the position of the lines in the intermediate frame. Figure 11 shows the second face distorted to the same intermediate position. The lines in the top and bottom picture are in the same position. We have distorted the two images to the same "shape".

Note that outside the outline of the faces. the grids are warped very differently in the two images. but because this is the background. it is not important. If there were background features that needed to be matched. lines could have been drawn over them as well.

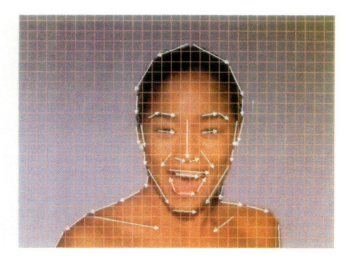

Figure 9

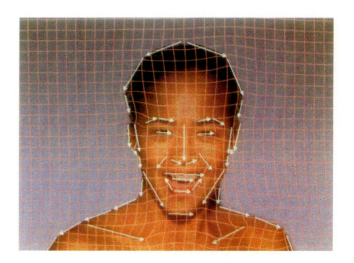

Figure 11

Figure 12

Figure 14

Figure 12 is the first face distorted to the intermediate position, without the grid or lines. Figure 13 is the second face distorted toward that same position. Note that the blend between the two distorted images is much more life-like than the either of the distorted images themselves. We have noticed this happens very frequently.

The final sequence is figures 14, 15, and 16.

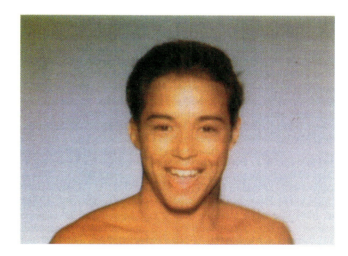

Figure 15

Figure 13

Figure 16

8 References

[1] Barr, A.H., Global and Local Deformations of Solid Primitives. In "Proc. SIGGRAPH '84" (Minneapolis, July 23-27, 1984). Published as "Computer Graphics", 18(3) (July 1984), pp. 21-30.

[2] Forsey, D. R., Bartels, R. H., Hierarchical B-Spline Refinement. In "Proc. SIGGRAPH '88" (Atlanta, August 1-5, 1988). Published as "Computer Graphics", 22(4) (August 1988), pp. 205-211

[3] Holzmann, G.J., PICO --- A Picture Editor. "AT&T Technical Journal", 66(2) (March/April 1987), pp. 2-13.

[4] Holzmann, G.J., "Beyond Photography: The Digital Darkroom". Prentice Hall, 1988.

[5] Kaul, A., Rossignac, J., "Solid-Interpolating Deformations: Constructions and Animation of PIPs," *Proceedings of EUROGRAPHICS '91*, September 1991, pp. 493-505

[6] Kent, J.,Parent, R., Carlson, W. "Establishing Correspondences by Topological Merging: A New Approach to 3-D Shape Transformation", *Proceedings of Graphics Interface '91*, June 1991, pp. 271-278

[7] Oakley, V., "Dictionary of Film and Television Terms". Barnes & Noble Books, 1983.

[8] Oka, M., Tsutsui, K., Akio, O., Yoshitaka, K., Takashi, T., Real-Time Manipulation of Texture-Mapped Surfaces. In "Proc. SIGGRAPH '87" (Anaheim, July 27-31, 1987). Published as "Computer Graphics", 21(4) (July 1987), pp. 181-188.

[9]Overveld, C.W.A.M. Van A Technique for Motion Specification."Visual Computer". March 1990

[10] Reeves, W.T., Particle Systems: A Technique for Modeling a Class of Fuzzy Objects. "ACM Transactions on Graphics", 2(2) (April 1983). (Reprinted in "Proc. SIGGRAPH '83" (Detroit, July 25-29, 1983). Published as "Computer Graphics", 17(3) (July 1983), pp. 359-376.)

[11] Rosenfeld, M., Special Effects Production with Computer Graphics and Video Techniques. In "SIGGRAPH '87 Course Notes #8 - Special Effects with Computer Graphics" (Anaheim, July 27-31, 1987).

[12] Sederberg, T.W. and Parry, S.R., Free-Form Deformation of Solid Geometric Models. In "Proc. SIGGRAPH '86" (Dallas, August 18-22, 1986). Published as "Computer Graphics", 20(4) (August 1986), pp. 151-160.

[13] Shay, J.D., Humpback to the Future. "Cinefex 29" (February 1987), pp. 4-19.

[14] Smith, A.R., Planar 2-Pass Texture Mapping and Warping. In "Proc. SIGGRAPH '87" (Anaheim, July 27-31, 1987). Published as "Computer Graphics", 21(4) (July 1987), pp. 263-272.

[15] Wolberg, G., "Digital Image Warping". IEEE Computer Society Press, 1990.

[16] Wolberg, G., Skeleton Based Image Warping, "Visual Computer", Volume 5, Number 1/2, March 1989. pp 95-108

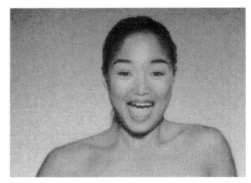

Figure 17
A sequence from Michael Jackson's *Black or White*
(Courtesy MJJ Productions)

View Interpolation for Image Synthesis

Shenchang Eric Chen, Lance Williams
Apple Computer, Inc.

ABSTRACT

Image-space simplifications have been used to accelerate the calculation of computer graphic images since the dawn of visual simulation. Texture mapping has been used to provide a means by which images may themselves be used as display primitives. The work reported by this paper endeavors to carry this concept to its logical extreme by using interpolated images to portray three-dimensional scenes. The special-effects technique of morphing, which combines interpolation of texture maps and their shape, is applied to computing arbitrary intermediate frames from an array of prestored images. If the images are a structured set of views of a 3D object or scene, intermediate frames derived by morphing can be used to approximate intermediate 3D transformations of the object or scene. Using the view interpolation approach to synthesize 3D scenes has two main advantages. First, the 3D representation of the scene may be replaced with images. Second, the image synthesis time is independent of the scene complexity. The correspondence between images, required for the morphing method, can be pre-determined automatically using the range data associated with the images. The method is further accelerated by a quadtree decomposition and a view-independent visible priority. Our experiments have shown that the morphing can be performed at interactive rates on today's high-end personal computers. Potential applications of the method include virtual holograms, a walkthrough in a virtual environment, image-based primitives and incremental rendering. The method also can be used to greatly accelerate the computation of motion blur and soft shadows cast by area light sources.

CR Categories and Subject Descriptors: I.3.3 [Computer Graphics]: Picture/Image Generation; I.3.7 [Computer Graphics]: Three-Dimensional Graphics and Realism.

Additional Keywords: image morphing, interpolation, virtual reality, motion blur, shadow, incremental rendering, real-time display, virtual holography, motion compensation.

1 INTRODUCTION

Generating a large number of images of an environment from closely spaced viewpoints is a very useful capability. A traditional application is a flight in the cabin of an aircraft simulator, whereas the contemporary model is perhaps a walk through a virtual environment; in both cases the same scene is displayed from the view of a virtual camera controlled by the user. The computation of global illumination effects, such as shadows, diffuse and specular inter-reflections, also requires a large number of visibility calculations. A typical approach to this problem is to rely on the computer to repetitively render the scene from different viewpoints. This approach has two major drawbacks. First, real-time rendering of complex scenes is computationally expensive and usually requires specialized graphics hardware. Second, the rendering time is usually not constant and is dependent on the scene complexity. This problem is particularly critical in simulation and virtual reality applications because of the demand for real-time feedback. Since scene complexity is potentially unbounded, the second problem will always exist regardless of the processing power of the computer.

A number of approaches have been proposed to address this problem. Most of these approaches use a preprocess to compute a subset of the scene visible from a specified viewing region[AIRE91, TELL92]. Only the potentially visible objects are processed in the walkthrough time. This approach does not completely solve the problem because there may be viewing regions from which all objects are visible. Greene and Kass[GREE93] developed a method to approximate the visibility at a location from adjacent environment maps. The environment maps are Z-buffered images rendered from a set of discrete viewpoints in 3D space. Each environment map shows a complete view of the scene from a point. An environment map can take the form of a cubic map, computed by rendering a cube of 90° views radiating from that point [GREE86]. The environment maps are pre-computed and stored with viewpoints arranged in a structured way, such as a 3D lattice. An image from a new viewpoint can be generated by re-sampling the environment maps stored in adjacent locations. The re-sampling process involves rendering the pixels in the environment maps as 3D polygons from the new viewpoint. The advantage of this approach is that the rendering time is proportional to the environment map resolutions and is independent of the scene complexity. However, this method requires Z-buffer hardware to render a relatively large number of polygons interactively, a feature still not available on most low-end computers.

This paper presents a fast method for generating intermediate images from images stored at nearby viewpoints. The method has advantages similar to those of Greene and Kass' method. The generation of a new image is independent of the scene complexity. However, instead of drawing every pixel as a 3D polygon, our method uses techniques similar to those used in image morphing[BEIE92]. Adjacent images are "morphed" to create a new image for an in-between viewpoint. The morphing makes use of pre-computed correspondence maps and, therefore, is very efficient. Our experiments with the new method have shown that it can be performed at interactive rates on inexpen-

---

Permission to copy without fee all or part of this material is granted provided that the copies are not made or distributed for direct commercial advantage, the ACM copyright notice and the title of the publication and its date appear, and notice is given that copying is by permission of the Association for Computing Machinery. To copy otherwise, or to republish, requires a fee and/or specific permission.
© 1993 ACM-0-89791-601-8/93/008/0279 $01.50

sive personal computers without specialized hardware.

The new method is based on the observation that a sequence of images from closely spaced viewpoints is highly coherent. Most of the adjacent images in the sequence depict the same objects from slightly different viewpoints. Our method uses the camera's position and orientation and the range data of the images to determine a pixel-by-pixel correspondence between images automatically. The pairwise correspondence between two successive images can be pre-computed and stored as a pair of morph maps. Using these maps, corresponding pixels are interpolated interactively under the user's control to create in-between images.

Pixel correspondence can be established if range data and the camera transformation are available. For synthetic images, range data and the camera transformation are easily obtainable. For natural images, range data can be acquired from a ranging camera [BESL88], computed by photogrammetry [WOLF83], or modeled by a human artist [WILL90]. The camera transformation can be found if the relative positions and orientations of the camera are known.

The idea of using images to represent a virtual environment has been presented previously. An earlier approach uses computer controlled videodiscs to perform surrogate travel [LIPP80]. A more recent approach uses digital movie technologies to construct a virtual museum [MILL92]. In both systems, a user navigates a finite set of routes and directions that have been pre-determined. Our method allows greater flexibility in the navigation because the stored frames can be interpolated smoothly to synthesize arbitrary intermediate points of view.

A static subject or environment portrayed by a restricted set of images indexed by the user's point of view supports a form of "desktop virtual reality" termed "virtual integral holography" [VENO90]. In this context also, our method permits smooth interpolation of the images to present a continuous display sequence, rather than quantizing the user's point of view and jumping to the closest prestored image.

The morphing method can be used to interpolate a number of different parameters, such as camera position, viewing angle, direction of view and hierarchical object transformation. The modeling and viewing transformations can be concatenated to compute the correspondence mapping between two images. Generally, the images can be arranged in an arbitrary graph structure. The nodes of the graph are the images. Each arc in the graph represents a correspondence mapping, which is bi-directional, and two maps are associated with each arc. The number of interpolation parameters determines the dimensionality of the graph. For instance, the graph for a virtual camera moving with two degrees of freedom (the latitudes and longitudes of a sphere bounding an object at a central "look-at" point, for example) is a simple polyhedron (rendering of objects rather than environments will be discussed in more detail in Section 4.4, Image-based Primitives.) The camera's location coordinates index a point on a face of the polyhedron, and the desired view is synthesized by interpolating the images and mappings stored with the vertices and edges of the face. Note that if each image is of the form of an environment map, view angle and direction also can be interpolated by re-projecting the environment map to the desired view orientation [MILL93] without increasing the dimensionality of the graph. Similarly, a camera moving in 3D is supported by a graph which takes the form of a 3D space lattice. The barycentric coordinates of the view location can be used to interpolate among the images attached to the vertices of the enclosing tetrahedron in a lattice of tetrahedra.

For the representation of scenes with objects moving or changes other than those consequent to a change in viewpoint, the graph becomes a general polytope. Generally, arbitrary distortions of surfaces are accommodated by the mapping, as are hierarchical motions of linkages or the limbs of animated characters[1]. To index such an elaborate set of mappings by the various parameters can be an arbitrarily complex process, requiring multivariate interpolation of a multidimensional graph.

Without loss of generality, this paper will concentrate on the interpolation of the camera position in 1D and 2D space (accommodating "virtual holograms" of objects as well as restricted navigation in 3D scenes). The scene is assumed to be static, and all the image changes are as a result of camera movement. Although the method can be applied to natural images, only synthetic ones have been attempted in the work described here. Interpolation of images accurately supports only view-independent shading. Reflection mapping or Phong specular reflection could be performed with separate maps for reflection map coordinates or normal components, but only diffuse reflection and texture mapping have been presented here.

Section 2 introduces the basic algorithms of the method as well as its limitations and optimizations. Section 3 gives implementation details and shows some examples. Section 4 shows applications of the method to virtual reality, temporal anti-aliasing, generating shadows from area lights, image-based display primitives and incremental rendering ("progressive refinement"). Conclusions and future directions are discussed in the last section.

2 VISIBILITY MORPHING

Image morphing is the simultaneous interpolation of shape and texture. The technique generally involves two steps. The first step establishes the correspondence between two images and is the most difficult part of most morphing methods. The correspondence is usually established by a human animator. The user might, for example, define a set of corresponding points or line segments within a pair or set of images. An algorithm is then employed to determine the correspondence (mapping) for the remainder of the images[BEIE92]. The second step in the process is to use the mapping to interpolate the shape of each image toward the other, according to the particular intermediate image to be synthesized, and to blend the pixel values of the two warped images by the same respective coefficients, completing the morph.

Our method uses the camera transformation and image range data to automatically determine the correspondence between two or more images. The correspondence is in the form of a "forward mapping." The mapping describes the pixel-by-pixel correspondence from the source to the destination image. The mapping is also bi-directional since each of the two images can act as the source and the destination. In the basic method, the corresponding pixels' 3D screen coordinates are interpolated and the pixels from the source image are moved to their interpolated locations to create an interpolated image. For pixels which map to the same pixel in the interpolated image, their Z-coordinates are compared to resolve visibility. Cross-dissolving the overlapping pixels' colors may be necessary if the image colors are not view-independent. This process is repeated for each of the source images.

This method is made more efficient by the following two properties. First, since neighboring pixels tend to move together in the mapping, a quadtree block compression is employed to exploit this coherence. Adjacent pixels which move in a similar manner are grouped in blocks and moved at the same time. This compression is particularly advantageous since a view-independent visible priority among the pixel blocks can be established. The pixel blocks are sorted once by their Z-co-

---

[1]Establishing such elaborate mappings is straightforward for synthetic images, a classic vision problem for natural ones.

ordinates, when the maps are created, and subsequently displayed from back to front to eliminate the overhead of a Z-buffer for visibility determination.

We will describe our method in terms of the morphing between two images first. Generalization of the method to more images is straightforward and will be discussed later.

2.1 Establishing Pixel Correspondence

As a camera moves, objects in its field of view move in the opposite direction. The speed of each object's apparent movement is dependent on the object's location relative to the camera. Since each pixel's screen coordinates (x, y and z) and the camera's relative location are known, a 4x4 matrix transformation establishes a correspondence between the pixels in each pair of images. The transformations can be pre-computed and reduced to a 3D spatial offset vector for each of the pixels. The offset vector indicates the amount each of the pixels moves in its screen space as a result of the camera's movement. The offset vectors are stored in a "morph map," which represents the forward mapping from one image to another. This map is similar in concept to a disparity map computed from a stereo pair[GOSH89], the field of offset vectors computed for "optical flow" analysis[NAGE86], or motion compensation in video compression and format conversion[MPEG90]. For a computed image or range image, an exact pixel-by-pixel map can be created. The mapping is many-to-one because many pixels from the first image may move to the same pixel in the second image. Therefore, the morph map is directional and two morph maps are needed for a pair of images.

The use of a pre-computed spatial look-up table for image warping has been presented in [WOLB89]. Wolberg used the look-up table to implement arbitrary forward mapping functions for image warping. Wolberg's maps contained absolute coordinates rather than offset vectors.

In a typical image morph, as described in the beginning of this section, a sparse correspondence provided by a human operator is used to perform strictly two-dimensional shape interpolation. Such a morph can also be used to interpolate stored images in order to represent 3D scenes or objects, as suggested in [POGG91]. The advantages of our method are that the correspondence is dense (every pixel has an explicitly computed map coordinate), the correspondence is automatic (rather than relying on human effort), and the explicit prestored maps permit the image deformations to be generated very quickly.

2.2 Interpolating Correspondences

To generate an in-between view of a pair of images, the offset vectors are interpolated linearly and the pixels in the source image are moved by the interpolated vector to their destinations. Figure 1 shows the offset vectors, sampled at twenty-pixel intervals, for the camera motion sequence in Figure 3.

The interpolation is an approximation to the transformation of the pixel coordinates by a perspective viewing matrix. A method which approximates the perspective changes with local frame shifting and scaling is presented in [HOFM88]. Perspective transformation requires multiplication of the pixel coordinates by a 4x4 matrix and division by the homogeneous coordinates, a rather computationally taxing process, although bounded by image resolution rather than scene complexity. Linear interpolation of pixel coordinates using the morph maps, on the other hand, is very efficient and can be performed incrementally using forward differencing.

If the viewpoint offset is small, the interpolation is very close to the exact solution. Moreover, quadratic or cubic interpolation, though slightly more expensive to perform, can be used to improve the accuracy of the approximation. When the viewpoint moves parallel to the viewing plane, the linear interpolation produces an exact solution. This case is demonstrated in Figure 2a, which traces the paths of mapped pixels in the interpolated image as the viewpoint traverses the four corners of a square parallel to the viewing plane. The squares in the figure are the extents of the pixel movement. Because the squares are parallel to the viewing plane, the linear interpolation of the square corners produces the same result as perspective transformation. Another special case is when the viewpoint moves perpendicular to the viewing plane along a square parallel to the ground(Figure 2b). The resulting pixel locations form trapezoids, which are the projections of squares parallel to the ground. The trapezoids can be interpolated linearly in the horizontal direction. The vertical direction requires perspective divisions. The divisions can be avoided if a look-up table indexed by the vertical offset is pre-computed for each possible integer height of the trapezoids. The second case can be generalized to include the case when the squares are perpendicular to both the ground and the viewing plane. If the viewpoints are aligned with a 3D lattice, the result will always fall into one of the above two cases, which allows us to use linear interpolation to generate an exact solution.

2.3 Compositing Images

The key problem with forward mapping is that overlaps and holes may occur in the interpolated image.

2.3.1 Overlaps

One reason overlaps occur is due to local image contraction. Local image contraction occurs when several samples in a local neighborhood of the source image move to the same pixel in the interpolated image. A typical example of this case is when our view of a plane moves from perpendicular to oblique. Perspective projection causes the image to contract as the plane moves away from the point of view. In the mapping, the samples on the far side of the plane contract while the samples on the near side expand. Contraction causes the samples to overlap in the target pixels.

Multiple layers of pixel depths also will cause the samples to overlap, as in the case of the foreground sculpture in Figure 3. Resolving this case is really a hidden surface problem. One way of solving this problem is to use the Z-buffer algorithm to determine the frontmost pixel. A more efficient way of determining the nearest pixel is presented in the Optimization Section.

2.3.2 Holes

Holes between samples in the interpolated image may arise from local image expansion when mapping the source image to the destination image. This case is shown in Figure 3 where a source image is viewed from viewpoints rotated to the right. The cyan regions indicate holes. Generally, a square pixel in the source image will map to a quadrilateral in the destination image. If we interpolate the four corners of the square instead of the pixel's center, the holes can be eliminated by filling and filtering the pixels in the destination quadrilateral.

A more efficient, though less accurate, method to fill the holes is to interpolate the adjacent pixels' colors or offset vectors. The holes are identified by filling the interpolated image with a reserved "background" color first. For those pixels which still retain the background color after the source to target mapping, new colors are computed by interpolating the colors of adjacent non-background pixels. Alternatively, we can interpolate the offset vectors of the adjacent pixels. The interpolated offset is used to index back to the source image to obtain the new sample color. Note that using a distinguished background color may not identify all the holes. Some of the holes may be created by a foreground object and are filled by a background object behind it (e.g., the holes in the sculpture in the rightmost image in Figure 3). This problem is alleviated, though not completely eliminated, when more source images are added as described below (e.g. Figure 5d).

Holes may also arise from sample locations invisible in each of the source images but visible in the interpolated image. The hole region, as shown in Figure 4, is the intersection of the umbra regions cast by viewpoints A and B and the visible region from point M. The small circle in the hole region is completely missed by the two source images from points A and B. One way of solving this problem is to use multiple source images to minimize the umbra region. Figure 5a shows the holes (cyan pixels) created by rotating one source image. Figure 5b shows that the number of holes is significantly less when two sources images are used. The number of holes can be reduced further if we place the two source viewpoints closer (Figure 5c). The remaining holes can be filled by interpolating the adjacent pixels(Figure 5d). If the images are computer-generated, a ray-tracing type of rendering can be used to render only those missing pixels.

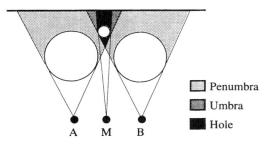

Fig. 4   Penumbra, umbra and hole regions

2.4   Optimization

The basic method is made more efficient by the following two steps.

2.4.1   Block Compression

Since adjacent pixels tend to move together in the mapping, a block compression scheme such as a quadtree can be applied to compress the morph map. The compression serves two purposes. First, it reduces the size of the morph map. Second, it allows us to interpolate offsets for entire blocks instead of pixel-by-pixel. The second aspect greatly accelerates the interpolation process as the main cost in the process is the interpolation of the offset vectors.

The compression ratio is related to the image depth complexity and the viewpoint movement. For images with high depth complexity, the compression ratio is usually low. The ratio is also lower if the viewpoint's movement results in greater pixel depth change. Figure 6 shows the quadtree decomposition of the morph map for the image sequence in Figure 3. The maximal offset threshold within a block is one pixel in Figure 6a and two pixels in Figure 6c, which means the offset vector coordinates within a block do not differ more than one or two pixel units. The compression ratio in Figure 6a is 15 to 1 and in Figure 6b is 29 to 1 (i.e., the number of blocks vs. the number of pixels).

The threshold provides a smooth quality degradation path for increased performance. Large threshold factors result in fewer quadtree blocks and, therefore, reduce the interpolation time. The performance gain is at the expense of increasing blockiness in the interpolated image. The interpolation times in Figure 6b and 6d are accelerated by a factor of 6 and 7 respectively. Note that the speedup factor does not grow linearly with the compression ratio because the same number of pixels still need to be moved.

2.4.2   View-Independent Visible Priority

In the basic method, the Z-buffer algorithm is used to resolve visibility. However, as shown in Figure 7, the A-closer-than-B priority established in View1 is still valid in View2, since Point A and Point B do not overlap in View2. The priority is incorrect in View3 when A and B overlap. As long as the angle θ in the figure is less than 90 degrees, the A-B priority does not need to be changed when the viewpoint is moved. This observation allows us to establish a view-independent visible priority for every source pixel for a viewing range. The pixels are ordered from back to front based on their original Z-coordinates when the morph maps are created, and are subsequently drawn in a back-to-front order in the interpolation process. This ordering of the samples, or sample blocks, eliminates the need for interpolating the Z-coordinates of every pixel and updating a Z-buffer in the interpolation process.

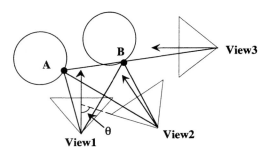

Fig. 7   View-independent visible priority

Note that the priority established here is for image pixels rather than for the underlying objects, unlike list-priority algorithms for hidden-surface removal[SCHU69].

This method applies to multiple source images as well. The source images' pixel Z-coordinates are transformed to a single coordinate system for establishing the Z-priority. All the pixels in the source images are sorted into the same priority list.

The priority can be assigned to every quadtree pixel block. With static objects and a moving camera, pixel offsets are directly related to Z-coordinates. Since the pixels within a block have similar offsets, they also have similar Z-coordinates. The Z-coordinates within a block are filtered to determine a Z value for the priority sort. The result is a sorted list of pixel blocks valid for the entire range between views.

3   IMPLEMENTATIONS

The method presented above can be summarized as follows.

3.1   Preprocessing

The preprocessing stage establishes the correspondence between each pair of source and destination images. As mentioned in Section 1, the source images are connected to form a graph structure. Each node of the graph contains a source image, its range data and camera parameters (i.e., camera's position, orientation). For each set of adjacent nodes in the graph, a sorted list of quadtree blocks is created (e.g., a block list is created for every triangle in a 2D lattice structure). Each block in the list contains a pointer to a pixel block in a source image, the size, the screen coordinates and the offset vectors of the block. The block list is created in the following steps:

Step 1. Get input data: a source node (image, range data and camera parameters), a destination node (only the camera parameters are needed) and a threshold factor for the quadtree decomposition.

Step 2. Create a morph map from the source to the destination (Section 2.1).

Step 3. Decompose the morph map into quadtree blocks and add the blocks to a block list (Section 2.4.1).

Step 4. Repeat Step 1 to 3 for each directional arc connecting the set of nodes.

5. Sort the block list from back to front by the blocks' Z-coordinates.

3.2 Interactive Interpolation

In the interactive interpolation stage, the block list corresponding to a new viewing location is retrieved. The parametric coordinates of the location with respect to the adjacent nodes are used as interpolation parameters. An interpolated image for the new location is generated in the following steps:

Step 1. Get input data: interpolation parameters and a sorted block list.

Step 2. Fill the interpolated image with a distinguished background color.

Step 3. For every block in the list in back-to-front order, compute its new location from the offset vectors and the interpolation parameters. Copy the pixel block from the source image to its new location in the interpolated image (Section 2.2).

Step 4. For every pixel in the interpolated image that still retains the background color, compute its color by filtering the colors of the adjacent non-background pixels (Section 2.3.2).

3.3 Examples

Figure 8 shows a sequence of images generated by moving the viewpoint to the right. The images were rendered at 256x256 resolution using progressive radiosity [COHE88] from a model created for the Virtual Museum project[MILL92].

Figure 9 shows two intermediate images created by morphing the leftmost and rightmost images. Each image took 0.17 second to generate (excluding the preprocessing time) on a Macintosh Quadra 950.

Note that for the interpolation to work properly, the source image cannot be anti-aliased. Anti-aliasing is view-dependent. It blends silhouette pixel colors from a particular viewpoint. Since the Z-buffer cannot be anti-aliased in the same way, the anti-aliased silhouette pixels may attach to either the foreground or the background objects depending on the quantization of the Z-buffer. This problem can be solved by morphing high-resolution unfiltered source images and then filtering the interpolated image.

The method can be applied to interpolating more than two source images. Figure 10 shows a sequence of images interpolated from the four source images in the corners. The viewpoints of the source images form a square parallel to the viewing plane. Therefore, as discussed before, linear interpolation is an exact solution to the perspective transformation. New images are computed from the nearest three corner images. The barycentric coordinates of the new viewpoint are used to interpolate the three images. Dividing the lattice into simplices minimizes the cost of interpolation.

4 APPLICATIONS

The morphing method can be used in a wide variety of applications which require fast visibility computations of a predefined static scene. Simulation and virtual reality applications typically require a scene to be displayed interactively from different viewpoints. Temporal anti-aliasing, or motion blur, can be accelerated by using morph maps to integrate image samples over time. The image samples are interpolated from key images using the morphing method. We also present an application of morph mapping to compute shadows from area lights using the shadow buffer method [WILL78]. The morphing method makes it possible to define a new class of graphic display primitives based on images. This approach is also useful in incremental rendering as it provides a way to reuse the pixels computed for previous images.

4.1 Virtual Reality

Instead of representing a virtual environment as a list of 3D geometric entities, the morphing method uses images (environment maps). To perform a walkthrough, the images adjacent to the viewpoint are interpolated to create the desired view.

In addition to supporting walkthroughs in virtual environments, the method can be used to create virtual holograms, where the display on the screen will change with respect to the user's viewpoint to provide 3D motion parallax. One existing approach uses 3D rendering to display the scene from the viewpoint obtained by a head location sensor[DEER92]. Another approach uses a finite set of pre-rendered frames, each corresponding to a particular viewing location[VENO90]. With the morphing method, only a few key images are required. The interpolation can generate the in-between frames. Figure 10 shows a sequence of images with vertical and horizontal motion parallax.

The image-based morphing method is inexpensive computationally and provides a smooth quality-speed tradeoff. Although the total storage requirement may be large, the amount of data needed to compute a frame is relatively small and can be read from secondary storage as needed. This approach is very appropriate for CD-ROM based devices because of their large storage capability. As the complexity of geometrical models increases, the advantage of image-based approaches will be more significant because of their bounded overhead.

Another advantage of using the image-based approach is that a real environment can be digitized by photographic means. Using a camera to capture the environment usually is much easier than modeling it geometrically. Although our method relies on range data to establish the correspondence between images, range data should be easier to obtain than the complete 3D geometry of the environment.

4.2 Motion Blur

If an image in a motion sequence is a sample at an instant of time instead of over a time interval, the motion will appear to be jerky and the image is said to be aliased in the temporal domain. One way to perform temporal anti-aliasing is super-sampling. The motion is sampled at a higher rate in the temporal domain and then the samples are filtered to the displayed rate. Super-sampling requires the computation of many more samples. For images which are expensive to render, this technique is very inefficient.

The morphing method allows additional temporal samples to be created by interpolation. The interpolation time is constant regardless of the rendering time for each frame. The sampling rate is determined by the largest offset vector from the morph map in order to perform proper anti-aliasing. Figure 11a is a motion blurred image computed from 32 source images for the camera motion in Figure 8. The images were first rendered at 512x512 resolution and then filtered down to 256x256 resolution before temporal anti-aliasing was performed. The temporal samples were anti-aliased with a box filter. Each image took around 5 seconds to render on a high-end workstation with 3D graphics hardware support. Figure 11b was computed from the same number of images interpolated from three of the source images. Each interpolated image took 0.6 second to compute on a Macintosh Quadra950. The only minor visible difference between the two images is the top of the inside loop of the foreground sculpture, due to the holes created from the interpolation as discussed previously.

The super-sampling approach requires the sampling rate to be determined based on the worst case. For images with fast moving objects and slowly moving backgrounds, this method is not very efficient. One way to solve this problem is to segment the images based on object movement and use different sampling rates for each segment. For instance, the foreground sculpture in this figure needs to be sampled at the highest rate while the wall behind it needs only a few samples. In the case of motion caused by viewpoint changes as in this figure, the segments can be sorted in order of depth as discussed in Section 2.4.2. Each segment is filtered independently and a temporal coverage value for each pixel is kept to indicate the ratio of background samples vs. all samples. The multiple segment layers are then composited in front-to-back order with each segment's pixel colors attenuated by the coverage value from the previous segment.

4.3 Shadows

A very general and efficient way of rendering shadows is the shadow buffer algorithm [WILL78]. The algorithm computes a Z-buffer (i.e., shadow map) from the point of view of the light source. To compute shadows, a surface point's coordinates are transformed to the light source's space and its Z-coordinate is compared to the corresponding Z-coordinate in the shadow map. If the point is further away then it is in shadow.

The algorithm only works for point light sources. To approximate a linear or an area source, many point lights may be needed [SHAP84]. The cost of computing the shadows is proportional to the number of point sources used.

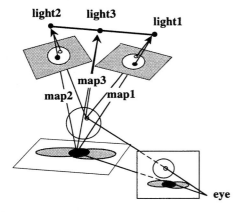

Fig. 12   Shadow buffer interpolation for a linear light source

The morphing method can be used to significantly reduce the cost of computing the shadow map for each of the point sources. Figure 12 illustrates the process of using the method to compute shadows from a linear light source. A shadow map is computed first for each of the two end points of the source (i.e., light1 and light2) using the conventional rendering method. A morph map from the viewpoint to each of the two end points is also computed to transform the screen coordinates to each point source's coordinate space (i.e., map1 and map2). The shadow map for an in-between point (e.g., light3) on the linear source is interpolated from the corner shadow maps using the morphing method. The same interpolation factor is used to interpolate the two morph maps (map1 and map2) to create a morph map from the viewpoint to the in-between light source point (map3). The standard shadow buffer algorithm is then used to compute shadows for the in-between point source. The process is repeated for all the in-between points at a desired interval. The resulting shadow images are composited to create the soft shadow of the linear source. This method can be generalized to any area or volume light source.

Figure 13 shows the result after compositing 100 in-between shadow images generated by randomly distributed points on a rectangular light source above the triangle. Four source shadow maps located at the corners of the rectangle were created for the interpolation. The shadow maps were rendered at 512x512 resolution and the shadow image resolution is 256x256. Percentage closer filtering [REEV87] was used to anti-alias the shadows for each image. Each shadow image took 1.5 seconds to compute. Shading for the illuminated pixels was computed by Lambert's Law weighted by the projected size of the rectangle source over the pixel.

4.4   Image-Based Primitives

A 3D object is perceived on a flat display screen through a series of 2D images. As long as we can generate the images from any viewpoint, it does not matter if a 3D description of the object is available. The morphing method permits any view of an object to be generated by interpolation from some key images. Therefore, a new class of primitives based on images can be defined. These image-based primitives are particularly useful for defining objects of very high complexity since the interpolation time is independent of the object complexity.

Figure 14 shows a sequence of images of a rotating teapot generated by the morphing method. The middle images were generated by interpolating the two key images at the extreme left and right. The key images were rendered with viewpoints rotated 22.5 degrees around the center of the teapot. A larger angular increment of the key images may result in holes and distortions as a result of the linear interpolation. Figure 15 is the same source images extrapolated to show the pixel blocks which compose the teapot.

Rendering an object using the morphing method is really not different from rendering a complete scene as described previously. The image-based object or scene can be treated as a "sprite" that can be composited with images generated by other means.

4.5   Incremental Rendering

Adjacent images in an animation sequence usually are highly coherent. Therefore, it's desirable to perform the rendering incrementally. Ideally, the rendering should be limited to only the pixels which are different from the previous frame. However, searching for the pixels that change is not always trivial. Some incremental rendering approaches which make use of frame-to-frame coherence were presented in [CHEN90], [JEVA92].

The morphing method provides a natural way of making use of frame coherence. For an animation sequence where the motion of every frame is known in advance, the frames can be rendered initially at a coarse temporal sampling rate. The remaining frames can then be computed by the morphing method. The missing samples or view-dependent shading, such as highlights, of the interpolated frames can be computed by additional rendering. If accuracy rather than speed is the main concern, the map-based interpolation or extrapolation of pixel coordinates can be replaced by perspective transformation.

5   CONCLUSIONS AND FUTURE DIRECTIONS

The interactive speed which the image-based display has achieved on modest computing platforms has fulfilled our primary goal in pursuing this research. In addition to this primary objective, we have demonstrated effective application of the view interpolation approach to computing some of the more complex rendering effects. Image-based computer graphics promises to be a productive area of research for some time. A number of intriguing research problems suggest themselves:

An automatic camera has been developed to record an array

of images of an object from viewpoints surrounding it [APPL92]. What are the prospects for automatic camera location selection to minimize the number of holes in the interpolated images? Similarly, what are good algorithmic criteria for dispensing with as many recorded images as possible, or selecting the best subset of images to represent the object?

By modeling the 3D transformation from one image to the next by a field of straight-line offsets, we introduce an approximation analogous to polygonization (except in the restricted cases mentioned in Section 2.2). Higher-dimensional, rather than linear, interpolation might be expected to better approximate the arcs traversed by objects rotating between views. Curved motion blur is another possible benefit of higher-order interpolation.

View-dependent shading such as specular reflection would extend the useful range of morphing as a display technique. One possibility mentioned previously is to define additional maps for specular surfaces, which specify normal components or reflection map coordinates.

Special-purpose image compression might profit greatly from morph-mapping algorithms. The resemblance of the morph maps to motion-compensation vectors commonly used in video sequence compression has been mentioned. These vectors, used in format conversion to address the interlace problem, and in compression to squeeze a little more redundancy out of the signal, also find application in optical flow algorithms for tracking objects in the visual field. The redundancy removed from the video sequence by motion compensation is limited, as it applies only between successive frames. In a morph mapping encoder, objects which appear and disappear repeatedly could be encoded with a small set of maps. The decoder, a hybrid of an image warper and a graphics pipeline, would use them as "sprites" from a catalog of maps.

The representation of objects and surfaces as sets of images and maps, possibly pyramidal maps, suggests the application of morph mapping to more general global illumination models. The approach of determining visibility to an area light source to compute soft shadows can be extended to treating all surfaces as sources of radiosity. For many global illumination problems, a few images and morph maps can serve to represent hundreds or thousands of computed images.

6. ACKNOWLEDGMENTS

Thanks to the Virtual Museum team for the museum model and images. Dan Venolia anticipated the use of range images as display primitives (without interpolation) in his virtual holography work. Ken Turkowski contributed the teapot images. Ned Greene, Nelson Max and members of the Advanced Technology Computer Graphics Group have offered useful ideas and criticism. Frank Crow and Apple Computer's continuous support of this research is highly appreciated.

REFERENCES

[AIRE91] Airey, J., J. Rohlf and F. Brooks. Towards Image Realism with Interactive Update Rates in Complex Building Environments. ACM SIGGRAPH Special Issue on 1990 Symposium on Interactive 3D Graphics, 41-50.

[APPL92] Apple Human Interface Group. Object Maker. [exhibit] In Interactive Experience, CHI'92, Monterey CA.

[BESL88] Besl, P.J. Active Optical Range Imaging Sensors. Machine Vision and Applications Vol. 1, 1988, 127-152.

[BEIE92] Beier, T. and S. Neely. Feature-Based Image Metamorphosis. SIGGRAPH'92 Proceedings, 35-42.

[CHEN90] Chen, S. E. Incremental Radiosity: An Extension of Progressive Radiosity to an Interactive Image Synthesis System. SIGGRAPH'90 Proceedings, 135-144.

[COHE88] Cohen, M. F., S. E. Chen, J. R. Wallace and D. P. Greenberg. A Progressive Refinement Approach to Fast Radiosity Image Generation. SIGGRAPH'88 Proceedings, 75-84.

[DEER92] Deering, M. High Resolution Virtual Reality. SIGGRAPH'92 Proceedings, 195-202, 1992.

[GOSH89] Goshtasby, A. Stereo Correspondence by Selective Search. Proc. Japan Computer Vision Conf., 1-10, July, 1989.

[GREE86] Greene, N. Environment Mapping and Other Applications of World Projections. IEEE CG&A, Vol. 6, No. 11, November, 1986.

[GREE93] Greene, N. and M. Kass. Approximating Visibility with Environment Maps. Technical Report 41, 1993, Apple Computer, Inc.

[HOFM88] Hofman, G. R. The Calculus of the Non-Exact Perspective Projection. Eurographics'88 Proceedings, 429-442

[JEVA92] Jevans, D. Object Space Temporal Coherence for Ray Tracing. Graphics Interface'92 Proceedings, 176-183, 1992.

[LIPP80] Lippman, A. Movie Maps: An Application of the Optical Videodisc to Computer Graphics. SIGGRAPH'80 Proceedings, 32-43.

[MILL92] Miller, G., E. Hoffert, S. E. Chen, E. Patterson, D. Blacketter, S. Rubin, S. A. Applin, D. Yim and J. Hanan. The Virtual Museum: Interactive 3D Navigation of a Multimedia Database. The Journal of Visualization and Computer Animation, Vol. 3, No. 3, 183-198, 1992.

[MILL93] Miller, G.and S. E. Chen. Real-Time Display of Surroundings Using Environment Maps. Technical Report 42, 1993, Apple Computer, Inc.

[MPEG90] MPEG Video Committee Draft, December, 1990.

[NAGE86] Nagel, H.-H. Image Sequences - Ten (octal) Years from Phenomenology to a Theoretical Foundation. Proc. 8th ICPR, Paris 1986, 1174-1185.

[POGG91] Poggio, T. and R. Brunelli. A Novel Approach to Graphics. MIT A.I. Memo No. 1354, C.B.I.P. Paper No. 71, February, 1992.

[REEV87] Reeves, W. T., D. H. Salesin and R. L. Cook. Rendering Antialiased Shadows with Depth Maps. SIGGRAPH'87 Proceedings, 283-291.

[SCHU69] Schumacker, R., B. Brand, M. Gilliland, and W. Sharp. Study for Applying Computer-Generated Images to Visual Simulation, Technical Report AFHRL-TR-69-14, NTIS AD700375, U.S. Air Force Human Resources Lab., Air Force Systems Command, Brooks AFB, TX, September, 1969.

[SHAP84] Shapiro, B. L., N. I. Badler. Generating Soft Shadows with a Depth Buffer Algorithm. IEEE CG&A, Vol. 4, No. 10, 5-38, 1984.

[TELL92] Teller, S and C. Sequin. Visibility Preprocessing for Interactive Walkthroughs. SIGGRAPH'91 Proceedings, pp.61-69, 1991.

[VENO90] Venolia, D. and L. Williams. Virtual Integral Holography. Proc. SPIE-Extracting Meaning from Complex Data: Processing, Display, Interaction (Santa Clara, CA, February, 1990), 99-105.

[WILL78] Williams, L. Casting Curved Shadows on Curved Surfaces. SIGGRAPH'78 Proceedings, 270-274.

[WILL90] Williams, L. 3D Paint. ACM SIGGRAPH Special Issue on 1990 Symposium on Interactive 3D Graphics, 225-233.

[WOLB89] Wolberg, G. and T. E. Boult. Separable Image Warping with Spatial Lookup Tables. SIGGRAPH'89 Proceedings, 369-377.

[WOLF83] Wolf, P. R. Elements of Photogrammetry, McGraw-Hill, New York, 1983.

Fig. 1 Offset vectors for the camera motion in Figure 3.

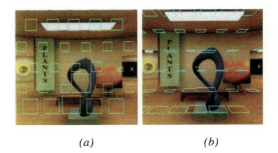

Fig. 2 Extents of pixel movement for 2D viewpoint motions: a) viewpoints parallel to the viewing plane, b) viewpoints parallel to the ground. (Source pixels are in the lower right corner of each extent.)

Fig. 3 A source image viewed from a camera rotated to the right.

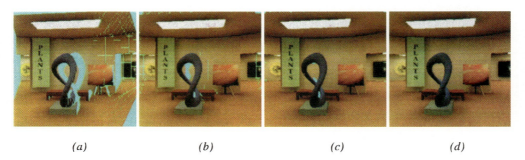

Fig. 5 (a) Holes from one source image, (b) holes from two source images, (c) holes from two closely spaced source images, (d) filling the holes with interpolation.

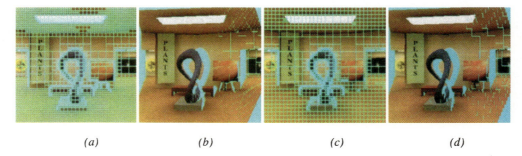

Fig. 6 Quadtree decompositions of a morph map: (a) compression ratio: 15 to 1, speedup factor: 6; (b) interpolated image from (a); (c) compression ratio: 29 to 1, speedup factor: 7; (d) interpolated image from (c).

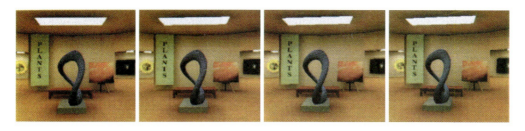

Fig. 8   Rendered Virtual Museum images.

Fig. 9   Interpolated Virtual Museum images (two middle ones).

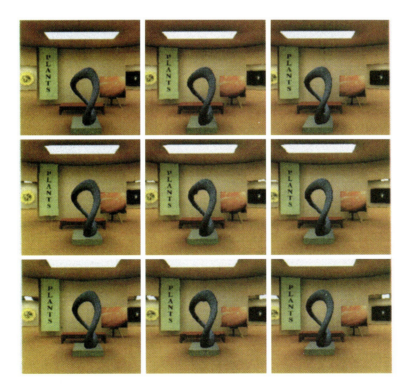

Fig. 10   2D interpolation. The source images are in the corners. All the other images are interpolated from their nearest three source images. (The center one is interpolated from the upper two and the lower left corners.)

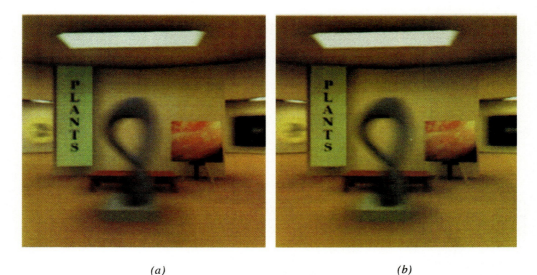

(a)   *(b)*

Fig.11   *(a) Motion blur computed from source images, (b) motion blur computed from interpolated images*[2].

Fig.13   Shadow from a rectangular area light computed with the shadow map interpolation.

Fig.15   Teapot extrapolated to show the quadtree pixel blocks.

Fig.14   Teapot images generated by interpolation (two middle ones).

---

[2]Figure 11 and 13 images were digitally enlarged 200% with bicubic interpolation.

SKETCHPAD
A MAN-MACHINE GRAPHICAL COMMUNICATION SYSTEM*

Ivan E. Sutherland
Consultant, Lincoln Laboratory**
Massachusetts Institute of Technology

I. INTRODUCTION

The Sketchpad system makes it possible for a man and a computer to converse rapidly through the medium of line drawings. Heretofore, most interaction between man and computers has been slowed down by the need to reduce all communication to written statements that can be typed; in the past, we have been writing letters to rather than conferring with our computers. For many types of communication, such as describing the shape of a mechanical part or the connections of an electrical circuit, typed statements can prove cumbersome. The Sketchpad system, by eliminating typed statements (except for legends) in favor of line drawings, opens up a new area of man-machine communication.

AN INTRODUCTORY EXAMPLE

To understand what is possible with the system at present let us consider using it to draw the hexagonal pattern in Figure 4. We will issue specific commands with a set of push buttons, turn functions on and off with switches, indicate position information and point to existing drawing parts with the light pen, rotate and magnify picture parts by turning knobs, and observe the drawing on the display system. This equipment as provided at Lincoln Laboratory's TX-2 computer[1] is shown in Figure 1. When our drawing is complete it may be inked on paper, as were all the drawings in this paper, by a PACE plotter.[15]

If we point the light pen at the display system and press a button called "draw," the computer will construct a straight line segment which stretches like a rubber band from the

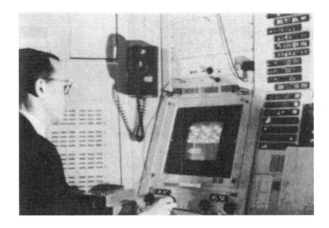

Figure 1. TX-2 operating area—Sketchpad in use. On the display can be seen part of a bridge similar to those of Figure 15. The Author is holding the light pen. The push buttons "draw," "move," etc., are on the box in front of the Author. Part of the bank of toggle switches can be seen behind the Author. The size and position of the part of the total picture seen on the display are controlled by the four black knobs just above the tables.

---

* This paper is based in part on a thesis submitted to the Department of Electrical Engineering, M.I.T., in partial fulfillment of the requirements for the Degree of Doctor of Philosophy.
** Operated with the support of the U.S. Army, Navy, and Air Force.

Reprinted with permission from *Proceedings of the AFIPS Spring Joint Computer Conference* Washington, D.C.: Spartan Books, 1963. 329-346.

initial to the present location of the pen as shown in Figure 2. Additional presses of the button will produce additional lines, leaving the closed irregular hexagon shown in Figure 3A.

To make the hexagon regular, we can inscribe it in a circle. To draw the circle we place the light pen where the center is to be and press the button "circle center," leaving behind a center point. Now, choosing a point on the circle (which fixes the radius) we press the button "draw" again, this time getting a circle arc whose angular length only is controlled by light pen position as shown in Figure 2.

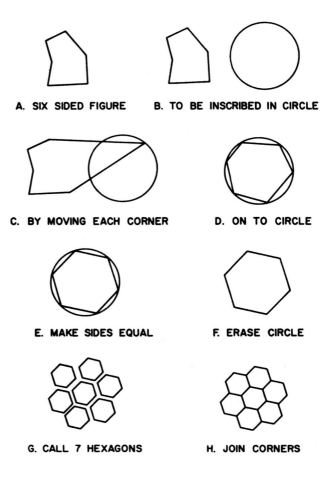

Figure 3. Illustrative example, see text.

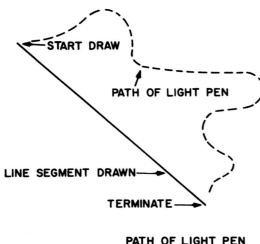

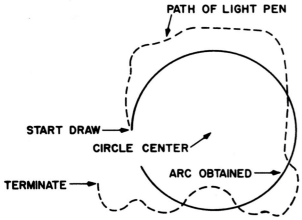

Figure 2. Steps for drawing straight lines and circle arcs.

Next we move the hexagon into the circle by pointing to a corner of the hexagon and pressing the button "move" so that the corner follows the light pen, stretching two rubber band line segments behind it. By pointing to the circle and terminating, we indicate that the corner is to lie on the circle. Each corner is in this way moved onto the circle at roughly equal spacing as shown in Figure 3D.

We have indicated that the vertices of the hexagon are to lie on the circle, and they will remain on the circle throughout our further manipulations. If we also insist that the sides of the hexagon be of equal length, a regular hexagon will be constructed.

With Sketchpad we can say, in effect, make *this* line equal in length to *that* line, pointing to the lines with the light pen. The computer satisfies all existing conditions (if it is possible) whenever we turn on a toggle switch. This done, we have a complete regular hexagon inscribed in a circle. We can erase the entire circle by pointing to any part of it and pressing the "delete" button. The completed hexagon is shown in Figure 3F.

To make the hexagonal pattern in Figure 4 we wish to attach a large number of hexagons together by their corners, and so we designate the six corners of our hexagon as attachment points by pointing to each and pressing a button. We now file away the basic hexagon and begin work on a fresh "sheet of paper" by changing a switch setting. On the new sheet we assemble, by pressing a button to create each hexagon as an "instance" or subpicture, six hexagons around a central seventh in approximate position as shown in Figure 3G. A subpicture may be positioned with the light pen, rotated or scaled by turning the knobs, or fixed in position by a termination signal, but its internal shape is fixed.

By pointing to the corner of one hexagon, pressing a button, and then pointing to the corner of another hexagon, we can fasten those corners together, because these corners have been designated as attachment points. If we attach two corners of each outer hexagon to the appropriate corners of the inner hexagon, the seven are uniquely related, and the computer will reposition them as shown in Figure 3H. An entire group of hexagons, once assembled, can be treated as a symbol. An "instance" of the entire group can be called up on another "sheet of paper" as a subpicture and assembled with other groups or with single hexagons to make a very large pattern.

INTERPRETATION OF INTRODUCTORY EXAMPLE

In the introductory example above we used the light pen both to position parts of the drawing and to point to existing parts. We also saw in action the very general *subpicture, constraint,* and *definition copying* capabilities of the system.

Subpicture:

The original hexagon might just as well have been anything else: a picture of a transistor, a roller bearing, or an airplane wing. Any number of different symbols may be drawn, in terms of other simpler symbols if desired, and any symbol may be used as often as desired.

Constraint:

When we asked that the vertices of the hexagon lie on the circle we were making use of a basic relationship between picture parts that is built into the system. Basic relationships (atomic constraints) to make lines vertical, horizontal, parallel, or perpendicular; to make points lie on lines or circles; to make symbols appear upright, vertically above one another or be of equal size; and to relate symbols to other drawing parts such as points and lines have been included in the system. Specialized constraint types may be added as needed.

Definition Copying:

We made the sides of the hexagon be equal in length by pressing a button while pointing to the side in question. Had we defined a composite operation such as to make two lines both parallel and equal in length, we could have applied it just as easily.

IMPLICATIONS OF INTRODUCTORY EXAMPLE

As we have seen, a Sketchpad drawing is entirely different from the trail of carbon left on a piece of paper. Information about how the drawing is tied together is stored in the computer as well as the information which gives the drawing its particular appearance. Since the drawing is tied together, it will keep a useful appearance even when parts of it are moved. For example, when we moved the corners of the hexagon onto the circle, the lines next to each corner were automatically moved so that the closed topology of the hexagon was preserved. Again, since we indicated that the corners of the hexagon were to lie on the circle, they remained on the circle throughout our further manipulations.

As well as storing how the various parts of the drawing are related, Sketchpad stores the structure of the subpictures used. For example, the storage for the hexagonal pattern of Figure 4 indicates that this pattern is made of smaller patterns which are in turn made of smaller patterns which are composed of single hexagons. If the master hexagon is changed, the entire appearance but not the structure of the hexagonal pattern will be changed. For example, if we change the basic hexagon into a semicircle, the fish scale pattern shown in Figure 4 instantly results.

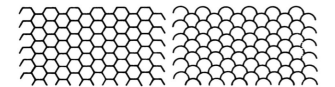

Figure 4. Hexagonal lattice with half hexagon and semicircle as basic elements.

SKETCHPAD AND THE DESIGN PROCESS

Construction of a drawing with Sketchpad is *itself* a model of the design process. The locations of the points and lines of the drawing model the variables of a design, and the geometric constraints applied to the points and lines of the drawing model the design constraints which limit the values of design variables. The ability of Sketchpad to satisfy the geometric constraints applied to the parts of a drawing models the ability of a good designer to satisfy all the design conditions imposed by the limitations of his materials, cost, etc. In fact, since designers in many fields produce nothing themselves but a drawing of a part, design conditions may well be thought of as applying to the drawing of a part rather than to the part itself. When such design conditions are added to Sketchpad's vocabulary of constraints, the computer will be able to assist a user not only in arriving at a nice looking drawing, but also in arriving at a sound design.

PRESENT USEFULNESS

As more and more applications have been made, it has become clear that the properties of Sketchpad drawings make them most useful in four broad areas:

For Storing and Updating Drawings:

Each time a drawing is made, a description of that drawing is stored in the computer in a form that is readily transferred to magnetic tape. A library of drawings will thus develop, parts of which may be used in other drawings at only a fraction of the investment of time that was put into the original drawing.

For Gaining Scientific or Engineering Understanding of Operations That Can Be Described Graphically:

A drawing in the Sketchpad system may contain explicit statements about the relations between its parts so that as one part is changed the implications of this change become evident throughout the drawing. For instance, Sketchpad makes it easy to study mechanical linkages, observing the path of some parts when others are moved.

As a Topological Input Device for Circuit Simulators, etc.:

Since the storage structure of Sketchpad reflects the topology of any circuit or diagram, it can serve as an input for many network or circuit simulating programs. The additional effort required to draw a circuit completely from scratch with the Sketchpad system may well be recompensed if the properties of the circuit are obtainable through simulation of the circuit drawn.

For Highly Repetitive Drawings:

The ability of the computer to reproduce any drawn symbol anywhere at the press of a button, and to recursively include subpictures within subpictures makes it easy to produce drawings which are composed of huge numbers of parts all similar in shape.

II. RING STRUCTURE

The basic n-component element structure described by Ross[10] has been somewhat expanded in the implementation of Sketchpad so that all references made to a particular n-component element or block are collected together by a string of pointers which originates within that block. For example, not only may the end points of a line segment be found by following pointers in the line block (n-component element), but also all the line segments which terminate on a particular point may be found by following a string of pointers which starts within the point block. This string of pointers closes on itself; the last pointer points back to the first, hence the name "ring." The ring points both ways to make it easy to find both the next and the previous member of the ring in case, as when deleting, some change must be made to them.

BASIC OPERATIONS

The basic ring structure operations are:
1. Inserting a new member into a ring at

some specified location on it, usually first or last.
2. Removing a member from a ring.
3. Putting all the members of one ring, in order, into another at some specified location in it, usually first or last.
4. Performing some auxiliary operation on each member of a ring in either forward or reverse order.

These basic ring structure operations are implemented by short sections of program defined as MACRO instructions in the compiler language. By suitable treatment of zero and one member rings, the basic programs operate without making special cases.

Subroutines are used for setting up new n-component elements in free spaces in the storage structure. As parts of the drawing are deleted, the registers which were used to represent them become free. New components are set up at the end of the storage area, lengthening it, while free blocks are allowed to accumulate. Garbage collection periodically compacts the storage structure by removal of the free blocks.

GENERIC STRUCTURE, HIERARCHIES

The main part of Sketchpad can perform basic operations on any drawing part, calling for help from routines specific to particular types of parts when that is necessary. For example, the main program can show any part on the display system by calling the appropriate display subroutine. The big power of the clearcut separation of the general and the specific is that it is easy to change the details of specific parts of the program to get quite different results without any need to change the general parts.

In the data storage structure the separation of general and specific is accomplished by collecting all things of one type together in a ring under a generic heading. The generic heading contains all the information which makes this type of thing different from all other types of things. Thus the data storage structure itself contains all the specific information. The generic blocks are further gathered together under super-generic or generic-generic blocks, as shown in Figure 5.

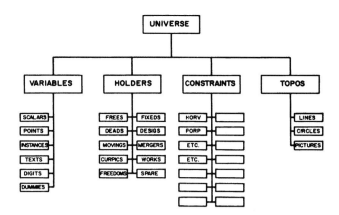

Figure 5. Generic structure. The n-component elements for each point or line, etc., are collected under the generic blocks "lines," "points," etc., shown.

EXPANDING SKETCHPAD

Addition of new types of things to the Sketchpad system's vocabulary of picture parts requires only the construction of a new generic block (about 20 registers) and the writing of appropriate subroutines for the new type. The subroutines might be easy to write, as they usually are for new constraints, or difficult to write, as for adding ellipse capability, but at least a finite, well-defined task faces one to add a new ability to the system. Without a generic structure it would be almost impossible to add the instructions required to handle a new type of element.

III. LIGHT PEN

In Sketchpad the light pen* is time shared between the functions of coordinate input for positioning picture parts on the drawing and demonstrative input for pointing to existing picture parts to make changes. Although almost any kind of coordinate input device could be used instead of the light pen for positioning, the demonstrative input uses the light pen optics as a sort of analog computer to remove from consideration all but a very few picture parts which happen to fall within its field of view, saving considerable program time. Drawing systems using storage display devices of the Memotron type may not be practical because of the loss of this analog computation feature.

___
* The reader unacquainted with light pens should refer to the paper on Man-Machine Console Facilities by Stotz[12] in this issue.

PEN TRACKING

To initially establish pen tracking,* the Sketchpad user must inform the computer of an initial pen location. This has come to be known as "inking-up" and is done by "touching" any existing line or spot on the display, whereupon the tracking cross appears. If no picture has yet been drawn, the letters INK are always displayed for this purpose. Sketchpad uses loss of tracking as a "termination signal" to stop drawing. The user signals that he is finished drawing by flicking the pen too fast for the tracking program to follow.

DEMONSTRATIVE USE OF PEN

During the 90% of the time that the light pen and display system are free from the tracking chore, spots are very rapidly displayed to exhibit the drawing being built, and thus the lines and circles of the drawing appear. The light pen is sensitive to these spots and reports any which fall within its field of view. Thus, a table of the picture parts seen by the light pen is assembled during each complete display cycle. At the end of a display cycle this table contains all the picture parts that could even remotely be considered as being "aimed at."

The one-half inch diameter field of view of the light pen, although well suited to tracking, is relatively large for pointing. Therefore, the Sketchpad system will reject any seen part which is further from the center of the light pen than some small minimum distance; about $\frac{1}{8}$ inch was found to be suitable. For every kind of picture part some method must be provided for computing its distance from the light pen center or indicating that this computation cannot be made.

After eliminating all parts seen by the pen which lie outside the smaller effective field of view, the Sketchpad system considers objects topologically related to the ones actually seen. End points of lines and attachment points of instances (subpictures) are especially important. One can thus aim at the end point of a line even though only the line is displayed. Figure 6 outlines the various regions within which the pen must lie to be considered aimed at a line segment, a circle arc, their end points, or their intersection.

PSEUDO PEN LOCATION

When the light pen is aimed at a picture part, the exact location of the light pen is ignored in favor of a "pseudo pen location" exactly on the part aimed at. If no object is aimed at, the pseudo pen location is taken to be the actual pen location. The pseudo pen location is displayed as a bright dot which is used as the "point of the pencil" in all drawing operations. As the light pen is moved into the areas outlined in Figure 6 the dot will lock onto the existing parts of the drawing, and any moving picture parts will jump to their new locations as the pseudo pen location moves to lie on the appropriate picture part.

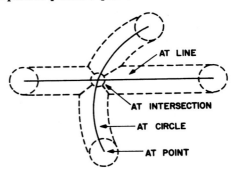

Figure 6. Areas in which pen must lie to "aim at" existing drawing parts (solid lines).

With just the basic drawing creation and manipulation functions of "draw," "move," and "delete," and the power of the pseudo pen location and demonstrative language programs, it is possible to make fairly extensive drawings. Most of the constructions normally provided by straight edge and compass are available in highly accurate form. Most important, however, the pseudo pen location and demonstrative language give the means for entering the topological properties of a drawing into the machine.

IV. DISPLAY GENERATION

The display system, or "scope," on the TX-2 is a ten bit per axis electrostatic deflection system able to display spots at a maximum rate of about 100,000 per second. The coordinates of the spots which are to be seen on the display are stored in a large table so that computation and display may proceed independently. If, instead of displaying each spot successively, the display program displays them in a random order or with interlace, the flicker of the display is reduced greatly.

MARKING OF DISPLAY FILE

Of the 36 bits available to store each display spot in the display file, 20 give the coordinates of that spot for the display system, and the remaining 16 give the address of the n-component element which is responsible for adding that spot to the display. Thus, all the spots in a line are tagged with the ring structure address of that line, and all the spots in an instance (subpicture) are tagged as belonging to that instance. The tags are used to identify the particular part of the drawing being aimed at by the light pen.

If a part of the drawing is being moved by the light pen, its display spots will be recomputed as quickly as possible to show it in successive positions. The display spots for such moving parts are stored at the end of the display file so that the display of the many non-moving parts need not be disturbed. Moving parts are made invisible to the light pen.

MAGNIFICATION OF PICTURES

The shaft position encoder knobs below the scope (see Figure 1) are used to tell the program to change the display scale factor or the portion of the page displayed. The range of magnification of 2000 available makes it possible to work, in effect, on a 7-inch square portion of a drawing about ¼ mile on a side.

For a magnified picture, Sketchpad computes which portion(s) of a curve will appear on the display and generates display spots for those portions only. The "edge detection" problem is the problem of finding suitable end points for the portion of a curve which appears on the display.

In concept the edge detection problem is trivial. In terms of program time for lines and circles the problem is a small fraction of the total computational load of the system, but in terms of program logical complexity the edge detection problem is a difficult one. For example, the computation of the intersection of a circle with any of the edges of the scope is easy, but computation of the intersection of a circle with all four edges may result in as many as eight intersections, some pairs of which may be identical, the scope corners. Now which of these intersections are actually to be used as starts of circle arcs?

LINE AND CIRCLE GENERATION

All of Sketchpad's displays are generated from straight line segments, circle arcs, and single points. The generation of the lines and circles is accomplished by means of the difference equations:

$$x_i = x_{i-1} + \Delta x \qquad y_i = y_{i-1} + \Delta y \qquad (1)$$

for lines, and

$$x_i = x_{i-2} + \frac{2}{R}(y_{i-1} - y_c)$$
$$y_i = y_{i-2} - \frac{2}{R}(x_{i-1} - x_c) \qquad (2)$$

for circles, where subscripts i indicate successive display spots, subscript c indicates the circle center, and R is the radius of the circle in Scope Units. In implementing these difference equations in the program, the fullest possible use is made of the coordinate arithmetic capability of the TX-2 so that both the x and y equation computations are performed in parallel on 18 bit subwords. Even so, about ¾ of the total Sketchpad computation time is spent in line and circle generation. A vector and circle generating display would materially reduce the computational load of Sketchpad.

For computers which do only one addition at a time, the difference equations:

$$x_i = x_{i-1} + \frac{1}{R}(y_{i-1} - y_c)$$
$$y_i = y_{i-1} - \frac{1}{R}(x_i - x_c) \qquad (3)$$

should be used to generate circles. Equations (3) approximate a circle well enough and are known to close exactly both in theory and when implemented, because the x and y equations are dissimilar.

DIGITS AND TEXT

Text, to put legends on a drawing, is displayed by means of special tables which indicate the locations of line and circle segments to make up the letters and numbers. Each piece of text appears as a single line of not more than 36 equally spaced characters which can be changed by typing. Digits to display the value of an indicated scalar at any position and in any size and rotation are formed from the same type face as text. It is possible to display up to five decimal digits with sign; binary to decimal conversion is provided, and leading zeros are suppressed.

Subpictures, whose use was seen in the introductory example above, are each represented in storage as a single n-component element. A subpicture is said to be an "instance" of its "master picture." To display an instance, all of the lines, text, etc. of its master picture must be shown in miniature on the display. The instance display program makes use of the line, circle, number, and text display programs and *itself* to expand the internal structure of the instance.

DISPLAY OF ABSTRACTIONS

The usual picture for human consumption displays only lines, circles, text, digits, and instances. However, certain very useful abstractions which give the drawing the properties desired by the user are represented in the ring structure storage. For example, the fact that the start and end points of a circle arc should be equidistant from the circle's center point is represented in storage by a "constraint" block. To make it possible for a user to manipulate these abstractions, each abstraction must be able to be seen on the display if desired. Not only does displaying abstractions make it possible for the human user to know that they exist, but also makes it possible for him to aim at them with the light pen and, for example, erase them. To avoid confusion, the display for particular types of objects may be turned on or off selectively by toggle switches. Thus, for example, one can turn on display of constraints as well as or instead of the lines and circles which are normally seen.

If their selection toggle switch is on, constraints are displayed as shown in Figure 7. The central circle and code letter are located at the average location of the variables constrained. The four arms of a constraint extend from the top, right side, bottom, and left side of the circle to the first, second, third, and fourth variables constrained, respectively. If fewer than four variables are constrained, ex-

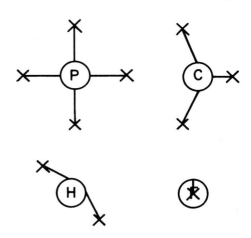

Figure 7. Display of constraints.

cess arms are omitted. In Figure 7 the constraints are shown applied to "dummy variables," each of which shows as an X.

Another abstraction that can be displayed if desired is the value of a set of digits. For example, in Figure 8 are shown three sets of digits all displaying the same scalar value, -5978. The digits themselves may be moved, rotated, or changed in size, without changing the value displayed. If we wish to change the value, we point at its abstract display, the # seen in Figure 8. The three sets of digits in Figure 8 all display the same value, as indicated by the lines connecting them to the #; changing this value would make all three sets of digits change. Constraints may be applied independently to either the position of the digits or their value as indicated by the two constraints in the figure.

V. RECURSIVE FUNCTIONS

In the process of making the Sketchpad system operate, a few very general functions were developed which make no reference at all to the specific types of entities on which they oper-

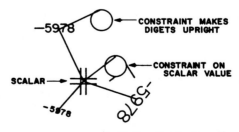

Figure 8. Three sets of digits displaying the same scalar value.

ate. These general functions give the Sketchpad system the ability to operate on a wide range of problems. The motivation for making the functions as general as possible came from the desire to get as much result as possible from the programming effort involved. For example, the general function for expanding instances makes it possible for Sketchpad to handle any fixed geometry subpicture. The power obtained from the small set of generalized functions in Sketchpad is one of the most important results of the research.

In order of historical development, the recursive functions in use in the Sketchpad system are:

1. Expansion of instances, making it possible to have subpictures within subpictures to as many levels as desired.
2. Recursive deletion, whereby removal of certain picture parts will remove other picture parts in order to maintain consistency in the ring structure.
3. Recursive merging, whereby combination of two similar picture parts forces combination of similarly related other picture parts, making possible application of complex definitions to an object picture.

RECURSIVE DELETING

If a thing upon which other things depend is deleted, the dependent things must be deleted also. For example, if a point is to be deleted, all lines which terminate on the point must also be deleted. Otherwise, since the *n*-component elements for lines contain no positional information, where would these lines end? Similarly, deletion of a variable requires deletion of all constraints on that variable; a constraint must have variables to act on.

RECURSIVE MERGING

If two things of the same type which are independent are merged, a single thing of that type results, and all things which depended on either of the merged things depend on the result* of the merger. For example, if two points are merged, all lines which previously terminated on either point now terminate on the single resulting point. In Sketchpad, if a thing is being moved with the light pen and the termination flick of the pen is given while aiming at another thing of the same type, the two things will merge. Thus, if one moves a point to another point and terminates, the points will merge, connecting all lines which formerly terminated on either. This makes it possible to draw closed polygons.

If two things of the same type which do depend on other things are merged, the things depended on by one will be forced to merge, respectively, with the things depended on by the other. The result* of merging two dependent things depends, respectively, on the results* of the mergers it forces. For example, if two lines are merged, the resultant line must refer to only two end points, the results of merging the pairs of end points of the original lines. All lines which terminated on any of the four original end points now terminate on the appropriate one of the remaining pair. More important and useful, all constraints which applied to any of the four original end points now apply to the appropriate one of the remaining pair. This makes it possible to speak of line segments as being parallel even though (because line segments contain no numerical information to be constrained) the parallelism constraint must apply to their end points and not to the line segments themselves. If we wish to make two lines both parallel and equal in length, the steps outlined in Figure 9 make it possible. More obscure relationships between dependent things may be easily defined and applied. For example, constraint complexes can be defined to make line segments be collinear, to make a line be tangent to a circle, or to make the values represented by two sets of digits be equal.

RECURSIVE DISPLAY OF INSTANCES

The block of registers which represents an instance is remarkably small considering that it may generate a display of any complexity. For the purposes of display, the instance block makes reference to its master picture. The instance will appear on the display as a figure geometrically similar to its master picture at a location, size, and rotation indicated by the four numbers which constitute the "value" of the instance. The value of an instance is considered numerically as a four dimensional vector. The

---

* The "result" of a merger is a single thing of the same type as the merged things.

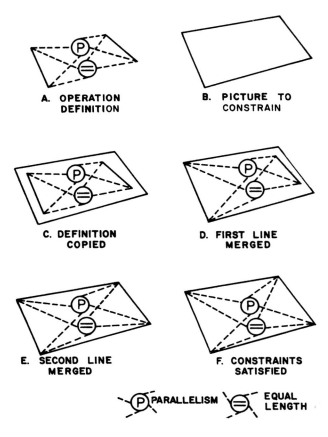

Figure 9. Applying a two-constraint definition to turn a quadrilateral into a parallelogram.

components of this vector are the coordinates of the center of the instance and its actual size as it appears on the drawing times the sine and cosine of the rotation angle involved.

In displaying an instance of a picture, reference is made to the master picture to find out what picture parts are to be shown. The master picture referred to may contain instances, however, requiring further reference, and so on until a picture is found which contains no instances. At each stage in the recursion, any picture parts displayed must be relocated so that they will appear at the correct position, size and rotation on the display. Thus, at each stage of the recursion, some transformation is applied to all picture parts before displaying them. If an instance is encountered, the transformation represented by its value must be adjoined to the existing transformation for display of parts within it. When the expansion of an instance within an instance is finished, the transformation must be restored for continuation at the higher level.

ATTACHERS AND INSTANCES

Many symbols must be integrated into the rest of the drawing by attaching lines to the symbols at appropriate points, or by attaching the symbols directly to each other. For example, circuit symbols must be wired up, geometric patterns made by fitting shapes together, or mechanisms composed of links tied together appropriately. An instance may have any number of attachment points, and a point may serve as attacher for any number of instances. The light pen has the same affinity for the attachers of an instance that it has for the end point of a line.

An "instance-point" constraint, shown with code T in Figure 10C, is used to relate an instance to each of its attachment points. An instance-point constraint is satisfied only when the point bears the same relationship to the instance that a master point in the master picture for that instance bears to the master picture coordinate system.

Any point may be an attacher of an instance, but the point must be designated as an attacher in the master drawing of the instance. For example, when one first draws a resistor, the ends of the resistor must be designated as attachers if wiring is to be attached to instances of it. At each level of building complex pictures, the attachers must be designated anew. Thus of the three attachers of a transistor it is possible to select one or two to be the attachers of a flip-flop.

VI. BUILDING A DRAWING, THE COPY FUNCTION

At the start of the Sketchpad effort certain ad hoc drawing functions were programmed as the atomic operations of the system. Each such operation, controlled by a push button, creates in the ring structure a specific set of new drawing parts. For example, the "draw" button creates a line segment and two new end points (unless the light pen happens to be aimed at a point in which case only one new point need be created). Similarly, there are atomic operations for drawing circles, applying a horizontal or vertical constraint to the end points of a line aimed at, and for adding a "point-on-line" constraint whenever a point is moved onto a line and left there.

The atomic operations described above make it possible to create in the ring structure new picture components and relate them topologically. The atomic operations are, of course, limited to creating points, lines, circles, and two or three types of constraints. Since implementation of the copy function it has become possible to create in the ring structure any predefined combination of picture parts and constraints at the press of a button. The recursive merging function makes it possible to relate the copied set of picture parts to any existing parts. For example, if a line segment and its two end points are copied into the object picture, the action of the "draw" button may be exactly duplicated in every respect. Along with the copied line, however, one might copy as well a constraint, Code H, to make the line horizontal as shown in Figure 10A, or two constraints to make the line both horizontal and three inches long, or any other variation one cares to put into the ring structure to be copied.

When one draws a definition picture to be copied, certain portions of it to be used in relating it to other object picture parts are designated as "attachers." Anything at all may be designated: for example, points, lines, circles, text, even constraints! The rules used for combining points when the "draw" button is pressed are generalized so that:

For copying a picture, the last-designated attacher is left moving with the light pen. The next-to-last-designated attacher is recursively merged with whatever object the pen is aimed at when the copying occurs, if that object is of like type. Previously designated attachers are recursively merged with previously designated object picture parts, if of like type, until either the supply of designated attachers or the supply of designated object picture parts is exhausted. The last-designated attacher may be recursively merged with any other object of like type when the termination flick is given.

Normally only two designated attachers are used because it is hard to keep track of additional ones.

If the definition picture consists of two line segments, their four end points, and a constraint, Code M, on the points which makes the lines equal in length, with the two lines designated as attachers as shown in Figure 10B, copying enables the user to make any two lines equal in length. If the pen is aimed at a line when "copy" is pushed, the first of the two copied lines merges with it (taking its position and never actually being seen). The other copied line is left moving with the light pen and will merge with whatever other line the pen is aimed at when termination occurs. Since merging is recursive, the copied equal-length constraint, Code M, will apply to the end points of the desired pair of object picture lines.

COPYING INSTANCES

As we have seen above, the internal structure of an instance is entirely fixed. The internal structure of a copy, however, is entirely variable. An instance always retains its identity as a single part of the drawing; one can only delete an entire instance. Once a definition picture is copied, however, the copy loses all identity as a unit; individual parts of it may be deleted at will.

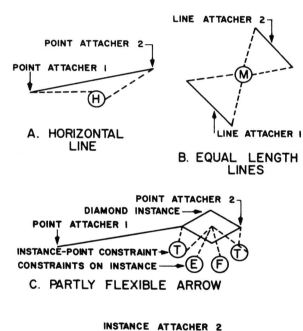

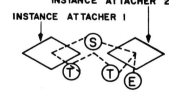

Figure 10. Definition pictures to be copied, see text.

One might expect that there was intermediate ground between the fixed-internal-structure instance and the loose-internal-structure copy. One might wish to produce a collection of picture parts, some of which were fixed internally and some of which were not. *The entire range of variation between the instance and the copy can be constructed by copying instances.*

For example, the arrow shown in Figure 10C can be copied into an object picture to result in a fixed-internal-structure diamond arrowhead with a flexible tail. As the definition in Figure 10C is set up, drawing diamond-arrowheaded lines is just like drawing ordinary lines. One aims the light pen where the tail is to end, presses "copy," and moves off with an arrowhead following the pen. The diamond arrowhead in this case will not rotate (constraint Code E), and will not change size (constraint Code F).

Copying pre-joined instances can produce vast numbers of joined instances very easily. For example, the definition in Figure 10D, when repetitively copied, will result in a row of joined, equal size (constraint Code S) diamonds. In this case the instances themselves are attachers. Although each press of the "copy" button copies two new instances into the object picture, one of these is merged with the last instance in the growing row. In the final row, therefore, each instance carries all constraints which are applied to either of the instances in the definition. This is why only one of the instances in Figure 10D carries the erect constraint, Code E.

VII. CONSTRAINT SATISFACTION

The major feature which distinguishes a Sketchpad drawing from a paper and pencil drawing is the user's ability to specify to Sketchpad mathematical conditions on already drawn parts of his drawing which will be automatically satisfied by the computer to make the drawing take the exact shape desired. The process of fixing up a drawing to meet new conditions applied to it after it is already partially complete is very much like the process a designer goes through in turning a basic idea into a finished design. As new requirements on the various parts of the design are thought of, small changes are made to the size or other properties of parts to meet the new conditions. By making Sketchpad able to find new values for variables which satisfy the conditions imposed, it is hoped that designers can be relieved of the need of much mathematical detail. The effort expended in making the definition of constraint types as general as possible was aimed at making design constraints as well as geometric constraints equally easy to add to the system.

DEFINITION OF A CONSTRAINT TYPE

Each constraint type is entered into the system as a generic block indicating the various properties of that particular constraint type. The generic block tells how many variables are constrained, which of these variables may be changed in order to satisfy the constraint, how many degrees of freedom are removed from the constrained variables, and a code letter for human reference to this constraint type.

The definition of what a constraint type does is a subroutine which will compute, for the existing values of the variables of a particular constraint of that type, the error introduced into the system by that particular constraint. For example, the defining subroutine for making points have the same x coordinate (to make a line between them vertical) computes the difference in their x coordinates. What could be simpler? The computed error is a scalar which the constraint satisfaction routine will attempt to reduce to zero by manipulation of the constrained variables. The computation of the error may be non-linear or time dependent, or it may involve parameters not a part of the drawing such as the setting of toggle switches, etc.

When the one pass method of satisfying constraints to be described later on fails, the Sketchpad system falls back on the reliable but slow method of relaxation[11] to reduce the errors indicated by various computation subroutines to smaller and smaller values. For simple constructions such as the hexagon illustrated in Figure 3, the relaxation procedure is sufficiently fast to be useful. However, for complex systems of variables, especially directly connected instances, relaxation is unacceptably slow. Fortunately it is for just such directly connected instances that the one pass method shows the most striking success.

ONE PASS METHOD

Sketchpad can often find an order in which the variables of a drawing may be re-evaluated to completely satisfy all the conditions on them in just one pass. For the cases in which the one pass method works, it is far better than relaxation: it gives correct answers at once; relaxation may not give a correct solution in any finite time. Sketchpad can find an order in which to re-evaluate the variables of a drawing for most of the common geometric constructions. Ordering is also found easily for the mechanical linkages shown in Figures 13 and 14. Ordering cannot be found for the bridge truss problem in Figure 15.

The way in which the one pass method works is simple in principle and was easy to implement as soon as the nuances of the ring structure manipulations were understood. To visualize the one pass method, consider the variables of the drawing as places and the constraints relating variables as passages through which one might pass from one variable to another. Variables are adjacent to each other in the maze formed by the constraints if there is a single constraint which constrains them both. Variables are totally unrelated if there is no path through the constraints by which to pass from one to the other.

Suppose that some variable can be found which has so few constraints applying to it that it can be re-evaluated to completely satisfy all of them. Such a variable we shall call a "free" variable. As soon as a variable is recognized as free, the constraints which apply to it are removed from further consideration, because the free variable can be used to satisfy them. Removing these constraints, however, may make adjacent variables free. Recognition of these new variables as free removes further constraints from consideration and may make other adjacent variables free, and so on throughout the maze of constraints. The manner in which freedom spreads is much like the method used in Moore's algorithm[8] to find the shortest path through a maze. Having found that a collection of variables is free, Sketchpad will re-evaluate them in reverse order, saving the first-found free variable until last. In re-evaluating any particular variable, Sketchpad uses only those constraints which were present when that variable was found to be free.

VIII. EXAMPLES AND CONCLUSIONS

The examples in this section were all taken from the library tape and thus serve to illustrate not only how the Sketchpad system can be used, but also how it actually has been used so far. We conclude from these examples that Sketchpad drawings can bring invaluable understanding to a user. For drawings where motion of the drawing, or analysis of a drawn problem is of value to the user, Sketchpad excels. For highly repetitive drawings or drawings where accuracy is required, Sketchpad is sufficiently faster than conventional techniques to be worthwhile. For drawings which merely communicate with shops, it is probably better to use conventional paper and pencil.

PATTERNS

The instance facility enables one to draw any symbol and duplicate its appearance anywhere on an object drawing at the push of a button. This facility made the hexagonal pattern we saw in Figure 4 easy to draw. It took about one half hour to generate 900 hexagons, including the time taken to figure out how to do it. Plotting them takes about 25 minutes. The drafting department estimated it would take two days to produce a similar pattern.

The instance facility also made it easy to produce long lengths of the zig-zag pattern shown in Figure 11. As the figure shows, a single "zig" was duplicated in multiples of five and three, etc. Five hundred zigs were generated in a single row. Four such rows were plotted one-half inch apart to be used for producing a printed circuit delay line. Total time taken was about 45 minutes for constructing the figure and about 15 minutes to plot it.

A somewhat less repetitive pattern to be used for encoding the time in a digital clock is shown in Figure 12. Each cross in the figure marks the position of a hole. The holes are placed so that a binary coded decimal (BCD) number will in-

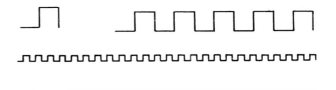

Figure 11. Zig-Zag for delay line.

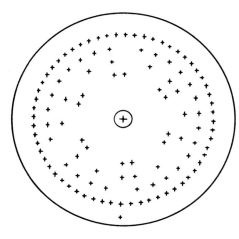

Figure 12. Binary coded decimal encoder for clock. Encoder was plotted exactly 12 inches in diameter for direct use as a layout.

dicate the time. Total time for placing crosses was 20 minutes, most of which was spent trying to interpret a pencil sketch of their positions.

LINKAGES

By far the most interesting application of Sketchpad so far has been drawing and moving linkages. The ability to draw and then move linkages opens up a new field of graphical manipulation that has never before been available. It is remarkable how even a simple linkage can generate complex motions. For example, the linkage of Figure 13 has only three moving parts. In this linkage a central ⊥ link is suspended between two links of different

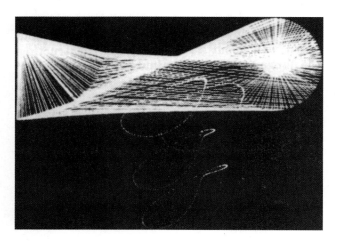

Figure 13. Three bar linkage. The paths of four points on the central link are traced. This is a 15 second time exposure of a moving Sketchpad drawing.

lengths. As the shorter link rotates, the longer one oscillates as can be seen in the multiple exposure. The ⊥ link is not shown in Figure 13 so that the motion of four points on the upright part of the ⊥ may be seen. These are the four curves at the top of the figure.

To make the three bar linkage, an instance shaped like the ⊥ was drawn and given 6 attachers, two at its joints with the other links and four at the places whose paths were to be observed. Connecting the ⊥ shaped subpicture onto a linkage composed of three lines with fixed length created the picture shown. The driving link was rotated by turning a knob below the scope. Total time to construct the linkage was less than 5 minutes, but over an hour was spent playing with it.

A linkage that would be difficult to build physically is shown in Figure 14 A. This link-

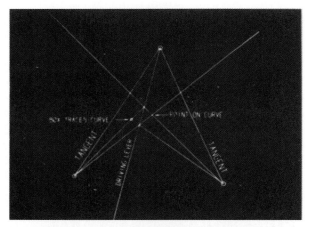

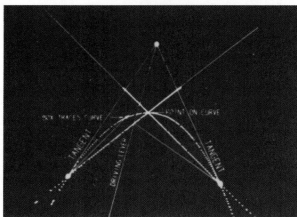

Figure 14. Conic drawing linkage. As the "driving lever" is moved, the point shown with a box around it (in A) traces a conic section. This conic can be seen in the time exposure (B).

age is based on the complete quadrilateral. The three circled points and the two lines which extend out of the top of the picture to the right and left are fixed. Two moving lines are drawn from the lower circled points to the intersections of the long fixed lines with the driving lever. The intersection of these two moving lines (one must be extended) has a box around it. It can be shown theoretically that this linkage produces a conic section which passes through the place labeled "point on curve" and is tangent to the two lines marked "tangent." Figure 14 B shows a time exposure of the moving point in many positions. At first, this linkage was drawn and working in 15 minutes. Since then we have rebuilt it time and again until now we can produce it from scratch in about 3 minutes.

DIMENSION LINES

To make it possible to have an absolute scale in drawings, a constraint is provided which forces the value displayed by a set of digits to indicate the distance between two points on the drawing. This distance-indicating constraint is used to make the number in a dimension line correspond to its length. Putting in a dimension line is as easy as drawing any other line. One points to where one end is to be left, copies the definition of the dimension line by pressing the "copy" button, and then moves the light pen to where the other end of the dimension line is to be. The first dimension line took about 15 minutes to construct, but that need never be repeated since it is a part of the library.

BRIDGES

One of the largest untapped fields for application of Sketchpad is as an input program for other computation programs. The ability to place lines and circles graphically, when coupled with the ability to get accurately computed results pictorially displayed, should bring about a revolution in computer application. By using Sketchpad's relaxation procedure we were to demonstrate analysis of the force distribution in the members of a pin connected truss.

A bridge is first drawn with enough constraints to make it geometrically accurate. These constraints are then deleted and each member is made to behave like a bridge beam.

A bridge beam is constrained to maintain constant length, but any change in length is indicated by an associated number. Under the assumption that each bridge beam has a cross-sectional area proportional to its length, the numbers represent the forces in the beams. The basic bridge beam definition (consisting of two constraints and a number) may be copied and applied to any desired line in a bridge picture by pointing to the line and pressing the "copy" button.

Having drawn a basic bridge shape, one can experiment with various loading conditions and supports to see what the effect of making minor modifications is. For example, an arch bridge is shown in Figure 15 supported both as a three-hinged arch (two supports) and as a cantilever (four supports). For nearly identical loading conditions the distribution of forces is markedly different in these two cases.

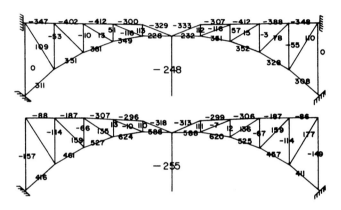

Figure 15. Cantilever and arch bridges. The numbers indicate the forces in the various members as computed by Sketchpad. Central load is not exactly vertical

ARTISTIC DRAWINGS

Sketchpad need not be applied exclusively to engineering drawings. For example, the girl "Nefertite" shown in Figure 16 can be made to wink by changing which of the three types of eyes is placed in position on her otherwise eyeless face. In the same way that linkages can be made to move, a stick figure could be made to pedal a bicycle or Nefertite's hair could be made to swing. The ability to make moving drawings suggests that Sketchpad might be used for making animated cartoons.

Figure 16. Winking girl, "Nefertite," and her component parts.

ELECTRICAL CIRCUIT DIAGRAMS

Unfortunately, electrical circuits require a great many symbols which have not yet been drawn properly with Sketchpad and therefore are not in the library. After some time is spent working on the basic electrical symbols it may be easier to draw circuits. So far, however, circuit drawing has proven difficult.

The circuits of Figure 17 are parts of an analog switching scheme. You can see in the figure that the more complicated circuits are made up of simpler symbols and circuits. It is very difficult, however, to plan far enough ahead to know what composites of circuit symbols will be useful as subpictures of the final circuit. The simple circuits shown in Figure 17 were compounded into a big circuit involving about 40 transistors. Including much trial and error, the time taken by a new user (for the big circuit not shown) was ten hours. At the end of that time the circuit was still not complete in every detail and he decided it would be better to draw it by hand after all.

CONCLUSIONS

The circuit experience points out the most important fact about Sketchpad drawings. It is only worthwhile to make drawings on the computer if you get something more out of the drawing than just a drawing. In the repetitive

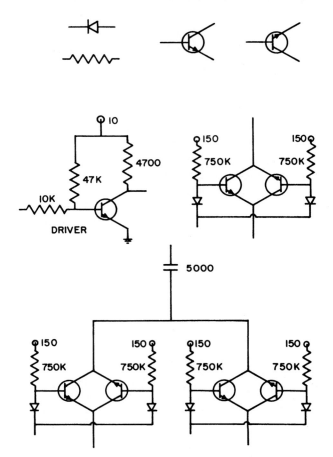

Figure 17. Circuit diagrams. These are parts of the large circuit mentioned in the text.

patterns we saw in the first examples, precision and ease of constructing great numbers of parts were valuable. In the linkage examples, we were able to gain an understanding of the behavior of a linkage as well as its appearance. In the bridge examples we got design answers which were worth far more than the computer time put into them. If we had had a circuit simulation program connected to Sketchpad so that we would have known whether the circuit we drew worked, it would have been worth our while to use the computer to draw it. We are as yet a long way from being able to produce routine drawings economically with the computer.

FUTURE WORK

The methods outlined in this paper generalize nicely to three dimensional drawing. In fact, the work reported in "Sketchpad III" by Timothy Johnson[3] will let the user communicate solid objects to the computer. Johnson is completely bypassing the problem of converting several two dimensional drawings into a three dimensional shape. Drawing will be directly in three dimensions from the start. No two dimensional representation will ever be stored.

Work is also proceeding in direct conversion of photographs into line drawings. Roberts reports a computer program[9] able to recognize simple objects in photographs well enough to produce three dimensional line drawings for them. Roberts is storing his drawings in the ring structure described here so that his results will be compatible with the three dimensional version of Sketchpad.

Major improvements to Sketchpad of the same order and power as the existing definition copying capability can be foreseen. At present Sketchpad is able to add defined relationships to an existing object drawing. A method should be devised for defining and applying changes which involve removing some parts of the object drawing as well as adding new ones. Such a capability would permit one to define, for example, what rounding off a corner means. Then, one could round off any corner by pointing to it and applying the definition.

ACKNOWLEDGEMENTS

The author is indebted to Professors Claude E. Shannon, Marvin Minsky and Steven A. Coons of the Massachusetts Institute of Technology for their help and advice throughout the course of this research.

The author also wishes to thank Douglas T. Ross and Lawrence G. Roberts for their help and answers to his many questions.

BIBLIOGRAPHY

1. CLARK, W. A., FRANKOVICH, J. M., PETERSON, H. P., FORGIE, J. W., BEST, R. L., OLSEN, K. H., "The Lincoln TX-2 Computer," Technical Report 6M-4968, Massachusetts Institute of Technology, Lincoln Laboratory, Lexington, Mass., April 1, 1957, *Proceedings of the Western Joint Computer Conference,* Los Angeles, California, February 1957.
2. COONS, S. A., *Notes on Graphical Input Methods,* Memorandum 8436-M-17, Dynamic Analysis and Control Laboratory, Massachusetts Institute of Technology, Department of Mechanical Engineering, Cambridge, Mass., May 4, 1960.
3. JOHNSON, T. E., "Sketchpad III, Three Dimensional Graphical Communication with a Digital Computer," *Proceedings of the Spring Joint Computer Conference,* Detroit, Michigan, May 21-23, 1963, (this issue).
4. JOHNSTON, L. E., *A Graphical Input Device and Shape Description Interpretation Routines,* Memorandum to Prof. Mann, Massachusetts Institute of Technology, Department of Mechanical Engineering, Cambridge, Mass., May 4, 1960.
5. LICKLIDER, J. C. R., "Man-Computer Symbiosis," *I.R.E. Trans. on Human Factors in Electronics,* vol. HFE, pp. 4-10, March 1960.
6. LICKLIDER, J. C. R., and CLARK, W., "Online Man-Computer Communication," *Proceedings of the Spring Joint Computer Conference,* San Francisco, California, May 1-3, 1962, vol. 21, pp. 113-128.
7. LOOMIS, H. H. JR., Graphical Manipulation Techniques Using the Lincoln TX-2 Computer, Group Report 51G-0017, Massachusetts Institute of Technology, Lincoln Laboratory, Lexington, Mass., November 10, 1960.
8. MOORE, E. F., "On the Shortest Path Through a Maze," *Proceedings of the International Symposium on the Theory of Switching,* Harvard University, Harvard Annals, vol. 3, pp. 285-292, 1959.
9. ROBERTS, L. G., *Machine Perception of Three Dimensional Solids,* Ph.D. Thesis, Massachusetts Institute of Technology, Electrical Engineering Department, Cambridge, Mass., February 1963.
10. ROSS, D. T., RODRIGUEZ, J. E., "Theoretical Foundations for the Computer-Aided Design System," *Proceedings of the Spring Joint Computer Conference,* Detroit, Michigan, May 21-23, 1963, (this issue).
11. SOUTHWELL, R. V., *Relaxation Methods in Engineering Science,* Oxford University Press, 1940.

12. STOTZ, R., "Man-Machine Console Facilities for Computer-Aided Design," *Proceedings of the Spring Joint Computer Conference*, Detroit, Michigan, May 21-23, 1963, (this issue).
13. VANDERBURGH, A. JR., *TX-2 Users Handbook*, Lincoln Manual No. 45, Massachusetts Institute of Technology, Lincoln Laboratory, Lexington, Mass., July 1961.
14. WALSH, J. F., and SMITH, A. F., "Computer Utilization," *Interim Engineering Report 6873-IR-10 and 11*, Electronic Systems Laboratory, Massachusetts Institute of Technology, Cambridge, Mass., pp. 57-70, November 30, 1959.
15. Handbook for Variplotter Models 205S and 205T, PACE, Electronic Associates Incorporated. Long Branch, New Jersey, June 15, 1959.

A system for interactive graphical programming*

by WILLIAM M. NEWMAN**

Harvard University
Cambridge, Massachusetts

INTRODUCTION

A system is described in this paper for developing graphical problem-oriented languages. This topic is of great importance in computer-aided design, but has hitherto received only sketchy documentation, with few attempts at a comparative study. Meanwhile displays are beginning to be used for design, and the results of such a study are badly needed. What has held back experimentation with computer graphics has been the difficulty of specifying new graphic techniques using the available programming languages; the method described in this paper appears to avoid this difficulty.

Defining a problem-oriented language

Notation

Any description of an interactive process must define the response of the system to each input. For this reason it is convenient to describe graphical problem-oriented languages in terms of *actions* and *reactions*. An *action* is simply an input which may produce a response; the corresponding *reaction* defines this response, and in addition any unmanifested effect of the action on the state of the machine. The same action may cause a different reaction on different occasions: for example, movement of the light pen may affect the display in a number of different ways. It is therefore convenient to treat the system as a finite-state automaton, and to say that the reaction is determined by the *state* of the program as well as by the action. In other words, the actions are *inputs* to the automaton, which cause it to change state; reactions are the *outputs*.

Just how convenient this is for describing interactive processes is illustrated by the following example. A 'rubber-band' line[1] can be created by means of a light pen and one push-button, in a sequence of five operations:
 1) press button to start pen tracking;
 2) track pen to starting point of line;
 3) press button to fix starting point;
 4) track pen to end point;
 5) press button to fix end point and stop tracking.

The 'rubber-band' effect is created by displaying a line joining the starting point to the pen position throughout stage 4.

Figure 1 shows a state-diagram representing this sequence. Each branch represents an action, and the resultant reaction is specified in the "arrowhead." Only valid actions are included; for example, pen movements are meaningless in state 1 and are therefore omitted. The inclusion or exclusion of an action may add semantic properties to the diagram. This is shown by the 'pen movement' branches on states 2 and 3, which imply pen tracking during those states and make explicit reference to tracking unnecessary.

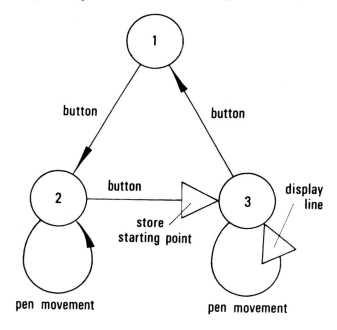

Figure 1 – A state-diagram representing rubber-bank line-drawing

---

*The work described in this report was supported by a Science Research Council Contract, No. B/SR/2071, "Computer Processing of Three-Dimensional Shapes."

**Formerly at the Centre for Computing and Automation, Imperial College, London.

Reprinted with permission from *Proceedings of the AFIPS Spring Joint Computer Conference* Washington, D.C.: Thompson Books, 1968. 47-54.

The state-diagram has been used in this way as the basis of a method for defining problem-oriented languages. A particular advantage of this technique is the way an *immediate* reaction can be associated with each action in a sequence; this is of great importance in graphical programs. On the other hand the state-diagram offers no direct method of attaching semantic functions to groups of actions, and is therefore of little use for describing phrase-structured grammars. This is less of a drawback than it seems. An interactive problem-oriented language need not possess a complex structure to function efficiently, and benefit can often be gained from simplifying the language as much as possible. Roos, for example, has noted the difficulty experienced by some engineers in using the relatively simple languages of the ICES System.[2]

The basic function of the state-diagram, as illustrated in Figure 1, is to indicate the actions which may validly occur during each state, and the reactions and changes of state which they will cause. A number of additions have been made to this basic notation. Normally, branching takes place when a user action matches an action defined in the diagram. Branching may however be over-ridden by the result of a *test routine* included in the branch definition. Furthermore, branching may be initiated by the program itself by means of *system actions*: thus the result of a procedure may determine to which of several states the program will branch. A procedure of this kind is called a *program block* and is attached to a state rather than to a branch; it is executed every time the corresponding state is entered. Program blocks need not terminate in a system action, but may instead be used to provide some sort of continuous background activity.

These are the essential additions to the notation. One other has been included for convenience in programming 'conversational' systems, in which each input message produces a predetermined output message. This message can be coded within the reaction procedure or program block, but it is convenient to be able to state it separately as an output string or *response*. States therefore possess a response as well as a program block, and reactions are similarly defined as two components, a response and a procedure. The procedure is represented as an *instruction for execution* or *IEX*.

The suggested form of these additions to the notation is shown in Figure 2; a somewhat similar notation has been used by Phillips[3] to describe real-time control programs. Figure 2 illustrates how the first example could be entended to permit the removal of lines and initialization of the program. These two functions are controlled by the commands DELETE and RESTART; as explained below, commands may be typed at the console typewriter, or may be arranged to appear on the screen as light-buttons. After giving the command DELETE, the user points the light pen at each line to be removed. Deletion is carried out by a test routine DLAST, which also tests whether any other lines remain on the screen. When none remains, or the user gives the command DRAW, the program changes state. RESTART causes the program to enter the initial state 4, execute its program block PBGO and return to state 1 when initialization is complete.

The language

A *Network Definition Language* has been developed so that problem-oriented languages, defined in the form of state-diagrams, can be compiled into interactive programs. W. R. Sutherland[4] has shown that programs can be described directly to the computer in graphical form, and this technique has obvious applications to the input of state-diagrams. However, much of the information in these diagrams is in character form, and would be difficult to describe in purely graphical terms. For this reason, and because it is more suited to off-line preparation, a character-based language was preferred. The following remarks and examples are intended to give a general impression of this language, which is described elsewhere in some detail.[5]

The state-diagram is described by defining each state in turn; each such *state definition* is followed by a list of the branches from that state and their properties. The ordering of the state definitions, and of the *branch definitions* within a list, is immaterial. State and branch definitions are constructed from *statements*, each defining one property as in the following examples:

```
RESP   PRESS BUTTON
PB     PB22
IEX    REPROG
```

These define a response "Press button," a program block called PB22 and an instruction for execution named REPROG, respectively.

Each state has three properties (name, response and program block) and each branch has seven. For convenience, however, the language permits certain statements to be omitted if the value of the property is null, meaningless or zero. The only statements which are syntactically necessary are those defining the names of states and the actions of branches. The remaining statements in a state or branch definition must follow these, but can be given in any order.

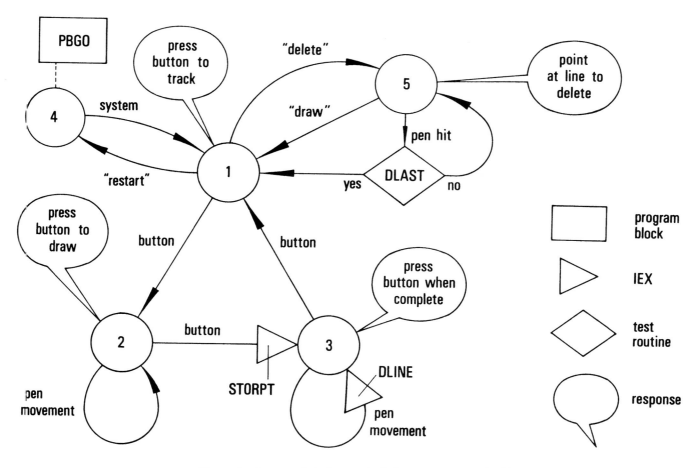

Figure 2 — An extended diagram including responses, and with provision for drawing and deleting lines and for initialization

Some care has been taken to avoid explicit references to peripherals in the language. As a result, state-diagrams are largely *device-independent* and compile into similarly device-independent programs. For example, a 'pen movement' action may originate as movement of a light pen or tracker ball, as a pair of typed coordinated, or even as two numbers read off a tape. Any such compatible set of actions is called a *category*, and the definition of an action must include the category name in the first statement. Some actions, such as typed commands, require a further property to define the message content. A command "restart" would be defined thus:

ACT 0

MES RESTART

The first statement indicates an action of category 0, which includes light-button hits as well as typed commands; the second defines the message content. Numerical names have been used for categories so that extensions to the category list can be made more easily.

Table I shows the state-diagram of Figure 2 coded by means of the language into a *network definition* and illustrates the use of the *state entry* to define a change of state. If no state entry is mentioned in a branch definition the state remains unaltered.

Compiling and executing an interactive program

Bilingual programming

The Network Definition Language contains no facilities for coding the procedures named in state diagrams. It is intended rather to be used in conjunction with a procedure-oriented language, each language being used for the tasks to which it is most suited. Some readers may disagree with this approach, which requires the programmer to be bilingual. The fact remains that procedure-oriented languages on to which powerful control facilities have been grafted rarely make for easy programming. It therefore seems reasonable that interactive programs should be written in two languages, one procedure-oriented and the other *control-oriented*.

STAT	1	Comment:	State definition, state 1
RESP	PRESS BUTTON TO TRACK		State 1 response, "Press button to track"
ACT	0		Branch definition, action of category 0 (command)
MES	RESTART		Message "restart"
SE	4		State entry, i.e. branch leads to state 4
ACT	0		Branch definition; command "delete" leads to state 5
MES	DELETE		
SE	5		
ACT	10		Branch definition, category 10 (button)
SE	2		Pressing button leads to state 2
STAT	2		State 2 definition
RESP	PRESS BUTTON TO DRAW		State 2 response
ACT	7		Branch definition, category 7 (pen movement)
ACT	10		Branch definition; pressing button leads to state 3
IEX	STORPT		STORPT stores pen position as starting point when button is pressed
SE	3		
STAT	3		State 3 definition
RESP	PRESS BUTTON WHEN COMPLETE		
ACT	10		Branch definition; pressing button leads to state 1
SE	1		
ACT	7		Branch definition, pen movement
IEX	DLINE		DLINE computes and displays fresh line at every pen movement
STAT	4		State 4 definition
INIT			Initial state, program starts here
PB	PBGO		Program block PBGO, executed on entering state 4
ACT	5		Branch definition, category 5 (system)
SE	1		Completion of PBGO leads to state 1
STAT	5		State 5 definition
RESP	POINT AT LINE TO DELETE		
ACT	0		Branch definition; command "draw" leads to state 1
MES	DRAW		
SE	1		
ACT	6		Branch definition: category 6 (pen hit)
TEST	DLAST		Test routine DLAST deletes indicated line
SE	1		If last line, branch to state 1
END			

TABLE I: The example of Figure 2 coded into Network Definition Language

This bilingual approach permits an interactive program to be created as three separate components, namely the *control component, procedure component* and *supervisor*. The supervisor contains routines for handling interrupts and maintaining the display; at its nucleus is a program which analyses and interprets inputs. This program, the *Reaction Handler,* is basically a table-driven syntax analyser.[5] The tables to which it refers are ring-structures and include a model of the state-diagram, created by compiling the network definition with a *Network Compiler*. These tables form the control component of the program. They contain references to the test routines, program blocks and instructions for execution, which constitute the procedure component and are compiled separately.

The decision to use ring-structures for the Reaction Handler tables was made for a number of reasons. It permitted null-valued entries to be omitted from the tables, and others such as message and response definitions to be of variable length. It meant that a package of routines would be available for building data structures for computer-aided design. It also allowed a much more flexible approach to the design of the Reaction Handler, since the tables could be easily extended or rearranged. The ring-processing package, which has been described in another paper, was based on the ASP language of J. C. Gray.[8] It differs from the earlier ring languages of Roberts[9] and others in the ease with which dynamic alterations can be made to the structure. In particular, elements can be attached to rings or removed from them without altering the element size, since the connections are made by *ring starts* and *associators* which need not be contiguous with the element. This flexibility has made it possible to write an on-line, incremental Network Compiler.

The network compiler

The essence of an incremental compiler, as described by Lock,[10] is that each statement is independently compiled into executable form, and can later be modified without complete recompilation. Normally this means assigning a number to each statement so that it can be referenced. In the Network Compiler it was found sufficient to assign names to the states and branches; individual statements could then be referenced by the property name. Branch naming has since been discarded in order to save space, and it is therefore no longer possible to refer back to individual branch definition statements. Users have not found this to be a great disadvantage.

The first statement in a state or branch definition causes the Network Compiler to set up a corresponding ring element; the two classes of element are called *state elements* and *branch elements*. An extra word is provided in the state element to hold the state name. Each further statement in a definition has the effect of attaching to the element a *definition ring* defining the named property. The manner in which rings define properties is shown diagrammatically in Figure 3. The value of any property of an element can be found by selecting the definition ring with the appropriate *attribute* in the associator, and ascending it to the ring start; the element attached to this ring start contains the value.

Statements defining state entries are treated in the same fashion: the ring to which the branch element is attached leads to the named state element. Each state element has such a *state entry ring*, whose constituent elements define the set of branches leading to this state. A second ring, the *permitted action ring*, starts from each state element, and defines the set of branches leading from that state; this set includes branches which return to the same state and therefore possess no state entry. Figure 4 shows part of the ring-structure resulting from compiling the network definition of Table I.

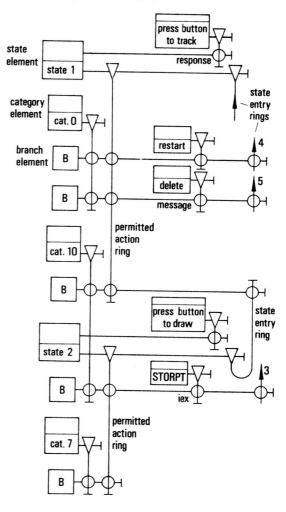

Figure 4 — Part of the ring-structure resulting from compiling the network definition of Table I

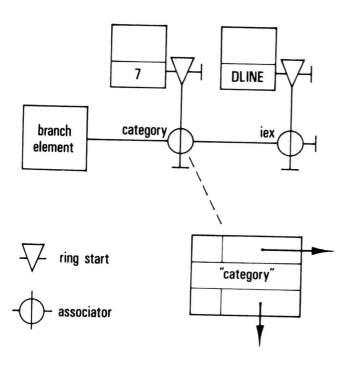

Figure 3 — Defining properties by means of definition rings. This shows the ring structure defining a branch of category 7 with an IEX called DLINE. An assocator is shown in detail

As mentioned above, the Network Compiler is designed for on-line use, and may be operated from the teleprinter or from the display using light-buttons. The teleprinter has proved the more convenient for on-line compilation, but the light-buttons and displayed responses provide a valuable aid, particularly to the novice. The compiler will also accept paper tapes prepared off-line. It has error-checking facilities, and will halt at any erroneous command on the tape until the correct version is typed.

The reaction handler: modes

A program under the control of the Reaction Handler may be in one of three modes: these are *interrupted mode, reaction handling* (or *RH*) *mode* and *waiting mode*. *Waiting mode* does not imply inactivity, but that the program has reached one of the states in the state-diagram and is ready for an action to occur. It may therefore be engaged in computation (user waiting for computer) or looping on a dynamic stop)computer waiting for user).

During waiting mode any action by the user will cause the program to switch to *interrupted mode*, and a *stimulus* to be passed to the Reaction Handler. The stimulus specifies the device involved and may also refer to a block of data or *message*, such as a teleprinter character or a pair of light pen coordinates. Device name and message address are stored in a five-word element which forms the head of a queue of stimuli.

The program then enters *RH mode* and the Reaction Handler processes the first stimulus in the queue. Stimulus processing is a form of syntax analysis, whose goal is to match the stimulus to an entry in the appropriate table. If this goal cannot be reached, the stimulus represents an ungrammatical action. If however the goal is reached, the table may specify a fresh goal to be attained. Eventually the process stops, either when it fails to reach a goal or when it arrives at an *ultimate goal* where no further goal is specified. The Reaction Handler then fetches the next stimulus from the queue and processes it; when the queue is empty the program returns to waiting mode.

At any time the Reaction Handler may be interrupted by a user action, and a further stimulus may be added to the end of the queue. To prevent the queue from growing uncontrollably, software flip-flops or *latches* are used to govern the rate at which each device generates stimuli. The light pen latch, for example, is set when a pen stimulus enters the queue and cleared when it has been processed; while it is set, all fresh pen positions are ignored.

Stimulus processing

The first task of the Reaction Handler on receiving a fresh stimulus is to establish what category of action, if any, the stimulus represents. This it does by referring to a *category table*. Once an action has been recognised in this way, it is matched against descriptions in a *branch table* of the branches leading from the current state. This second phase determines what reaction and change of state should occur, and it is convenient to describe this phase first.

The branch table is in fact the ring structure created by the Network Compiler, as described above and illustrated in Figure 4. The Reaction Handler's first goal is to find a branch of the appropriate category which belongs to the current state. This can be done by searching in parallel the permitted action ring and the category definition ring. If any branch elements belong to both rings, the next goal is to find among them an element whose message definition matches the stimulus message. A series of message comparisons therefore takes place; before carrying out a comparison on a branch element, the test routine is executed.

If a matching element is found, the corresponding reaction takes place: the reaction response is displayed, and the IEX is executed. If no match can be achieved, the Reaction Handler will accept any branch element with a 'null' message. The final goal is the branch's state entry. If none exists, there is no change of state. If on the other hand the branch element is attached to a state entry ring, the new state's response is displayed, and the program block address is used as a transfer address when the program eventually returns to waiting mode. This address may be modified by a *jump displacement* included in the branch definition: this is a method of achieving multiple entries to a program block. If the state has no program block, the program transfers to a standard dynamic stop address.

The most time-consuming part of this process is the parallel ring search, which becomes particularly undesirable when repeated actions such as pen movements are taking place very frequently. The parallel search is therefore avoided by scanning through the permitted action ring at every change of state. At each branch element on the ring an *activity bit* is set which allows a simple search through the category definition ring to be carried out whenever an action of that category occurs.

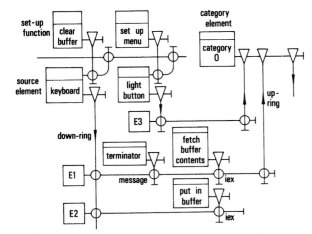

Figure 5 – A category table ring-structure, capable of dealing with typed commands and light-button commands

The first phase of the reaction handling process, in which an input stimulus may be recognized as a particular category of action, is carried out in a similar fashion to the second. During this phase the Reaction Handler uses the *category table*, a fragment of which is shown in Figure 5. When a stimulus is received, it is first matched with a *source element* containing the same device name as the stimulus. A search is then carried out along the *down-ring* from this element, in an identical fashion to the second-phase search along the category ring. If a matching element is found on this ring, its IEX is executed. The next goal is to find an *up-ring* from this element, leading to a *category element*: this ring is treated in the same fashion as the state entry ring in the second phase. The category element forms a link between the category table and the branch table, and the down-ring which starts at this element is in fact the category definition ring used in the second-phase search.

The first phase of reaction handling performs two important functions. It is capable of concatenating stimuli so that the combined input string can be treated as a single action by the second phase; it is also responsible for grouping together actions of the same category. Both functions are illustrated by Figure 5, which depicts the ring-structure for dealing with input commands. Typed commands originate as a string of characters, each of which matches with element E2 and is stored in a buffer. When the terminating character is typed, the IEX of element E1 exchanges the single-character stimulus message for the complete buffer contents, and the second phase of reaction handling commences from the "Category 0" element. Light-button hits produce stimuli containing the complete command as an input message. These match with element E3 and lead immediately to the second phase.

When the program changes state, the old activity bits must be cleared and the new ones set. The Reaction Handler must also carry out various *set-up functions*, defined as properties of the source elements. These functions include such operations as clearing buffers, starting pen-tracking and setting up the light-button 'menu.' Source elements are themselves held on a ring, whose members define the set of active devices. The display is treated as a number of different 'devices': light pen interrupts are separated into light-button hits, tracking interrupts and so forth, and passed to the Reaction Handler under different device names.

In its general layout, the category table closely resembles the branch table, and is set up by a very similar compiler. This *Category Compiler* is also incremental, and accepts table descriptions written in the *Category Definition Language*,[5] which differs only slightly from the Network Definition Language. In general, a complete category table suits most programs, but it is convenient to be able to edit out unwanted categories with the aid of the Category Compiler in order to save space.

CONCLUSION

At the time of writing, the Reaction Handler system has been in use for only a few months. Nevertheless it has during this brief period demonstrated a number of valuable features. In particular, the Network Definition Language provides a very efficient means of writing graphical programs, and simple experiments with graphical techniques can now be carried out in a matter of hours instead of weeks. Both the language and the underlying state-diagram concept are extremely simple, and can be used by those with very little programming experience.

The adoption of a bilingual approach has undoubtedly helped to make this possible, and it is interesting to compare other systems of a similar nature. The use of a separate language to define a program's control sequence has been proposed before, but it is rare to find explicit reference to the need for two languages in interactive programming. The ICES System employs what amounts to a bilingual method, in which a *Command Definition Language* is used to define the control sequence. The language is designed around the use of card-image input, however, and is not particularly suitable for interactive programming. *Command Flow Graphs* are used in a similar fashion to state-diagrams, but the concept of program states is not employed.

A much more powerful facility for treating problem-oriented languages of a very general nature is provided in the AED System.[11] Language syntax can be described by means of the AEDJR Command Language,[12] the extreme generality which this system permits is attractive, but is probably unnecessary in graphical programs. The Command Language is very complex, and its efficient use obviously requires considerable experience.

The processing of basic characters by the AED System is carried out by the RWORD System. This system is particularly interesting, as it employs the concept of representing programs as finite-state automata. It possesses many of the features of the Reaction Handler, but avoids the explicit definition of program states, a feature which has been found valuable in practice. RWORD instead uses a very neat regular-expression language for defining vocabulary words, and avoids the use of tables in order to speed up program execution. It is clearly capable of producing more efficient programs than is possible using the

Reaction Handler's ring-structured category network.

Nevertheless, the Reaction Handler has performed quite satisfactorily as a real-time supervisor. It provides a fast response to all types of user action, including pen movement where a good response is essential. It does so at the expense of a high system overhead, which may reach as much as 20% during pen-tracking. In a display processor, which is idle most of the time, this is quite acceptable.

Less acceptable is the space consumed by the supervisor. The system was developed on an 8K DEC PDP-7 computer and Type 340 display, and in this machine the supervisor occupies nearly 4K. Besides the Reaction Handler, this includes the ring-processing package, a full set of interrupt-handling and output routines, and a software character generator. Some difficulty was experienced in coding the ring-processing routines as pure procedures, due to the lack of index registers on the PDP-7. It seems likely that the size of the supervisor could be greatly reduced by using a machine equipped with index registers and a hardware character generator.

ACKNOWLEDGMENTS

I wish to thank Mr. C. B. Jones for his extensive assistance in programming the system. I am also grateful to Mr. Alan Tritter for suggesting including the test routine; and to many members of staff of the Centre for Computing and Automation, Imperial College, and of the Cambridge University Engineering and Mathematical Laboratories, including Professor W. S. Elliott and Messrs G. F. Coulouris, C. A. Lang and R. J. Pankhurst, for their advice and encouragement.

REFERENCES

1 I E SUTHERLAND
Sketchpad: a man-machine graphical communication system
Proceedings of the 1963 Spring Joint Computer Conference

2 D ROOS
ICES system design
MIT Press Cambridge Massachusetts 1966 p 25

3 C S E PHILLIPS
Networks for real-time programming
Computer Journal Volume 10 May 1967 p 46

4 W R SUTHERLAND
On-line graphical specification of computer procedures
MIT Lincoln Laboratory Technical Report No 405
Lincoln Laboratory Lexington Massachusetts

5 W M NEWMAN
Definition languages for use with the reaction handler
Computer Technology Group Report 67/9 Imperial College London October 1967

6 T E CHEATHAM K SATTLEY
Syntax-directed compiling
Proceedings of the 1964 Spring Joint Computer Conference

7 W M NEWMAN
The ASP-7 ring structure processor
Computer Technology Group Report 67/8 Imperial College London October 1967

8 J C GRAY
Compound data structures for computer aided design: a survey
Proceedings of the ACM 20th Anniversary Conference 1967

9 L G ROBERTS
Graphical communication and control languages
Information System Sciences Spartan Books 1964

10 K LOCK
Structuring programs for multiprogram time-sharing on-line applications
Proceedings of the 1965 Fall Joint Computer Conference

11 D T ROSS
The AED approach to generalized computer-aided design
Proceedings of the ACM 20th Anniversary Conference 1967

12 D T ROSS
AEDJR: An experimental language processor
MIT Electronic Systems Laboratory Memorandum 211, 1964

The Art of Natural Man-Machine Conversation

JAMES D. FOLEY, MEMBER, IEEE, AND VICTOR L. WALLACE, MEMBER, IEEE

Abstract — The design of interactive graphic systems whose aim is good symbiosis between man and machine involves numerous factors. Many of those factors can be judged from the perspective of natural spoken conversation between two people.

Guiding rules and principles for design of such systems are presented as a framework for a survey of design techniques for man-machine conversation. Attention is especially focused on ideas of action syntax structuring, logical equivalences among action devices, and avoidance of psychological blocks to communication.

I. INTRODUCTION

The dictionary provides two meanings for the word "graphic." One is "pertaining to the drawing of marks, lines or characters on a surface" [1]. Although the traditional usage of the term "computer graphics" clearly derives from this meaning, it is by no means accidental that the alternate meaning is given by the phrase "clearly and vividly described." It is precisely because graphics (first definition) are graphic (second definition) that they are used as a medium of communication between man and machine.

Nevertheless, the clarity and vividness of computer graphic communication is not an automatic consequence of the mere use of drawings. Conscious design effort must be applied by an "application programmer" to provide clarity and vividness in the user's communication with his machine. In computer graphics, the effort must be applied to designing the action sequences by which the user communicates his desires to the machine, and the pictures by which the machine communicates responses. The objective is to make both paths of communication *natural* to the user to increase his productivity in technical or artistic tasks. This design effort is sometimes described as *human factors design* or *ergonomic design*.

The purpose of this paper is to review and organize those ideas and techniques useful in ergonomic design of computer graphics applications. Our primary concern is with what is natural in man-machine graphic communication, and how naturalness can be achieved.

As an object of systematic study, natural man-machine dialogue suffers a common affliction with natural language communication between persons: nearly every rule has its exceptions, and the final arbiter of "correctness" of usage must be its acceptance by lively participants. Nevertheless, studying actions and pictures for grammatical principles is certainly no less useful than studying gestures and speech in interpersonal communication. It is also considerably less well understood. This paper represents a beginning.

Manuscript received December 12, 1973.
The authors are with the department of Computer Science, the University of North Carolina, Chapel Hill, N. C. 27514

II. CONVERSATIONAL FACTORS

One of the principal goals of interactive systems, graphic or otherwise, is the symbiosis between man and machine. When a terminal user is able to interact with a computer so that he is unaware either of the computer or of the medium of communication, this interaction can be said to be conversational. Then the capabilities of the two partners, man and computer, become as one working on a single task.

While this ideal is rarely completely obtained, it represents the goal which, through skillful design of the machine and the medium of communication, can be met in large measure today.

The particular concerns of such a design are referred to here as conversational factors. Considerable understanding of these factors is

gained by analogy to the psychology of normal spoken conversations. The patterns of speaking and listening which have evolved from our need to converse deeply, without self-consciousness, with our fellow man must be respected, and inspected, to accomplish the same goals with computer graphics.

One can express two guiding principles in skillful design of conversational graphic systems, relating to language and to psychology, respectively.

A. Language Principles

The language in computer graphics communication is not one of spoken or even written words, but rather one of pictures, and of actions such as button pushes, lightpen indications, and joystick movements which serve as words.

The language and context of the conversation must be the language of the man and must be natural to him. When a Frenchman and a German converse intensely, at least one of them must be fluent in the other's language. In our case, either the computer graphics system must "learn" the user's language, or the user must learn the computer's. Clearly the former should be the design's goal. In Sackman's words, "the need (is) to adapt the machine to the man rather than the man to the machine" [2]. A biochemist studying protein conformations wants to speak to the computer in terms of atoms, bonds, dihedral angles, residues, and bonding forces, not in terms of linked lists, iterations, and subpictures. The former are words in his vocabulary. The latter are words in a foreign language which he has neither time nor inclination to master.

However, it is essential also that the language be efficient, complete and have a natural grammar. An efficient language is one which conveys ideas effectively and concisely. A complete language permits expression of any idea relevant to the domain of discourse. A natural grammar offers few awkward constraints to the expression of ideas using the fundamental devices and symbols which are available. Natural grammar also permits the system to be useful with a minimum of user training. An interaction language should allow the user to concentrate on the semantics of what he intends to express. The distractions and discontinuities injected into his conscious thought processes by the language's syntax and vocabulary must be minimal or nonexistent. Only if this goal is achieved can a user become engrossed in productive man-machine communications.

Few systematic guidelines for the design of such language exist. Hornbuckle [3] suggests that "observing what man does normally during his creative efforts can provide a starting point for the [language] designer. In particular" he says, "a mathematician does not manipulate equations at a typewriter, nor does a circuit designer prefer a keypunch." Hansen [4] is even more succinct: KNOW THE USER he says. Watch him, study him, interact with him, learn to understand how he thinks, why he does what he does.

Irani and Wallace [5] suggest following up this start with a detailed axiomatic abstraction of the elements of the man's discourse in algebraic terms, with a systematic definition of the mathematical meaning of those elements through algebraic elaboration, and with a definition of operations imposed on them by procedural "productions." Their methodology has been applied only to generalized networks, but offers potential in other areas. Experience indicates that the designer must know the underlying theory of the user's discipline to a considerable degree if complete and efficient languages are to be achieved.

Section III will expand upon principles of designing a language's syntax, while Section IV will expand upon various design details.

B. Psychological Principles

The second guiding principle is that the system should avoid psychological blocks that often prevent full user involvement in an interaction. The most typical of these blocks are boredom panic, frustration, confusion and discomfort.

Boredom is a consequence of improper pacing. The maintenance of adequate response times is the critical concern. Response time depends upon hardware characteristics and the design of algorithms used for responses. However, not all user actions require the same speed of response. Miller [6] suggests that there may be a hierarchy of required response, corresponding to various levels of psychological "closure" – the feeling of having completed a certain task. The smaller or less significant the job, the sooner the response is expected, because the feeling of closure will be less.

It appears likely that human action occurs at three quite distinct levels of closure. We call them lexical, syntactic, and semantic. At the lexical level are those things which are done by reflex, either natural or trained. It appears that our time to perform such actions goes down to about 50 ms, which approximates the period between key depressions for a very fast typist. (This figure loosely corresponds to one provided by Miller). To be useful, system response to lexical actions must be within the same time interval, since human psychology does not tolerate the interruption of reflex actions.

At the syntactic level are the semiconscious actions by which sentences, or complete thoughts, are constructed. The basic elements meaning "add a 5-Ω resistor between this node and that node" would be constructed more deliberately than the lexical construction, because the user is forming his "idea" as he works. Time intervals of approximately 1 s seem most characteristic of syntactic actions. The system's responses to them are correspondingly less exacting, with a half-second delay being entirely adequate, while often even 2- to 4- s delays are tolerated.

The semantic level involves requests of major import for which the user expects "thoughtful' answers. Semantic actions are completely conscious actions, and may take tens of seconds and more. The tolerable response time appears to be highly variable. If the action were the sentence "Hello, I'm Joe," it would be disconcerting to wait more than 2 s for the response "Hi." On the other hand, a request to display the minimal energy bond in a complex molecule could take 10 s or more without a user losing his train of thought. In fact, he would probably use the delay to think about what he will do with the answer.

Users are usually more comfortable if the response time for an action, be it lexical, syntactic, or semantic, is about the same each time the action is performed, rather than being highly variable. This can avoid the next psychological block.

Panic is the consequence of unexpectedly long delays, wherein a conversational partner gives no reply to a statement or question over a prolonged period of time. Questions, irrelevant to the conversation, are forced to his attention. Has the system encountered problems? Is it down? Am I in a loop? Is the program faulty? The remedy, when the real delay cannot be reduced, is to introduce some form of placebo – a trivial system response providing assurance and perhaps a modicum of information. The DAC-1 system [7] provided displayed sequence numbers, indicating the progress of the program. Other remedies are to display partial answers as they are obtained. The SELMA system [8] retrieved large pictures slowly because of hardware limitations, but constructed them piece by piece as a placebo. At the very least, a positive indication of acceptance of the command, of the beginning of processing, and the completion of processing should be provided.

Frustration results from an inability to easily convey intentions to the computer and, consequently, eliciting an unexpected result or none at all. Frustration is further compounded if the unexpected response cannot be undone, or if one cannot determine what response actually took place.

Frustration is caused by inflexible and unforgiving systems. For example, many graphics systems expect the user to at least occasionally enter text strings from a keyboard. What happens f he makes a typing mistake while entering the string? A completely unforgiving system would offer no choice but to continue typing the text string and to enter it into the system. Then another command must be used to enter a modified text string, replacing the old, incorrect one. A somewhat better system would allow the user to immediately start re-entering the text string, without it ever having been accepted by the system. Finally, the best system would provide a combined backspace and character delete key, making the correction a trivial matter indeed.

Nearly all system designers recognize the desirability of the third approach. But too few designers recognize that this is just a special case of a more general system requirement; namely, the ability to recover from incorrect or unwanted actions. If a picture can be changed in some way, it must be possible to conveniently and easily undo the change.

A corollary is to force the user to think twice and reconfirm his request whenever and action from which recovery would be difficult is to be executed. Deleting a picture or emptying a file are examples of actions which should, and usually do, require confirmation. A related capability is to let the user preview the result of a change to the picture without making the change permanent. If he likes the change, he goes on, and the change is made permanent. If not, he rejects the change and it is automatically undone. This is equivalent to providing the ability to "back up" by one operation whenever desired.

The so-called "rubber band" line drawing is an example of this situation. Once the starting point of a line is established, the line is drawn to the endpoint indicated by a lightpen or joystick. As the endpoint moves, so moves the rubber band line. When the user has placed the line where he wants it he so indicates to the system, and the line is fixed in place.

Another means of recovery from incorrect actions is the ability to respecify some operand. By improper placement the lightpen might have detected the wrong object. When the detected object is intensified, the user quickly realizes it to be the wrong one. He should then be able to simply lightpen another object. It should intensify and the old one should deintensify. This assumes that only one such object is needed for the action being performed: more complicated situations require more complicated dialogues.

What happens if midway through the specification of an action like adding to a drawing, the user decides he really wants to do something else? As with the typing case, a poorly designed system would give the user no choice but to finish defining the line and then to delete the line, or to use the backup facility previously described. A forgiving system would instead let the user cancel in midstream so he can immediately proceed with what he really wants to do. The clear implication of canceling a partially specified action is that the application program and display must return exactly to their state before the aborted action was initiated. This cancellation capability can then be viewed as an extension of the backup capability.

There are other aspects of a flexible system. In man-man communication we usually have several ways of expressing a thought or asking a question. Yet how many graphics systems allow the user several paths to a given end? Precious few. Drafting systems offer an exception, because they typically offer several ways to construct a line such as two endpoints, or point, angle and length. The underlying question for system designers is whether one's attitude toward the users will be "this is how you *must* express yourself on the system," or "here are several ways to express yourself, choose whichever you prefer." Pursuit of Hansen's KNOW THE USER dictum can help to determine the appropriate attitude in each circumstance.

Another component of flexibility is extensibility. An extensible system provides users with the capability of extending the command language with a procedure definition capability. The basic command language would include a set of *primitives*. These primitives can be combined into a procedure which is then identified with a newly defined syntactic element of the command language. Then, using the new syntactic element as a command language element, the entire procedure can be invoked. As with subroutines or macros in programming languages, these user-defined procedures provide both economy of discourse, and the opportunity to apply basic general instructions to the special needs of an individual user.

While the programming technology needed to provide extensible graphics command languages is well known, it is regrettably infrequently used. Successful applications include the Culler-Fried System [9], Wright's protein molecule display and manipulation system [10], [11], and Armit's shape design system [12].

Confusion is the consequence of perceived structure being overwhelmed by detail. For example, the user may be offered many poorly defined command options at once, or may face too much undifferentiated detail in a displayed picture. The remedy for such confusion is to increase the amount of underlying structure, to improve the perception of the structure of the structure already present, or to reduce unnecessary detail.

Structure can be increased by organizing a series of command options in a hierarchical form, and presenting command options sequentially down the structure. It can also be increased by carefully grouping visible objects on the screen according to function.

TABLE I

Coding Method	Maximum Number of Codes for Essentially Error-Free Recognition by Normal Individuals
Color	6
Geometric shapes	10
Linewidth	2
Line type	5
Intensities	2

The perception of command structure can be enhanced by prompting the user, telling him which tasks he can do next. However, since prompts are usually distracting to an experienced user, a good system provides simple means for disabling or selectively enabling them. One method for prompting is via commentary in a standard area on the screen. Other forms of prompting include: selectively illuminating function keys, brightening light buttons, displaying a prominent tracking cross when a position is required, providing a blinking cursor when a text string is needed, and providing a scale or dial when a numerical value is expected.

The perception of structure among objects on the screen can be enhanced by using different line types (solid, dotted, dot-dash), widths, intensity levels, or geometric shapes. These all help make a display more meaningful. Martin [13] briefly summarizes what can be done with these techniques, and Barmack and Sinaiko [14] give a more detailed discussion.

The latter two references provide more specific information concerning the usefulness of various distinguishing features, as shown in Table I. For each technique, the number of easily distinguished codes is listed. They are listed in approximately decreasing effectiveness, with color providing the most useful distinction. It is relatively expensive, however, and unacceptable for the color-blind user. The other techniques are easily programmed, and are often available inexpensively as hardware options.

The user's attention can best be directed to an area of interest on the screen by displaying objects in the area in a bright color (orange or red is preferred [14]) blinking them (at 2 or 3 Hz with a flash duration of at least 50 ms [14]) or pointing to them with a large blinking arrow.

The perception of displayed structure can also be enhanced through the use of three-dimensional displays, and by augmenting the sense of sight with other senses. Gregory's *The Intelligent Eye* [15] offers an excellent analysis of perception in three dimensions. Batter and Brooks [16] have studied the effect of the kinesthetic sense (sense of force) on the perception of force fields simultaneously displayed in vector form. Noll [17] has studied the use of the tactile sense in perceiving the shape of surface and objects. Sound also has a potential for enhancing perception.

The obvious means of decreasing visual detail is selective display. A network is shown in Figs. 1 and 2 with and without annotations. If one's primary interest is in the topology of the network, Fig. 2 is much preferred. Alternatively, a zoom capability permits a user to enlarge a small area of the display to expose details not otherwise distinguishable. Efficiency of the interactive command language is also a major factor in the degree of detail presented.

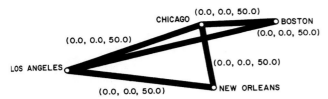

Fig. 1. Network with annotations.

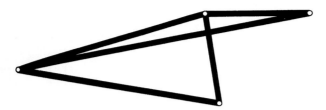

Fig. 2. Network without annotations.

Discomfort comes from providing an inappropriate physical environment for the graphics workstation. This psychological block to effective conversation is all too often neglected when designing conversational systems.

The optical faceplate of most cathode-ray tubes (CRT's) are very annoying when reflecting such distractions as overhead lights and bright windows. It is necessary to position the CRT away from windows or install blackout shades, and to shield overhead lights. A nonglare glass faceplate on the CRT, a partial hood around it, and a low ambient room illumination are other solutions.

Large work areas are needed for spreading out working papers. Surprisingly, few display systems provide satisfactory arrangements. An uncomfortable chair, and improperly placed work surface, or a high ambient noise causes discomfort and distraction from the task at hand. Operator interaction devices should be located on the work surface where they can be reached quickly. One arrangement is to place the alphanumeric keyboard in front of the screen so touch-typists can easily place both hands on it. Right-handed users normally handle the lightpen with the right hand, so the pen should have a holder or bracket to the right of the screen. By placing the programmed function keyboard (if one is used) to the left of the screen, a user can easily reach it with his left hand while holding the pen in his right hand. If a tablet is used, a different arrangement becomes necessary. Regrettably, not all systems allow the pen and function keyboard to be interchanged to accommodate left-handed users! These, and many other general considerations, have been discussed by McCormick [18].

III. THE ACTION LANGUAGE

There are two distinct languages in the communication between the man and the graphic machine [19]. One is the language of display by which the machine presents information regarding the state of its data and the options available for further action by the user. The other is the language of *actions* using input devices, by which the man relates his intended transformations of machine-stored data with references to objects in the displayed picture.

The goals of language design, both action and picture are to provide a language format which is natural, and which does not add to the boredom, panic, frustration, and confusion of the user. Assuming that the required response times can be achieved, that the apparatus and environment have been properly constructed, that the semantics of the intended conversation are understood, and that the suitable tutorial material can be developed, there remains a need for well-designed sequences of input actions coordinated with output pictures to permit symbiotic communication.

A number of syntactic principles of naturalness for action sequences can be abstracted from experience. The important ones, in our judgment, are sentence structure, visual continuity, tactile continuity, and contextual continuity.

An action language is sentence structured if, within a given phase or subdomain of discourse, each complete user thought can be expressed in a continuous sequence of input device manipulations with standard patterns of beginning and termination. Upon termination, the machine returns to a state from which similar actions sequences, other sentences, can begin.

The essential features of this sentence structure are indivisible, complete thought; unbroken action; a well-defined "home state"; regularity of pattern. Obviously, these properties are modeled after spoken discourse.

A complete thought reflects a graphic or semantic intent, such as "draw a line from this point to that one," or "apply this constraint to that object," or "rotate this object about that axis by the following amount." It must be sufficiently circumscribed that an interruption in its flow implies uncertainty, and a deliberate break before completion (as in beginning another "sentence") implies an intention to cancel the incomplete thought, and return all data to their presentence state. As in spoken discourse, a proper terminator of the sentence normally implies confirmation of intent, with important (or dangerous) sentences perhaps reinforced by a "handshake" of confirmation. Virtually any meaningful sentence should be eligible for expression upon termination of another sentence.

The notion of sentence structure does not preclude the possibility of paragraphing, whereby a particular local domain of thought can be delimited, as evidenced by multiple "phases" in many systems, such as construction, solution, labeling, etc.

The idea of visual continuity is that, within a given sentence, the eye should focus on a single area which moves in a continuous manner throughout the expression of the sentence. For example, a lightpen or cursor often provides the visual cue to actions, or a sequence of flashing objects may direct attention from one area on the screen to another. Contrarily, a *need* to scan a displaced prompt field during an action is undesirable and unnatural, as is the provision of error messages on a separate device.

Tactile continuity refers to the need to avoid groping or searching with hands or feet once a sentence has begun. None but a touch-typist should be required to use a typewriter keyboard as an input device within the expression of a sentence. When programmed function keys are used by the left hand, it should be possible to keep the hand in a standard position for striking keys "by feel" throughout a sentence. It should not be necessary to move the hand to an independent device during the sequence, most especially not one like the lightpen which might not be found in a fixed position. Input languages which adopt a one-device philosophy, using a lightpen or tablet as the sole hand-activated device for action sequences, emphasize tactile continuity and have great attractiveness when they can be applied.

Differentiated key shapes, and a more mnemonic arrangement like the keys of a touch-tone phone are desirable attributes of keyboards, enhancing one's ability to develop tactile continuity in an action language. So also are footswitches or kneeswitches, but not both, because the foot or knee can remain nearby throughout an action.

Contextual continuity refers to the absence of unrecognized side effects resulting from a user's actions. It is best achieved by providing only immediately perceivable responses to reinforce the effect of every step in the action sentence. If the reinforcement, or feedback, is visual, it should be within the primary field of vision (focus) for that part of the sentence. Nevertheless, at the expense of decreased visual continuity, contextual continuity can be preserved if the user is trained to look at some standard place for special reinforcements, such as diagnostics. This place may be elsewhere on the same screen, on a second display, or it may be on an adjacent Teletypewriter. The reinforcement may, however, be nothing more than an audible click, a change in force on a manipulator, or a vibration in a joystick.

While these virtues are sometimes countervailing, and often difficult to achieve, successful graphic conversational languages include these properties in large measure and deny them grudgingly. Often, when a system fails to provide continuity at the syntactic level, experienced users will train themselves to compensate, just as typists have trained themselves at touch-typing to regain tactile continuity from an inherently clumsy nontactile device. So also will a user unconsciously train himself to anticipate locations of actions to recover visual continuity, or to keep abreast of discontinuous context changes. Nevertheless, the goal must be to provide systems for which only minimal compensations and self-training are necessary. This goal is particularly important where accessibility by many users is important, or where each user accesses the system infrequently.

The characterization of syntactic goals for naturalness of actions has not been subjected to intensive study, and is a prime area for future research. English, Englebart, and Bertman [20] have studied factors for selecting devices for pointing at text on the screen of a CRT. They have observed the importance of what we call tactile continuity to the quality of user performance. Their paper is one of the few sources of experimental evidence comparing graphic input devices.

The notion of a sentence depends upon the view of a conversational system as an event-driven finite state machine [21]. In this view, each action represents a symbol which asynchronously causes the control state of the machine to change, consequently, changing its response to subsequent actions. For every context, or "phase," of user work, we have assumed a special home state corresponding to the wait-for-next-action condition. Within an action, the system enters a number of new states, none of which permit the beginning of a new sentence without first aborting or terminating the old sentence and returning to the home state.

A partial state diagram of the action sequences associated with diagram construction of the SELMA system [8] is shown in Fig. 3. In that system, during the construction phase, every sentence begins with a lightpen hit on a displayed object. Identification of the type of the object picked determines the alternative next actions, which in some cases could be the tracing of geometric patterns with the lightpen.

In Fig. 3, each intermediate state is shown by a circle containing a description of the activity executed continually while the system is in that state. That activity could in turn be described in a more detailed state diagram. The standard state between sentences is shown by the long oval in the center. Each branch between states has two labels: the first is an identifier of the stimulus which must occur before the transition is permitted, the second identifies the system response during the transition. In some cases the response is null, signifying that the change in state is the only result of the stimulus.

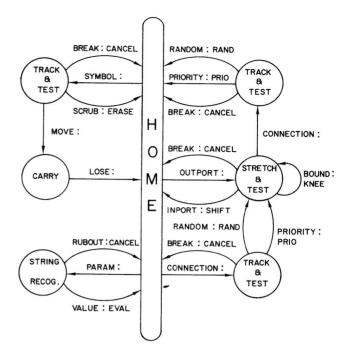

Fig. 3. SELMA state diagram.

For the simple system represented there are just five possible sentence forms. They begin by the stimuli "symbol" "outport," "parameter," "connection," and "escape," each of which is identified by the act of pointing with a lightpen to an object of the class specified. "Escape" is actually a light *button* which causes a change in state to the home state of another *phase* of discourse.

To illustrate one sentence form, suppose a connection was picked. The system will track the lightpen, continuously seeking patterns (described in Section IV) to the motion. If it recognizes the motion associated with one type of branching (e.g., random), it creates a symbol at the originally selected point on the connection, and proceeds to accept the creation of a segmented connection line, successively stretching rubber bands and recognizing corners of the connection, until it terminates on an "input port." If tracking is broken during any part of this sequence, the CANCEL response program is invoked causing all construction since the start of the sentence to disappear, followed by a return to the home state.

IV. DEVICES AND VIRTUAL DEVICES

The user's communication to the computer is in the form of action with devices. The diverse devices available at a given terminal may include typewriter keyboard, function keys, lightpen, tablet, joystick, and dials. Each device can be treated as a physical realization of one or several of just four distinct virtual devices, the pick, the button, the locator, and the valuator.

A *pick* is used to designate *user defined* objects, like a line, resistor, window, or curve. The lightpen is the prototype pick, and was developed in direct response to the user's needs to point at displayed objects.

A *button* is for selecting a *system defined* object such as an action to be performed or a character to be entered. Prototypes for this device are the programmed function keyboard which typically contains 16 to 32 such buttons, and the alphanumeric keyboard, often with over 100 buttons.

A *locator* is used to indicate a location and/or orientation in the user's *conceptual drawing space*. It is typified by the tablet joystick, and mouse.

A *valuator* in contrast is a device to determine a single value in the *real number space*. A potentiometer is the classical valuator.

This section discusses our classification of devices, shows its usefulness in designing interaction languages, and suggests ways to overcome inherent device limitations.

A. Pick

In contradistinction to written language, interactive graphic language can accommodate picking without first naming the picked object. This gives graphic language a unique power, and is also responsible for some of the data structuring problems and opportunities which are distinctive to graphics.

Nearly every graphics program either requires or allows the user to indicate displayed objects so they can be operated upon. But not every graphics terminal has a lightpen. How can physical devices other than picks be used to pick?

A locator is used to move a cursor close to the object of interest. Then the cursor's position is compared to that of each displayed object. Whichever is closest to the cursor is picked. Implemented in software [22], this process can be slow if many objects are displayed. When done with hardware [23], [24], there is no perceivable delay.

Three buttons can be used to simulate a pick. Each displayed entity is successively increased in intensity for a short period. When the entity to be picked brightens, the user activates one button. In the brief moment between the entity's brightening and the responding button activation several subsequent entities are likely to have brightened, so the second button is used to reverse the brightening sequence, one step at a time. When the correct entity is again brightened, the user activates the third button, and proceeds. This brightening method has been successfully used to pick a single molecular bond from several thousand on the screen---a case where the proximity of individual bonds precludes use of any other method. It is also a useful pick in stereoscopic three-dimensional displays [25].

A group of buttons (such as a keyboard) can be used as a pick. If names (either numeric or alphanumeric) are displayed next to each entity, the user need only type the name of the entity to be picked. By restricting the names of numerics, a valuator with sufficient resolution to specify any name could be used in place of the buttons.

These last two examples may seem farfetched. They do illustrate the interchangeability of devices through suitable software.

Picks are often used with a hierarchical picture structure, allowing the user to pick a basic object (like a house window), a collection of basic objects (all the windows in a particular house) are perhaps a collection of collections (all the windows in all the houses). A pick has no inherent notion of hierarchy, yet the user's intent must somehow be made known to the machine.

The best way to achieve this is to design the action language so that the intent can be inferred from the current state phase without explicit action. If this is impossible, then the action language must provide the user explicit means for conveying his purpose.

Commands like "move window" and "move house's windows" illustrate such means. If the hierarchical level at which the user operates is changed relatively infrequently, continuity can be better preserved with a separate command to set the level at which all ensuing picks will be made. The user respecifies the level whenever necessary.

If the number of hierarchical levels is unknown to the system designer and is potentially large, as in a drafting system where "templates" can be defined as containing other templates as well as basic objects like lines, points, and arcs, another approach is necessary. Two user commands are required: "travel up the hierarchy," and "come back down." When the user picks something, the system intensifies the lowest level object seen. If this is what the user wanted to pick he can proceed. If not, he uses the first of the two commands, "travel up the hierarchy." The entire first level object, of which the detected object is a part, is intensified. Either this is what he wants, or he travels up again and still more of the picture is intensified. If he should accidentally travel too far up the hierarchy, the "come back down" command will cause a step back down the hierarchy each time it is used.

B. Button

Buttons are ubiquitous in graphics applications. They are used to enter text by providing for selection among characters in a prespecified alphabet, and to specify an action command by selecting among alternative commands specified by the application program. The switch on most lightpens is often used as a button to tell the system that the picked entity is now to be operated upon, or that the tracking cross is now positioned at its final location. Switches on tablet styli are used in a like manner.

If commands are selected with a function keyboard, either single or multiple physical keys (a chord) can be used to invoke a command. Coded overlays, if available, can further expand the number of distinct buttons provided. So that at least trained users can enter some commands without looking away from the display and losing visual continuity; the most frequently used commands should be assigned to keys clustered in an area where they can be located by feel. If several overlays must be used, careful assignment of commands to overlays can minimize overlay changes. Commands which are frequently used together should be grouped together on an overlay. The goal should be to have no more than one overlay per phase of the interactive application, even after accommodating the small nucleus of often-used commands which are made available on every overlay. These latter commands are of course always invoked with the same key to avoid confusion.

A pick such as a lightpen can be used to simulate physical buttons. A "menu" of system-defined "light buttons" is displayed. The pen is used to pick the desired action from the collection of alternatives. The selection can also be effected by using a locator to move the cursor close to a light button. Even a valuator can be used as a button activator, by indicating a numeric value which has been associated with each button.

Menus can be used in two ways. Fig. 4 shows one which has temporarily replaced whatever had been displayed, while Fig. 5 shows one displayed with other material. Its items are more abbreviated than those in the first example, but are always displayed. With the first method the buttons can be more self-explanatory, but the user may be forced to frequently flip back and forth between the menu and his application display, destroying visual continuity.

If the interaction language has more commands than the screen has space for light buttons, the frequently used commands can be assigned to light buttons, with the remaining commands relegated to physical buttons. Otherwise, a hierarchical selection can be made. A command category is selected from an initially displayed menu, and the desired specific command is chosen from the subsequently displayed menu. Compared to function keyboards, a category is an

```
SET END POINTS
SET INPUT VALUES
ORIENTATION - WITHOUT FORCE
ORIENTATION - WITH FORCE
DIRECT LINEAR FORCE
INVERSE LINEAR FORCE
DIRECT SQUARE FORCE
INVERSE SQUARE FORCE
DIRECT CUSE FORCE
INVERSE CUSE FORCE
VELOCITY DEPENDENT FORCE
PERPENDICULAR VELOCITY DEPENDENT FD
ARBITRARY CHARGE DISTRIBUTION
CAPACITOR
DIODE
TRIODE
NUCLEAR FORCE
TWO PLANETS
PLANE CAPACITOR
CYLINDRICAL CAPACITOR
SPHERICAL CAPACITOR
METER-FINE
METER-COARSE
SET INPUT VALUES
CHANGE PROPORTIONALITY CONSTANT
DOUBLE PROPORTIONALITY CONSTANT
HALVE PROPORTIONALITY CONSTANT
REPULSIVE FORCE
ATTRACTIVE FORCE
FIND POSITION OF GROPE DEVICE
TERMINATE
```

Fig. 4. Full-screen menu.

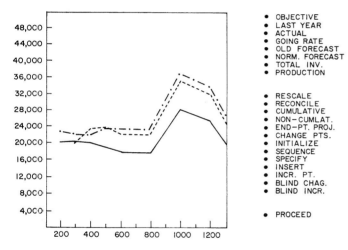

Fig. 5. Partial-screen menu.

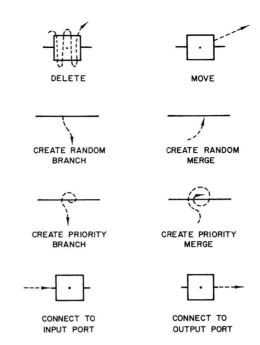

Fig. 6. Movements recognized as buttons.

overlay, and a command is a key. This has the advantage over keyboards that the changing buttons are immediately seen at or near a point of visual focus, and the user need not interrupt his thinking to change overlays.

A good way to cope with a large number of commands is to follow the state notion suggested in Section III and display light buttons for only those commands which the current state will accept. Analogously with keyboards, frequently used light buttons should always be displayed in the same place.

A powerful use of locators is to recognize certain combinations or sequences of movements as button activations. In the system whose state diagram was outlined in Section II, a small and hence easily recognized set of just seven specialized motions (symbols) is used. Some of their meanings are "delete," "move," "create branch," and "create priority branch." The latter two meanings are specialized to the queuing networks for whose design and analysis the system is meant. The motions are shown in Fig. 6 as dotted lines, with the entities operated upon shown as solid lines. Because the motions are made with the lightpen while pointing at the element to be operated upon, both the command and operand are simultaneously specified!

In the more general case, the set of symbols accepted might include all the alphanumerics, along with punctuation and control (erase, insert) characters or motions. On-line character recognizers were described as early as 1964 [26]-[28]. They are easily used in a minicomputer satellite or in a responsive time-sharing system. Program and data typically occupy less than 4000 bytes. Their input rate is not limited by computation time for recognition, but rather by the need for a pause between each character so that the end of the character is clearly detected. The pause can be as little as 300 s, a small burden for the average user.

Character input with a tablet and recognizer has several advantages. No typing skills are required, tactile continuity is preserved, and it is faster than selecting characters from a displayed keyboard. Furthermore, a character's position is implicit upon entry: no cursor need be positioned first.

The work of Negroponte on inference making, reported elsewhere in this special issue, is in some ways an extension of character recognition. The notion is that a graphics system should be able to infer a user's intent by measuring parameters such as his speed in performing actions, or how firmly he presses with a stylus while entering a sketch. For example, a slowly and firmly drawn line is likely meant to exactly trace whatever path the stylus followed, while a nearly straight path traversed quickly and lightly is probably meant to be a straight line. In this particular example, one of two virtual buttons is being activated as a function of spatial, temporal, and pressure inputs. At the same time, the positions needed by either command have also been recorded.

C. Locator

While the prototype locators are joysticks and tablets, the lightpen with its tracking cross is perhaps the more frequently used. The tracking cross consists of a number of individual entities arranged as a cross. When one or more of these entities are picked by the pen, the cross is moved as a unit so as to continue to be picked by the pen. Details of tracking algorithms are discussed in several reference works [22], [29].

Important tracking considerations are tracking initiation, speed, and loss. To start tracking, the cross must be on the screen. It might always be displayed at the screen's boundary, or a raster scan of the screen (using dots, letters, or lines) can be used to find the pen's position. The cross is then displayed beneath the pen, enhancing visual and tactile continuity by not forcing the user to look for and move to the cross.

The speed at which the cross can move with the lightpen must accommodate fast hand movements. A pen velocity of 10 in/s seems slow (try it), while 50 in/s seems quite fast. Prince [29] suggests that 25 in/s velocity is sufficient. If tracking is "lost" because the tracking algorithm cannot keep up with the pen's motion, the user may want the option to resume tracking by moving the pen back to the cross. Alternatively, another raster scan can be used to relocate the pen. If it cannot be found, the user has presumably removed it from the screen as an implicit signal that the cross is at its intended position.

In lieu of a pick or conventional locator, buttons can be easily used. With just four buttons, a cursor can be moved up, down, left, and right. Continuous button depression can be used to cause rapid continuous cursor movement, with a short activation causing a unit move. This method is attractive to preserve tactile continuity if the action language is keyboard-oriented.

A tablet with cursor feedback is usually a convenient locator, but accurately specifying a position to within a hundredth of an inch or more, as may be required in precise engineering applications, is difficult. Positioning accuracy can be helped by displaying, in numeric form, the cursor's current position in the application's coordinate system. If necessary, the area in which a position is to be marked can be scaled up. This means a unit move of the cursor in display coordinates can correspond to a much finer unit in application coordinates, and will work well if the user can maintain his orientation while viewing a very small part of his drawing space. If not, a keyboard of buttons can be used to enter pairs or triples of valuators, thus providing whatever resolution is needed.

Locators have dimensionality. They can, depending on their design, locate positions in one, two, or three dimensions. Moreover, some can even represent orientation of a rigid body, providing six dimensions corresponding to, for example, x, y, z, pitch, roll, and yaw. Furthermore, they can represent orientation of articulated bodies exhibiting even higher dimensionality. For example, seven dimensions are provided by a manipulator arm of the type used in handling radioactive materials. The hand represents a rigid body, articulated to provide "pinch." One such device also provides force output in all seven dimensions [30], [31].

D. Valuators

Graphics applications often require the user to enter numeric values which are unrelated to the drawing space. A resistor's value, Young's modulus for a beam and a shock absorber's damping factor are all examples.

While a potentiometer or a single axis of a joystick or tablet can be used directly as a low resolution valuator, other devices can simulate one. A keyboard of either physical buttons or light buttons can be used to form a digit string. One of the variety of dials and scales illustrated in Fig. 7 can be displayed.

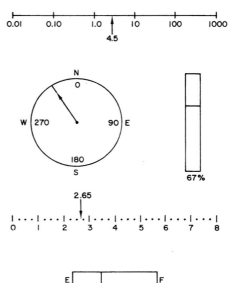

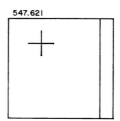

Fig. 7. Scales and dials.

Fig. 8. Light handle.

A lightpen is then used to manipulate them in various ways, such as dragging the pointer to a new position or picking a new tick mark on the scale. The usefulness of any of these valuators is often enhanced by displaying in numeric form whatever value is currently indicated. All such gauges or dials should be laid out in a natural way. We usually associate left to right, bottom to top, or clockwise movements with in creased values, and the opposite directions with decreased values [18].

An interesting approach is found in Newman's "light handle" [32]. A lightpen tracking cross, a number, and a work area (perhaps 2 or 3 in square) are displayed as shown in Fig. 8. To change the number, the cross is moved with the lightpen.

Upward movements of the cross cause the number to increase; downward, decrease. Movements in the left part of the work area cause larger changes than movements in the right part. Horizontal movements have no effect on the value. "All vertical movements, except those in the right-hand column cause changes proportional to the square of the change in y. In the right-hand column, the number's changes are proportional to the change in y, so that a "fine tuning" mechanism exists. Clockwise circular motions of the cross result in an increased value; counterclockwise, decreased.

Newman nicely summarizes the concept's usefulness:

"The principal asset of the Light Handle is that it provides the programmer with a shaft encoder without the expense of extra hardware. It also offers him a number of advantages over the typewriter which compensate for its relative slowness. For example, it avoids the need to check each character for validity; limits can easily be set on the displayed value; and the value may be incremented by any desired step size. It has the added advantage to the user of not diverting his attention from the display screen. For these reasons it appears to be a valuable tool for the display programmer."

An important consideration with valuators, as with locators, is their limited resolution. The light handle illustrated one way of overcoming the problem. Another useful approach for potentiometers (usually limited to 10 or 12 bits of accuracy) is to use the potentiometer's rate of change to specify a value. A displayed number can be "cranked up" by alternating fast clockwise rotations to cause large increases in the number with slow counter clockwise rotations to cause only small decreases. The counterclockwise rotations are unnecessary if the potentiometer can be continually rotated in one direction. Homing in on a final value is done with a slow rotation.

E. Utility of the Virtual Device Concept

The real usefulness of virtual devices far transcends the mere recognition that user interaction devices can be neatly categorized. There are several important advantages to writing application programs in terms of virtual picks, buttons, locators, and valuators, and using a few basic routines to couple the virtual devices to a terminal's physical devices.

Most important from this paper's viewpoint is the attendant flexibility of interchanging one physical device for another, thus facilitating easy experimentation and optimization of those interaction language aspects related to visual and tactile continuity. While any physical device can be used as any one or more virtual devices, such experimentation is necessary because physical devices are not necessarily psychologically equivalent and interchangeable. To be sure, they can be substituted, but often at the cost of additional user compensation and self-training, which increase the psychological distance between man and computer. Such experimentation, which we call human factors fine tuning, would not be necessary were the design of interaction languages an exacting science rather than somewhat of an art form. But is not, and once a poorly designed interaction language is embedded in an application program, fine tuning can be slow and expensive, and may not even get done. The authors know of a drafting system which took 18 man-months to develop and debug, and another 18 man-months to refine and enhance the human factors. Using virtual devices can help reduce these fine-tuning costs, and in addition can simplify accommodation of individual user preferences for different physical devices.

Virtual devices are crucial to transportability of graphics programs between terminals with dissimilar physical devices. This much-neglected consideration has forced many new users of graphics to reinvent already existing wheels, thus contributing to already high costs.

That the proposed classification is reasonable is testified to by Cotton [33], who proposed essentially identical schema for use in a computer network.

The basic concept of virtual devices is simply the concept of device independence, as exemplified by the independence most operating systems allow between logical files and physical storage. In the graphics area, the first effort in this direction was by Newman [21] who postulated a group of seven user input categories: text strings with and without embedded carriage return, decimal and octal valuators, pick, locator, and keyboard push buttons. These are all subsumed by our picks, buttons, locators, and valuators.

V. CONCLUSION

Many aspects of human factors design in graphics which do not bear directly upon enhancing conversational qualities of discourse through improved naturalness were deliberately omitted. Specifically excluded have been the factors involved in the physical design of the hardware devices. These have long been the traditional province of "human factors" specialists. Also excluded is the separable but nonetheless important influence of software and hardware architecture on responsiveness, availability, reliability, and cost of graphic interaction. Very little attention was given to the formal syntactic design of picture or display languages, the specific language used to communicate from the machine to the user, and its relation to semantics. Finally, the subject of perception enhancement, particularly regarding three-dimensional objects, is a major separate topic necessarily ignored here.

The study and design of graphic man-machine conversation is a fledgling discipline. There is a large body of lore dealing with specific techniques for specific problems, but there have been few guiding rules and principles. This paper has surveyed that lore and has attempted to construct a perspective to encourage the development of such guiding rules and principles. The heritage of natural spoken language and its conventions has been used as a model to judge graphic man-machine communication. Hopefully, the structures offered for exploiting that model in the design of graphic language conventions will prove useful.

A designer of conversational graphic systems should be concerned with: guaranteeing *complete* and *efficient* discourse, reducing the psychological distance by avoiding unnecessary *trauma*, improving the naturalness of the discourse by imposing syntactic regularity on the action language (notably, *sentence structuring* and *continuity*), using the *logical equivalences* among action devices to exploit their *psychological differences*, and choosing *implementation* of action language constructs to suit the context.

The idea of *sentence structuring* for graphics systems appears to be the most fruitful new principle presented here.

REFERENCES

[1] C. L. Barnhart, Ed., *The American College Dictionary*. New York: Wise & Co., 1952.
[2] H. Sackman, *Computers, System Science, and Evolving Society*. New York: Wiley, 1967.
[3] G. D. Hornbuckle, "The computer graphics user/machine interface," *IEEE Trans Hum. Factors Electron.*, vol. HFE-8, pp. 17-20. Mar. 1967.
[4] W. J. Hansen, "User engineering principles for interactive systems," in *1971 Fall Joint Computer Conf., AFIPS Conf.*, Proc., vol. 39. Montvale, N. J.: AFIPS Press, 1971, pp. 523-532.
[5] K. B. Irani and V.L. Wallace, "On network linguistics and the conversational design of queuing networks," *J. Ass. Comput. Mach.*, vol. 18, pp. 616-629, Oct. 1971.
[6] R. B. Miller, "Response time in man-computer conversational transaction," in *1968 Fall Joint Computer Conf., AFIPS Conf. Proc.*, vol. 33, pt. 1. Montvale, N. J.: AFIPS Press, 1968, pp. 267-277.
[7] E. L. Jacks, "A laboratory for the study of graphical man-machine communications," in *1964 Fall Joint Computer Conf., AFIPS*

Conf., Proc., vol. 26. Montvale, N. J.: AFIPS Press, 1968, pp. 363-386.

[8] K. B. Irani, V.L. Wallace, and J.H. Jackson, "Conversational design of stochastic service systems from a graphical terminal," in *Proc. Of the 1970 Int. Symp. On Computer Graphics*, R. D. Parslow and R. E. Green, Eds. New York: Plenum, 1971, pp. 91-107.

[9] B. Fried, "On the user's point of view," in *Interactive Systems for Experimental Applied Mathematics*. M. Klerer and J. Reinfields, Eds. New York: Academic Press 1968, pp. 11-21.

[10] W. V. Wright, "An interactive computer graphic system for molecular studies," Ph.D. dissertation. Dep. Comput. Sci., Univ. of North Carolina, Chapel Hill, 1972.

[11] ____, "The two dimensional interface of an interactive system for molecular studies," *SIGPLAN Notic.*, vol.7, pp. 76-84, Oct. 1972.

[12] A. P. Armit, "A language for interactive shape design," in *Graphic Languages*, F. Nake and A. Rosenfeld, Eds. Amsterdam, The Netherlands: North-Holland, 1972, pp. 369-380.

[13] J. Martin, *Design of Man-Computer Dialogues*. Englewood Cliffs, N. J.: Prentice Hall, 1973.

[14] J. Barmack and H. Sinaiko, "Human factors problems in computer-generated graphic displays," Inst. for Defense Analysis Study, CFSTI ASTIA Doc. AD636170, Vol. 5-234, Apr. 1966.

[15] R. L. Gregory, *The Intelligent Eye*. New York: McGraw-Hill, 1970.

[16] J. J. Batter and F. P. Brooks, Jr., "GROPE-1: A computer display to the sense of feel," in *Proc. 1971 IFIP Congr.*, booklet TA-7, pp. 135-140.

[17] A. M. Noll, "Man-machine tactile communication," Ph.D. dissertation, Dep. Elec. Eng., Polytech. Inst. of Brooklyn, Brooklyn, N. Y., 1971.

[18] E. J. McCormick, "Visual displays," in *Human Engineering*. New York: McGraw-Hill, 1957, ch.4.

[19] W. R. Sutherland, "The on-line graphical specification of computer procedures," Ph.D. dissertation, Dep. Elec. Eng., M.I.T., Cambridge, 1966.

[20] W. K. English, D. C. Engelbart, and M. L. Berman, "Display-selection techniques for text manipulation," *IEEE Trans. Hum. Factors Electron.*, vol. HFE-8, pp. 5-15, Mar. 1967.

[21] W. M. Newman, "A system for interactive graphical programming," in *1968 Spring Joint Computer Conf., AFIPS Conf. Proc.*, vol. 32. Montvale, N. J.: AFIPS Press, 1968, pp. 47-54.

[22] W. M. Newman and R. F. Sproull, *Principles of Interactive Computer Graphics*. New York: McGraw-Hill, 1973.

[23] R. F. Sproull and I. E. Sutherland, "A clipping divider," in *1968 Fall Joint Computer Conf., AFIPS Conf. Proc.*, vol. 33. Montvale, N. J.: AFIPS Press, 1968, pp. 765-775.

[24] K. H. Konkle, "An analog comparator as a pseudo-light pen for computer displays," *IEEE Trans. Comput.* (Short Notes), vol. C-17, pp. 54-55, Jan. 1968.

[25] A. Ortony, "A system for stereo viewing," *Comput. J.*, vol. 14, pp. 140-149, May 1971.

[26] M. Bernstein, "Computer recognition of on-line, handwritten characters," Rand Corp. Rep. RM-3753-ARPA, 1964.

[27] R. M. Brown, "On-line computer recognition of handprinted characters," *IEEE Trans. Electron. Comput.* (Short Notes), vol. EC-13, pp. 750-752, Dec. 1964.

[28] W. Teitelman, "Real-time recognition of hand-printed characters," in *1964 Fall Joint Computer Conf., AFIPS Conf. Proc.*, vol. 26. Washington, D. C.: Spartan, 1964, pp.559-575.

[29] M. D. Prince, *Interactive Graphics for Computer-Aided Design*. Reading, Mass.: Addison Wesley, 1971.

[30] F. P. Brooks, Jr., "An investigation of a system for displaying computer outputs to the kinesthetic sense: 1970-1971 progress report," Comput. Sci. Dep., Univ. of North Carolina, Chapel Hill, 1971.

[31] J. J. Capowski, "Remote manipulators as a computer input device," M. S. thesis, Dep. Comput. Sci., Univ. of North Carolina, Chapel Hill, 1971.

[32] W. M. Newman, "A graphical technique for computer input," *Comput. J.*, vol. 11, pp. 63-64, May 1968.

[33] I. Cotton, "Network graphic attention handling," in *Online 72 Int. Conf.* (Brunel Univ., Uxbridge, England, Sept. 1972), pp. 465-490.

PAINT

Alvy Ray Smith
Lucasfilm
San Rafael, CA 94912

Introduction

Paint is a menu-driven computer program for handpainting two-dimensional images in full color. It is a highly interactive software package with which a human artist may employ the power of a digital computer to compose paintings that are entirely of his own creation. The "canvas" is actually a large piece of digital computer memory that is displayed for the artist on a conventional color television monitor. His "brush" is an electronic stylus resembling an ordinary pen. Its shape can be any two-dimensional shape he desires, so long as it fits into the canvas memory space. He may choose any color he desires from a "palette" of 256 colors. If this is an inadequate selection, he may mix his own set of colors from a vast set of possibilities.

The main purpose of this tutorial is to describe in detail how an artist accomplishes these acts and what his choices are. In fact, the tutorial is designed to be read as a textbook for Paint users.

A secondary purpose is a careful description of a successful human-engineering design. Paint is designed to have a "natural feel" and to be readily usable by computer-naive people. There are detailed descriptions of the techniques which make this possible. A more computer-science oriented description of the equipment used by Paint can be found in [2].

Paint includes routines for defining and selecting brushes, automatic filling and clearing large areas, saving and restoring pictures, magnifying the canvas temporarily for detail work, and recording histories of picture composition. These functions will be described fully. Subsidiary routines available to the artist include such graphic aids as straight-line, ellipse, circle, and spline generators, mirroring, rotation, etc. These programs will not be described here, nor will be the large overseeing program, Bigpaint, of which Paint is a principal component. Bigpaint (see Figure 1) permits the artist to work on a canvas so large that it cannot all be displayed simultaneously. It will be described elsewhere

There have been several versions of Paint at NYIT (New York Institute of Technology). Each version exists or existed for a specific configuration of equipment. Appendix A gives the various configurations that have been tried, with appraisals of each.

One version of Paint represents increased sophistication rather than mere equipment reconfiguration. This version is called Paint3. It is superior to Paint described here in its use of 24 bits rather than 8 bits for representation of each point in the canvas memory. Appendix B explains the extension of Paint to Paint3.

Appendix C gives a brief history of painting programs, emphasizing those which most directly influenced Paint.

The Artist's View

An artist at a typical paint station (Figure 2) faces a color display, a menu display, and a tablet with its stylus. The *color display* is an RGB (red-green-blue) full-color standard television monitor. The *menu display* is a monochrome line-drawing monitor (sometimes called a "vector display" or a "calligraphic display"). The *tablet* is a flat, rectangular device that continually sends to the computer the current location of the tip of the stylus. The *stylus* resembles a pencil or ballpoint pen with a thin flexible wire connecting its top end to the computer. In fact, it is frequently called a *pen*. When a user presses the tip of the stylus (typically but not necessarily against the tablet surface), a switch closes and the stylus is said to be *in pressure*. The artist can feel this because the stylus moves through a short distance, its *throw,* as the switch closes. The state of this switch is continually fed to the computer. The tablet can also detect whether the stylus is near the tablet (*in proximity*) or not, and passes this information to the computer. So pen location and pen *status* are always available to Paint.

The artist would also find two devices of secondary importance to Paint: a keyboard for interaction with the system (e.g., to command the computer to start the Paint program) and a small monochrome monitor used for error display and other miscellaneous messages.

The artist starts Paint by typing "paint <return>" at the keyboard. He then takes up the stylus and begins tracking it on the menu display. *Tracking* is the process of sliding the stylus lightly over the tablet (in proximity but not in pressure) while watching a cursor on the display. The *cursor* is a small symbol indicating the position of the stylus. (The favored cursor at NYIT is an up-side-down V, or arrowhead, its apex the sensitive point.) Other computer programs ensure that every time the stylus

```
paint                              current window switch
                                   state of the world
create canvas
open canvas                        write all rough
delete canvas                      write some rough

select window                      rotate
select grid window                 append
display window                     dissect
select & display
select & display grid              tablet mapping
                                   transparency switch
update window
update colormap                    exit
update transparency

display all
display all xparent
```

Figure 1. Bigpaint menu.

moves, so does the cursor on the menu display—in the same direction, at the same speed, and through a distance in direct proportion to that moved by the artist on the tablet. To him, the cursor movement appears to happen instantaneously. It feels to him as if the cursor is in direct, physical, mechanically rigid contact with the stylus. To complete the illusion, when he lifts the stylus off the tablet, the cursor disappears.

Frequently I have found that, to the uninitiated, tracking seems unnatural, since "you can't see your hands." If the cursoring routines are written as described above, tracking begins to feel natural within two to five minutes after first exposure. Children and professional artists have all adapted to it quickly. A benefit derived from separating the eye focus from the finger focus is that one's hands are never in the way while painting.

Paint is designed so that the artist never has to lay down the stylus (e.g., to type at the keyboard) once he has entered the program. This not only maintains the flow of the interaction but is convenient for using Paint in darkened rooms, where hand placement on an ill-illuminated keyboard is difficult.

When entered, Paint first displays its *menu* on the menu display. A typical menu is shown in Figure 3 with the cursor in an arbitrary position. It is a list of *buttons* of which only the labels are visible. The artist "pushes a button" by moving the cursor over the label he wants and pressing down momentarily on the stylus.

The sequence of events initiated by pushing the "full paint" button will be described in detail below. "Full paint" is the regular painting mode—nothing fancy. The many variations on basic painting will be described briefly afterwards.

Immediately upon a push of the "full paint" button a *palette* appears on the color monitor that serves to display the artist's canvas. The palette is a display of the 256 currently available colors (see Figure 4). (Paint3 has more than 16 million currently available colors, an improvement with many consequences. See Appendix B.) Although only 256 colors are available at any one time they are selected from a colorspace comprised of over 68 billion colors—more than a human can distinguish. The *colorspace* is a perceptual continuum of colors for practical purposes. How the artist makes his selection from this colorspace will be described later.

The appearance of the palette is a cue to the artist that he can select a color to paint with. He may choose a color from the palette or from anywhere on the color display. As soon as he chooses a color, the palette disappears.

He makes the color selection with the following procedure: He begins tracking in the color display by sliding the stylus from one half of the tablet to the other half. On the displays, this action appears as a movement of the cursor from the menu display to the color display. (Other arrangements are required for some of the configurations discussed in Appendix A.) He positions the cursor over the desired color and presses down momentarily to complete color selection.

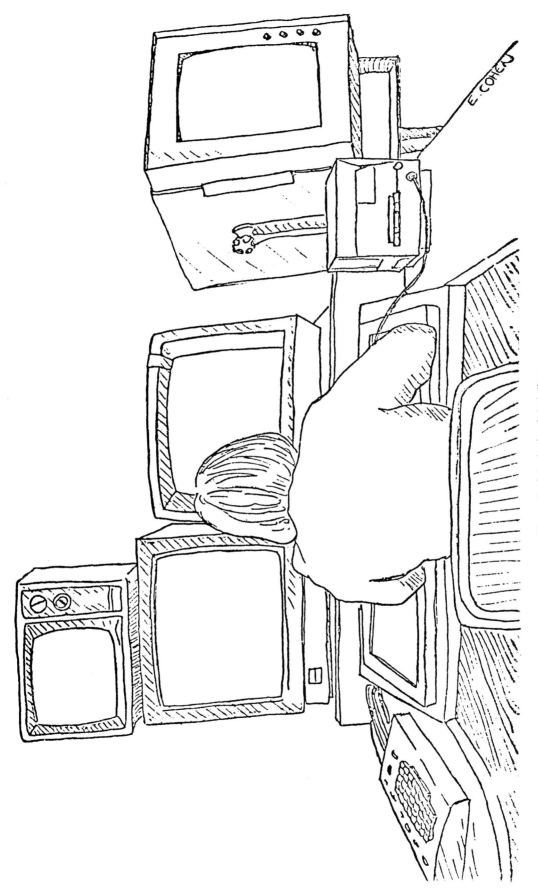

Figure 2. A typical paint station.

```
full paint              save picture
cycle paint             get picture
tint paint
value paint             color maker
picture paint           get colormap
filter paint
                        palette
                        magnify
sketch                  cursor

pick brush              history
make brush
                        remove
fill
tint fill               run any program

full clear              redraw menu
clear window            exit
```

Figure 3. Paint menu.

He makes the color selection with the folowing procedure: He begins tracking the color display by sliding the stylus from one half of the tablet to the other half. On the displays, this action appears as a movement of the cursor from the menu display to the color display. (Other arrangements are required for some of the configurations discussed in Appendix A.) He positions the cursor over the desired color and presses down momentarily to complete color selection.

The palette's disappearance is a cue to the artist that he may proceed to paint. However, should he desire a new color, he may call up the palette again, with a simple flick of the wrist, by momentarily sliding (no pressure) the cursor off-screen below the color display. We henceforth assume the reader identifies a cursor movement on the displays with the simultaneous and "similar" stylus movement on the tablet.

The artist "paints" with his chosen color by moving the cursor to the desired position and then pressing down while moving the stylus. Painting begins with pressure and ends with release of pressure on the stylus. This constitutes one *stroke*. While painting a stroke (with stylus in pressure), he may move the stylus off-screen in any direction without interrupting the stroke. At the end of a stroke the artist is again tracking in the color display. He may begin a new stroke, select a new color (by sliding off-screen-below), or return to the menu display (by sliding off-screen toward the menu display).

What the artist sees while painting a stroke is a succession of copies of a *brush* he has previously selected with the "pick brush" menu button (see below). For example, a brush might be a disk about one-half inch in diameter. It can, in fact, be any picture that use of Paint can produce, but artists do not use the very large brushes because they make painting too slow. The copies of the brush are written into the color display so rapidly as to appear to flow onto the screen. The brush is always written into the display in the color previously chosen. Figure 5 shows some typical strokes and the brushes used to make them.

To select a different brush or to exercise any of a number of other options, the artist returns to the menu by sliding off-screen toward the menu display. A return to the menu erases the palette if it is visible. Thus, the palette is never left in the color display to mar the composition.

Options Available

This completes our brief description of basic painting behavior in Paint. We will now list the sixteen options available and the menu buttons used to elicit them. Then we will describe the ten available variations on simple painting.

make brush

As indicated, the artist may define a brush of arbitrary shape. He does this by painting the desired brush shape, then pressing the "make brush" button. The menu is erased and a keyboard drawn in its place. The computer then instructs him to name the brush. (All instructions are displayed in the menu display.) He "types" on the keyboard by moving the menu display cursor over the desired key and pressing down momentarily (Figure 6). The "done" key indicates the end of the name and causes issuance of the next instruction.

This next instruction is a request for a window around the desired brush. A *window* is a rectangular subset of the color of display plus an *origin*, a point which may be thought of as where the stylus is to be attached to the brush. The artist designates the window by sliding to the color display and selecting a lower-left corner, an upper-right corner, and an origin, much as he chooses a color when painting. He slides the cursor to the desired location and presses down momentarily.

As cued, the cursor changes shape. First, it is L-shaped to indicate lower-left corner selection. This is replaced by the upper-right corner cursor, which is the L-shaped cursor rotated 180 degrees around the intersection of the two arms of the L. And this is replaced by the standard arrowhead or triangle cursor described previously for origin designation.

The final step in brush creation is the specification of a transparent color. This is a color in the chosen window which is not to be displayed as part of the brush. The reappearance of the Paint menu is the cue that "make brush" has been completed.

Figure 4. 256-color palette in a typical position.

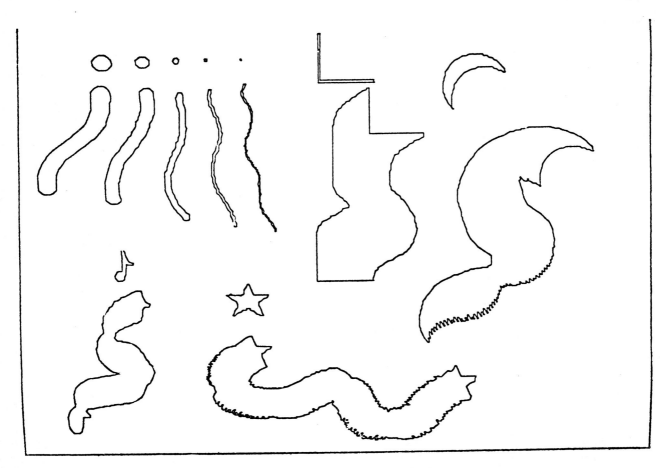

Figure 5. Several brushes and strokes created with them.

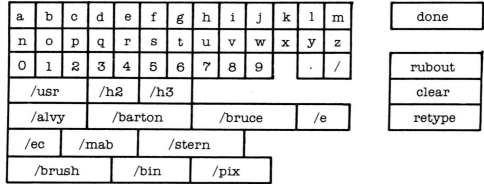

Figure 6. The virtual keyboard.

pick brush

Whenever an artist creates a brush (see "make brush"), its name is added to a list. When the artist presses the "pick brush" button, his action erases the Paint menu and displays this list in the menu display instead (Figure 7). He selects the brush he desires by name in the usual way (by sliding the cursor over the name and pressing down momentarily). The next time he paints, the selected brush will be used. Redisplay of the Paint menu signals completion of this operation.

color maker

The artist may mix his own palette of 256 colors with the set of routines invoked by this button. He can change the color of each *paint pot* in the palette directly by varying each pot's red, green, and blue primary components or indirectly by varying its hue, saturation, and value. The algorithms used are described in [1].

Routines provide for setting the colors of several paint pots simultaneously (Figure 8). For example, the first twenty paint pots might be set to a linearly spaced set of colors varying smoothly from red to blue (Figure 9). Or the first ten colors could be reversed in order.

Once the artist has the palette set up as desired, he usually saves it for future use. "Color maker" provides a means for saving the set of colors assigned to the paint pots of the palette. The artist supplies a name (as in "make brush"), and the current set of colors is saved in the auxiliary memory of the computer (as a disk file). These saved sets of colors are called *colormaps*. Redisplay of the Paint menu signifies a return from "color maker" to Paint.

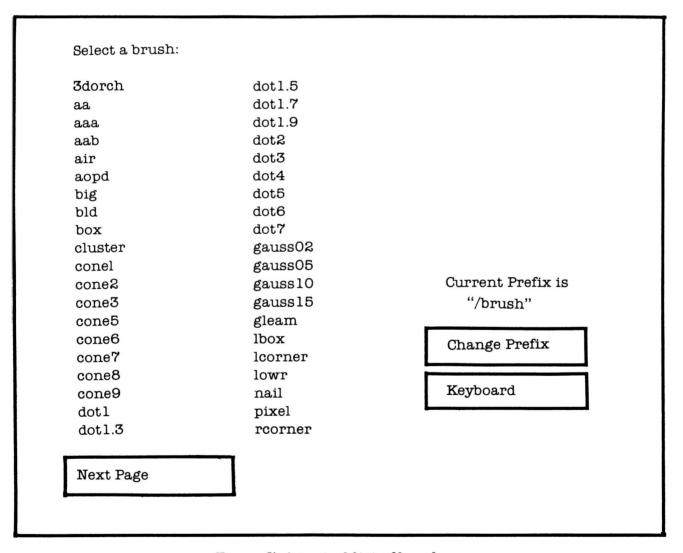

Figure 7. A typical list of brushes.

```
set one RGB          split range RGB
set one HSV          split range HSV
set range RGB
set range HSV        fly RGB

number switch
palette switch

get colormap
save colormap

match color

return
```

Figure 8. Color maker menu.

get colormap

Most often, an artist chooses a new set of palette colors by selecting a colormap previously defined and saved (see "color maker"). The "get colormap" button provides the colormap selection facility, which is similar to "pick brush." A list of available colormaps is displayed, and the artist selects one. The signal for completion of this operation is a sudden change of colors in the color display (as the new colormap replaces the old) and a redisplay of the Paint menu.

full clear

To initialize the color display or to erase its contents, the artist selects "full clear" from the menu. It causes a palette to appear in the color display, the cue that the artist is to select a color, as in the regular painting mode, "full paint." The color display is completely cleared to this color. After each clear, the palette reappears so that the artist can clear again to a different color if he so desires. He signals Paint that he is finished with clearing by sliding back to the menu, which causes the palette to disappear from the color display.

clear window

This button is similar to "full clear" except that it requires a window to be specified in the color display (see "make brush"). Only this window is cleared to the specified color.

save picture

At any time the artist may wish to permanently save his painting, either as a finished piece or as a safeguard. "Save picture" causes all of the current color display or a window of it to be saved as a disk file. The operation is very similar to "make brush," since a brush is just a little picture. This operation, however, is slightly more powerful than "make brush," for in one step it allows the artist to save the current colormap with the current picture. It also allows him to specify any number of transparent colors, whereas "make brush" allows only one. The Paint menu is redisplayed to signify completion of picture saving.

get picture

Any picture saved with "save picture" (or with "make brush") can be recalled into the color display with this button. The menu display offers a list of pictures, and selection proceeds as in "pick brush." When the artist has selected picture name, Paint asks him where he wants the picture to be restored. (This query appears in the menu display, as do all text messages.) The artist indicates the location of the picture origin by sliding to the color display and pressing down momentarily at the desired location. Or he may opt for the default origin location by simply sliding back to the menu display without pressing down. The *default origin* is that of the picture as it was originally saved. Thus, to restore to the same position a picture that originally filled the color display, the artist simply flicks his wrist toward the color display from the menu display. He is also given the options of changing the current colormap to that saved with the picture (if one was saved with it) or of leaving it unchanged. The Paint menu is redisplayed at the end of this operation.

cursor

This option selects the cursor displayed in the color display while the artist is tracking there in preparation for painting a stroke. Either the currently selected brush or the standard arrowhead may be used as a cursor. Whichever is the artist's choice remains in effect until he pushes the "cursor" button again. Redisplay of the Paint menu indicates completion of this choice.

magnify

To do detail work, the artist may magnify the color display by a factor of 1, 2, 4, or 8 (Figure 10). (A factor of 1 is equivalent to turning magnification off.) After he makes his selection, the Paint menu reappears. No magnification occurs until he pushes one of the "paint" buttons (e.g., "full paint").

The following modification of the basic painting behavior occurs: After the artist makes his color selection and the palette disappears, he is cued to select a portion of the color display for magnification. The cue is a box-shaped cursor, the size of the box depending on the magnification factor. The contents of the box is the portion of the color display that will be magnified to fill the entire screen when the artist presses down. Thus, he tracks the box-shaped cursor until it covers the portion he wishes to have magnified. Then he presses down momentarily to make the selection. The magnification occurs immediately.

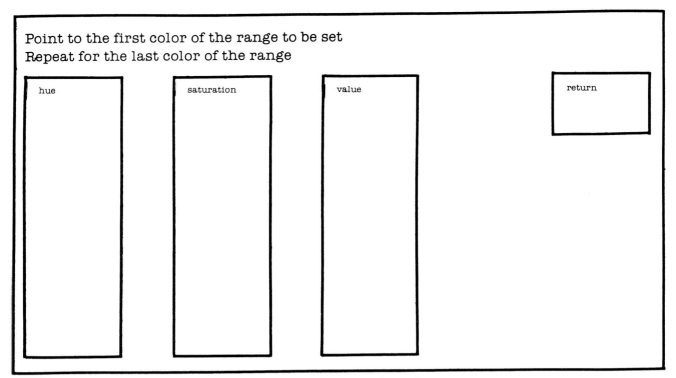

Figure 9. Sliders for setting color.

It is important to understand that this is only a temporary magnification that in no way alters the picture stored in the computer memory. The artist can proceed to paint on the magnified picture. The magnification occurs in such a way that his cursor does not change position during the magnification, and a motion of the stylus on the tablet corresponds to the same distance on the color display after magnification as before.

To demagnify, the artist either slides off-screen-below (which is also the signal for palette display) or off-screen toward the menu display (which is the signal for return to menu selection). This implies that he must remagnify (with the box-shaped cursor) after each color selection. He can opt for "constant" magnification, which does not demagnify for color selection. The disadvantage in doing so, however, is that the palette is not fully visible. Constant magnification, therefore, is only used when the colors of possible interest all lie within the magnified area. (Recall that a color may be selected from anywhere in the display, not just from the palette.)

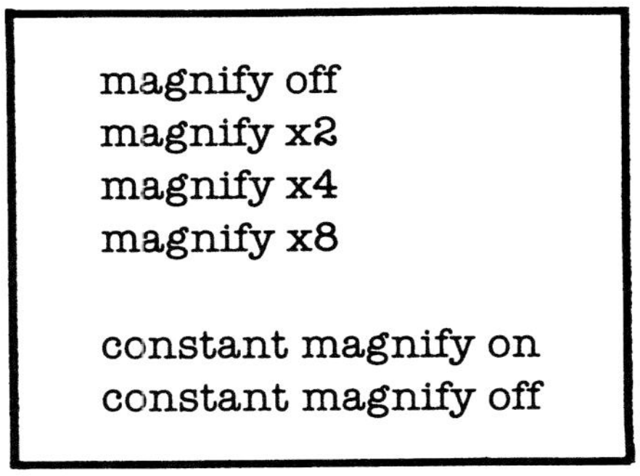

The magnification step is added to the basic painting behavior until the artist pushes the "magnify" button a second time and turns off magnification. The step is added to the behaviors required for all the "paints" and all the "fills" (see below).

sketch

This button invokes a set of routines which the artist may use to draw *antialiased,* or antijagged, curves or straight lines. A line drawn into a digital computer memory such as used by Paint will have an unpleasant "stairstep" appearance (see Figure 11). It is said to have the *jaggies*. "Sketch" uses a computer graphics technique which removes these unwanted jaggies for someone standing at a typical viewing distance. Figure 11 shows what the technique does to a jagged line in closeup.

"Sketch" also allows the artist to select the width of the "smooth" line he wishes to draw with. He draws with the chosen line width by sliding to the color display and stroking just as he would for painting. An antirastered stroke of the chosen width appears instead of a painted strip. He may not change the color of the line (see, however, the discussion of Paint3 in Appendix B). He returns to menu selection in Paint by simply sliding to menu display from the color display and

Figure 10. Magnify menu.

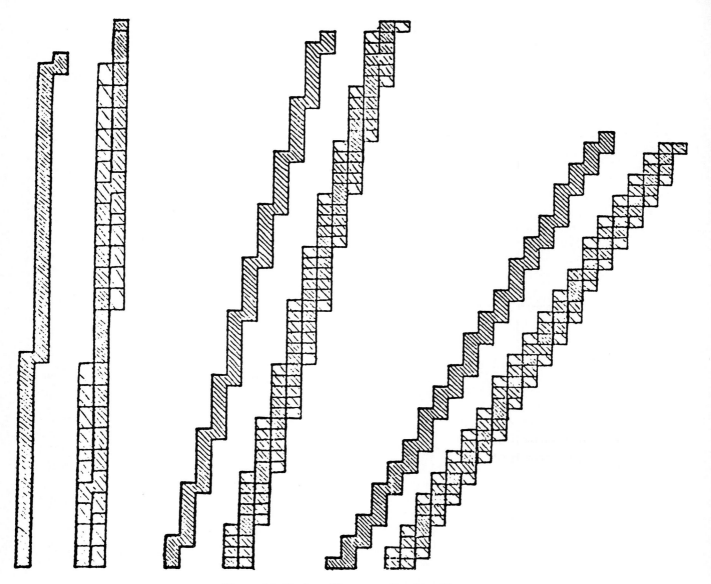

Figure 11. Rastered line vs. antirastered line.

pressing the "return" button of the sketch menu (Figure 12). Reappearance of the Paint menu signals an end to sketching.

fill

To change the color of an irregularly shaped area in the color display, the artist presses this button. The behavior expected of him is much like that for painting. A palette appears to cue color selection. Then, if magnification is on, the box-shaped cursor cues selection of the area to be magnified. But instead of painting a stroke, he selects a point in the area he wishes to fill with the new color. This point is called the *seedpoint*. The area is filled quickly using the algorithm explained in [2]. The artist may then fill another area with the same color or choose another color (as in "full paint," by sliding off-screen-below to cause palette display). Return to menu selection in Paint is the same as for "full paint."

```
smooth draw
smooth lines

change width

return
```

Figure 12. Sketch menu.

tint fill

This version of filling is more sophisticated than that used in "fill" in that it knows about antirastered lines (see "sketch"). It is used exactly like the version described in "fill," with two differences. The main difference the artist will notice is that in color selection, a restricted palette of only sixteen colors is displayed, because sixteen shades of each color are used to do the antirastering depicted in Figure 11, and 16 x 16 = 256, the total number of colors available at any one time. The restricted palette is called the *tint palette.* The other difference he will notice is a slower speed of filling. The more complex algorithm used by "tint fill" is described in [2].

palette

The "palette" menu (Figure 13) replaces the Paint menu when the artist presses this button. It allows him to select several options concerning the palette displayed for color selection (e.g., in "full paint," "fill," or "full clear"). Return to Paint menu selection is signaled by display of the Paint menu.

```
full palette
tint palette
value palette
standard palette
move palette

dot switch on
dot switch off
clear dots
```

Figure 13. Palette menu.

The artist uses the "move palette" button to change the location of the palette when it is displayed for color selection. Pressing this button causes the palette to appear in the color display. The artist moves the palette by sliding to the color display, selecting a point in the usual way, and aligning the palette so that its vertical position is the same as that of the point selected. It is centered horizontally at this position.

There are three types of palettes in Paint. The one most commonly used is the "full palette" of 256 paint pots used in "full paint." Another is the "tint palette" of sixteen colors used in "tint fill." The third is the "value palette," the sixteen shades that each of the sixteen colors in the tint palette may assume in antirastering (see "sketch"). The artist can force the display of any one of these palettes during color selection by pressing the corresponding button in this menu. The usual request, however, is "standard palette," which causes the display of the palette most appropriate to the situation (full palette for full paint, tint palette for tint fill, etc.).

Sometimes an artist finds it convenient to know exactly which colors he has selected in a painting. Keeping track of the last color used in a palette of 256 paint pots can be quite tedious. By pressing "dot switch on," the artist causes to be displayed on each paint pot a small dot corresponding to a color he picks during color selection, regardless of which routine he is performing. To turn off this option, he must press "palette" again and then press "dot switch off" in its menu. "Clear dots" removes all dots from a palette during color selection but does not turn off (or on) the dot option.

history

A *history* is a list of actions performed in Paint between two times selected by the artist. By pressing the "history" button, he can start the recording of such a history or stop it. These options are available to him on the "history" menu (Figure 14). When he starts the recording of a history, he is asked to supply a name for it. This name is added to a list of history names. From this moment until he returns to the history menu and presses the "cease recording history" button, the computer records each button he pushes, each brush he selects, each color he selects, each stroke he paints, etc. Thus, a history is a way of saving a painting permanently as well as the sequence of events which composed it.

```
begin history
cease history
playback history
return
```

Figure 14. History menu.

The artist can reconstruct a painting at a later time by pressing the "history" button in the Paint menu, then pressing the "playback history" button in the history menu. The computer will present him with a list of histories that have been recorded, from which he may select one in the usual way (see "pick brush"). The computer will then replay the exact sequence of events as they were recorded.

remove

Paint permanently stores in the computer disk memory as disk files: pictures, brushes, colormaps, and histories. The artist stores these items, and he can remove them by pressing this button. He requests which type of file he wishes to remove by pressing a button in the "remove" menu (Figure 15). A list of the files stored is displayed on the menu display, from which he may select one in the usual way (see "pick brush"). He is then asked to confirm the deletion before the file is

```
remove brush
remove picture
remove 3 picture
remove colormap
remove history
return
```

Figure 15. Remove menu.

actually deleted from the computer memory. He makes or does not make the confirmation by pressing yet another button on a two-item "confirmation" menu (Figure 16). The "return" button of the remove menu causes redisplay of the Paint menu.

```
push here to confirm deletion of
usr/h8/alvy/runcode/uuuuu


push here for no deletion
```

Figure 16. Confirmation menu.

Variations on Simple Painting

This concludes our brief overview of the options available to the artist in Paint to assist him while painting. To complete the survey of Paint options, we now list the variations on simple painting which are available to him. All the options listed above are, of course, available for these variations also.

cycle paint

"Cycle paint" is a simple variation on full paint, wherein the color of the brush is not constant but cycles through the paint pots in the palette. As each copy of the brush is laid down, the next color in the palette is used. The effect is a cycle of colors along the stroke instead of a constant color. No palette is displayed for cycle paint.

tint paint

In pictures composed with the special sixteen-tint colormaps mentioned above in "tint fill," tint painting can be used just like full painting, but only the tint of the paint selected is used to change only the tint of pixels under the brush. (A *pixel*, for picture element, is one point in the digital canvas used by Paint.) Pictures created with "sketch," for example, can be tint painted without destroying the antijaggied curves created by sketching. The standard palette for tint paint is the tint palette.

value paint

Value painting is the complement of tint painting. Only the value, or blackness, of the selected color is used, changing only the value of the pixels under the brush. The effect leaves the tints unchanged but varies their darkness to that of the color selected. The standard palette for value paint is the value palette.

picture paint

No palette is displayed for this type of painting because the brush is restored exactly as it was saved (see "make brush"). The effect is to "rubberstamp" the picture that is the brush along the path of the artist's stroke.

z picture paint

This is like "picture paint," except that a color in the brush is painted into the canvas space only if its position in the palette is greater than that of the color under it in the canvas space. (The positions of paint pots in a palette are assumed to be numbered; hence, there is a number associated with each color.) If the brush is a picture of a smooth-shaded sphere, for example, then z picture paint has the effect of intersecting the spheres with one another as they are laid down in the canvas space along the stroke.

tincture paint

This is a combination of "tint paint" and "picture paint." The tint is selected from the tint palette, the standard palette displayed for this option. Then the tints of all pixels in the brush are changed to the selected tint, and the resulting picture is picture painted into the canvas.

z paint

The full palette is displayed normally for this option. The color chosen is painted into the canvas space at only those pixels under the brush which contain colors with lower numbers (see "z picture paint"). The effect is to paint over some colors and under others.

filter paint

At every pixel in the canvas under the brush "filter paint" takes a weighted average of the 3 x 3 neighborhood of pixels originally there and writes that average into the central pixel. This average is formed from the numbers associated with the colors, i.e., their respective positions in the palette. The effect is dependent on the colormap currently in use. For colormaps composed of smooth ramps of color, the effect is to smooth rough edges. No palette is necessary for filter paint.

smear paint

Smearing is similar to filtering, but the local average is written into a pixel in the direction of motion of the artist's hand. The effect is to smear the canvas contents in the direction of motion. No palette is necessary.

slide paint

Slide paint is just like smear paint without averaging. The portion of the canvas under the brush is simply shifted in the direction of motion. Again no pallette is necessary.

REFERENCES

1. Alvy Ray Smith, "Color Gamut Transform Pairs," *Computer Graphics,* Vol. 12, No. 3, August 1978, pp. 12–19, (SIGGRAPH 78).

2. Alvy Ray Smith, "Tint Fill," *Computer Graphics,* Vol. 13, No. 2, August. 1979, pp. 276–283, (SIGGRAPH 79).

Figure 17. Author at work.

Appendix A: Equipment Configurations

Following is a list of various equipment configurations which have been used at New York Institute of Technology for painting stations, together with a brief analysis of each one.

I. line-drawing device: Evans and Sutherland (E&S) Picture System I
   tablet: Summagraphics 22" x 22"
   frame buffer: one E&S, 512 x 512 x 8 bits
   computer: one Digital Equipment Corporation (DEC) PDP 11/45
   remarks: one stand-alone station
   advantages: very sophisticated line-drawing device; stand alone
   disadvantages: only one station; Picture System monitor very noisy; only 8 bits; Picture System very expensive

II. line-drawing device: Tektronix 4014
   tablet: Summagraphics 16" x 30"
   frame buffer: six E&S, 512 x 512 x 8 bits (or, equivalently, two 512 x 512 x 24-bit RGB buffers)
   computer: DEC PDP 11/45 and 11/70 (one each)
   remarks: five time-shared stations
   advantages: double-width tablet feels "natural" and easy to explain; RGB frame buffers; several stations; cheap line-drawing device
   disadvantages: time-sharing and interactive tablet manipulation do not mix well; Tektronix 4014 flashes for screen clear

III. line-drawing device: 3 Rivers Graphic Wonder
   tablet: Talos 16" x 16"
   frame buffer: six E&S, 512 x 512 x 8 bits (=2 E&S RGB), and 12 Genisco, 512 x 512 x 8 bits (= 4 Genisco (RGB)
   computer: DEC PDP 11/34 (five of them)
   remarks: five stand-alone stations
   advantages: high-resolution tablet; no time-sharing; cheap, sophisticated, quiet line-drawing device; cheaper computer; RGB frame buffers
   disadvantages: slower computer

Equipment configuration I is no longer used, and II is being phased out.

Appendix B: Paint3, The RGB Version of Paint

Only 256 colors are available at any one time in Paint, although they can be selected from a vast number (4096^3) of possibilities and the selection can be changed very rapidly (by changing only the colormap). This limitation is due to there being only 8 bits per pixel. Paint3 assumes 24 bits per pixel—8 for red, 8 for green, and 8 for blue. The colormap mechanism is not used, or, equivalently, it is assumed fixed at a ramp—i.e., a direct mapping of pixel values into gun voltages (with perhaps a curve in the mapping to compensate for nonlinearities). Thus 256^3 colors are always available in Paint3. This large number of colors permits many types of painting not possible in Paint. Some of these are briefly described below:

tint paint

This is a true tint paint as opposed to that described for Paint, which required the use of special colormaps. The tint of the color chosen to paint with is extracted using a color transform [1]. Then this tint is substituted for that of every pixel under the brush, also using the color transforms.

hue, value, luminance, . . . paints

As for "tint paint," but the color attribute substituted at each pixel under the brush is hue, value, luminance, etc., respectively, instead of tint.

wet paint

The (8-bit) values of the brush are used as "wetness" weights. The higher the weight w in the brush, the more dominant is the color A, the color selected to paint with, over the color B at a pixel under the brush. The computation is the familiar "lerp" function (linear interpolation): $w*A+(1-w)*B$. If the brush is shaped as a random distribution over a circular radius, clustering toward the center with higher weights there, then wet painting simulates airbrushing.

intensity paint

As in "wet paint," the three-dimensional shape of the brush is used, where the values in the brush represent points in the third dimension. The computation at each pixel under the brush is as follows: The values of the brush are assumed to weight the colors under the brush. For a weight w from 0 to say, 200 (the *knee* k), the weighting is direct. The new color at a pixel is the old color times w/255—i.e., it is weighted toward black. For a weight w from the knee to 255, the weighting is toward white instead: $a*W+(1-a)*C$, the lerp of the old color C and white W, where $a =(w-k)/(255-k)$. The effect is to map the painting onto the surface represented by the brush shape, or to pass the brush under the surface of the painting, deforming it to the shape of the brush.

The structure of Paint3 is essentially that of Paint. The routines called by the menu buttons have either been rewritten for 24 bits when that makes sense (e.g., for fill and sketch) or replaced with items which were not possible in 8 bits (e.g., wet paint).

Although the frame buffer colormap is not altered in Paint3, there is still a "get colormap" button. This is used to select a set of 256 "convenient" colors to be displayed as the palette. For example, in tint paint, 256 pure hues spanning the spectrum are convenient.

There is one additional "get picture" button ("get 1 picture") which fetches 8-bit paintings, created with Paint, and displays them in 24 bits. The "get 3 picture" button restores 24-bit paintings created with Paint3.

Appendix C: Brief History Of Paint Programs

The following history is restricted to color paint programs. There are several black-and-white or gray "paint" programs not included in this short survey.

The earliest paint program with which I am acquainted is that of Joan Miller [1], implemented at Bell Labs in 1969-70 on a 3-bit frame buffer. The user could draw lines and then alter the colors by turning potentiometers. More or less simultaneously, the "tricolor cartograph" [2] came into existence with eight fixed colors, including black and white.

The first 8-bit frame buffer paint program that I know of, and certainly the first I personally used, is that written by Dick Shoup (assisted by Bob Flegal and Patrick Baudelaire) at Xerox Palo Alto Research Center in 1972-73. This program is a direct predecessor of the New York Institute of Technology (NYIT) Paint program and influenced it greatly. It is implemented on a frame buffer designed and built by Dick Shoup. Another direct influence on the current Paint is the paint program written by Garland Stern at the University of Utah for the same (Evans & Sutherland) 8-bit frame buffer first used at NYIT. He wrote his program in 1974-75 and brought it with him to NYIT when he joined the Computer Graphics Lab in 1975. Yet another University of Utah paint program used at NYIT briefly was that written by Jim Blinn, also in the 1974-75 period. Duane Palyka wrote another paint program during this time, but I have not used it. The NYIT Paint was written in 1975-76 and has been in constant use ever since. It has undergone quite a few modifications, however, mostly to accommodate equipment reconfigurations (see Appendix A). A similar program was implemented at the Massachusetts Institute of Technology shortly thereafter. See [3, 4] for descriptions of the equipment used there. More recently, Marc Lavoy programmed an 8-bit paint at Cornell University and is currently at work on an RGB paint (awaiting only the acquisition of 16 additional bits per pixel in the Cornell frame buffer). A 24-bit, or RGB, version of paint at NYIT was certainly the first of this variety. It was implemented in 1977.

The Paint program was sold to CBS and Ampex* in 1977 and implemented on an equipment configuration specified by NYIT (configuration II of Appendix A) under my supervision. Junaid Sheikh and Larry Evans of Ampex made slight modifications to the program. For example, a history editing facility was added. Then it was used by Leroy Niemann at the Super Bowl in January 1978 and subsequently written up in several publications: *The New York Times, New Times, Videography,* and *Playboy*.

References
1. Joan E. Miller, personal communication, Bell Labs, Murray Hill, N.J., July 1978.
2. W. J. Kubitz and W.J. Poppelbaum, "The Tricolor Cartograph: A Display System with Automatic Coloring Capabilities," *Information Display,* November/December, 1969, pp.76-79.
3. Jeffrey Entwisle, "An Image Processing Approach to Computer Graphics", *Comput. & Graphics,* Vol. 2, pp. 111-117, Pergamon Press, 1977.
4. Nicholas Negroponte, "Raster Scan Approaches to Computer Graphics", *Comput. & Graphics,* Vol. 2, pp. 179-193, Pergamon Press, 1977.

Figures

Figures 1 and 17 were sketched (with ordinary pencil) by Ephraim Cohen. All of the menus were generated directly off a Tektronix 4014 using a Tektronix hard-copy unit. The type was then reset for this publication. Figures 4, 5, and 11 were generated by contouring the contents of the canvas space into a Tektronix 4014 using a program by Garland Stern. Then the hardcopy unit was again used to get the line drawings shown here.

---

*Currently being marketed under the name AVA (Ampex Video Art), with additions and modifications by Tom Porter.

Bibliography

[APPE 67] Appel, Arthur. The Notion of Quantitative Invisibility and the Machine Rendering of Solids. *Proceedings of the ACM National Conference* 1967. 387-393.

[BARR 84] Barr, Alan H. Global and Local Deformations of Solid Primitives. *Computer Graphics (SIGGRAPH '84 Proceedings)* 18(3) July 1984. 21-30.

[BEIE 92] Beier, Thaddeus and Shawn Neely. Feature-Based Image Metamorphosis. *Computer Graphics (SIGGRAPH '92 Proceedings)* 26(2) July 1992. 35-42.

[BLIN 76] Blinn, James F. and Martin E. Newell. Texture and Reflection in Computer Generated Images. *Communications of the ACM* 19(10) October 1976. 542-546.

[BLIN 77] Blinn, James F. Models of Light Reflection for Computer Synthesized Pictures. *Computer Graphics (SIGGRAPH '77 Proceedings)* 11(2) July 1977. 192-198.

[BLIN 78] Blinn, James F. Simulation of Wrinkled Surfaces. *Computer Graphics (SIGGRAPH '78 Proceedings)* 12(3) August 1978. 286-292.

[BRES 65] Bresenham, J. E. Algorithm for Computer Control of a Digital Plotter. *IBM Systems Journal* 4(1) 1965. 25-30.

[BUIT 75] Bui-Tuong, Phong. Illumination for Computer Generated Pictures. *Communications of the ACM* 18(6) June 1975. 311-317.

[BURT 76] Burtnyk, N. and M. Wein. Interactive Skeleton Techniques for Enhancing Motion Dynamics in Key Frame Animation. *Communications of the ACM* 19(10) October 1976. 564-569.

[CATM 72] Catmull, Edwin. A System for Computer Generated Movies. *Proceedings of the ACM National Conference* August 1972. 422-431.

[CATM 75] Catmull, Edwin. Computer Display of Curved Surfaces. *Proceedings of the IEEE Conference on Computer Graphics, Pattern Recognition and Data Structures* (IEEE Cat. No. 75CH0981-1C) 1975. 11-17.

[CATM 78] Catmull, E. and J. Clark. Recursively Generated B-spline Surfaces on Arbitrary Topological Meshes. *Computer Aided Design* 19(6) November 1978. 350-354.

[CHEN 93] Chen, Shenchang Eric and Lance Williams. View Interpolation for Image Synthesis. *Computer Graphics (SIGGRAPH '93 Proceedings)* 1993. 279-288.

[CLAR 76] Clark, James H. Hierarchical Geometric Models for Visible Surface Algorithms. *Communications of the ACM* 19(10) October 1976. 547-554.

[CLAR 82] Clark, James H. The Geometry Engine: A VLSI Geometry System for Graphics. *Computer Graphics (SIGGRAPH '82 Proceedings)* 16(3) July 1982. 127-133.

[COHE 88] Cohen, Michael F., Shenchang Eric Chen, John R. Wallace and Donald P. Greenberg. A Progressive Refinement Approach to Fast Radiosity Image Generation. *Computer Graphics (SIGGRAPH '88 Proceedings)* 22(4) August 1988. 75-84.

[COOK 84a] Cook, Robert L. Shade Trees. *Computer Graphics (SIGGRAPH '84 Proceedings)* 18(3) July 1984. 223-231.

[COOK 84b] Cook, Robert L., Thomas Porter and Loren Carpenter. Distributed Raytracing. *Computer Graphics (SIGGRAPH '84 Proceedings)* 18(3) July 1984. 137-145.

[CROW 77] Crow, F. The Antialiasing Problem in Computer-Generated Shaded Images. *Communications of the ACM* 20(11) November 1977. 799-805.

[DOO 78] Doo, D. and M. Sabin. Behaviour of Recursive Division Surfaces Near Extraordinary Points. *Computer Aided Design* 10(6) November 1978. 356-360.

[DREB 88] Drebin, Robert A., Loren Carpenter and Pat Hanrahan. Volume Rendering. *Computer Graphics (SIGGRAPH '88 Proceedings)* 22(4) August 1988. 65-74.

[FOLE 74] Foley, James D. and Victor L. Wallace. The Art of Natural Graphic Man-Machine Conversation. *Proceedings of the IEEE* 62(4) April 1974. 462-471.

[FOUR 82] Fournier, Alain, Don Fussell and Loren Carpenter. Computer Rendering of Stochastic Models. *Communications of the ACM* 25(6) June 1982. 371-384.

[FUCH 77] Fuchs, Henry. Distributing A Visible Surface Algorithm Over Multiple Processors. *Proceedings of the ACM National Conference* 1977. 449-451.

[GIRA 85] Girard, Michael and A. A. Maciejewski. Computational Modeling for the Computer Animation of Legged Figures. *Computer Graphics (SIGGRAPH '85 Proceedings)* 19(3) July 1985. 263-270.

[GORA 84] Goral, Cindy M., Kenneth E. Torrence, Donald P. Greenberg and Bennett Battaile. Modelling the Interaction of Light Between Diffuse Surfaces. *Computer Graphics (SIGGRAPH '84 Proceedings)* 18(3) July 1984. 213-222.

[GOUR 71] Gouraud, Henri. Continuous Shading of Curved Surfaces. *IEEE Transactions on Computers* C-20(6) June 1971. 623-29.

[HECK 82] Heckbert, Paul. Color Image Quantization for Frame Buffer Display. *Computer Graphics (SIGGRAPH '82 Proceedings)* 16(3) July 1982. 297-307.

[HECK 87] Heckbert, Paul S. Ray Tracing JELL-O® Brand Gelatin. *Computer Graphics (SIGGRAPH '87 Proceedings)* 21(4) July 1987. 73-74.

[KAJI 75] Kajiya, James T., Ivan E. Sutherland and Edward Cheadle. A Random-Access Video Frame Buffer. *Proceedings of the IEEE Conference on Computer Graphics, Pattern Recognition and Data Structures* (IEEE Cat. No. 75CH0981-1C) 1975. 1-6.

[KAJI 86] Kajiya, James T. The Rendering Equation. *Computer Graphics (SIGGRAPH '86 Proceedings)* 20(4) August 1986. 143-150.

[LASS 87] Lasseter, John. Principles of Animation as Applied to 3D Character Animation. *Computer Graphics (SIGGRAPH '87 Proceedings)* 21(4) July 1987. 35-44.

[LORE 87] Lorensen, William and Harvey E. Cline. Marching Cubes: A High Resolution 3D Surface Construction Algorithm. *Computer Graphics (SIGGRAPH '87 Proceedings)* 21(4) July 1987. 163-170.

[MYER 68] Myer, T. H. and I. E. Sutherland. On the Design of Display Processors. *Communications of the ACM* 11(6) June 1968. 410-414.

[NEWE 72] Newell, M. E., R. G. Newell and T. L. Sancha. A Solution to the Hidden Surface Problem. *Proceedings of the ACM National Conference* 1972. 443-50.

[NEWM 68] Newman, William M. A System for Interactive Graphical Programming. *Proceedings of the AFIPS Spring Joint Computer Conference* Washington, D.C.: Thompson Books, 1968. 47-54.

[NOLL 71] Noll, A. Michael. Scanned-Display of Computer Graphics. *Communications of the ACM* 14(3) March 1971. 143-150.

[PARK 72] Parke, Frederic I. Computer Generated Animation of Faces. *Proceedings of the ACM National Conference* 1972. 451-457.

[PERL 85] Perlin, Ken. An Image Synthesizer. *Computer Graphics (SIGGRAPH '85 Proceedings)* 19(3) July 1985. 287-296.

[PORT 84] Porter, Thomas and Tom Duff. Compositing Digital Images. *Computer Graphics (SIGGRAPH '84 Proceedings)* 18(3) July 1984. 253-259.

[REEV 83] Reeves, William T. Particle Systems: A Technique for Modeling a Class of Fuzzy Objects. *Computer Graphics (SIGGRAPH '83 Proceedings)* 17(3) July 1983. 359-376.

[REYN 87] Reynolds, Craig W. Flocks, Herds and Schools: A Distributed Behavior Model. *Computer Graphics (SIGGRAPH '87 Proceedings)* 21(4) July 1987. 25-34.

[ROMN 68] Romney, Gordon, Gary S. Watkins and David C. Evans. Real Time Display of Computer Generated Half-Tone Perspective Pictures. *Proceedings of the IFIP Congress* 1968. 973-978.

[SMIT 82] Smith, Alvy Ray. Paint. *IEEE Tutorial on Computer Graphics*, 2nd. Ed. Beatty and Booth, eds. 1982. 501-515.

[SUTH 63] Sutherland, Ivan E. Sketchpad: A Man-Machine Graphical Communication System. *Proceedings of the AFIPS Spring Joint Computer Conference* Washington, D.C.: 1963. 329-346.

[SUTH 68] Sutherland, Ivan E. A Head-Mounted Three-Dimensional Display. *Proceedings of the AFIPS Fall Joint Computer Conference* Washington, D.C.: Thompson Books, 1968. 757-764.

[WEIS 66] Weiss, Ruth E. BE VISION, a Package of IBM 7090 FORTRAN Programs to Drive Views of Combinations of Plane and Quadric Surfaces. *Journal of the ACM* 13(4) April 1966. 194-204.

[WHIT 80] Whitted, Turner. An Improved Illumination Model for Shaded Display. *Communications of the ACM* 23(6) June 1980. 343-349.

[WILL 78] Williams, Lance. Casting Curved Shadows on Curved Surfaces. *Computer Graphics (SIGGRAPH '78 Proceedings)* 12(3) August 1978. 270-274.

[WILL 83] Williams, Lance. Pyramidal Parametrics. *Computer Graphics (SIGGRAPH '83 Proceedings)* 17(3) July 1983. 1-11.

Author Index

Appel, A.	19	Smith, A.	427
Barr, A.	221	Sutherland, I.	289, 295, 315, 391
Battaile, B.	137	Torrence, K.	137
Beier, T.	373	Wallace, J.	167
Blinn, J.	103, 111, 329	Wallace, V.	417
Bresenham, J.	1	Watkins, G.	283
Bui-Tuong, Phong	95	Wein, M.	249
Burtnyk, N.	249	Weiss, R.	7
Carpenter, L.	77, 189, 363	Whitted, T.	119
Catmull, E.	35, 183, 231	Williams, L.	51, 65, 381
Cheadle, E.	315		
Chen, S.	167, 381		
Clark, J.	43, 183, 321		
Cline, H.	347		
Cohen, M.	167		
Cook, R.	77, 127		
Crow, F.	57		
Doo, D.	177		
Drebin, R.	363		
Duff, T.	355		
Evans, D.	283		
Foley, J.	417		
Fournier, A.	189		
Fuchs, H.	311		
Fussell, D.	189		
Girard, M.	255		
Goral, C.	137		
Gouraud, H.	87		
Greenberg, D.	137, 167		
Hanrahan, P.	363		
Heckbert, P.	165, 335		
Kajiya, J.	157, 315		
Lasseter, J.	263		
Lorensen, W.	347		
Maciejewski, A.	255		
Myer, T.	89		
Neely, S.	373		
Newell, M.	27, 329		
Newell, R.	27		
Newman, W.	409		
Noll, M.	303		
Parke, F.	241		
Perlin, K.	147		
Porter, T.	77, 355		
Reeves, W.	203		
Reynolds, C.	273		
Romney, G.	283		
Sabin, M.	177		
Sancha, T.	27